MW01253605

MIDWIFERY CASEBOOK
A PRACTICAL RECORD OF MATERNAL AND NEWBORN NURSING
FOR GNM STUDENTS

MIDWIFERY CASEBOOK

A PRACTICAL RECORD OF MATERNAL AND NEWBORN NURSING

FOR GNM STUDENTS

WITH IMPORTANT NOTES ON CARE OF MOTHER AND NEWBORN

Fourth Edition

Prepared by

Annamma Jacob MSc (N)
Former Principal
Bhagwan Mahaveer Jain College of Nursing
Bengaluru, Karnataka, India
Formerly
Professor
St Philomenas College of Nursing, Bengaluru
Principal
Graduate School for Nurses, Board of Nursing Education
South India Branch Christian Medical Association of India, Bengaluru
Nurse Supervisor
Suburban Medical Center
Paramount, Southern California, USA
Assistant Director of Nursing
AL-Sabah Hospital, Ministry of Public Health
Kuwait, Arab, Western Asia
Sister Tutor
Leelabai Thackersey College of Nursing
Shreemati Nathibai Damodar Thackersey Women's University
Mumbai, Maharashtra, India
Junior Tutor
College of Nursing, Christian Medical College and Hospital
Vellore, Tamil Nadu, India

Edited by

Jadhav Sonali Tarachand
PhD MSc (N) PGDMLE
Principal
MS Ramaiah Institute of Nursing Education and Research, Bengaluru, Karnataka, India
Formerly

- Lecturer in Medical Surgical Nursing, St Martha's College of Nursing, Bengaluru
- Assistant Lecturer, Bharati Vidyapeeth's College of Nursing, Pune, Maharashtra

JAYPEE BROTHERS MEDICAL PUBLISHERS
The Health Sciences Publisher
New Delhi | London | Panama

Jaypee Brothers Medical Publishers (P) Ltd

Headquarters

Jaypee Brothers Medical Publishers (P) Ltd
4838/24, Ansari Road, Daryaganj
New Delhi 110 002, India
Phone: +91-11-43574357
Fax: +91-11-43574314
Email: jaypee@jaypeebrothers.com

Overseas Offices

J.P. Medical Ltd
83 Victoria Street, London
SW1H 0HW (UK)
Phone: +44 20 3170 8910
Fax: +44 (0)20 3008 6180
Email: info@jpmedpub.com

Jaypee-Highlights Medical Publishers Inc
City of Knowledge, Bld. 235, 2nd Floor
Clayton, Panama City, Panama
Phone: +1 507-301-0496
Fax: +1 507-301-0499
Email: cservice@jphmedical.com

Jaypee Brothers Medical Publishers (P) Ltd
Bhotahity, Kathmandu, Nepal
Phone: +977-9741283608
Email: kathmandu@jaypeebrothers.com

Website: www.jaypeebrothers.com
Website: www.jaypeedigital.com

Midwifery Casebook: A Practical Record of Maternal and Newborn Nursing for GNM Students

First Edition: 2007

Second Edition: 2013

Third Edition: 2018

Fourth Edition: **2019**

ISBN 978-93-5270-513-9

Printed at Sanat Printers

Preface to the Fourth Edition

The fourth edition of the casebook retains all the content and features of the previous edition of the book with few modifications in the nursing care pages. These pages are included in different sections with more space for each column of the nursing process format for students to document the nursing care they plan and provide to care study clients – mothers and newborns. The modifications are made as desired by a large number of student midwives. I hope and trust that GNM students will find it the best format to write all aspects of nursing care of their patients.

Annamma Jacob

Preface to the First Edition

Practice of obstetric nursing has become an interesting and challenging experience for practicing nurses as well as students of midwifery. In order to keep pace with the expansion and advancement of knowledge and to master the skills needed for practice, nurse educators and midwifery students require adequate theoretical information and practice guidelines.

The "Midwifery Casebook for GNM Students" includes an outline of learning requirements according to the Revised Indian Nursing Council Syllabus, for undergraduate nursing students in the country. Formats for entering client data and notes on nursing process to be carried out for clients in various stages of childbearing experience, are included.

Brief notes on maternal newborn care and nursing diagnoses are part of the casebook for reference of undergraduate students as they engage in planning, implementing and evaluating nursing care to such clients.

This practical record book, I feel will be of much help to midwifery nursing students of GNM course to provide comprehensive care to their maternal and newborn clients as well as record the information in a systematic manner.

Annamma Jacob

Notes on Midwifery

The nursing profession tends to attract those who desire to help others and ability to think critically in every situation. But today's nurses care are more challenging to make quick, yet critical and informed decisions and also highly trained, well-educated and to face many challenges within their working environment. Knowledge of all aspects of childbirth is an essential requirement for all, as they start learning clinically. Having a reference source ready in hand often proves helpful.

In order to meet such a need, brief notes on important topics in obstetric nursing are included in this casebook. The content of this section covers notes on maternal pelvis and fetal skull, the process of labor and delivery as well as care of mothers and newborns. A few nursing diagnoses for maternal and newborn are also included in order to provide guidelines for students to plan and provide relevant and need-based nursing care to their clients.

Annamma Jacob

CLINICAL EXPERIENCE RECORD

Photograph

Name of Student: --

Registration Number: --

Age and Date of Birth: --

Name and Address of the Institution: --

Signature of Student **Signature of Class Coordinator** **Signature of Principal**

Date .... **Date** .... **Date** ....

Signature of Examiners

1. **Internal** ....
2. **External**...............................

ESSENTIAL REQUIREMENTS OF CLINICAL PRACTICE AS PER INDIAN NURSING COUNCIL SYLLABUS (REVISED)

S. No.	Title of Requirement	Total Requirement	Completed Requirement
1.	Antenatal Examinations Performed	20	
2.	Normal Deliveries Witnessed	15	
3.	Normal Deliveries Conducted	10	
4.	Vaginal Examinations Performed in Labor	10	
5.	Episiotomies and Suturing of 1st Degree Lacerations Performed	10	
6.	Abnormal Deliveries Witnessed (Forceps/Ventouse)	10	
7.	IUCD Insertions Carried Out	05	
8.	Cesarean Sections Witnessed	05	
	Care Studies		
1.	Prenatal Mothers Nursed	10	
2.	Intranatal Mothers Nursed	10	
3.	Postnatal Mothers and Newborns Nursed including Cesarean Mothers	10	
4.	Neonates Nursed	10	

Signature of Student

Signature of Class Coordinator

Contents

Notes on Midwifery

STRUCTURE OF FEMALE PELVIS (FIGURE 1)

The pelvis is a skeletal ring often referred to as pelvic girdle formed by two innominate bones, the sacrum and the coccyx.

Innominate Bones

Each innominate bone is made up of three bones—(1) ilium, (2) ischium, and (3) pubis.

Sacrum

The sacrum is a wedge-shaped bone consisting of five fused vertebrae and lies between the two ilia. The prominent upper margin of the first sacral vertebra is called the sacral promontory. The anterior surface of the sacrum is concave from above downward and from side to side and is referred to as the hollow of sacrum. There are four pairs of foramina through which the sacral nerves pass.

Coccyx

The coccyx is a small triangular bone which articulates with the lower end of the sacrum.

Pelvic Joints

- **Sacroiliac joints:** These are two slightly movable joints formed where the ilium joins with the first two sacral vertebrae on either side.
- **Symphysis pubis:** It is a cartilaginous joint between the two pubic bones.
- **Sacrococcygeal joint:** It is a hinge joint between the sacrum and the coccyx.

Pelvic Ligaments

The pelvic girdle requires great strength and stability in order to fulfill its function of support. The pelvic joints are reinforced by powerful ligaments.

- **Sacroiliac ligaments:** These ligaments pass in front of and behind each sacroiliac joint.
- **Pubic ligaments:** The superior pubic ligament connects the top portion of the pubic bones. The arcuate pubic ligament runs under the symphysis pubis and connects the lower portion.
- **Sacrotuberous ligaments:** One ligament on each side runs from sacrum to the ischial tuberosity.
- **Sacrospinous ligaments:** One ligament on each side runs between the sacrum and ischial spine.
- **Sacrococcygeal ligaments:** One ligament on each side from the sacrum to the coccyx.

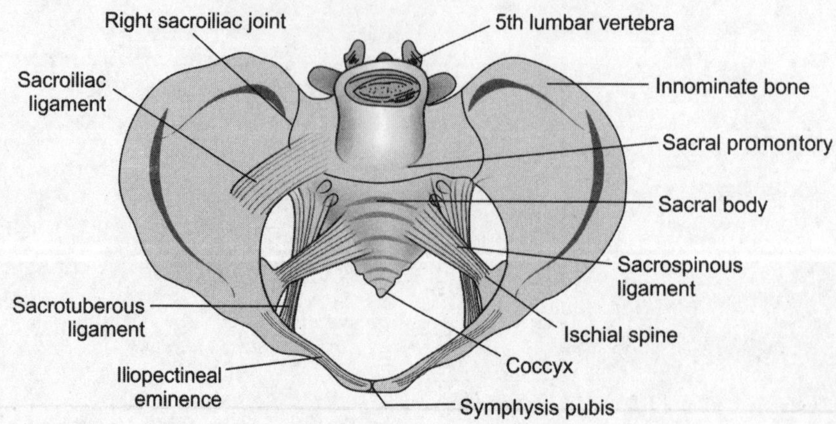

Figure 1: Normal female pelvis

Division of the Pelvis

1. **False pelvis:** Lies above an imaginary line called linea terminalis at the level of brim. Function of the false pelvis is to support the enlarged uterus.
2. **True pelvis:** Lies below the linea terminalis or pelvic brim. It is the bony canal through which the fetus must pass. It is divided into three planes (Figure 2).

   a. **Brim or inlet**

   It is the upper boundary of true pelvis. The brim is bounded by upper margin of symphysis pubis in front, linea terminalis on sides and sacral promontory in the back. Largest diameter of the inlet is transverse and smallest diameter is anteroposterior.

   i. *Anteroposterior diameter* of the inlet is measured clinically by *diagonal conjugate,* the distance from the lower margin of symphysis pubis to the sacral promontory and usually measures 13.5 cm.

   Obstetric or true conjugate is the distance between the inner surface of symphysis and sacral promontory. The measurement is obtained by subtracting 1.5–2.0 cm (thickness of symphysis pubis) from diagonal conjugate. Adequate diameter is usually 11.5 cm.

   ii. *Oblique diameters:* Right and left oblique diameters are measured from the sacroiliac joint on the one side to the iliopectineal eminence on the opposite side. It is named in relation to the mother's anatomical position. Right oblique is from right sacroiliac joint and measures 12 cm.

   iii. *Transverse diameter:* It is the maximum distance between two farthest points of pelvic brim. This diameter is nearest the sacrum than the pubis. It measures 13 cm.

   b. **Cavity**

   Cavity is circular in shape and is the space between the plane of brim and that of outlet. It is a curved canal with shallow anterior and deep posterior wall. Anterior wall measures 4 cm and posterior wall 12 cm and curved. Diameters of the inlet cannot be measured clinically. Clinical evaluation of adequacy is made by noting the ischial spines. All the diameters are considered to be 12 cm.

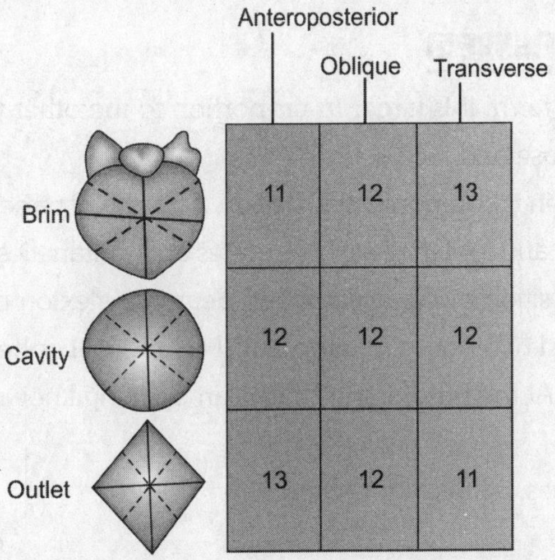

Figure 2: Measurements of the pelvic canal in centimeters

   c. **Outlet**

   Outlet is diamond shaped, bounded by lower margin of symphysis pubis in front, ischial tuberosities on sides and tip of sacrum posteriorly.

   i. *Anteroposterior diameter* extends from the apex of the pubic arch to the tip of the coccyx. This diameter increases by half an inch during labor by the coccyx being displaced backwards as the head descends, and measures 13 cm.

ii. *Transverse diameters:* There are two transverse diameters *Bi-spinous* 10 cm, at the upper boundary of outlet and *intertuberischial* 11 cm at the lower border of outlet, distance between the inner borders of ischial tuberosities.

Shapes of the Pelvis (Figure 3)

There are four types of pelvic shapes-based essentially on the shape of the brim.

1. Gynecoid (normal female pelvis)
   Has optimal diameters in all three planes. Seen in 50% of women.
2. Android (normal male pelvis)
   Posterior segments are decreased in all three planes. Deep transverse arrest and failure of rotation of the fetus are common. Seen in 20% of all women.
3. Anthropoid (apelike pelvis)
   Anteroposterior diameter is longer, may allow for easy delivery of an occiput posterior presentation of fetus. Seen in 25% of all women.
4. Platypelloid (flat female pelvis with wide transverse diameter)
   Arrest of fetal descend at the pelvic inlet is common. This type of pelvis is seen in 5% of all women.

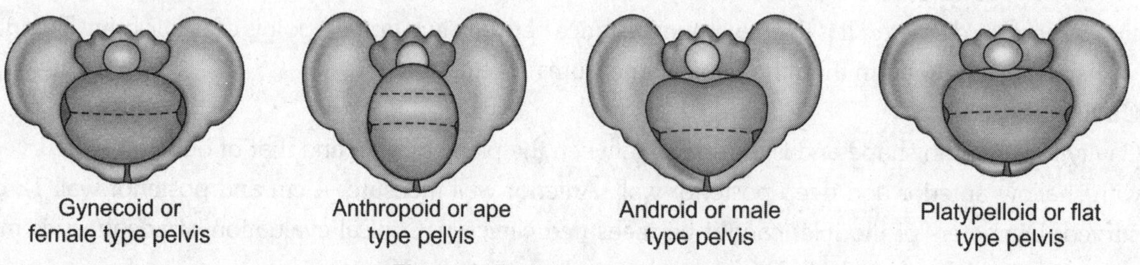

Figure 3: The four types of pelvis

PARTS OF THE FETAL SKULL (REFER FIGURE 5)

The fetal skull is ovoid in shape. At term, it is larger in proportion to the other parts of the skeleton. The skull may be divided into three parts: vault, base and face.

1. The vault which contains the brain is composed of 5 bones: 2 frontal, 2 parietal and 1 occipital. These are united by membranes known as sutures and fontanelles. The sutures and fontanelles may be felt on vaginal examination during labor and indicate the position of the occiput and degree of flexion of the head.
2. The base of the skull is composed of 5 bones: 2 temporal, 1 ethmoid, 1 sphenoid and part of the occipital bone. These are firmly fused together. At the base of the skull is an opening known as *the foramen magnum*, through which passes the spinal cord.
3. The face is composed of 14 bones, all fused together.

Sutures (Figure 4)

There are four sutures of obstetrical importance. They are composed of soft, fibrous tissue and allow mobility between the cranial bones. Sutures are very useful landmarks while making a vaginal examination.

1. *Sagittal suture*: Between two parietal bones
2. *Frontal suture*: Between two frontal bones

FEATURES OF THE FOUR TYPES OF PELVIS

Plane of pelvis	*Features*	*Gynecoid*	*Android*	*Anthropoid*	*Platypelloid*
Brim	Forepelvis Brim	Wide Rounded	Narrow Heart-shaped	Narrow Oval anteroposteriorly	Wide Oval transversely (kidney-shaped)
Cavity	Side walls Sacrum	Straight Well-curved	Convergent Straight	Straight Deep concave	Divergent Flat
Outlet	Ischial spines Subpubic arch	Blunt Wide, 90 degrees	Prominent Narrow, <90 degrees	Blunt Wide >90 degrees	Blunt Wide >90 degrees
Bone structure		Medium	Heavy	Medium	Medium
Incidence		50%	20%	25%	5%

3. *Coronal suture*: Between the frontal bone on one side and the parietal bones on the other side.
4. *Lambdoidal suture*: Between the parietal and occipital bones.

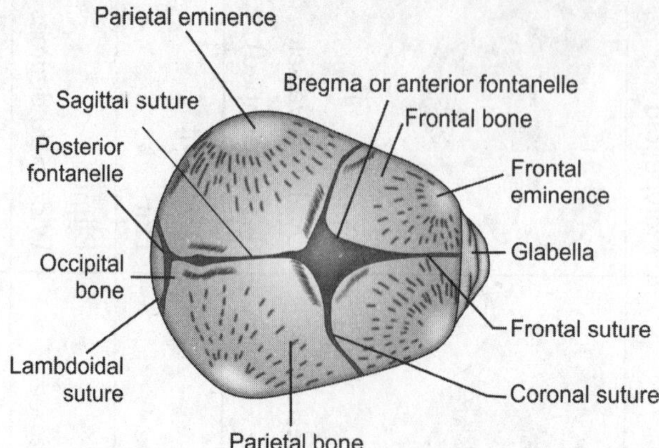

Figure 4: Fetal skull at term showing fontanelles and sutures

Fontanelles

Membranous spaces between the cranial bones of the fetus or newborn baby. There are six fontanelles on the skull, but only two are of obstetrical importance, the anterior and the posterior.

1. *Anterior fontanelle:* The largest fontanelle. It is the junction of the sagittal, frontal and coronal sutures. It is diamond shaped, 2.5 cm long and 1.5 cm wide. Pulsations of the cerebral vessels can be felt through it. The fontanelle closes by 18 months of age.
2. *Posterior fontanelle:* This is located where the sagittal suture meets the lambdoidal suture. It is triangle shaped and smaller than anterior fontanelle. This fontanelle can be recognized as the junction of three sutures in vaginal examination during labor. It closes by six weeks of age.

Regions of Fetal Skull (Figure 5)

1. Vertex: It is a quadrilateral area bounded by the anterior fontanelle and the coronal suture in front, the posterior fontanelle and the lambdoidal suture behind, and longitudinal lines through the parietal eminences laterally.
2. Brow or sinciput: It is the area bounded by the supraorbital ridges in front, the anterior fontanelle and the coronal sutures behind and longitudinal lines passing through the frontal eminences laterally.
3. Face: It is the area bounded by the orbital ridges and the root of the nose to the junction of the chin and neck.

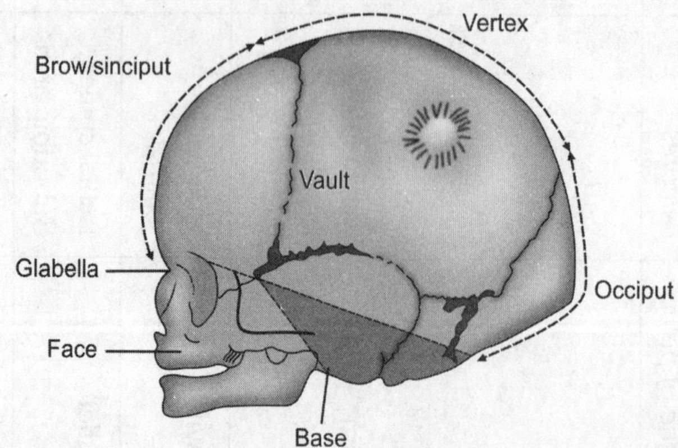

Figure 5: Regions of the fetal skull showing vault, face and base

4. Occiput: This is the region that lies between the foramen magnum and the posterior fontanelle. The part below the occipital protuberance is known as the suboccipital region.

Diameters of the Fetal Skull (Figure 6)

The engaging diameter of the fetal skull depends on the degree of flexion present.

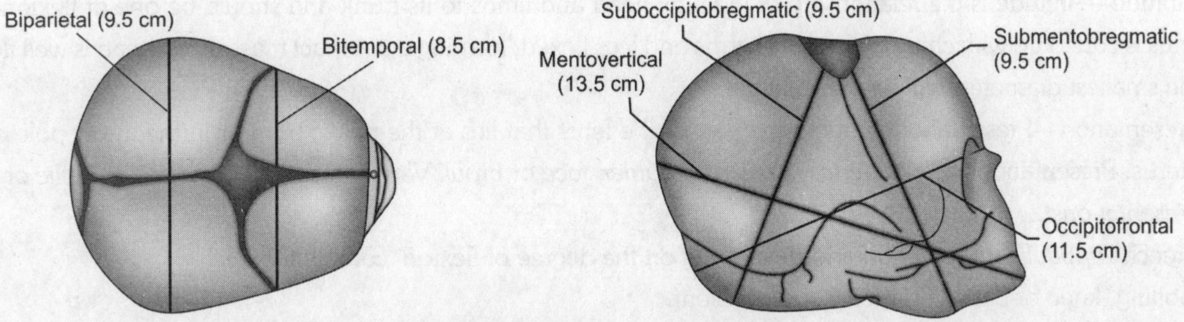

Figure 6: Diameters of the fetal skull

Diameters of the fetal skull

Sl. No.	*Diameter*	*Measurement*	*Presentation*
1	Suboccipitobregmatic Measured from below the occipital protuberance to the center of the anterior fontanelle or bregma	9. 5 cm	Vertex well flexed
2.	Suboccipitofrontal Measured from below the suboccipital protuberance to the center of the frontal suture	10 cm	Vertex deflexed
3.	Occipitofrontal Measured from the occipital protuberance to the root of the nose (glabella)	11.5 cm	Vertex extremely deflexed in occipito-posterior position
4.	Submentobregmatic Measured from the point where the chin joins the neck to the center of the bregma	9.5 cm	Face completely extended
5.	Submentovertical Measured from the point where the chin joins the neck to the highest point on the vertex	11.5 cm	Face incompletely extended
6.	Mentovertical Measured from midpoint of the chin to the highest point on the vertex, slightly nearer to the posterior than to the anterior fontanelle	13.5 cm	Brow midway between flexion and extention
7.	Biparietal Transverse diameter, measured between the two parietal eminences	9.5 cm	
8.	Bitemporal Transverse diameter, measured between the furthest points of the coronal suture at the temples	8.2 cm	

Relationship of the Fetus to the Uterus and Pelvis

Relationship of the fetus to the uterus and pelvis are expressed using certain terms. These determine which part of the fetus enters the pelvic brim first and governs the mechanism of labor.

1. Lie—The lie of the fetus is the relationship between the long axis of the fetus to the long axis of the uterus. Lie may be longitudinal, transverse or oblique.
2. Attitude—Attitude is the relationship of the fetal head and limbs to its trunk and should be one of flexion. The fetus is curled up with chin on chest and arms and legs flexed, forming a compact mass. If the head is well flexed, the smallest diameters will be presenting.
3. Presentation—Presentation refers to the part of the fetus that lies at the pelvic brim or in the lower pole of the uterus. Presentations can be *vertex, breech, shoulder, face* or *brow*. Vertex, face and brow are *cephalic* or *head presentations*.

   Breech is *podalic presentation* and depending on the degree of flexion, complete breech, footling, knee or extended breech may present.

   In transverse presentation, the fetus lies across the pelvis and there may be shoulder, arm or any part of the trunk presenting.
4. Denominator

   Denominator is the part of presentation that indicates or determines the position. Each presentation has different denominator and these are as follows:
   - In vertex presentation, the occiput is the denominator
   - In breech presentation, the sacrum is the denominator
   - In face presentation, the mentum is the denominator
   - In shoulder presentation, the acromion process is the denominator
   - In brow presentation, no denominator is used.
5. Position

   Position is the relationship between the denominator of the presentation and six areas of the pelvic brim:

   i. Right anterior ii. Left anterior
   iii. Right posterior iv. Left posterior
   v. Right lateral vi. Left lateral.

   In addition, when the denominator is found in the midline either anteriorly or posteriorly, it is described as direct anterior or direct posterior.

Engagement of the Fetal Head

Engagement of the fetal head is said to have occurred when the widest presenting transverse diameter has passed through the brim of the pelvis.

A head is not engaged when its greatest diameter is still above the plane of inlet. If freely movable, it is called a floating head. A head is said to be deeply engaged when the largest diameter has passed into the cavity. A head is at the outlet when the largest diameter is lying at the bony outlet and the perineum is beginning to bulge.

Presenting Part

The presenting part of the fetus is the part that lies over the cervical os during labor and on which the caput succedaneum forms and thus first to be felt per vagina during internal examination.

PREGNANCY

Pregnancy is the state of a female after conception and until the termination of gestation. Conception is the act of conceiving—the implantation of a blastocyst in the endometrium. The human conceptus from fertilization through eight weeks of pregnancy is termed as an *embryo*, from 9th week till delivery, it is called a *fetus.*

The duration of pregnancy is approximately 280 days or 40 weeks. Gestational age is expressed in completed weeks. Fertilization takes place at the time of ovulation, approximately 14 days after the first day of last menstrual period (in a 28 day cycle) and the period of gestation is thus 266 days or 38 weeks.

Gravidity is the total number of pregnancies regardless of their duration. *Parity* is the number of viable newborns live or dead that a woman has delivered regardless of the number of children involved. (e.g. the birth of twins or triplets increases the parity only by one).

Calculation of the Expected Date of Delivery (EDD) and Duration of Pregnancy

The expected date of delivery is calculated from the first day of the last menstrual period (LMP) by counting 9 calendar months and adding 7 days to it. The number of days counted from the first day of the last menstrual period to the date of examination will give the duration of pregnancy at that particular date.

Estimation of Gestational Period from the Height of the Fundus of Uterus

The fundus assumes different heights in the abdomen at different periods of gestation (Figure 7).

12	Level of the symphysis pubis
16	Half-way between symphysis pubis and umbilicus
20	1–2 fingerbreadths below the umbilicus
22–24	1–2 fingerbreadths above the umbilicus
28–30	1/3 of the way between umbilicus and xiphoid process. (3 fingerbreadths above the umbilicus)
32	2/3 of the way between umbilicus and xiphoid process. (3–4 fingerbreadths below the xiphoid process)
38	Level of the xiphoid process
40	2–3 fingerbreadths below the xiphoid process if lightening occurs.

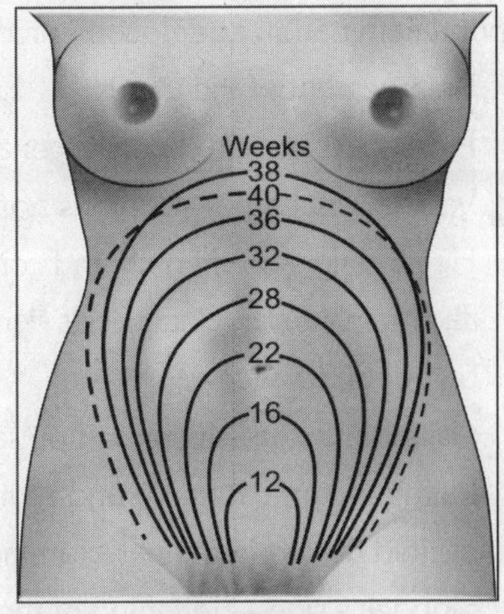

Figure 7: The level of fundus of uterus at different weeks

Diagnosis of Pregnancy

Pregnancy may be diagnosed by the woman herself even before she has missed a period because she feels different. Changes in breasts can occur as early as 5 to 6 weeks after conception. Several fast and easy pregnancy test kits are presently available in drug stores, which work by detecting the presence of human chorionic gonadotropin (hCG) in the woman's urine. Few drops of urine placed on a test strip will give the result in 1–2 minutes.

Diagnosis of pregnancy in the first trimester and early second trimester is based on a combination of presumptive and probable signs of pregnancy. Pregnancy is self-evident later in gestation when the positive signs are readily observed.

Presumptive Signs of Pregnancy

These are the maternal physiological changes which the woman experiences.

- Amenorrhea at 4th week (cessation of menstruation)
- Nausea and vomiting (morning sickness) from 4th to 14th week
- Tingling, tenseness and enlargement of breasts from 3rd to 4th week
- Frequency of micturition—6th to 12th weeks
- Fatigue
- Breast changes—Darkening of nipples, primary and secondary areolar changes and appearance of Montgomery's tubercles.
- Presence of colostrum in the nipples
- Excessive salivation
- Quickening—The first movement of fetus felt by the mother around 18th to 20th week
- Skin pigmentation and conditions such as chloasma, breast and abdominal striae, linea nigra and palmar erythema.

Probable Signs

Probable signs of pregnancy are maternal physiological changes other than presumptive signs which are detected upon examination and documented by the examiner.

- Enlargement of the uterus.
- Presence of human chorionic gonadotropin (hCG) in blood from 4th to 12th week and in urine from 6th to 12th week.
- Vaginal discharge—Copious non-irritating mucoid discharge which appears at 6th week.
- Hegar's sign—Softening and compressibility of the isthmus from 6th to 10th week.
- Jacquemiers sign/Chadwick's sign—Violet-Blue discoloration of the vaginal membrane due to increased vascularity by about 8th week.
- Osiander's sign—Increased pulsation felt in the lateral fornices from 8th week onwards.
- Palmer's sign—Regular and rhythmic uterine contractions resembling systole and diastole of heart that can be elicited during bimanual examination as early as 8 weeks.
- Goodell's sign—Softening of the cervix from a nonpregnant state of firmness similar to the tip of a nose to the softness of lips of mouth in the pregnant state by sixth week
- Globular enlargement of uterus with a soft feel.
- Palpation of Braxton Hicks contractions.
- Ballottement of fetus from 16th to 28th week.

Positive Signs

Positive signs are those directly attributable to the fetus as detected and documented by the examiner.

- Visualization of fetus by ultrasound from 6th week onwards
- Visualization of fetal skeleton by 16th week
- Fetal heart sounds by ultrasound from 6th week onwards
- Palpable fetal movements from 22nd week onwards

- Visible fetal movements late in pregnancy
- Palpation of fetal parts from 24th week onwards.

Pregnancy Tests

1. Immunologic test

This test is based on the production of chorionic gonadotropin (hCG) by the syncytiotrophoblastic cells during early pregnancy. hCG is secreted into the maternal bloodstream and then excreted in mother's urine.

Specific antisera are mixed with urine from the woman suspected of being pregnant. If the urine contains hCG, it will neutralize the antibodies in the antiserum and inhibit agglutination indicating a positive pregnancy test.

If the urine does not contain hCG, agglutination will occur—a negative pregnancy test.

Pregnancy test kits for home use.

Several self-use pregnancy test kits are now available. These FDA (Food and Drug Administration) approved products are easy to use (urine drops placed on test strip) and give quick results. The result seen on the test strip indicates if the test is positive or negative for pregnancy or needs to be repeated. Some of the pregnancy test strips presently available in drug stores are: '*i can*' one-step pregnancy test kit, '*First response*' pregnancy test kit, '*velocit eazy*' pregnancy detection kit and '*Pregakem*' pregnancy test kit.

2. Radioimmunoassay test

Blood is tested to detect the hCG beta subunit. These are extremely sensitive tests, able to detect hCG at far lower levels than other tests. The test known as *beta pregnancy* can be used as early as one week after conception, if laboratory facilities are available.

3. Biological tests of pregnancy

Biological tests were done in the past using mice and frogs. The tests included Aschheim Zondek test, Friedman test, Frank test and Hogben test.

ANTENATAL CARE

Antenatal care refers to the care given to an expectant mother from the time the conception is confirmed until the beginning of labor.

Objectives

The objectives of prenatal care are to:

- Promote, protect and maintain the health of the mother during pregnancy.
- Detect high-risk pregnancies and give special attention
- Foresee complications and take preventive measures
- Remove anxiety and fear associated with pregnancy
- Reduce maternal and infant morbidity and mortality
- Teach the mother elements of nutrition, personal hygiene and newborn care.
- Sensitize the mother to the need of family planning

The importance of regular visits to the prenatal clinic must be emphasized to help the mother have an optimum outcome of pregnancy that is "healthy mother and healthy baby".

Frequency of Visits to the Antenatal Clinic

Ideally the mother should visit the antenatal clinic once a month during the first seven months (28 weeks) twice a month during the eight month (up to 32 weeks) and thereafter once a week if everything is normal.

Antenatal Examination

The first visit irrespective of when it occurs should include the client's health history, obstetric history, physical and pelvic examinations and laboratory examinations.

1. Health history

- Personal history: Patient name, age, religion and occupation
  Spouse: Name, age, occupation, family income and address.
- Medical history: Medical conditions that require special care
  - Urinary tract infection
  - Essential hypertension
  - Asthma, epilepsy
  - Diabetes
  - Cardiac condition.
- Family history: History: of conditions that are genetic in origin, familial or racial
  - Diabetes in first degree relative
  - Hypertension
  - Multiple pregnancies
  - Sickle cell anemia, thalassemia
  - Congenital anomalies.
- Menstrual history
  - Age at menarche
  - Frequency, duration and amount of menstrual flow
  - Dysfunctional uterine bleeding.

2. Obstetric history

- Prenatal health
- Past pregnancy
  - Labor and delivery: Mode of delivery, duration of labor, postpartum hemorrhage (PPH)
  - Puerperium: Sepsis, mastitis, hypertension
  - Babies: Condition at birth, sex, weight
  - Lactation: Breastfeeding, any complication.
- Present pregnancy
  - Duration of amenorrhea
  - Eating and sleeping habits
  - Bowel and bladder pattern
  - Minor disorders.

3. Physical examination

A complete screening physical examination is done during the initial antepartal examination in order to ascertain if the woman has any medical disease or abnormalities.

The components of physical examination are:

- Physical measurements: temperature, pulse, respirations and blood pressure.
- General observations: appearance, emotional state, posture and apparent state of health
- Review of systems.

4. Assessments and laboratory tests

- Height and weight
- Urinalysis
- Blood tests—ABO blood group and Rh factor, hemoglobin and hematocrit, venereal disease research laboratory (VDRL), human immunodeficiency virus (HIV) and Rubella immune status.

5. Abdominal examination

An abdominal examination of the pregnant woman should be done in addition to the physical examination and assessment. The examination includes inspection, palpation and auscultation.

- Inspection is done to note
  - Skin condition of abdomen
  - Incisional scars
  - Contour of abdomen which give clue to lie of the fetus presenting part and to determine if it is engaged or floating.
  - Size of abdomen.
- Palpation is done using Leopold's maneuvers
  - First maneuver (Fundal palpation) is performed to detect the height of fundus and presentation.
  - Second maneuver (Lateral palpation) helps to identify the position, lie and variety.
  - Third maneuver (Pawlick's grip/second pelvic grip) is done to identify the presenting part and to determine if it is engaged or floating.
  - Fourth maneuver (Pelvic palpation/first pelvic grip) to determine the degree of flexion of the presenting part as well as the extent of its descend into the pelvic cavity.
- Auscultation—of fetal heart sounds helps in the diagnosis of a live fetus and its location of maximum intensity which provides information about the presentation.

6. Vaginal examination

Vaginal examination is performed in early pregnancy to detect the condition of vagina, presence of scars, prolapse of uterus or cervical fibroids. In late pregnancy, the examination is done to make pelvic assessment.

Ultrasonography

Ultrasonographic examination has almost replaced the radiological examination during pregnancy. This painless procedure is useful for detecting and confirming:

- The pregnancy
- Gestational age
- Abnormalities of pregnancy
- Fetal anomalies
- Fetal well-being.

Prenatal Education

Every mother needs advice regarding the importance of regular prenatal check-ups and measures to be taken to maintain or improve her health status during pregnancy in order to have a normal delivery and healthy baby.

In order to remove the fear of unknown and to help them approach the event of childbirth without undue anxiety, 'child birth preparation' through explanation of physiological changes and methods of coping during labor and delivery and puerperium must be explained .

Rest and Sleep

Pregnant women may continue her usual activities throughout pregnancy.

Hard and strenuous activities should be avoided in the first trimester and last six weeks. The woman should have an average of 10 hours of sleep (8 hours at night and 2 hours at noon) especially in the last trimester.

In late pregnancy, lateral position in bed would be more comfortable.

Diet

The diet during pregnancy should be adequate to maintain maternal health, meet the needs of growing fetus and provide strength during labor. During pregnancy, the calorie requirement is increased by about 300. The diet should be light, nutritious, easily digestable and rich in protein, minerals and vitamins. In addition to the principal food, the mother needs additional quantity of milk, egg, green vegetables and fruits. 2400 calories is generally recommended.

Exercise

Day-to-day domestic and social activities to be continued during pregnancy. Brisk walk in the morning and evening and specific antenatal exercises to prepare the mother's body for labor and delivery are recommended.

Bathing and Clothing

Daily bath and wearing loose comfortable clothes are advised for the comfort of pregnant women. Wearing high heeled shoes should be avoided in late pregnancy when the center of balance alters.

Care of Breasts and Nipples

If the nipples are anatomically normal, nothing beyond ordinary cleaning is needed. If the nipples are flat or retracted, rolling of the nipples and drawing them out between thumb and forefinger, twice daily for 5 minutes must be explained. Drawing the nipples and rolling them between fingers is recommended after cleansing.

Dental Care

Tendency to dental caries is high in pregnancy and consulting a dentist and taking required treatment must be emphasized.

Alcohol and smoking—should be avoided in pregnancy since nicotine is harmful for the growing fetus and mother. Growth retardation and maldevelopment of fetus are the possible complications to be prevented.

Care of Bowels

Regulation of diet to include food containing roughage, fluids and vegetables as well as extra quantity of water are to be explained to mother.

Coitus—should be avoided in the first three months to prevent abortion and in the 3rd trimester to prevent premature labor and puerperal infection.

Travel—by vehicles having jerks are better avoided in first trimester and last six weeks. Rail journey is preferable to bus travel and travel by aircraft offers no risk.

Immunization—against tetanus is essential for mothers in developing countries to protect them as well as their neonates. Two doses of tetanus toxoid between 16 and 24 weeks are generally recommended.

General Advice

The mother should be instructed to go to the hospital in the following circumstances:

- Active vaginal bleeding even if small amount
- Severe and continuous headache
- Swelling of face, fingers and toes
- Persistent vomiting
- Dimness or blurred vision
- Painful uterine contractions at interval of about 10 minutes or less for at least one hour
- Sudden gush of watery fluid per vagina
- Pain in abdomen
- Fever with chills.

MINOR DISORDERS OF PREGNANCY

At various times during the course of pregnancy, women will experience problems due to physiological changes occurring in their body.

- **Nausea and vomiting**

  Nausea and vomiting upon getting up in the morning are experienced by some women, especially primigravidae in their first trimester. Advice to stay in bed longer, avoiding fatty foods and fluids in empty stomach are generally sufficient to relieve symptoms.
- **Backache**

  A problem experienced in the last trimester by some women. Relaxation of pelvic joints, faulty posture, muscle spasm and urinary infection are some of the causes for backache.

  Advice regarding more rest in hard bed, massaging back muscles and wearing a well—fitting pelvic girdle belt while walking may be given.
- **Constipation**

  This is a common problem in pregnancy due to the effect of progesterone on the gut and diminished physical activity.

  Regular bowel habits, taking fluids and including vegetables and fruits in diet are to be explained to mothers having problem of constipation.

- **Heartburn**

  Restriction of greasy and spicy foods and avoiding fats often help to reduce the problem. Remaining upright for 1 to 2 hours after meals reduces the possibility acid reflux. Taking small, frequent meals to avoid overloading the stomach is helpful. Antacids if prescribed by the physician can be taken for relief of symptoms.
- **Leg cramps**

  Leg cramps often occur due to deficiency of serum calcium and elevation of serum phosphorus. Instruct patient to elevate her legs periodically and avoid lying with toes pointed. Increasing milk intake, taking warm baths at bedtime and regular exercises prevent the occurrence of leg cramps.
- **Urinary frequency and dysuria**

  Taking more fluids during day time, avoiding distension of bladder and early treatment for any urinary tract infection are the measures to help women with urinary problems in pregnancy.
- **Varicose veins**

  Varicose veins in the legs, vulva or rectum appear in the later months of pregnancy. Elevation of legs while resting and elastic crepe bandage during movements can give symptomatic relief. For hemorrhoids, local application of hydrocortisone ointment and prescribed laxatives to keep the bowels soft are recommended.

LABOR

A process that involves a series of integrated uterine contractions that occur over time, and work to propel the products of conception (fetus, placenta and amniotic fluid) out of the uterus through the birth canal.

Normal Labor or Eutocia

Labor is normal when a fetus of 38 to 42 weeks presenting by the vertex, is delivered within 24 hours, spontaneously, uncomplicated and with minimal aid in case of both mother and baby.

Causes of Onset of Labor

The precise mechanism of initiation of labor is still unclear. Some of the hypotheses are as listed below:

- Uterine distension. The stretching effect on the myometrium by the growing fetus and liquor amni.
- Pressure of the presenting part on the nerve endings in the cervix. Pressure stimulates a nerve plexus known as the cervical ganglion. Labor is more likely to start on time when the head is engaged.
- Over distension of uterus in case of multiple pregnancy and hydramnios, over distension tends to induce premature labor.
- Oxytocin stimulation theory—The uterus becomes increasingly sensitive to oxytocin as pregnancy progresses.
- Progesterone withdrawal theory—A decrease in progesterone production may stimulate prostaglandin synthesis and enhance the effect of estrogen which has a stimulating effect on uterine muscle.
- Estrogen stimulation theory—Estrogen stimulates irritability of uterine muscles and enhances uterine contractions.
- Fetal cortisol theory—Estrogen level increases due to the effects of fetal cortisol in late pregnancy.
- Prostaglandin stimulation theory—Initiation and maintenance of labor due to synthesis of prostaglandins in late pregnancy.

SIGNS OF LABOR

1. Prelabor or premonitory signs of labor may begin two to three weeks prior to the onset of true labor in primigravidae and a few days before in multiparae.

- Lightening—In primigravidae, the presenting part sinks into the true pelvis due to active pulling up of the lower segment of the uterus around the presenting part. This minimizes the fundal height and hence relieves the pressure on diaphragm making breathing easier for the mother.
- Frequency of micturition and constipation—The mother may experience urinary frequency and constipation due to pressure from the engaged presenting part.
- Cervical changes—The cervix becomes ripe. A ripe cervix is soft, less than 1.3 cm in length, admits one finger and is dilatable.
- Taking up of cervix—The cervix becomes shorter as it gets drawn up and merged into the lower uterine segment.
- Appearance of false pains or spurious labor—False pains are erratic and irregular. The uterus contracts and relaxes and the discomfort remains stationary at the lower abdomen.

2. True labor

   The features of true labor pains are:

   - Painful, rhythmic uterine contractions with hardening of uterus.
   - Progressive dilatation and effacement of cervix
   - Appearance of "show"—blood stained mucoid discharge
   - Formation of the bag of waters.

Features of True and False Labor Pains

True labor pains	*False labor pains*
• The pain arises in the back, radiates to the front of abdomen and thighs	• Pain occurs in the lower abdomen and groin only and remains stationary in the lower abdomen
• Intermittent in nature with increase in intensity, frequency and duration	• Pain is continuous without any rhythmicity
• Associated with hardening of uterus due to retraction of muscle fibers	• There is no hardening of uterus
• Expulsion of "Show" which is the mucus plug mixed with blood from the ruptured capillaries of the cervix	• No effect on dilatation of cervix and no "show"
• Dilatation of internal os and taking up of cervix	• No dilatation and taking up of cervix
• Formation of "bag of waters" due to stretching of the lower uterine segment and detachment of membranes from the decidua	• No formation of bag of waters
• Pain increases after administration of an enema	• Pain diminishes after enema
• Pain occurs due to uterine contraction	• Pain occurs due to a loaded rectum

STAGES OF LABOR AND PHYSIOLOGICAL CHANGES DURING THE DIFFERENT STAGES

1. First Stage—Stage of Dilatation

First stage of labor begins with regular, rhythmic contractions and completes when the cervix is fully dilated.

Average duration is 12 hours in primigravida and 8 hours in multigravida.

Physiological changes

- Contraction and retraction of uterine muscle
- Formation of upper and lower segments

- Development of the retraction ring
- Polarity which is the neuromuscular harmony between the two poles or segments of uterus
- Dilatation and effacement of cervix
- Fetal axis pressure
- Formation of bag of water
- Rupture of membranes.

2. Second Stage—Stage of Expulsion

Second stage of labor begins with the complete dilatation of the cervix and ends with the expulsion of the fetus through the birth canal. Average duration is 1–1½ hours in primigravida and ½ hour in multigravida.

Physiological changes

- Stronger, frequent contractions
- Voluntary contractions of the abdominal muscles–bearing down efforts
- Expulsive, downward force of uterine contractions
- Displacement of pelvic floor (soft tissue displacement)
- Expulsion of the fetus.

Mechanism of Normal Labor

Definition

The mechanisms of labor are the positional movements that the fetus undergoes to accommodate itself to the maternal pelvis as it negotiates the birth canal.

Positional movements

There are several basic movements which take place when the fetus is in a cephalic or vertex presentation.

- Engagement
- Descend throughout
- Flexion
- Internal rotation of the head
- Crowning
- Birth of the head by extension
- Restitution
- Internal rotation of the shoulders
- External rotation of the head as the shoulders rotate internally
- Birth of the shoulders and body by lateral flexion.

Principles

The principles are common to all mechanisms.

- Descend occurs throughout
- The part that leads and first meets the resistance of the pelvic floor will rotate forwards until it comes under the symphysis pubis.
- The part that escapes under the symphysis pubis will pivot around the pubic bone.
- During the mechanism, the fetus turns slightly to take advantage of the widest available space in each plane of the pelvis, i.e. transverse at the brim and anteroposterior at the outlet.

Summary of mechanisms in left occipitoanterior position

- The lie is longitudinal
- The presentation is cephalic
- The position is left occipitoanterior
- The attitude is one of flexion
- The denominator is occiput
- The presenting part is the posterior part of the anterior parietal bone.

Positional movements

- Engagement takes place with sagittal suture of the fetal head in the right oblique diameter of the pelvic inlet and the biparietal diameter in the left oblique. The occiput points to the left iliopectineal eminence and sinciput to the right sacroiliac joint.
- Descend occurs throughout.
- Flexion substitutes the suboccipitobregmatic diameter for the suboccipito-frontal which entered the pelvic inlet.
- Internal rotation takes place as the occiput turns 1/8th of a circle (45 degrees) to the right and sagittal suture comes to the anteroposterior diameter of the pelvis (outlet).
- The occiput escapes under the symphysis pubis and crowning occurs when the head no longer recedes between contractions.
- The head is born by extension, pivoting on the suboccipital-region around the pubic arch.
- Restitution: The occiput turns 1/8th of a circle (45 degrees) to the left to undo the twist on the neck.
- Internal rotation of the shoulders.
  The anterior shoulder reaches the pelvic floor and rotates anteriorly to lie under the symphysis pubis. This movement can be seen as the head turns at the same time in external rotation.
- External rotation of the head.
  The head turns 1/8th of a circle (45 degrees) to the mother's left. The bisacromial diameter comes into the anteroposterior diameter of the maternal pelvis. This occurs in the same direction as restitution and at the same time as internal rotation of shoulders.
- The anterior shoulder escapes under the symphysis pubis and the body is born by lateral flexion.

3. Third Stage—Stage of Placental Delivery

Third stage of labor comprises the phase of placental separation, its descend to the lower segment and finally its expulsion with the membranes. The time begins upon completion of the birth of the baby and ends with the expulsion of placenta. Average duration of third stage is 30 minutes in both primigravidae and multipara.

Physiological changes

- Contraction and retraction of uterus
- Expulsion of placenta and membranes.

Signs of placental separation:

- Sudden trickle or gush of blood
- Lengthening of the umbilical cord visible on the introitus
- Change in the shape of the uterus from discoid to globular
- Change in the position of the uterus as it rises in the abdomen.

Method of separation of the placenta may be central (Schultz method) or marginal (Mathews Duncan method).

4. Fourth Stage

Fourth stage of labor begins with the birth of the placenta and ends one hour later. The first postpartal hour is a critical time of initial recovery from the stress of labor and delivery and requires close observation of the mother.

Physiological changes

- Uterus becomes firm and retracted (hard to touch)
- When contracted, the entwining muscle fibers of the myometrium serve as ligatures to the open blood vessels at the placental site and bleeding is controlled naturally.
- Thrombi form in the distal blood vessels in the decidua do not get released into systemic circulation.

NURSING MANAGEMENT DURING LABOR AND DELIVERY

First Stage of Labor

- Admit the mother in labor room and complete the procedures such as changing to hospital gown, applying identification band, obtaining history and completing chart forms.
- Orient patient to labor and delivery rooms
- Explain admission protocol, labor process and management plans
- Carry out perineal shave and administer enema if not contraindicated
- Start an IV line if indicated and administer fluids
- Provide bodily care and attend to comfort needs.
- Monitor and evaluate maternal well-being, fetal well-being and progress of labor (vital signs of mother, fetal heart sounds, uterine contractions, cervical dilation and fetal descend).
- Encourage to use coping skills such as breathing, relaxation and positioning.
  - During latent phase (1–4 cm dilation): Review breathing technique she can use as labor progresses and encourage ambulation and comfortable position.
  - During active phase (4–8 cm dilation): Provide comfortable position, assist with breathing exercises, provide backup and sacral pressure and analgesia.
  - During transitional phase (8–10 cm dilation): Assist with deep breathing during contractions and shallow breathing and relaxation between contractions.
- Provide information about progress of labor, fetal well-being and how she is coping.

Second Stage of Labor

- Continue to monitor maternal well-being including vital signs, bladder care, hydration and analgesia
- Encourage maternal pushing efforts
- Evaluate perineal integrity and perform episiotomy if appropriate
- Deliver the baby and reassure mother about neonate's condition.

Third Stage of Labor

- Encourage patient to maintain position to facilitate delivery of placenta
- Allow mother to hold and feed the baby if she desires
- Deliver placenta and membranes
- Monitor maternal vital signs, bleeding and consistency of uterus
- Administer oxytocin if required

- Examine placenta and membranes for completeness
- Perform episiotomy suturing if one was made.

Fourth Stage of Labor

- Provide clean gown, perineal pads and comfortable position
- Check vital signs regularly
- Palpate fundus of uterus for contractility
- Massage the fundus and express any clots present
- Inspect the perineum, bladder and change pads
- Offer food and fluids if not contraindicated.

ABNORMAL LABOR (DYSTOCIA)

Dystocia means abnormal or difficult labor or delivery.

Difficulty in labor and delivery may be due to

- Fetal causes such as fault in
  - Attitude, e.g. deficient flexion
  - Position, e.g. posterior positions
  - Presentation, e.g. breech, shoulder
- Maternal causes such as
  - Fault in the force, e.g. abnormal uterine action
  - Fault in passage, e.g. Pelvic abnormalities
  - Poor maternal health, e.g. poor general condition.

MALPOSITIONS AND PRESENTATIONS

1. Occipitoposterior Position

An abnormal position of the vertex which gives rise to difficulty in delivery of the fetus with a normal gynecoid pelvis.

Causes

- Shape of the pelvic inlet. Android or anthropoid pelvis with wide posterior segment favors occipitoposterior position.
- Deflexion of the fetal head—Factors affecting flexion of the head are high pelvic inclination and attachment of placenta in the anterior wall of the uterus.
- Abnormal uterine contraction—This could be the cause or effect of deflexion.

Possible difficulties in occipitoposterior position

- Difficulty in engagement of head
- Premature rupture of membranes
- Prolonged labor with increased risk of fetal asphyxia
- Formation of constriction ring and hypertonic uterine contractions
- Extension of head resulting in brow or face presentation
- Excessive moulding.

Possible outcomes of labor

Favorable outcome

- Long anterior rotation of the head (3/8th of a circle/135 degrees) and delivery as in an anterior position.
- Short posterior rotation and vaginal delivery as face to pubis.

Unfavorable outcomes

- Arrested occipitoposterior position
- Arrest in occipitotransverse or oblique position.

Alternative methods of delivery

- Rotation of head and extraction using Keilland's forceps if the pelvis is adequate and the obstetrician is skilled.
- Application of ventouse. In cases where the pelvis is adequate and nonrotation is due to weak contractions, ventouse is applied to promote flexion, achieve rotation and to extract the head.

Special needs during labor and nursing care

- Occipitoposterior position may lead to disorganized labor especially in primigravidae.
- Monitor the uterine contractions, maternal vital signs, fetal heart sounds and maternal condition at regular intervals.
- Prolonged labor accompanied by marked backache.
- Analgesia, back rub and comfort measures need to be provided.
- Encourage mother to lie on the side, which the fetus faces and to walk about.
- Retention of urine: Catheterization may be required.
- The urge to bear down may present before second stage.

  Examination to confirm dilatation and instructions for appropriate action are indicated.

2. Brow Presentation

Brow presents when the head is midway between full flexion and full extension. The engaging diameter is mentovertical 13.0 cm and is the longest diameter of fetal head.

Causes

- Faults in passage such as contracted pelvis, obliquity of uterus, pendulous abdomen and tumors of the lower uterine segment.
- Faults in the passenger—tumor on the neck of the fetus, cord round the neck, anencephaly.

Outcome of labor

- If the position is unstable it may get converted to either vertex or face presentation.
- If no conversion occurs, there is no mechanism of labor for an average size baby with normal pelvis.

Management

- If brow presentation is diagnosed during pregnancy and there is no contraindications such as contracted pelvis and congenital malformation of the fetus, one may wait for spontaneous correction to occur until one week prior to the expected date of delivery.
- Elective cesarean section, if brow presentation persists with complicating factors such as elderly primigravida and contracted pelvis.
- If diagnosed during labor, with mother and baby in good condition, cesarean section is the best method.
- If obstructed labor with dead baby, craniotomy may be the choice for management.

3. Face Presentation

A cephalic presentation where the presenting part is the face. The attitude of the fetus shows complete flexion of the limbs with extension of the spine. There is complete extension of the head so that the occiput is in contact with the back. The denominator is mentum.

Causes

Maternal

- Minor degree of disproportion particularly in flat type of pelvis
- Multiparity with pendulous abdomen
- Lateral obliquity of the uterus.

Fetal

- Anencephaly
- Congenital goiter
- Dolichocephalic head with long anteroposterior diameter
- Short umbilical cord round the neck of the fetus several times
- Increased tone of the extensor group of neck muscles.

Diagnosis

- Antenatal diagnosis is seldom made
- Intranatal diagnosis: mentoposterior is easier to diagnose
- Vaginal examination:

  Early in labor—diagnosis is difficult as the head is high and the parts are difficult to feel through the bulging membranes.

  Late in labor—after rupture of membranes the following features can be palpated:

  - Mouth and malar eminences
  - Sucking effect of mouth
  - Hard alveolar margins
  - Absence of meconium staining on the examining finger.

  However, the facial parts are often obscured due to edema. The findings must be clearly distinguished from those of breech presentation in which case:

  - Ischial tuberosities can be felt in line with the anus
  - Absence of alveolar margins
  - Meconium is always present on the examining finger
  - Grip of the anal sphincter may be felt on the finger.

Management

- Sonography should be done to confirm the diagnosis, to exclude bony, congenital malformation of the fetus and to note the size of the baby.
- If the pelvis is normal and adequate, labor is allowed to proceed, taking care to prevent exhaustion from prolonged labor.
- If the pelvis is contracted and the patient is an elderly primigravida or multigravida with bad obstetric history, treatment is cesarean section.

4. Transverse or Shoulder Presentation

When the long axis of the fetus lies perpendicular to the maternal spine, it is called a transverse lie. The shoulder is most likely to present over the cervical opening during labor.

Shoulder presentation is about 5 times greater in multigravidae than in primigravidae

Causes

- Contracted pelvis
- Uterine deformities
- Prematurity
- Lax abdomen in multigravidae
- Hydramnios
- Multiple pregnancy
- Hydrocephalus and anencephalus
- Placenta previa.

Types

- Dorsoanterior
- Dorsoposterior.

Diagnosis

- Inspection: The uterus appears broader and asymmetrical with the height of fundus less than the period of amenorrhea.
- Transverse bulging of the abdomen with bulging of flanks.

Palpation

- Hard, ballotable, rounded head on one iliac fossa, at a lower level than breech.
- Soft, broad and irregular breech to one side of midline.
- The back is felt anteriorly across the long axis in dorsoanterior or irregular, small parts are felt anteriorly in dorsoposterior.
- The lower pole of the uterus is found empty in the prenatal period, (During labor, it may be occupied by the shoulder).

Auscultation

Fetal heart sounds are heard much below the umbilicus. It is quite distinct in dorsoanterior position and indistinct in dorsoposterior.

Vaginal examination (During labor)

Elongated bag of membranes can be felt if it does not rupture prematurely. Presenting part may be high up and floating.

After rupture of membranes, the shoulder can be indentified by palpating the following parts—the acromion process, the scapula, the clavicle and axilla. Palpating the ribs and intercostal spaces is the characteristic landmark.

Occasionally an arm is found prolapsed. Hand can be differentiated from a foot and an elbow from a knee.

Ultrasonography can diagnose transverse lie and position of placenta.

Management

There is no mechanism of labor in transverse lie/shoulder presentation and an average size baby fails to pass through an average size pelvis. If diagnosed early and the fetus is alive, cesarean section is done.

If labor is advanced with follicle stimulating hormone (FHS) absent and mother exhausted, resuscitation of mother is done with IV fluids. When her condition improves, destructive operations such as decapitation or evisceration is done depending upon the position of the neck. If the fetus is large, even cesarean section is done for maternal safety.

5. Breech Presentation (Figure 8)

It is the presentation in which the lie of the fetus is longitudinal and the podalic pole presents at the pelvic brim.

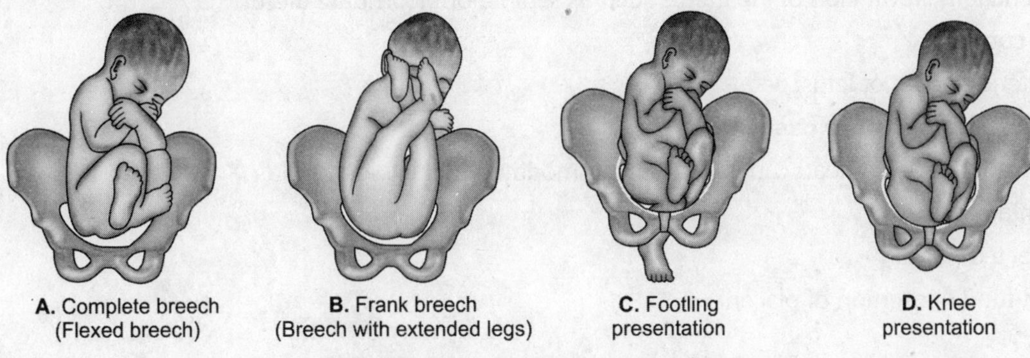

Figure 8: Types of breech presentation

Varieties

- Complete breech (Flexed breech)
  The normal attitude of full flexion is present. The thighs are flexed at the hips, legs are flexed at the knees, and arms flexed over chest. The presenting part consists of the two buttocks and external genitalia and two feet. It is commonly present in multiparae.
- Incomplete breech
  Occurs due to varying degrees of extension of thighs or legs at the podalic pole. Three varieties are possible.
  a. Breech with extended legs or frank breech
     In this condition, the thighs are flexed on the trunk and the legs are extended at the knee joints. The presenting part consists of the two buttocks and external genitalia only.
     It is commonly present in primigravidae.
  b. Footling presentation
     One or both feet present because neither hips nor knees are fully flexed. The feet are lower than the buttocks.
  c. Knee presentation
     Thighs are extended but the knees are flexed, bringing the knees down to present at the brim.

Clinical varieties

a. Uncomplicated breech
   Breech presentation with no other associated obstetric complications.
b. Complicated breech
   The presentation is associated with conditions which adversely influence the prognosis such as prematurity, twins, contracted pelvis, placenta previa, etc.

Causes

- **Prematurity**
  There is higher incidence of breech in earlier weeks of pregnancy. Smaller size of the fetus and comparatively larger volume of amniotic fluid allow the fetus to undergo spontaneous version by kicking movements until 36th week when the position becomes stabilized.
- **Factors preventing spontaneous version such as**
  - Breech with extended legs
  - Twins
  - Oligohydramnios
  - Congenital malformation of the uterus such as septate or bicornuate uterus
  - Short cord
  - Intrauterine death of fetus.
- **Favorable adaptation in cases like**
  - Hydrocephalus—big head can be well accommodated in the wide fundus
  - Placenta previa
  - Contracted pelvis
  - Cornu-fundal insertion of placenta.

Diagnosis

- Abdominal palpation reveals the cephalic pole at the fundus and podalic pole below
- Auscultation—FHS is heard above the umbilicus
- Ultrasonography—diagnosis can be confirmed by sonography
- Vaginal examination
  In early labor, vaginal examination will reveal the following:
  - Presenting part high
  - Slow dilatation of the cervix
  - Sausage-shaped, elongation of forewater
  - Sometimes presenting part (foot) can be felt in the bag of water
  - Premature rupture of membranes.

Management

Delivery of fetus in breech presentation occurs in three phases

- Delivery of the breech or buttocks
- Delivery of the shoulder
- Delivery of the head.

Selection for vaginal delivery or elective cesarean section is done at term. The woman is admitted into hospital at 39 to 40 weeks for cesarean section.

Women with breech in labor anticipating vaginal delivery requires special attention.

- Enema is restricted to reduce the chance of rupture of membranes.
- Mother is kept in bed to preserve the membranes intact and to allow the cervix to dilate fully.
- Hydration is maintained with IV fluids.

- Arrangements to be made for forceps application and resuscitation of newborn.
- Oxytocics to be kept ready to treat possible postpartum hemorrhage.

Management of Arrest of Breech

- Arrest of after coming head

  The after coming head can get arrested due to:

  - Hydrocephalus
  - Contracted pelvis
  - Deflexed head
  - Posteriorly-rotated head
  - Contraction ring around neck
  - Rigid perineum (arrest at the outlet).

Methods of delivering the after coming head

- Burns Marshall's method
- Mauriceau Smellie Veit method (Jaw flexion and shoulder traction)
- Pinard's maneuver for extended legs
- Extraction using forceps.

If the head is arrested and the fetus dead, craniotomy may be done.

Principles involved in the delivery of after coming head

- Cervix should be fully dilated
- Head should be in flexed position
- Effective suprapubic pressure should be provided
- The head should be delivered within 5 to 8 minutes, after the delivery of the trunk.

6. Compound Presentation

Presence of a hand or foot or both alongside the head or both hands by the side of the breech is called compound presentation.

The commonest compound presentation is head with the hand

The rarest is the head with a hand and foot.

Causes

Conditions preventing engagement of the head where a hand or foot slips by the side of the head.

- Prematurity
- Contracted pelvis
- Pelvic tumors
- Multiple pregnancy
- Macerated fetus
- High head with early rupture of membranes
- Hydramnios.

Diagnosis

Feeling the limb alongside head when cervix is sufficiently dilated.

Management

Management depends on the stage of labor, maturity of the fetus, number of fetuses, (singleton or twins) pelvic adequacy and associated cord prolapse. In cases of single, live fetus with contracted pelvis or cord prolapse delivery by cesarean section is the choice. In uncomplicated cases, if there is a favorable sign of elevation of prolapsed limb during uterine contraction in the first stage and the condition of fetus is good, replacement of the prolapsed limb is done under general anesthesia in the second stage followed by forceps delivery.

7. Cord Prolapse

Abnormal descend of the umbilical cord by the side of the presenting part.

Types of cord prolapse

- Occult prolapse—The cord lies alongside but not in front of the presenting part and is not felt by the fingers on internal examination.
- Cord presentation—The cord is slipped down below the presenting part and lies in front of it in the intact bag of membranes.
- Cord prolapse—The cord lies in front of the presenting part inside the vagina or outside the vulva following rupture of the membranes.

Predisposing factors

Any situation where the presenting part is neither well applied to the lower uterine segment nor well down in the pelvis allowing a loop of cord to slip down in front of the presenting part. These include:

- Malpresentations
- Prematurity
- Multiple pregnancy
- Polyhydramnios
- High head
- High parity.

Diagnosis

Occult prolapse

- Peristence of variable deceleration of fetal heart rate pattern on continuous fetal monitoring in an otherwise normal labor.
- Persistent funic soufflé with irregular heart sounds.

Cord presentation

- Feeling the pulsation of the cord through the intact membranes
- Evidence of decelerations in fetal heart monitoring.

Cord prolapse

- The cord is felt below or beside the presenting part on vaginal examination
- A loop of cord visible at the vulva
- Cord is felt at the cervical os if the presenting part is high
- Pulsation can be felt between contractions if the fetus is alive.

Management

- Discontinue vaginal examinations to reduce the risk of rupturing the membranes
- Obtain continuous or frequent fetal heart sounds
- Keep patient in exaggerated Sim's position to minimize cord compression
- Cesarean section is the most likely method of delivery.

FORCEPS DELIVERY

Forceps delivery is a means of extracting the fetus with the aid of obstetric forceps when it is inadvisable or impossible for the mother to complete the delivery by her own efforts.

Forceps are also used to assist the delivery of the after coming head of the breech and on occasion to withdraw the head up and out of the pelvis at cesarean section.

Types of Obstetric Forceps Currently Used

Three varieties are commonly used in present day obstetric practice

1. Long curved forceps with or without axis traction device
2. Short curved forceps
3. Kielland's forceps.

Classification According to Level of Application

1. High forceps operation
   Application of forceps on a fetal head where the biparietal diameter has not yet passed the pelvic brim that is a nonengaged head. In present day practice, cesarean is preferred to this type of forceps application.
2. Midforceps operation
   Application of the forceps on a head, the biparietal diameter of which has passed the pelvic brim but not reached the level of ischial spines.
3. Low forceps operation
   Application of the forceps on a head, the biparietal diameter of which has passed the level of ischial spines.
4. Outlet forceps
   Application on a fetal head lying on the perineum and is visible at the introitus between contractions.

Indications of Forceps Application

Maternal indications

Delay in the second stage that is head on the perineum for 20 to 30 minutes without advancement as in following conditions:

1. Maternal distress
2. Preeclampsia or eclampsia
3. Heart disease
4. Failure to bear down due to regional blocks, paraplegia or psychiatric disorders
5. Vaginal birth after cesarean delivery (VBAC).

Fetal indications

1. Fetal distress in the second stage
2. Cord prolapse
3. Aftercoming head of breech
4. Low birth weight baby
5. Postmaturity.

Prerequisites for forceps delivery

1. Cervix fully dilated and effaced
2. Membranes ruptured
3. Suitable presentation and position of head for application of forceps blades to the sides of head.
4. Fetal head engaged
5. No appreciable CPD
6. Bladder emptied
7. Good uterine contractions.

Preparation of the mother

- Adequate explanation of the procedure and the need for it
- Adequate and appropriate analgesia
- Lithotomy position as the obstetrician gets ready to apply the forceps.

Preparation to receive the baby

- Resuscitation equipment and medications
- Presence of pediatrician.

VACUUM EXTRACTION (VENTOUSE DELIVERY)

Ventouse is an instrumental device designed to assist the delivery by creating a vacuum between it and the fetal scalp.

Indications

1. Deep transverse arrest with adequate pelvis
2. Delay in descend of the second twin baby
3. Occiput posterior or occiput lateral position
4. Delay in the second stage or late first stage
5. As an alternative to forceps operation except in face presentation, aftercoming head of breech, fetal distress and prematurity
6. Maternal exhaustion.

Conditions to be Fulfilled

1. No bony resistance below the head
2. Engaged head of a singleton baby
3. Cervix dialated at least 6 cm.

Preparation of the Mother and Articles

1. Adequate explanation to mother
2. Preparation and position as for forceps delivery
3. Appropriate size cup for application on fetal head
4. Pudendal block or perineal infiltration
5. Ventous in good working condition.

NORMAL PUERPERIUM

Puerperium is the period following childbirth during which the body tissues especially the pelvic organs revert back approximately to the prepregnant state both anatomically and physiologically. Retrogressive changes occur in reproductive organs with the exception of mammary glands which show features of activity.

Involution is the process whereby genital organs revert back approximately to the state as they were before pregnancy.

Duration of Puerperium

Puerperium begins as soon as the placenta is expelled and lasts for approximately six weeks. The postpartum period is divided into:

- Immediate puerperium—the first 24 hours
- Early puerperium up to 7 days
- Remote puerperium up to 6 weeks

The remote puerperium includes the period of involution. Majority of nonlactating women resume menstrual cycles at this time or soon thereafter.

Anatomical and Physiological Changes during Puerperium

Uterus

Immediately following delivery, the uterus weighs about 1 kg and its size approximately 20 weeks of pregnancy. Height of fundus is about 5” from the symphysis pubis. Daily, the height of uterus comes down by ½ an inch. By 12th day the fundus is at the level of symphysis pubis. Uterine involution is complete by 6 weeks at which time the organ weighs less than 100 g, slightly larger following pregnancy. The placental site contracts rapidly to a size less than half the diameter of placenta. This contraction causes constriction and permits occlusion of underlying blood vessels. The resulting hemostasis leads to endometrial necrosis. Endometrial regeneration is completed by 6 to 8 weeks.

Lower uterine segment

Immediately following delivery, the lower segment becomes a thin, flabby, collapsed structure. It reverts back to normal size and shape in few weeks.

Cervix

The cervix contracts slowly, the external os admits two fingers for a few days and narrows down to admit the tip of a finger by the end of first week. The external os never reverts back to nulliparous state.

Vagina

The distensible vagina seen soon after birth takes 4 to 8 weeks to involute. It regains its tone but never to the virginal state. The rugae reappear partially by 3rd week, but not to the prepregnant state. Hymen is lacerated and is represented by nodular rags called the carunculae myrtiformes. Broad ligaments and round ligaments recover from stretching and laxation after several weeks. Pelvic floor and pelvic fascia also take long time to involute from the stretching effect during delivery.

Lochia

Lochia is the vaginal discharge during puerperium containing blood, mucus, shreds of epithelium, decidual membranes and cholesterin crystals and is usually present for two weeks. It has a peculiar offensive, fishy smell and is alkaline in reaction.

Depending on the variation of color, it is named as:

- Lochia rubra—red in color and contains shreds of epithelium and blood. Its duration is 3 to 4 days.
- Lochia serosa—serous color discharge (yellowish or pink or pale brownish) which contains mostly WBC. Its duration is 5 to 9 days.
- Lochia alba—pale white in color contains decidual cells, leukocytes and granular epithelial cells. Its duration is 10 to 15 days.

Normal duration may extend up to 3 weeks.

Excessive lochia discharge is due to retained products of conception, infection, defective suckling of baby.

The discharge may be excessive following cesarean delivery, twin delivery and hydramnios. It may be scanty following premature labor.

Persistence of red color beyond the normal limit indicates subinvolution or retained bits of conceptus.

Duration of the lochia alba beyond 3 weeks suggests local genital lesion.

General Physiological Changes

Temperature

There may be slight reactionary rise of temperature following delivery by 0.5 degree F.

Temperature normally comes down within 12 hours. On the 3rd day, there may be slight rise of temperature due to breast engorgement which usually does not last for more than 24 hours. If the temperature stays high for longer period, genitourinary tract infection should be ruled out.

Pulse

Pulse rate is likely to be raised for few hours after normal delivery and settles down to normal by second postpartum day. The pulse rate is quite unstable during puerperium—it may be raised when the mother gets excited or has after pains and may be lowered due to rest and increased fluid excretion.

Urinary tract

The bladder may be overdistended without any desire to pass urine. Stagnation of urine along with devitalized bladder wall contribute to urinary tract infection in puerperium.

The insensitivity of bladder resulting from trauma during labor and dilatation of ureters and renal pelvis return to normal by 8 weeks.

Gastrointestinal tract

In early puerperium, women experience increased thirst due to loss of fluid during labor (diuresis, perspiration and bleeding). Constipation may be present due to slight intestinal paresis. Lack of tone of the perineal and abdominal muscles and pain in the perineal region are common.

Weight loss

In addition to the weight loss as a consequence of the expulsion of the uterine contents, a further loss of about 2 kg occurs during puerperium because of diuresis.

Blood values

Immediately following delivery, there is slight decrease in blood volume due to dehydration and blood loss. The blood volume returns to the nonpregnant level by the second week. RBC count, hematocrit level and platelet count are decreased and WBC count is elevated until second week. ESR remains elevated and a state of hypercoagulability persists for a week after delivery.

Menstruation and Ovulation

Menstruation returns by 6th week in 40% and by 12th week in 80% of nonbreastfeeding mothers.

In breastfeeding mothers, menstruation may be suspended until the baby stops breastfeeding in about 70% and for others it may start earlier. Ovulation may occur as early as 4 weeks in non-lactating mothers and about 10 weeks after delivery in lactating mothers.

Ovulation may precede the first menstrual period in about 1/3rd and it is possible for the woman to become pregnant before she menstruated following her delivery.

Lactation

Preparation for lactation starts during pregnancy although lactation starts following delivery.

The physiological basis of lactation is divided into 4 phases:

- Preparation of breasts—mammogenesis
- Synthesis and secretion from the breast alveoli—lactogenesis
- Ejection of milk—galactokinesis
- Maintenance of lactation—galactopoiesis.

In the first postpartum week, the total amount of milk yield in 24 hours is calculated to be 60 multiplied by the number of postpartum days and is expressed in milliliters. Thus, the milk yield on 3rd postpartum day will be about 180 mL. By the end of second week the milk yield per feeding will become 120 to 180 mL.

NURSING MANAGEMENT OF POSTPARTAL CLIENTS

The principles in management of postpartal clients are to:

1. Restore the health of mother
2. Prevent infection
3. Promote and maintain lactation
4. Help the mother take care of the baby
5. Motivate the mother for contraceptive acceptance.

Immediate Attention

In the immediate hours following delivery, the mother's temperature, pulse, respiration and blood pressure must be checked regularly to monitor her general condition.

She may be given a drink or something to eat if she is hungry. Measures to promote sleep must be instituted.

Rest and Ambulation

Physician's order for rest and ambulation may depend on the intrapartal course, the mother's condition and the type of analgesia and anesthesia used. A woman who had a long, difficult labor, is exhausted. Those who hemorrhaged or groggy from medication may need rest for several hours.

A woman who entered labor rested, progressed normally and is alert may be ambulated as required with assistance at first. Early ambulation provides a sense of wellbeing, promotes better drainage of lochia and hastens involution of uterus.

Additional benefits of early ambulation include faster healing of episiotomy, regular bowel movement and reduced chance of postpartum thrombophlebitis and urinary tract infection. The range of activities should be increased gradually.

Eight hours sleep during night and two hours after noon are recommended.

Diet

The woman must be given regular diet and plenty of fluids after delivery. For a woman who hemorrhaged, high protein diet and iron supplements are recommended. Women who breastfeed require high calories, adequate protein, plenty of fluids, minerals and vitamins.

Perineal Care

Immediately after delivery, cold compress may be applied to the perineum to decrease traumatic edema and discomfort. Perineal area should be gently cleaned with plain soap or antiseptic solution 2 to 3 times a day and after voiding and defecation.

Episiotomy wound should be inspected daily. Instructions regarding handwashing, cleansing of perineum and careful application and removal of perineal pads must be given.

Care of Bladder and Bowel

The woman should be encouraged to pass urine 6 to 8 hours following delivery and thereafter at 4 to 6 hours interval. Failure to empty the bladder 8 hours after delivery or incomplete emptying evidenced by presence of residual urine of more than 60 mL requires evacuation of the bladder by catheterization.

Constipation may occur in most women following delivery. For those who do not move their bowels, stool softeners or tap water enema may be prescribed on the 2nd postpartum day.

Care of Breasts

The breasts should be examined daily regardless of the feeding method. Presence of redness or soreness to be noted and mother given instructions regarding handwashing, cleaning of breasts before and after feeding and wearing of wellfitting brassiers for comfort and support.

Postpartum Immunization for Rh Negative Mothers

For Rh negative mothers who deliver Rh positive babies, if the coombs test on cord blood is negative, 1 mL (300 mg) Rh (D) immunoglobulin is given after cross matching. (Mother's RBCs are crossmatched with 1:1000 dilution of Rh immunoglobulin before preparing the injection).

The injection is given intramuscularly within 72 hours after delivery.

Postpartum Exercises

Postnatal exercises should be started as soon after delivery as possible in order to improve circulation, strengthen pelvic floor and abdominal muscles.

Circulatory Exercises

Foot and leg exercises must be performed very frequently in the immediate postpartum period to improve circulation, reduce edema and prevent deep vein thrombosis.

Pelvic Floor Exercises

Mothers should be encouraged to do perineal exercises as often as possible in order to regain full bladder control, prevent uterine prolapse and ensure normal sexual satisfaction in future. For this exercise, the mother may sit, stand or halflie with legs slightly apart. Close and draw up around the anal passage as though preventing a bowel action, then repeat for front passages (vagina and urethra) as if to stop the flow of urine in midstream. Hold for as long as possible up to 10 seconds,(to a count of six) breathing normally, then relax. Repeat up to ten times. Pelvic floor exercises should be continued for 2 to 3 months.

Abdominal Exercises

These help abdominal muscles to regain tone as soon as possible after delivery in order to prevent backache and regain former figure. Abdominal exercises include abdominal breathing, head and shoulder raising, leg raising, pelvic tilt, knee rolling, hip hitching and sit ups.

Mothers who had cesarean deliveries can start abdominal tightening, pelvic tilting and knee rolling exercises gently after 24 hours. Pelvic floor exercises, head raising and hip hitching can be started after 4 to 5 days.

Health Education

Mothers should receive the following instructions before they leave the hospital.

- Postpartum check-up six weeks later
- Problems to be reported to physician in the postpartum period
- Methods of contraception
- Physiology of puerperium and return of menstruation
- Diet for lactating mothers
- Breastfeeding
- Immunization for the baby
- Management of minor newborn problems
- Care of eyes and umbilical cord
- Diet in postpartum period and for lactation.

NATIONAL IMMUNIZATION SCHEDULE

Age	*Vaccine*	*Dosage*	*Route of Administration*
At birth	BCG (For institutional deliveries) OPU zero dose (For institutional deliveries)	0.05 mL 2 drops	Intradermal Oral
6 weeks	BCG if not given at birth DPT1 and OPV1	0.05 mL 0.5 mL 2 drops/0.5 mL	Intradermal Deep intramuscular Oral
10 weeks	DPT2 OPV2	0.5 mL 2 drops	Deep IM Oral
14 weeks	DPT3 OPV3	0.5 mL 2 drops	Deep IM Oral
9 months	M M R	0.5 mL	Subcutaneous
16–24 months	DPT (Booster dose) OPV (Booster dose)	0.5 mL 2 drops	Deep IM Oral
5–6 years	DT (A second dose of DT after 4 weeks if no evidence of previous immunization with DPT)	0.5 mL	Deep IM
10–16 years	Tetanus Toxoid (A second dose of TT after 4 weeks if no evidence of previous immunization with DPT, DT or TT)	0.5 mL	Deep IM
For pregnant women	TT1 in early pregnancy TT2 after 4 weeks	0.5 mL	Intramuscular

NEWBORN BABY

Definitions and Terms

- Newborn/Neonate

  The term used for a baby from birth through the first 28 days of life.
- Term baby

  A baby born at term (between 38–42 weeks), has an average birth weight for the country, has breathed and cried immediately following birth, established independent rhythmic respiration and adapted quickly to the extrauterine environment.
- Low birth weight baby

  A newborn weighing less than 2.5 kg (normal birth weight in India) at birth irrespective of gestational age.
- Very low birth weight baby

  Newborns weighing 1500 g or less at birth
- Extremely low birth weight baby

  Newborns weighing 1000 g or less at birth
- Preterm baby

  A baby born before 37 completed weeks of gestation (calculating from the first day of last menstruation).
- Small for gestational age (SGA) baby

  A newborn with low birth weight for its gestational age
- Post-term baby

  A baby born after 42 weeks of gestation

- Stillborn baby

  A baby born after 28th completed week of gestation with no sign of life and absence of breathing.

Immediate Care of the Newborn

The primary concern for the baby at the time of delivery is the establishment of respiration. Prompt onset of breathing is essential to subsequent mental and physical development. When the head is delivered, suctioning of the mouth and nares is done with a bulb syringe or mucus sucker to prevent aspiration of mucus or amniotic fluid.

Soon after birth rubbing of the back or flicking of the sole of the foot is done to provide stimulation for respiration. The newborn must be dried and wet linen removed at the earliest followed by wrapping in warm blanket to prevent heat loss.

Apgar scoring at 1 minute and at 5 minutes to be recorded.

The cord is to be clamped and cut as soon as convenient following birth of the baby. Early clamping should be done in case of Rh incompatibility, to prevent antibody transfer from the mother to baby.

If a radiant warmer is available the newborn may be placed under the warmer until temperature stabilizes.

A quick check must be made at this stage to detect any gross abnormality. Identification tags are to be tied on the wrists of mother and newborn.

- **Apgar scoring**

  Sixty seconds after the complete birth of the baby, the following five objective signs are evaluated and each given a score of 0, 1 or 2. A score of 10 indicates that the baby is in best possible condition. A normal infant in good condition at birth will achieve an Apgar score of 7 to 10.

  If the score is less than 7 medical aid is necessary.

  Apgar score evaluated at one minute is useful to decide on resuscitation. Apgar score at 5 minutes is useful to assess the effectiveness of resuscitative measures taken.

APGAR SCORE

Sign		***Score***		
		0	***1***	***2***
1.	Heart rate	Absent	Less than 100 bpm	More than 100 bpm
2.	Respiratory effort	Absent	Slow, irregular	Good, crying
3.	Muscle tone	Limp	Some flexion of limbs	Active
4.	Reflex response to stimulus (to catheter in nostrils)	None	Minimal grimace	Cough or sneeze
5.	Color	Blue, pale	Body pink, extremities blue	Completely pink

FEATURES OF A NORMAL NEWBORN

Posture

A newborn baby assumes a posture of general flexion

- Flexion of limbs, spine and head resembling the posture during intrauterine life.

Head

- The shape of the head depends on the mode of presentation and moulding of the head during labor. Head circumference varies from 33 to 35 cm. Moulding and caput succedaneum disappears within a day or two after birth.
- Temperature, Respiration, Heart rate and blood pressure. The temperature shows variations as the heat regulation mechanism is not well developed in newborn. The rectal temperature varies from 97° to 99°F.

  Breathing varies from 40 to 60 per minute with an average of 44 per minute and regular.

  Heart rate varies from 120 to 140 per minute.

  The blood pressure varies from systolic 60 to 80 and diastolic below 50 mm of Hg.

Skin

The skin color is pinkish red. Lanugo present at birth gradually disappears. Non-specific rashes may appear. The skin may show yellowish tinge on 2nd or 3rd day and gradually disappear by 7th day. This is the physiological jaundice which appears in about 10% of newborns and is due to excessive bilirubin production following rapid breakdown of red cells and imperfect excretion of bile pigments by the neonatal liver.

Abdomen

The cord becomes dry and shriveled up by 5th day and falls off by 7th day by a process of dry gangrene that sets in it.

Genitalia

Vulval engorgement, leukorrhea or at times, slight vaginal bleeding may occur during the first week in female newborns. It is due to the withdrawal of maternal estrogen from the newborn.

Urine

The baby usually passes urine during or immediately after delivery. During the first week, urinary output is very low to the extent of 60 mL in 24 hours and thereafter the amount increases. The color is at first dark and soon becomes colorless with low specific gravity.

Stools

Meconium is normally passed 3 to 4 times a day for 2–3 days. A delay in the initial passage of meconium for more than 12 hours after birth requires observation to rule out obstruction in the alimentary tract. Meconium is sticky, dark green and odorless. Transitional stool occurs gradually from 3rd day and is yellowish brown in color with a characteristic smell due to the development of bacterial flora in the lower intestine. Milk stools are passed by the end of first week.

In breastfed babies, the stools are soft and golden yellow in color, sour smelling and acid in reaction. In bottle-fed babies, the stools are hard, pale in color, foul smelling and alkaline in reaction. Stool frequency varies from one or two to 5 to 6 in 24 hours.

Weight

In normal full-term babies, there is a loss of approximately 10% of body weight in the first 4 to 5 days. The loss is due to loss of water through the skin, lungs, urine and bowel while intake is very little. In bigger babies, the loss is more. After the first week, the baby makes a regular gain of 40 to 60 g per day. After the second week, the rate of weight gain is about 25 to 30 g per day for the first three months.

Measurements

Variations in measurements may be seen, but relationships are consistent. Average newborn measurements are–head circumference 35 cm, chest circumference 32 cm, crown–rump length 35 cm and crown–heel length 51 cm.

Behavior and Reflexes of Neonates

- Crying and sleeping
  A healthy newborn baby usually sleeps during most part of the day and night. The baby usually cries when hungry or wet.
- Sucking and swallowing reflexes are present at birth. Yawning and sneezing at intervals may be present in the neonatal period.
- Rooting reflex—it is the movement of the mouth for sucking of the nipple when corner of the infant's mouth is lightly touched.
- The grasp reflex—when any object like finger or pencil is grasped by the flexed palm of the infant, it is called palmar reflex. This reflex is present in a healthy term baby and weak in a preterm baby.
- The moro reflex/startle reflex
  This reflex is elicited by sudden jerking of the cot or even a loud noise. The newborn suddenly throws his arms upwards and outwards with the hands and fingers extended with a vigorous extensor tremor of the forelimbs which rapidly subsides.
- Tonic neck reflex—the baby is placed on his/her back and the head is turned to one side. The arm and leg on the same side extend and the opposite arm and leg flex and the baby assumes a fencing position. If the head is turned to the opposite side, same reaction occurs. This reflex is present for 2 to 3 months. If it persists longer than this time. It usually indicates neurological dysfunction.
- Walking/stepping reflex—the baby is held so that the soles of the feet touches a flat surface. This stimulates the baby to a stepping or dancing movement with both legs. This reflex is present at birth and disappears after 3 to 4 weeks.
- Traction response/head lag reflex—when pulled to an upright position by the wrists to a sitting position, the head will lag initially and then right itself momentarily before falling foreward on to the chest.
- Ventral suspension—when held prone suspended over the examiner's arm, the baby shortly holds his head level with his body and flexes his limbs.
- Babinski reflex—the lateral aspect of the sole of the infant's foot is scratched, going from heel to toes. The reflex shows a dorsal flexion of the big toe. The reflex is present until 9th or 10th month. Poor response may be due to nervous system immaturity and absence may be due to defects in the lower spinal cord.

Daily Care and Observation of the Newborn

Daily assessment is important for identification of early problems. For a normal newborn, the following care and observations should be carried out every day.

- **Vital signs check**
  - Respirations are to be regular, smooth and quiet with a rate about 40 per minute.
  - Temperature by axilla or groin to be within normal range.

- **Weight**

  Weight to be checked and evaluated daily. Loss of 10% of body weight in the first week is normal. Most babies regain their birth weight in 7 to 10 days.
- **Color**

  Any cyanosis should be reported to the pediatrician immediately. Jaundice may be noted from the third day. It is abnormal if jaundice appears earlier, deepens or persists beyond 7th day.
- **The head**

  Assessment of the anterior fontanelle which should be level with the scalp (not bulging or depressed), resolution of caput succedaneum and moulding are important. Appearance of any swelling such as cephalhematoma should also be noted.
- **The mouth**

  Mouth should be clean and moist. Adherent white patch indicates oral thrush.
- **Umbilical cord**

  The base of umbilical cord is inspected and cleaned with alcohol daily.
- **Elimination**

  The stools are observed and compared with expected normal in relation to the neonate's age and feeding. Constipation, loose stools or sore buttocks to be noted. The frequency of passing urine in 24 hours should be noted.
- **Bath**

  Cleansing the skin may be done daily or as frequently as required, especially the face, skin flexures and napkin area to prevent excoriation. Daily bath is recommended if the baby is at home. As the baby is undressed, skin is inspected for rashes, septic spots or abrasions.

INFANT FEEDING

Majority of women decide when they conceive that they want to breastfeed their babies. Some may not take a decision early. However, it is important to teach all pregnant women about the benefits of breastfeeding. Preparation for breastfeeding must begin when pregnancy starts altering the breasts and nipples. All pregnant women must be given the following instructions:

- Wear a comfortable brassier that does not compress the breasts and support the increasing weight.
- Cleanse the breasts daily with water and wipe with a soft clean cloth followed by careful cleansing.
- If the nipples are flat or inverted, nipple rolling to be done to bring them out with lightly lubricated thumb and index fingers. Roll the nipple of each breast for approximately 30 seconds every day in the 9th month.
- The importance and benefits of breast milk and exclusive breastfeeding.

Benefits of Breastfeeding

- It is always available at right temperature
- It is free of bacterial contamination
- It is easily digestable and nourishing. Breastfed babies thrive much better and are less susceptible to infection.
- Breastfed infants become less obese
- Breast milk contains the essential vitamins and necessary food factors in proper proportion.

- Breastfeeding helps in faster involution of uterus for the mother
- Mother gets more opportunity to bond with the baby and baby gets a feeling of security
- Milk allergy is very rare with breast milk
- Breast milk is a more effective rehydration fluid than plain water
- In the immediate postpartum period frequent sucking at the breasts, is the best stimulus for milk production
- Breast milk offers protection against infection and deficiency states as it contains:
  - Vitamin D which offers protection against rickets
  - Lactoferrin which hinders the growth of *E. coli* and provides protection against gastroenteritis
  - Bifidus factor which promotes *Lactobacillus* and inhibits growth of *E. coli*
  - Lysozyme which offers protection against infection
- Breast milk gives passive immunity to the baby as it contains protective antibodies
- Breast milk has a laxative action and offers no danger of allergy.

Hormonal Control of Milk Production and Ejection

When the placenta is delivered, estrogen and progesterone levels fall and cause prolactin levels to rise in the mother. Prolactin which is secreted from the anterior pituitary gland stimulates the production of milk in the alveoli cells of the breasts. The 'let down' reflex occurs when the baby begins to suckle at the breast.

As the baby sucks, the nerve endings in the nipple and areola stimulate the posterior pituitary which in turn secretes oxytocin. Oxytocin causes the myoepithelial cells in the alveoli and lactiferous sinuses to contract and eject milk. The hind milk that is ejected after the let-down is rich in fats and nutrients. The pituitary gland is controlled by the hypothalamus and hence the let-down reflex is influenced by emotions such as fear, pain, anxiety and environment.

Management of Breastfeeding

- Time of first feeding

  The baby can be put to mother's breast within an hour after birth. The sucking reflex is strongest in the first half hour after birth.
- Feeding schedule
  - The baby should be permitted to suck freely at the breast frequently and without any fixed time table (demand feeding).
  - This will ensure that the newborn has the full benefit of colostrum. The baby takes feed frequently in the beginning but gradually settles to a 3 to 4 hour schedule.
  - As regards night feeds, it is desirable that at least one feed is given for first three months. Later the baby may not need night feeds.
- Duration of each feed

  On the first day 2 to 3 minutes on each breast may be sufficient and the duration may be increased by a minute per breast per day. After the initial week the baby should be fed for 7 to 10 minutes at each breast when he indicates he is hungry. Most babies will settle down to feeding every 3 to 4 hours and gain weight satisfactorily.
- Beginning breastfeeding
  - Instruct mother to clean her nipple and areola with wet swab or soft cloth before and after each feed.
  - Advice mother to keep clean hands, short nails and wear clean clothes.

- Teach the technique of breastfeeding:
  - Assume comfortable position–sitting or lying in bed
  - Place the nipple and areola into baby's mouth
  - Relax and give full attention to baby while feeding and keep the baby awake while feeding.
  - Rotate breasts as the starting and ending breast to provide for complete emptying of both breasts.
- Burping (breaking the wind)

  At the end of feeding from each breast, burping is done for five minutes to prevent regurgitation and vomiting. Burping helps the baby to bring out swallowed air from stomach. For burping, hold the baby in upright position either on the shoulder or lap and gently pat the back upwards until the swallowed air is expelled.
- Identifying the baby who is well-fed

  A baby who takes adequate quantity of milk will:
  - not cry after feeding
  - fall asleep and have uninterrupted sleep
  - refuse to drink any more milk
  - not have constipation
  - have progressive weight gain
- The baby-friendly hospital initiative

  In 1992, UNICEF and WHO launched the baby-friendly initiative to promote, protect and support breastfeeding. The objective is to establish the superiority of breastfeeding in order to protect the newborn's health by becoming baby friendly. The steps of the initiative laid down are:
  - There must be a written breastfeeding policy.
  - All pregnant women must be informed about the benefits of breastfeeding.
  - Mothers must be helped to initiate breastfeeding within half an hour of birth.
  - Mothers must be taught the correct technique of breastfeeding.
  - Unless medically indicated, the newborn should be given no food or drink other than breast milk.
  - To practice rooming in by allowing mothers and babies to remain together 24 hours a day.
  - To encourage breastfeeding on demand.
  - To encourage exclusive breastfeeding.
  - No artificial teats should be given to babies.
  - Breastfeeding support groups are to be established and mothers must be referred to them on discharge.
  - A baby-friendly hospital should also provide other preventive care services such as immunization, rehydration salts against diarrheal dehydration and baby's growth and development surveillance.
- Contraindications to breastfeeding
  - Mothers on drugs that can be harmful to baby such as cytotoxics, certain hormones and radioactive isotopes
  - Infectious diseases such as typhoid fever, human immune deficiency infection and pulmonary tuberculosis
  - Chronic medical illnesses such as heart disease, severe anemia and poorly controlled epilepsy
  - Puerperal psychosis
  - Mothers taking high doses of antiepileptic, anticoagulant and antithyroid drugs
  - Babies with harelip and cleft palate
  - Preterm and very ill babies.

Nursing Diagnoses (Selected Few)

NURSING DIAGNOSES FOR MATERNAL-NEONATAL CLIENTS

Description

Nursing diagnosis is a clinical judgment about individual, family or community responses to actual or potential health problems/life processes. Nursing diagnosis provides the basis for selection of nursing interventions to achieve outcomes for which the nurse is accountable (NANDA).

Use of Nursing Diagnosis

- Nursing diagnosis is used as the second step of the nursing process. In the second step, the data collected during the assessment of the client's health status is analyzed and problems are identified. Some of the conclusions resulting from data analysis will lead to nursing diagnoses.
- Nursing diagnoses are used as diagnostic labels which describe health states that a nurse could legally diagnose and treat. These labels are concise descriptors of a cluster of signs and symptoms.
- Nursing diagnosis is used to describe a two-part or three-part statement about an individual's, family's or a group's response to a situation or a health problem.

Types of Nursing Diagnoses

1. *Actual Nursing Diagnoses*

   An actual nursing diagnosis represents a state that has been clinically validated by identifiable, major, defining characteristics. The actual nursing diagnosis statement begins with a precise qualifier such as 'altered', 'impaired', 'deficit', or 'ineffective'.

   The defining characteristics refer to clinical cues—subjective and objective signs or symptoms that point to the nursing diagnoses. For example, Impaired skin integrity related to immobility as evidenced by erythematous sacral lesions.
2. *High-risk Nursing Diagnoses*

   A high-risk nursing diagnosis is a clinical judgment that an individual, family or community is more vulnerable to develop the problem than others in the same or similar situation. The statement of nursing diagnosis will begin with 'High-risk for'. For example, A postoperative high-risk nursing diagnosis statement could be as 'High-risk for impaired skin integrity related to immobility secondary to pain'.
3. *Possible Nursing Diagnoses*

   A possible nursing diagnosis is a statement describing a suspected problem for which additional data are needed. The word possible is used to describe problems that may be present but that require additional data to be confirmed or ruled out. The word possible serves to alert nurses to the need for additional data. Possible nursing diagnoses are two-part statements.

   For example, Possible feeding self-care deficit related to fatigue and IV in right hand.
4. *Wellness Nursing Diagnoses*

   A wellness nursing diagnosis is a clinical judgment about an individual, group or community in transition from a specific level of wellness to a higher level or wellness. For such a nursing diagnosis, two cues should be present.

   i. Desire for a higher level of wellness.

   ii. Effective present status or function.

   These are one part statements containing the label only. The label begins with 'potential for enhanced' followed by the higher level of wellness that the individual or group desires.

For example:

- Potential for enhanced family process.
- Potential for enhanced marital relationship.
- Potential for enhanced parenting.

5. *Syndrome Nursing Diagnoses*

   A syndrome diagnosis comprises a cluster of actual or high-risk nursing diagnoses that are predicted to be present because of a certain event or situation. Syndrome nursing diagnoses are one-part diagnostic statements because the etiology or contributing factors for the diagnosis are contained in the diagnostic label.

   For example:

   - Rape trauma syndrome.
   - Disuse syndrome.

Types of Diagnostic Statements

Diagnostic statements can have one, two or three parts. One-part statements contain only the diagnostic label. Wellness and syndrome nursing diagnoses are written as one-part statements.

Two-part statements contain the label and factors that have contributed or could contribute to a health status change. Possible nursing diagnoses and high-risk nursing diagnoses are written as two-part statements.

For writing actual nursing diagnoses, three-part statements are used. They contain the label, the contributing factors and the defining characteristics (signs and symptoms) of the health state alteration.

Three-part statements

- Actual nursing diagnoses statements consist of three parts.
- Diagnostic label + contributing factors + defining characteristics.
- Gordon identified the PES format for recording the three-part diagnosis. Problem, etiology and signs and symptoms (PES).

Problem = Diagnostic category/Diagnostic label

related to

Etiology = Contributing factors

as evidenced by

Signs and symptoms/Defining characteristics.

The format cannot be used for high-risk or possible diagnoses because signs and symptoms are not present in those instances.

Writing Actual and High-risk Diagnostic Statements

- Ineffective coping related to labor and delivery as evidenced by fatigue and expressed inability to cope. 'I cannot go on anymore'.
- Hypothermia related to cold stress as evidenced by body temperature below normal, cool pale skin and acrocyanosis.
- Deficient fluid volume related to postpartum hemorrhage as evidenced by decreased pulse volume and pressure, increased pulse rate and decreased urinary output.
- Risk for infection related to neonate's immature immune system.
- Risk for infection related to labor and delivery.

NURSING DIAGNOSES FOR PRENATAL CLIENTS (Selected Few)

1. Deficient Knowledge Related to Self-care Activities during Pregnancy

Definition

Inadequate understanding of information needed to practice health-related behaviors during pregnancy.

Assessment

- Age of patient.
- Psychosocial aspects such as health beliefs, knowledge regarding pregnancy, learning ability, previous obstetric history, support system and coping pattern.
- Mental status and orientation and memory.

Defining characteristics

- Inability to follow through with instructions
- Inappropriate or exaggerated behaviors such as hostility, apathy and agitation
- Inadequate knowledge of care to be taken during pregnancy
- Verbalization of problems.

Expected outcomes

- Patient will communicate need for more information
- Patient will demonstrate understanding of information taught
- Patient will demonstrate ability to perform new bahaviors learned
- Patient will continue to practice appropriate health-related behaviors after pregnancy.

Nursing interventions

- Establish a trusting relationship and respect so that patient will relax and be receptive to learning
- Communicate and negotiate realistic learning goals with the patient
- Assess patient's knowledge of pregnancy to establish a basis for nursing care plans
- Provide information/teaching tailoring the content to suit the patient's level of understating
- Provide instructions to seek appropriate resource persons for obtaining comprehensive care during pregnancy
- Review exercise routines designed for pregnant women to enhance well-being and improve muscle tone in preparation for child birth.
- Review dietary intake during pregnancy based on physician's recommendations. Explain to patient that she needs an extra 300 calories per day, for a total of 2100 to 2400 calories per day.
- Instruct patient to avoid wearing constrictive clothing, using high-heeled shoes and taking nonprescription drugs. Constrictive clothing can obstruct venous circulation and high-heeled shoes can increase the likelihood of back strain.
- Discuss dangers of exposure to toxic chemicals or gases to avoid possible teratogenic effects on fetus.
- Instruct the woman to contact physician or go to hospital if she experiences any danger sign or symptom
  - Severe vomiting
  - Frequent and severe headache
  - Epigastric pain
  - Vision disturbances

- Swelling of fingers and face
- Altered or absent fetal movements after quickening
- Signs of vaginal tract or urinary infection
- Unusual or severe abdominal pain
- Fluid discharge from vagina
- Vaginal bleeding.

Evaluations for expected outcomes

- Patient expresses need for more information about self-care
- Patient establishes realistic goals
- Patient demonstrates understanding of matters taught
  - Follows appropriate exercises
  - Limits or stops smoking and/or consumption of alcohol if indicated
  - Obtains sufficient rest
  - Avoids areas that may contain toxic chemicals or gases
  - Stops wearing constrictive clothing and high-heeled shoes
  - Reports danger signals to physician promptly
  - Takes prenatal vitamins as prescribed
- Patient demonstrates ability to perform health-related behaviors learned
- Patient continues to practice health-related behaviors after pregnancy.

Documentation

- Patient's knowledge of self-care activities
- Expressions indicating motivation to learn
- Teaching carried out and methods of teaching used
- Dietary intake reported or seen
- Demonstration or return demonstration of skills
- Response to teaching observed.

2. Nausea and Vomiting Related to Physiological Changes of Pregnancy

Definition

A minor disorder of pregnancy experienced by pregnant women between 4th and 16th week of gestation.

Assessment

- Characteristics and pattern of occurrence of nausea and vomiting
- Types of food and smell to which patient has intolerance
- Physical health status
- Patient's understanding of the physiological changes of pregnancy
- Support system available.

Defining characteristics

- Change in appetite and pattern of eating
- Vomiting in the morning and/or later in the day
- Increased salivation
- Inability to retain food and fluids
- Fatigue and signs of dehydration.

Expected outcomes

- Patient will identify the factors that aggravate vomiting
- Patient will appreciate the physiological changes of pregnancy that cause vomiting
- Patient will modify her habits of eating
- Patient will adopt appropriate measures to obtain relief
- Patient will experience cessation of vomiting and improvement of general health.

Nursing interventions

- Assess and document the extent of nausea and vomiting to have a database.
- Reassure patient that nausea will usually subside by the 4th month of pregnancy in order to reduce her anxiety.
- Instruct patient to eat dry, unsalted crackers before rising in the morning to prevent nausea from an empty stomach.
- Instruct patient to avoid greasy or spicy food, which irritate the stomach. Fats with meals depress gastric motility and secretion of digestive enzyme and slow intestinal peristalsis causing gastroesophageal reflux.
- Advise patient to avoid cooking odors that precipitate nausea.
- Advise mothers to eat six small meals instead of three large ones to avoid overloading the stomach.
- Advise mothers to eat foods high in carbohydrates as they are easier to digest.
- Instruct her to take iron pills and vitamins after meals to avoid irritating the stomach.
- Advise to take frequent walks outside as fresh air reduces nausea and helps reinforce a positive outlook.
- Instruct to separate food and fluid intake by half an hour. Drinking excessive fluids with food distends stomach, predisposing to nausea.
- Advise client to avoid very cold food and fluids at meal times as they may cause nausea and abdominal cramping.
- Instruct her to consult physician before taking over-the-counter medications for nausea and vomiting to avoid harmful effects on fetus.

Evaluations for expected outcomes

- Patient identifies factors and food habits that aggravate nausea and vomiting
- Patient modifies her habits of eating

- Patient adopts measures to obtain relief from nausea
- Patient experiences reduction in nausea and cessation of vomiting
- Patient experiences improvement of general health.

Documentation

- Patient's description of nausea, vomiting and aggravating factors
- Patient's general health observed
- Instructions given to patient and her response to teaching
- Change in eating and drinking habits observed and reported by patient
- Expected outcomes evaluated.

3. Urinary Frequency and Dysuria Related to Physiological Changes of Pregnancy

Definition

Frequency, urgency and pain on urination experienced by some women during pregnancy.

Assessment

- Nature and duration of urinary frequency
- Daily fluid intake
- Symptoms of UTI such as pain on urination, and fever
- Patients understanding of the physiological changes in pregnancy.

Defining characteristics

- Frequency and urgency of urination
- Dysuria if associated infection present
- Sleep disturbance due to urinary frequency
- Occurrence of complaints in the early and late months of pregnancy.

Expected outcomes

- Patient will experience relief from frequency of urination and dysuria
- Patient will increase her fluid intake during day time
- Patient will practice measures to prevent bladder distention and urinary stasis
- Patient will learn to report signs of developing urinary tract infections.

Nursing interventions

- Reassure patient that urinary frequency is normal in the early and late months of pregnancy because, the enlarging uterus places pressure on the bladder.
- Instruct patient to avoid drinking large amounts of fluids within 2 to 3 hours of bedtime to prevent nocturnal urination and sleep loss.
- Instruct client to ingest the required amount of fluid early in the day to reduce the need for evening liquids.
- Instruct client to void when the urge occurs to prevent bladder distention and urinary stasis which may predispose to urinary tract infection.
- Teach patient signs and symptoms of UTI.
- Teach patient to report signs and symptoms of UTI promptly.
  Early detection of UTI allows early treatment and helps prevent complications such as pyelonephritis.

Evaluations for expected outcome

- Patient develops knowledge of the causes of urinary frequency.
- Patient adapts and adjusts to the change in urinary elimination.
- Patient modifies her fluid intake pattern.
- Patient learns to identify and report signs of UTI if she develops it.
- Patient experiences more rest during night and relaxation during day time.

Documentation

- Patient's description of urinary frequency and dysuria
- Measures of relief explained and response of patient
- Relief measures observed and reported
- Health instructions given.

NURSING DIAGNOSES FOR LABOR AND DELIVERY CLIENTS (Selected Few)

1. Acute Pain Related to Physiological Response to Labor

Definition

An unpleasant sensory and emotional experience arising from actual or potential tissue damage; pain may be sudden or slow in onset, vary in intensity from mild to severe and constant or recurring.

Assessment

- Characteristics of pain including location, intensity and source of relief.
- Physiological variables including age, and pain tolerance.
- Psychological variables including personality, previous experience with pain and anxiety.
- Sociocultural variables such as cognitive style, culture, attitudes and values.
- Knowledge and expectations of labor and delivery.

Defining characteristics

- Alteration is muscle tone-listless to rigid.
- Autonomic response such as diaphoresis, change in blood pressure and respiratory rate, dilated pupils.
- Change in appetite.
- Communication of pain.
- Behavior such as pacing and seeking out other people.
- Expressions of pain such as moaning and crying.
- Grimacing and other facial expressions.
- Guarding or protective behavior.
- Narrowed focus such as altered perception, impaired thought process and withdrawal from people.
- Self-focusing.
- Sleep disturbance.

Expected outcomes

- Patient will identify characteristics of pain
- Patient will describe factors that intensify pain.
- Patient will modify behavior to decrease pain.
- Patient will express decrease in intensity of pain.
- Patient will express satisfaction of her performance during labor and delivery.

Nursing interventions

- Orient patient to labor and delivery rooms on admission.
- Explain admission protocol and labor process.
- Show patient her room, bed and facilities such as call bell, toilet, television, etc., to allay her fear and anxiety.
- Assess patient's knowledge of labor process to plan nursing interventions.
- Explain availability of analgesics and/or anesthesia (epidural) to patient and family for reducing anxiety.
- Encourage support person or family member to remain with patient if hospital policy permits.
- Instruct patient and support person in techniques to decrease the discomfort of labor.
  - Discuss techniques of conscious relaxation.
  - Instruct to concentrate on an internal or external focal point.

- Instruct in deep chest breathing during contractions.
- Instruct in shallow chest breathing and slow panting like breathing between contractions which will avoid hyperventilations.
- Instruct patient in effleurage.

- In early labor provide patient with diversional activities such as watching television if possible to reduce anxiety.
- As labor progresses to active phase, modify environment to reduce distractions and promote concentration, e.g. close curtains and door, turn off television.
- Apply sacral pressure if needed to decrease back pain.
- Assist to change position and provide additional pillow to reduce stiffness and promote comfort.
- Assess bladder for distention and encourage to void every two hours to reduce discomfort during contractions and facilitate fetal descend.
- Provide frequent mouth care. Provide ice chips or wet gauze for dry lips caused by breathing techniques and nil-by-mouth.
- Apply cool, damp wash cloth to forehead to relieve diaphoresis.
- Provide clean gown and bed linen as needed. Diaphoresis and vaginal discharge can dampen bed linen and gown.
- Encourage patient to rest and relax between contractions to decrease discomfort.
- Discuss with patient and support person that pain medications are available if alternate pain control methods provide inadequate relief.
- When required, administer prescribed analgesics to cope with labor process.

Evaluations

- Patient identifies characteristics of pain and describes factors that intensify it.
- Patient modifies behaviors to decrease pain and discomfort such as using breathing techniques, asking for analgesia and assuming comfortable position.
- Patient reports decrease in discomfort.
- Patient expresses satisfaction with her performance during childbirth.

Documentation

- Patient's childbirth preparation
- Patient's description of pain and discomfort
- Observation of patient's response to labor
- Nursing interventions carried out to decrease discomfort
- Patient's response to nursing interventions.

2. Deficient Knowledge Related to Information about Birth Process

Definition

Inadequate understanding of or inability to perform skills needed to cope effectively with the process of labor.

Assessment

- Age of patient.
- Psychosocial status such as expectations of the birth process and interest in learning.
- Current knowledge about pregnancy, birth and recovery.
- Ability to learn and attention span.
- Support system including presence of support person interested in helping the patient.

Defining characteristics

- Inability to follow through with instructions.
- Inappropriate or exaggerated behaviors such as hysteria hostility, agitation and apathy.
- Verbalization of problems.

Expected outcomes

- Patient will recognize that increased knowledge and skill will help her cope better with birth process.
- Patient will demonstrate understanding of what is taught.
- Patient will demonstrate ability to perform skills needed for coping with labor.
- Patient will express realistic expectations about birth process.
- Patient will express satisfaction with her increased knowledge.

Nursing interventions

- Find a quiet, private place to teach the patient.
- Establish a trusting relationship with the patient and develop mutual goals for learning.
- Select appropriate teaching methods and materials such as discussions and demonstrations using audiovisual aids.
- Teach information and skills needed for understanding and coping during birth to increase the patient's sense of competence.

Evaluations for expected outcomes

- Patient expresses desire to put knowledge into practice during labor.
- Patient describes birth process in her own words.
- Patient responds to labor without undue anxiety and uses breathing, relaxation and position changes.
- Patient voices satisfaction with newly acquired knowledge and skills.

Documentation

- Patient's understanding about birth process.
- Patient's expression of need for better understanding.
- Learning goals established with the patient.
- Information and skills taught to patient.
- Teaching methods used.
- Patient's response to teaching.
- Patient's mastery of knowledge and skills demonstrated.
- Evaluation of expected outcomes observed.

3. Ineffective Coping Related to Labor and Delivery

Definition

Inability to use adaptive behaviors in response to labor and delivery.

Assessment

- Age, health beliefs, feelings about pregnancy, decision-making ability, motivation to learn and obstacles to learning.
- Pain threshold, perception of pain and response to analgesia.
- Stage and length of labor, complications, ability to concentrate and use techniques, presence and effectiveness of support person.
- Mode of delivery
- Previous experience with pregnancy, labor and delivery and knowledge of birth process.
- Preexisting pregnancy-induced or medical conditions.

Defining characteristics

- Expressed inability to cope
- Fatigue
- Inability to meet basic needs and role expectations
- Poor concentration and problem-solving abilities
- Destructive behavior towards self or others.

Expected outcomes

- Patient will express need to develop better coping behaviors.
- Patient will set realistic learning goals
- Patient will use learned coping skills
- Patient will communicate feelings about pregnancy, labor and delivery.
- Patient will maintain appropriate sense of control throughout the course of labor and delivery.
- Patient will demonstrate ability to cope with unexpected changes.

Nursing Interventions

- Establish a relationship of mutual trust and respect to enhance patient's learning.
- Develop learning goals with the patient to foster a sense of control.
- Select appropriate teaching strategies to encourage compliance.
- Teach skills that the patient can use during labor and delivery and have her give a return demonstration of each skill.
- During the latent phase of labor (dilation 1 to 4 cm).
  - Encourage patient to participate in her own care.
  - Review breathing techniques she can use during labor.
  - Involve support person in care and comfort measures.
  - Provide continuous or frequent monitoring to identify any deviation from normal.
- During the active phase of labor (dilation 4 to 8 cm).
  - Encourage patient to assume comfortable position to promote relaxation between contractions.
  - Assist patient with breathing techniques to reduce anxiety and prevent hyperventilation.

- Encourage the support person to participate in patient care such as changing soiled linen, providing sacral pressure, back rub and offering ice chips to moisten lips.
- Administer analgesia as ordered to reduce pain.
- Reassure patient about fetal status.

- During the transitional phase of labor (dilatation 8 to 10 cm).
  - Assist patient with breathing during contractions.
  - Encourage rest between contractions.
  - Explain all procedures and treatments and answer patient's questions to allay fears.
- During delivery of the placenta.
  - Encourage patient to maintain her position to facilitate delivery of placenta.
  - Show the neonate to the patient and reassure about the neonate's condition to provide emotional support.
  - Allow the patient to hold the neonate if permitted.
  - Allow her to breastfeed neonate if she desires to promote bonding.
- In a delivery, allow the patient to express her feelings and explain to her the care being provided to enable her cope with the task of motherhood.

Evaluation for expected outcomes

- Patient participate in establishing learning goals.
- Patient successfully uses breathing and relaxation techniques during labor and delivery.
- Patient maintains appreciable sense of control during labor and delivery.
- Nurses and support persons provide effective comfort to patient during labor and delivery.
- Patient demonstrates ability to cope with unexpected changes.

Documentation

- Patient's knowledge of labor and delivery.
- Patient's expressions of motivation to learn.
- Methods used to teach patient.
- Information taught and skills demonstrated.
- Patient's level of satisfaction with delivery.
- Evaluation for expected outcomes.

4. Anxiety Related to Hospitalization and Birth Process

Definition

Feeling of threat or danger to self, related to pregnancy or delivery.

Assessment

- Expressed worries, fears and concerns
- Expectations of labor experience
- Reactions to uterine activity, fatal movement, and interactions with nurse and significant others
- Ability to concentrate, learn and remember
- Physiologic status
- Usual coping methods
- Mood and personality
- Progress of labor.

Defining characteristics

- Excessive attention to uterine activity and fetal movements.
- Excessive reaction to uterine contractions
- Expressed concern about childbirth
- Expressed fear of unspecified negative outcomes
- Expressed feelings of helplessness
- Fear and apprehension
- Inability to concentrate and remember
- Increased muscle tension in body
- Increased perspiration
- Rapid pulse rate
- Restlessness, shakiness and trembling.

Expected outcomes

- Patient will express feelings of anxiety
- Patient will identify causes of anxiety
- Patient will make use of available emotional support
- Patient will show fewer signs of anxiety
- Patient will identify positive aspects of her efforts to cope during childbirth.
- Patient will acquire increased knowledge about childbirth.
- Patient will be better prepared to cope with future births.

Nursing interventions

- Assess the patient's knowledge and expectations of labor to identify the precise source of anxiety.
- Discuss normal labor progression with patient and explain what to expect during labor to help her understand her own experience.
- Involve the patient in making decisions about care to reduce the sense of powerlessness.
- Share information about progress of labor and neonate's condition with patient to provide reassurance and to increase her sense of participation.

- Interpret to patient sights and sounds in labor room such as fetal heart sounds, fetal monitor strip and activities to reduce anxiety and increase confidence.
- Attend to the patient's comfort needs to increase her trust.
- Encourage patient to use coping skills such as breathing relaxation and positioning to increase her sense of power and control.
- Spend as much time as possible with the patient to provide comfort and assistance, thereby promoting the patient's sense of security.
- Allow family member to participate in care to promote comfort and help patient cope with labor.

Evaluation for expected outcomes

- Patient expresses feelings of anxiety about pregnancy and childbirth.
- Patient identifies causes of anxiety.
- Patient communicates with nurse and family members, to gain reassurance and emotional support.
- Patient's physiologic and behavioral signs return to normal.
- Patient expresses satisfaction with her behavior while giving birth.

Documentation

- Patient's expression of anxiety
- Patient's statement of reasons for anxiety
- Observations of physical and behavioral signs of anxiety
- Interventions to assist patient with coping
- Patient's response to interventions
- Evaluations of expected outcomes observed.

NURSING DIAGNOSIS FOR POSTPARTUM CLIENTS (Selected Few)

1. Deficient Knowledge Related to Postpartum Care

Definition

Inadequate understanding of postpartum self-care activities or inability to perform skills needed to practice health-related behaviors.

Assessment

- Age and learning ability
- Decision-making ability
- Interest in learning
- Knowledge and skill regarding postpartum self-care
- Obstacles to learning
- Support systems and usual coping pattern
- Physical abilities to perform self-care activities.

Defining characteristics

- Inability to follow through with instructions.
- Inappropriate or exaggerated behaviors such as hostility, agitation or apathy.
- Poor knowledge level.
- Verbalization of problem.

Expected outcomes

- Patient will express desire to learn how to care for herself after delivery.
- Patient will verbalize or demonstrate understanding of what she has learned about self-care.
- Patient will incorporate newly learned skills into daily routine.
- Patient will make changes in postpartum routine.
- Patient will seek help from health care professional, if required.

Nursing interventions

- Establish mutual trust and respect to enhance patient's learning.
- Assess patient's level of understanding of postpartum self-care activities to establish a baseline for learning.
- Assist patient in making decisions regarding target dates for mastering postpartum self-care skills.
- Select teaching strategies best suited for patient's individual learning style to enhance learning.
- Teach skills which the patient can incorporate into her daily life such as perineal care, sitz bath, application and removal of perineal pads and breast care.
- Teach patient about the process of involution to help her understand postpartum changes.
- Teach patient the importance of adequate nutrition and hydration to ensure proper urinary and bowel elimination.
- Discuss the importance of adequate rest to promote emotional and physical stability.
- Help the patient to incorporate learned skills into her daily routine during hospitalization.
- Encourage patient to continue hygienic practices even after discharge from hospital.

Evaluation for expected outcomes

- Patient expresses motivation to learn
- Patient establishes realistic learning goals
- Patient demonstrates understanding of what she has learned.

- Patient incorporates what she has learned into her daily routine such as breast care, perineal care and obtaining adequate rest and sleep.
- Patient states intention of making changes in daily routine.
- Patient expresses intention to seek help from health professional if required.

Documentation

- Patient's understanding and skill in postpartum self-care.
- Patient's expressions which indicate her motivation to learn.
- Methods used to teach patient
- Information taught to patient
- Skills demonstrated to patient
- Patient's response to teaching
- Evaluation of expected outcomes.

2. Pain Related to Postpartum Physiological Changes

Definition

An unpleasant sensory and emotional experience that arises from actual or potential tissue damage.

Assessment

- Patient's description of pain
- Patient's age, parity and pain tolerance
- Previous experience with pain in post-delivery period.
- Presence of physical factors such as breast engorgement, cracked nipples and hemorrhoids.

Defining characteristics

- Alteration in vital signs, diaphoresis, etc.
- Communication of pain in verbal and nonverbal forms.
- Behavior changes such as pacing and repetitive actions.
- Expressions of pain such as crying, groaning and grimacing.
- Sleep disturbance.

Expected outcomes

- Patient will identify characteristics of pain and describe the factors that intensify it.
- Patient will carry out appropriate interventions for pain relief.
- Patient will express relief from pain and comfort.

Nursing interventions

- Assess patient's pain symptoms and plan appropriate nursing interventions.
- Discuss the reasons for pain and its expected duration to reduce the patient's anxiety.
- Inspect the presence of hemorrhoids and provide instructions for hemorrhoid care if indicated.
- Assess for uterine tenderness and presence and frequency of afterbirth pains every 4 hours for first 24 hours and every shift thereafter as indicated. Oxytocin administration, multiparity and breastfeeding are factors that may intensify uterine contractions.
- Instruct breastfeeding mother to wear supportive bra to increase comfort.
- If breastfeeding mother's breasts are engorged instruct her to use warm compress or take warm shower to simulate the flow of milk and help relieve stasis and discomfort.
- If nipples become sore, instruct mother to air dry the nipples for 20 to 30 minutes after feeding to roughen the nipples.
- Apply breast cream as ordered to soften nipples and relieve pain.
- Instruct nonbreastfeeding mother to wear tight, supportive bra or breast binder and apply ice packs as needed to prevent or reduce lactation.

Evaluations for expected outcomes

- Patient describes pain and factors that intensify it.
- Patient carries out appropriate interventions for pain relief as instructed.
- Patient expresses relief of pain and discomfort.
- Patient's breasts remain soft and lactation continues to be adequate.
- Patient expresses understanding of instructions and follows through.

Documentation

- Patient's description of pain and discomfort
- Observations of pain manifestations
- Comfort measures and medications provided for pain relief
- Effectiveness of interventions carried out
- Instructions provided to patient about pain and pain relief measures
- Evaluations of expected outcome.

3. Deficient Fluid Volume Related to Postpartum Hemorrhage

Definition

Excessive fluid and electrolyte loss resulting from excessive postpartum bleeding.

Assessment

- History of problems that can cause fluid loss such as hemorrhage, vomiting and diarrhea.
- Vaginal signs such as visible bleeding, laceration, etc.
- Fluid and electrolyte status including weight, intake and output, urine specific gravity, skin turgor, mucous membranes and serum electrolytes and blood urea nitrogen levels.
- Laboratory values such as hemoglobin (Hb) level and hematocrit (HCT) value.
- Risk factors such as grand multiparty, overdistended uterus, prolonged labor, previous history of postpartum hemorrhage, traumatic delivery, uterine fibroids, and bleeding disorders.

Defining characteristics

- Decreased pulse volume and pressure
- Decreased urine output and increased concentration
- Dry skin and mucous membranes
- Increased hematocrit
- Increased pulse rate
- Low blood pressure
- Poor skin turgor
- Thirst
- Weakness
- Change in mental status.

Expected outcomes

- Patient's vital signs will remain stable.
- Patient's hematology values will be within normal range.
- Patient's uterus will remain firm and contracted.
- Signs of shock will be identified quickly and treatment initiated immediately by medical personnel.
- Patient's blood volume will return to normal.
- Patient's urinary output will return to normal.

Nursing interventions

- Following delivery, monitor the color, amount, and consistency of lochia every 15 minutes for one hour, every 4 hours for 24 hours and then every shift until discharge.
- Count or weigh sanitary pads if lochia is excessive.
- Monitor and record vital signs every 15 minutes for one hour, every hour for 4 hours and every 4 hours for 24 hours to detect signs of hemorrhage and shock.
- Immediately after delivery, palpate the fundus every 15 minutes for one hour, every hour for 4 hours, every 4 hours for 24 hours and then every shift until discharge to note its location and muscle tone. Lack of uterine muscle tone or strength (atony) is the most common cause of postpartum hemorrhage.
- Gently massage a boggy fundus, to make it become firm (over stimulation can cause relaxation).

- Teach patient to assess and gently massage the fundus and notify if bogginess persists.
- Explain to patient the process of involution and the need to palpate the fundus to decrease her anxiety and increase cooperation.
- Evaluate postpartum hematology studies and report abnormal values to plan required interventions.
- Administer fluids, blood or blood products or plasma expanders as ordered to replace lost blood volume.
- Monitor patient's intake and output every shift.
- Note bladder distention and catheterize as ordered as distended bladder interferes with the involution of uterus.
- Administer oxytocic agents such as ergometrine as ordered as distended bladder interferes with involution of uterus.
- Assess patient regularly for signs and symptoms of shock such as rapid thready pulse, increased respiratory rate, decreased blood pressure and urine output and cold, clammy, pale, skin.

Evaluations for expected outcomes

- Patient's vital signs remain stable
- Results of hematology studies are within normal range.
- Patient's uterus remains firm
- Patient does not develop distended bladder.
- Patient's blood loss after delivery is less than 500 mL.
- Patient's blood volume is replenished.
- Quick identification and prompt treatment are provided if patient develops shock.

Documentation

- Estimation of blood loss
- Location and tone of fundus
- Laboratory results
- Replacement of lost fluid
- Nursing interventions to control active blood loss
- Vital signs, intake and output
- Patient's response to nursing interventions.

4. Pain Related to Episiotomy or Cesarean Incision

Definition

Unpleasant sensory and emotional experiences arising from tissue damage which vary in intensity from mild to severe and be constant or recurring.

Assessment

- Patient's description of pain including quality and intensity.
- Patient's age and pain tolerance
- Patient's anxiety level and any symptoms of secondary gain.

Defining characteristics

- Alteration in vital signs, diaphoresis or dilated pupils
- Change in appetite and eating
- Communication of pain in verbal and nonverbal forms
- Expressions of pain such as crying moaning and grimacing
- Guarding or protective activities
- Sleep disturbance.

Expected outcomes

- Patient will describe nature of pain and intensity
- Patient will understand and carry out appropriate interventions for pain relief.
- Patient will express comfort and relief from pain.

Nursing interventions

- Examine the episiotomy site for redness, edema, ecchymosis, drainage and approximation to detect trauma to perineal tissues or developing complications.
- Discuss reasons for pain and discomfort and measures to be carried out for relief.
- Apply ice pack to the episiotomy site for the first 24 hours to increase vasoconstriction and reduce edema and discomfort.
- Provide warm sitz bath (temperature 100° to 105° F/37.8 to 40.6°C) from 2nd postpartum day. Instruct patient to take sitz baths three times a day with each lasting for 20 minutes. Sitz bath increases circulation, reduces edema and promotes healing.
- Provide infrared light to perineum if ordered to reduce discomfort.
- Apply any prescribed sprays, creams or ointments for reduction of swelling and discomfort.
- Instruct patient to tighten buttocks before sitting and to sit on flat firm surface. This reduces stress and direct pressure on the perineum.
- Administer prescribed pain medications to provide pain relief.
- For postcesarean patients, provide an additional pillow and teach to splint the incision site when moving or coughing to provide support for the abdominal muscles.

Evaluations for expected outcomes

- Patient reports characteristics and intensity of pain.
- Patient carries out appropriate interventions for pain relief as instructed.

- Patient expresses relief of pain and discomfort.
- Episiotomy or cesarean incision heals normally.
- Patient expresses understanding of instructions given and implements care activities.

Documentation

- Patient's description of pain and pain relief experienced.
- Nurse's observation of patient's response to interventions for pain relief.
- Comfort measures and medications provided for pain relief.
- Instructions provided to patient for self-care activities.

NURSING DIAGNOSIS FOR NEONATAL CLIENTS

1. Ineffective Breastfeeding Related to Difficulty with Breastfeeding Process

Definition

State in which mother or neonate experiences dissatisfaction or difficulty with breastfeeding process.

Assessment

- Maternal status such as age, parity, previous bonding history and breastfeeding preparation in prenatal period.
- Adequacy of milk supply, nipple shape and perceptions about breastfeeding.
- Neonate's growth rate and age-weight relationship.

Defining characteristics

- Inadequate milk supply
- Arching and crying when at breast
- Evidence of inadequate milk intake
- Fussiness and crying within an hour of breastfeeding
- Inability to latch on to nipple correctly
- Lack of sustained sucking at breast
- Insufficient emptying of breasts
- Lack of response to other comfort measures
- Sore nipples for mother after first week of breastfeeding.

Expected outcomes

- Mother will express satisfaction with breastfeeding techniques and practice.
- Mother will show decreased anxiety and apprehension.
- Neonate will feed well on both breasts and appear satisfied for at least two hours after feeding.
- Neonate will grow and thrive.

Nursing interventions

- Educate mother in breast care and breastfeeding techniques
- Be available and encourage mother during initial breastfeeding episodes.
- Teach techniques for encouraging the let-down reflex such as warm shower before feeding, breast massage and holding the neonate close to the breasts.
- Provide quiet, private, comfortable, environment for mother and baby to promote successful breastfeeding
- Encourage mother to clarify questions regarding successful breastfeeding.

Evaluations for expected outcomes

- Mother expresses satisfaction with breastfeeding practices
- Mother exhibits decreased anxiety and apprehension
- Neonate feeds successfully on both breasts and appears satisfied for at least 2 hours after feeding.
- Neonate grows and thrives.

Documentation

- Mother's expressions of satisfaction and comfort with breastfeeding ability.
- Observations of bonding and breastfeeding processes

- Teaching and instructions given
- Neonates weight and growth
- Expected outcomes evaluated.

2. Hypothermia Related to Cold Stress or Sepsis

Definition

State in which neonate's body temperature is below normal range.

Assessment

- Gestational age
- Intrapartal history
- Presence of maternal risk factors such as fever, diabetes mellitus, dystocia and perinatal asphyxia.
- Vital signs including core temperature, heart rate, respiration and blood pressure.
- Lab values such as blood gas, serum glucose and electrolytes
- Skin color: central and peripheral
- Birth weight.

Defining characteristics

- Body temperature below normal level
- Cool, pale skin
- Cyanotic nailbeds
- Increased heart rate and blood pressure
- Piloerection
- Shivering
- Slow capillary refill.

Expected outcomes

- Neonate will exhibit normal body temperature
- Neonate will have warm, dry skin and normal capillary refill
- Neonate will not develop complications of hypothermia
- Neonate will not shiver
- Neonate will maintain normal temperature
- Mother will verbalize knowledge of how hypothermia develops and will state measures to prevent recurrence of hypothermia.

Nursing interventions

- Monitor body temperature every hour by axillary route. If using a radiant warmer, monitor the device's temperature reading hourly and compare it with the neonates body temperature.
- Monitor and record vital signs every 1 to 4 hours. Perform continuous electronic cardiorespiratory monitoring as appropriate.
- *For mild hypothermia*, dress the baby with a shirt, diaper, stockinet or knitted hat and wrap in double blankets.
- Change wet diapers promptly
- Perform all procedures under a radiant warmer, if possible
- Postpone bathing
- *For severe hypothermia*, place the neonate in an isolette or overhead radiant warmer bed, and provide supportive measures.

- Keep the neonate undressed
- Set the isolette temperature at 36° to 36.6°C (96.8° to 97.8° F)
- Attach a skin probe to the right upper quadrant of the neonate's abdomen.
- Monitor carefully for evaporative and insensible fluid loss

- Carry out prescribed treatment regimen such as administering IV fluids and small frequent feeding.
- Discuss precipitating factors with mother and family members to prevent recurrence.
- Instruct family members in preventive measures such as dressing the neonate appropriately and providing adequate nutrition for neonates growth needs.

Evaluations for expected outcomes

- Neonate's temperature returns to normal
- Neonate exhibits warm, dry skin and normal capillary refill time.
- Neonate does not develop complications of hypothermia
- Neonate does not demonstrate signs of hyperthermia related to radiant heat source.
- Neonate is successfully weaned from isolette or radiant warmer
- Parents verbalize understanding of causes of hypothermia and preventive measures.
- Mother demonstrates proper temperature measurement technique.

Documentation

- Neonate's physical findings such as cardiovascular status and temperature.
- Nursing interventions carried out
- Neonate's response to interventions
- Mother's and family member's willingness and ability to provide adequate care at home.
- Expected outcomes evaluated.

3. Risk for Infection Related to Neonate's Immature Immune System

Definition:

Presence of internal or external hazards that threaten neonate's health.

Assessment:

- Gestational age of neonate
- Temperature, heart rate and respirations
- Labor and delivery record including maternal fever, premature rupture of membranes and foul smelling amniotic fluid.
- Recent or current maternal infections
- Signs of infection of umbilical cord and skin at base of cord such as redness, odor and discharge.
- Signs and symptoms of developing infections such as lethargy, jaundice, skin lesions, thrush, unstable body temperature, hypoglycemia, diarrhea, vomiting, poor feeding patterns, cyanosis and mottling of skin.
- Signs of respiratory distress such as grunting, retractions, nasal flaring and cyanosis.
- Evidence of chronic intrauterine infections such as growth retardation and hepatosplenomegaly.

Risk factors

- Early rupture of amniotic membranes
- Environmental exposure to pathogens during birth process
- Inadequate primary responses such as broken skin
- Invasive procedures
- Poor feeding pattern
- Tissue destruction
- Trauma
- Medication use.

Expected outcomes

- Neonate's vital signs will remain within normal range
- Neonate will be alert and active
- Neonate will remain free from signs and symptoms of infection
- Neonate's umbilical cord will remain free of infection and heal properly.
- Mother and family members will practice good handwashing technique before handling neonate.

Nursing interventions

- Review the maternal chart and delivery record to detect risk factors that predispose the neonate to infection
- Assess the neonate's gestational age. [As passive immunity via the placenta increases significantly in last trimester, premature neonates are more susceptible to infection].
- Follow sterile technique
  Remove, rings, wrist watches and bracelets before handling the neonate.
- Scrub hands and arms with antimicrobial preparation before entering nursery and after contact with contaminated material.
- Wash hands after handling the neonate and instruct parents in handwashing techniques.
- Perform umbilical cord care with each diaper change or as facility policy dictates in order to promote healing.

- Assess respirations, heart rate and temperature every 15 minutes for first hour, then every hour for four hours, then every four hours for 24 hours, then every shift or as indicated. [Unstable vital signs, persistent elevations in temperature or hypothermia may indicate neonatal infection].
- Observe neonate for signs and symptoms of infection and notify physician if signs and symptoms of infection appear.
- Observe standard precautions: Wear gloves for neonate's first bath and when in contact with blood and body secretions. [These actions prevent cross-contamination and transmission of pathogens].
- Encourage mother to begin breastfeeding early. Colostrum and breast milk provide passive immunity and helps reduce infection.

Evaluations for expected outcomes

- Neonate's vital signs remain within normal range
- Neonate remains alert and active
- Neonate is free from signs and symptoms of infection
- Umbilical cord is clean, dry and healing
- Mother and family members demonstrate proper handwashing technique before handling neonate.

Documentation

- Vital signs
- Appearance of umbilical cord
- Feeding pattern and weight gain
- Condition of oral mucosa
- Skin color and rashes
- Elimination pattern
- Activity pattern
- Interventions performed to reduce risk of infection
- Neonates response to nursing interventions
- Evaluation of outcomes observed.

4. Ineffective Breastfeeding Related to Limited Maternal Experience

Definition

State in which mother or neonate experiences dissatisfaction or difficulty with breastfeeding process.

Assessment

- Age and maturity of mother
- Previous bonding history—parity
- Level of prenatal breastfeeding preparation
- Previous breastfeeding experience
- Actual or perceived inadequate milk supply
- Nipple shape such as inverted nipple
- Stressors such as family and career
- Views on breastfeeding
- Support from spouse and family members
- Satisfaction and contentment of neonate.

Defining characteristics

Mother

- Actual or perceived inadequate supply of milk
- Insufficient emptying of each breast
- Lack of observable signs of oxytocin release
- Sore nipples after first week of breastfeeding.

Baby

- Arching and crying when at breast
- Evidence of inadequate intake of milk
- Fussing and crying within one hour after feeding
- Inability to latch on to nipple correctly
- Lack of response to comfort measures and efforts at pacifying
- Lack of sustained sucking at breast
- Resistance to latch on to breast
- Unsatisfactory breastfeeding process.

Expected outcomes

- Mother will express understanding of breastfeeding techniques and practice.
- Mother will display decreased anxiety and apprehension
- Mother and baby will experience successful breastfeeding
- Neonate's initial weight loss will be within accepted norms
- Neonates nutritional needs will be met adequately.

Nursing interventions

- Assess mother's knowledge of breastfeeding
- Educate mother in breast care and breastfeeding techniques
- Provide written materials and audio-visual aids which illustrate proper feeding technique.

- Teach techniques for encouraging the let-down reflex such as: warm shower, breast massage, relaxation, holding neonate close to the breasts and infant sucking.
- Stay with mother during feeding and encourage to ask questions to increase understanding.
- Evaluate nipple position in neonate's mouth and sucking motion
- Ensure that the neonate is awake and alert when feeding, unwrap as needed
- Evaluate neonate for anomalies that may interfere with breastfeeding ability such as cleft lip or palate
- When ready to start feeding, let a drop or two of breast milk fall on baby's lips. The neonate may open his mouth on tasting the milk
- Instruct the mother in breast care techniques such as wearing supportive bra, washing and air drying nipples to prevent cracking, soreness and bleeding which interfere with feeding.
- Teach mother on ways to prevent breast engorgement
- Teach mother the factors that enhance milk production as well as those that can alter production and quality of milk.
- Provide positive reinforcement for the mother's efforts in order to decrease her anxiety and increase her confidence and self-esteem.

Evaluations for expected outcomes

- Mother properly positions baby during breastfeeding
- Uses appropriate techniques to encourage attachment to nipple
- Mother expresses decreased anxiety and increased enthusiasm for breastfeeding.
- Neonate feeds successfully on both breasts and appears satisfied for at least 2 hours after feeding.
- Neonate's nutritional needs are met
- Neonate's initial weight loss remains within accepted norms.

Documentation

- Mother's level of knowledge related to breastfeeding
- Mother's expression of dissatisfaction with breastfeeding ability
- Mother's breastcare practices
- Maternal conditions that interfere with breastfeeding such as inverted nipples.
- Mother's and neonate's behavior during and after breastfeeding such as positioning on breasts an baby's level of satisfaction.
- Frequency and duration of breastfeeding
- Teaching and instructions given and mother's response to teaching
- Neonates weight and growth
- Mother's and neonate's response to nursing interventions.

BIBLIOGRAPHY

1. Annamma J. A comprehensive Textbook of Midwifery, Jaypee Brothers; New Delhi; 2005.
2. Diane FM, Margaret CA. Myles Textbook for Midwives. 14th edition, Churchill Livingstone, Edinburgh; 2003.
3. Dutta DC. Textbook of Obstetrics, 5th edition, New Central Brook Company, Kolkata; 2001.
4. Helen V, Jan KM, Carolyin G. Text book of Nurse Midwifery, 4th edition, All India Publishers and Distributors Regd, New Delhi; 2005.
5. Lynda CJ. "Nursing Diagonosis, Application to Clinical Practice", 4th edition, JB. Lippineot Company, Philadelphia, 1992.
6. Marilyan DE, Mary MF, Joseph BT, "Application of Nursing Process and Nursing Diagnosis, 2nd edition, Jaypee Brothers, New Delhi; 1995.
7. Sheila SR, Cynthia TM. "Spark's and Tailor's Nursing Diagnosis" Reference Mannal, 6th edition, Lippincott Williams and Wilkins, Philadelphia; 2005.

Clinical Nursing Procedures (Selected Few)

PERFORMING AN ANTENATAL ABDOMINAL EXAMINATION AND PALPATION

Definition

Examination of a pregnant woman to determine the normalcy of fetal growth in relation to the gestational age, position of the fetus in uterus and its relationship to the maternal pelvis.

Purposes

1. To measure the abdominal girth and fundal height.
2. To determine the abdominal muscle tone
3. To determine the fetal lie, presentation, position, variety (anterior or posterior) and engagement.
4. To determine the possible location of the fetal heart tones.
5. To observe the signs of pregnancy
6. To detect any deviation from normal.

Articles

1. Fetoscope/stethoscope/Doppler machine
2. Measuring tape/pelvimeter.

Procedure

Sl. No.	Nursing Action	Rationale
1.	Explain to the woman what will be done and how she may cooperate	Reduces anxiety and promotes relaxation during the procedure
2.	Instruct the woman to empty her bladder	Avoids discomfort during palpation
3.	Draw curtains around the bed	Provides privacy
	INSPECTION	
4.	Position the woman for examination • Place a pillow under her head muscles, and upper shoulders • Have her arms by her sides • Expose her abdomen from below the breasts to the symphysis pubis	Promotes relaxation of abdominal muscles Enables visualization of the whole abdomen
5.	Inspect abdomen for the following: Scars, Diastasis recti, Hernia, Linea nigra, Striae gravidarum, Contour of the abdomen, State of umbilicus and skin condition	

Sl. No.	Nursing Action	Rationale
6.	Determine the fundal height using the ulnar side of the palm. • 12 weeks: Level of the symphysis pubis • 16 weeks: Halfway between symphysis pubis and umbilicus • 20 weeks: 1–2 fingerbreadths below the umbilicus • 22–24 weeks: 1–2 fingerbreadths above the umbilicus • 28–30 weeks: 1/3rd of the way between umbilicus and xiphoid process • 32 weeks: 2/3rd of the way between umbilicus and xiphoid process • 38 weeks: Level of the xiphoid process • 40 weeks: 2–3 fingerbreadths below the xiphoid process after lightening	In order to estimate if fetal growth corresponds to the gestational period 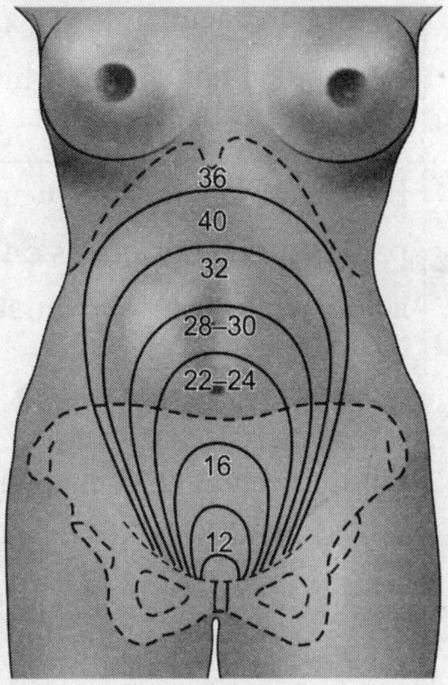 36 40 32 28–30 22–24 16 12 Fundal height at various weeks of pregnancy
7.	Measure fundal height using any one of the following methods: a. Using measuring tape • Place zero line of the tape measure on the superior border of the symphysis pubis • Stretch the tape across the contour of the abdomen to the top of the fundus along the midline b. Caliper method (Pelvimeter) • Place one tip of the caliper on the superior border of the symphysis pubis and the other tip at the top of the fundus. Both placements are in the midline • Read the measurement on the centimeter scale located on the arc, close to the joint. The number of centimeters should be equal approximately to the weeks of gestation after about 22 to 24 weeks	The number of centimeters measured should be approximately equal to the weeks of gestation after about 22 to 24 weeks This method is more accurate
8.	Measure the abdominal girth by encircling the woman's abdomen with a tape measure at the level of the umbilicus	Normally the measurement is 2 inches (5 cm) less than the weeks of gestation. e.g. 32 inches at 34 weeks gestation. Measurements more than 100 cm (39 ½ inches) is abnormal at any week of gestation

Sl. No.	Nursing Action	Rationale
	ABDOMINAL PALPATION FOR LEOPOLD'S MANEUVERS	
9.	Instruct the woman to relax her abdominal muscles by bending her knees slightly and doing relaxation breathing	These steps reduce the stretching and tension of abdominal muscles
10.	Be sure your hands are warm before beginning to palpate, rest your hands on the mother's abdomen lightly while giving explanation about the procedure	Cold hands may cause muscle contraction and discomfort. Resting hands on mother's abdomen would help her to become accustomed to your touch and dissipate muscle tightening
11.	For the technique of palpation, • Use the flat palmar surface of fingers and not finger tips. Keep fingers of hands together and apply smooth deep pressure as firm as is necessary to obtain accurate findings	These measures would aid in gathering greatest amount of information with least discomfort to the woman
12.	Perform the first maneuver (fundal palpation) • Face the woman's head • Place your hands on the sides of the fundus and curve the fingers around the top of the uterus • Palpate for size, shape, consistency and mobility of the fetal part in the fundus	Round, hard, readily, movable part, ballotable between the fingers of both hands is indicative of head Irregular, bulkier, less firm and not well-defined or movable part is indicative of breech Neither of the above is indicative if transverse lie
13.	Do the second maneuver (lateral palpation) • Continue to face the woman's head • Place your hands on both sides of the uterus about midway between the symphysis pubis and the fundus • Apply pressure with one hand against the side of the uterus pushing the fetus to the other side and stabilizing it there • Palpate the other side of the abdomen with the examining finger from the midline to the lateral side and from the fundus using smooth pressure and rotatory movements • Repeat the procedure for examination of opposite side of the abdomen	A firm convex, continuously smooth and resistant mass extending from breech to neck is indicative of fetal back. Small knobby, irregular mass, which move when, pressed or may kick or hit your examining hand is indicative of the fetal small parts. Small parts all over the abdomen are indicative of a posterior position

Sl. No.	Nursing Action	Rationale
*14.	Third maneuver (Pawlik's grip) • Continue to face the woman's head and make sure the woman has her knees bent • Grasp the portion of the lower abdomen immediately above the symphysis pubis between the thumb and middle finger of your outstretched hand. Press gently into the abdomen in order to feel the presenting part between your thumb and finger • As in the first maneuver, palpate for size, shape, consistency and mobility in order to differentiate if it is the head or breech in the lower pole of the uterus	Avoids discomfort If the fetal head is above the brim, it will be readily movable and ballotable. If not readily movable, it is indicative of an engaged head
*15.	Fourth maneuver (pelvic palpation) • Turn and face the woman's feet (make sure the woman's knees are bent) • Place your hands on the sides of the uterus, with the palm of your hands just below the level of umbilicus and your fingers directed towards the symphysis pubis • Press deeply with your finger tips into the lower abdomen and move them toward the pelvic inlet • The hands converge around the presenting part when head is not engaged • The hands will diverge away from the presenting part and there will have no give or mobility if the presenting part is engaged or dipping	Avoids pain with the maneuver Cephalic prominence on the same side as the fetal small parts indicates vertex presentation with well-flexed head Cephalic prominence on the same side as the fetal back may be occiput in a face presentation with extended head Prominences are felt on both sides in military position with deflected head (brow presentation)

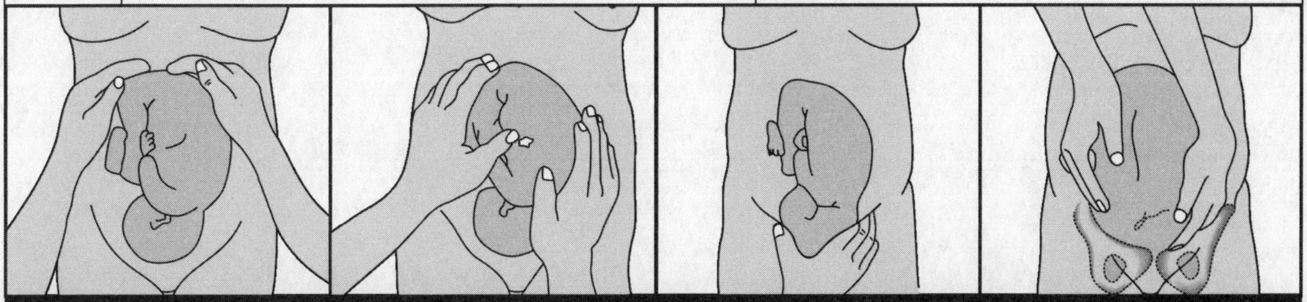

i First maneuver (Fundal palpation)

ii Second maneuver (Lateral palpation)

iii Third maneuver (Pawlik's grip)

iv Fourth maneuver (Pelvic palpation)

Sl. No.	Nursing Action	Rationale
	AUSCULTATION	
16.	Place fetoscope or stethoscope over the convex portion of the fetus closest to the anterior uterine wall	Fetal heart sounds are heard over fetal back (scapula region) in vertex and breech presentation. Over chest in face presentation.
17.	Inform the mother of your findings. Make her comfortable	
18.	Replace articles and wash hands	
19.	Record in the patient's chart the time, findings and remarks, if any	

Location of the maximum intensity of the fetal heart tones

Sl. No.	Presentation and positional varieties	Location
1.	Cephalic	Midway between umbilicus and level of anterior superior iliac spine
2.	Breech	Level with or above umbilicus
3.	Anterior	Close to the abdominal midline
4.	Transverse	In lateral abdominal area
5.	Posterior	In flank area

* Note : Pelvic palpation may be performed as the 3rd maneuver to feel for the cephalic prominances and to confirm the presentation, before performing Pawlick's grip.

Pawlick's grip as the 3rd maneuver is recommended as this sequence has advantages of completing the three maneuvers which require the nurse to be facing the client's head and then turning to her feet for pelvic palpation (4th maneuver) without taking her hands off the mothers abdomen.

CONDUCTING A NORMAL VAGINAL DELIVERY

Definition

Conducting or managing a normal vaginal delivery involves the hand maneuvers used to assist the baby's birth, immediate care of the newborn and the delivery of the placenta.

Purposes

1. To have the childbirth event take place in a prepared and safe environment.
2. To conduct delivery with least trauma to mother and baby.
3. To assist mother go through the process without undue stress, injury or complication.
4. To promote transition to the extrauterine life of the newborn, smooth and safe.
5. To avoid complications.

Articles:

For mother:

A Sterile delivery pack containing:

a. Articles for cutting and suturing an episiotomy.
   - A pair of straight, blunt ended scissors
   - Episiotomy scissors
   - Artery clamps—3
   - Tissue forceps—1
   - Needle holder— 1
   - Syringe and needle for infiltration—10 mL

b. Scissors for cutting the cord
c. Bowl for cleaning solution
d. Basin to receive placenta
e. Cotton balls
f. 4 x 4 gauze pieces
g. Towel to cover the hand supporting the perineum
h. Sterile gown
i. Leggings for the mother
j. Apron, gloves and mask for staff.

For newborn:

1. Baby blanket or flannel cloth—2, one to receive and dry the baby of excess secretions and another to wrap the baby.
2. Neonatal resuscitation equipment checked and ready for use.
3. Oxygen source with tubing.

4. Suction apparatus and mucous extractor.
5. Cord clamp.
6. Bulb syringe for nasal and oropharyngeal suctioning of the baby.

Clean tray with :

- Antiseptic lotion—savlon or dettol
- Suture material
- Perineal pads for the mother
- Oxytocic drugs
- Sterile gloves
- Methergine
- Lignocaine 2%
- Syringes and needles for injection.

Points to remember:

- Follow strict aseptic technique
- Never ask the mother to bear down before full dialatation
- Always give episiotomy at the peak of a uterine contraction
- Check that the resuscitation set, suction apparatus and other equipments are in good working condition
- Record any alteration in uterine contraction or FHR. Record the time of rupture of membranes and color of amniotic fluid
- Note FHR when the uterine contractions are not present.

Preparation:

1. Provide local preparation as per agency policy.
2. Administer enema.

Procedure:

Sl. No.	Nursing Action	Rationale
1.	Transfer mother to the labor room	
2.	Change her clothings into hospital gown	
3.	Monitor uterine contraction and PV findings	Helps in assessing progress of labor
4.	Assess the presentation, lie, position, attitude, station, cervical dilatation, effacement, etc.	Helps in assessing progress of labor
5.	Maintain labor progress chart	Helps in determining abnormalities
6.	Note the color of the liquor if the membranes rupture	Meconuim stained liquor indicates fetal distress.
7.	Note the fetal heart rate every 10–15 minutes, if not on continuous fetal monitoring	Detects fetal distress at an early stage
8.	Avoid giving solid foods	During labor emptying time of the stomach is delayed and may cause regurgitation

Sl. No.	Nursing Action	Rationale
9.	Give her fluids in the form of lemon juice or fruit juice (If an operative delivery is anticipated keep mother on NPO)	
10.	Instruct her to follow the breathing technique	Ensures more oxygen supply to the fetus and promotes relaxation
11.	Instruct mother to lie down in left lateral position	Enhances more blood supply to the fetus as well as prevents supine hypotensive syndromes
12.	Give adequate explanation regarding breathing, relaxation and pushing (bearing down) to mother	Obtains her cooperation and participation during the process
13.	Once the onset of second stage has been confirmed place the woman in dorsal position with knees bent at lower end of the delivery bed. Ensure that bladder is empty	Gives view to the perineum and to assess the progress clearly
14.	Open the delivery pack, arrange the articles and pour cleansing solution in the bowl	For convenience and timely use
15.	Perform a surgical hand scrub and put on sterile gown and gloves	
16.	Drape the mother's perineum and delivery area	Obtains a sterile field for delivery
17.	Clean the perineum in the following manner using one cotton ball separately for each stroke a) Mons pubis in *zigzag* manner from level of clitoris upward b) Clitoris to fourchette-one downward stroke c) Farther labia minora and then near side d) Labia majora farther side first and then near side e) Thighs in long strokes away from the perineum f) Anus in one circular stroke	Proper cleansing makes the perineum free from microorganism
18.	Delivery of the head As the head becomes visible at the introitus, place the pads of your fingertips on the portion of the vertex at vaginal introitus	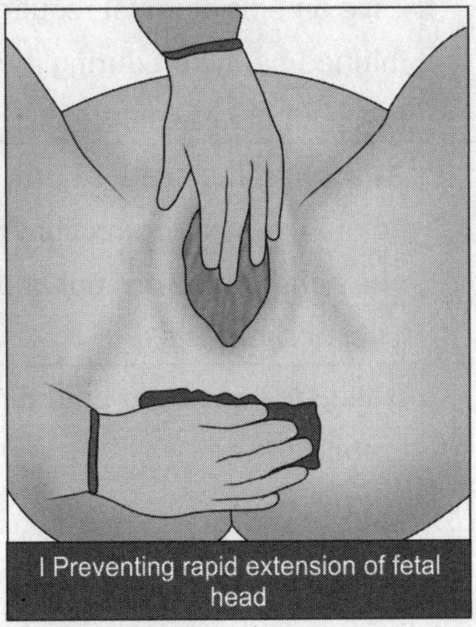 I Preventing rapid extension of fetal head

Sl. No.	Nursing Action	Rationale
19.	As more of the head is visible, spread your fingers over the vertex of the baby's head, with fingertips pointing towards the unseen face of the fetus and the elbow pointing upwards, towards the mother 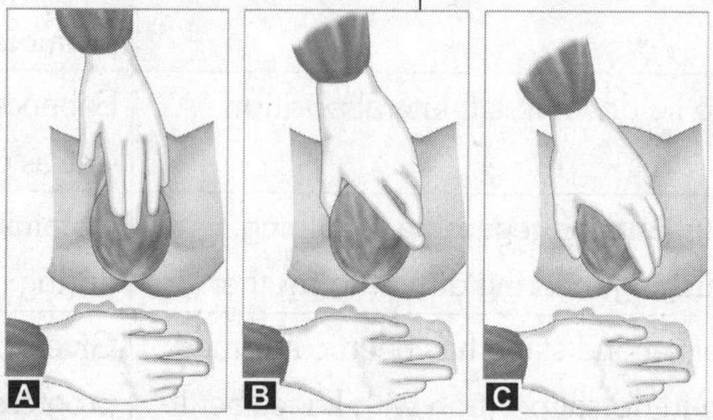 **Developing fetal head:** (A) Preventing too rapid extension; (B) Controlling the crowning; (C) Easing the perineum to release the face	Gives pressure against the fetal head to keep it well flexed.
20.	Cover the hand not used on baby's head with a towel and place the thumb in the crease of the groin midway on one side of the perineum. Place the middle finger in the same way on the other side of perineum	Prevent contamination from the anus
21.	As the head advances allow it to gradually extend beneath your hand by exerting control but not prohibitive pressure	Control of the head in this manner will prevent explosive crowning and pressure on the perineum
22.	With the hand over the perineum, apply pressure downward and inward towards each other across the perineal body at the same time	This support will prevent rapid birth of head causing intracranial damage to baby and laceration to perineum
23.	Observe the perineum in the space between the thumb and middle finger while offering head control and perineal support	Detects signs of impending tear such as stretch marks beneath the perineal skin
24.	Give an episiotomy if required when there is bulging thinned perineum during the peak of a contraction or just prior to crowning	Avoids injury to the anal sphincter and spontaneous laceration of the perineum
25.	As soon as the head is born, during the resting phase, before the next contraction, place the fingertips of one hand on the occiput and slide them down to the level of shoulders	
26.	Sweep the fingers in both directions to feel for the umbilical cord	Detects the presence of nuchal cord, which can prevent the descend of the fetus and delivery of the body

Sl. No.	Nursing Action	Rationale
27.	If the cord is felt and if it is loose, slip it over the baby's head. If the cord is tight apply clamps about 3 cm apart and cut the cord at the middle of the neck (mother must be instructed to pant while clamping, cutting and unwinding the cord).	Prevents the cord from becoming tightened around the neck
28.	Wipe the baby's face and wipe off fluid from nose and mouth.	Facilitates breathing
29.	Suction the oral and nasal passage with a bulb syringe	Prevents aspiration of the fluid
30.	Delivery of shoulders: - Wait for a contraction and watch for restitution and external rotation of head.	Allows time for shoulders to rotate to the anteroposterior diameter of the outlet
31.	When the shoulders reach the anteroposterior diameter of the pelvic outlet, proceed to deliver one shoulder at a time in the following manner: ♦ Place a hand on each side of the head over the ears and apply downward traction to deliver the anterior shoulder ♦ When the axillary crease is seen, guide the head and trunk in an upward curve to allow the posterior shoulder to escape over the posterior vaginal wall	Avoids overstretching of the perineum

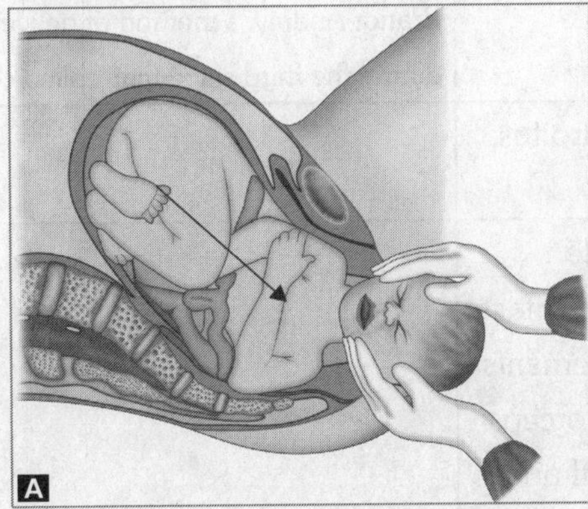

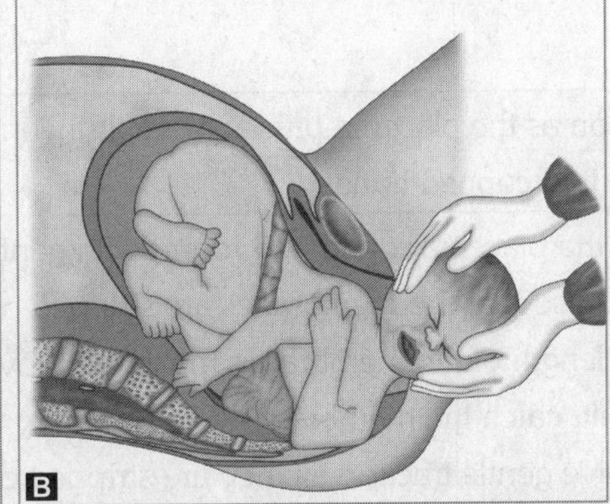

Normal vaginal delivery (illustrated): (A) Downward traction of fetal head; (B) Delivery of posterior shoulder

Sl. No.	Nursing Action	Rationale
32.	Grasp the baby around the chest and lift the baby towards the mother's abdomen	This allows the mother to immediately see her baby and have close physical contact
33.	Note the time of birth	
34.	Place two clamps on the cord about 8–10 cm from the umbilicus and cut it while covering it with a gauze	Covering with a gauze while cutting prevents spraying the delivery field with blood

Sl. No.	Nursing Action	Rationale
35.	Give the baby to the nursery nurse who will place him in the designated area, dry him and carry out the assessment and care	
36.	Place the placenta receiver against the perineum	For receiving the placenta and membranes
37.	Place one hand over the fundus to feel the contraction of the uterus	
38.	Watch for signs of placental separation: lengthening of cord, gush of bleeding, fundus becoming round and placenta descending into the vagina	Contraction and placental separation may occur in minutes
39.	When placental descend is confirmed ask the patient to beardown as the uterus contracts, as she did during the second stage of labor (controlled cord traction can be used to deliver placenta)	Bearing down simultaneously with a contraction aids expulsion of the placenta 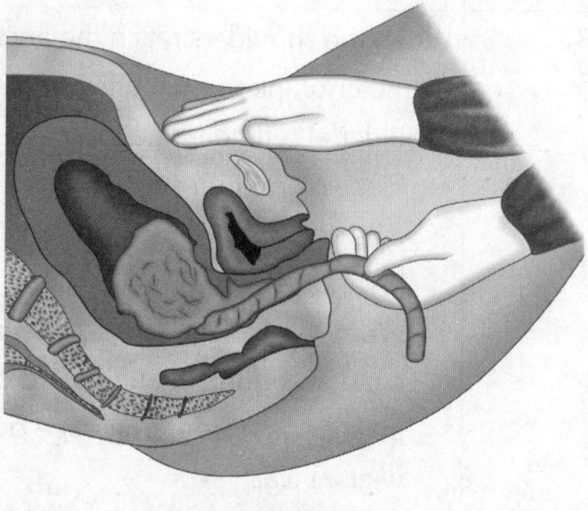 Brandt-Andrew's method of delivering the placenta during the third stage (controlled cord traction)
40.	As soon as the placenta passes through the introitus, grasp it in cupped hands	
41.	Twist the placenta round and round with gentle traction so that the membranes are stripped off intact. If the length of the membranes make the movements difficult, catch the membranes with an artery forceps and give gentle traction till they are stripped off and expelled intact	
42.	If spontaneous expulsion fails to occur in 20–30 minutes, perform controlled cord traction or Brandt-Andrews method	
43.	Examine the patient's vulva, vagina and perineum for any laceration	

Sl. No.	Nursing Action	Rationale
44.	Massage the uterus to make it contract for expulsion of any retained blood clots	
45.	Suture the episiotomy layer by layer if one was made	
46.	Clean the vulva and surrounding area with antiseptic solution and place perineal pad	
47.	Straighten mother's legs, cross them and make her comfortable	Reduces bleeding
48.	Clean and replace articles	
49.	Remove gloves and wash hands	Prevents spread of microorganisms
50.	Record the details of delivery and condition of the mother and baby in the patient's chart	

PERFORMING AN EXAMINATION OF PLACENTA

Definition:

A thorough inspection and examination of the placenta and membranes, soon after expulsion, for its completeness and normalcy.

Purposes:

1. To ensure that the entire placenta and membranes have been expelled and no part has been retained.
2. To make sure that placenta is of normal size, shape, consistency and weight.
3. To detect abnormalities such as infarctions, calcification or additional lobes.
4. To ascertain the length of the cord, number of blood vessels and site of insertion of the cord.
5. To prevent PPH and infection.
6. To check weight of placenta and measure cord length.

Equipments:

1. Placenta in a bowl.
2. A washable surface to lay the placenta.
3. A weighing machine.
4. Measuring tape.
5. Kidney tray.
6. Pair of gloves.

Procedure:

Sl. No.	Nursing Action	Rationale
1.	Don gloves	Protects nurse from contamination
2.	Using gloved hands hold the placenta by the cord allowing the membranes to hang (twisting the cord twice around the fingers will provide a firm grip)	Hanging membranes will provide a better view to check its completeness
3.	Identify the hole through which the baby was delivered	If the membrances are not torn into pieces, a single round hole can be identified clearly
4.	Insert hand through the hole and spread out the fingers to view the membranes and the blood vessels	The position of cord insertion and the course of blood vessels can be noted in this position  Examination of the membranes

Sl. No.	Nursing Action	Rationale
5.	Remove the hand from inside the membranes and lay the placenta on a flat surface with the fetal surface up. Identify the site of cord insertion	Normally the cord is inserted in the center of placenta Lateral or velamentous insertion may be noted 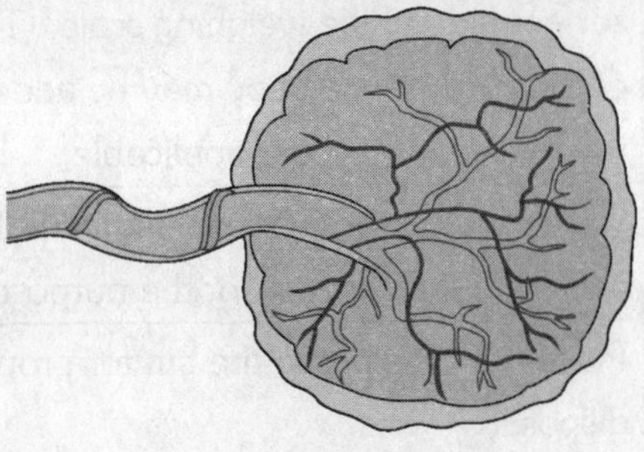 Fetal surface of placenta
6.	Examine the two membranes, amnion and chorion for completeness and presence of abnormal vessels indicating succenturiate lobe	Amnion is shiny and chorion is shaggy. Amnion can be peeled from the chorion upto the umbilical cord
7.	Invert the placenta, expose the maternal surface and remove any clots present	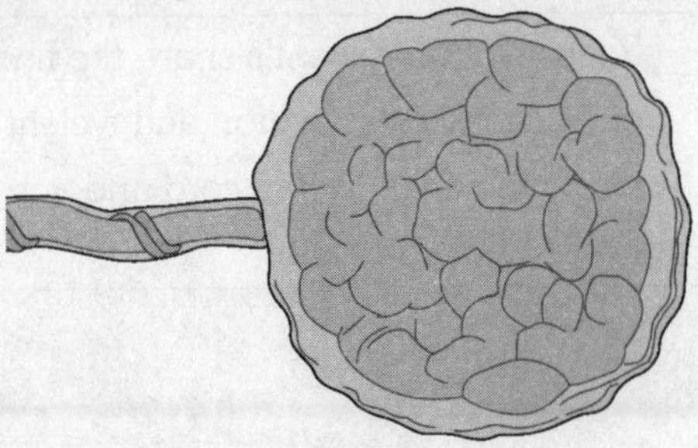 Maternal surface of placenta
8.	Examine the maternal surface by spreading it in the palms of your two hands and placing the cotyledons in close approximation (any broken fragments must be replaced before accurate assessment is made)	Ensures that no part of the placenta or membranes is left inside the uterus
9.	Assess for presence of abnormalities such as infarctions, calcifications or succenturiate lobes	
10.	Inspect the cut end of the umblical cord for presence of three umbilical vessels	Two arteries and one vein should normally be seen Absence of an artery may be associated with renal abnormalities 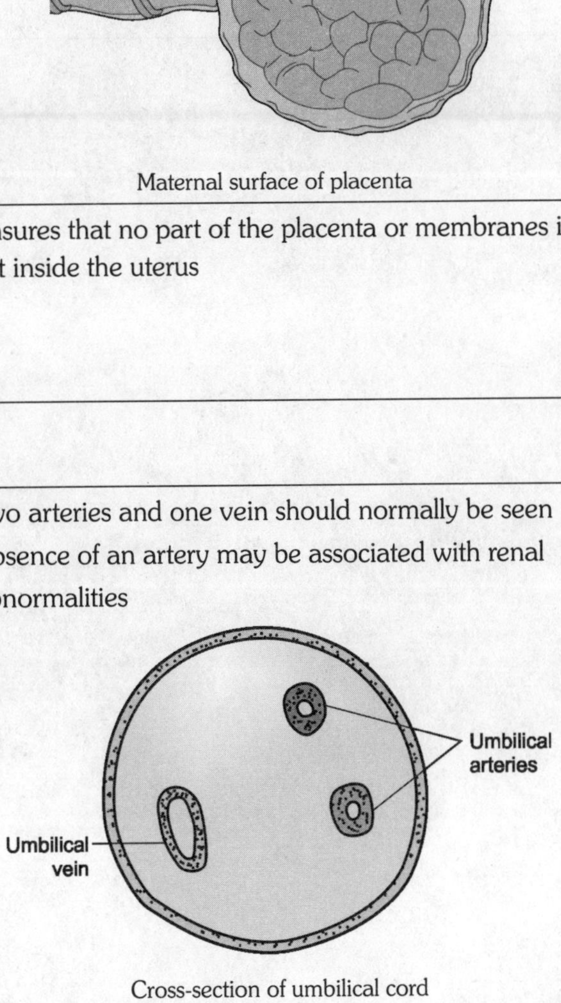 Umbilical arteries Umbilical vein Cross-section of umbilical cord

Sl. No.	Nursing Action	Rationale
11.	Measure the length of the umbilical cord by holding it extended against a graduated surface/side of the weighing scale. (The length of the cord on the baby may be added to get the total length where applicable)	Average length of the cord is 50 cm
12.	Weigh the placenta by placing it on the weighing scale meant for the purpose	Normally the placenta weighs about 1/6th of the baby's weight
13.	Place the placenta in the bin for proper disposal	
14.	Clean the area used for examination of the placenta and membranes, the weighing scale and the bowl	
15.	Remove gloves and wash hands	
16.	Record in the patient's chart, the findings of placental examination and weight of the placenta, length of the cord and any special observations made	Acts as a communication between staff members

GIVING A PERINEAL CARE

Definition:

Cleansing the patient's external genitalia and surrounding skin using an antiseptic solution

Purposes:

1. To cleanse the perineal skin.
2. To reduce chances of infection of episiotomy wound.
3. To stimulate circulation.
4. To reduce body odor and improve self-image.
5. To promote the feeling of well being.

Equipment:

a. A clean tray containing

1. Sterile antiseptic lotion—2% dettol or savlon.
2. Sterile normal saline in a bottle.
3. Cheatle forceps.
4. Antiseptic or antibiotic medication if ordered.
5. Sterile sanitary pad.
6. Kidney tray.
7. Sterile gloves.
8. Mackintosh.

b. Sterile pack or tray containing

1. Artery forceps—2
2. Dissecting forceps—1
3. Cotton balls
4. Gauze pieces
5. Sterile towel to wipe hands after surgical scrub.

c. Additional items

1. Infrared light.
2. Bedpan (if procedure is done at bedside).

Procedure:

Sl. No.	Nursing Action	Rationale
1.	Explain the procedure to patient, the purpose and how she has to cooperate	Gains confidence and cooperation of the patient
2.	Assemble articles at the bedside or in the treatment room	Saves time and effort

Sl. No.	Nursing Action	Rationale
3.	Ask the patient to empty her bowel and bladder and wash the perineal area before coming for perineal care	Ensures cleanliness and reduces number of organisms in the perineal area
4.	Screen the bed or close the doors as appropriate	Providing privacy reduces embarrassment
5.	Assist the patient to assume dorsal recumbent position with knees bend and drape the area using diamond draping method	Dorsal position facilitates better viewing of the perineum
6.	Open sterile tray, arrange articles with cheatle forceps and pour antiseptic solution in the sterile gallipot in this tray	
7.	Adjust the position of the infrared light so that it shines on the perineum at a distance of 45–50 cm	
8.	Scrub hands and dry with the sterile towel	
9.	Put on sterile gloves	
10.	Take the cotton swabs with artery forceps, dip in savlon and squeeze excess lotion with dissecting forceps into the kidney tray	Maintains asepsis
11.	With the swab clean from urethra towards anus. Clean the area from midline outward in the following order until clean and discard the swab after each stroke. Strokes are to be in the following order: • Separate the vestibule with non-dominant hand and clean vestibule starting from clitoris to fourchette • Inside of labia minora downward, farther side first then nearer side • Take off the non-dominant hand • Labia majora downward farthest side and then nearer side • Discard the used forceps (if a second one is available) • Using the second forceps clean the episiotomy wound from center outwards and outside of episiotomy both sides	Cleaning from more cleaner area to least clean area prevents contamination

Sl. No.	Nursing Action	Rationale
12.	Wipe all traces of antiseptic away with sterile normal saline swabs in the same manner as described above using thumb forceps	
13.	Dry the episiotomy with gauze pieces	Cotton fibers are likely to get caught while drying
14.	Provide perineal light/infrared light for 10 minutes, if indicated	Provides soothing effect from heat
15.	Put prescribed medication on a gauze piece and apply to the episiotomy	Prevents entry of pathogenic organisms
16.	Place sanitary pad from front to back. Do not shift position of the pad once it is applied	Avoids chances of contamination
17.	Discard gloves and used items in the kidney tray, wash forceps and tray and keep ready for sterilization	Reduces chances of contamination
18.	Replace other articles in designated places	
19.	Make the patient comfortable and leave the unit clean	
20.	Record procedure in the patient's chart including details regarding status of lochia and condition of episiotomy wound	Documentation helps for communication between staff members and provides evidence of care given and observations made

Special Considerations:

1. If a sitz bath is indicated, give it before perineal care.
2. If patient has urinary catheter, provide catheter care along with perineal care.

Studies have shown that healing takes place effectively even when patients practice perineal hygiene by themselves.

PROVIDING IMMEDIATE NEWBORN CARE

Definition :

Care provided to baby soon after birth.

Purposes :

1. To clear air passage and facilitate breathing.
2. To observe for any external anomalies.
3. To provide adequate warmth.
4. To help the newborn to adapt to the extrauterine environment.
5. To prevent injury and infections.
6. To keep baby clean.

Equipments :

1. Suction machine.
2. Mucous sucker.
3. Radiant warmer.
4. Cord clamp.
5. Sterile cotton balls.
6. Sterile cord cutting scissors.
7. Measuring tape.
8. Rectal thermometer.
9. Baby cloth (frock)
10. Baby sheet.
11. Identification tag.
12. Alcohol swabs/alcohol solution and cotton balls.

General instructions :

1. The emergency equipment for neonatal resuscitation is to be always kept ready in neonatal area.
2. Injection Naloxane to be kept ready in case mother was sedated prior to delivery.
3. Do not stimulate baby (rubbing the back or suctioning nose) and avoid bagging if amniotic fluid is meconium stained.
4. If there is any deviation from normal, a neonatologist is to be informed. If mother has diabetes mellitus and is on insulin, and if the baby's weight is less than 2 kg or more than 3.8 kg transfer to nursery.

Procedure

Sl. No.	Nursing Action	Rationale
I	**Immediate care:**	
1.	Place the baby soon after delivery on a tray covered with sterile linen with the head slightly downward (15 degrees)	Facilitates drainage by gravity of the mucus accumulated in the tracheobronchial tree

Sl. No.	Nursing Action	Rationale
2.	Place the tray between the legs of the mother at a lower level than the uterus	Facilitates gravitational flow of blood from the placenta to the fetus
3.	Clear the air passage of mucus using a mucus extractor or bulb syringe	Maintains patent airway
4.	Check Apgar rating at 1 minute and 5 min and record	Assesses the health status of newborn
5.	Clamp and ligate the cord. Cord is to be clamped and divided, following birth of the baby	
6.	Tie identification tag which has mother's name and hospital number on wrist of both mother and baby	Avoids confusion between staff and chances of wrong identification
II	**Care of the umbilical cord:**	
1.	Clean with spirit/alcohol around umbilicus, from center outward upto 10 cm away from umbilicus or according to institutional policy	Reduces risk of infection If the cord is exposed to the air, without any application of dusting powder, it dries up and falls of much earlier
III	**Care of eyes:**	
1.	Clean the eyes with sterile cotton balls soaked in normal saline	
2.	Instill soframycin eyedrops (erythromycin eye ointment) to each eye	Acts as a prophylaxis against ophthalmia neonatorum and chlamydia trachomatis
IV	**Clothings:**	
1.	Clothe the baby using a dress that is appropriate for the climate. Extremities should be free for movement. Apply a napkin which should be changed periodically	Moisture increases chances of microorganisms colonising in the skin and crevices
2.	Check patency of rectum by introducing lubricated rectal thermameter	Identifies imperforated anus
3.	Check the weight and length of the baby, the baby should be weighed naked	Normal measurements – weight—Indian baby 2.5–3.0 kg – length—50 cm
4.	Check vital signs	Identifies any deviation from normal
5.	Administer vitamin K 1 mg intramuscularly	Minimizes risk of hemorrhage
6.	Administer prophylactic antibiotic therapy if ordered in conditions like – delivery following premature rupture of membranes – instrumentation in delivery	Prevents secondary infection
7.	Observe the baby frequently atleast for 4–8 hours	Identifies any abnormal signs developing in newborn.
8.	Fill babycard and antenatal folder and document any abnormality	Acts as a communication between staff members

BATHING A NEWBORN

Purposes:

1. To keep the baby's skin clean.
2. To refresh the baby.
3. To stimulate circulation.

Equipments:

1. Big basin.
2. A soft wash cloth or absorbent pad for sponging and drying.
3. Mild, nonperfumed soap in a container.
4. Cotton balls.
5. A towel to place under the baby during bath.
6. Bath blanket or towel to cover the newborn during bath.
7. Nylon brush/soft brush for cleaning newborn's scalp.
8. Sterile water to clean the eyes of baby.
9. Diaper.
10. Baby cloth (shirt or gown).
11. Baby oil or mild lotion.
12. Tissue paper.

Procedure:

Sl. No.	Nursing Action	Rationale
1.	Explain the procedure to mother	Helps in obtaining cooperation
2.	Ensure that the room is warm and free of draughts. This is particularly important when caring for newborns	Temperature regulating mechanisms are not completely developed in newborn
3.	Remove the infant's diaper, and wipe away any faeces on the baby's perineum with the tissues	
4.	Reassure the infant before and during the bath by holding the infant firmly but gently	
5.	Undress the infant and place him or her in a supine position on a towel and cover	
6.	Place small articles such as safety pins out of the infant's reach	Prevents injury
7.	Ascertain the infant's weight and vital signs	

Sl. No.	Nursing Action	Rationale
8.	Clean the baby's eyes with sterile water only, using clean cotton swabs. Use separate swab for each eye wipe from inner to outer canthus. (In some agencies, the infant's eyes and scalp are cleaned before the infant is undressed)	Using separate cotton balls prevent the transmission of microorganisms from one eye to the other. Wiping away from the inner canthus avoids entry debris into the nasolacrimal duct
9.	Wash and dry the baby's face using water only. Soap is used to clean the ears	Soap can be irritating to the eyes, if used on face
10.	Pick the baby up using the foot ball hold (that is hold the baby against your side supporting the body with your forearm and the head with the palm of your hand). Position the baby's head over the wash basin and lather the scalp with a mild soap. Massage the lather over the scalp using finger tips	Loosens any dry scales from the scalp and helps to prevent cradle cap. If cradle cap is present it may be treated with baby oil, a dandruff shampoo or ointment prescribed by physician
11.	Rinse and dry the scalp well. Place the baby supine again	
12.	Apply soap, wash, rinse and dry each arm and hand paying particular attention to the axilla. Avoid using soap to the palmar surface and avoid excessive rubbing. Dry thoroughly	Rubbing can cause irritation and moisture can cause excoriation of the skin. Avoiding soap on palms prevents baby putting soapy fingers in mouth
13.	Apply soap, wash, rinse and dry the baby's chest and abdomen. Keep the baby covered with the bath blanket or towel between washing and rinsing	Covering the infant prevents chilling
14.	Apply soap and rinse the legs and feet. Dry it. Expose only one leg and foot at a time. Give special attention to the area between toes	Keeping exposure to a minimum maintains the baby's warmth
15.	Turn the baby on her/his stomach or side, wash, rinse and dry the back	
16.	Place the baby on his/her back. Clean and dry the genitals and anterior perineal area from front to back. a. Clean the folds of the groin. b. For females, separate the labia and clean them. Clean the genital area from front to back using moistened cotton balls. Use a clean swab for each stroke	The rectal area is cleaned last since it is most contaminated The smegma that collects between the folds of the labia and under the foreskin in males, facilitates bacterial growth and must be removed

Sl. No.	Nursing Action	Rationale
	c. If a male infant is uncircumcised, retract the foreskin if possible and clean the glans penis using a moistened cotton ball. If the foreskin is tight, do not forcibly retract it. Gentle pressure on a tight foreskin over a period of days or weeks may accomplish eventual retraction. After swabbing, replace the foreskin to prevent edema of the glans penis. Clean the shaft of the penis and scrotum (In some agencies foreskin is not retracted) d. If a male infant has been recently circumcised, clean the glans penis by gently squeezing a cotton ball moistened with sterile water over the site. Note any signs of bleeding or infection. Petroleum jelly or bacteriocidal ointment is applied to the circumcision site. Avoid applying excessive quantities of ointment	Lotions, powders and dirt can accumulate between the labia under the foreskin and need to be removed Excess ointment may obstruct the urinary meatus
17.	Clean the posterior perineum and buttocks, grasp both of the baby's ankles, raise the feet and elevate the buttocks Wash and rinse the area with the wash cloth. Dry the area and apply ointment. Do not apply powder	
18.	Clean the base of the umbilical cord with a cotton ball dipped in 70% ethyl alcohol. (Some agencies use other antiseptics such as povidone-iodine)	Alcohol promotes drying and prevents infection
19.	Check for dry, cracked or peeling skin and apply a mild baby oil or lotion	
20.	Cloth the baby with a clean dress and the diaper below the cord site	Exposing the cord site to air will promote healing
21.	Until the umbilicus and circumcision site are healed, position the baby on his side in the crib with a rolled towel or diaper behind the back for support	This position allows more air to circulate around the cord site
22.	Swaddle wrap the baby	Gives the baby a sense of security as well as keeps him warm
23.	Return the baby to mother and provide needed instructions	Mother continues care and observation of the baby
24.	Clean and replace/discard used articles as appropriate	
25.	Record any significant observation such as reddened area or skin rashes, the color and the consistency of the stool and the state of the cord stump	Helps in planning treatment

PARTOGRAPH

Definition

The partograph is a graphical presentation of the progress of labor and of fetal and maternal condition during labor. It is the best tool to detect whether labor is progressing normally or abnormally and to warn if there are signs of fetal distress or if the mother's vital signs deviate from the normal range.

Purposes

1. To record the clinical observations accurately during the period of labor.
2. To monitor the progress of labor and to organize the need for action at the appropriate time for timely referral.
3. To interpret the recorded partograph and to identify any deviation from normal.
4. To monitor the wellbeing of mother as she goes through labor.
5. To clearly identify the different stages of labor for providing appropriate attention and care.

Principal Features

1. The partograph is a valuable tool to assess the progress of labor.
2. Partograph is useful to detect deviations from normal such as abnormal progress, fetal distress, or maternal exhaustion.
3. The partograph is designed for recording maternal identification data, fetal heart rate, color of amniotic fluid, moulding of the fetal skull, cervical dilatation, fetal descend, uterine contractions, whether oxygen was administered or intravenous fluids were given, maternal vital signs and urine output.
4. Partograph reading to be started when labor is in active stage (4 cm cervical dilation or above).
5. Cervical dilatation, descend of the fetal head and uterine contractions are used in assessing the progress of labor. About 1 cm/hour cervical dilation and 1 cm descend in 4 hours indicate good progress in active first-stage.
6. Fetal heart rate and uterine contractions are recorded every 30 minutes if they are in the normal range. Assess cervical dilatation, fetal descend, color of amniotic fluid (if membranes have ruptured) and the degree of moulding or caput every 4 hours.
7. Perform a digital vaginal examination immediately if the membranes rupture and gush of amniotic fluid comes out while the woman is in any stage of labor.
8. Fetal heart rate below 120/minute or above 160/minute for more than 10 minutes is an urgent indication to inform the physician unless labor is progressing too fast.
9. Immediate reference to physician is required in case where the cervical dilatation mark crosses the Alert line, moulding is +3 with poor progress of labor and if amniotic fluid is lightly stained in latent first stage or moderately stained in active first stage or thick amniotic fluid in any stage of labor.
10. The latent phase of labor should last no longer than 8 hours.

Components of the Partograph

- Identification section

  This portion of the partograph at the top, to write the name and age of the mother, her 'gravida', 'para' status, her hospital registration number, the date and time when she was first attended for delivery and the time, the fetal membranes ruptured.
- The graph section

  The features of the fetus and mother are to be recorded in different areas of the chart. This includes the graph to record fetal heart rate, initially and then every 30 minute. The scale for fetal heart rate covers the range from 80 to 200 beats per minute. In the second stage of labor, if the liquor contains thick green or black meconium, the fetal heart rate is counted and recorded every five minutes. Each square for fetal heart on the partograph represents 30 minutes.
- Liquor and moulding

  The rows placed below the heart rate section are to record liquor (amniotic fluid) if the membranes have ruptured and the moulding of fetal skull. The status of liquor is recorded using certain letters of the alphabet.

  I: intact membranes

  A: membranes have ruptured and liquor is absent

  C: clear liquor

  B: blood stained liquor

  M_1 : lightly meconium stained

  M_2 : little bit thick meconium stained

  M_3 : very thick liquor with meconium which has soup-like appearance.

  The color of liquor should be recorded every four hours.
- **Moulding**

  Moulding denotes the extent to which the bones of the fetal skull are overlapping each other as the head is forced down the birth canal. The degree of moulding to be recorded every 4 hours. Moulding is recorded in the partograph as degrees 1 to 3.

  "O" making indicates no moulding. Bones are separated and sutures can be palpated easily.

  Degree 1 moulding is '+1' and refers to; sutures apposed, skull bones touching each other but not overlapping.

  Degree 2 is '+2' and refers to; one skull bone is overlapping another, but when pushed gently, the overlapped bone goes back easily.

  Degree 3 moulding is recorded as '+3'. One skull bone is overlapping another but when tried to push the overlapped bone, it does not go back. Degree 3 moulding indicates that the labor is at increased risk for becoming obstructed.
- **Dilatation of cervix and descend of fetal head**

  The portion of partograph labeled cervix (cm), and marked 'X' is for recording cervical dilatation, i.e. the diameter of the cervix in centimeters. This portion of the partograph is for recording descend of the fetal head (cm) marked 'O' which denotes how far down the birth canal the baby has progressed. The measurements are marked 'X' or 'O' every 4 hours. There are two rows at the bottom of this section of the partograph to write the number of hours of monitoring the labor and time on the clock.

Components of the WHO Model Partograph

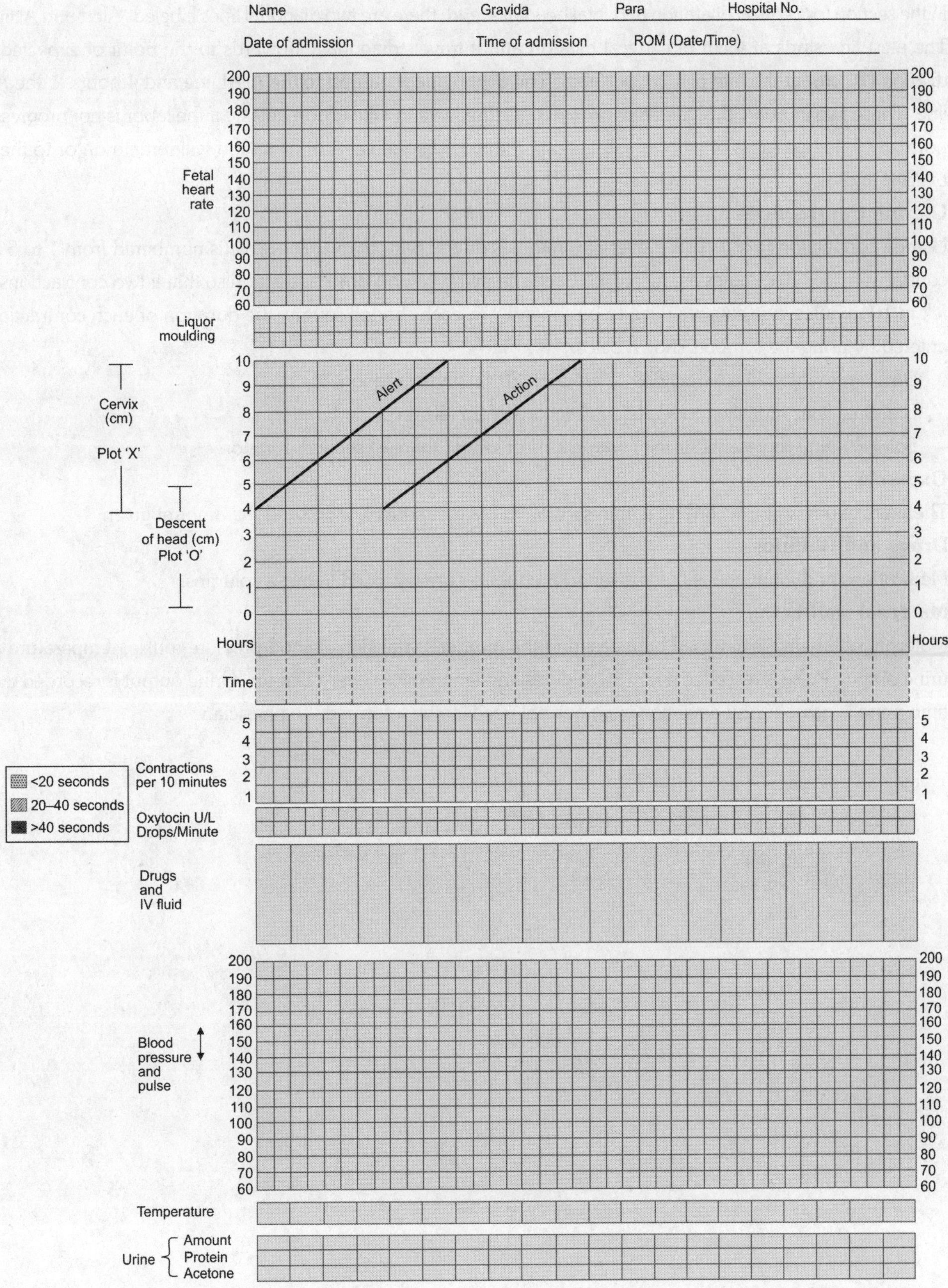

Source: WHO model partograph. Opoku Research Journal of Women's Health, 2015, www.hoagonline.com

- **Alert and Action lines**

  In the section for cervical dilatation and fetal head descend, there are two diagonal lines labeled "Alert and Action". The alert line starts at 4 cm of cervical dilation and it travels diagonally upwards to the point of expected full dilation (10 cm) at the rate of 1 cm per hour. The action line is parallel to the Alert line and 4 hours to the Alert line. These two lines are designed to warn the nurse/midwife to take action quickly if the labor is not progressing normally. If the progress of labor is satisfactory, the recording of cervical dilatation will remain on or to the left of Alert line.
- **Uterine Contractions**

  Uterine contractions are recorded every 30 minutes on the partograph. The scale is numbered from 1 to 5 and contractions per 10 minutes are recorded. Each square represents one contraction so that if two contractions are felt in 10 minutes, two squares need to be shaded. On each shaded square, the duration of each contraction is entered by using the symbols shown below:

  – Dots represent mild contractions of less than 20 seconds duration

  – Diagonal lines indicate moderate contractions of 20–40 seconds duration

  – Solid shading represents strong contractions of longer than 40 second duration
- **Oxytocin**

  There are two rows for recording administration of oxytocin during labor and the amount given
- **Drugs and IV fluids**

  Medications and intravenous fluids given to the mother are recorded in these columns.
- **Maternal well-being**

  Maternal well-being is assessed by measuring the mother's vital signs; blood pressure, pulse, temperature and urine output. Pulse is recorded every 30 minutes and temperature every 2 hours. Urine output is recorded every time urine is passed. Any deviation from normal needs to be informed the physician.

Midwifery Record

ANTENATAL EXAMINATIONS

Sl. No.	Name of the Patient	Register Number	Date of Examination	Age	Obst Score	LMP	EDD	Weeks of Gestation		
								Fundal height		Abd girth
								Weeks	Cm	
1.										
2.										
3.										
4.										
5.										
6.										
7.										
8.										
9.										
10.										
11.										
12.										
13.										
14.										
15.										
16.										
17.										
18.										
19.										
20.										

Signature of Student

PERFORMED

Presen-tation	Position	Engage-ment	Hb%	Blood Glucose	Urine	FHS	BP	Maternal weight	Treatment Advised	Signature of Supervisor

Signature of Supervisor

NORMAL DELIVERIES

Sl. No.	Name of the Patient	Register Number	Age	Obst Score	Date and Time of Delivery	LMP	EDD	Weeks of Gestation		Presentation
								Weeks	Cm	
1.										
2.										
3.										
4.										
5.										
6.										
7.										
8.										
9.										
10.										
11.										
12.										
13.										
14.										
15.										

Signature of Student

WITNESSED

Position	Baby			Condition of Baby	Medications used	Conducted by	Supervised by
	Sex	Weight	Apgar Score				

Signature of Supervisor

NORMAL DELIVERIES

Sl. No.	Name of the Patient	Register Number	Age	Obst Score	Date and Time of Delivery	LMP	EDD	Weeks of Gestation		Presentation
								Weeks	Cm	
1.										
2.										
3.										
4.										
5.										
6.										
7.										
8.										
9.										
10.										

Signature of Student

CONDUCTED

Position	Baby			Condition of Baby	Medications used	Conducted by	Supervised by
	Sex	Weight	Apgar Score				

Signature of Supervisor

VAGINAL EXAMINATIONS PERFORMED

Sl. No.	Name of the Patient	Date of Admission	Register Number	Age	Obst Score	Weeks of Gestation
1.						
2.						
3.						
4.						
5.						
6.						
7.						
8.						
9.						
10.						

Signature of Student

IN LABOR

Cervix		Membranes	Presentation Position	Station of Pr Part	Pelvis	Remarks	Signature of Supervisor
Effacement	Dilation						

Signature of Supervisor

EPISIOTOMIES AND SUTURING

Sl. No.	Name of the Patient	Register Number	Date of Delivery	Age	Obst Score
1.					
2.					
3.					
4.					
5.					
6.					
7.					
8.					
9.					
10.					

Signature of Student

PERFORMED/ASSISTED

Type of Episiotomy	No. of Sutures	Condition	Remarks	Signature of Supervisor

Signature of Supervisor

ABNORMAL DELIVERIES

Sl. No.	Name of the Patient	Date	Register Number	Age	Weeks of Gestation	Presentation Position
1.						
2.						
3.						
4.						
5.						
6.						
7.						
8.						
9.						
10.						

Signature of Student

WITNESSED (FORCEPS/VENTOUSE)

Indication	Nature of Delivery	Baby			Remarks on Delivery	Condition of		By whom Performed
		Sex	Weight	Apgar Score		Mother	Baby	

Signature of Supervisor

IUCD INSERTIONS

Sl. No.	Name of the Patient	Date	Register Number	Age	Para	Date of last Delivery	Presentation Position
1.							
2.							
3.							
4.							
5.							
6.							
7.							
8.							
9.							
10.							

Signature of Student

ASSISTED/CARRIED OUT

Contraceptive used before	LMP	Duration of LMP	Type of IUCD Inserted	Remarks	Performed by

Signature of Supervisor

CESAREAN SECTIONS

Sl. No.	Name of the Patient	Date	Register Number	Age	Obst Score	LMP	EDD	Weeks of Gestation
1.								
2.								
3.								
4.								
5.								
6.								
7.								
8.								
9.								
10.								

Signature of Student

WITNESSED

Presentation	Position	Indication	Type of IUCD Inserted			Condition		Performed by
			Sex	Weight	Apgar Score	Mother	Baby	

Signature of Supervisor

PRENATAL MOTHERS

Sl. No.	Name of the Patient	Register Number	Date of Admission	Dates of Care	Age	Obst Score	LMP	EDD	Period of Gestation
1.									
2.									
3.									
4.									
5.									
6.									
7.									
8.									
9.									
10.									

Signature of Student

NURSED (NORMAL AND HIGH RISK)

Presentation	Position	BP	Blood Exam	Urine Exam	FHR	Maternal Condition	Treatment	Signature of Supervisor

Signature of Supervisor

INTRANATAL MOTHERS

Sl. No.	Name of the Patient	Register Number	Date of Admission	Dates of Delivery	Age	Obst Score	LMP	EDD	Period of Gestation
1.									
2.									
3.									
4.									
5.									
6.									
7.									
8.									
9.									
10.									

Signature of Student

NURSED

Presentation	Position	BP	Blood Exam	FHR	Duration of Labor	Type of Delivery	Condition		Signature of Supervisor
							Mother	Baby	

Signature of Supervisor

POSTNATAL MOTHERS AND NEWBORNS

Sl. No.	Name of the Patient	Date of Admission	Register Number	Age	Obst Score	LMP	EDD	Date of Delivery	Type of Delivery
1.									
2.									
3.									
4.									
5.									
6.									
7.									
8.									
9.									
10.									

Signature of Student

NURSED INCLUDING CESAREAN MOTHERS

Perineum	Lochia	Fundus	Condition			Treatment and Remarks	Signature of Supervisor
			Mother	Baby	Apgar Score		

Signature of Supervisor

NEONATES

Sl. No.	Name of the Patient	Register Number	Date of Admission	Dates of Delivery	Age	Obst Score	LMP	EDD	Period of Gestation
1.									
2.									
3.									
4.									
5.									
6.									
7.									
8.									
9.									
10.									

Signature of Student

NURSED

Presentation	Position	BP	Blood Exam	Urine Exam	FHR	Maternal Condition	Treatment	Signature of Supervisor

Signature of Supervisor

PRENATAL MOTHER NURSED (NORMAL AND HIGH RISK)–1

Name ....Age..............................Gravida................................Para...................

Hospital Number.....................................

Date of Admission...................................

Weeks of Gestation ....

Date of Discharge...................................

- **Prenatal Record**
  Date of booking .... LMP ....
  Gestation at 1st visit .... EDD ....
- **Medical History/Chief complaints**
  Chronic illness .... Allergy...
  Surgery .... Communicable disease ....
- **Family History**
  Type of Family Nuclear/Joint .... No. of Persons...

  Diseases Chronic illness: Hypertension .... Diabetes ....
  Genetic disorders.................................... Other specify ....
  Psychiatric disorder ....

History of Multiple Births

- **Socioeconomic Background**
  Religion .... Family Income ....
  Education: Husband .... Wife ....
  Occupation: Husband .... Wife ....
- **Menstrual History**
  Age at Menarchy .... Duration ....
  Interval .... Flow...
- **Marital History**
  Age of Marriage.. Years Married ....
  Consanguineous: Yes/No
- **Dietary Pattern**
  Vegetarian... Non-vegetarian..
  Likes.. Dislikes ....
  Habits: Smoking/Drinking/Chewing Pan/Tobacco
- **Present pregnancy**
  Duration..weeks Trimester: First/second/third

PAST OBSTETRICAL HISTORY

Sl. No.	Year	Full-term	Pre-term	Abortion	Type of Delivery	Baby				Remarks
						Sex	Alive	Stillborn	Weight	

PRENATAL VISITS

Date	Height	Weight	Urine	BP	FHR	Gestation Weeks	Ht of Fundus	Abd girth	Presentation	Position	Treatment and Remarks

- **Admission Notes**

Date of Admission .... Diagnosis ....

General Condition: Good/Fair/Satisfactory/Poor

Heart .... Lungs .... Mouth ....

Abdomen .... Breasts .... Nipples ....

Edema: Ankles .... Hands .... Legs .... Face ....

Abdomen .... Vulva .... All over body

Blood Pressure .... TPR ....

Digestion .... Micturition .... Bowels ....

Pain .... Vaginal Discharge .... Others ....

- **Obstetrical Examination**

Period of Gestation .... Presentation .... Position ....

Height of Fundus .... Engaged/Not Engaged/Floating ....

Fetal Heart Rate .... Abdominal Girth ....

Remarks ....

- **Investigations**

Blood Group .... Rh .... Hb ....

VDRL .... HIV .... Other ....

Ultrasound ....

Diet Ordered ....

Medications Ordered ....

....

....

....

Treatment ....

Remarks ....

PRENATAL CLINICAL CHART

Name .... Age .... Obs Score																	
Date																	
Days																	
Temperature		M	E	M	E	M	E	M	E	M	E	M	E	M	E	M	E
F	C																
106.6	41.5																
105.8	41.0																
104.9	40.5																
104.0	40.0																
103.1	39.5																
102.2	39.0																
101.3	38.5																
100.4	38.0																
99.5	37.5																
98.6	37.0																
97.7	36.5																
96.8	36.0																
BP																	
Pulse																	
Respiration																	
FHR																	
Urine																	
Motion																	

- **HEALTH EDUCATION**

....

....

....

....

....

....

- **LIST OF NURSING DIAGNOSES**

....

....

....

....

....

....

Signature of Student

Signature of Clinical Instructor

PRENATAL NURSING CARE

Nursing Diagnosis Statements Prioritized	Nursing Care Plans Listed	Nursing Care Implemented and Evaluated

PRENATAL NURSING CARE

Nursing Diagnosis Statements Prioritized	Nursing Care Plans Listed	Nursing Care Implemented and Evaluated

PRENATAL NURSING CARE

Nursing Diagnosis Statements Prioritized	Nursing Care Plans Listed	Nursing Care Implemented and Evaluated

PRENATAL MOTHER NURSED (NORMAL AND HIGH RISK)–2

Name .... Age .... Gravida .... Para ....

Hospital Number ....

Date of Admission ....

Weeks of Gestation ....

Date of Discharge ....

- **Prenatal Record**
  Date of booking .... LMP ....
  Gestation at 1st visit .... EDD ....

- **Medical History/Chief complaints**
  Chronic illness .... Allergy ....
  Surgery .... Communicable disease ....

- **Family History**
  Type of Family Nuclear/Joint .... No. of Persons ....

  Diseases Chronic illness: Hypertension .... Diabetes ....
  Genetic disorders .... Other specify ....
  Psychiatric disorder ....

History of Multiple Births

- **Socioeconomic Background**
  Religion .... Family Income ....
  Education: Husband .... Wife ....
  Occupation: Husband .... Wife ....

- **Menstrual History**
  Age at Menarchy .... Duration ....
  Interval .... Flow ....

- **Marital History**
  Age of Marriage .... Years Married ....
  Consanguineous: Yes/No

- **Dietary Pattern**
  Vegetarian .... Non-vegetarian ....
  Likes .... Dislikes ....
  Habits: Smoking/Drinking/Chewing Pan/Tobacco

- **Present pregnancy**
  Duration .... weeks Trimester: First/second/third

PAST OBSTETRICAL HISTORY

Sl. No.	Year	Full-term	Pre-term	Abortion	Type of Delivery	Baby				Remarks
						Sex	Alive	Stillborn	Weight	

PRENATAL VISITS

Date	Height	Weight	Urine	BP	FHR	Gestation Weeks	Ht of Fundus	Abd girth	Presentation	Position	Treatment and Remarks

- **Admission Notes**

Date of Admission .... Diagnosis ....

General Condition: Good/Fair/Satisfactory/Poor

Heart .... Lungs .... Mouth ....

Abdomen .... Breasts .... Nipples ....

Edema: Ankles .... Hands .... Legs .... Face ....

Abdomen .... Vulva .... All over body

Blood Pressure .... TPR ....

Digestion .... Micturition .... Bowels ....

Pain .... Vaginal Discharge .... Others ....

- **Obstetrical Examination**

Period of Gestation .... Presentation .... Position ....

Height of Fundus .... Engaged/Not Engaged/Floating ....

Fetal Heart Rate .... Abdominal Girth ....

Remarks ....

- **Investigations**

Blood Group .... Rh .... Hb ....

VDRL .... HIV .... Other ....

Ultrasound ....

Diet Ordered ....

Medications Ordered ....

....

....

....

Treatment ....

Remarks ....

PRENATAL CLINICAL CHART

Name .... Age .... Obs Score																	
Date																	
Days																	
Temperature		M	E	M	E	M	E	M	E	M	E	M	E	M	E	M	E
F	C																
106.6	41.5																
105.8	41.0																
104.9	40.5																
104.0	40.0																
103.1	39.5																
102.2	39.0																
101.3	38.5																
100.4	38.0																
99.5	37.5																
98.6	37.0																
97.7	36.5																
96.8	36.0																
BP																	
Pulse																	
Respiration																	
FHR																	
Urine																	
Motion																	

- **HEALTH EDUCATION**

....

....

....

....

....

....

- **LIST OF NURSING DIAGNOSES**

....

....

....

....

....

....

------------------------------ **Signature of Student**

------------------------------ **Signature of Clinical Instructor**

PRENATAL NURSING CARE

Nursing Diagnosis Statements Prioritized	Nursing Care Plans Listed	Nursing Care Implemented and Evaluated

PRENATAL NURSING CARE

Nursing Diagnosis Statements Prioritized	Nursing Care Plans Listed	Nursing Care Implemented and Evaluated

PRENATAL NURSING CARE

Nursing Diagnosis Statements Prioritized	Nursing Care Plans Listed	Nursing Care Implemented and Evaluated

PRENATAL MOTHER NURSED (NORMAL AND HIGH RISK)–3

Name ....Age...............................Gravida................................Para...................

Hospital Number......................................

Date of Admission....................................

Weeks of Gestation ....

Date of Discharge....................................

- **Prenatal Record**
  Date of booking .... LMP ....
  Gestation at 1st visit .... EDD ....

- **Medical History/Chief complaints**
  Chronic illness .... Allergy..
  Surgery .... Communicable disease ....

- **Family History**
  Type of Family Nuclear/Joint .... No. of Persons...

  Diseases Chronic illness: Hypertension .... Diabetes ....
  Genetic disorders.................................. Other specify ....
  Psychiatric disorder ....

History of Multiple Births

- **Socioeconomic Background**
  Religion .... Family Income ....
  Education: Husband .... Wife ....
  Occupation: Husband .... Wife ....

- **Menstrual History**
  Age at Menarchy .... Duration ....
  Interval .... Flow ....

- **Marital History**
  Age of Marriage... Years Married ....
  Consanguineous: Yes/No

- **Dietary Pattern**
  Vegetarian... Non-vegetarian ....
  Likes... Dislikes ....
  Habits: Smoking/Drinking/Chewing Pan/Tobacco

- **Present pregnancy**
  Duration...weeks Trimester: First/second/third

PAST OBSTETRICAL HISTORY

Sl. No.	Year	Full-term	Pre-term	Abortion	Type of Delivery	Baby				Remarks
						Sex	Alive	Stillborn	Weight	

PRENATAL VISITS

Date	Height	Weight	Urine	BP	FHR	Gestation Weeks	Ht of Fundus	Abd girth	Presentation	Position	Treatment and Remarks

- **Admission Notes**

Date of Admission .... Diagnosis..

General Condition: Good/Fair/Satisfactory/Poor

Heart .... Lungs .... Mouth ....

Abdomen.. Breasts.. Nipples ....

Edema: Ankles .... Hands.......................... Legs .... Face...........

Abdomen .... Vulva .... All over body

Blood Pressure.................................... TPR..

Digestion .... Micturition.................................... Bowels..............................

Pain .... Vaginal Discharge.......................... Others..............................

- **Obstetrical Examination**

Period of Gestation .... Presentation.................................. Position.............................

Height of Fundus .... Engaged/Not Engaged/Floating...

Fetal Heart Rate.................................. Abdominal Girth ....

Remarks...

- **Investigations**

Blood Group .... Rh .... Hb..................................

VDRL .... HIV .... Other ....

Ultrasound...

Diet Ordered...

Medications Ordered..

....

....

....

Treatment...

Remarks...

PRENATAL CLINICAL CHART

Name .... Age .... Obs Score																	
Date																	
Days																	
Temperature		M	E	M	E	M	E	M	E	M	E	M	E	M	E	M	E
F	C																
106.6	41.5																
105.8	41.0																
104.9	40.5																
104.0	40.0																
103.1	39.5																
102.2	39.0																
101.3	38.5																
100.4	38.0																
99.5	37.5																
98.6	37.0																
97.7	36.5																
96.8	36.0																
BP																	
Pulse																	
Respiration																	
FHR																	
Urine																	
Motion																	

- **HEALTH EDUCATION**

....

....

....

....

....

....

- **LIST OF NURSING DIAGNOSES**

....

....

....

....

....

....

Signature of Student

Signature of Clinical Instructor

PRENATAL NURSING CARE

Nursing Diagnosis Statements Prioritized	Nursing Care Plans Listed	Nursing Care Implemented and Evaluated

PRENATAL NURSING CARE

Nursing Diagnosis Statements Prioritized	Nursing Care Plans Listed	Nursing Care Implemented and Evaluated

PRENATAL NURSING CARE

Nursing Diagnosis Statements Prioritized	Nursing Care Plans Listed	Nursing Care Implemented and Evaluated

PRENATAL MOTHER NURSED (NORMAL AND HIGH RISK)–4

Name ....Age.............................Gravida.................................Para...................

Hospital Number......................................

Date of Admission....................................

Weeks of Gestation ....

Date of Discharge....................................

- **Prenatal Record**
  Date of booking .... LMP ....
  Gestation at 1st visit .... EDD ....

- **Medical History/Chief complaints**
  Chronic illness .... Allergy..
  Surgery .... Communicable disease ....

- **Family History**
  Type of Family Nuclear/Joint .... No. of Persons...

  Diseases Chronic illness: Hypertension .... Diabetes ....
  Genetic disorders.................................. Other specify ....
  Psychiatric disorder ....

History of Multiple Births

- **Socioeconomic Background**
  Religion .... Family Income ....
  Education: Husband .... Wife ....
  Occupation: Husband .... Wife ....

- **Menstrual History**
  Age at Menarchy .... Duration..
  Interval .... Flow..

- **Marital History**
  Age of Marriage.. Years Married ....
  Consanguineous: Yes/No

- **Dietary Pattern**
  Vegetarian.. Non-vegetarian...
  Likes... Dislikes ....
  Habits: Smoking/Drinking/Chewing Pan/Tobacco

- **Present pregnancy**
  Duration...weeks Trimester: First/second/third

PAST OBSTETRICAL HISTORY

Sl. No.	Year	Full-term	Pre-term	Abortion	Type of Delivery	Baby				Remarks
						Sex	Alive	Stillborn	Weight	

PRENATAL VISITS

Date	Height	Weight	Urine	BP	FHR	Gestation Weeks	Ht of Fundus	Abd girth	Presentation	Position	Treatment and Remarks

- **Admission Notes**

Date of Admission .... Diagnosis ....

General Condition: Good/Fair/Satisfactory/Poor

Heart .... Lungs .... Mouth ....

Abdomen .... Breasts .... Nipples ....

Edema: Ankles .... Hands .... Legs .... Face ....

Abdomen .... Vulva .... All over body

Blood Pressure .... TPR ....

Digestion .... Micturition .... Bowels ....

Pain .... Vaginal Discharge .... Others ....

- **Obstetrical Examination**

Period of Gestation .... Presentation .... Position ....

Height of Fundus .... Engaged/Not Engaged/Floating ....

Fetal Heart Rate .... Abdominal Girth ....

Remarks ....

- **Investigations**

Blood Group .... Rh .... Hb ....

VDRL .... HIV .... Other ....

Ultrasound ....

Diet Ordered ....

Medications Ordered ....

....

....

....

Treatment ....

Remarks ....

PRENATAL CLINICAL CHART

Name	Age	Obs Score														
Date																
Days																
Temperature		M	E	M	E	M	E	M	E	M	E	M	E	M	E	M	E
F	C																
106.6	41.5																
105.8	41.0																
104.9	40.5																
104.0	40.0																
103.1	39.5																
102.2	39.0																
101.3	38.5																
100.4	38.0																
99.5	37.5																
98.6	37.0																
97.7	36.5																
96.8	36.0																
BP																	
Pulse																	
Respiration																	
FHR																	
Urine																	
Motion																	

- **HEALTH EDUCATION**

....

....

....

....

....

....

- **LIST OF NURSING DIAGNOSES**

....

....

....

....

....

....

....

Signature of Student

Signature of Clinical Instructor

PRENATAL NURSING CARE

Nursing Diagnosis Statements Prioritized	Nursing Care Plans Listed	Nursing Care Implemented and Evaluated

PRENATAL NURSING CARE

Nursing Diagnosis Statements Prioritized	Nursing Care Plans Listed	Nursing Care Implemented and Evaluated

PRENATAL NURSING CARE

Nursing Diagnosis Statements Prioritized	Nursing Care Plans Listed	Nursing Care Implemented and Evaluated

PRENATAL MOTHER NURSED (NORMAL AND HIGH RISK)–5

Name .... Age............................ Gravida.............................. Para..................

Hospital Number.....................................

Date of Admission...................................

Weeks of Gestation ....

Date of Discharge...................................

- **Prenatal Record**
  Date of booking .... LMP ....
  Gestation at 1st visit .... EDD ....

- **Medical History/Chief complaints**
  Chronic illness .... Allergy...
  Surgery .... Communicable disease ....

- **Family History**
  Type of Family   Nuclear/Joint .... No. of Persons...

  Diseases   Chronic illness: Hypertension .... Diabetes ....
  Genetic disorders.................................. Other specify ....
  Psychiatric disorder ....

History of Multiple Births

- **Socioeconomic Background**
  Religion .... Family Income ....
  Education: Husband .... Wife ....
  Occupation: Husband .... Wife ....

- **Menstrual History**
  Age at Menarchy .... Duration ....
  Interval .... Flow ....

- **Marital History**
  Age of Marriage... Years Married ....
  Consanguineous: Yes/No

- **Dietary Pattern**
  Vegetarian.. Non-vegetarian..
  Likes... Dislikes ....
  Habits: Smoking/Drinking/Chewing Pan/Tobacco

- **Present pregnancy**
  Duration...weeks Trimester: First/second/third

PAST OBSTETRICAL HISTORY

Sl. No.	Year	Full-term	Pre-term	Abortion	Type of Delivery	Baby				Remarks
						Sex	Alive	Stillborn	Weight	

PRENATAL VISITS

Date	Height	Weight	Urine	BP	FHR	Gestation Weeks	Ht of Fundus	Abd girth	Presentation	Position	Treatment and Remarks

- **Admission Notes**

Date of Admission .... Diagnosis ....
General Condition: Good/Fair/Satisfactory/Poor
Heart .... Lungs .... Mouth ....
Abdomen .... Breasts .... Nipples ....
Edema: Ankles .... Hands .... Legs .... Face ....
Abdomen .... Vulva .... All over body
Blood Pressure .... TPR ....
Digestion .... Micturition .... Bowels ....
Pain .... Vaginal Discharge .... Others ....

- **Obstetrical Examination**

Period of Gestation .... Presentation .... Position ....
Height of Fundus .... Engaged/Not Engaged/Floating ....
Fetal Heart Rate .... Abdominal Girth ....
Remarks ....

- **Investigations**

Blood Group .... Rh .... Hb ....
VDRL .... HIV .... Other ....
Ultrasound ....

Diet Ordered ....
Medications Ordered ....
....
....
....

Treatment ....
Remarks ....

PRENATAL CLINICAL CHART

Name .... Age .... Obs Score																
Date																
Days																
Temperature		M	E	M	E	M	E	M	E	M	E	M	E	M	E	M	E
F	C															
106.6	41.5															
105.8	41.0															
104.9	40.5															
104.0	40.0															
103.1	39.5															
102.2	39.0															
101.3	38.5															
100.4	38.0															
99.5	37.5															
98.6	37.0															
97.7	36.5															
96.8	36.0															
BP																
Pulse																
Respiration																
FHR																
Urine																
Motion																

- **HEALTH EDUCATION**

....
....
....
....
....
....

- **LIST OF NURSING DIAGNOSES**

....
....
....
....
....
....

Signature of Student

Signature of Clinical Instructor

PRENATAL NURSING CARE

Nursing Diagnosis Statements Prioritized	Nursing Care Plans Listed	Nursing Care Implemented and Evaluated

PRENATAL NURSING CARE

Nursing Diagnosis Statements Prioritized	Nursing Care Plans Listed	Nursing Care Implemented and Evaluated

PRENATAL NURSING CARE

Nursing Diagnosis Statements Prioritized	Nursing Care Plans Listed	Nursing Care Implemented and Evaluated

PRENATAL MOTHER NURSED (NORMAL AND HIGH RISK)–6

Name ....Age..............................Gravida.................................Para..................

Hospital Number......................................

Date of Admission...................................

Weeks of Gestation ....

Date of Discharge...................................

- **Prenatal Record**
  Date of booking .... LMP ....
  Gestation at 1st visit .... EDD ....

- **Medical History/Chief complaints**
  Chronic illness .... Allergy...
  Surgery .... Communicable disease ....

- **Family History**
  Type of Family Nuclear/Joint .... No. of Persons..

  Diseases Chronic illness: Hypertension .... Diabetes ....
  Genetic disorders.................................. Other specify ....
  Psychiatric disorder ....

History of Multiple Births

- **Socioeconomic Background**
  Religion .... Family Income ....
  Education: Husband .... Wife ....
  Occupation: Husband .... Wife ....

- **Menstrual History**
  Age at Menarchy .... Duration ....
  Interval .... Flow ....

- **Marital History**
  Age of Marriage.. Years Married ....
  Consanguineous: Yes/No

- **Dietary Pattern**
  Vegetarian.. Non-vegetarian...
  Likes.. Dislikes ....
  Habits: Smoking/Drinking/Chewing Pan/Tobacco

- **Present pregnancy**
  Duration...weeks Trimester: First/second/third

PAST OBSTETRICAL HISTORY

Sl. No.	Year	Full-term	Pre-term	Abortion	Type of Delivery	Baby				Remarks
						Sex	Alive	Stillborn	Weight	

PRENATAL VISITS

Date	Height	Weight	Urine	BP	FHR	Gestation Weeks	Ht of Fundus	Abd girth	Presentation	Position	Treatment and Remarks

- **Admission Notes**

Date of Admission .... Diagnosis..

General Condition: Good/Fair/Satisfactory/Poor

Heart .... Lungs .... Mouth ....

Abdomen.................................... Breasts.................................... Nipples ....

Edema: Ankles .... Hands........................ Legs .... Face............

Abdomen .... Vulva .... All over body

Blood Pressure.................................... TPR..

Digestion .... Micturition.................................... Bowels..........................

Pain .... Vaginal Discharge.................................... Others..........................

- **Obstetrical Examination**

Period of Gestation .... Presentation.................................... Position..........................

Height of Fundus .... Engaged/Not Engaged/Floating..

Fetal Heart Rate.................................... Abdominal Girth ....

Remarks..

- **Investigations**

Blood Group.................................... Rh .... Hb..........................

VDRL .... HIV.................................... Other ....

Ultrasound..

Diet Ordered..

Medications Ordered..

....

....

....

Treatment..

Remarks..

PRENATAL CLINICAL CHART

Name		Age										Obs Score				
Date																
Days																
Temperature		M	E	M	E	M	E	M	E	M	E	M	E	M	E	M	E
F	C															
106.6	41.5															
105.8	41.0															
104.9	40.5															
104.0	40.0															
103.1	39.5															
102.2	39.0															
101.3	38.5															
100.4	38.0															
99.5	37.5															
98.6	37.0															
97.7	36.5															
96.8	36.0															
BP																
Pulse																
Respiration																
FHR																
Urine																
Motion																

- **HEALTH EDUCATION**

....

....

....

....

....

....

- **LIST OF NURSING DIAGNOSES**

....

....

....

....

....

....

Signature of Student

Signature of Clinical Instructor

PRENATAL NURSING CARE

Nursing Diagnosis Statements Prioritized	Nursing Care Plans Listed	Nursing Care Implemented and Evaluated

PRENATAL NURSING CARE

Nursing Diagnosis Statements Prioritized	Nursing Care Plans Listed	Nursing Care Implemented and Evaluated

PRENATAL NURSING CARE

Nursing Diagnosis Statements Prioritized	Nursing Care Plans Listed	Nursing Care Implemented and Evaluated

PRENATAL MOTHER NURSED (NORMAL AND HIGH RISK)–7

Name ....Age..............................Gravida................................Para...................

Hospital Number.....................................

Date of Admission...................................

Weeks of Gestation ....

Date of Discharge...................................

- **Prenatal Record**
  Date of booking .... LMP ....
  Gestation at 1st visit .... EDD ....
- **Medical History/Chief complaints**
  Chronic illness .... Allergy...
  Surgery .... Communicable disease ....
- **Family History**
  Type of Family Nuclear/Joint .... No. of Persons..

  Diseases Chronic illness: Hypertension .... Diabetes ....
  Genetic disorders................................... Other specify ....
  Psychiatric disorder ....

History of Multiple Births

- **Socioeconomic Background**
  Religion .... Family Income ....
  Education: Husband .... Wife ....
  Occupation: Husband .... Wife ....
- **Menstrual History**
  Age at Menarchy .... Duration ....
  Interval .... Flow ....
- **Marital History**
  Age of Marriage.. Years Married ....
  Consanguineous: Yes/No
- **Dietary Pattern**
  Vegetarian.. Non-vegetarian..
  Likes... Dislikes ....
  Habits: Smoking/Drinking/Chewing Pan/Tobacco
- **Present pregnancy**
  Duration..weeks Trimester: First/second/third

PAST OBSTETRICAL HISTORY

Sl. No.	Year	Full-term	Pre-term	Abortion	Type of Delivery	Baby				Remarks
						Sex	Alive	Stillborn	Weight	

PRENATAL VISITS

Date	Height	Weight	Urine	BP	FHR	Gestation Weeks	Ht of Fundus	Abd girth	Presentation	Position	Treatment and Remarks

- **Admission Notes**

Date of Admission .... Diagnosis ....
General Condition: Good/Fair/Satisfactory/Poor
Heart .... Lungs .... Mouth ....
Abdomen .... Breasts .... Nipples ....
Edema: Ankles .... Hands .... Legs .... Face ....
Abdomen .... Vulva .... All over body
Blood Pressure .... TPR ....
Digestion .... Micturition .... Bowels ....
Pain .... Vaginal Discharge .... Others ....

- **Obstetrical Examination**

Period of Gestation .... Presentation .... Position ....
Height of Fundus .... Engaged/Not Engaged/Floating ....
Fetal Heart Rate .... Abdominal Girth ....
Remarks ....

- **Investigations**

Blood Group .... Rh .... Hb ....
VDRL .... HIV .... Other ....
Ultrasound ....

Diet Ordered ....
Medications Ordered ....
....
....
....

Treatment ....
Remarks ....

PRENATAL CLINICAL CHART

Name .... Age .... Obs Score																
Date																
Days																
Temperature		M	E	M	E	M	E	M	E	M	E	M	E	M	E	M	E
F	C															
106.6	41.5															
105.8	41.0															
104.9	40.5															
104.0	40.0															
103.1	39.5															
102.2	39.0															
101.3	38.5															
100.4	38.0															
99.5	37.5															
98.6	37.0															
97.7	36.5															
96.8	36.0															
BP																
Pulse																
Respiration																
FHR																
Urine																
Motion																

- **HEALTH EDUCATION**

....

....

....

....

....

....

- **LIST OF NURSING DIAGNOSES**

....

....

....

....

....

....

Signature of Student

Signature of Clinical Instructor

PRENATAL NURSING CARE

Nursing Diagnosis Statements Prioritized	Nursing Care Plans Listed	Nursing Care Implemented and Evaluated

PRENATAL NURSING CARE

Nursing Diagnosis Statements Prioritized	Nursing Care Plans Listed	Nursing Care Implemented and Evaluated

PRENATAL NURSING CARE

Nursing Diagnosis Statements Prioritized	Nursing Care Plans Listed	Nursing Care Implemented and Evaluated

PRENATAL MOTHER NURSED (NORMAL AND HIGH RISK)–8

Name ....Age..............................Gravida...............................Para...................

Hospital Number.....................................

Date of Admission...................................

Weeks of Gestation ....

Date of Discharge....................................

- **Prenatal Record**
  Date of booking .... LMP ....
  Gestation at 1st visit .... EDD ....
- **Medical History/Chief complaints**
  Chronic illness .... Allergy..
  Surgery .... Communicable disease ....
- **Family History**
  Type of Family Nuclear/Joint .... No. of Persons ....

  Diseases Chronic illness: Hypertension .... Diabetes ....
  Genetic disorders.................................. Other specify ....
  Psychiatric disorder ....

History of Multiple Births

- **Socioeconomic Background**
  Religion .... Family Income ....
  Education: Husband .... Wife ....
  Occupation: Husband .... Wife ....
- **Menstrual History**
  Age at Menarchy .... Duration ....
  Interval .... Flow ....
- **Marital History**
  Age of Marriage... Years Married ....
  Consanguineous: Yes/No
- **Dietary Pattern**
  Vegetarian.. Non-vegetarian ....
  Likes.. Dislikes ....
  Habits: Smoking/Drinking/Chewing Pan/Tobacco
- **Present pregnancy**
  Duration..weeks Trimester: First/second/third

PAST OBSTETRICAL HISTORY

Sl. No.	Year	Full-term	Pre-term	Abortion	Type of Delivery	Baby				Remarks
						Sex	Alive	Stillborn	Weight	

PRENATAL VISITS

Date	Height	Weight	Urine	BP	FHR	Gestation Weeks	Ht of Fundus	Abd girth	Presentation	Position	Treatment and Remarks

- **Admission Notes**

Date of Admission .... Diagnosis ....

General Condition: Good/Fair/Satisfactory/Poor

Heart .... Lungs .... Mouth ....

Abdomen.. Breasts.. Nipples ....

Edema: Ankles .... Hands.......................... Legs .... Face ....

Abdomen .... Vulva .... All over body

Blood Pressure.. TPR..

Digestion .... Micturition.. Bowels.................................

Pain .... Vaginal Discharge .... Others.................................

- **Obstetrical Examination**

Period of Gestation .... Presentation...................................... Position...............................

Height of Fundus .... Engaged/Not Engaged/Floating...

Fetal Heart Rate.. Abdominal Girth ....

Remarks..

- **Investigations**

Blood Group.. Rh .... Hb.......................................

VDRL .... HIV.. Other ....

Ultrasound..

Diet Ordered...

Medications Ordered..

....

....

....

Treatment..

Remarks...

PRENATAL CLINICAL CHART

Name .... Age .... Obs Score ....

Date																	
Days																	
Temperature		M	E	M	E	M	E	M	E	M	E	M	E	M	E	M	E
F	C																
106.6	41.5																
105.8	41.0																
104.9	40.5																
104.0	40.0																
103.1	39.5																
102.2	39.0																
101.3	38.5																
100.4	38.0																
99.5	37.5																
98.6	37.0																
97.7	36.5																
96.8	36.0																
BP																	
Pulse																	
Respiration																	
FHR																	
Urine																	
Motion																	

- **HEALTH EDUCATION**

....

....

....

....

....

....

- **LIST OF NURSING DIAGNOSES**

....

....

....

....

....

....

Signature of Student

Signature of Clinical Instructor

PRENATAL NURSING CARE

Nursing Diagnosis Statements Prioritized	Nursing Care Plans Listed	Nursing Care Implemented and Evaluated

PRENATAL NURSING CARE

Nursing Diagnosis Statements Prioritized	Nursing Care Plans Listed	Nursing Care Implemented and Evaluated

PRENATAL NURSING CARE

Nursing Diagnosis Statements Prioritized	Nursing Care Plans Listed	Nursing Care Implemented and Evaluated

PRENATAL MOTHER NURSED (NORMAL AND HIGH RISK)–9

Name ....Age............................Gravida..............................Para...................

Hospital Number....................................

Date of Admission...................................

Weeks of Gestation ....

Date of Discharge....................................

- **Prenatal Record**
  Date of booking .... LMP ....
  Gestation at 1st visit .... EDD..
- **Medical History/Chief complaints**
  Chronic illness .... Allergy...
  Surgery .... Communicable disease ....
- **Family History**
  Type of Family Nuclear/Joint .... No. of Persons...

  Diseases Chronic illness: Hypertension .... Diabetes ....
  Genetic disorders.................................. Other specify ....
  Psychiatric disorder ....

History of Multiple Births

- **Socioeconomic Background**
  Religion .... Family Income ....
  Education: Husband .... Wife ....
  Occupation: Husband .... Wife ....
- **Menstrual History**
  Age at Menarchy .... Duration ....
  Interval .... Flow ....
- **Marital History**
  Age of Marriage... Years Married ....
  Consanguineous: Yes/No
- **Dietary Pattern**
  Vegetarian... Non-vegetarian..
  Likes... Dislikes ....
  Habits: Smoking/Drinking/Chewing Pan/Tobacco
- **Present pregnancy**
  Duration...weeks Trimester: First/second/third

PAST OBSTETRICAL HISTORY

Sl. No.	Year	Full-term	Pre-term	Abortion	Type of Delivery	Baby				Remarks
						Sex	Alive	Stillborn	Weight	

PRENATAL VISITS

Date	Height	Weight	Urine	BP	FHR	Gestation Weeks	Ht of Fundus	Abd girth	Presentation	Position	Treatment and Remarks

- **Admission Notes**

Date of Admission .... Diagnosis ....
General Condition: Good/Fair/Satisfactory/Poor
Heart .... Lungs .... Mouth ....
Abdomen.. Breasts.. Nipples ....
Edema: Ankles .... Hands.......................... Legs .... Face..........
Abdomen .... Vulva .... All over body
Blood Pressure.. TPR..
Digestion .... Micturition.. Bowels..................................
Pain .... Vaginal Discharge .... Others..................................

- **Obstetrical Examination**

Period of Gestation .... Presentation.................................. Position..................................
Height of Fundus .... Engaged/Not Engaged/Floating..................................
Fetal Heart Rate.................................. Abdominal Girth ....
Remarks..

- **Investigations**

Blood Group .... Rh .... Hb..................................
VDRL .... HIV .... Other ....
Ultrasound..

Diet Ordered..
Medications Ordered..
....
....
....

Treatment..
Remarks..

PRENATAL CLINICAL CHART

Name .... Age .... Obs Score ....

Date																	
Days																	
Temperature		M	E	M	E	M	E	M	E	M	E	M	E	M	E	M	E
F	C																
106.6	41.5																
105.8	41.0																
104.9	40.5																
104.0	40.0																
103.1	39.5																
102.2	39.0																
101.3	38.5																
100.4	38.0																
99.5	37.5																
98.6	37.0																
97.7	36.5																
96.8	36.0																
BP																	
Pulse																	
Respiration																	
FHR																	
Urine																	
Motion																	

- **HEALTH EDUCATION**

....

....

....

....

....

....

- **LIST OF NURSING DIAGNOSES**

....

....

....

....

....

....

Signature of Student

Signature of Clinical Instructor

PRENATAL NURSING CARE

Nursing Diagnosis Statements Prioritized	Nursing Care Plans Listed	Nursing Care Implemented and Evaluated

PRENATAL NURSING CARE

Nursing Diagnosis Statements Prioritized	Nursing Care Plans Listed	Nursing Care Implemented and Evaluated

PRENATAL NURSING CARE

Nursing Diagnosis Statements Prioritized	Nursing Care Plans Listed	Nursing Care Implemented and Evaluated

PRENATAL MOTHER NURSED (NORMAL AND HIGH RISK)–10

Name ....Age.............................Gravida................................Para..................

Hospital Number....................................

Date of Admission...................................

Weeks of Gestation ....

Date of Discharge..................................

- **Prenatal Record**
  Date of booking .... LMP ....
  Gestation at 1st visit .... EDD ....

- **Medical History/Chief complaints**
  Chronic illness .... Allergy...
  Surgery .... Communicable disease ....

- **Family History**
  Type of Family   Nuclear/Joint .... No. of Persons...

  Diseases   Chronic illness: Hypertension .... Diabetes ....
  Genetic disorders.................................... Other specify ....
  Psychiatric disorder ....

History of Multiple Births

- **Socioeconomic Background**
  Religion .... Family Income ....
  Education: Husband .... Wife ....
  Occupation: Husband .... Wife ....

- **Menstrual History**
  Age at Menarchy .... Duration ....
  Interval .... Flow ....

- **Marital History**
  Age of Marriage.. Years Married ....
  Consanguineous: Yes/No

- **Dietary Pattern**
  Vegetarian .... Non-vegetarian...
  Likes.. Dislikes ....
  Habits: Smoking/Drinking/Chewing Pan/Tobacco

- **Present pregnancy**
  Duration..weeks   Trimester: First/second/third

PAST OBSTETRICAL HISTORY

Sl. No.	Year	Full-term	Pre-term	Abortion	Type of Delivery	Baby				Remarks
						Sex	Alive	Stillborn	Weight	

PRENATAL VISITS

Date	Height	Weight	Urine	BP	FHR	Gestation Weeks	Ht of Fundus	Abd girth	Presentation	Position	Treatment and Remarks

- **Admission Notes**

Date of Admission .... Diagnosis ....

General Condition: Good/Fair/Satisfactory/Poor

Heart .... Lungs .... Mouth ....

Abdomen .... Breasts .... Nipples ....

Edema: Ankles .... Hands .... Legs .... Face ....

Abdomen .... Vulva .... All over body

Blood Pressure .... TPR ....

Digestion .... Micturition .... Bowels ....

Pain .... Vaginal Discharge .... Others ....

- **Obstetrical Examination**

Period of Gestation .... Presentation .... Position ....

Height of Fundus .... Engaged/Not Engaged/Floating ....

Fetal Heart Rate .... Abdominal Girth ....

Remarks ....

- **Investigations**

Blood Group .... Rh .... Hb ....

VDRL .... HIV .... Other ....

Ultrasound ....

Diet Ordered ....

Medications Ordered ....

....

....

....

Treatment ....

Remarks ....

PRENATAL CLINICAL CHART

Name .... Age .... Obs Score ....

Date

Days

Temperature		M	E	M	E	M	E	M	E	M	E	M	E	M	E	M	E
F	C																
106.6	41.5																
105.8	41.0																
104.9	40.5																
104.0	40.0																
103.1	39.5																
102.2	39.0																
101.3	38.5																
100.4	38.0																
99.5	37.5																
98.6	37.0																
97.7	36.5																
96.8	36.0																
BP																	
Pulse																	
Respiration																	
FHR																	
Urine																	
Motion																	

- **HEALTH EDUCATION**

....

....

....

....

....

....

- **LIST OF NURSING DIAGNOSES**

....

....

....

....

....

....

Signature of Student

Signature of Clinical Instructor

PRENATAL NURSING CARE

Nursing Diagnosis Statements Prioritized	Nursing Care Plans Listed	Nursing Care Implemented and Evaluated

PRENATAL NURSING CARE

Nursing Diagnosis Statements Prioritized	Nursing Care Plans Listed	Nursing Care Implemented and Evaluated

PRENATAL NURSING CARE

Nursing Diagnosis Statements Prioritized	Nursing Care Plans Listed	Nursing Care Implemented and Evaluated

INTRANATAL MOTHER NURSED–1

Name.. Age .... Gravida............................ Para..............................

Hospital Number...

Date of Admission..

Date of Delivery ....

Discharge
Condition of Mother......................................
Baby...

- **Antenatal Record**

Date of Booking .... LMP...
Gestation at 1st visit .... EDD ....

- **Medical History**

Chronic Illness .... Allergy..
Surgery .... Communicable Disease.................................

- **Family History**

Type of Family: Single .... No. of Persons ....
Joint .... No. of Persons ....

Diseases: Chronic Illness: Hypertension:........................ Diabetes...
Genetic Disorders...
Psychiatric Disorders...
Other...

Multiple Births: ....

- **Socioeconomic Background**

Religion .... Family Income ....
Education: Husband .... Wife...
Occupation: Husband .... Wife...

- **Menstrual History**

Menarchy...Duration......................................Interval ....
Flow..

- **Marital History**

Age of Marriage .... Years Married...
Consanguineous: Yes/No

- **Dietary Pattern**

Vegetarian .... Non-vegetarian ....
Likes .... Dislikes ....
Habits: Smoking/Drinking/Chewing pan

PAST OBSTETRICAL HISTORY

Sl. No.	Year	Full-term	Pre-term	Abortion	Type of Delivery	Sex of Baby	Alive	SB	Weight	Remarks

Present Pregnancy

- **Admission Notes**

Admitted on ....at ....am/pm
Contractions commenced on ....at ....am/pm
Period of Gestation .... Membranes: Intact ....
Ruptured on ....at ....am/pm
Height of Fundus... Contractions ....
Presentation .... Position ....
Engaged/Not Engaged/Free .... FHR ....
Bladder .... Bowels ....
Special Observations ....

PRENATAL VISITS

Date of Booking	Weight	Height	Urine		BP	FHR	Weeks of Gestation	Height of fundus	Position	Treatment
			Protein	Glucose						

- **General Condition**

BP .... TPR ....
Urine: Sp Gravity .... Reaction ....
Protein ....Glucose ....Acetone ....

- **Examinations and Investigations**

Blood Group..................................... Rh ....Hemoglobin ....
VDRL... HIV..................................Other ....
Heart .... Lungs ....Breasts ....
Abdomen... Perineum..

Components of the WHO Model Partograph

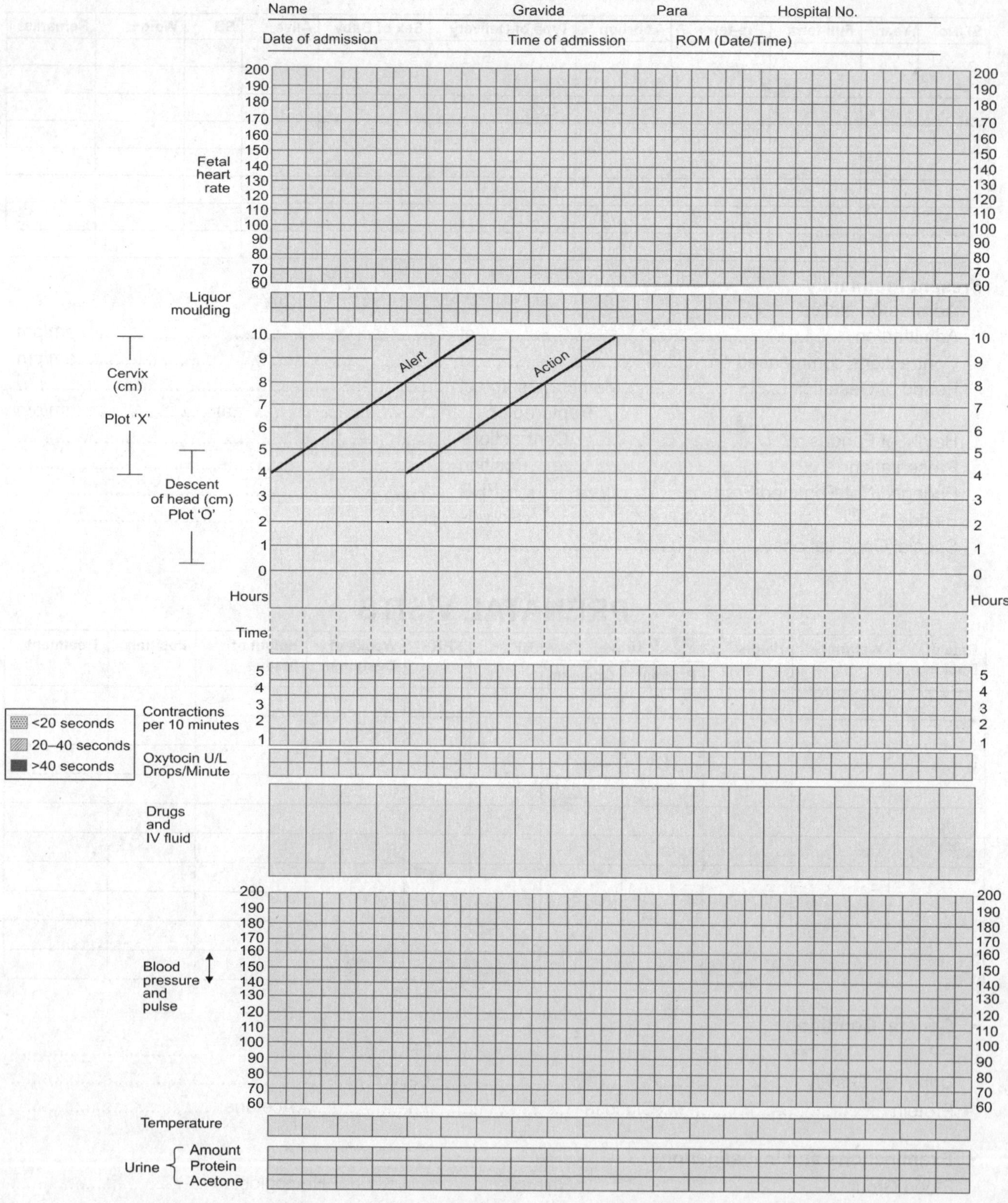

Source: WHO model partograph. Opoku Research Journal of Women's Health, 2015, www.hoagonline.com

Delivery Record

Onset of true labor: Date .... Time ....
Time of full dilation: Date .... Time ....
Membranes ruptured at .... Spontaneous/Artificial ....
PROM..

a. Delivery of Baby

Baby born at ....am/pm, Male/Female.............................., Mode of Delivery..............................
Condition of Baby Active/Limp/Asphyxiated

APGAR SCORING

Sl. No.	Sign	0	Neonate's score	1	Neonate's score	2	Neonate's score
1.	Respiratory effort	Absent		Slow, irregular, weak cry		Strong cry	
2.	Heart rate	Absent		Slow, less than 100		Over 100	
3.	Muscle tone	Limp		Some flexion of limbs		Active movement	
4.	Reflex response to flicking of foot	Absent		Facial grimace		Cry	
5.	Color	Blue-Pale		Body pink, Limbs blue		Completely pink	

0–2 Severe asphyxia
3–4 Moderate asphyxia
5–7 Mild asphyxia
8–10 No asphyxia

Score at one minute ....
Score at five minutes ....

Stillborn/Macerated..
Cause ....
Treatment at birth ....

b. Delivery of placenta and membranes

Delivered at ....am/pm
Spontaneously/Helped out/Manually removed..
Type of Placenta..
Placenta and membranes: Complete/Incomplete..
Weight..............................Cord length..............................Cord insertion ....
Any abnormality..

c. Blood loss: (Approximate total amount)

Before delivery of the Placenta.. mL
During delivery of the Placenta .... mL
After delivery of the Placenta.. mL
Total .... mL

d. Perineum:

Intact ....Episiotomy..............................Laceration..............................
Repair..

e. Medications given ....

....

....

f. Length of Labor

Mode of Delivery..
Duration of Labor. First stage: .... Hours ....Minutes
Second stage: .... Hours ....Minutes
Third stage: .... Hours ....Minutes
Total: .... Hours ....Minutes

Condition of Mother following delivery

Pulse..BP..Uterus ....
Vaginal bleeding ....
Breastfeeding initiated at..

INTRANATAL MOTHER NURSED

Nursing Diagnosis Statements Prioritized	Nursing Care Plans Listed	Nursing Care Implemented and Evaluated

INTRANATAL MOTHER NURSED

Nursing Diagnosis Statements Prioritized	Nursing Care Plans Listed	Nursing Care Implemented and Evaluated

INTRANATAL MOTHER NURSED

Nursing Diagnosis Statements Prioritized	Nursing Care Plans Listed	Nursing Care Implemented and Evaluated

INTRANATAL MOTHER NURSED

Nursing Diagnosis Statements Prioritized	Nursing Care Plans Listed	Nursing Care Implemented and Evaluated

INTRANATAL MOTHER NURSED–2

Name.. Age ....Gravida............................Para...............................

Hospital Number..

Date of Admission..

Date of Delivery..

Discharge
Condition of Mother.......................................
Baby..

- **Antenatal Record**

Date of Booking .... LMP...

Gestation at 1st visit .... EDD ....

- **Medical History**

Chronic Illness .... Allergy..

Surgery .... Communicable Disease ....

- **Family History**

Type of Family: Single .... No. of Persons ....

Joint .... No. of Persons ....

Diseases: Chronic Illness: Hypertension:....................... Diabetes...

Genetic Disorders...

Psychiatric Disorders...

Other..

Multiple Births: ....

- **Socioeconomic Background**

Religion .... Family Income ....

Education: Husband .... Wife..

Occupation: Husband .... Wife..

- **Menstrual History**

Menarchy..Duration....................................Interval.................................. . ..

Flow...

- **Marital History**

Age of Marriage .... Years Married..

Consanguineous: Yes/No

- **Dietary Pattern**

Vegetarian .... Non-vegetarian ....

Likes .... Dislikes ....

Habits: Smoking/Drinking/Chewing pan

PAST OBSTETRICAL HISTORY

Sl. No.	Year	Full-term	Pre-term	Abortion	Type of Delivery	Sex of Baby	Alive	SB	Weight	Remarks

Present Pregnancy

- **Admission Notes**

Admitted on ....at ....am/pm
Contractions commenced on ....at ....am/pm
Period of Gestation ....Membranes: Intact ....
Ruptured on ....at ....am/pm
Height of Fundus.......................................Contractions ....
Presentation ....Position ....
Engaged/Not Engaged/Free .... FHR ....
Bladder ....Bowels ....
Special Observations ....

PRENATAL VISITS

Date of Booking	Weight	Height	Urine		BP	FHR	Weeks of Gestation	Height of fundus	Position	Treatment
			Protein	Glucose						

- **General Condition**

BP .... TPR...
Urine: Sp Gravity .... Reaction ....
Protein ....Glucose ....Acetone ....

- **Examinations and Investigations**

Blood Group... Rh ....Hemoglobin ....
VDRL.. HIV ....Other ....
Heart .... Lungs ....Breasts ....
Abdomen.. Perineum...

Components of the WHO Model Partograph

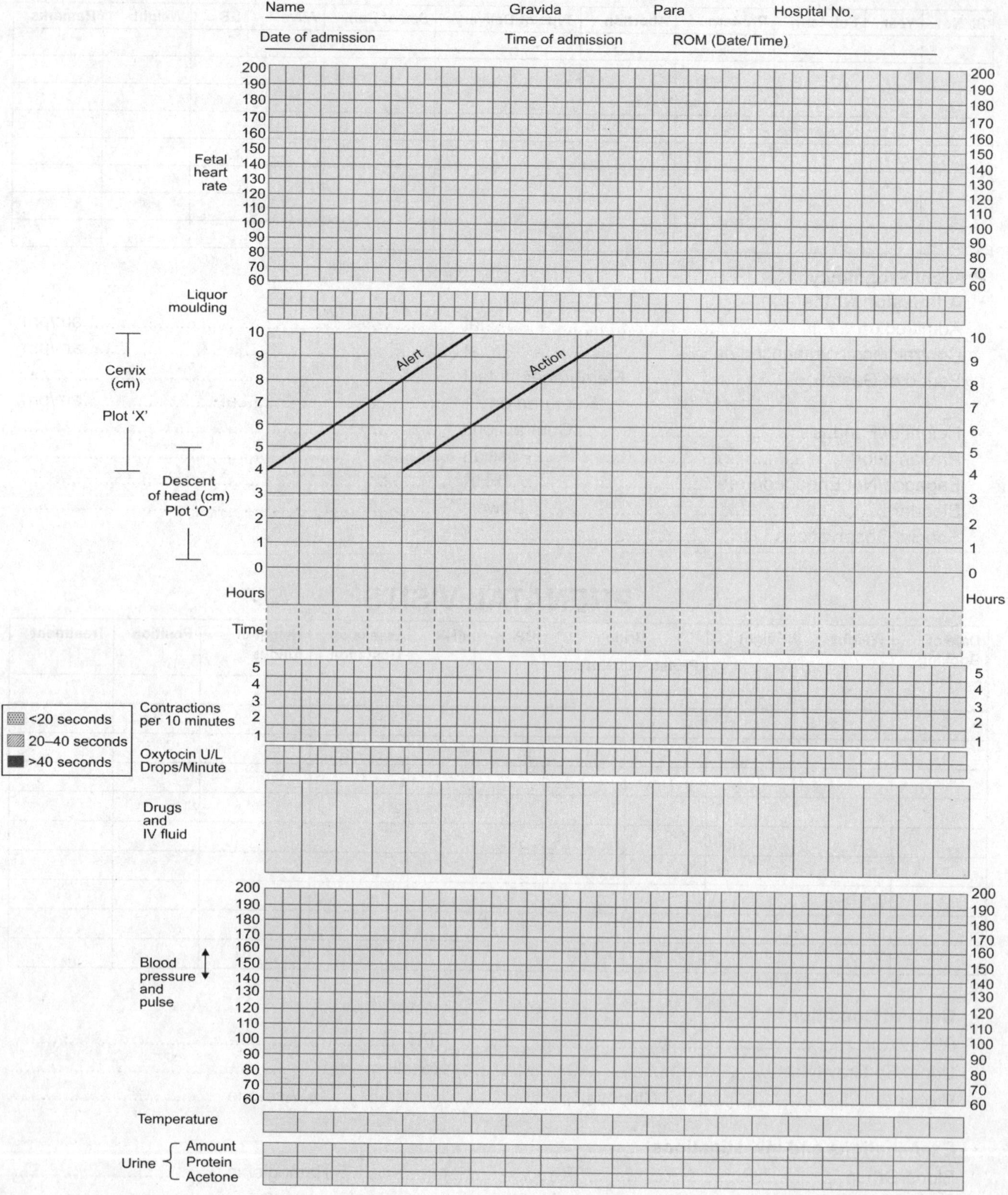

Source: WHO model partograph. Opoku Research Journal of Women's Health, 2015, www.hoagonline.com

Delivery Record

Onset of true labor: Date .... Time ....

Time of full dilation: Date .... Time ....

Membranes ruptured at .... Spontaneous/Artificial ....

PROM..

a. Delivery of Baby

Baby born at ....am/pm, Male/Female...................................., Mode of Delivery.............................

Condition of Baby Active/Limp/Asphyxiated

APGAR SCORING

Sl. No.	Sign	0	Neonate's score	1	Neonate's score	2	Neonate's score
1.	Respiratory effort	Absent		Slow, irregular, weak cry		Strong cry	
2.	Heart rate	Absent		Slow, less than 100		Over 100	
3.	Muscle tone	Limp		Some flexion of limbs		Active movement	
4.	Reflex response to flicking of foot	Absent		Facial grimace		Cry	
5.	Color	Blue-Pale		Body pink, Limbs blue		Completely pink	

0–2 Severe asphyxia

3–4 Moderate asphyxia

5–7 Mild asphyxia

8–10 No asphyxia

Score at one minute ....

Score at five minutes ....

Stillborn/Macerated..

Cause ....

Treatment at birth ....

b. Delivery of placenta and membranes

Delivered at ....am/pm

Spontaneously/Helped out/Manually removed..

Type of Placenta..

Placenta and membranes: Complete/Incomplete..

Weight.............................Cord length.........................Cord insertion ....

Any abnormality..

c. Blood loss: (Approximate total amount)

Before delivery of the Placenta.. mL

During delivery of the Placenta .... mL

After delivery of the Placenta.. mL

Total .... mL

d. Perineum:

Intact ....Episiotomy....................................Laceration....................................

Repair ....

e. Medications given ....

....

....

f. Length of Labor

Mode of Delivery..

Duration of Labor. First stage: .... Hours ....Minutes

Second stage: .... Hours ....Minutes

Third stage: .... Hours ....Minutes

Total: .... Hours ....Minutes

Condition of Mother following delivery

Pulse...................................BP....................................Uterus ....

Vaginal bleeding ....

Breastfeeding initiated at..

INTRANATAL MOTHER NURSED

Nursing Diagnosis Statements Prioritized	Nursing Care Plans Listed	Nursing Care Implemented and Evaluated

INTRANATAL MOTHER NURSED

Nursing Diagnosis Statements Prioritized	Nursing Care Plans Listed	Nursing Care Implemented and Evaluated

INTRANATAL MOTHER NURSED

Nursing Diagnosis Statements Prioritized	Nursing Care Plans Listed	Nursing Care Implemented and Evaluated

INTRANATAL MOTHER NURSED

Nursing Diagnosis Statements Prioritized	Nursing Care Plans Listed	Nursing Care Implemented and Evaluated

INTRANATAL MOTHER NURSED–3

Name.. Age ....Gravida...........................Para...............................

Hospital Number...

Date of Admission..

Date of Delivery ....

Discharge
Condition of Mother....................................
Baby.......................................

- **Antenatal Record**

Date of Booking .... LMP..

Gestation at 1st visit .... EDD ....

- **Medical History**

Chronic Illness .... Allergy...

Surgery .... Communicable Disease ....

- **Family History**

Type of Family: Single .... No. of Persons ....

Joint .... No. of Persons ....

Diseases: Chronic Illness: Hypertension:...................... Diabetes...

Genetic Disorders...

Psychiatric Disorders..

Other...

Multiple Births: ....

- **Socioeconomic Background**

Religion .... Family Income ....

Education: Husband .... Wife...

Occupation: Husband .... Wife...

- **Menstrual History**

Menarchy..Duration..................................Interval...............................

Flow..

- **Marital History**

Age of Marriage .... Years Married..

Consanguineous: Yes/No

- **Dietary Pattern**

Vegetarian .... Non-vegetarian ....

Likes .... Dislikes ....

Habits: Smoking/Drinking/Chewing pan

PAST OBSTETRICAL HISTORY

Sl. No.	Year	Full-term	Pre-term	Abortion	Type of Delivery	Sex of Baby	Alive	SB	Weight	Remarks

Present Pregnancy

- **Admission Notes**

Admitted on ....at ....am/pm
Contractions commenced on ....at ....am/pm
Period of Gestation ....Membranes: Intact ....
Ruptured on ....at ....am/pm
Height of Fundus...Contractions ....
Presentation ....Position ....
Engaged/Not Engaged/Free .... FHR ....
Bladder ....Bowels ....
Special Observations ....

PRENATAL VISITS

Date of Booking	Weight	Height	Urine		BP	FHR	Weeks of Gestation	Height of fundus	Position	Treatment
			Protein	Glucose						

- **General Condition**

BP .... TPR ....
Urine: Sp Gravity .... Reaction ....
Protein ....Glucose ....Acetone ....

- **Examinations and Investigations**

Blood Group .... Rh ....Hemoglobin ....
VDRL.. HIV .... Other ....
Heart .... Lungs ....Breasts ....
Abdomen.. Perineum...

Components of the WHO Model Partograph

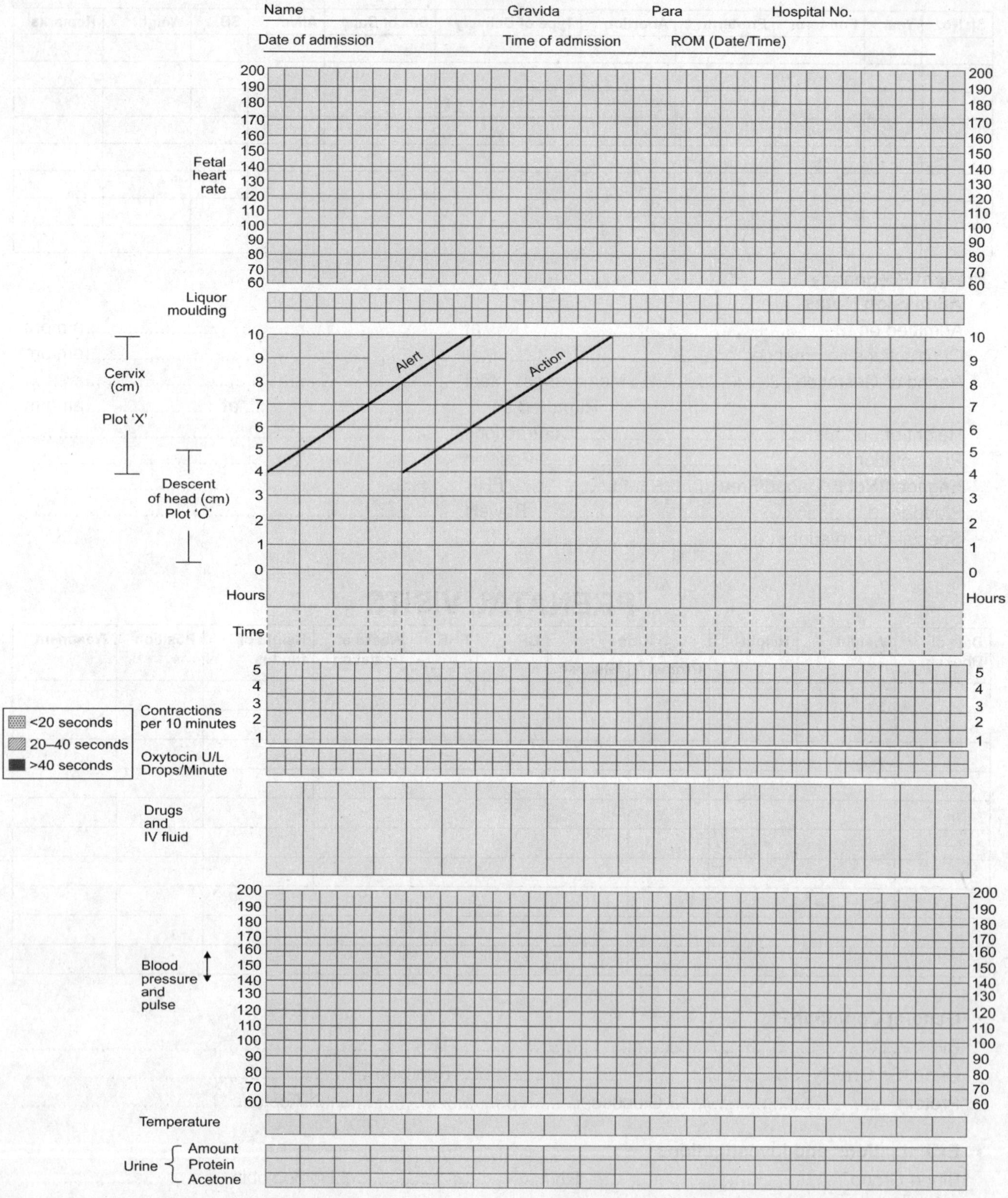

Source: WHO model partograph. Opoku Research Journal of Women's Health, 2015, www.hoagonline.com

Delivery Record

Onset of true labor: Date .... Time ....

Time of full dilation: Date .... Time ....

Membranes ruptured at .... Spontaneous/Artificial ....

PROM...

a. Delivery of Baby

Baby born at ....am/pm, Male/Female.., Mode of Delivery...............................

Condition of Baby Active/Limp/Asphyxiated

APGAR SCORING

Sl. No.	Sign	0	Neonate's score	1	Neonate's score	2	Neonate's score
1.	Respiratory effort	Absent		Slow, irregular, weak cry		Strong cry	
2.	Heart rate	Absent		Slow, less than 100		Over 100	
3.	Muscle tone	Limp		Some flexion of limbs		Active movement	
4.	Reflex response to flicking of foot	Absent		Facial grimace		Cry	
5.	Color	Blue-Pale		Body pink, Limbs blue		Completely pink	

0–2 Severe asphyxia

3–4 Moderate asphyxia

5–7 Mild asphyxia

8–10 No asphyxia

Score at one minute ....

Score at five minutes ....

Stillborn/Macerated...

Cause ....

Treatment at birth ....

b. Delivery of placenta and membranes

Delivered at ....am/pm

Spontaneously/Helped out/Manually removed...

Type of Placenta...

Placenta and membranes: Complete/Incomplete...

Weight..............................Cord length.............................Cord insertion ....

Any abnormality...

c. Blood loss: (Approximate total amount)

Before delivery of the Placenta... mL

During delivery of the Placenta .... mL

After delivery of the Placenta... mL

Total .... mL

d. Perineum:

Intact ....Episiotomy.....................................Laceration.....................................

Repair...

e. Medications given ....

....

....

f. Length of Labor

Mode of Delivery...

Duration of Labor. First stage: .... Hours ....Minutes

Second stage: .... Hours ....Minutes

Third stage: .... Hours ....Minutes

Total: .... Hours ....Minutes

Condition of Mother following delivery

Pulse...BP...Uterus ....

Vaginal bleeding ....

Breastfeeding initiated at...

INTRANATAL MOTHER NURSED

Nursing Diagnosis Statements Prioritized	Nursing Care Plans Listed	Nursing Care Implemented and Evaluated

INTRANATAL MOTHER NURSED

Nursing Diagnosis Statements Prioritized	Nursing Care Plans Listed	Nursing Care Implemented and Evaluated

INTRANATAL MOTHER NURSED

Nursing Diagnosis Statements Prioritized	Nursing Care Plans Listed	Nursing Care Implemented and Evaluated

INTRANATAL MOTHER NURSED

Nursing Diagnosis Statements Prioritized	Nursing Care Plans Listed	Nursing Care Implemented and Evaluated

INTRANATAL MOTHER NURSED–4

Name.. Age ....Gravida..........................Para..............................

Hospital Number..

Date of Admission..

Date of Delivery ....

Discharge
Condition of Mother.......................................
Baby...

- **Antenatal Record**

Date of Booking .... LMP...

Gestation at 1st visit .... EDD ....

- **Medical History**

Chronic Illness .... Allergy..

Surgery .... Communicable Disease ....

- **Family History**

Type of Family: Single .... No. of Persons ....

Joint .... No. of Persons ....

Diseases: Chronic Illness: Hypertension:...................... Diabetes...

Genetic Disorders ....

Psychiatric Disorders ....

Other...

Multiple Births: ....

- **Socioeconomic Background**

Religion .... Family Income ....

Education: Husband .... Wife..

Occupation: Husband .... Wife..

- **Menstrual History**

Menarchy...Duration...................................Interval.................................

Flow..

- **Marital History**

Age of Marriage .... Years Married..

Consanguineous: Yes/No

- **Dietary Pattern**

Vegetarian .... Non-vegetarian ....

Likes .... Dislikes ....

Habits: Smoking/Drinking/Chewing pan

PAST OBSTETRICAL HISTORY

Sl. No.	Year	Full-term	Pre-term	Abortion	Type of Delivery	Sex of Baby	Alive	SB	Weight	Remarks

Present Pregnancy

- **Admission Notes**

Admitted on ....at ....am/pm
Contractions commenced on ....at ....am/pm
Period of Gestation ....Membranes: Intact ....
Ruptured on ....at ....am/pm
Height of Fundus......................................Contractions ....
Presentation ....Position ....
Engaged/Not Engaged/Free .... FHR ....
Bladder .... Bowels ....
Special Observations ....

PRENATAL VISITS

Date of Booking	Weight	Height	Urine		BP	FHR	Weeks of Gestation	Height of fundus	Position	Treatment
			Protein	Glucose						

- **General Condition**

BP .... TPR ....
Urine: Sp Gravity .... Reaction ....
Protein ....Glucose ....Acetone ....

- **Examinations and Investigations**

Blood Group.. Rh ....Hemoglobin ....
VDRL.. HIV..Other ....
Heart .... Lungs ....Breasts ....
Abdomen.. Perineum..

Components of the WHO Model Partograph

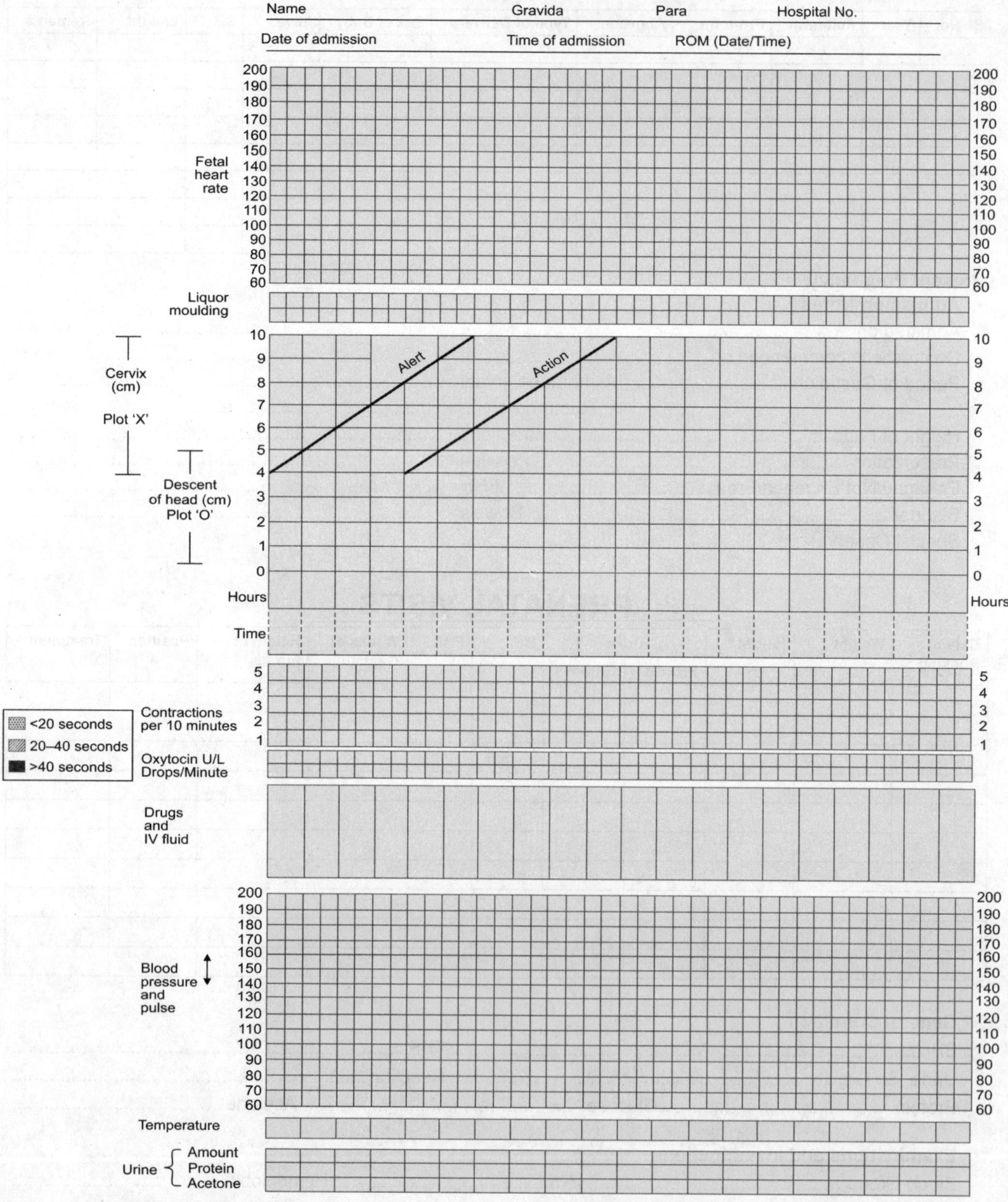

Source: WHO model partograph. Opoku Research Journal of Women's Health, 2015, www.hoagonline.com

Delivery Record

Onset of true labor: Date .... Time ....

Time of full dilation: Date .... Time ....

Membranes ruptured at .... Spontaneous/Artificial ....

PROM..

a. Delivery of Baby

Baby born at ....am/pm, Male/Female....................................., Mode of Delivery............................

Condition of Baby Active/Limp/Asphyxiated

APGAR SCORING

Sl. No.	Sign	0	Neonate's score	1	Neonate's score	2	Neonate's score
1.	Respiratory effort	Absent		Slow, irregular, weak cry		Strong cry	
2.	Heart rate	Absent		Slow, less than 100		Over 100	
3.	Muscle tone	Limp		Some flexion of limbs		Active movement	
4.	Reflex response to flicking of foot	Absent		Facial grimace		Cry	
5.	Color	Blue-Pale		Body pink, Limbs blue		Completely pink	

0–2 Severe asphyxia

3–4 Moderate asphyxia

5–7 Mild asphyxia

8–10 No asphyxia

Score at one minute ....

Score at five minutes ....

Stillborn/Macerated..

Cause ....

Treatment at birth ....

b. Delivery of placenta and membranes

Delivered at ....am/pm

Spontaneously/Helped out/Manually removed ....

Type of Placenta...

Placenta and membranes: Complete/Incomplete..

Weight............................Cord length...........................Cord insertion ....

Any abnormality..

c. Blood loss: (Approximate total amount)

Before delivery of the Placenta...mL

During delivery of the Placenta ....mL

After delivery of the Placenta...mL

Total ....mL

d. Perineum:

Intact ....Episiotomy...............................Laceration.................................

Repair..

e. Medications given ....

....

....

f. Length of Labor

Mode of Delivery..

Duration of Labor. First stage: .... Hours ....Minutes

Second stage: .... Hours ....Minutes

Third stage: .... Hours ....Minutes

Total: .... Hours ....Minutes

Condition of Mother following delivery

Pulse...BP...Uterus ....

Vaginal bleeding ....

Breastfeeding initiated at..

INTRANATAL MOTHER NURSED

Nursing Diagnosis Statements Prioritized	Nursing Care Plans Listed	Nursing Care Implemented and Evaluated

INTRANATAL MOTHER NURSED

Nursing Diagnosis Statements Prioritized	Nursing Care Plans Listed	Nursing Care Implemented and Evaluated

INTRANATAL MOTHER NURSED

Nursing Diagnosis Statements Prioritized	Nursing Care Plans Listed	Nursing Care Implemented and Evaluated

INTRANATAL MOTHER NURSED

Nursing Diagnosis Statements Prioritized	Nursing Care Plans Listed	Nursing Care Implemented and Evaluated

INTRANATAL MOTHER NURSED–5

Name.. Age .... Gravida........................... Para..............................

Hospital Number...

Date of Admission..

Date of Delivery...

Discharge
Condition of Mother.......................................
Baby...

- **Antenatal Record**

Date of Booking .... LMP..

Gestation at 1st visit .... EDD ....

- **Medical History**

Chronic Illness .... Allergy...

Surgery .... Communicable Disease.................................

- **Family History**

Type of Family: Single .... No. of Persons ....

Joint .... No. of Persons ....

Diseases: Chronic Illness: Hypertension:...................... Diabetes..

Genetic Disorders...

Psychiatric Disorders...

Other..

Multiple Births: ....

- **Socioeconomic Background**

Religion .... Family Income ....

Education: Husband .... Wife..

Occupation: Husband .... Wife..

- **Menstrual History**

Menarchy..Duration.......................................Interval.................................

Flow..

- **Marital History**

Age of Marriage .... Years Married...

Consanguineous: Yes/No

- **Dietary Pattern**

Vegetarian .... Non-vegetarian ....

Likes .... Dislikes ....

Habits: Smoking/Drinking/Chewing pan

PAST OBSTETRICAL HISTORY

Sl. No.	Year	Full-term	Pre-term	Abortion	Type of Delivery	Sex of Baby	Alive	SB	Weight	Remarks

Present Pregnancy

- **Admission Notes**

Admitted on ....at ....am/pm
Contractions commenced on ....at ....am/pm
Period of Gestation ....Membranes: Intact ....
Ruptured on ....at ....am/pm
Height of Fundus.....................................Contractions ....
Presentation ....Position ....
Engaged/Not Engaged/Free .... FHR ....
Bladder .... Bowels ....
Special Observations ....

PRENATAL VISITS

Date of Booking	Weight	Height	Urine		BP	FHR	Weeks of Gestation	Height of fundus	Position	Treatment
			Protein	Glucose						

- **General Condition**

BP .... TPR ....
Urine: Sp Gravity .... Reaction ....
Protein ....Glucose ....Acetone ....

- **Examinations and Investigations**

Blood Group .... Rh ....Hemoglobin ....
VDRL... HIV ....Other ....
Heart .... Lungs ....Breasts ....
Abdomen... Perineum..

Components of the WHO Model Partograph

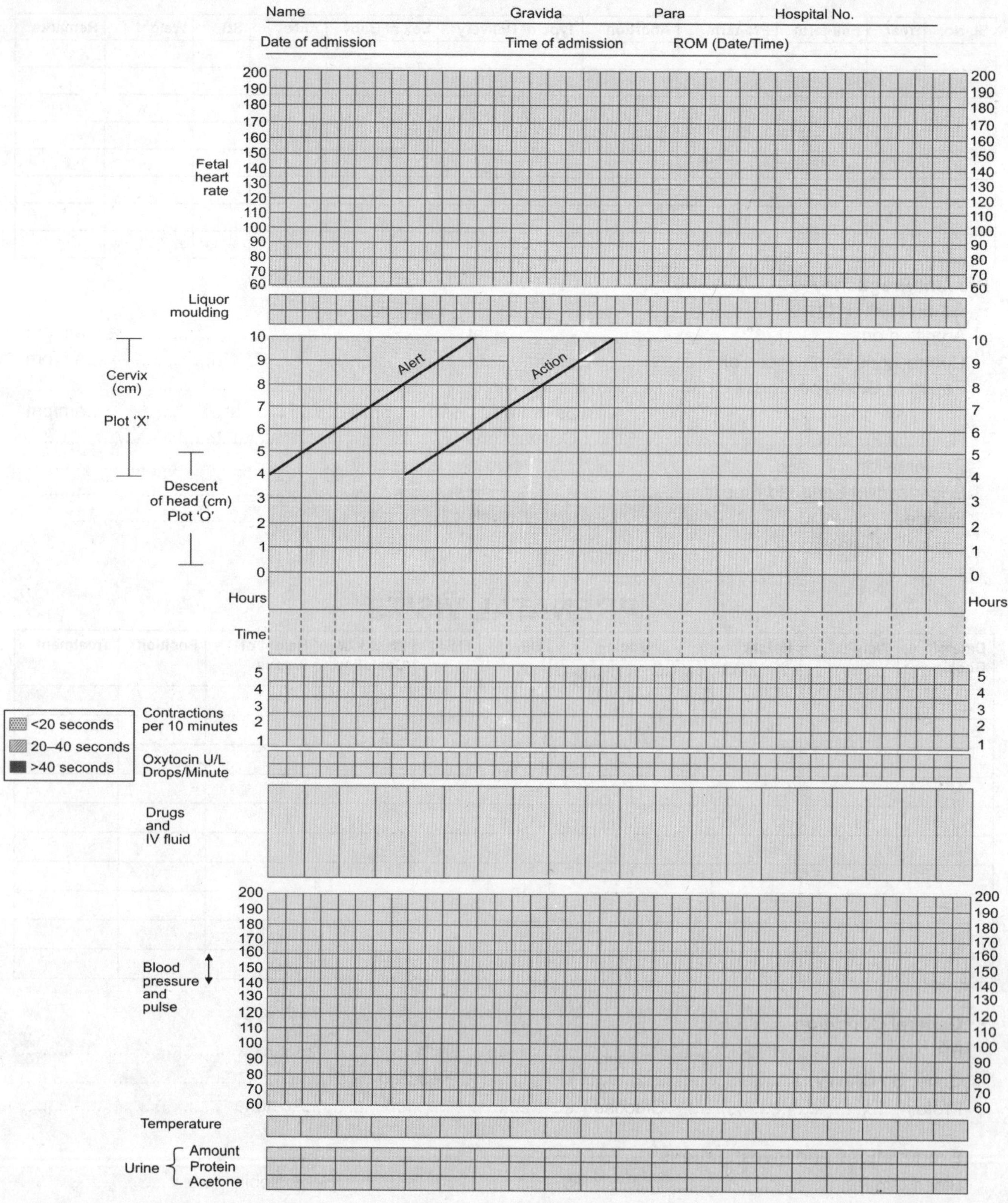

Source: WHO model partograph. Opoku Research Journal of Women's Health, 2015, www.hoagonline.com

Delivery Record

Onset of true labor: Date .... Time ....

Time of full dilation: Date .... Time ....

Membranes ruptured at .... Spontaneous/Artificial ....

PROM ....

a. Delivery of Baby

Baby born at ....am/pm, Male/Female......................................, Mode of Delivery............................

Condition of Baby Active/Limp/Asphyxiated

APGAR SCORING

Sl. No.	Sign	0	Neonate's score	1	Neonate's score	2	Neonate's score
1.	Respiratory effort	Absent		Slow, irregular, weak cry		Strong cry	
2.	Heart rate	Absent		Slow, less than 100		Over 100	
3.	Muscle tone	Limp		Some flexion of limbs		Active movement	
4.	Reflex response to flicking of foot	Absent		Facial grimace		Cry	
5.	Color	Blue-Pale		Body pink, Limbs blue		Completely pink	

0–2 Severe asphyxia

3–4 Moderate asphyxia

5–7 Mild asphyxia

8–10 No asphyxia

Score at one minute ....

Score at five minutes ....

Stillborn/Macerated..

Cause ....

Treatment at birth ....

b. Delivery of placenta and membranes

Delivered at ....am/pm

Spontaneously/Helped out/Manually removed..

Type of Placenta..

Placenta and membranes: Complete/Incomplete..

Weight............................Cord length..........................Cord insertion ....

Any abnormality..

c. Blood loss: (Approximate total amount)

Before delivery of the Placenta.. mL

During delivery of the Placenta .... mL

After delivery of the Placenta.. mL

Total .... mL

d. Perineum:

Intact ....Episiotomy....................................Laceration....................................

Repair..

e. Medications given ....

....

....

f. Length of Labor

Mode of Delivery..

Duration of Labor. First stage: .... Hours ....Minutes

Second stage: .... Hours ....Minutes

Third stage: .... Hours ....Minutes

Total: .... Hours ....Minutes

Condition of Mother following delivery

Pulse....................................BP....................................Uterus ....

Vaginal bleeding..

Breastfeeding initiated at..

INTRANATAL MOTHER NURSED

Nursing Diagnosis Statements Prioritized	Nursing Care Plans Listed	Nursing Care Implemented and Evaluated

INTRANATAL MOTHER NURSED

Nursing Diagnosis Statements Prioritized	Nursing Care Plans Listed	Nursing Care Implemented and Evaluated

INTRANATAL MOTHER NURSED

Nursing Diagnosis Statements Prioritized	Nursing Care Plans Listed	Nursing Care Implemented and Evaluated

INTRANATAL MOTHER NURSED

Nursing Diagnosis Statements Prioritized	Nursing Care Plans Listed	Nursing Care Implemented and Evaluated

INTRANATAL MOTHER NURSED–6

Name... Age .... Gravida............................. Para.................................

Hospital Number..

Discharge
Condition of Mother.......................................
Baby..

Date of Admission...

Date of Delivery ....

- **Antenatal Record**

Date of Booking .... LMP...

Gestation at 1st visit .... EDD ....

- **Medical History**

Chronic Illness .... Allergy...

Surgery .... Communicable Disease ....

- **Family History**

Type of Family: Single .... No. of Persons ....

Joint .... No. of Persons ....

Diseases: Chronic Illness: Hypertension:........................ Diabetes...

Genetic Disorders ....

Psychiatric Disorders ....

Other..

Multiple Births: ....

- **Socioeconomic Background**

Religion .... Family Income ....

Education: Husband .... Wife...

Occupation: Husband .... Wife...

- **Menstrual History**

Menarchy...Duration....................................Interval...................................

Flow..

- **Marital History**

Age of Marriage .... Years Married..

Consanguineous: Yes/No

- **Dietary Pattern**

Vegetarian .... Non-vegetarian ....

Likes .... Dislikes ....

Habits: Smoking/Drinking/Chewing pan

PAST OBSTETRICAL HISTORY

Sl. No.	Year	Full-term	Pre-term	Abortion	Type of Delivery	Sex of Baby	Alive	SB	Weight	Remarks

Present Pregnancy

- **Admission Notes**

Admitted on ....at ....am/pm
Contractions commenced on ....at ....am/pm
Period of Gestation ....Membranes: Intact ....
Ruptured on ....at ....am/pm
Height of Fundus..Contractions ....
Presentation ....Position ....
Engaged/Not Engaged/Free .... FHR ....
Bladder ....Bowels ....
Special Observations ....

PRENATAL VISITS

Date of Booking	Weight	Height	Urine		BP	FHR	Weeks of Gestation	Height of fundus	Position	Treatment
			Protein	Glucose						

- **General Condition**

BP .... TPR ....
Urine: Sp Gravity .... Reaction ....
Protein ....Glucose ....Acetone ....

- **Examinations and Investigations**

Blood Group .... Rh ....Hemoglobin ....
VDRL... HIV ....Other ....
Heart .... Lungs ....Breasts ....
Abdomen.. Perineum...

Components of the WHO Model Partograph

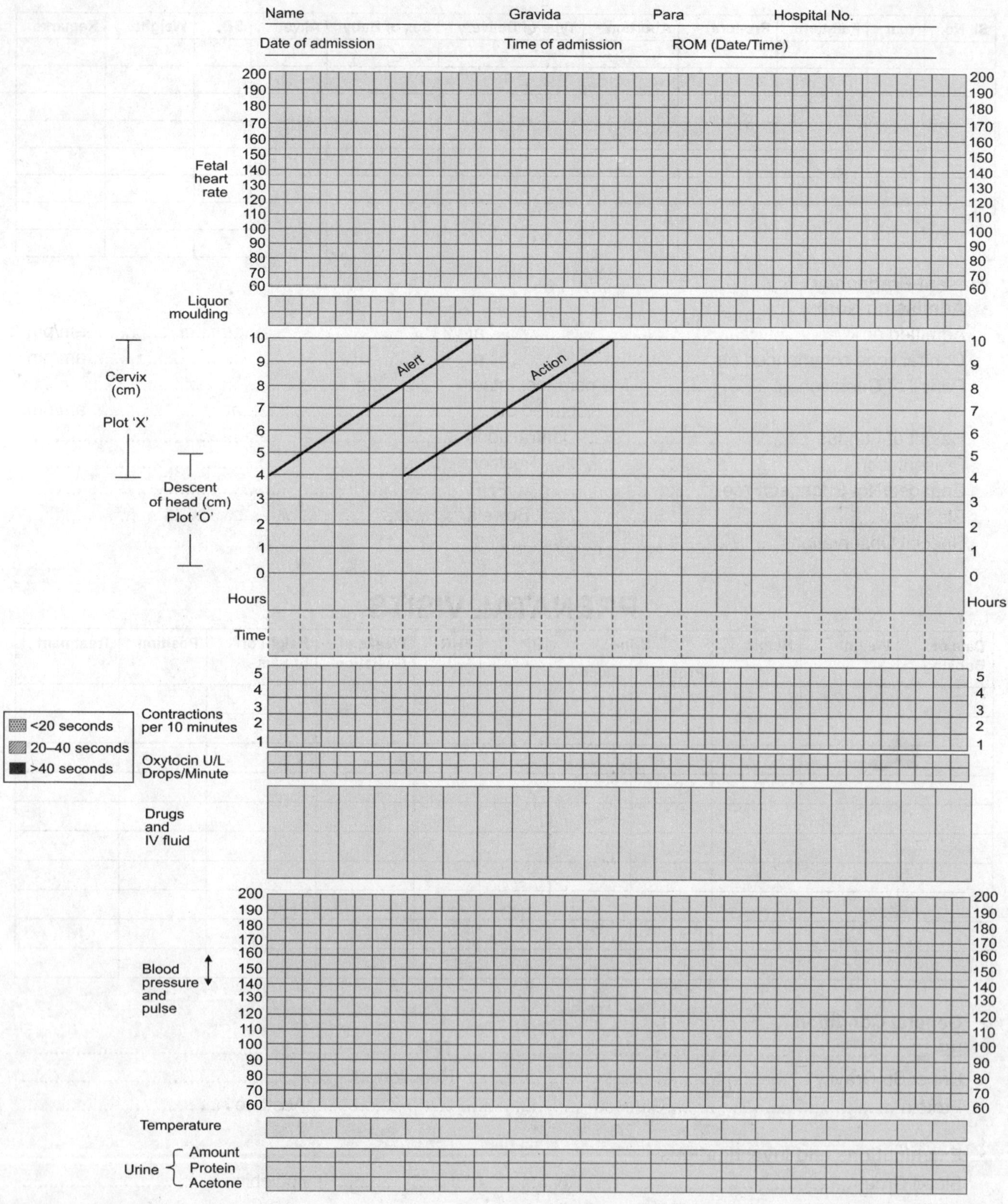

Source: WHO model partograph. Opoku Research Journal of Women's Health, 2015, www.hoagonline.com

Delivery Record

Onset of true labor: Date .... Time ....
Time of full dilation: Date .... Time ....
Membranes ruptured at .... Spontaneous/Artificial ....
PROM..

a. Delivery of Baby

Baby born at ....am/pm, Male/Female............................., Mode of Delivery.............................
Condition of Baby Active/Limp/Asphyxiated

APGAR SCORING

Sl. No.	Sign	0	Neonate's score	1	Neonate's score	2	Neonate's score
1.	Respiratory effort	Absent		Slow, irregular, weak cry		Strong cry	
2.	Heart rate	Absent		Slow, less than 100		Over 100	
3.	Muscle tone	Limp		Some flexion of limbs		Active movement	
4.	Reflex response to flicking of foot	Absent		Facial grimace		Cry	
5.	Color	Blue-Pale		Body pink, Limbs blue		Completely pink	

0–2 Severe asphyxia
3–4 Moderate asphyxia
5–7 Mild asphyxia
8–10 No asphyxia

Score at one minute ....
Score at five minutes ....

Stillborn/Macerated..
Cause ....
Treatment at birth ....

b. Delivery of placenta and membranes

Delivered at ....am/pm
Spontaneously/Helped out/Manually removed..
Type of Placenta..
Placenta and membranes: Complete/Incomplete..
Weight.............................Cord length.............................Cord insertion ....
Any abnormality..

c. Blood loss: (Approximate total amount)

Before delivery of the Placenta.. mL
During delivery of the Placenta .... mL
After delivery of the Placenta.. mL
Total .... mL

d. Perineum:

Intact ....Episiotomy.............................Laceration.............................
Repair..

e. Medications given ....

....

....

f. Length of Labor

Mode of Delivery..
Duration of Labor. First stage: .... Hours ....Minutes
Second stage: .... Hours ....Minutes
Third stage: .... Hours ....Minutes
Total: .... Hours ....Minutes

Condition of Mother following delivery

Pulse.............................BP.............................Uterus ....
Vaginal bleeding ....
Breastfeeding initiated at..

INTRANATAL MOTHER NURSED

Nursing Diagnosis Statements Prioritized	Nursing Care Plans Listed	Nursing Care Implemented and Evaluated

INTRANATAL MOTHER NURSED

Nursing Diagnosis Statements Prioritized	Nursing Care Plans Listed	Nursing Care Implemented and Evaluated

INTRANATAL MOTHER NURSED

Nursing Diagnosis Statements Prioritized	Nursing Care Plans Listed	Nursing Care Implemented and Evaluated

INTRANATAL MOTHER NURSED

Nursing Diagnosis Statements Prioritized	Nursing Care Plans Listed	Nursing Care Implemented and Evaluated

INTRANATAL MOTHER NURSED–7

Name.. Age ....Gravida...........................Para...............................

Hospital Number...

Date of Admission...

Date of Delivery..

Discharge
Condition of Mother....................................
Baby..

- **Antenatal Record**

Date of Booking .... LMP...

Gestation at 1st visit .... EDD ....

- **Medical History**

Chronic Illness .... Allergy..

Surgery .... Communicable Disease.....................................

- **Family History**

Type of Family: Single .... No. of Persons ....

Joint .... No. of Persons ....

Diseases: Chronic Illness: Hypertension:...................... Diabetes...

Genetic Disorders...

Psychiatric Disorders...

Other...

Multiple Births: ....

- **Socioeconomic Background**

Religion .... Family Income ....

Education: Husband .... Wife..

Occupation: Husband .... Wife..

- **Menstrual History**

Menarchy...Duration.................................Interval..............................

Flow..

- **Marital History**

Age of Marriage .... Years Married...

Consanguineous: Yes/No

- **Dietary Pattern**

Vegetarian .... Non-vegetarian ....

Likes .... Dislikes ....

Habits: Smoking/Drinking/Chewing pan

PAST OBSTETRICAL HISTORY

Sl. No.	Year	Full-term	Pre-term	Abortion	Type of Delivery	Sex of Baby	Alive	SB	Weight	Remarks

Present Pregnancy

- **Admission Notes**

Admitted on ....at ....am/pm
Contractions commenced on ....at ....am/pm
Period of Gestation ....Membranes: Intact ....
Ruptured on ....at ....am/pm
Height of Fundus..Contractions ....
Presentation ....Position ....
Engaged/Not Engaged/Free .... FHR ....
Bladder ....Bowels ....
Special Observations ....

PRENATAL VISITS

Date of Booking	Weight	Height	Urine		BP	FHR	Weeks of Gestation	Height of fundus	Position	Treatment
			Protein	Glucose						

- **General Condition**

BP .... TPR ....
Urine: Sp Gravity .... Reaction ....
Protein ....Glucose ....Acetone ....

- **Examinations and Investigations**

Blood Group .... Rh ....Hemoglobin ....
VDRL... HIV ....Other ....
Heart .... Lungs ....Breasts ....
Abdomen.. Perineum..

Components of the WHO Model Partograph

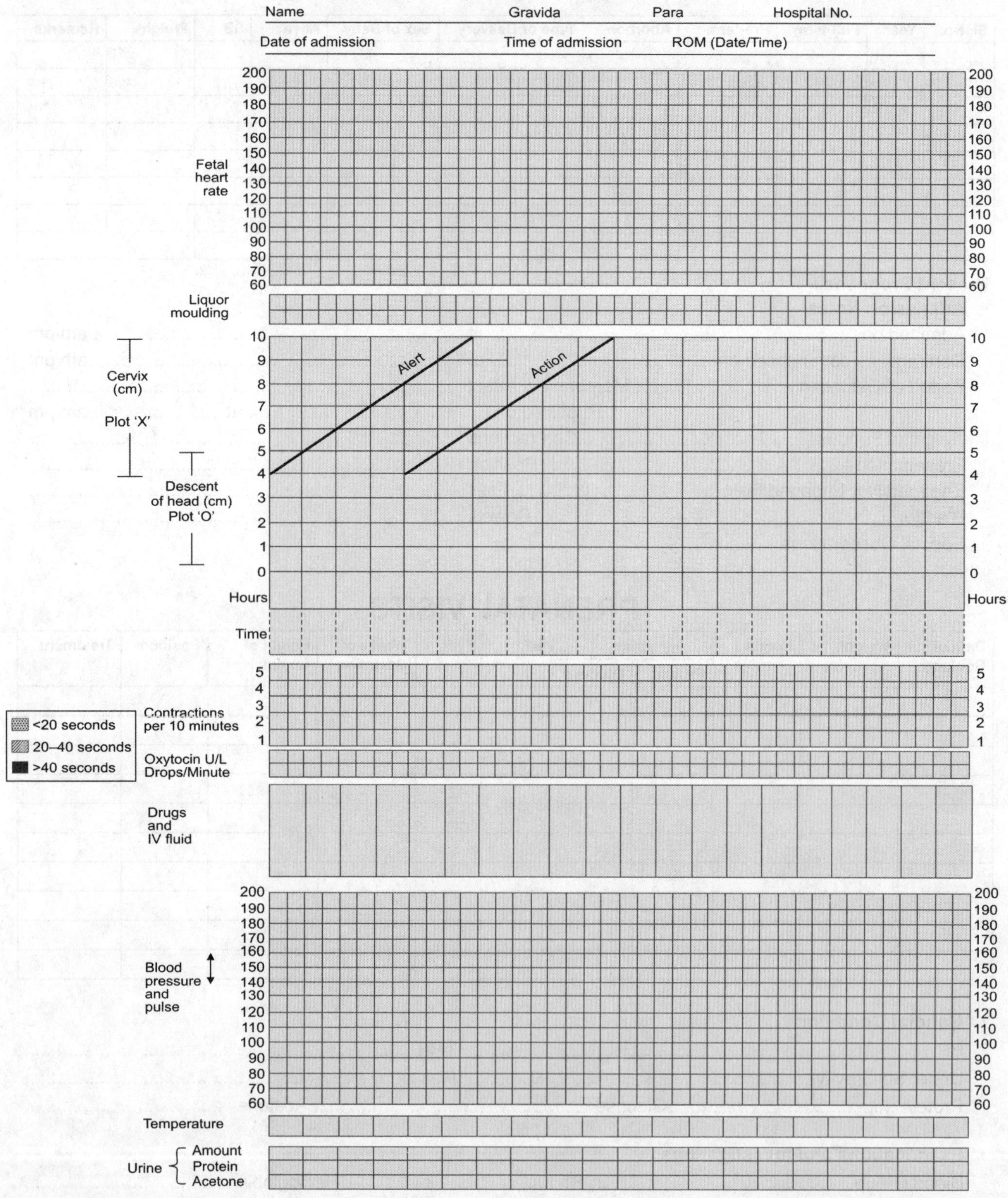

Source: WHO model partograph. Opoku Research Journal of Women's Health, 2015, www.hoagonline.com

Delivery Record

Onset of true labor: Date .... Time ....

Time of full dilation: Date .... Time ....

Membranes ruptured at .... Spontaneous/Artificial ....

PROM..

a. Delivery of Baby

Baby born at ....am/pm, Male/Female....................................., Mode of Delivery..............................

Condition of Baby Active/Limp/Asphyxiated

APGAR SCORING

Sl. No.	Sign	0	Neonate's score	1	Neonate's score	2	Neonate's score
1.	Respiratory effort	Absent		Slow, irregular, weak cry		Strong cry	
2.	Heart rate	Absent		Slow, less than 100		Over 100	
3.	Muscle tone	Limp		Some flexion of limbs		Active movement	
4.	Reflex response to flicking of foot	Absent		Facial grimace		Cry	
5.	Color	Blue-Pale		Body pink, Limbs blue		Completely pink	

0–2 Severe asphyxia

3–4 Moderate asphyxia

5–7 Mild asphyxia

8–10 No asphyxia

Score at one minute ....

Score at five minutes..

Stillborn/Macerated..

Cause ....

Treatment at birth ....

b. Delivery of placenta and membranes

Delivered at ....am/pm

Spontaneously/Helped out/Manually removed..

Type of Placenta..

Placenta and membranes: Complete/Incomplete..

Weight.............................Cord length...........................Cord insertion ....

Any abnormality..

c. Blood loss: (Approximate total amount)

Before delivery of the Placenta.. mL

During delivery of the Placenta .... mL

After delivery of the Placenta.. mL

Total .... mL

d. Perineum:

Intact ....Episiotomy..................................Laceration..................................

Repair..

e. Medications given ....

....

....

f. Length of Labor

Mode of Delivery..

Duration of Labor. First stage: .... Hours ....Minutes

Second stage: .... Hours ....Minutes

Third stage: .... Hours ....Minutes

Total: .... Hours ....Minutes

Condition of Mother following delivery

Pulse...BP..Uterus ....

Vaginal bleeding..

Breastfeeding initiated at..

INTRANATAL MOTHER NURSED

Nursing Diagnosis Statements Prioritized	Nursing Care Plans Listed	Nursing Care Implemented and Evaluated

INTRANATAL MOTHER NURSED

Nursing Diagnosis Statements Prioritized	Nursing Care Plans Listed	Nursing Care Implemented and Evaluated

INTRANATAL MOTHER NURSED

Nursing Diagnosis Statements Prioritized	Nursing Care Plans Listed	Nursing Care Implemented and Evaluated

INTRANATAL MOTHER NURSED

Nursing Diagnosis Statements Prioritized	Nursing Care Plans Listed	Nursing Care Implemented and Evaluated

INTRANATAL MOTHER NURSED–8

Name.. Age ....Gravida..........................Para..............................

Hospital Number..

Date of Admission...

Date of Delivery...

Discharge
Condition of Mother....................................
Baby.......................................

- **Antenatal Record**

Date of Booking .... LMP...

Gestation at 1st visit .... EDD ....

- **Medical History**

Chronic Illness .... Allergy ....

Surgery .... Communicable Disease ....

- **Family History**

Type of Family: Single .... No. of Persons ....

Joint .... No. of Persons ....

Diseases: Chronic Illness: Hypertension:...................... Diabetes..

Genetic Disorders..

Psychiatric Disorders...

Other...

Multiple Births: ....

- **Socioeconomic Background**

Religion .... Family Income ....

Education: Husband .... Wife...

Occupation: Husband .... Wife...

- **Menstrual History**

Menarchy...Duration..................................Interval..................................

Flow...

- **Marital History**

Age of Marriage .... Years Married...

Consanguineous: Yes/No

- **Dietary Pattern**

Vegetarian .... Non-vegetarian ....

Likes .... Dislikes ....

Habits: Smoking/Drinking/Chewing pan

PAST OBSTETRICAL HISTORY

Sl. No.	Year	Full-term	Pre-term	Abortion	Type of Delivery	Sex of Baby	Alive	SB	Weight	Remarks

Present Pregnancy

- **Admission Notes**

Admitted on ....at ....am/pm
Contractions commenced on ....at ....am/pm
Period of Gestation ....Membranes: Intact ....
Ruptured on ....at ....am/pm
Height of Fundus..Contractions ....
Presentation ....Position ....
Engaged/Not Engaged/Free .... FHR ....
Bladder ....Bowels ....
Special Observations ....

PRENATAL VISITS

Date of Booking	Weight	Height	Urine		BP	FHR	Weeks of Gestation	Height of fundus	Position	Treatment
			Protein	Glucose						

- **General Condition**

BP .... TPR ....
Urine: Sp Gravity .... Reaction ....
Protein ....Glucose ....Acetone ....

- **Examinations and Investigations**

Blood Group .... Rh ....Hemoglobin ....
VDRL.. HIV ....Other ....
Heart .... Lungs ....Breasts ....
Abdomen.. Perineum...

Components of the WHO Model Partograph

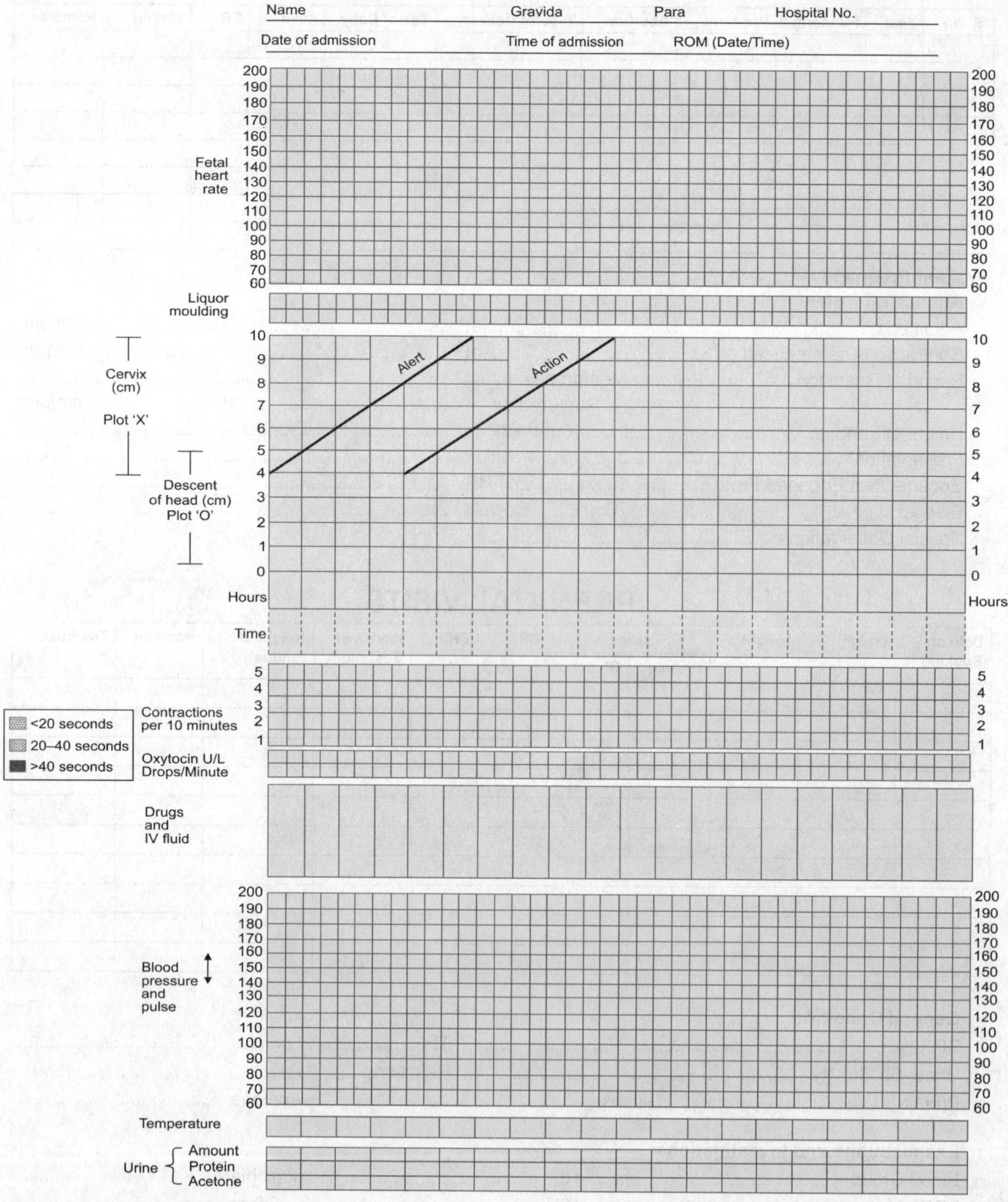

Source: WHO model partograph. Opoku Research Journal of Women's Health, 2015, www.hoagonline.com

Delivery Record

Onset of true labor: Date .... Time ....

Time of full dilation: Date .... Time ....

Membranes ruptured at .... Spontaneous/Artificial ....

PROM..

a. Delivery of Baby

Baby born at ....am/pm, Male/Female......................................, Mode of Delivery...............................

Condition of Baby Active/Limp/Asphyxiated

APGAR SCORING

Sl. No.	Sign	0	Neonate's score	1	Neonate's score	2	Neonate's score
1.	Respiratory effort	Absent		Slow, irregular, weak cry		Strong cry	
2.	Heart rate	Absent		Slow, less than 100		Over 100	
3.	Muscle tone	Limp		Some flexion of limbs		Active movement	
4.	Reflex response to flicking of foot	Absent		Facial grimace		Cry	
5.	Color	Blue-Pale		Body pink, Limbs blue		Completely pink	

0–2 Severe asphyxia

3–4 Moderate asphyxia

5–7 Mild asphyxia

8–10 No asphyxia

Score at one minute ....

Score at five minutes ....

Stillborn/Macerated..

Cause ....

Treatment at birth ....

b. Delivery of placenta and membranes

Delivered at ....am/pm

Spontaneously/Helped out/Manually removed ....

Type of Placenta..

Placenta and membranes: Complete/Incomplete..

Weight............................Cord length..........................Cord insertion ....

Any abnormality..

c. Blood loss: (Approximate total amount)

Before delivery of the Placenta.. mL

During delivery of the Placenta .... mL

After delivery of the Placenta.. mL

Total .... mL

d. Perineum:

Intact ....Episiotomy..................................Laceration...............................

Repair..

e. Medications given ....

....

....

f. Length of Labor

Mode of Delivery..

Duration of Labor. First stage: .... Hours ....Minutes

Second stage: .... Hours ....Minutes

Third stage: .... Hours ....Minutes

Total: .... Hours ....Minutes

Condition of Mother following delivery

Pulse.................................BP...Uterus ....

Vaginal bleeding..

Breastfeeding initiated at..

INTRANATAL MOTHER NURSED

Nursing Diagnosis Statements Prioritized	Nursing Care Plans Listed	Nursing Care Implemented and Evaluated

INTRANATAL MOTHER NURSED

Nursing Diagnosis Statements Prioritized	Nursing Care Plans Listed	Nursing Care Implemented and Evaluated

INTRANATAL MOTHER NURSED

Nursing Diagnosis Statements Prioritized	Nursing Care Plans Listed	Nursing Care Implemented and Evaluated

INTRANATAL MOTHER NURSED

Nursing Diagnosis Statements Prioritized	Nursing Care Plans Listed	Nursing Care Implemented and Evaluated

INTRANATAL MOTHER NURSED–9

Name... Age .... Gravida............................ Para...............................

Hospital Number..

Date of Admission...

Date of Delivery..

Discharge
Condition of Mother.....................................
Baby..

- **Antenatal Record**

Date of Booking .... LMP...

Gestation at 1st visit .... EDD ....

- **Medical History**

Chronic Illness .... Allergy..

Surgery .... Communicable Disease.....................................

- **Family History**

Type of Family: Single .... No. of Persons ....

Joint .... No. of Persons ....

Diseases: Chronic Illness: Hypertension:....................... Diabetes..

Genetic Disorders ....

Psychiatric Disorders..

Other...

Multiple Births: ....

- **Socioeconomic Background**

Religion .... Family Income ....

Education: Husband .... Wife...

Occupation: Husband .... Wife...

- **Menstrual History**

Menarchy...Duration...................................Interval....................................

Flow...

- **Marital History**

Age of Marriage .... Years Married...

Consanguineous: Yes/No

- **Dietary Pattern**

Vegetarian .... Non-vegetarian ....

Likes .... Dislikes ....

Habits: Smoking/Drinking/Chewing pan

PAST OBSTETRICAL HISTORY

Sl. No.	Year	Full-term	Pre-term	Abortion	Type of Delivery	Sex of Baby	Alive	SB	Weight	Remarks

Present Pregnancy

- **Admission Notes**

Admitted on ....at ....am/pm
Contractions commenced on ....at ....am/pm
Period of Gestation ....Membranes: Intact ....
Ruptured on ....at ....am/pm
Height of Fundus...Contractions ....
Presentation ....Position ....
Engaged/Not Engaged/Free ....FHR ....
Bladder ....Bowels ....
Special Observations ....

PRENATAL VISITS

Date of Booking	Weight	Height	Urine		BP	FHR	Weeks of Gestation	Height of fundus	Position	Treatment
			Protein	Glucose						

- **General Condition**

BP .... TPR...
Urine: Sp Gravity .... Reaction..
Protein ....Glucose ....Acetone ....

- **Examinations and Investigations**

Blood Group.. Rh ....Hemoglobin ....
VDRL... HIV..Other ....
Heart .... Lungs ....Breasts ....
Abdomen.. Perineum...

Components of the WHO Model Partograph

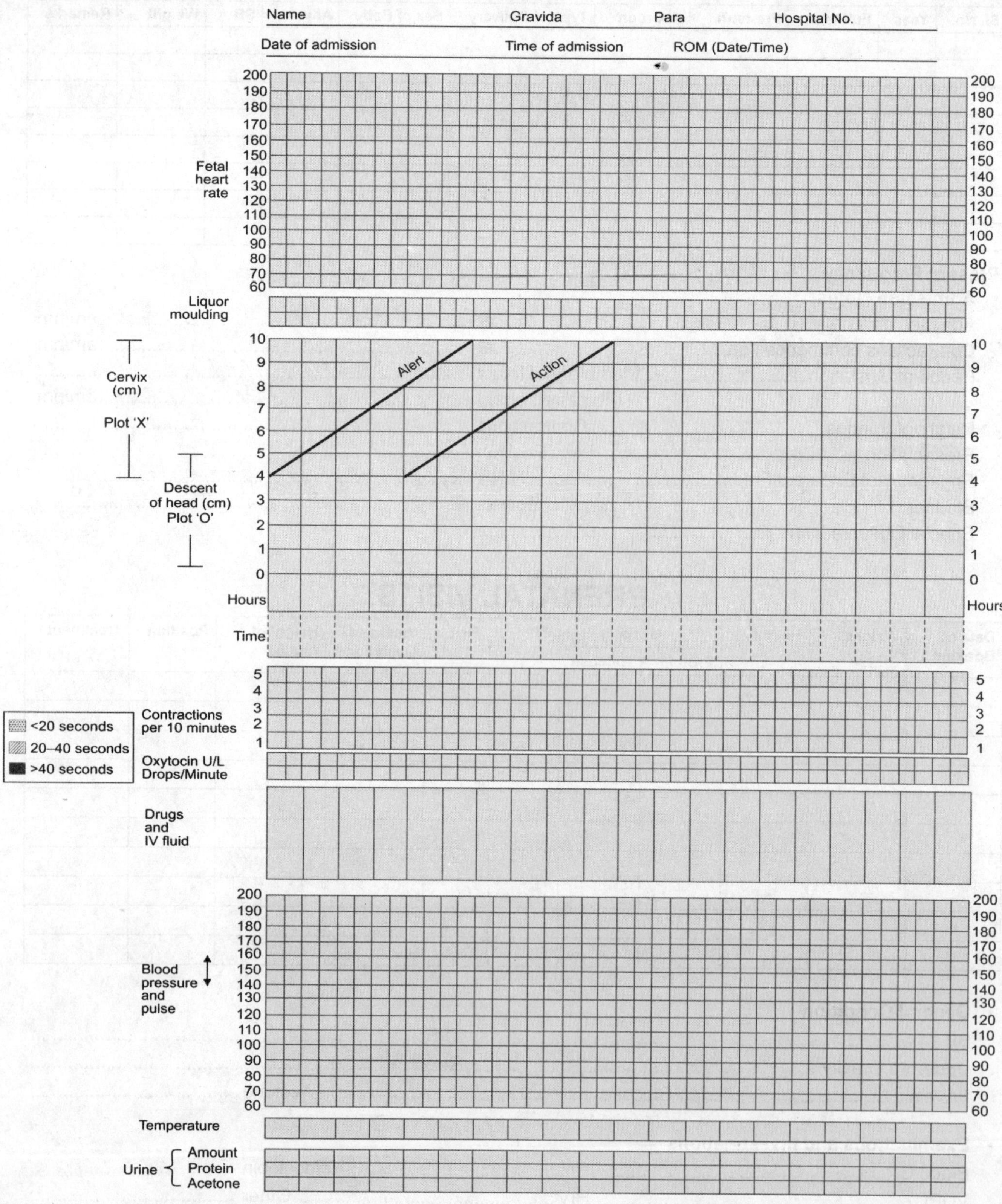

Source: WHO model partograph. Opoku Research Journal of Women's Health, 2015, www.hoagonline.com

Delivery Record

Onset of true labor: Date .... Time ....

Time of full dilation: Date .... Time ....

Membranes ruptured at .... Spontaneous/Artificial ....

PROM ....

a. Delivery of Baby

Baby born at ....am/pm, Male/Female...................................., Mode of Delivery....................................

Condition of Baby Active/Limp/Asphyxiated

APGAR SCORING

Sl. No.	Sign	0	Neonate's score	1	Neonate's score	2	Neonate's score
1.	Respiratory effort	Absent		Slow, irregular, weak cry		Strong cry	
2.	Heart rate	Absent		Slow, less than 100		Over 100	
3.	Muscle tone	Limp		Some flexion of limbs		Active movement	
4.	Reflex response to flicking of foot	Absent		Facial grimace		Cry	
5.	Color	Blue-Pale		Body pink, Limbs blue		Completely pink	

0–2 Severe asphyxia

3–4 Moderate asphyxia

5–7 Mild asphyxia

8–10 No asphyxia

Score at one minute ....

Score at five minutes ....

Stillborn/Macerated....................................

Cause ....

Treatment at birth ....

b. Delivery of placenta and membranes

Delivered at ....am/pm

Spontaneously/Helped out/Manually removed....................................

Type of Placenta....................................

Placenta and membranes: Complete/Incomplete....................................

Weight....................................Cord length....................................Cord insertion ....

Any abnormality....................................

c. Blood loss: (Approximate total amount)

Before delivery of the Placenta.................................... mL

During delivery of the Placenta .... mL

After delivery of the Placenta.................................... mL

Total .... mL

d. Perineum:

Intact ....Episiotomy....................................Laceration....................................

Repair....................................

e. Medications given ....

....

....

f. Length of Labor

Mode of Delivery....................................

Duration of Labor. First stage: .... Hours ....Minutes

Second stage: .... Hours ....Minutes

Third stage: .... Hours ....Minutes

Total: .... Hours ....Minutes

Condition of Mother following delivery

Pulse....................................BP....................................Uterus ....

Vaginal bleeding....................................

Breastfeeding initiated at....................................

INTRANATAL MOTHER NURSED

Nursing Diagnosis Statements Prioritized	Nursing Care Plans Listed	Nursing Care Implemented and Evaluated

INTRANATAL MOTHER NURSED

Nursing Diagnosis Statements Prioritized	Nursing Care Plans Listed	Nursing Care Implemented and Evaluated

INTRANATAL MOTHER NURSED

Nursing Diagnosis Statements Prioritized	Nursing Care Plans Listed	Nursing Care Implemented and Evaluated

INTRANATAL MOTHER NURSED

Nursing Diagnosis Statements Prioritized	Nursing Care Plans Listed	Nursing Care Implemented and Evaluated

INTRANATAL MOTHER NURSED–10

Name.. Age .... Gravida............................ Para...............................

Hospital Number..

Date of Admission..

Date of Delivery..

Discharge
Condition of Mother.......................................
Baby.......................................

- **Antenatal Record**

  Date of Booking .... LMP..

  Gestation at 1st visit .... EDD ....

- **Medical History**

  Chronic Illness .... Allergy..

  Surgery .... Communicable Disease..

- **Family History**

  Type of Family: Single .... No. of Persons ....

  Joint .... No. of Persons ....

  Diseases: Chronic Illness: Hypertension:....................... Diabetes..

  Genetic Disorders..

  Psychiatric Disorders..

  Other..

  Multiple Births: ....

- **Socioeconomic Background**

  Religion .... Family Income ....

  Education: Husband .... Wife..

  Occupation: Husband .... Wife..

- **Menstrual History**

  Menarchy.. Duration.................................... Interval................ ....

  Flow..

- **Marital History**

  Age of Marriage .... Years Married..

  Consanguineous: Yes/No

- **Dietary Pattern**

  Vegetarian .... Non-vegetarian ....

  Likes .... Dislikes ....

  Habits: Smoking/Drinking/Chewing pan

PAST OBSTETRICAL HISTORY

Sl. No.	Year	Full-term	Pre-term	Abortion	Type of Delivery	Sex of Baby	Alive	SB	Weight	Remarks

Present Pregnancy

- **Admission Notes**

Admitted on .... at .... am/pm
Contractions commenced on .... at .... am/pm
Period of Gestation .... Membranes: Intact ....
Ruptured on .... at .... am/pm
Height of Fundus .... Contractions ....
Presentation .... Position ....
Engaged/Not Engaged/Free .... FHR ....
Bladder .... Bowels ....
Special Observations ....

PRENATAL VISITS

Date of Booking	Weight	Height	Urine		BP	FHR	Weeks of Gestation	Height of fundus	Position	Treatment
			Protein	Glucose						

- **General Condition**

BP .... TPR ....
Urine: Sp Gravity .... Reaction ....
Protein .... Glucose .... Acetone ....

- **Examinations and Investigations**

Blood Group .... Rh .... Hemoglobin ....
VDRL .... HIV .... Other ....
Heart .... Lungs .... Breasts ....
Abdomen .... Perineum ....

Components of the WHO Model Partograph

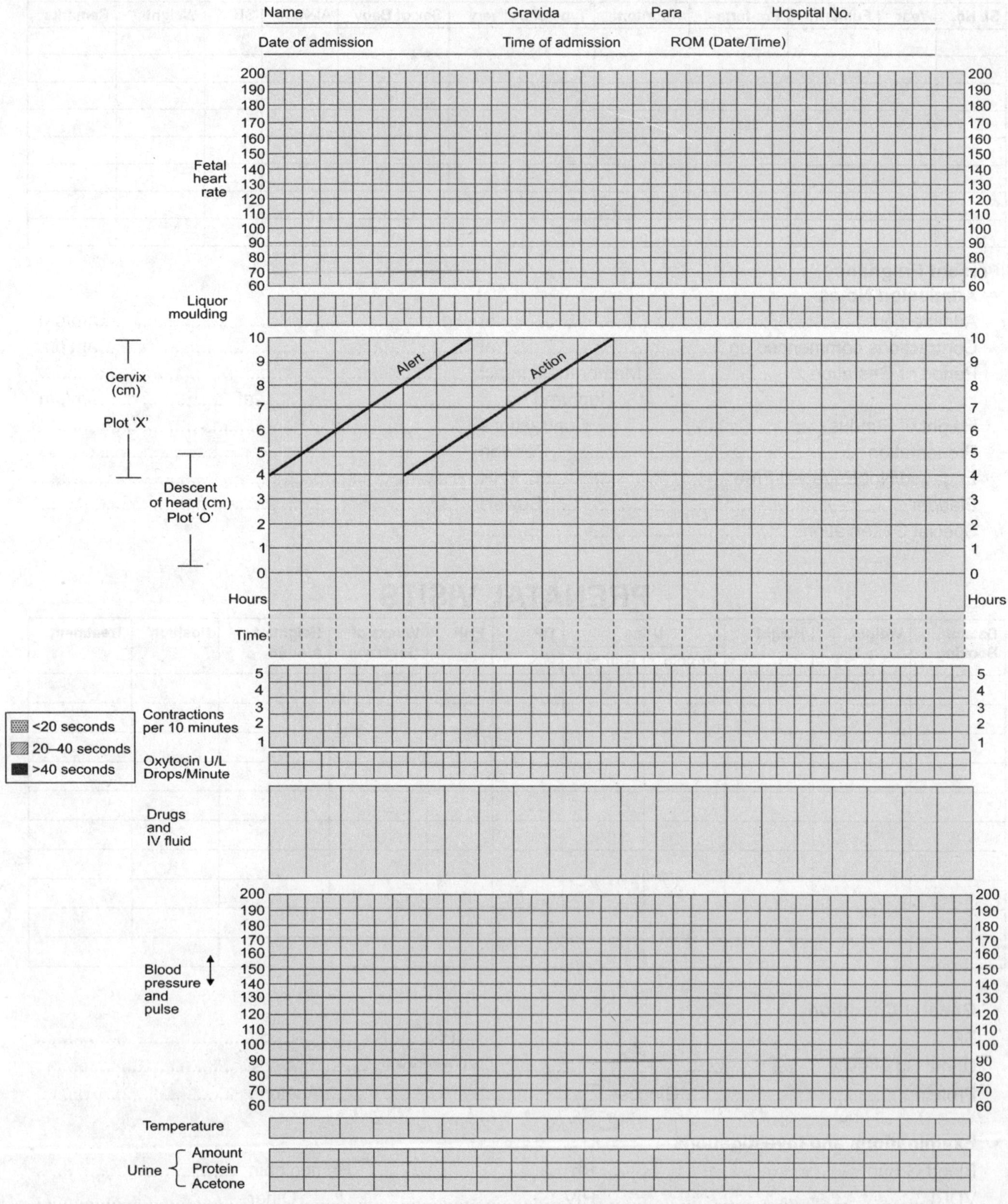

Source: WHO model partograph. Opoku Research Journal of Women's Health, 2015, www.hoagonline.com

Delivery Record

Onset of true labor: Date .... Time ....

Time of full dilation: Date .... Time ....

Membranes ruptured at .... Spontaneous/Artificial ....

PROM..

a. Delivery of Baby

Baby born at ....am/pm, Male/Female..., Mode of Delivery...............................

Condition of Baby Active/Limp/Asphyxiated

APGAR SCORING

Sl. No.	Sign	0	Neonate's score	1	Neonate's score	2	Neonate's score
1.	Respiratory effort	Absent		Slow, irregular, weak cry		Strong cry	
2.	Heart rate	Absent		Slow, less than 100		Over 100	
3.	Muscle tone	Limp		Some flexion of limbs		Active movement	
4.	Reflex response to flicking of foot	Absent		Facial grimace		Cry	
5.	Color	Blue-Pale		Body pink, Limbs blue		Completely pink	

0–2 Severe asphyxia

3–4 Moderate asphyxia

5–7 Mild asphyxia

8–10 No asphyxia

Score at one minute ....

Score at five minutes ....

Stillborn/Macerated..

Cause ....

Treatment at birth ....

b. Delivery of placenta and membranes

Delivered at ....am/pm

Spontaneously/Helped out/Manually removed ....

Type of Placenta..

Placenta and membranes: Complete/Incomplete..

Weight.............................Cord length...........................Cord insertion ....

Any abnormality..

c. Blood loss: (Approximate total amount)

Before delivery of the Placenta.. mL

During delivery of the Placenta .... mL

After delivery of the Placenta.. mL

Total .... mL

d. Perineum:

Intact ....Episiotomy....................................Laceration....................................

Repair..

e. Medications given ....

....

....

f. Length of Labor

Mode of Delivery..

Duration of Labor. First stage: .... Hours ....Minutes

Second stage: .... Hours ....Minutes

Third stage: .... Hours ....Minutes

Total: .... Hours ....Minutes

Condition of Mother following delivery

Pulse.......................................BP...Uterus ....

Vaginal bleeding ....

Breastfeeding initiated at..

INTRANATAL MOTHER NURSED

Nursing Diagnosis Statements Prioritized	Nursing Care Plans Listed	Nursing Care Implemented and Evaluated

INTRANATAL MOTHER NURSED

Nursing Diagnosis Statements Prioritized	Nursing Care Plans Listed	Nursing Care Implemented and Evaluated

INTRANATAL MOTHER NURSED

Nursing Diagnosis Statements Prioritized	Nursing Care Plans Listed	Nursing Care Implemented and Evaluated

INTRANATAL MOTHER NURSED

Nursing Diagnosis Statements Prioritized	Nursing Care Plans Listed	Nursing Care Implemented and Evaluated

POSTNATAL MOTHERS AND NEWBORNS NURSED INCLUDING CESAREAN MOTHERS–1

Name.. Age ....Gravida............................Para...............................

Hospital Number..

Date of Admission...

Date of Delivery..

Date of Discharge..

Discharge
Condition of Mother.....................................
Baby..

- **Prenatal Record**
  Date of booking .... LMP ....
  Gestation at 1st visit .... EDD..
- **Medical History**
  Chronic Illness .... Allergy ....
  Surgery .... Communicable Disease ....
- **Family History**
  Type of Family: Nuclear .... No. of Persons..
  Joint .... No. of Persons..

Diseases Chronic illness: ....
Genetic disorders..
Psychiatric disorders..

History of Multiple Births..

- **Socioeconomic Background**
  Religion .... Family Income..
  Education: Husband .... Wife ....
  Occupation: Husband .... Wife ....
- **Menstrual History**
  Menarchy .... Duration..
  Interval .... Flow..
- **Marital History**
  Age of Marriage.. Years Married ....
  Consanguineous: Yes/No ....
- **Dietary Pattern**
  Vegetarian .... Non-Vegetarian ....
  Likes .... Dislikes..
  Habits: Smoking/Drinking/Chewing Pan/Tobacco

PAST OBSTETRICAL HISTORY

Sl. No.	Year	Full-term	Pre-term	Abortion	Type of Delivery	Baby				Remarks
						Sex	Alive	Stillborn	Weight	

Present Pregnancy

- **Admission Notes**

Admitted on .... at ....am/pm
Contractions commenced on .... at ....am/pm
Height of Fundus... Contractions..
Presentation .... Position ....
Engaged/Not Engaged/Free .... FHR..
Bladder .... Bowels ....
Special Observations ....

PRENATAL VISITS

Date of Booking	Weight	Height	Urine		BP	FHR	Weeks of Gestation	Height of fundus	Position	Treatment
			Protein	Glucose						

- **General Condition**

BP .... TPR ....
Urine: Sp Gravity .... Reaction ....
Protein ....Glucose ....Acetone ....

- **Examinations and Investigations**

Blood Group .... Rh ....Hemoglobin ....
VDRL... HIV ....Other ....
Heart .... Lungs ....Breasts ....
Abdomen.. Perineum..

Delivery Record

Onset of true labor: Date .... Time ....
Time of full dilation: Date .... Time ....
Membranes ruptured at .... Spontaneous/Artificial ....
PROM..

a. Delivery of Baby

Baby born at ....am/pm, Male/Female ....
Mode of Delivery..
Condition of Baby: Active/Limp/Asphyxiated
Stillbirth/Macerated

Apgar Score ....
Treatment at Birth..

b. Delivery of placenta and membranes

Delivered at ....am/pm
Spontaneously/Helped out/Manually removed..
Type of Placenta..
Placenta and membranes: Complete/Incomplete..
Weight..Cord length.....................Cord insertion ....
Any abnormality..
Total blood loss..mL
Perineum: Intact/Episiotomy..
Laceration..
Medications given..
....

c. Length of Labor

Mode of Delivery..

Duration of Labor

First stage: .... Hours ....Minutes
Second stage: .... Hours ....Minutes
Third stage: .... Hours ....Minutes
Total: .... Hours ....Minutes

Condition of Mother following delivery

Pulse..BP..
Uterus: Hard/Soft..
Vaginal bleeding..
Breastfeeding initiated at..

CLINICAL CHART OF BABY

Date															
Temperature		M	E	M	E	M	E	M	E	M	E	M	E	M	E
F	C														
104.0	40														
103.1	39.5														
102.2	39														
101.3	38.5														
100.4	38														
99.5	37.5														
98.6	37														
97.7	36.5														
96.8	36														
Heart Rate															
Respiration															
Urine															
Stool															
Vomit															
Jaundice															
Weight															

CLINICAL CHART OF PUERPERIUM

Date																
Temperature		M	E	M	E	M	E	M	E	M	E	M	E	M	E	Fundus in cm
F	C															
104.9	40.5															20
104.0	40															17.5
103.1	39.5															15
102.2	39															12.5
101.3	38.5															10
100.4	38															7.5
99.5	37.5															5
98.6	37															2.5
97.7	36.5															
96.8	36															
95.9	35.5															
Pulse	M															
	E															
Respiration	M															
	E															
Blood Pressure	M															
	E															
Lochia																
Urine																
Motion																

POSTNATAL MOTHER AND NEWBORNS NURSED

Nursing Diagnosis Statements Prioritized	Nursing Care Plans Listed	Nursing Care Implemented and Evaluated

POSTNATAL MOTHER AND NEWBORNS NURSED

Nursing Diagnosis Statements Prioritized	Nursing Care Plans Listed	Nursing Care Implemented and Evaluated

POSTNATAL MOTHER AND NEWBORNS NURSED

Nursing Diagnosis Statements Prioritized	Nursing Care Plans Listed	Nursing Care Implemented and Evaluated

POSTNATAL MOTHER AND NEWBORNS NURSED

Nursing Diagnosis Statements Prioritized	Nursing Care Plans Listed	Nursing Care Implemented and Evaluated

Health Education:

Signature of Student

Signature of Supervisor

POSTNATAL MOTHERS AND NEWBORNS NURSED INCLUDING CESAREAN MOTHERS–2

Name.. Age .... Gravida............................. Para................................

Hospital Number..

Date of Admission...

Date of Delivery ....

Date of Discharge..

Discharge
Condition of Mother.......................................
Baby.......................................

- **Prenatal Record**

  Date of booking .... LMP ....

  Gestation at 1st visit .... EDD..

- **Medical History**

  Chronic illness .... Allergy ....

  Surgery .... Communicable disease ....

- **Family History**

  Type of Family: Nuclear .... No. of Persons...................................

  Joint .... No. of Persons...................................

Diseases Chronic illness: ....

Genetic disorders...

Psychiatric disorders...

History of Multiple Births...

- **Socioeconomic Background**

  Religion .... Family Income....................................

  Education: Husband .... Wife ....

  Occupation: Husband .... Wife ....

- **Menstrual History**

  Menarchy .... Duration..

  Interval .... Flow..

- **Marital History**

  Age of Marriage.. Years Married ....

  Consanguineous: Yes/No ....

- **Dietary Pattern**

  Vegetarian .... Non-Vegetarian ....

  Likes .... Dislikes ....

  Habits: Smoking/Drinking/Chewing Pan/Tobacco

PAST OBSTETRICAL HISTORY

Sl. No.	Year	Full-term	Pre-term	Abortion	Type of Delivery	Baby				Remarks
						Sex	Alive	Stillborn	Weight	

Present Pregnancy

- **Admission Notes**

Admitted on .... at ....am/pm
Contractions commenced on .... at ....am/pm
Height of Fundus.. Contractions ....
Presentation .... Position ....
Engaged/Not Engaged/Free .... FHR...
Bladder .... Bowels ....
Special Observations ....

PRENATAL VISITS

Date of Booking	Weight	Height	Urine		BP	FHR	Weeks of Gestation	Height of fundus	Position	Treatment
			Protein	Glucose						

- **General Condition**

BP .... TPR...
Urine: Sp Gravity .... Reaction ....
Protein ....Glucose ....Acetone ....

- **Examinations and Investigations**

Blood Group .... Rh ....Hemoglobin ....
VDRL.. HIV ....Other ....
Heart .... Lungs ....Breasts ....
Abdomen... Perineum...

Delivery Record

Onset of true labor: Date .... Time ....

Time of full dilation: Date .... Time ....

Membranes ruptured at .... Spontaneous/Artificial ....

PROM..

a. **Delivery of Baby**

Baby born at ....am/pm, Male/Female ....

Mode of Delivery..

Condition of Baby: Active/Limp/Asphyxiated

Stillbirth/Macerated

Apgar Score ....

Treatment at Birth..

b. **Delivery of placenta and membranes**

Delivered at ....am/pm

Spontaneously/Helped out/Manually removed ....

Type of Placenta..

Placenta and membranes: Complete/Incomplete..

Weight..Cord length.......................Cord insertion ....

Any abnormality..

Total blood loss..mL

Perineum: Intact/Episiotomy..

Laceration..

Medications given..

....

c. **Length of Labor**

Mode of Delivery..

Duration of Labor

First stage: .... Hours ....Minutes

Second stage: .... Hours ....Minutes

Third stage: .... Hours ....Minutes

Total: .... Hours ....Minutes

Condition of Mother following delivery

Pulse..BP..

Uterus: Hard/Soft..

Vaginal bleeding..

Breastfeeding initiated at..

CLINICAL CHART OF BABY

Date															
Temperature		M	E	M	E	M	E	M	E	M	E	M	E	M	E
F	C														
104.0	40														
103.1	39.5														
102.2	39														
101.3	38.5														
100.4	38														
99.5	37.5														
98.6	37														
97.7	36.5														
96.8	36														
Heart Rate															
Respiration															
Urine															
Stool															
Vomit															
Jaundice															
Weight															

CLINICAL CHART OF PUERPERIUM

Date																
Temperature		M	E	M	E	M	E	M	E	M	E	M	E	M	E	Fundus in cm
F	C															
104.9	40.5															20
104.0	40															17.5
103.1	39.5															15
102.2	39															12.5
101.3	38.5															10
100.4	38															7.5
99.5	37.5															5
98.6	37															2.5
97.7	36.5															
96.8	36															
95.9	35.5															
Pulse	M															
	E															
Respiration	M															
	E															
Blood Pressure	M															
	E															
Lochia																
Urine																
Motion																

POSTNATAL MOTHER AND NEWBORNS NURSED

Nursing Diagnosis Statements Prioritized	Nursing Care Plans Listed	Nursing Care Implemented and Evaluated

POSTNATAL MOTHER AND NEWBORNS NURSED

Nursing Diagnosis Statements Prioritized	Nursing Care Plans Listed	Nursing Care Implemented and Evaluated

POSTNATAL MOTHER AND NEWBORNS NURSED

Nursing Diagnosis Statements Prioritized	Nursing Care Plans Listed	Nursing Care Implemented and Evaluated

POSTNATAL MOTHER AND NEWBORNS NURSED

Nursing Diagnosis Statements Prioritized	Nursing Care Plans Listed	Nursing Care Implemented and Evaluated

Health Education:

Signature of Student **Signature of Supervisor**

POSTNATAL MOTHERS AND NEWBORNS NURSED INCLUDING CESAREAN MOTHERS–3

Name.. Age .... Gravida........................... Para...............................

Hospital Number...

Date of Admission...

Date of Delivery..

Date of Discharge...

Discharge
Condition of Mother......................................
Baby...

- **Prenatal Record**
  Date of booking .... LMP ....
  Gestation at 1st visit .... EDD...
- **Medical History**
  Chronic illness .... Allergy ....
  Surgery .... Communicable disease ....
- **Family History**
  Type of Family: Nuclear .... No. of Persons......................................
  Joint .... No. of Persons......................................

  Diseases Chronic illness: ....
  Genetic disorders...
  Psychiatric disorders..

  History of Multiple Births...
- **Socioeconomic Background**
  Religion .... Family Income ....
  Education: Husband .... Wife ....
  Occupation: Husband .... Wife ....
- **Menstrual History**
  Menarchy .... Duration...
  Interval .... Flow...
- **Marital History**
  Age of Marriage.. Years Married ....
  Consanguineous: Yes/No ....
- **Dietary Pattern**
  Vegetarian .... Non-Vegetarian ....
  Likes .... Dislikes ....
  Habits: Smoking/Drinking/Chewing Pan/Tobacco

PAST OBSTETRICAL HISTORY

Sl. No.	Year	Full-term	Pre-term	Abortion	Type of Delivery	Baby				Remarks
						Sex	Alive	Stillborn	Weight	

Present Pregnancy

- **Admission Notes**

Admitted on .... at .... am/pm
Contractions commenced on .... at .... am/pm
Height of Fundus .... Contractions ....
Presentation .... Position ....
Engaged/Not Engaged/Free .... FHR ....
Bladder .... Bowels ....
Special Observations ....

PRENATAL VISITS

Date of Booking	Weight	Height	Urine		BP	FHR	Weeks of Gestation	Height of fundus	Position	Treatment
			Protein	Glucose						

- **General Condition**

BP .... TPR ....
Urine: Sp Gravity .... Reaction ....
Protein .... Glucose .... Acetone ....

- **Examinations and Investigations**

Blood Group .... Rh .... Hemoglobin ....
VDRL .... HIV .... Other ....
Heart .... Lungs .... Breasts ....
Abdomen .... Perineum ....

Delivery Record

Onset of true labor: Date .... Time ....

Time of full dilation: Date .... Time ....

Membranes ruptured at .... Spontaneous/Artificial ....

PROM..

a. Delivery of Baby

Baby born at ....am/pm, Male/Female ....

Mode of Delivery..

Condition of Baby: Active/Limp/Asphyxiated
Stillbirth/Macerated

Apgar Score ....

Treatment at Birth..

b. Delivery of placenta and membranes

Delivered at ....am/pm

Spontaneously/Helped out/Manually removed..

Type of Placenta..

Placenta and membranes: Complete/Incomplete..

Weight..Cord length..Cord insertion ....

Any abnormality..

Total blood loss..mL

Perineum: Intact/Episiotomy..

Laceration..

Medications given..

....

c. Length of Labor

Mode of Delivery..

Duration of Labor

First stage: .... Hours ....Minutes

Second stage: .... Hours ....Minutes

Third stage: .... Hours ....Minutes

Total: .... Hours ....Minutes

Condition of Mother following delivery

Pulse.. ....BP..

Uterus: Hard/Soft..

Vaginal bleeding..

Breastfeeding initiated at..

CLINICAL CHART OF BABY

Date															
Temperature		M	E	M	E	M	E	M	E	M	E	M	E	M	E
F	C														
104.0	40														
103.1	39.5														
102.2	39														
101.3	38.5														
100.4	38														
99.5	37.5														
98.6	37														
97.7	36.5														
96.8	36														
Heart Rate															
Respiration															
Urine															
Stool															
Vomit															
Jaundice															
Weight															

CLINICAL CHART OF PUERPERIUM

Date																
Temperature		M	E	M	E	M	E	M	E	M	E	M	E	M	E	Fundus in cm
F	C															
104.9	40.5															20
104.0	40															17.5
103.1	39.5															15
102.2	39															12.5
101.3	38.5															10
100.4	38															7.5
99.5	37.5															5
98.6	37															2.5
97.7	36.5															
96.8	36															
95.9	35.5															
Pulse	M															
	E															
Respiration	M															
	E															
Blood Pressure	M															
	E															
Lochia																
Urine																
Motion																

POSTNATAL MOTHER AND NEWBORNS NURSED

Nursing Diagnosis Statements Prioritized	Nursing Care Plans Listed	Nursing Care Implemented and Evaluated

POSTNATAL MOTHER AND NEWBORNS NURSED

Nursing Diagnosis Statements Prioritized	Nursing Care Plans Listed	Nursing Care Implemented and Evaluated

POSTNATAL MOTHER AND NEWBORNS NURSED

Nursing Diagnosis Statements Prioritized	Nursing Care Plans Listed	Nursing Care Implemented and Evaluated

POSTNATAL MOTHER AND NEWBORNS NURSED

Nursing Diagnosis Statements Prioritized	Nursing Care Plans Listed	Nursing Care Implemented and Evaluated

Health Education:

Signature of Student

Signature of Supervisor

POSTNATAL MOTHERS AND NEWBORNS NURSED INCLUDING CESAREAN MOTHERS–4

Name.................................... Age .... Gravida............................ Para................................

Hospital Number..

Date of Admission..

Date of Delivery..

Date of Discharge..

Discharge
Condition of Mother...
Baby...

- **Prenatal Record**
  Date of booking .... LMP ....
  Gestation at 1st visit .... EDD ....
- **Medical History**
  Chronic illness .... Allergy ....
  Surgery .... Communicable disease ....
- **Family History**
  Type of Family: Nuclear .... No. of Persons..
  Joint .... No. of Persons..

Diseases Chronic illness: ....
Genetic disorders..
Psychiatric disorders..

History of Multiple Births..

- **Socioeconomic Background**
  Religion .... Family Income ....
  Education: Husband .... Wife ....
  Occupation: Husband .... Wife ....
- **Menstrual History**
  Menarchy .... Duration ....
  Interval .... Flow ....
- **Marital History**
  Age of Marriage .... Years Married ....
  Consanguineous: Yes/No ....
- **Dietary Pattern**
  Vegetarian .... Non-Vegetarian ....
  Likes .... Dislikes ....
  Habits: Smoking/Drinking/Chewing Pan/Tobacco

PAST OBSTETRICAL HISTORY

Sl. No.	Year	Full-term	Pre-term	Abortion	Type of Delivery	Baby				Remarks
						Sex	Alive	Stillborn	Weight	

Present Pregnancy

- **Admission Notes**

Admitted on .... at .... am/pm
Contractions commenced on .... at .... am/pm
Height of Fundus .... Contractions ....
Presentation .... Position ....
Engaged/Not Engaged/Free .... FHR ....
Bladder .... Bowels ....
Special Observations ....

PRENATAL VISITS

Date of Booking	Weight	Height	Urine		BP	FHR	Weeks of Gestation	Height of fundus	Position	Treatment
			Protein	Glucose						

- **General Condition**

BP .... TPR ....
Urine: Sp Gravity .... Reaction ....
Protein .... Glucose .... Acetone ....

- **Examinations and Investigations**

Blood Group .... Rh .... Hemoglobin ....
VDRL .... HIV .... Other ....
Heart .... Lungs .... Breasts ....
Abdomen .... Perineum ....

Delivery Record

Onset of true labor: Date .... Time ....

Time of full dilation: Date .... Time ....

Membranes ruptured at .... Spontaneous/Artificial ....

PROM..

a. **Delivery of Baby**

Baby born at ....am/pm, Male/Female ....

Mode of Delivery..

Condition of Baby: Active/Limp/Asphyxiated
Stillbirth/Macerated

Apgar Score ....

Treatment at Birth..

b. **Delivery of placenta and membranes**

Delivered at ....am/pm

Spontaneously/Helped out/Manually removed ....

Type of Placenta..

Placenta and membranes: Complete/Incomplete..

Weight..Cord length........................Cord insertion ....

Any abnormality..

Total blood loss..mL

Perineum: Intact/Episiotomy..

Laceration..

Medications given..

....

c. **Length of Labor**

Mode of Delivery..

Duration of Labor

First stage: .... Hours ....Minutes

Second stage: .... Hours ....Minutes

Third stage: .... Hours ....Minutes

Total: .... Hours ....Minutes

Condition of Mother following delivery

Pulse..BP..

Uterus: Hard/Soft..

Vaginal bleeding ....

Breastfeeding initiated at..

CLINICAL CHART OF BABY

Date															
Temperature		M	E	M	E	M	E	M	E	M	E	M	E	M	E
F	C														
104.0	40														
103.1	39.5														
102.2	39														
101.3	38.5														
100.4	38														
99.5	37.5														
98.6	37														
97.7	36.5														
96.8	36														
Heart Rate															
Respiration															
Urine															
Stool															
Vomit															
Jaundice															
Weight															

CLINICAL CHART OF PUERPERIUM

Date																
Temperature		M	E	M	E	M	E	M	E	M	E	M	E	M	E	Fundus in cm
F	C															
104.9	40.5															20
104.0	40															17.5
103.1	39.5															15
102.2	39															12.5
101.3	38.5															10
100.4	38															7.5
99.5	37.5															5
98.6	37															2.5
97.7	36.5															
96.8	36															
95.9	35.5															
Pulse	M															
	E															
Respiration	M															
	E															
Blood Pressure	M															
	E															
Lochia																
Urine																
Motion																

POSTNATAL MOTHER AND NEWBORNS NURSED

Nursing Diagnosis Statements Prioritized	Nursing Care Plans Listed	Nursing Care Implemented and Evaluated

POSTNATAL MOTHER AND NEWBORNS NURSED

Nursing Diagnosis Statements Prioritized	Nursing Care Plans Listed	Nursing Care Implemented and Evaluated

POSTNATAL MOTHER AND NEWBORNS NURSED

Nursing Diagnosis Statements Prioritized	Nursing Care Plans Listed	Nursing Care Implemented and Evaluated

POSTNATAL MOTHER AND NEWBORNS NURSED

Nursing Diagnosis Statements Prioritized	Nursing Care Plans Listed	Nursing Care Implemented and Evaluated

Health Education:

Signature of Student **Signature of Supervisor**

POSTNATAL MOTHERS AND NEWBORNS NURSED INCLUDING CESAREAN MOTHERS–5

Name.. Age .... Gravida.............................. Para...............................

Hospital Number..

Date of Admission...

Date of Delivery..

Date of Discharge..

Discharge
Condition of Mother.....................................
Baby...

- **Prenatal Record**
  Date of booking .... LMP ....
  Gestation at 1st visit .... EDD..
- **Medical History**
  Chronic illness .... Allergy ....
  Surgery .... Communicable disease ....
- **Family History**
  Type of Family: Nuclear .... No. of Persons...............................
  Joint .... No. of Persons...............................

  Diseases Chronic illness: ....
  Genetic disorders..
  Psychiatric disorders..

  History of Multiple Births..
- **Socioeconomic Background**
  Religion .... Family Income ....
  Education: Husband .... Wife ....
  Occupation: Husband .... Wife ....
- **Menstrual History**
  Menarchy .... Duration ....
  Interval .... Flow ....
- **Marital History**
  Age of Marriage .... Years Married ....
  Consanguineous: Yes/No ....
- **Dietary Pattern**
  Vegetarian .... Non-Vegetarian ....
  Likes .... Dislikes ....
  Habits: Smoking/Drinking/Chewing Pan/Tobacco

PAST OBSTETRICAL HISTORY

Sl. No.	Year	Full-term	Pre-term	Abortion	Type of Delivery	Baby				Remarks
						Sex	Alive	Stillborn	Weight	

Present Pregnancy

- **Admission Notes**

Admitted on .... at ....am/pm
Contractions commenced on .... at ....am/pm
Height of Fundus.. Contractions...
Presentation .... Position ....
Engaged/Not Engaged/Free .... FHR...
Bladder .... Bowels ....
Special Observations ....

PRENATAL VISITS

Date of Booking	Weight	Height	Urine		BP	FHR	Weeks of Gestation	Height of fundus	Position	Treatment
			Protein	Glucose						

- **General Condition**

BP .... TPR ....
Urine: Sp Gravity .... Reaction ....
Protein ....Glucose ....Acetone ....

- **Examinations and Investigations**

Blood Group .... Rh ....Hemoglobin ....
VDRL.. HIV...Other ....
Heart .... Lungs ....Breasts ....
Abdomen.. Perineum...

Delivery Record

Onset of true labor: Date .... Time ....

Time of full dilation: Date .... Time ....

Membranes ruptured at .... Spontaneous/Artificial ....

PROM..

a. **Delivery of Baby**

Baby born at ....am/pm, Male/Female ....

Mode of Delivery..

Condition of Baby: Active/Limp/Asphyxiated
Stillbirth/Macerated

Apgar Score ....

Treatment at Birth..

b. **Delivery of placenta and membranes**

Delivered at ....am/pm

Spontaneously/Helped out/Manually removed..

Type of Placenta..

Placenta and membranes: Complete/Incomplete..

Weight..Cord length..............................Cord insertion ....

Any abnormality..

Total blood loss..mL

Perineum: Intact/Episiotomy..

Laceration..

Medications given..

....

c. **Length of Labor**

Mode of Delivery..

Duration of Labor

First stage: .... Hours ....Minutes

Second stage: .... Hours ....Minutes

Third stage: .... Hours ....Minutes

Total: .... Hours ....Minutes

Condition of Mother following delivery

Pulse.. ....BP..

Uterus: Hard/Soft..

Vaginal bleeding ....

Breastfeeding initiated at..

CLINICAL CHART OF BABY

Date															
Temperature		M	E	M	E	M	E	M	E	M	E	M	E	M	E
F	C														
104.0	40														
103.1	39.5														
102.2	39														
101.3	38.5														
100.4	38														
99.5	37.5														
98.6	37														
97.7	36.5														
96.8	36														
Heart Rate															
Respiration															
Urine															
Stool															
Vomit															
Jaundice															
Weight															

CLINICAL CHART OF PUERPERIUM

Date																
Temperature		M	E	M	E	M	E	M	E	M	E	M	E	M	E	Fundus in cm
F	C															
104.9	40.5															20
104.0	40															17.5
103.1	39.5															15
102.2	39															12.5
101.3	38.5															10
100.4	38															7.5
99.5	37.5															5
98.6	37															2.5
97.7	36.5															
96.8	36															
95.9	35.5															
Pulse	M															
	E															
Respiration	M															
	E															
Blood Pressure	M															
	E															
Lochia																
Urine																
Motion																

POSTNATAL MOTHER AND NEWBORNS NURSED

Nursing Diagnosis Statements Prioritized	Nursing Care Plans Listed	Nursing Care Implemented and Evaluated

POSTNATAL MOTHER AND NEWBORNS NURSED

Nursing Diagnosis Statements Prioritized	Nursing Care Plans Listed	Nursing Care Implemented and Evaluated

POSTNATAL MOTHER AND NEWBORNS NURSED

Nursing Diagnosis Statements Prioritized	Nursing Care Plans Listed	Nursing Care Implemented and Evaluated

POSTNATAL MOTHER AND NEWBORNS NURSED

Nursing Diagnosis Statements Prioritized	Nursing Care Plans Listed	Nursing Care Implemented and Evaluated

Health Education:

Signature of Student

Signature of Supervisor

POSTNATAL MOTHERS AND NEWBORNS NURSED INCLUDING CESAREAN MOTHERS–6

Name.................................... Age .... Gravida............................ Para..............................

Hospital Number..

Date of Admission..

Date of Delivery..

Date of Discharge..

Discharge
Condition of Mother...
Baby...

- **Prenatal Record**
  Date of booking .... LMP ....
  Gestation at 1st visit .... EDD..
- **Medical History**
  Chronic illness .... Allergy ....
  Surgery .... Communicable disease ....
- **Family History**
  Type of Family: Nuclear .... No. of Persons..
  Joint .... No. of Persons..

Diseases Chronic illness: ....
Genetic disorders..
Psychiatric disorders..

History of Multiple Births..

- **Socioeconomic Background**
  Religion .... Family Income ....
  Education: Husband .... Wife ....
  Occupation: Husband .... Wife ....
- **Menstrual History**
  Menarchy .... Duration..
  Interval .... Flow..
- **Marital History**
  Age of Marriage.. Years Married ....
  Consanguineous: Yes/No ....
- **Dietary Pattern**
  Vegetarian .... Non-Vegetarian ....
  Likes .... Dislikes ....
  Habits: Smoking/Drinking/Chewing Pan/Tobacco

PAST OBSTETRICAL HISTORY

Sl. No.	Year	Full-term	Pre-term	Abortion	Type of Delivery	Baby				Remarks
						Sex	Alive	Stillborn	Weight	

Present Pregnancy

- **Admission Notes**

Admitted on .... at ....am/pm
Contractions commenced on .... at ....am/pm
Height of Fundus .... Contractions ....
Presentation .... Position ....
Engaged/Not Engaged/Free .... FHR ....
Bladder .... Bowels ....
Special Observations ....

PRENATAL VISITS

Date of Booking	Weight	Height	Urine		BP	FHR	Weeks of Gestation	Height of fundus	Position	Treatment
			Protein	Glucose						

- **General Condition**

BP .... TPR ....
Urine: Sp Gravity .... Reaction ....
Protein ....Glucose ....Acetone ....

- **Examinations and Investigations**

Blood Group .... Rh ....Hemoglobin ....
VDRL .... HIV ....Other ....
Heart .... Lungs ....Breasts ....
Abdomen .... Perineum ....

Delivery Record

Onset of true labor: Date .... Time ....

Time of full dilation: Date .... Time ....

Membranes ruptured at .... Spontaneous/Artificial ....

PROM..

a. Delivery of Baby

Baby born at ....am/pm, Male/Female ....

Mode of Delivery..

Condition of Baby: Active/Limp/Asphyxiated
Stillbirth/Macerated

Apgar Score ....

Treatment at Birth..

b. Delivery of placenta and membranes

Delivered at ....am/pm

Spontaneously/Helped out/Manually removed ....

Type of Placenta..

Placenta and membranes: Complete/Incomplete..

Weight..Cord length..........................Cord insertion ....

Any abnormality..

Total blood loss..mL

Perineum: Intact/Episiotomy..

Laceration..

Medications given..

....

c. Length of Labor

Mode of Delivery..

Duration of Labor

First stage: .... Hours ....Minutes

Second stage: .... Hours ....Minutes

Third stage: .... Hours ....Minutes

Total: .... Hours ....Minutes

Condition of Mother following delivery

Pulse.. ....BP..

Uterus: Hard/Soft..

Vaginal bleeding ....

Breastfeeding initiated at..

CLINICAL CHART OF BABY

Date															
Temperature		M	E	M	E	M	E	M	E	M	E	M	E	M	E
F	C														
104.0	40														
103.1	39.5														
102.2	39														
101.3	38.5														
100.4	38														
99.5	37.5														
98.6	37														
97.7	36.5														
96.8	36														
Heart Rate															
Respiration															
Urine															
Stool															
Vomit															
Jaundice															
Weight															

CLINICAL CHART OF PUERPERIUM

Date																
Temperature		M	E	M	E	M	E	M	E	M	E	M	E	M	E	Fundus in cm
F	C															
104.9	40.5															20
104.0	40															17.5
103.1	39.5															15
102.2	39															12.5
101.3	38.5															10
100.4	38															7.5
99.5	37.5															5
98.6	37															2.5
97.7	36.5															
96.8	36															
95.9	35.5															
Pulse	M															
	E															
Respiration	M															
	E															
Blood Pressure	M															
	E															
Lochia																
Urine																
Motion																

POSTNATAL MOTHER AND NEWBORNS NURSED

Nursing Diagnosis Statements Prioritized	Nursing Care Plans Listed	Nursing Care Implemented and Evaluated

POSTNATAL MOTHER AND NEWBORNS NURSED

Nursing Diagnosis Statements Prioritized	Nursing Care Plans Listed	Nursing Care Implemented and Evaluated

POSTNATAL MOTHER AND NEWBORNS NURSED

Nursing Diagnosis Statements Prioritized	Nursing Care Plans Listed	Nursing Care Implemented and Evaluated

POSTNATAL MOTHER AND NEWBORNS NURSED

Nursing Diagnosis Statements Prioritized	Nursing Care Plans Listed	Nursing Care Implemented and Evaluated

Health Education:

Signature of Student

Signature of Supervisor

POSTNATAL MOTHERS AND NEWBORNS NURSED INCLUDING CESAREAN MOTHERS–7

Name.. Age .... Gravida............................ Para.................................

Hospital Number...

Date of Admission..

Date of Delivery..

Date of Discharge..

Discharge
Condition of Mother......................................
Baby...

- **Prenatal Record**
  Date of booking .... LMP ....
  Gestation at 1st visit .... EDD ....
- **Medical History**
  Chronic illness .... Allergy ....
  Surgery .... Communicable disease ....
- **Family History**
  Type of Family: Nuclear .... No. of Persons..
  Joint .... No. of Persons..

  Diseases Chronic illness: ....
  Genetic disorders..
  Psychiatric disorders..

  History of Multiple Births..
- **Socioeconomic Background**
  Religion .... Family Income ....
  Education: Husband .... Wife ....
  Occupation: Husband .... Wife ....
- **Menstrual History**
  Menarchy .... Duration..
  Interval .... Flow..
- **Marital History**
  Age of Marriage.. Years Married ....
  Consanguineous: Yes/No ....
- **Dietary Pattern**
  Vegetarian .... Non-Vegetarian ....
  Likes .... Dislikes ....
  Habits: Smoking/Drinking/Chewing Pan/Tobacco

PAST OBSTETRICAL HISTORY

Sl. No.	Year	Full-term	Pre-term	Abortion	Type of Delivery	Baby				Remarks
						Sex	Alive	Stillborn	Weight	

Present Pregnancy

- **Admission Notes**

Admitted on .... at ....am/pm
Contractions commenced on .... at ....am/pm
Height of Fundus.. Contractions ....
Presentation .... Position ....
Engaged/Not Engaged/Free .... FHR...
Bladder .... Bowels ....
Special Observations ....

PRENATAL VISITS

Date of Booking	Weight	Height	Urine		BP	FHR	Weeks of Gestation	Height of fundus	Position	Treatment
			Protein	Glucose						

- **General Condition**

BP .... TPR ....
Urine: Sp Gravity .... Reaction ....
Protein ....Glucose ....Acetone ....

- **Examinations and Investigations**

Blood Group .... Rh ....Hemoglobin ....
VDRL.. HIV ....Other ....
Heart .... Lungs ....Breasts ....
Abdomen.. Perineum..

Delivery Record

Onset of true labor: Date .... Time ....

Time of full dilation: Date .... Time ....

Membranes ruptured at .... Spontaneous/Artificial ....

PROM..

a. Delivery of Baby

Baby born at ....am/pm, Male/Female ....

Mode of Delivery..

Condition of Baby: Active/Limp/Asphyxiated
Stillbirth/Macerated

Apgar Score ....

Treatment at Birth..

b. Delivery of placenta and membranes

Delivered at ....am/pm

Spontaneously/Helped out/Manually removed ....

Type of Placenta..

Placenta and membranes: Complete/Incomplete..

Weight...Cord length............................Cord insertion ....

Any abnormality..

Total blood loss..mL

Perineum: Intact/Episiotomy..

Laceration..

Medications given..

....

c. Length of Labor

Mode of Delivery..

Duration of Labor

First stage: .... Hours ....Minutes

Second stage: .... Hours ....Minutes

Third stage: .... Hours ....Minutes

Total: .... Hours ....Minutes

Condition of Mother following delivery

Pulse.. BP..

Uterus: Hard/Soft..

Vaginal bleeding..

Breastfeeding initiated at..

CLINICAL CHART OF BABY

Date															
Temperature		M	E	M	E	M	E	M	E	M	E	M	E	M	E
F	C														
104.0	40														
103.1	39.5														
102.2	39														
101.3	38.5														
100.4	38														
99.5	37.5														
98.6	37														
97.7	36.5														
96.8	36														
Heart Rate															
Respiration															
Urine															
Stool															
Vomit															
Jaundice															
Weight															

CLINICAL CHART OF PUERPERIUM

Date																
Temperature		M	E	M	E	M	E	M	E	M	E	M	E	M	E	Fundus in cm
F	C															
104.9	40.5															20
104.0	40															17.5
103.1	39.5															15
102.2	39															12.5
101.3	38.5															10
100.4	38															7.5
99.5	37.5															5
98.6	37															2.5
97.7	36.5															
96.8	36															
95.9	35.5															
Pulse	M															
	E															
Respiration	M															
	E															
Blood Pressure	M															
	E															
Lochia																
Urine																
Motion																

POSTNATAL MOTHER AND NEWBORNS NURSED

Nursing Diagnosis Statements Prioritized	Nursing Care Plans Listed	Nursing Care Implemented and Evaluated

POSTNATAL MOTHER AND NEWBORNS NURSED

Nursing Diagnosis Statements Prioritized	Nursing Care Plans Listed	Nursing Care Implemented and Evaluated

POSTNATAL MOTHER AND NEWBORNS NURSED

Nursing Diagnosis Statements Prioritized	Nursing Care Plans Listed	Nursing Care Implemented and Evaluated

POSTNATAL MOTHER AND NEWBORNS NURSED

Nursing Diagnosis Statements Prioritized	Nursing Care Plans Listed	Nursing Care Implemented and Evaluated

Health Education:

Signature of Student

Signature of Supervisor

POSTNATAL MOTHERS AND NEWBORNS NURSED INCLUDING CESAREAN MOTHERS–8

Name.. Age .... Gravida................................ Para...............................

Hospital Number..

Date of Admission..

Date of Delivery..

Date of Discharge..

Discharge
Condition of Mother.......................................
Baby.......................................

- **Prenatal Record**

Date of booking .... LMP ....
Gestation at 1st visit .... EDD..

- **Medical History**

Chronic illness .... Allergy ....
Surgery .... Communicable disease ....

- **Family History**

Type of Family: Nuclear .... No. of Persons..
Joint .... No. of Persons..

Diseases Chronic illness: ....
Genetic disorders..
Psychiatric disorders..

History of Multiple Births..

- **Socioeconomic Background**

Religion .... Family Income ....
Education: Husband .... Wife ....
Occupation: Husband .... Wife ....

- **Menstrual History**

Menarchy .... Duration..
Interval .... Flow..

- **Marital History**

Age of Marriage.. Years Married ....
Consanguineous: Yes/No ....

- **Dietary Pattern**

Vegetarian .... Non-Vegetarian ....
Likes .... Dislikes ....
Habits: Smoking/Drinking/Chewing Pan/Tobacco

PAST OBSTETRICAL HISTORY

Sl. No.	Year	Full-term	Pre-term	Abortion	Type of Delivery	Baby				Remarks
						Sex	Alive	Stillborn	Weight	

Present Pregnancy

- **Admission Notes**

Admitted on .... at .... am/pm
Contractions commenced on .... at .... am/pm
Height of Fundus .... Contractions ....
Presentation .... Position ....
Engaged/Not Engaged/Free .... FHR ....
Bladder .... Bowels ....
Special Observations ....

PRENATAL VISITS

Date of Booking	Weight	Height	Urine		BP	FHR	Weeks of Gestation	Height of fundus	Position	Treatment
			Protein	Glucose						

- **General Condition**

BP .... TPR ....
Urine: Sp Gravity .... Reaction ....
Protein .... Glucose .... Acetone ....

- **Examinations and Investigations**

Blood Group .... Rh .... Hemoglobin ....
VDRL .... HIV .... Other ....
Heart .... Lungs .... Breasts ....
Abdomen .... Perineum ....

Delivery Record

Onset of true labor: Date .... Time ....

Time of full dilation: Date .... Time ....

Membranes ruptured at .... Spontaneous/Artificial ....

PROM..

a. **Delivery of Baby**

Baby born at ....am/pm, Male/Female ....

Mode of Delivery..

Condition of Baby: Active/Limp/Asphyxiated
Stillbirth/Macerated

Apgar Score ....

Treatment at Birth..

b. **Delivery of placenta and membranes**

Delivered at ....am/pm

Spontaneously/Helped out/Manually removed..

Type of Placenta..

Placenta and membranes: Complete/Incomplete..

Weight..Cord length.........................Cord insertion ....

Any abnormality..

Total blood loss..mL

Perineum: Intact/Episiotomy..

Laceration..

Medications given..

....

c. **Length of Labor**

Mode of Delivery..

Duration of Labor

First stage: .... Hours ....Minutes

Second stage: .... Hours ....Minutes

Third stage: .... Hours ....Minutes

Total: .... Hours ....Minutes

Condition of Mother following delivery

Pulse..BP..

Uterus: Hard/Soft..

Vaginal bleeding ....

Breastfeeding initiated at..

CLINICAL CHART OF BABY

Date															
Temperature		M	E	M	E	M	E	M	E	M	E	M	E	M	E
F	C														
104.0	40														
103.1	39.5														
102.2	39														
101.3	38.5														
100.4	38														
99.5	37.5														
98.6	37														
97.7	36.5														
96.8	36														
Heart Rate															
Respiration															
Urine															
Stool															
Vomit															
Jaundice															
Weight															

CLINICAL CHART OF PUERPERIUM

Date																
Temperature		M	E	M	E	M	E	M	E	M	E	M	E	M	E	Fundus in cm
F	C															
104.9	40.5															20
104.0	40															17.5
103.1	39.5															15
102.2	39															12.5
101.3	38.5															10
100.4	38															7.5
99.5	37.5															5
98.6	37															2.5
97.7	36.5															
96.8	36															
95.9	35.5															
Pulse	M															
	E															
Respiration	M															
	E															
Blood Pressure	M															
	E															
Lochia																
Urine																
Motion																

POSTNATAL MOTHER AND NEWBORNS NURSED

Nursing Diagnosis Statements Prioritized	Nursing Care Plans Listed	Nursing Care Implemented and Evaluated

POSTNATAL MOTHER AND NEWBORNS NURSED

Nursing Diagnosis Statements Prioritized	Nursing Care Plans Listed	Nursing Care Implemented and Evaluated

POSTNATAL MOTHER AND NEWBORNS NURSED

Nursing Diagnosis Statements Prioritized	Nursing Care Plans Listed	Nursing Care Implemented and Evaluated

POSTNATAL MOTHER AND NEWBORNS NURSED

Nursing Diagnosis Statements Prioritized	Nursing Care Plans Listed	Nursing Care Implemented and Evaluated

Health Education:

Signature of Student

Signature of Supervisor

POSTNATAL MOTHERS AND NEWBORNS NURSED INCLUDING CESAREAN MOTHERS–9

Name.. Age .... Gravida............................ Para...............................

Hospital Number..

Date of Admission..

Date of Delivery..

Date of Discharge..

Discharge
Condition of Mother.....................................
Baby.......................................

- **Prenatal Record**

Date of booking .... LMP ....

Gestation at 1st visit .... EDD..

- **Medical History**

Chronic illness .... Allergy ....

Surgery .... Communicable disease ....

- **Family History**

Type of Family: Nuclear .... No. of Persons...

Joint .... No. of Persons...

Diseases Chronic illness: ....

Genetic disorders...

Psychiatric disorders...

History of Multiple Births...

- **Socioeconomic Background**

Religion .... Family Income ....

Education: Husband .... Wife ....

Occupation: Husband .... Wife ....

- **Menstrual History**

Menarchy .... Duration...

Interval .... Flow...

- **Marital History**

Age of Marriage... Years Married ....

Consanguineous: Yes/No ....

- **Dietary Pattern**

Vegetarian .... Non-Vegetarian ....

Likes .... Dislikes ....

Habits: Smoking/Drinking/Chewing Pan/Tobacco

PAST OBSTETRICAL HISTORY

Sl. No.	Year	Full-term	Pre-term	Abortion	Type of Delivery	Baby				Remarks
						Sex	Alive	Stillborn	Weight	

Present Pregnancy

- **Admission Notes**

Admitted on .... at .... am/pm
Contractions commenced on .... at .... am/pm
Height of Fundus .... Contractions ....
Presentation .... Position ....
Engaged/Not Engaged/Free .... FHR ....
Bladder .... Bowels ....
Special Observations ....

PRENATAL VISITS

Date of Booking	Weight	Height	Urine		BP	FHR	Weeks of Gestation	Height of fundus	Position	Treatment
			Protein	Glucose						

- **General Condition**

BP .... TPR ....
Urine: Sp Gravity .... Reaction ....
Protein .... Glucose .... Acetone ....

- **Examinations and Investigations**

Blood Group .... Rh .... Hemoglobin ....
VDRL .... HIV .... Other ....
Heart .... Lungs .... Breasts ....
Abdomen .... Perineum ....

Delivery Record

Onset of true labor: Date .... Time ....

Time of full dilation: Date .... Time ....

Membranes ruptured at .... Spontaneous/Artificial ....

PROM..

a. Delivery of Baby

Baby born at ....am/pm, Male/Female ....

Mode of Delivery..

Condition of Baby: Active/Limp/Asphyxiated
Stillbirth/Macerated

Apgar Score ....

Treatment at Birth..

b. Delivery of placenta and membranes

Delivered at ....am/pm

Spontaneously/Helped out/Manually removed..

Type of Placenta..

Placenta and membranes: Complete/Incomplete..

Weight....................................Cord length..........................Cord insertion ....

Any abnormality..

Total blood loss..mL

Perineum: Intact/Episiotomy..

Laceration..

Medications given..

....

c. Length of Labor

Mode of Delivery..

Duration of Labor

First stage: .... Hours ....Minutes

Second stage: .... Hours ....Minutes

Third stage: .... Hours ....Minutes

Total: .... Hours ....Minutes

Condition of Mother following delivery

Pulse.. BP..

Uterus: Hard/Soft..

Vaginal bleeding..

Breastfeeding initiated at..

CLINICAL CHART OF BABY

Date															
Temperature		M	E	M	E	M	E	M	E	M	E	M	E	M	E
F	C														
104.0	40														
103.1	39.5														
102.2	39														
101.3	38.5														
100.4	38														
99.5	37.5														
98.6	37														
97.7	36.5														
96.8	36														
Heart Rate															
Respiration															
Urine															
Stool															
Vomit															
Jaundice															
Weight															

CLINICAL CHART OF PUERPERIUM

Date																
Temperature		M	E	M	E	M	E	M	E	M	E	M	E	M	E	Fundus in cm
F	C															
104.9	40.5															20
104.0	40															17.5
103.1	39.5															15
102.2	39															12.5
101.3	38.5															10
100.4	38															7.5
99.5	37.5															5
98.6	37															2.5
97.7	36.5															
96.8	36															
95.9	35.5															
Pulse	M															
	E															
Respiration	M															
	E															
Blood Pressure	M															
	E															
Lochia																
Urine																
Motion																

POSTNATAL MOTHER AND NEWBORNS NURSED

Nursing Diagnosis Statements Prioritized	Nursing Care Plans Listed	Nursing Care Implemented and Evaluated

POSTNATAL MOTHER AND NEWBORNS NURSED

Nursing Diagnosis Statements Prioritized	Nursing Care Plans Listed	Nursing Care Implemented and Evaluated

POSTNATAL MOTHER AND NEWBORNS NURSED

Nursing Diagnosis Statements Prioritized	Nursing Care Plans Listed	Nursing Care Implemented and Evaluated

POSTNATAL MOTHER AND NEWBORNS NURSED

Nursing Diagnosis Statements Prioritized	Nursing Care Plans Listed	Nursing Care Implemented and Evaluated

Health Education:

Signature of Student

Signature of Supervisor

POSTNATAL MOTHERS AND NEWBORNS NURSED INCLUDING CESAREAN MOTHERS–10

Name.. Age .... Gravida.............................. Para...............................

Hospital Number..

Date of Admission..

Date of Delivery..

Date of Discharge..

Discharge
Condition of Mother..
Baby..

- **Prenatal Record**

Date of booking .... LMP ....
Gestation at 1st visit .... EDD..

- **Medical History**

Chronic illness .... Allergy ....
Surgery .... Communicable disease ....

- **Family History**

Type of Family: Nuclear .... No. of Persons..
Joint .... No. of Persons..

Diseases Chronic illness: ....
Genetic disorders..
Psychiatric disorders..

History of Multiple Births..

- **Socioeconomic Background**

Religion .... Family Income..
Education: Husband .... Wife ....
Occupation: Husband .... Wife ....

- **Menstrual History**

Menarchy .... Duration..
Interval .... Flow..

- **Marital History**

Age of Marriage.. Years Married ....
Consanguineous: Yes/No ....

- **Dietary Pattern**

Vegetarian .... Non-Vegetarian ....
Likes .... Dislikes ....
Habits: Smoking/Drinking/Chewing Pan/Tobacco

PAST OBSTETRICAL HISTORY

Sl. No.	Year	Full-term	Pre-term	Abortion	Type of Delivery	Baby				Remarks
						Sex	Alive	Stillborn	Weight	

Present Pregnancy

- **Admission Notes**

Admitted on .... at .... am/pm
Contractions commenced on .... at .... am/pm
Height of Fundus .... Contractions ....
Presentation .... Position ....
Engaged/Not Engaged/Free .... FHR ....
Bladder .... Bowels ....
Special Observations ....

PRENATAL VISITS

Date of Booking	Weight	Height	Urine		BP	FHR	Weeks of Gestation	Height of fundus	Position	Treatment
			Protein	Glucose						

- **General Condition**

BP .... TPR ....
Urine: Sp Gravity .... Reaction ....
Protein .... Glucose .... Acetone ....

- **Examinations and Investigations**

Blood Group .... Rh .... Hemoglobin ....
VDRL .... HIV .... Other ....
Heart .... Lungs .... Breasts ....
Abdomen .... Perineum ....

Delivery Record

Onset of true labor: Date .... Time ....

Time of full dilation: Date .... Time ....

Membranes ruptured at .... Spontaneous/Artificial ....

PROM..

a. Delivery of Baby

Baby born at ....am/pm, Male/Female ....

Mode of Delivery..

Condition of Baby: Active/Limp/Asphyxiated

Stillbirth/Macerated

Apgar Score ....

Treatment at Birth ....

b. Delivery of placenta and membranes

Delivered at ....am/pm

Spontaneously/Helped out/Manually removed..

Type of Placenta..

Placenta and membranes: Complete/Incomplete..

Weight......................................Cord length......................Cord insertion ....

Any abnormality..

Total blood loss..mL

Perineum: Intact/Episiotomy..

Laceration..

Medications given..

....

c. Length of Labor

Mode of Delivery..

Duration of Labor

First stage: .... Hours ....Minutes

Second stage: .... Hours ....Minutes

Third stage: .... Hours ....Minutes

Total: .... Hours ....Minutes

Condition of Mother following delivery

Pulse.. BP..

Uterus: Hard/Soft..

Vaginal bleeding..

Breastfeeding initiated at..

CLINICAL CHART OF BABY

Date															
Temperature		M	E	M	E	M	E	M	E	M	E	M	E	M	E
F	C														
104.0	40														
103.1	39.5														
102.2	39														
101.3	38.5														
100.4	38														
99.5	37.5														
98.6	37														
97.7	36.5														
96.8	36														
Heart Rate															
Respiration															
Urine															
Stool															
Vomit															
Jaundice															
Weight															

CLINICAL CHART OF PUERPERIUM

Date																
Temperature		M	E	M	E	M	E	M	E	M	E	M	E	M	E	Fundus in cm
F	C															
104.9	40.5															20
104.0	40															17.5
103.1	39.5															15
102.2	39															12.5
101.3	38.5															10
100.4	38															7.5
99.5	37.5															5
98.6	37															2.5
97.7	36.5															
96.8	36															
95.9	35.5															
Pulse	M															
	E															
Respiration	M															
	E															
Blood Pressure	M															
	E															
Lochia																
Urine																
Motion																

POSTNATAL MOTHER AND NEWBORNS NURSED

Nursing Diagnosis Statements Prioritized	Nursing Care Plans Listed	Nursing Care Implemented and Evaluated

POSTNATAL MOTHER AND NEWBORNS NURSED

Nursing Diagnosis Statements Prioritized	Nursing Care Plans Listed	Nursing Care Implemented and Evaluated

POSTNATAL MOTHER AND NEWBORNS NURSED

Nursing Diagnosis Statements Prioritized	Nursing Care Plans Listed	Nursing Care Implemented and Evaluated

POSTNATAL MOTHER AND NEWBORNS NURSED

Nursing Diagnosis Statements Prioritized	Nursing Care Plans Listed	Nursing Care Implemented and Evaluated

Health Education:

Signature of Student

Signature of Supervisor

NEONATES NURSED–1

Name .... Sex .... Date of Birth .... Hospital No. ....
Date of Discharge .... Condition on Discharge ....

- **Mother's Obstetric History**

  Gravida .... Para .... Abortion ....
  Full-term Delivery .... Preterm Delivery ....
  Babies Born Alive .... Stillborn ....
  Babies Dead .... Cause of Death ....

- **Present Pregnancy**

  Antenatal Care: Yes/No .... Anemia: Yes/No ....
  Antepartal Hemorrhage: Yes/No .... Diabetes: Yes/No ....
  Pregnancy-induced Hypertension: Yes/No .... Any other Medical Condition, specify ....

- **Labor**

  Type of Delivery: Normal/Abnormal, specify: ....
  Duration of Labor: 1st stage .... 2nd Stage .... 3rd Stage ....
  Fetal Distress Present: Yes/No ....
  Membranes Ruptured: Spontaneously/Artificially ....
  Character of Amniotic Fluid: Clear/Meconium stained/foul smelling ....
  Amount: Normal/Excessive/scanty ....
  Placenta and Membranes: Healthy/Unhealthy ....
  Retroplacental Clots: Yes/No ....
  Umbilical Core: Normal/Around Neck/Around Body ....
  Drugs and Treatment Given....... ....

- **Baby**

  Date and Time of Birth: ....
  Condition at Birth: Active/Limp/Asphyxiated ....
  Apgar Score: ....
  Treatment for Eyes and Umbilicus: ....
  Medication Given: ....
  Time of Breastfeeding: ....

- **General Examination**

  Weight: .... Height: .... Head Circumference: ....
  Moulding: Normal/Excessive/Nil: ....
  Caput: Present/Not present: ....
  Eyes: .... Skin: ....
  Mouth: .... Limbs: ....
  Chest: .... Genitalia: ....
  Abdomen: .... Anus: ....
  Heart: .... Lungs: ....

  Other Findings Significant: ....

Feeding: Breastfeeding/Formula feeding

- **Elimination: Urine:**..**Stool:**..
- **Bonding**..
....
- **Investigations:**..
....
- **Treatment:**..
....

List of Nursing Diagnosis

....
....
....
....
....
....
....
....
....
....

Health Education to Mother

....
....
....
....
....
....
....
....
....
....

Signature of Student

Signature of Supervisor

CLINICAL CHART OF BABY

Date															
Temperature		M	E	M	E	M	E	M	E	M	E	M	E	M	E
F	C														
104.0	40														
103.1	39.5														
102.2	39														
101.3	38.5														
100.4	38														
99.5	37.5														
98.6	37														
97.7	36.5														
96.8	36														
Heart Rate/Min															
Respiration/Min															
Urine															
Stool															
Vomit															
Jaundice															
Weight (kg)															

CLINICAL CHART OF PUERPERIUM

Date	1	2	3	4	5	6	7	8	9	10	11	12	
Daily weight													Grams
													360
													330
													300
													270
													240
													210
													180
													150
													120
													90
													60
													30
													Birth weight
													–30
													–60
													–90
													–120
													–150
													–180
													–210
													–240
													–270
													–300
													–330
													–360

NEONATES NURSED

Nursing Diagnosis Statements Prioritized	Nursing Care Plans Listed	Nursing Care Implemented and Evaluated

NEONATES NURSED

Nursing Diagnosis Statements Prioritized	Nursing Care Plans Listed	Nursing Care Implemented and Evaluated

NEONATES NURSED

Nursing Diagnosis Statements Prioritized	Nursing Care Plans Listed	Nursing Care Implemented and Evaluated

NEONATES NURSED–2

Name .... Sex .... Date of Birth .... Hospital No. ....

Date of Discharge.......................... Condition on Discharge..

- **Mother's Obstetric History**

  Gravida .... Para .... Abortion ....

  Full-term Delivery .... Preterm Delivery ....

  Babies Born Alive .... Stillborn ....

  Babies Dead.. Cause of Death ....

- **Present Pregnancy**

  Antenatal Care: Yes/No .... Anemia: Yes/No..

  Antepartal Hemorrhage: Yes/No.. Diabetes: Yes/No...

  Pregnancy-induced Hypertension: Yes/No .... Any other Medical Condition, specify ....

- **Labor**

  Type of Delivery: Normal/Abnormal, specify:...

  Duration of Labor: 1st stage .... 2nd Stage .... 3rd Stage ....

  Fetal Distress Present: Yes/No...

  Membranes Ruptured: Spontaneously/Artificially...

  Character of Amniotic Fluid: Clear/Meconium stained/foul smelling...

  Amount: Normal/Excessive/scanty ....

  Placenta and Membranes: Healthy/Unhealthy ....

  Retroplacental Clots: Yes/No...

  Umbilical Core: Normal/Around Neck/Around Body ....

  Drugs and Treatment Given....... ....

- **Baby**

  Date and Time of Birth:...

  Condition at Birth: Active/Limp/Asphyxiated ....

  Apgar Score:..

  Treatment for Eyes and Umbilicus:..

  Medication Given:..

  Time of Breastfeeding:...

- **General Examination**

  Weight: .... Height:.. Head Circumference: ....

  Moulding: Normal/Excessive/Nil: ....

  Caput: Present/Not present: ....

  Eyes:... Skin: ....

  Mouth:.. Limbs:..

  Chest: .... Genitalia: ....

  Abdomen: .... Anus: ....

  Heart: .... Lungs: ....

  Other Findings Significant: ....

Feeding: Breastfeeding/Formula feeding

- **Elimination: Urine:**...**Stool:** ....
- **Bonding** ....
  ....
- **Investigations:** ....
  ....
- **Treatment**: ....
  ....

List of Nursing Diagnosis

....

....

....

....

....

....

....

....

....

....

Health Education to Mother

....

....

....

....

....

....

....

....

....

....

Signature of Student

Signature of Supervisor

CLINICAL CHART OF BABY

Date															
Temperature		M	E	M	E	M	E	M	E	M	E	M	E	M	E
F	C														
104.0	40														
103.1	39.5														
102.2	39														
101.3	38.5														
100.4	38														
99.5	37.5														
98.6	37														
97.7	36.5														
96.8	36														
Heart Rate/Min															
Respiration/Min															
Urine															
Stool															
Vomit															
Jaundice															
Weight (kg)															

CLINICAL CHART OF PUERPERIUM

Date	1	2	3	4	5	6	7	8	9	10	11	12	
Daily weight													Grams
													360
													330
													300
													270
													240
													210
													180
													150
													120
													90
													60
													30
													Birth weight
													–30
													–60
													–90
													–120
													–150
													–180
													–210
													–240
													–270
													–300
													–330
													–360

NEONATES NURSED

Nursing Diagnosis Statements Prioritized	Nursing Care Plans Listed	Nursing Care Implemented and Evaluated

NEONATES NURSED

Nursing Diagnosis Statements Prioritized	Nursing Care Plans Listed	Nursing Care Implemented and Evaluated

NEONATES NURSED

Nursing Diagnosis Statements Prioritized	Nursing Care Plans Listed	Nursing Care Implemented and Evaluated

NEONATES NURSED–3

Name .... Sex .... Date of Birth .... Hospital No. ....
Date of Discharge .... Condition on Discharge ....

- **Mother's Obstetric History**

Gravida .... Para .... Abortion ....
Full-term Delivery .... Preterm Delivery ....
Babies Born Alive .... Stillborn ....
Babies Dead .... Cause of Death ....

- **Present Pregnancy**

Antenatal Care: Yes/No .... Anemia: Yes/No ....
Antepartal Hemorrhage: Yes/No .... Diabetes: Yes/No ....
Pregnancy-induced Hypertension: Yes/No .... Any other Medical Condition, specify ....

- **Labor**

Type of Delivery: Normal/Abnormal, specify: ....
Duration of Labor: 1st stage .... 2nd Stage .... 3rd Stage ....
Fetal Distress Present: Yes/No ....
Membranes Ruptured: Spontaneously/Artificially ....
Character of Amniotic Fluid: Clear/Meconium stained/foul smelling ....
Amount: Normal/Excessive/scanty ....
Placenta and Membranes: Healthy/Unhealthy ....
Retroplacental Clots: Yes/No ....
Umbilical Core: Normal/Around Neck/Around Body ....
Drugs and Treatment Given....... ....

- **Baby**

Date and Time of Birth: ....
Condition at Birth: Active/Limp/Asphyxiated ....
Apgar Score: ....
Treatment for Eyes and Umbilicus: ....
Medication Given: ....
Time of Breastfeeding: ....

- **General Examination**

Weight: .... Height: .... Head Circumference: ....
Moulding: Normal/Excessive/Nil: ....
Caput: Present/Not present: ....
Eyes: .... Skin: ....
Mouth: .... Limbs: ....
Chest: .... Genitalia: ....
Abdomen: .... Anus: ....
Heart: .... Lungs: ....

Other Findings Significant: ....

Feeding: Breastfeeding/Formula feeding

- **Elimination: Urine:**..**Stool:** ....
- **Bonding** ....
  ....
- **Investigations:** ....
  ....
- **Treatment:** ....
  ....

List of Nursing Diagnosis

....
....
....
....
....
....
....
....
....
....

Health Education to Mother

....
....
....
....
....
....
....
....
....
....

Signature of Student

Signature of Supervisor

CLINICAL CHART OF BABY

Date															
Temperature		M	E	M	E	M	E	M	E	M	E	M	E	M	E
F	C														
104.0	40														
103.1	39.5														
102.2	39														
101.3	38.5														
100.4	38														
99.5	37.5														
98.6	37														
97.7	36.5														
96.8	36														
Heart Rate/Min															
Respiration/Min															
Urine															
Stool															
Vomit															
Jaundice															
Weight (kg)															

CLINICAL CHART OF PUERPERIUM

Date	1	2	3	4	5	6	7	8	9	10	11	12	
Daily weight													Grams
													360
													330
													300
													270
													240
													210
													180
													150
													120
													90
													60
													30
													Birth weight
													–30
													–60
													–90
													–120
													–150
													–180
													–210
													–240
													–270
													–300
													–330
													–360

NEONATES NURSED

Nursing Diagnosis Statements Prioritized	Nursing Care Plans Listed	Nursing Care Implemented and Evaluated

NEONATES NURSED

Nursing Diagnosis Statements Prioritized	Nursing Care Plans Listed	Nursing Care Implemented and Evaluated

NEONATES NURSED

Nursing Diagnosis Statements Prioritized	Nursing Care Plans Listed	Nursing Care Implemented and Evaluated

NEONATES NURSED–4

Name.................................... Sex .... Date of Birth .... Hospital No. ....

Date of Discharge.......................... Condition on Discharge...

- **Mother's Obstetric History**

  Gravida .... Para .... Abortion ....

  Full-term Delivery .... Preterm Delivery ....

  Babies Born Alive .... Stillborn ....

  Babies Dead.. Cause of Death ....

- **Present Pregnancy**

  Antenatal Care: Yes/No .... Anemia: Yes/No...

  Antepartal Hemorrhage: Yes/No.. Diabetes: Yes/No...

  Pregnancy-induced Hypertension: Yes/No .... Any other Medical Condition, specify ....

- **Labor**

  Type of Delivery: Normal/Abnormal, specify:...

  Duration of Labor: 1st stage .... 2nd Stage .... 3rd Stage ....

  Fetal Distress Present: Yes/No...

  Membranes Ruptured: Spontaneously/Artificially..

  Character of Amniotic Fluid: Clear/Meconium stained/foul smelling...

  Amount: Normal/Excessive/scanty ....

  Placenta and Membranes: Healthy/Unhealthy ....

  Retroplacental Clots: Yes/No...

  Umbilical Core: Normal/Around Neck/Around Body ....

  Drugs and Treatment Given........ ....

- **Baby**

  Date and Time of Birth:...

  Condition at Birth: Active/Limp/Asphyxiated ....

  Apgar Score:...

  Treatment for Eyes and Umbilicus:..

  Medication Given:..

  Time of Breastfeeding:..

- **General Examination**

  Weight: .... Height:.. Head Circumference: ....

  Moulding: Normal/Excessive/Nil: ....

  Caput: Present/Not present: ....

  Eyes:.. Skin: ....

  Mouth:... Limbs:...

  Chest: .... Genitalia: ....

  Abdomen: .... Anus: ....

  Heart: .... Lungs: ....

  Other Findings Significant: ....

Feeding: Breastfeeding/Formula feeding

- **Elimination: Urine:**..**Stool:** ....
- **Bonding**...
  ....
- **Investigations:** ....
  ....
- **Treatment:** ....
  ....

List of Nursing Diagnosis

....
....
....
....
....
....
....
....
....
....

Health Education to Mother

....
....
....
....
....
....
....
....
....
....

Signature of Student

Signature of Supervisor

CLINICAL CHART OF BABY

Date															
Temperature		M	E	M	E	M	E	M	E	M	E	M	E	M	E
F	C														
104.0	40														
103.1	39.5														
102.2	39														
101.3	38.5														
100.4	38														
99.5	37.5														
98.6	37														
97.7	36.5														
96.8	36														
Heart Rate/Min															
Respiration/Min															
Urine															
Stool															
Vomit															
Jaundice															
Weight (kg)															

CLINICAL CHART OF PUERPERIUM

Date	1	2	3	4	5	6	7	8	9	10	11	12	
Daily weight													Grams
													360
													330
													300
													270
													240
													210
													180
													150
													120
													90
													60
													30
													Birth weight
													–30
													–60
													–90
													–120
													–150
													–180
													–210
													–240
													–270
													–300
													–330
													–360

NEONATES NURSED

Nursing Diagnosis Statements Prioritized	Nursing Care Plans Listed	Nursing Care Implemented and Evaluated

NEONATES NURSED

Nursing Diagnosis Statements Prioritized	Nursing Care Plans Listed	Nursing Care Implemented and Evaluated

NEONATES NURSED

Nursing Diagnosis Statements Prioritized	Nursing Care Plans Listed	Nursing Care Implemented and Evaluated

NEONATES NURSED–5

Name.................................Sex.........................Date of Birth.........................Hospital No. ....

Date of Discharge.........................Condition on Discharge..

- **Mother's Obstetric History**

  Gravida .... Para ....Abortion..

  Full-term Delivery..Preterm Delivery ....

  Babies Born Alive...Stillborn ....

  Babies Dead..Cause of Death ....

- **Present Pregnancy**

  Antenatal Care: Yes/No ....Anemia: Yes/No...

  Antepartal Hemorrhage: Yes/No..Diabetes: Yes/No...

  Pregnancy-induced Hypertension: Yes/No ....Any other Medical Condition, specify ....

- **Labor**

  Type of Delivery: Normal/Abnormal, specify:...

  Duration of Labor: 1st stage ....2nd Stage........................3rd Stage ....

  Fetal Distress Present: Yes/No...

  Membranes Ruptured: Spontaneously/Artificially...

  Character of Amniotic Fluid: Clear/Meconium stained/foul smelling...

  Amount: Normal/Excessive/scanty...

  Placenta and Membranes: Healthy/Unhealthy ....

  Retroplacental Clots: Yes/No..

  Umbilical Core: Normal/Around Neck/Around Body ....

  Drugs and Treatment Given....... ....

- **Baby**

  Date and Time of Birth:..

  Condition at Birth: Active/Limp/Asphyxiated ....

  Apgar Score:...

  Treatment for Eyes and Umbilicus:..

  Medication Given:..

  Time of Breastfeeding:...

- **General Examination**

  Weight: .... Height:.......................................Head Circumference: ....

  Moulding: Normal/Excessive/Nil:...

  Caput: Present/Not present:..

  Eyes:..Skin: ....

  Mouth:..Limbs:...

  Chest: ....Genitalia: ....

  Abdomen: ....Anus: ....

  Heart: ....Lungs: ....

  Other Findings Significant: ....

Feeding: Breastfeeding/Formula feeding

- **Elimination: Urine:**...**Stool:** ....
- **Bonding** ....

 ....
- **Investigations:** ....

 ....
- **Treatment:** ....

 ....

List of Nursing Diagnosis

....

....

....

....

....

....

....

....

....

....

Health Education to Mother

....

....

....

....

....

....

....

....

....

....

Signature of Student **Signature of Supervisor**

CLINICAL CHART OF BABY

Date															
Temperature		M	E	M	E	M	E	M	E	M	E	M	E	M	E
F	C														
104.0	40														
103.1	39.5														
102.2	39														
101.3	38.5														
100.4	38														
99.5	37.5														
98.6	37														
97.7	36.5														
96.8	36														
Heart Rate/Min															
Respiration/Min															
Urine															
Stool															
Vomit															
Jaundice															
Weight (kg)															

CLINICAL CHART OF PUERPERIUM

Date	1	2	3	4	5	6	7	8	9	10	11	12	
Daily weight													Grams
													360
													330
													300
													270
													240
													210
													180
													150
													120
													90
													60
													30
													Birth weight
													–30
													–60
													–90
													–120
													–150
													–180
													–210
													–240
													–270
													–300
													–330
													–360

NEONATES NURSED

Nursing Diagnosis Statements Prioritized	Nursing Care Plans Listed	Nursing Care Implemented and Evaluated

NEONATES NURSED

Nursing Diagnosis Statements Prioritized	Nursing Care Plans Listed	Nursing Care Implemented and Evaluated

NEONATES NURSED

Nursing Diagnosis Statements Prioritized	Nursing Care Plans Listed	Nursing Care Implemented and Evaluated

NEONATES NURSED–6

Name .... Sex .... Date of Birth .... Hospital No. ....

Date of Discharge .... Condition on Discharge ....

- **Mother's Obstetric History**

Gravida .... Para .... Abortion ....

Full-term Delivery .... Preterm Delivery ....

Babies Born Alive .... Stillborn ....

Babies Dead .... Cause of Death ....

- **Present Pregnancy**

Antenatal Care: Yes/No .... Anemia: Yes/No ....

Antepartal Hemorrhage: Yes/No .... Diabetes: Yes/No ....

Pregnancy-induced Hypertension: Yes/No .... Any other Medical Condition, specify ....

- **Labor**

Type of Delivery: Normal/Abnormal, specify: ....

Duration of Labor: 1st stage .... 2nd Stage .... 3rd Stage ....

Fetal Distress Present: Yes/No ....

Membranes Ruptured: Spontaneously/Artificially ....

Character of Amniotic Fluid: Clear/Meconium stained/foul smelling ....

Amount: Normal/Excessive/scanty ....

Placenta and Membranes: Healthy/Unhealthy ....

Retroplacental Clots: Yes/No ....

Umbilical Core: Normal/Around Neck/Around Body ....

Drugs and Treatment Given ....

- **Baby**

Date and Time of Birth: ....

Condition at Birth: Active/Limp/Asphyxiated ....

Apgar Score: ....

Treatment for Eyes and Umbilicus: ....

Medication Given: ....

Time of Breastfeeding: ....

- **General Examination**

Weight: .... Height: .... Head Circumference: ....

Moulding: Normal/Excessive/Nil: ....

Caput: Present/Not present: ....

Eyes: .... Skin: ....

Mouth: .... Limbs: ....

Chest: .... Genitalia: ....

Abdomen: .... Anus: ....

Heart: .... Lungs: ....

Other Findings Significant: ....

Feeding: Breastfeeding/Formula feeding

- **Elimination: Urine:**..**Stool:** ....
- **Bonding** ....
  ....
- **Investigations:** ....
  ....
- **Treatment**: ....
  ....

List of Nursing Diagnosis

....
....
....
....
....
....
....
....
....
....

Health Education to Mother

....
....
....
....
....
....
....
....
....
....

Signature of Student

Signature of Supervisor

CLINICAL CHART OF BABY

Date															
Temperature		M	E	M	E	M	E	M	E	M	E	M	E	M	E
F	C														
104.0	40														
103.1	39.5														
102.2	39														
101.3	38.5														
100.4	38														
99.5	37.5														
98.6	37														
97.7	36.5														
96.8	36														
Heart Rate/Min															
Respiration/Min															
Urine															
Stool															
Vomit															
Jaundice															
Weight (kg)															

CLINICAL CHART OF PUERPERIUM

Date	1	2	3	4	5	6	7	8	9	10	11	12	
Daily weight													Grams
													360
													330
													300
													270
													240
													210
													180
													150
													120
													90
													60
													30
													Birth weight
													–30
													–60
													–90
													–120
													–150
													–180
													–210
													–240
													–270
													–300
													–330
													–360

NEONATES NURSED

Nursing Diagnosis Statements Prioritized	Nursing Care Plans Listed	Nursing Care Implemented and Evaluated

NEONATES NURSED

Nursing Diagnosis Statements Prioritized	Nursing Care Plans Listed	Nursing Care Implemented and Evaluated

NEONATES NURSED

Nursing Diagnosis Statements Prioritized	Nursing Care Plans Listed	Nursing Care Implemented and Evaluated

NEONATES NURSED–7

Name .... Sex .... Date of Birth .... Hospital No. ....

Date of Discharge .... Condition on Discharge..

- **Mother's Obstetric History**

  Gravida .... Para .... Abortion ....

  Full-term Delivery .... Preterm Delivery ....

  Babies Born Alive .... Stillborn ....

  Babies Dead... Cause of Death ....

- **Present Pregnancy**

  Antenatal Care: Yes/No .... Anemia: Yes/No..

  Antepartal Hemorrhage: Yes/No.. Diabetes: Yes/No..

  Pregnancy-induced Hypertension: Yes/No .... Any other Medical Condition, specify ....

- **Labor**

  Type of Delivery: Normal/Abnormal, specify:..

  Duration of Labor: 1st stage .... 2nd Stage .... 3rd Stage ....

  Fetal Distress Present: Yes/No..

  Membranes Ruptured: Spontaneously/Artificially...

  Character of Amniotic Fluid: Clear/Meconium stained/foul smelling..

  Amount: Normal/Excessive/scanty ....

  Placenta and Membranes: Healthy/Unhealthy ....

  Retroplacental Clots: Yes/No..

  Umbilical Core: Normal/Around Neck/Around Body ....

  Drugs and Treatment Given....... ....

- **Baby**

  Date and Time of Birth:...

  Condition at Birth: Active/Limp/Asphyxiated ....

  Apgar Score:...

  Treatment for Eyes and Umbilicus:...

  Medication Given:..

  Time of Breastfeeding:..

- **General Examination**

  Weight: .... Height:.. Head Circumference: ....

  Moulding: Normal/Excessive/Nil: ....

  Caput: Present/Not present: ....

  Eyes:.. Skin: ....

  Mouth:.. Limbs:..

  Chest: .... Genitalia: ....

  Abdomen: .... Anus: ....

  Heart: .... Lungs: ....

  Other Findings Significant: ....

Feeding: Breastfeeding/Formula feeding

- **Elimination: Urine:**..**Stool:** ....
- **Bonding** ....
....
- **Investigations:** ....
....
- **Treatment:** ....
....

List of Nursing Diagnosis

....
....
....
....
....
....
....
....
....
....

Health Education to Mother

....
....
....
....
....
....
....
....
....
....

Signature of Student **Signature of Supervisor**

CLINICAL CHART OF BABY

Date															
Temperature		M	E	M	E	M	E	M	E	M	E	M	E	M	E
F	C														
104.0	40														
103.1	39.5														
102.2	39														
101.3	38.5														
100.4	38														
99.5	37.5														
98.6	37														
97.7	36.5														
96.8	36														
Heart Rate/Min															
Respiration/Min															
Urine															
Stool															
Vomit															
Jaundice															
Weight (kg)															

CLINICAL CHART OF PUERPERIUM

Date	1	2	3	4	5	6	7	8	9	10	11	12	
Daily weight													Grams
													360
													330
													300
													270
													240
													210
													180
													150
													120
													90
													60
													30
													Birth weight
													–30
													–60
													–90
													–120
													–150
													–180
													–210
													–240
													–270
													–300
													–330
													–360

NEONATES NURSED

Nursing Diagnosis Statements Prioritized	Nursing Care Plans Listed	Nursing Care Implemented and Evaluated

NEONATES NURSED

Nursing Diagnosis Statements Prioritized	Nursing Care Plans Listed	Nursing Care Implemented and Evaluated

NEONATES NURSED

Nursing Diagnosis Statements Prioritized	Nursing Care Plans Listed	Nursing Care Implemented and Evaluated

NEONATES NURSED–8

Name .... Sex .... Date of Birth .... Hospital No. ....

Date of Discharge........................... Condition on Discharge...

- **Mother's Obstetric History**

  Gravida .... Para .... Abortion...

  Full-term Delivery.. Preterm Delivery ....

  Babies Born Alive... Stillborn ....

  Babies Dead.. Cause of Death ....

- **Present Pregnancy**

  Antenatal Care: Yes/No .... Anemia: Yes/No..

  Antepartal Hemorrhage: Yes/No.. Diabetes: Yes/No..

  Pregnancy-induced Hypertension: Yes/No.. Any other Medical Condition, specify ....

- **Labor**

  Type of Delivery: Normal/Abnormal, specify:..

  Duration of Labor: 1st stage .... 2nd Stage .... 3rd Stage ....

  Fetal Distress Present: Yes/No...

  Membranes Ruptured: Spontaneously/Artificially..

  Character of Amniotic Fluid: Clear/Meconium stained/foul smelling...

  Amount: Normal/Excessive/scanty ....

  Placenta and Membranes: Healthy/Unhealthy ....

  Retroplacental Clots: Yes/No...

  Umbilical Core: Normal/Around Neck/Around Body ....

  Drugs and Treatment Given...

- **Baby**

  Date and Time of Birth:...

  Condition at Birth: Active/Limp/Asphyxiated ....

  Apgar Score:..

  Treatment for Eyes and Umbilicus:..

  Medication Given:...

  Time of Breastfeeding:...

- **General Examination**

  Weight: .... Height:... Head Circumference: ....

  Moulding: Normal/Excessive/Nil: ....

  Caput: Present/Not present:...

  Eyes:.. Skin: ....

  Mouth:.. Limbs:...

  Chest: .... Genitalia: ....

  Abdomen:.. Anus: ....

  Heart: .... Lungs: ....

  Other Findings Significant: ....

Feeding: Breastfeeding/Formula feeding

- **Elimination: Urine:**...**Stool:** ....
- **Bonding**..
....
- **Investigations:** ....
....
- **Treatment:** ....
....

List of Nursing Diagnosis

....
....
....
....
....
....
....
....
....
....

Health Education to Mother

....
....
....
....
....
....
....
....
....
....

Signature of Student **Signature of Supervisor**

CLINICAL CHART OF BABY

Date															
Temperature		M	E	M	E	M	E	M	E	M	E	M	E	M	E
F	C														
104.0	40														
103.1	39.5														
102.2	39														
101.3	38.5														
100.4	38														
99.5	37.5														
98.6	37														
97.7	36.5														
96.8	36														
Heart Rate/Min															
Respiration/Min															
Urine															
Stool															
Vomit															
Jaundice															
Weight (kg)															

CLINICAL CHART OF PUERPERIUM

Date	1	2	3	4	5	6	7	8	9	10	11	12	
Daily weight													Grams
													360
													330
													300
													270
													240
													210
													180
													150
													120
													90
													60
													30
													Birth weight
													–30
													–60
													–90
													–120
													–150
													–180
													–210
													–240
													–270
													–300
													–330
													–360

NEONATES NURSED

Nursing Diagnosis Statements Prioritized	Nursing Care Plans Listed	Nursing Care Implemented and Evaluated

NEONATES NURSED

Nursing Diagnosis Statements Prioritized	Nursing Care Plans Listed	Nursing Care Implemented and Evaluated

NEONATES NURSED

Nursing Diagnosis Statements Prioritized	Nursing Care Plans Listed	Nursing Care Implemented and Evaluated

NEONATES NURSED–9

Name .... Sex .... Date of Birth .... Hospital No. ....

Date of Discharge.......................... Condition on Discharge...

- **Mother's Obstetric History**

  Gravida .... Para .... Abortion ....

  Full-term Delivery .... Preterm Delivery ....

  Babies Born Alive .... Stillborn ....

  Babies Dead.. Cause of Death ....

- **Present Pregnancy**

  Antenatal Care: Yes/No .... Anemia: Yes/No...

  Antepartal Hemorrhage: Yes/No... Diabetes: Yes/No...

  Pregnancy-induced Hypertension: Yes/No .... Any other Medical Condition, specify ....

- **Labor**

  Type of Delivery: Normal/Abnormal, specify:...

  Duration of Labor: 1st stage .... 2nd Stage......................... 3rd Stage ....

  Fetal Distress Present: Yes/No...

  Membranes Ruptured: Spontaneously/Artificially..

  Character of Amniotic Fluid: Clear/Meconium stained/foul smelling..

  Amount: Normal/Excessive/scanty ....

  Placenta and Membranes: Healthy/Unhealthy ....

  Retroplacental Clots: Yes/No...

  Umbilical Core: Normal/Around Neck/Around Body ....

  Drugs and Treatment Given....... ....

- **Baby**

  Date and Time of Birth:...

  Condition at Birth: Active/Limp/Asphyxiated ....

  Apgar Score:...

  Treatment for Eyes and Umbilicus:...

  Medication Given:...

  Time of Breastfeeding:...

- **General Examination**

  Weight: .... Height:... Head Circumference: ....

  Moulding: Normal/Excessive/Nil: ....

  Caput: Present/Not present: ....

  Eyes:.. Skin: ....

  Mouth:.. Limbs:...

  Chest: .... Genitalia: ....

  Abdomen: .... Anus: ....

  Heart: .... Lungs: ....

  Other Findings Significant: ....

Feeding: Breastfeeding/Formula feeding

- **Elimination: Urine:**..**Stool:** ....
- **Bonding** ....
....
- **Investigations:** ....
....
- **Treatment**: ....
....

List of Nursing Diagnosis

....
....
....
....
....
....
....
....
....
....

Health Education to Mother

....
....
....
....
....
....
....
....
....
....

Signature of Student **Signature of Supervisor**

CLINICAL CHART OF BABY

Date															
Temperature		M	E	M	E	M	E	M	E	M	E	M	E	M	E
F	C														
104.0	40														
103.1	39.5														
102.2	39														
101.3	38.5														
100.4	38														
99.5	37.5														
98.6	37														
97.7	36.5														
96.8	36														
Heart Rate/Min															
Respiration/Min															
Urine															
Stool															
Vomit															
Jaundice															
Weight (kg)															

CLINICAL CHART OF PUERPERIUM

Date	1	2	3	4	5	6	7	8	9	10	11	12	
Daily weight													Grams
													360
													330
													300
													270
													240
													210
													180
													150
													120
													90
													60
													30
													Birth weight
													–30
													–60
													–90
													–120
													–150
													–180
													–210
													–240
													–270
													–300
													–330
													–360

NEONATES NURSED

Nursing Diagnosis Statements Prioritized	Nursing Care Plans Listed	Nursing Care Implemented and Evaluated

NEONATES NURSED

Nursing Diagnosis Statements Prioritized	Nursing Care Plans Listed	Nursing Care Implemented and Evaluated

NEONATES NURSED

Nursing Diagnosis Statements Prioritized	Nursing Care Plans Listed	Nursing Care Implemented and Evaluated

NEONATES NURSED–10

Name .... Sex .... Date of Birth .... Hospital No. ....

Date of Discharge .... Condition on Discharge ....

- **Mother's Obstetric History**

Gravida .... Para .... Abortion ....

Full-term Delivery .... Preterm Delivery ....

Babies Born Alive .... Stillborn ....

Babies Dead .... Cause of Death ....

- **Present Pregnancy**

Antenatal Care: Yes/No .... Anemia: Yes/No ....

Antepartal Hemorrhage: Yes/No .... Diabetes: Yes/No ....

Pregnancy-induced Hypertension: Yes/No .... Any other Medical Condition, specify ....

- **Labor**

Type of Delivery: Normal/Abnormal, specify: ....

Duration of Labor: 1st stage .... 2nd Stage .... 3rd Stage ....

Fetal Distress Present: Yes/No ....

Membranes Ruptured: Spontaneously/Artificially ....

Character of Amniotic Fluid: Clear/Meconium stained/foul smelling ....

Amount: Normal/Excessive/scanty ....

Placenta and Membranes: Healthy/Unhealthy ....

Retroplacental Clots: Yes/No ....

Umbilical Core: Normal/Around Neck/Around Body ....

Drugs and Treatment Given....... ....

- **Baby**

Date and Time of Birth: ....

Condition at Birth: Active/Limp/Asphyxiated ....

Apgar Score: ....

Treatment for Eyes and Umbilicus: ....

Medication Given: ....

Time of Breastfeeding: ....

- **General Examination**

Weight: .... Height: .... Head Circumference: ....

Moulding: Normal/Excessive/Nil: ....

Caput: Present/Not present: ....

Eyes: .... Skin: ....

Mouth: .... Limbs: ....

Chest: .... Genitalia: ....

Abdomen: .... Anus: ....

Heart: .... Lungs: ....

Other Findings Significant: ....

Feeding: Breastfeeding/Formula feeding

- **Elimination: Urine:**...**Stool:** ....
- **Bonding** ....
  ....
- **Investigations:** ....
  ....
- **Treatment:** ....
  ....

List of Nursing Diagnosis

....

....

....

....

....

....

....

....

....

....

Health Education to Mother

....

....

....

....

....

....

....

....

....

....

Signature of Student **Signature of Supervisor**

CLINICAL CHART OF BABY

Date															
Temperature		M	E	M	E	M	E	M	E	M	E	M	E	M	E
F	C														
104.0	40														
103.1	39.5														
102.2	39														
101.3	38.5														
100.4	38														
99.5	37.5														
98.6	37														
97.7	36.5														
96.8	36														
Heart Rate/Min															
Respiration/Min															
Urine															
Stool															
Vomit															
Jaundice															
Weight (kg)															

CLINICAL CHART OF PUERPERIUM

Date	1	2	3	4	5	6	7	8	9	10	11	12	
Daily weight													Grams
													360
													330
													300
													270
													240
													210
													180
													150
													120
													90
													60
													30
													Birth weight
													–30
													–60
													–90
													–120
													–150
													–180
													–210
													–240
													–270
													–300
													–330
													–360

NEONATES NURSED

Nursing Diagnosis Statements Prioritized	Nursing Care Plans Listed	Nursing Care Implemented and Evaluated

NEONATES NURSED

Nursing Diagnosis Statements Prioritized	Nursing Care Plans Listed	Nursing Care Implemented and Evaluated

NEONATES NURSED

Nursing Diagnosis Statements Prioritized	Nursing Care Plans Listed	Nursing Care Implemented and Evaluated

ADVANCES IN PSYCHOLOGY RESEARCH. VOLUME 88

ADVANCES IN PSYCHOLOGY RESEARCH

Additional books in this series can be found on Nova's website under the Series tab.

Additional E-books in this series can be found on Nova's website under the E-book tab.

ADVANCES IN PSYCHOLOGY RESEARCH

ADVANCES IN PSYCHOLOGY RESEARCH. VOLUME 88

ALEXANDRA M. COLUMBUS
EDITOR

Nova Science Publishers, Inc.
New York

For permission to use material from this book please contact us:
Telephone 631-231-7269; Fax 631-231-8175
Web Site: http://www.novapublishers.com

Library of Congress Cataloging-in-Publication Data

ISSN: 1532-723X

ISBN: 978-1-62100-591-9

Published by Nova Science Publishers, Inc. † New York

CONTENTS

PREFACE

This continuing series presents original research results on the leading edge of psychology. This book reviews research on new perspectives in the treatment of mania; social aspects of mood disorders; the role of parental discipline and family environments during childhood and in cluster B personality symptoms in adulthood; behavior therapy in Tourette Syndrome; depression and its impact on osteoarthritis outcomes; gender differences in bipolar disorder; the relation between premenstrual dysphoric disorder, panic attacks, and panic disorder; the psychology of cravings to predict relapse in substance abuse patients and family relationships and ADHD. (Imprint: Nova)

Chapter 1 - There has been a recent increase in the treatment options for mania; however, despite pharmacological advances, this disorder continues to be difficult to treat. Lithium, a mood stabilizing drug, is still the gold standard for the treatment of acute mania, controlling symptoms and preventing new episodes, although this therapy is associated with several drawbacks. New insights and advances on the neurobiological basis and therapeutic approaches to mania will arise from understanding more precisely the putative molecular mechanisms of drugs that have clinical efficacy or developing therapies based on knowledge obtained regarding the pathophysiology of mania. This chapter reviews research on new targets/compounds that have shown antimanic effects in subjects with mood disorders or in preclinical animal models. These include glycogen synthase kinase-3, protein kinase C and histone deacetylase inhibitors, modulators of glutamatergic and purinergic systems, antioxidants, compounds that act on bioenergetic parameters, and other putative antimanic agents. Considering the drawbacks of the conventional pharmacotherapy for the treatment of mania, research dealing with the molecular mechanisms underlying this disorder, and the development of more specific and more effective novel compounds for its management, is welcome.

Chapter 2 - Mood disorders are among the most prevalent mental disorders with almost twice as many women as men afflicted by them. They can lead to occupational impairment, disruption in interpersonal and family relationships, poor health and suicide. Thus, they represent a significant burden to individuals and society. Moreover, although effective interventions for the treatment of mood disorders are available, most individuals who suffer from them do not seek medical treatment.

In this chapter, data from nationally representative surveys are used to identify demographic and socioeconomic factors associated with mood disorders. Secondly, the comorbidity of mood disorders with other psychological conditions, e.g. eating disorders and with chronic physical illness are examined. Thirdly, effects of mood disorders, alone and in

combination with anxiety disorders and/or physical illness on functional disability and quality of life are studied. Specifically, the hypothesis of a socioeconomic gradient in disability associated with mood disorders is explored. Lastly, Barriers to seeking medical help for mood disorders are examined and identified.

Chapter 3 - The work presented here uses a science-based approach to obtain new understandings on the mechanisms and the ramifications of competition in everyday life. Assuming competition of a Darwinian nature we can deduce an S-shaped pattern for growth in most competitive environments. Examples range from a rabbit population growing in a fenced-off grass field to scientists competing for Nobel-Prize awards. There are secrets embedded in the mathematical law that describes growth in competition. The rate of growth being proportional to the amount of growth already achieved makes beginnings difficult and sheds light on such proverbial wisdom as "you need goal to make gold". It also argues for the necessity to engage teachers in the learning process. Other revelations are linked to the symmetry of a life-cycle pattern, which possesses predictive power and demystifies the easy-come-easy-go phenomenon. Predictive power characterizes the rapid-growth phase of the S-shaped pattern (rheostasis) as well as the end of the pattern when growth reaches a ceiling (homeostasis) where supply and demand are in equilibrium. The latter phenomenon is best exemplified by society's tolerance of deadly car accidents because deaths from car accidents have remained at an invariant level for many decades reflecting equilibrium. The mathematical equation for growth in competition when cast in discrete form reveals fluctuations of chaotic nature before and after the rapid-growth phase. This can illuminate the turbulent times before and after the formation of the USSR as well as the tumultuous times of the 1930s in America. Extending the quantitative approach to two species competing in the same niche involves introducing coupling constants that account for how one species impacts the growth rate of the other. A celebrated example is the predator-prey relationship, which is only one of six possible interactions all of which can be encountered in the marketplace where products and companies compete like species. There are six possible dimensions for action in a two-species competitive struggle that can be exploited toward managing competition and setting one's role/image in the marketplace. An example dealt in detail is the evolution of the number of American Noble-Prize winners whose numbers are not about to begin diminishing. Americans are involved in a win-win competitive struggle with non-American scholars, but Americans are drawing more of a benefit.

Chapter 4 - Mood disorders (MD) affect approximately 10% of the general population determining significant functional impairment in sufferers and often leads to adverse social outcomes. Two main groups of MD are broadly recognized: the unipolar and the bipolar types. Major depressive disorder is the most common mood disorder being one of the leading sources of premature death and disability among all diseases and accounting for enormous health service utilization. Comorbid anxiety and depression occurs at a high rate, and is associated with higher costs from both an individual and societal perspective. Patients with MD most often present in primary care settings, have more severe symptoms, and require health care resources. Case identification and correct assessment are crucial steps. MD pose complicated diagnostic and treatment challenges, often leading to inadequate diagnosis and treatment resulting in unnecessary patient distress and increased utilization of health care services. Effective assessment, correct evaluation, diagnosis and treatment can lead to better treatment outcomes and improved quality of life (QOL) in care patients. **[key words:** mood disorders; health service utilization; societal impact; assessment; treatment]

Chapter 5 - The present study sought to establish that negative parental discipline practices, parental bonding, and family conflict would be associated with self esteem, emotional dysregulation, guilt and shame in predicting Cluster B personality disorder (PD) features, i.e.Histrionic (HPD), Narcissistic (NPD) Borderline (BPD) and Antisocial (ASPD). The predictor measures were the Parental Bonding Instrument, PBI, two brief measures of parental discipline, the Family Environment Scale, the Rosenberg Self Esteem Scale, the Test of Self-Conscious Affect–3, the General Emotional Dysregulation Measure, and the dependent variables were the Cluster B disorder features as measured by the Personality Diagnostic Questionnaire4+ (PDQ). The PDQ was not used as specifically diagnostic, but as an estimate of personality disorder symptoms. Multiple regressions to find the best fit models were run with the above variables regressed onto each personality disorder. The criterion for each was taken as a measure of the presence of more severe symptoms in GLM analyses of the four PDs with the same dependent variables as were predictors in the regression analyses. The main findings were that emotional dysregulation was a significant predictor for all disorders except ASPD in females. Maternal negative discipline was mostly associated with it, but the pattern of other significant predictors differed for the four personality disorders. The findings suggested that emotional dysregulation varies in quality according to other influencing factors such as parental discipline style. There were some gender differences in variables that suggested that, in this sample, recollections of early bonding experiences were influenced by gender.

Chapter 6 - Mania has long been considered as an abnormal behaviour indicative of mental illness. Manic states are generally characterized by abnormal elevated mood (euphoria) also including hyperactivity, hypersexuality, irritability, reduced need for sleep and cognitive deficits associated with negative functional outcome. According to the Diagnostic and Statistical Manual of Mental Disorders, Fourth Edition, Text Revision (DSM-IV-TR), a subject experiencing a state of elevated or irritable mood, as well as other invalidating symptoms for at least one week may be diagnosed as affected by bipolar disorder. However, manic symptoms and hypomanic symptoms challenge conventional diagnostic nomenclature and are often not adequately recognized in clinical practice. Individuals are commonly misdiagnosed due to the frequent coexisting psychiatric conditions such as frequent substance abuse. Recently, the fifth edition of the DSM proposes modifications of the actual diagnostic system. Overall, despite recent advances, efficacy and tolerability of current treatments are limited and additional interventions strategies are needed in order to develop new treatment strategies. Combining psychological, psychosocial and psychopharmacological approaches will presumably offer new operative models to better manage patients with different bipolar subtypes. [keywords: mania, bipolar disorder, diagnostic nomenclature, treatment, intervention]

Chapter 7 - Tourette syndrome (TS) is a chronic neurodevelopmental disorder characterized by the presence of multiple motor and phonic tics, and associated behavioural problems. While a range of pharmacological therapies have been shown to be effective in treating tic symptoms and co-morbid conditions such as obsessive compulsive disorder and attention-deficit hyperactivity disorder, drug treatment is complicated by side effects and potential toxicity in young individuals. Furthermore, some individuals with TS find that their symptoms do not respond favourably to such treatments, and exhibit difficulties for which behavioural treatments may be more appropriate or effective. Current behavioural treatments for tics include Habit Reversal Training, Exposure Response Prevention and Massed Negative

Practice. Other approaches, such as hypnotherapy and self-monitoring have also been trialled in TS. Interventions including psychotherapy and cognitive behavioural therapy can be applied to assist with co-morbid conditions, and related social or self esteem difficulties which can impact quality of life. In this chapter, we review behavioural treatments available for the symptoms of TS, providing an evaluation of efficacy and associated limitations. We discuss factors influencing treatment response, such as attention, insight, sensory awareness and compliance which implicate cognitive, physiological and psychosocial domains. Future longitudinal studies are crucial in order to determine the long term efficacy of behavioural treatments in TS, and establish whether certain approaches are more appropriate for individuals exhibiting particular clinical and behavioural profiles.

Chapter 8 - Psychological conditions are highly prevalent among adults in general, and among adults with chronic diseases, in particular. This chapter describes the literature and research evidence concerning the nature of depression, its prevalence among aging adults, and the impact of comorbid and/or concurrent depressive symptoms among adults with hip or knee osteoarthritis, a highly prevalent and painful disabling joint disease. It also advocates for improved efforts to identify and treat concomitant depression among adults with osteoarthritis in the context of the community as well as the surgical setting. To this end, the author reports data embedded in the relevant literature using PubMed, Scopus, Science Citation and PsychInfo data bases over the last twenty years, as well as data extracted from the records of 1,000 hip osteoarthritis surgical candidates and 100 community dwelling cases of knee osteoarthritis that highlight the magnitude and impact of the presence of a comorbid depression or depression/anxiety anxiety, as well as concurrent depressive symptoms on selected disease features and treatment outcomes. Based on this evidence, the author highlights the importance of comprehensive efforts to prevent, identify and treat comorbid depression among people with chronic pain due to osteoarthritis. The author's insights and analysis should be of specific interest to clinicians working in this area who seek to apply their skills towards reducing the immense burden of osteoarthritis and heightening their patients' life quality.

Chapter 9 - Cognitive restructuring is a therapeutic tool that is widely used by clinicians, specially the Socratic Method, that is considered its main therapeutic component. There are many contradictions that accompany the application of the Socratic Method and the research studies on the processes of this technique have not been clear, so virtually no progress has been made since it was initially proposed by Ellis and Beck. Some years ago our group started a research line on the mechanisms of change that occur when cognitive-behavioral therapy is applied in clinical contexts. Therefore we believe that we must know *which* techniques works, but also we must research on *how* or *why* certain changes take place. In this sense we began a study on cognitive techniques, specifically on the cognitive restructuring technique, based on the observation and analysis of the interaction between therapist and client. The aim of this work is to present three measuring instruments that we have developed to study this technique: (1) the *Coding System for the Study of Therapist-Patient Interaction* (SISC-INTER), that allows the analysis of the therapist's and the client's verbal behavior and finally the interaction between them; (2) the *Coding System of Patient Verbal Behavior Based on Therapeutic Goals* (SISC-COT), that allows classifying the clients' verbalizations according to their degree of approximation to the therapeutic objectives pursued by the psychologist during the Socratic Method; (3) the *Assessment Scale of Effectiveness of the Socratic Method in Cognitive Restructuring* (*EVED-RC*), that allows to assign to each

fragment of Socratic Method a single category based on its level of effectiveness. This work has two objectives: first, to present the process of developing the measuring instruments; second, to discuss their possible applications for the research giving examples of studies performed by our group. Therefore, although the chapter is devoted primarily to explain the process of developing the observation instruments, we will briefly discuss some of the results already found with their application.

Chapter 10 - Interest in epidemiological and clinical gender differences in bipolar disorder have increased over the past few years. Most studies have found that women are at a higher risk of starting the bipolar disorder with a depressive episode and have more depressive episodes during the course of illness. When psychotic symptoms are associated with pure or mixed manic episodes, women show more paranoid and reference delusions than men, and more hallucinations. Moreover, women have a greater risk of mixed episodes and more tendency to rapid cycling than men. Anxiety and eating co-morbid disorders are more frequent in women whereas substance abuse disorders are more common in men. However, women with bipolar disorder have more drug problems than women of the general population. Other differences are more controversial, some studies have found that the age of onset is later among women, whereas others have found no significant differences. More women are hospitalised for manic episodes and it is controversial if they need more days for recovering. Longitudinal studies have shown that in women depressive episodes are more frequent than manic, mixed or euthymic episodes during the course of the illness. Moreover, women are at higher risk of suffering from depression. Treatment strategies specific for women in bipolar disorder are still scarce and will be discussed.

Chapter 11 - Premenstrual dysphoric disorder (PMDD) affects three to eight percent of women of reproductive age. The syndrome, which includes depressed mood, anxiety, irritability, mood fluctuations, and physical symptoms, occurs in the days prior to menstruation and remits a few days after the onset of menses. Women with PMDD suffer from a high rate of panic disorder (PD) and, like those with PD, demonstrate high fear reactivity to laboratory panic challenges. In this chapter, we examine prominent hypotheses for the high rate of panic attacks among women with PMDD. More specifically, we explore (a) physiological hypotheses, such as suffocation false alarm and neurotransmitter system dysfunction, and (b) psychological hypotheses, including those that invoke behavioral conditioning, catastrophic misinterpretation, and anxiety sensitivity. We conclude by proposing several lines of research that could shed additional light on this topic.

Chapter 12 - Clinical experts in drug dependence therapy must grasp patients' levels of craving to predict their propensity to relapse. Although craving is considered to lead to relapse, the findings have been mixed in supporting this hypothesis. The lack of robust associations may be attributable to (*i*) the inconsistency in the definition of craving across studies, (*ii*) limitations in measuring craving and drug use, and (*iii*) mismatched timeframes and timing in the measurement of craving. This chapter reviews the following possible solutions for these problems, including (*i*) multidimensional measurement of an extended concept of craving, (*ii*) methodological techniques to avoid response bias (e.g., social cognitive measurement), and (*iii*) real-time measurement of craving with Ecologically Momentary Assessment. Additionally, we developed the Relapse Risk Index (RRI), which is a set of assessment systems for predicting relapse. The use of conceptually and methodologically based assessments will lead to a more precise understanding of the directional relationship between a patient's level of craving and risk of relapse.

Chapter 13 - Clinical experts in drug dependence therapy must grasp patients' levels of craving to predict their propensity to relapse. Although craving is considered to lead to relapse, the findings have been mixed in supporting this hypothesis. The lack of robust associations may be attributable to (*i*) the inconsistency in the definition of craving across studies, (*ii*) limitations in measuring craving and drug use, and (*iii*) mismatched timeframes and timing in the measurement of craving. This chapter reviews the following possible solutions for these problems, including (*i*) multidimensional measurement of an extended concept of craving, (*ii*) methodological techniques to avoid response bias (e.g., social cognitive measurement), and (*iii*) real-time measurement of craving with Ecologically Momentary Assessment. Additionally, we developed the Relapse Risk Index (RRI), which is a set of assessment systems for predicting relapse. The use of conceptually and methodologically based assessments will lead to a more precise understanding of the directional relationship between a patient's level of craving and risk of relapse.

In: Advances in Psychology Research. Volume 88
Editor: Alexandra M. Columbus, pp. 1-23
ISBN: 978-1-62100-591-9

Chapter 1

New Perspectives in the Treatment of Mania

Morgana Moretti, Josiane Budni and Ana Lúcia Severo Rodrigues
Department of Biochemistry, Center of Biological Sciences,
Universidade Federal de Santa Catarina, Florianópolis, SC, Brazil

Abstract

There has been a recent increase in the treatment options for mania; however, despite pharmacological advances, this disorder continues to be difficult to treat. Lithium, a mood stabilizing drug, is still the gold standard for the treatment of acute mania, controlling symptoms and preventing new episodes, although this therapy is associated with several drawbacks. New insights and advances on the neurobiological basis and therapeutic approaches to mania will arise from understanding more precisely the putative molecular mechanisms of drugs that have clinical efficacy or developing therapies based on knowledge obtained regarding the pathophysiology of mania. This chapter reviews research on new targets/compounds that have shown antimanic effects in subjects with mood disorders or in preclinical animal models. These include glycogen synthase kinase-3, protein kinase C and histone deacetylase inhibitors, modulators of glutamatergic and purinergic systems, antioxidants, compounds that act on bioenergetic parameters, and other putative antimanic agents. Considering the drawbacks of the conventional pharmacotherapy for the treatment of mania, research dealing with the molecular mechanisms underlying this disorder, and the development of more specific and more effective novel compounds for its management, is welcome.

Introduction

Treatment of mania is still a challenge in spite of the recent increase in the treatment options for its clinical condition. Current therapies are associated with variable rates of

efficacy, high recurrence rates of mood episodes, residual symptoms, functional impairment, psychosocial disability and significant medical and psychiatric comorbidity.

Lithium was the first agent for bipolar disorder (BD) approved for clinical use. It is a mood stabilizer widely used in clinical practice, dampening both the manic and depressive phases of BD (Fountoulakis et al., 2008). Despite many other agents have been approved for clinical use in BD or suggested in preclinical studies for BD treatment since then, it should be considered that many patients, especially those in the classic form of the disease (type I), respond to lithium (Akiskal, 2006). However, some drawbacks of the lithium treatment are related to the side effects elicited by the treatment and the possibility of toxic effects. It needs medical vigilance, including the frequent determination of blood levels to adequate the dose (Fountoulakis et al., 2008).

Treatment of mania has focused on alleviating symptoms and preventing recurrence of episodes. In order to obtain novel effective agents for the treatment of mania, new insights and advances on the neurobiological basis of BD are necessary. This chapter highlights research on targets that have been shown to be involved in the pathophysiology of BD, as well as some novel compounds that have shown antimanic effects in BD patients or in preclinical animal models.

Glycogen Synthase Kinase-3 (GSK-3) Inhibitors

GSK-3 is a multifunctional serine/threonine kinase constitutively active in cells. It is found in all eukaryotes, and is deactivated by multiple signaling pathways, including Wnt and phosphoinositide 3-kinase, protein kinase A and protein kinase C (PKC) pathways (Embi et al., 1980; Goode et al., 1992; Siegfried et al., 1992; Cross et al., 1995; Grimes and Jope, 2001; Tanji et al., 2002). This protein is found in two isoforms (GSK-3α and GSK-3β) in mammals and they usually have similar biological function. GSK-3β is expressed in neuronal and glial cells (Woodgett, 1990; 1991; Sutherland and Cohen, 1994). This enzyme plays important roles in many cellular functions including neuroplasticity, neurotransmission, metabolic function, and neuronal growth (Pap and Cooper, 1998; Lesort et al., 1999; Li et al., 2004). Normally, the activation of GSK-3β is pro-apoptotic and it induces neuron death, whereas its inhibition attenuates or prevents apoptosis inducing neuron survival (Pap and Cooper, 1998). The inhibition of GSK-3β has been investigated as a pharmacological strategy for treating many disorders, including BD (Lesort et al., 1999; Pan et al., 2011).

There is mounting evidence indicating the important role of GSK-3β in the action of mood stabilizers and possibly in the pathophysiology of mania (Jope and Bijur, 2002; Du et al., 2004b; Gould et al., 2004b; Gould and Manji et al 2005; Rowe et al., 2007). A recent study indicated that GSK3 knockin mice may have increased vulnerability to BD, since they displayed increased susceptibility to amphetamine-induced hyperactivity, a putative model of mania (Polter et al., 2010). Moreover, another study performed by Ackermann et al. (2010) showed that mice carrying the mutation in serine within the PKB phosphorylation site, renders GSK-3 resistant to inactivation by protein kinase B/serum and glucocorticoid inducible kinase (two kinases activated through the phosphatidylinositol 3 kinase pathway) leading to altered food and fluid intake as well as manic-like behavior.

Interestingly, the activation of GSK3β has been shown to be involved in the amphetamine-induced hyperactivity in mice. In this model, the efficacy of several selective GSK3 inhibitors such as indirubin, alsterpaullone, TDZD-8, AR-A014418, SB-216763, and SB-627772 as well as mood stabilizers (lithium, valproate, and carbamazepine) and antipsychotic (olanzapine and ziprasidone) was evaluated. The GSK3 inhibitors prevented rearing hyperactivity, whereas the mood stabilizers and antipsychotic reduced the hyperactivity in this animal model of mania. These finding suggest that GSK3 inhibitors may be useful in the therapy of BD (Kalinichev and Dawson, 2011).

Further indicating the role of GSK-3β in BD pathophysiology, the electroconvulsive therapy, an effective treatment for BD indicated in more severe and refractory cases (Versiani et al., 2011), can induce Ser-9 phosphorylation of GSK-3β in the rat hippocampus, cerebral cortex and cerebellum, which is compatible with the effect of classical drugs used for the treatment of this disorder (Roh et al., 2003).

Lithium, the most well-established treatment for the manic phase of BD, inhibits GSK-3β in *vitro* in *Xenopus* embryos (Klein and Melton, 1996) *Drosophila* S2 cells, rat PC12 cells (Stambolic et al., 1996) and SH-SY5Y human neuroblastoma cells (Aubry et al., 2009). Preclinical studies also show this inhibitory effect of lithium on GSK-3β (Gurvich and Klein 2002; Gould et al., 2004a; O'Brien et al., 2004), however, the precise mechanism by which it exerts its therapeutic effects remains unclear (Gould and Manji, 2005).

The anticonvulsant valproate, another mood stabilizing agent, effective in the treatment of manic episodes of BD (Rosa et al., 2011), can also cause inhibition of GSK-3β activity in vitro and in vivo (Chen et al., 1999; Grimes and Jope, 2001; Gould et al 2004a). Moreover, clinical evidence has increasingly recognized that GSK-3β activity can be inhibited during the treatment with lithium, valproate and atypical antipsychotics such as olanzapine, quetiapine and risperidone, since these treatments are accompanied by a significant increase in the inhibitory phosphorylation of GSK-3β in manic subjects (Li et al., 2010).

Taken together, these studies suggest that pharmacological treatment used in BD cause an inhibition of GSK-3β, supporting the notion that the modulation of this enzyme is an important target for development of new drugs for the treatment of the manic phase of BD. Therefore, clinical trials with novel GSK-3β inhibitors are welcome.

Protein Kinase C (PKC) Inhibitors

Biological and pharmacological studies have increasingly investigated the PKC signaling pathway in the BD pathophysiology and treatment (Coyle and Duman, 2003). PKC is a major regulatory enzyme and an important component of the phosphoinositide signaling system. In this system, the interaction of an agonist with receptors causes the hydrolysis of the substrate phosphatidyl inositol 4,5-bisphosphate by the enzyme phospholipase C, resulting in the formation of inositol 1,4,5-tris phosphate (IP3) and diacylglycerol, two second messengers (Berridge and Irvine, 1989; Tanaka and Nishizuka, 1994). IP3, in turn, stimulates the release of intracellular calcium from intracellular stores (Nishizuka, 1988), and diacylglycerol is responsible for stimulating PKC, which, in the brain, exerts fundamental role in pre and post-synaptic neurotransmission, regulating neuronal excitability, neurotransmitter release and cellular plasticity (Manji and Lenox, 1999).

A study with drug-free bipolar subjects in the manic state found an increased ratio of membrane-bound to cytosolic PKC activities, which was attenuated by lithium treatment (Friedman et al., 1993). Additionally, in postmortem brains of bipolar patients, an altered subcellular distribution of PKC isozymes, compatible with increased activity of PKC, was also described (Wang and Friedman, 1996). Literature data also demonstrated that chronic lithium administration results in a decrease of phorbol ester (PKC activators)-mediated responses (Bitran et al., 1990), and a down-regulation of PKC-specific isozymes (α and ε) in limbic and limbic-related areas of the brain (Manji et al, 1993). In this context, Soares et al (2000) reported that lithium-treated bipolar patient had significantly lower levels of cytosolic PKC α isozyme and a trend toward reduced levels of cytosolic PKC βII compared to control subjects.

These findings are corroborated by in vitro data showing that lithium exposure inhibits the phosphoinositide pathway and alters PKC-mediated processes (Baraban et al., 1989; Wang and Friedman, 1989; Lenox and Watson, 1992; Manji et al., 1993; Bitran et al., 1995). Importantly, the other primary antimanic agent valproate, which acts via different sub-pathways and is structurally dissimilar to lithium, causes a very analogous effects to those of lithium on PKCα and ε isozymes and on myristoylated alanine-rich protein kinase C substrate (MARCKS), a key substrate of PKC (Chen et al., 1994; Watson et al., 1998; Manji and Lenox, 1999)

In animal models of mania, several studies have demonstrated that both acute and chronic amphetamine treatment alter PKC activity, PKC's relative cytosol to membrane distribution, and phosphorylation of GAP-43 (growth-associated protein of 43 kDa- implicated in neuronal differentiation, plasticity and neurotransmitter release) at the PKC site (Giambalvo, 1992a, b; Gnegy, 1993; Iwata et al., 1997). Furthermore, the knockout of PKC protein isoform in mice has demonstrated many cellular effects, including modulation of hippocampal neuroplasticity (Dempsey et al., 2000), which has been implicated in pathophysiology of BD.

The fact that PKC activity is altered in mania associated with the ability of both lithium and valproate to inhibit PKC-associated signaling in brain tissue, encourage development of PKC inhibitors as putative antimanic agents. Regarding this issue, more recently, studies have used specific PKC inhibitors to more directly assess the possible involvement of PKC inhibition in the reversion of manic-like behavior in animal models. It has been demonstrated that tamoxifen, a PKC inhibitor, significantly reduced the hyperactivity induced by amphetamine and normalized amphetamine-induced increase in risk-taking behavior (Einat et al., 2007, Sabioni et al., 2008; Moretti et al., 2011). Tamoxifen administration also decreased phosphorylation of GAP-43 induced by amphetamine, a result that is consistent with the reversion of manic symptoms in rats (Einat et al., 2007). Similarly, the administration of another inhibitor of PKC, Ro31-8220, in the nucleus accumbens, attenuated the motor response produced by amphetamine, an effect which was associated with the blockade of dopamine release (Browman et al., 1998).

Clinical experience with tamoxifen for the treatment of manic patients reported that it has a highly significant antimanic effects, similar in magnitude and timing to those reported for lithium and valproate (Bebchuk et al., 2000; Kulkarni et al., 2006; Yildiz et al., 2008). Moreover a recent double-blind, randomized, placebo-controlled 6-week study on the efficacy and safety of the tamoxifen adjunctive to lithium in acute bipolar mania demonstrated that the combination of tamoxifen with lithium was superior to lithium alone for the rapid reduction of manic symptoms (Amrollahi et al, 2011).

Further indicating the involvement of PKC inhibition in the mechanism of antimanic agents, a study reported that verapamil (a calcium channel blocker that has PKC inhibitory activity) plus lithium improved outcome in mania unresponsive to lithium, an effect that was suggested to be mediated by additive actions on PKC inhibition (Mallinger et al., 2008).

Taken together, these animal and human studies support the involvement of PKC, not only in the pathophysiology of BD, but also in the therapeutic mechanism of action of mood stabilizing drugs, thus reinforcing the need for the study of inhibitors of PKC as a possible target for new medications to BD.

Histone Deacetylase (HDAC) Inhibitors

Epigenetic regulatory mechanisms are reversible chromatin rearrangements, mostly related to decreased DNA methylation and increased acetylation of histones, which control gene expression without modifying DNA sequence (Kato et al., 2005; Santini et al., 2007). The acetylation of histones by histone acetyltransferase promotes access to DNA and docking sites for transcriptional factors, permitting transcriptional activation (Kurdistani et al., 2004). On the other hand, HDAC removes acetyl groups from lysine/arginine residues on the amino-terminal tails of core histones, preventing access of transcriptional activators to their target sites, resulting in transcriptional repression (Hsieh and Gage, 2005).

Aberrant transcriptional regulation and epigenetic modifications, such as changes in histone acetylation, has been suggested to be an important component of the pathophysiology of several neuropsychiatric disorders, including mood disorders, schizophrenia and drug addiction (Colvis et al., 2005; Tsankova et al., 2007). Considering these findings, some laboratories have sought to identify alterations in gene expression in post mortem brain samples and peripheral blood cells of bipolar patients. A study performed by Mill et al (2008) utilized frontal cortex brain tissue from bipolar patients to evaluate DNA methylation across approximately 12,000 regulatory regions of the genome. It was identified epigenetic changes in loci associated with glutamatergic and GABAergic neurotransmission, consistent with evidence indicating modification of these neurotransmitter pathways in BD pathogenesis (Benes and Berretta, 2001). More recently, Hobara and colleagues (2010) found different alteration pattern of HDACs mRNA expression levels in peripheral blood cells of bipolar subjects. Within this paradigm, it has been proposed that early life stressors may increase susceptibility to the first episode for individuals predisposed to BD, events which are in agreement with consequent deficits in chromatin plasticity (Leverich et al., 2003), indirectly supporting a role for chromatin remodeling as an important regulatory mechanism underlying BD pathophysiology and treatment.

Literature data demonstrated that chronic microinjection of valproate, characterized as an inhibitor of HDAC (Phiel et al., 2001), into the nucleus accumbens attenuated amphetamine-induced hyperlocomotor activity (Kim et al., 2008). In addition, intraperitoneal valproate administration reversed and prevented amphetamine-induced manic-like behaviors (Frey et al., 2006a, b), raising the possibility that HDAC inhibition by valproate may be one of the mechanisms associated with its therapeutic effect. Reinforcing these data, a study showed that inhibition of HDAC activity by sodium butyrate facilitated extinction of drug-seeking behavior in a rat model of cocaine-induced conditioned place preference (Schroeder et al.,

2008). In a model of mania induced by D-amphetamine, intracerebral microinjection of sodium butyrate and valproate in the ventricle, amygdala, striatum and prefrontal cortex blocked the hyperactivity induced by methamphetamine and inhibited HDAC activity, an effect that was dependent on the brain structure evaluated (Arent et al., 2011). A study performed by Wu et al. (2008) demonstrated that HDAC inhibitors (sodium butyrate and trichostatin A) were capable of promoting neuronal survival and protecting dopaminergic neurons from 1-methyl-4-phenylpyridinium (MPP+)-toxicity in neuron-glia culture, suggesting that this class of drugs protect neurons against oxidative stress-induced neuronal injury. Moreover, recent studies propose that inhibitors of HDAC including suberoylanilidehydroxamic acid and trichostatin A are effective for treating neurodegenerative disorders, or enhancing memory and synaptic plasticity, a mechanism that has been proposed to be involved in the pathophysiology and therapeutics of BD (Hockly et al., 2003; Vecsey et al., 2007).

Finally, it was demonstrated that HDAC inhibitors up-regulate glial cell-derived neurotrophic factor, brain-derived neurotrophic factors (necessary for long-term behavior and cognitive changes observed in neurons and glial cells) and protect dopaminergic neurons during episodes of mania (Yatham et al., 2002; Schroeder et al., 2007). Altogether, these findings raise the possibility that modulation of histone acetylation by HDAC inhibitors might represent a novel and promising therapeutic target in BD management. However, since little is known about the possible side effects and unspecific targets of HDAC inhibitors currently available, additional studies are essential to clarify the potential role of these agents in the BD pathophysiology and therapeutics.

Glutamatergic Modulators

Glutamate is considered the major excitatory neurotransmitter in the central nervous system in mammalian and regulates numerous physiological functions (Davies et al., 1979; Watkins and Evans, 1981; Obrenovitch and Urenjak, 1997; Maragakis and Rothstein, 2004). The glutamatergic system plays important roles in a wide range of neuronal physiological functions, including learning, memory, cognition, neurotrophic and neurotoxic actions, and neuronal plasticity (Verkhratsky and Kirchhoff, 2007).

Glutamate exerts its action at the presynaptic and postsynaptic level through the stimulation mediated by several classes of glutamate receptors, expressed in virtually all cells of neural origin and that can be classified by structural characteristics: ionotropic glutamate receptors (including NMDA [N-methyl-D-aspartate], AMPA [α-amino-3-hydroxy-5-methyl-4-isoxazolepropionic acid] and Kainate receptors); eight G-protein-coupled metabotropic receptors (mGluRs) (Verkhratsky and Kirchhoff, 2007).

It has been shown that patients with mania have elevate glutamate/glutamine ratio in dorsolateral prefrontal cortex (Cecil et al., 2002; Michael et al., 2003, 2009), anterior cingulated cortex (Moore et al., 2007; Öngür et al, 2008) and parieto-occipital cortex (Öngür et al., 2008), when compared with healthy subjects. This is consistent with glutamatergic overactivity, suggesting an increased glutamate release with the consequent impairment in neuronal-glial glutamate cycling in mania patients. These abnormalities in BD patients may represent targets for novel therapeutic interventions. Consistent with this proposal, mood

stabilizers indirectly or directly affect this system, down regulating glutamatergic activity (Zarate et al., 2010). It was reported that lithium protects cultured rat cerebellar, cerebral cortical and hippocampal neurons against glutamate-induced excitotoxicity (Nonaka et al., 1998). This neuroprotection in rat cerebral cortical neurons was mediated by suppression of NR2B phosphorylation, a subunit of NMDA receptor linked to the receptor activity (Hashimoto et al., 2002). The chronic administration of lithium, valproate and carbamazepine in rats downregulates the glutamatergic signaling through arachidonic acid (Basselin et al., 2005, 2008a, b). Moreover, postmortem studies demonstrated that patients with BD exhibited a decreased density of gamma-aminobutyric acid interneurons that express the NMDA NR(2A)subunit in the anterior cingulate cortex (Woo et al., 2004). Clinical studies indicated that the GRIN1 gene (glutamate receptor, ionotropic NMDA1) confers susceptibility to BD (Mundo et al., 2003; Liu et al., 2007). Recently, a lower protein and mRNA levels of the subunits of NMDA receptors, NR-1 and NR-3A in frontal cortex (Rao et al., 2010) and a decrease in NR-1 and NR-2A subunits in hippocampus (McCullumsmith et al., 2007) in postmortem brain from BD patients were reported, suggesting that an increased glutamate transmission is associated with decreased expression of NMDA receptor subunits.

AMPA receptors are also involved in the pathophysiology of mania, since chronic treatment with antimanic agents, lithium and valproate - *in vivo* and *in vitro* - induced synaptic plasticity by AMPA GluR1 receptors (Du et al., 2003, 2004a). Furthermore, a study from Du et al. (2008) also showed that chronic lithium and valproate, *in vitro* and *in vivo,* significantly downregulated AMPA GluR1/2 synaptic and surface in the hippocampus, suggesting that hippocampal AMPA GluR1/2 receptors may play an important role in the pathophysiology and treatment of mania. Moreover, this study indicates that treatment with lithium and AMPA antagonist attenuated hippocampal synaptic AMPA receptors and reduced amphetamine-induced hyperactivity, an animal model of mania. These findings provide compelling behavioral support for the notion that AMPA receptors also play important roles in the pathophysiology of BD.

Memantine is a low-affinity NMDA receptor antagonist used in the treatment of Alzheimer disease (Winslow et al., 2011). Recently, it was demonstrated that this drug administered for 7 days prevented the ouabain-induced hyperlocomotion, an animal model of mania in rats (Gao et al., 2011). Moreover, a clinical study with bipolar I disorder (manic or mixed episode, with and without psychotic features) patients indicated that memantine can be effective and safe in the treatment of mania (Keck et al., 2009). A study of Koukopoulos et al. (2011) also indicated antimanic and mood-stabilizing effect of memantine. However, more controlled clinical studies are necessary to confirm the efficacy and safety of memantine for the treatment of mania.

A preclinical study indicated that magnesium, a noncompetitive antagonist of NMDA receptor, exerts antimanic effect in an animal model of mania induced by methylphenidate in mice (Barbosa et al., 2011). This report is consistent with a clinical study which showed that intravenous magnesium sulphate can be an effective supplementary therapy in the clinical management of severe manic agitation (Heiden et al., 1999). In addition, combined magnesium plus verapamil therapy may increase antimanic efficacy of verapamil, an antiarrhythmic agent, suggesting that this combination may be useful in therapeutic maintenance of mania (Giannini et al., 2000).

Altogether, these findings show a critical role for the glutamatergic system in manic behavior and indicate an important target for development of novel medication for manic phase of BD.

Purinergic System

The purinergic system typically relates to the adenine nucleotides ATP, ADP, and AMP, and nucleoside adenosine. The purinergic receptor family contains some of the most abundant receptors in living organisms and, apart from its key role in energy metabolism, purines can modulate neuronal activity, and additionally connect to other extracellular messenger systems (Burnstock, 2008). Studies have proposed that the complex network of changes on neurotransmitters pathways correlated to manic state can be connected with reduced adenosinergic activity, mostly at adenosine A_1 receptors (Machado-Vieira et al., 2002).

Adenosine, recognized as an inhibitory neuromodulator and an endogenous anticonvulsant, acts mostly through A_1 and A_{2A} receptors. The activation of A_1 receptors leads to membrane hyperpolarization, decreases uric acid levels (the ultimate step in the metabolism of the purinergic system) and reduces calcium influx in postsynaptic neurons (Machado-Vieira et al., 2002). Indeed, adenosine agonists induce sedative, anticonvulsant, anti-aggressive, and antipsychotic-like effects in rats, whereas some adenosine receptor antagonists, like caffeine, exert behavioral and neuronal stimulant effects which include changes in motor activity, alertness, performance, and sleep (Waldeck, 1975; Sawyer et al., 1982; Zwyguizen-Doorenbos et al., 1990; Lara et al., 2006).

A role for purinergic system in mood disorder has been suggested since 19th century due to the reported association between manic symptoms, uric acid excretion, hyperuricemia and gout (Kraeplin, 1921). Later, an increased renal clearance of uric acid during the remission of mania was observed (Anumonye et al., 1968), a result reinforced by the reported cases of refractory mania associated with hyperuricemia (Machado-Vieira et al., 2001). In agreement with these data, in animal models, uric acid has been shown to increase locomotor activity (Hunter et al., 1990). Additionally, it was demonstrated that lithium might exert its effects on mood stabilization targeting the uric acid metabolism per se, which was its main indication before used in BD (Cade, 1949). Literature data also show that carbamazepine treatment induces an upregulation at adenosine A_1 receptors in brain cells (Biber et al., 1999), indicating that the mechanism of action of carbamazepine also seems to involve an adenosinergic modulation. Altogether, these results suggest that the antimanic effects of some mood stabilizers might be associated, at least in part, with the adenosine neuromodulatory effects, mainly through actions at A_1 receptors.

Although there are relatively few reports on the effects of treatments with purinergic modulator in manic patients, abnormalities in the purinergic system are definitely observed in this disorder, as previously described, and certain purinergic agents exhibit antimanic effects in patients. Allopurinol, a clinically available drug, has been described to regulate the brain purinergic metabolism and to reduce manic symptoms in bipolar subjects (Machado-Vieira et al., 2001; Akhondzadeh et al., 2006; Machado-Vieira et al., 2008). Allopurinol and its active metabolite oxypurinol are inhibitors of xanthine oxidase and have been proposed as hypouricemic agents that might produce therapeutic effects by decreasing the production of

superoxide, and hydrogen peroxide (Pacher et al., 2006).The antimanic efficacy of allopurinol as adjunct therapy to haloperidol plus lithium was shown in a double-blind, placebo-controlled study (Akhondzadeh et al., 2006). Additionally, in a randomized, placebo-controlled, double-blind study performed in adult patients by Machado-Vieira et al. (2008), allopurinol was shown to be clinically effective and well-tolerated adjunctively with lithium in manic episodes. Moreover, a significant positive association between antimanic effects and decreased plasma uric acid levels in the allopurinol group was shown in this study.

Since there are no direct adenosine agonists available for human use, purinergic modulation by allopurinol may be conceived as a possible strategy in the treatment of acute mania. Moreover the efficacy of allopurinol to obtain a greater improvement in these patients seems to support the purinergic dysfunction in mania.

Oxidative Stress and Bioenergetics

Mitochondria have the well-known function of regulating energy production through the tricarboxylic acid cycle and oxidative phosphorylation. Under normal conditions, mitochondria are the major source of reactive oxygen species (ROS), which are produced in the electron transport chain (Mattiasson et al., 2003). In conditions in which the production of ROS exceeds the capacity of antioxidant defense, the oxidative stress may cause direct damage to cellular proteins, DNA and lipids, thereby affecting cellular function (Cochrane, 1991). Many lines of evidence have implicated oxidative stress mechanisms in the BD pathogenesis (Steckert et al., 2010). Moreover, several studies have provided evidence for BD as a disease of mitochondrial energy metabolism (Konradi et al., 2004). Despite oxidative stress and bioenergetics studies do not completely clarify the pathophysiology of BD, they are targets for drugs that can be useful as alternative treatment for this disorder. In addition, these targets have been proposed as biological markers (in plasma samples) to assist in the diagnosis of BD (Yumru et al., 2009).

In vivo magnetic resonance spectroscopy studies have demonstrated alteration in brain compounds related to energy production, oxidative phosphorylation and phospholipid metabolism in bipolar patients (Stork and Renshaw, 2005). Moreover, neuroimaging (Cecil et al, 2002; Bertolino et al, 2003; Deicken et al, 2003) and postmortem brain studies (Konradi et al., 2004; Vawter et al., 2006) suggest that the decrease in mitochondrial function with the consequent impairment in cell energy production is implicated in the pathophysiology of BD. Corroborating these data, levels of creatine kinase mRNA are reported to be decreased in bipolar postmortem subjects, especially in the hippocampus (MacDonald et al, 2006). Conversely, serum creatine kinase activity was higher in manic patients as compared to healthy control or depressed subjects (Segal et al., 2007; Feier et al., 2011). In addition, studies with animal models of mania suggest that amphetamine administration promoted a decrease in brain energy metabolism in rats by inhibiting citrate synthase, creatine kinase and mitochondrial respiratory chain activity. Mood stabilizers exerted protective effect against these amphetamine-induced impairments (Corrêa et al., 2007; Streck et al., 2008, Valvassori et al., 2010). Altogether, these observations suggest that enhancing mitochondrial function may represent an important strategy for the optimal long-term treatment of BD (Quiroz et al., 2008).

Studies dealing with the role of oxidative stress in the pathophysiology of BD have consistently reported increased products of lipid peroxidation and alterations in the antioxidant enzyme activities in serum of bipolar subjects. For example, a study with bipolar patients at various phases of the illness indicated raised thiobarbituric acid reactive substances (TBARS) levels, a direct index of cell lipid peroxidation, regardless of illness phase, whereas glutathione peroxidase activity was elevated in euthymia, but not in depressed or manic phases (Andreazza et al., 2007). The same study found that superoxide dismutase (SOD) activity was increased during the manic and depressed phases of BD, but not in euthymia, whereas catalase (CAT) was reduced during mania and euthymia, but not in depression (Andreazza et al., 2007). Similarly, plasma levels of TBARS and SOD activity were increased in unmedicated manic patients compared to controls (Machado-Vieira et al., 2007). In agreement with these findings, a study which investigated the oxidative stress profile in two monozygotic twins during a manic episode found higher TBARS levels and SOD activity, and lower CAT activity than healthy controls (Frey et al., 2007). Besides, decreased levels of glutathione, the most abundant antioxidant substrate in all tissues, have been described in bipolar subjects (Andreazza et al., 2008; Gawryluk et al., 2011), reinforcing the idea that oxidative stress may play a role in the pathophysiology of BD. It is important to be mentioned that manic patients treated with lithium show lower levels of TBARS and SOD than unmedicated patients (Frey et al., 2007; Machado-Vieira et al., 2007), indicating a possible corrective property of this mood stabilizer on oxidative parameters and indirectly supporting the pathophysiological role of oxidative stress in BD.

Comparable results with those of bipolar patients were obtained from animal models of mania. Injections of D-amphetamine in rats are associated with increased protein and lipid oxidative damage in brain tissues following both single and repeated dosing (Frey et al., 2006b, c). Alteration in the activities of SOD and CAT, as well as increased superoxide production in submitochondrial particles in the rat brain were also found after D-amphetamine exposure (Frey et al., 2006b, c, d, e). Moreover, it was reported that amphetamine promotes time-dependent and brain region selective elevation of protein carbonyls and TBARS in mice (Gluck et al., 2001). Intracerebroventricular (icv) injection of ouabain, a potent Na(+)/K(+)-ATPase inhibitor, in rats, also resulted in manic-like behavior and increased TBARS levels and protein carbonyl generation in the prefrontal cortex and hippocampus. Moreover, the activity of the antioxidants enzymes were altered in several areas of the rat brain and cerebrospinal fluid of ouabain-treated rats (Brocardo et al., 2010; Riegel et al., 2010), supporting the view that oxidative stress is occurring during a manic-like state. Similar to clinical findings, in animal models of mania several evidence support that lithium and valproate have antioxidant effects in parallel with the reversion of the manic-like symptoms (Frey et al., 2006a, c; Andreazza et al., 2008; Brocardo et al., 2010; Jornada et al., 2011). Furthermore, preclinical studies have shown that the pretreatment with the antioxidant deferoxamine also protects against methamphetamine-induced neuronal damage by decreasing the level of oxidative stress in rat brain (Park et al., 2006; Valvassori et al., 2008).

Considering that oxidative stress and bioenergetic play an important function in the manic phase of BD and that these target may have a direct role in some aspects of mood stabilizers therapeutic effects, recent studies have explored compounds which antioxidant properties as putative candidate to assist in the treatment of mania.

N-acetyl-L-cysteine (NAC), a precursor for glutathione synthesis, is a well-known thiolic antioxidant that acts through mechanisms against cellular degeneration. The reducing thiol

group in NAC acts directly against reactive oxygen species, protecting neurons against oxidative damage (Aruoma et al., 1989). In preclinical studies with rat model of mania, NAC significantly prevented methamphetamine-induced hyperactivity, behavioral sensitization and attenuated in a dose-dependent fashion long-term dopaminergic depletion and lipid peroxidation formation in the rat striatum following striatal amphetamine infusion (Fukami et al., 2004; Wan et al., 2006). In agreement with these results, Valvassori et al. (2008) suggest that NAC treatment can prevent against oxidative stress damage induced by amphetamine. In line with this, in a recent randomized, placebo-controlled trial of adjunctive NAC in the treatment of a small subset of subjects with bipolar II disorder, this antioxidant demonstrated an interesting pattern of efficacy after 6 months of treatment. Six out of seven participants achieved full remission of both depressive and manic symptoms; this was true for only two participants in the placebo (Magalhães et al., 2011). Taken together, these data suggest that antioxidant compounds may be useful in the treatment of BD. This hypothesis deserves further studies.

Alternative Treatments in Mania

There has been growing interest in the use of complementary and alternative treatments for the management of the manic phase of BD.

Some nutritional interventions have been proposed to ameliorate manic symptoms, as it is expected that these approaches would lack some of the limiting side effects observed with conventional mood stabilizers.

A study reported that branched-chain amino acid drink administered for seven days to patients with mania lowered mania ratings acutely over the first 6 h of treatment (Scarna et al., 2003). Moreover, some studies with 36-ingredient micronutrient formula (14 vitamins, 16 minerals, 3 aminoacids, and 3 antioxidants) have suggested that this intervention can be beneficial for the reduction of symptoms of BD (Rucklidge et al., 2010; Rucklidge and Harrison, 2010). The symptoms improvement is argued to be due to the array of nutrients available in the formulation required for effective neurotransmitter synthesis.

Noteworthy, one of the ingredients of the mentioned 36-ingredient micronutrient formula is folic acid (folate), a water-soluble vitamin that plays an essential role in one-carbon metabolism which is crucial for neurological function (Kronenberg et al., 2009). Clinical studies suggest that folic acid may play a role in manic phase of BD, since reduced folate levels in the erythrocytes (Hasanah et al., 1997) and serum (Ozbek et al., 2008) of manic patients are reported. Moreover, beneficial effects of folic acid administration in enhancing the prophylactic effects of lithium on affective morbidity have been reported (Coppen and Abou-Saleh, 1982; Coppen et al., 1986). Noteworthy, a clinical study showed that folic acid may be an effective adjuvant to mood stabilizer valproate in the treatment of the manic phase of patients with BD (Behzadi et al., 2009). Interestingly, a preclinical study showed that folic acid, similarly to lithium, prevented biochemical and behavioral alterations in an ouabain-induced animal model of mania in rats (Brocardo et al., 2010). Therefore, folic acid might a putative candidate to therapy of BD, but further preclinical and clinical studies are necessary to confirm this hypothesis.

Finally, it is important to recognize the fundamental role of the antipsychotics in the treatment of mania. First-generation (chlorpromazine and haloperidol) and second-generation antipsychotics (olanzapine, quetiapine, aripiprazole, risperidone, ziprasidone and asenapine) have proven efficacy against acute mania alone or in combination with mood stabilizers (Fountoulakis et al., 2011). This class of drugs is widely used considering that psychotic symptoms often occur in the manic phase of BD. They are also frequently utilized to reduce manic symptoms until mood stabilizers can take full effect and, in some cases, these may be used for long-term maintenance of stability (McElroy et al., 1996).

Cariprazine (RGH-188) is a novel putative antipsychotic drug that exerts partial agonism at dopamine D2/D3 receptors, with preferential binding to D3 receptors, and partial agonism at serotonin 5-HT1A receptors. A recent study showed that this drug has antipsychotic and antimanic properties that are superior to placebo when tested in phase II trials in patients (Gründer, 2010). The molecular mechanisms through which cariprazine exerts its therapeutic effect remain to be elucidate, however future work dissecting the cellular and molecular pathways involved in its antimanic effect should provide some insight into the its therapeutic action and may lead to the identification of new candidate pharmacological targets to improve therapeutic armamentarium for affective disorders.

Conclusion

Medical and research findings support a view of BD as a chronic, progressive, multisystem disorder. In this chapter, we present basic research data combined with clinical studies in an attempt to help to the understanding the neuropsychobiology of BD, paving the way for new breakthroughs for therapeutics. Although lithium remains the gold standard for the treatment of mania, novel approaches include inhibitors of the enzymes glycogen synthase kinase-3, protein kinase C and histone deacetylase, modulators of glutamatergic and purinergic systems, antioxidants, compounds that act on bioenergetic parameters, and folic acid. However, there is need of more intense research with these agents to confirm their efficacy and safety in order to determine which therapy should be applied in the therapeutic arsenal to optimize mania treatment. Considering that the majority of novel compounds are still based on limited data, additional studies are necessary to clarify their actual role in the clinical management of this condition.

References

Ackermann, TF; Kempe, DS; Lang, F; Lang, UE. Hyperactivity and enhanced curiosity of mice expressing PKB/SGK-resistant glycogen synthase kinase-3 (GSK-3). *Cell Physiol Biochem,* 2010 25, 775-86.

Akhondzadeh, S; Milajerdi, MR; Amini, H; Tehrani-Doost, M. Allopurinol as an adjunct to lithium and haloperidol for treatment of patients with acute mania: a double-blind; randomized; placebo-controlled trial. *Bipolar Disord,* 2006 5, 485-9.

Akiskal, HS. The Scope of Bipolar Disorders. In: Akiskal HS, Tohen M. Bipolar *Psychopharmacotherapy: Caring for the Patient.* John Wiley & Sons, Ltd; 2006; 1-8.

Amrollahi, Z; Rezaei, F; Salehi, B; Modabbernia, AH; Maroufi, A; Esfandiari, GR; Naderi, M; Ghebleh, F; Ahmadi-Abhari, SA; Sadeghi, M; Tabrizi, M; Akhondzadeh, S. Double-blind; randomized; placebo-controlled 6-week study on the efficacy and safety of the tamoxifen adjunctive to lithium in acute bipolar mania. *J Affect Disord*, 2011 129, 327-31.

Andreazza, AC; Cassini, C; Rosa, AR; Leite, MC; de Almeida, LM; Nardin, P; Cunha, AB; Cereser, KM; Santin, A; Gottfried C; Salvador, M; Kapczinski, F; Goncalves, CA. Serum S100B and antioxidant enzymes in bipolar patients. *J Psychiatr Res*, 2007 41, 523-9.

Andreazza, AC; Kauer-Sant'anna, M; Frey, BN; Bond, DJ; Kapczinski, F; Young, LT; Yatham, LN. Oxidative stress markers in bipolar disorder: a meta-analysis. *J Affect Disord,* 2008 111, 135-44.

Anumonye, A; Reading, HW; Knight, F; Ashcroft, GW. Uric-acid metabolism in manic-depressive illness and during lithium therapy. *Lancet*, 1968 7555, 1290-3.

Arent, CO; Valvassori, SS; Fries, GR; Stertz, L; Ferreira, CL; Lopes-Borges, J; Mariot, E; Varela, RB; Ornell, F; Kapczinski, F; Andersen, ML; Quevedo, J. Neuroanatomical profile of antimaniac effects of histone deacetylase inhibitors. *Mol Neurobiol*, 2011 43, 207-14.

Aruoma, OI; Halliewell, B; Hoey, BM; Butler, J. The antioxidant action of N-acetylcysteine: its reaction with hydrogen peroxide, hydroxyl radical, superoxide, and hypochlorous acid. *Free Radic Biol Med*, 1989 6, 593-7.

Aubry, JM; Schwald, M; Ballmann, E; Karege, F. Early effects of mood stabilizers on the Akt/GSK-3beta signaling pathway and on cell survival and proliferation. *Psychopharmacology* (Berl), 2009 205, 419-29.

Baraban, JM; Worley, PF; Snyder, SH. Second messenger systems and psychoactive drug action: focus on the phosphoinositide system and lithium. *Am J Psychiatry*, 1989 146, 1251-60.

Barbosa, FJ; Hesse, B; de Almeida, RB; Baretta, IP; Boerngen-Lacerda, R; Andreatini, R. Magnesium sulfate and sodium valproate block methylphenidate-induced hyperlocomotion, an animal model of mania. *Pharmacol Rep*, 2011 63, 64-70.

Basselin, M; Chang, L; Bell, JM; Rapoport, SI. Chronic lithium chloride administration to unanesthetized rats attenuates brain dopamine D2-like receptor-initiated signaling via arachidonic acid. *Neuropsychopharmacology*, 2005 30, 1064-75.

Basselin, M; Chang, L; Chen, M; Bell, JM; Rapoport, SI. Chronic administration of valproic acid reduces brain NMDA signaling via arachidonic acid in unanesthetized rats. *Neurochem Res,* 2008b 33, 2229-40.

Basselin, M; Chang, L; Chen, M; Bell, JM; Rapoport, SI. Chronic carbamazepine administration attenuates dopamine D2-like receptor-initiated signaling via arachidonic acid in rat brain. *Neurochem Res,* 2008a 33, 1373-83.

Bebchuk, JM; Arfken, CL; Dolan-Manji, S; Murphy, J; Hasanat, K; Manji, HK. A preliminary investigation of a protein kinase C inhibitor in the treatment of acute mania. *Arch Gen Psychiatry*, 2000 57, 95-7.

Behzadi, AH; Omrani, Z; Chalian, M; Asadi, S; Ghadiri, M. Folic acid efficacy as an alternative drug added to sodium valproate in the treatment of acute phase of mania in bipolar disorder: a double-blind randomized controlled trial. *Acta Psychiatr Scand*, 2009 120, 441-5.

Benes, FM; Berretta, S. GABAergic interneurons: implications for understanding schizophrenia and bipolar disorder. *Neuropsychopharmacology*, 2001 25, 1-27.

Berridge, MJ; Irvine, RF. Inositol phosphates and cell signaling. *Nature*, 1989 341, 197-205.

Bertolino, A; Frye, M; Callicott, JH; Mattay, VS; Rakow, R; Shelton- Repella, J; Post, R; Weinberger, DR. Neuronal pathology in the hippocampal area of patients with bipolar disorder: a study with proton magnetic resonance spectroscopic imaging. *Biol Psychiatry*, 2003 53, 906–13.

Biber, K; Fiebich, BL; Gebicke-Harter, P; van Calker, D. Carbamazepine-induced upregulation of adenosine A1-receptorsin astrocyte cultures affects coupling to the phosphoinositol signaling pathway. *Neuropsychopharmacology*, 1999 20, 271-8.

Bitran, JA; Manji, HK; Potter, WZ; Gusovsky, F. Down-regulation of PKC alpha by lithium in vitro. *Psychopharmacology Bulletin*, 1995 31, 449-52.

Bitran, JA; Potter, WZ; Manji, HK; Gusovsky, F. Chronic Li+ attenuates agonist- and phorbol ester-mediated Na+/H+ antiporter activity in HL-60 cells. *Eur J Pharmacol*, 1990 188, 193-202.

Brocardo, PS; Budni, J; Pavesi, E; Franco, JL; Uliano-Silva, M; Trevisan, R; Terenzi, MG; Dafre, AL; Rodrigues, ALS. Folic acid administration prevents ouabain-induced hyperlocomotion and alterations in oxidative stress markers in the rat brain. *Bipolar Disord,* 2010 12, 414-24.

Browman, KE; Kantor, L; Richardson, S; Badiani, A; Robinson, TE; Gnegy, ME. Injections of protein kinase C inhibitor Ro31-8220 into the nucleus accumbens attenuates the acute response to amphetamine: tissue and behavior studies. *Brain Res,* 1998 814, 112-9.

Burnstock, G. Purinergic signalling and disorders of the central nervous system. *Nat Rev Drug Discov* 2008 7, 575-90.

Cade, JF. Lithium salts in the treatment of psychotic excitement. Med J Aust, 1949 2,349-52.

Cecil, KM; DelBello, MP; Morey, R; Strakowski, SM. Frontal lobe differences in bipolar disorder as determined by proton MR spectroscopy. *Bipolar Disord*, 2002 4, 357-65.

Chen, G; Huang, LD; Jiang, YM; Manji, HK. The mood-stabilizing agent valproate inhibits the activity of glycogen synthase kinase-3. *J Neurochem,* 1999 72, 1327-30.

Chen, G; Manji, HK; Hawver, DB; Wright, CB; Potter, WZ. Chronic sodium valproate selectively decreases protein kinase C alpha and epsilon in vitro. *J Neurochem*, 1994 63, 2361-4.

Cochrane, CG. Mechanisms of oxidant injury of cells. *Mol Aspects Med*, 1991 12,137- 47.

Colvis, CM; Pollock, JD; Goodman, RH; Impey, S; Dunn, J; Mandel, G; Champagne, FA; Mayford, M; Korzus, E; Kumar, A; Renthal, W; Theobald, DE, Nestler, EJ. Epigenetic mechanisms and gene networks in the nervous system. *The Journal of Neuroscience,* 2005 25, 10379-89.

Coppen, A; Abou-Saleh, MT. Plasma folate and affective morbidity during long-term lithium therapy. *Br J Psychiatry*, 1982 141, 87-9.

Coppen, A; Chaudhry, S; Swade, C. Folic acid enhances lithium prophylaxis. *J Affect Disord,* 1986 10, 9-13.

Corrêa, C; Amboni, G; Assis, LC; Frey, BN; Kapczinksi, F; Streck, EL; Quevedo, J. Effects of lithium and valproate on hippocampus citrate synthase activity in an animal model of mania. *Prog Neuropsychopharmacol Biol Psychiatry*, 2007 31, 887-91.

Coyle, JT; Duman, RS. Finding the intracellular signaling pathways affected by mood disorder treatments. *Neuron*, 2003 38, 157-60.

Cross, DA; Alessi, DR; Cohen, P; Andjelkovich, M; Hemmings, BA. Inhibition of glycogen synthase kinase-3 by insulin mediated by protein kinase B. *Nature*, 1995 378, 785-9.

Davies, J; Evans, RH; Francis, AA; Watkins, JC. Excitatory amino acid receptors and synaptic excitation in the mammalian central nervous system. *J Physiol* (Paris), 1979 75, 641-54.

Deicken, RF; Pegues, MP; Anzalone, S; Feiwell, R; Soher, B. Lower concentration of hippocampal N-acetylaspartate in familial bipolar I disorder. *Am J Psychiatry*, 2003 160, 873-82.

Dempsey, EC; Newton, AC; Mochly-Rosen, D; Fields, AP; Reyland, ME; Insel, PA; Messing, RO. Protein kinase C isozymes and the regulation of diverse cell responses. *Am J Physiol Lung Cell Mol Physiol*, 2000 279, 429-38.

Du, J; Creson, TK; Wu, LJ; Ren, M; Gray, NA; Falke, C; Wei, Y; Wang, Y; Blumenthal, R; Machado-Vieira, R; Yuan, P; Chen, G; Zhuo, M; Manji, HK. The role of hippocampal GluR1 and GluR2 receptors in manic-like behavior. *J Neurosci*, 2008 28, 68-79.

Du, J; Gray, NA; Falke, C; Yuan, P; Szabo, S; Manji, HK. Structurally dissimilar antimanic agents modulate synaptic plasticity by regulating AMPA glutamate receptor subunit GluR1 synaptic expression. *Ann N Y Acad Sci*, 2003 1003, 378-80.

Du, J; Gray, NA; Falke, CA; Chen, W; Yuan, P; Szabo, ST; Einat, H; Manji, HK. Modulation of synaptic plasticity by antimanic agents: the role of AMPA glutamate receptor subunit 1 synaptic expression. *J Neurosci,* 2004a 24, 6578-89.

Du, J; Quiroz, J; Yuan, P; Zarate, C; Manji, HK. Bipolar disorder: involvement of signaling cascades and AMPA receptor trafficking at synapses. *Neuron Glia Biol,* 2004b 1, 231-43.

Einat, H; Yuan, P; Szabo, ST; Dogra, S; Manji, HK. Protein kinase C inhibition by tamoxifen antagonizes manic-like behavior in rats: implications for the development of novel therapeutics for bipolar disorder. *Neuropsychobiology*, 2007 55, 123-31.

Embi, N; Rylatt, DB; Cohen, P. Glycogen synthase kinase-3 from rabbit skeletal muscle. Separation from cyclic-AMP-dependent protein kinase and phosphorylase kinase. *Eur. J. Biochem,* 1980 107, 519-27.

Feier, G; Valvassori, SS; Rezin, GT; Búrigo, M; Streck, EL; Kapczinski, F; Quevedo, J. Creatine kinase levels in patients with bipolar disorder: depressive, manic, and euthymic phases. *Rev Bras Psiquiatr*, 2011, in press.

Fountoulakis, KN; Vieta, E; Bouras, C; Notaridis, G; Giannakopoulos, P; Kaprinis, G; Akiskal, H. A systematic review of existing data on long-term lithium therapy: neuroprotective or neurotoxic? *Int J Neuropsychopharmacol.* 2008 11, 269-87.

Frey, BN; Andreazza, AC; Cereser, KM; Martins, MR; Valvassori, SS; Réus, GZ; Quevedo, J; Kapczinski, F. Effects of mood stabilizers on hippocampus BDNF levels in an animal model of mania. *Life Sci,* 2006a 79, 281-6.

Frey, BN; Andreazza, AC; Kunz, M; Gomes, FA; Quevedo, J; Salvador, M; Gonçalves, CA; Kapczinski, F. Increased oxidative stress and DNA damage in bipolar disorder: a twin-case report. *Prog Neuropsychopharmacol Biol Psychiatry*, 2007 31, 283-5.

Frey, BN; Martins, MR; Petronilho, FC; Dal-Pizzol, F; Quevedo, J; Kapczinski, F. Increased oxidative stress after repeated amphetamine exposure: possible relevance as a model of mania. *Bipolar Disord*, 2006b 8, 275–80.

Frey, BN; Valvassori, SS; Gomes, KM; Martins, MR; Dal-Pizzol, F; Kapczinski, F; Quevedo, J. Increased oxidative stress in submitochondrial particles after chronic amphetamine exposure. *Brain Res,* 2006e 1097, 224-9.

Frey, BN; Valvassori, SS; Réus, GZ; Martins, MR; Petronilho, FC; Bardini, K; Dal-Pizzol, F; Kapczinski, F; Quevedo, J. Effects of lithium and valproate on amphetamine-induced oxidative stress generation in an animal model of mania. *J Psychiatry Neurosci*, 2006c 31, 326-32.

Frey, BN; Valvassori, SS; Réus, GZ; Martins, MR; Petronilho, FC; Bardini, K; Dal-Pizzol, F; Kapczinski, F; Quevedo, J. Changes in antioxidant defense enzymes after d-amphetamine exposure: implications as an animal model of mania. *Neurochem Res*, 2006d 31, 699-703.

Friedman, E; Wang, HY; Levinson, D; Connell, TA; Singh, H. Altered platelet protein kinase C activity in bipolar affective disorder; manic episode. *Biol Psychiatry*, 1993 33, 520-25.

Fukami, G; Hashimoto, K; Koike, K; Okama, N; Shimizu, E; Iyo, M. Effect of antioxidant N-acetyl-L-cysteine on behavioral changes and neurotoxicity in rats after administration of methamphetamine. *Brain Res*, 2004 1016, 90-5.

Gao, Y; Payne, RS; Schurr, A; Hougland, T; Lord, J; Herman, L; Lei, Z; Banerjee, P; El-Mallakh, RS. Memantine reduces mania-like symptoms in animal models. *Psychiatry Res*, 2011, in press.

Gawryluk, JW; Wang, JF; Andreazza, AC; Shao, L; Young, LT. Decreased levels of glutathione, the major brain antioxidant, in post-mortem prefrontal cortex from patients with psychiatric disorders. *Int J Neuropsychopharmacol*, 2011 14, 123-30.

Giambalvo, CT. Protein kinase C and dopamine transport--1. Effects of amphetamine in vivo. *Neuropharmacology*, 1992a 31,1201-10.

Giambalvo, CT. Protein kinase C and dopamine transport--2. Effects of amphetamine in vitro. *Neuropharmacology*, 1992b 31, 1211-22.

Giannini, AJ; Nakoneczie, AM; Melemis, SM; Ventresco, J; Condon, M. Magnesium oxide augmentation of verapamil maintenance therapy in mania. *Psychiatry Res*, 2000 93, 83-7.

Gluck, MR; Moy, LY; Jayatilleke, E; Hogan, KA; Manzino, L; Sonsalla, PK.. Parallel increases in lipid and protein oxidative markers in several mouse brain regions after methamphetamine treatment. *J Neurochem*, 2001 79, 152–60.

Gnegy, ME; Hong, P; Ferrell, ST. Phosphorylation of neuromodulin in rat striatum after acute and repeated, intermittent amphetamine. *Brain Res Mol Brain Res*, 1993 20, 289-98.

Goode, N; Hughes, K; Woodgett, JR; Parker, PJ. Differential regulation of glycogen synthase kinase-3 beta by protein kinase C isotypes. *J Biol Chem,* 1992 267, 16878-82.

Gould, TD; Chen, G; Manji, HK. In vivo evidence in the brain for lithium inhibition of glycogen synthase kinase-3. *Neuropsychopharmacology*, 2004a 29, 32-8.

Gould, TD; Manji, HK. Glycogen synthase kinase-3: a putative molecular target for lithium mimetic drugs. *Neuropsychopharmacology*, 2005 30, 1223-37.

Gould, TD; Quiroz, JA; Singh, J; Zarate, CA; Manji, HK. Emerging experimental therapeutics for bipolar disorder: insights from the molecular and cellular actions of current mood stabilizers. *Mol Psychiatry*, 2004b 9, 734-55.

Grimes, CA; Jope, RS. CREB DNA binding activity is inhibited by glycogen synthase kinase-3β and facilitated by lithium. *J Neurochem*, 2001 78, 1219-32.

Gründer, G. Cariprazine, an orally active D2/D3 receptor antagonist, for the potential treatment of schizophrenia, bipolar mania and depression. *Curr Opin Investig Drugs,* 2010 11, 823-32.

Gurvich, N; Klein, PS. Lithium and valproic acid: parallels and contrasts in diverse signaling contexts. *Pharmacol Ther,* 2002 96, 45-66.

Hasanah, CI; Khan, UA; Musalmah, M; Razali, SM. Reduced red-cell folate in mania. *J Affect Disord*, 1997 46, 95-9.

Hashimoto, R; Hough, C; Nakazawa, T; Yamamoto, T; Chuang DM. Lithium protection against glutamate excitotoxicity in rat cerebral cortical neurons: involvement of NMDA receptor inhibition possibly by decreasing NR2B tyrosine phosphorylation. *J Neurochem,* 2002 80, 589-97.

Heiden, A; Frey, R; Presslich, O; Blasbichler, T; Smetana, R; Kasper, S. Treatment of severe mania with intravenous magnesium sulphate as a supplementary therapy. *Psychiatry Res,* 1999 89, 239-46.

Hobara, T; Uchida, S; Otsuki, K; Matsubara, T; Funato, H; Matsuo, K; Suetsugi, M; Watanabe, Y. Altered gene expression of histone deacetylases in mood disorder patients. *J Psychiatr Res*, 2010 44, 263-70.

Hockly, E; Richon, VM; Woodman, B; Smith DL; Zhou X; Rosa, E; Sathasivam, K; Ghazi-Noori, S; Mahal, A; Lowden, PA; Steffan, JS; Marsh, JL; Thompson, LM; Lewis, CM; Marks, PA; Bates, GP. Suberoylanilidehydroxamic acid, a histone deacetylase inhibitor, ameliorates motor deficits in a mouse model of Huntington's disease. *Proc Natl Acad Sci U.S.A,* 2003 100, 2041-6.

Hsieh, J; Gage, FH. Chromatin remodeling in neural development and plasticity. *Curr Opin Cell Biol,* 2005 17, 664-71.

Hunter, RE; Barrera, CM; Dohanich, GP; Dunlap, WP. Effects of uric acid and caffeine on A1 adenosine receptor binding in developing rat brain. *Pharmacol Biochem Behav*, 1990 35, 791-5.

Iwata, SI; Hewlett, GH; Ferrell ST; Kantor, L; Gnegy, ME: Enhanced dopamine release and phosphorylation of synapsin I and neuromodulin in striatal synaptosomes after repeated amphetamine. *J Pharmacol Exp Ther*, 1997 283, 1445-52.

Jope, RS; Bijur, GN. Mood stabilizers, glycogen synthase kinase-3 and cell Survival. *Mol Psychiatry,* 2002 7, 35-45.

Jornada, LK; Valvassori, SS; Steckert, AV; Moretti, M; Mina, F; Ferreira, CL; Arent, CO; Dal-Pizzol, F; Quevedo, J. Lithium and valproate modulate antioxidant enzymes and prevent ouabain-induced oxidative damage in an animal model of mania. *J Psychiatr Res,* 2011 45, 162-8.

Kalinichev, M; Dawson, LA. Evidence for antimanic efficacy of glycogen synthase kinase-3 (GSK3) inhibitors in a strain-specific model of acute mania. Int J *Neuropsychopharmacol*, 2011 6, 1-17.

Kato, T; Iwamoto, K; Kakiuchi, C; Kuratomi, G; Okazaki, Y. Genetic or epigenetic difference causing discordance between monozygotic twins as a clue to molecular basis of mental disorders. *Mol Psychiatry*, 2005 10, 622–30.

Keck, PE Jr; Hsu, HA; Papadakis, K; Russo, J Jr. Memantine efficacy and safety in patients with acute mania associated with bipolar I disorder: a pilot evaluation. *Clin Neuropharmacol,* 2009 32, 199-204.

Kim, WY; Kim, S; Kim, JH. Chronic microinjection of valproic acid into the nucleus accumbens attenuates amphetamine-induced locomotor activity. *Neurosci Lett*, 2008 432, 54-7.

Klein, PS; Melton, DA. Amolecularmechanismfor the effect of lithium on development. *Proc Natl Acad Sci USA*, 1996 93, 8455-9.

Konradi, C; Eaton, M; Macdonald, ML; Walsh, J; Benes, FM; Heckers, S. Molecular evidence for mitochondrial dysfunction in bipolar disorder. *Arch Gen Psychiatry*, 2004 61, 300-8.

Koukopoulos, A; Reginaldi, D; Serra, G; Koukopoulos, A; Sani, G; Serra, G. Antimanic and mood-stabilizing effect of memantine as an augmenting agent in treatment-resistant bipolar disorder. *Bipolar Disord*, 2010 12, 348-9.

Kraeplin, E. *Manic-Depressive Insanity and Paranoia*. Edinburgh, Scotland: E & S Livingstone; 1921.

Kronenberg, G; Colla, M; Endres, M. Folic acid, neurodegenerative and neuropsychiatric disease. *Curr Mol Med,* 2009 9, 315-23.

Kulkarni, J; Garland, KA; Scaffidi, A; Headey, B; Anderson, R; de Castella, A; Fitzgerald, P; Davis, SR. A pilot study of hormone modulation as a new treatment for mania in women with bipolar affective disorder. *Psychoneuroendocrinology*, 2006 31, 543-47.

Kurdistani, SK; Tavazoie, S; Grunstein, M. Mapping global histone acetylation patterns to gene expression. *Cell*, 2004 117, 721-33.

Lara, DR; Dall'Igna, OP; Ghisolfi, ES; Brunstein, MG. Involvement of adenosine in the neurobiology of schizophrenia and its therapeutic implications. *Prog Neuropsychopharmacol Biol Psychiatry*, 2006 30, 617-29.

Lenox, RH; Watson, DGJP; Ellis, J. Chronic lithium administration alters a prominent PKC substrate in rat hippocampus. *Brain Res,* 1992 570, 333-40.

Lesort, M; Greendorfer, A; Stockmeier, C; Johnson, GV; Jope, RS. Glycogen synthase kinase-3beta, beta-catenin, and tau in postmortem bipolar brain. *J Neural Transm*, 1999 106, 1217-22.

Leverich, GS; Altshuler, LL; Frye, MA; Suppes, T; Keck, PE Jr; McElroy, SL; Denicoff, KD; Obrocea, G; Nolen, WA; Kupka, R; Walden, J; Grunze, H; Perez, S; Luckenbaugh, DA; Post, RM. Factors associated with suicide attempts in 648 patients with bipolar disorder in the Stanley Foundation Bipolar Network. *J Clin Psychiatry*, 2003 64, 506-15.

Li, X; Liu, M; Cai, Z; Wang, G; Li, X. Regulation of glycogen synthase kinase-3 during bipolar mania treatment. *Bipolar Disord*, 2010 12, 741-52.

Li, X; Zhu, W; Roh, MS; Friedman, AB; Rosborough, K; Jope, RS. In vivo regulation of glycogen synthase kinase-3beta (GSK3beta) by serotonergic activity in mouse brain. *Neuropsychopharmacology*, 2004 29, 1426-31.

Liu, M; Ling, SH; Li, WB; Wang, CY; Chen, DF; Wang, G. *An association study between GRIN1, BDNF genes and bipolar disorder*. Yi Chuan, 2007 29, 41-6.

MacDonald, ML; Naydenov, A; Chu, M; Matzilevich, D; Konradi C. Decrease in creatine kinase messenger RNA expression in the hippocampus and dorsolateral prefrontal cortex in bipolar disorder. *Bipolar Disord,* 2006 8, 255-64.

Machado-Vieira, R; Andreazza, AC; Viale, CI; Zanatto, V; Cereser Jr, V; da Silva Vargas, R; Kapczinski, F; Portela, LV; Souza, DO; Salvador, M; Gentil, V. Oxidative stress parameters in unmedicated and treated bipolar subjects during initial manic episode: a possible role for lithium antioxidant effects. *Neurosci Lett*, 2007 421, 33-6.

Machado-Vieira, R; Lara, DR; Souza, DO; Kapczinski, F. Therapeutic efficacy of allopurinol in mania associated with hyperuricemia. *J Clin Psychopharmacol*, 2001 21, 621-2.

Machado-Vieira, R; Lara, DR; Souza, DO; Kapczinski, F. Purinergic dysfunction in mania: an integrative model. *Med Hypotheses*, 2002 58, 297-304.

Machado-Vieira, R; Soares, JC; Lara, DR; Luckenbaugh, DA; Busnello, JV; Marca, G; Cunha, A; Souza, DO; Zarate, CA Jr; Kapczinski, F. A double-blind; randomized; placebo-controlled 4-week study on the efficacy and safety of the purinergic agents allopurinol and dipyridamole adjunctive to lithium in acute bipolar mania. *J Clin Psychiatry*, 2008 69, 1237-45.

Magalhães, PV; Dean, OM; Bush, AI; Copolov, DL; Malhi, GS; Kohlmann, K; Jeavons, S; Schapkaitz, I; Anderson-Hunt, M; Berk, M. N-acetyl cysteine add-on treatment for bipolar II disorder: a subgroup analysis of a randomized placebo-controlled trial. *J Affect Disord*, 2011 129, 317-20.

Mallinger, AG; Thase, ME; Haskett, R; Buttenfield, J; Luckenbaugh, DA; Frank, E; Kupfer, DJ; Manji, HK. Verapamil augmentation of lithium treatment improves outcome in mania unresponsive to lithium alone: preliminary findings and a discussion of therapeutic mechanisms. *Bipolar Disord,* 2008 10, 856-66.

Manji, HK; Etcheberrigaray, R; Chen, G; Olds, JL. Lithium decreases membrane-associated protein kinase C in hippocampus: selectivity for the alpha isozyme. *J Neurochem*, 1993 61, 2303-10.

Manji, HK; Lenox, RH. Protein kinase C signaling in the brain: molecular transduction of mood stabilization in the treatment of manic-depressive illness. *Biol Psychiatry,* 1999 46, 1328-51.

Maragakis, NJ; Rothstein, JD. Glutamate transporters: animal models to neurological disease. *Neurobiol Dis*, 2004 15, 461-73.

Mattiasson, G; Shamloo, M; Gido, G; Mathi, K; Tomasevic, G; Yi, S; Warden, CH; Castilho, RF; Melcher, T; Gonzalez-Zulueta, M; Nikolich, K; Wieloch, T. Uncoupling protein-2 prevents neuronal death and diminishes brain dysfunction after stroke and brain trauma. *Nat Med,* 2003 9, 1062-8.

McCullumsmith, RE; Kristiansen, LV; Beneyto, M; Scarr, E; Dean, B; Meador-Woodruff, JH. Decreased NR1, NR2A, and SAP102 transcript expression in the hippocampus in bipolar disorder. *Brain Res*, 2007 1127, 108-18.

McElroy, SL; Keck, PE Jr; Strakowski, SM. Mania, psychosis, and antipsychotics. *J Clin Psychiatry*, 1996 57, 14-26.

Michael, N; Erfurth, A; Ohrmann, P; Gossling, M; Arolt, V; Heindel, W; Pfleiderer, B. Acute mania is accompanied by elevated glutamate/glutamine levels within the left dorsolateral prefrontal cortex. *Psychopharmacology* (Berl), 2003 168, 344-6.

Michael, N; Erfurth, A; Pfleiderer, B. Elevated metabolites within dorsolateral prefrontal cortex in rapid cycling bipolar disorder. *Psychiatry Res,* 2009 172, 78-81.

Mill, J; Tang, T; Kaminsky, Z; Khare, T; Yazdanpanah, S; Bouchard, L; Jia, P; Assadzadeh, A; Flanagan, J; Schumacher, A; Wang, SC; Petronis, A. Epigenomic profiling reveals DNA-methylation changes associated with major psychosis. *Am J Hum Genet*, 2008 82, 696-711.

Moore, CM; Frazier, JA; Glod, CA; Breeze, JL; Dieterich, M; Finn, CT; Frederick, B; Renshaw, PF. Glutamine and glutamate levels in children and adolescents with bipolar disorder: A 4.0-T proton magnetic resonance spectroscopy study of the anterior cingulate cortex. *J Am Acad Child Adolesc Psychiatry*, 2007 46, 524-34.

Moretti, M; Valvassori, SS; Steckert, AV; Rochi, N; Benedet, J; Scaini, G; Kapczinski, F; Streck, EL; Zugno, AI; Quevedo, J. Tamoxifen effects on respiratory chain complexes

and creatine kinase activities in an animal model of mania. *Pharmacol Biochem Behav,* 2011 98, 304-10.

Mundo, E; Tharmalingham, S; Neves-Pereira, M; Dalton, EJ; Macciardi, F; Parikh, SV; Bolonna, A; Kerwin, RW; Arranz, MJ; Makoff, AJ; Kennedy, JL. Evidence that the N-methyl-D-aspartate subunit 1 receptor gene (GRIN1) confers susceptibility to bipolar disorder. *Mol Psychiatry,* 2003 8, 241-5.

Nishizuka, Y. The molecular heterogeneity of protein kinase C and its implications for cellular regulation. *Nature*, 1988 334, 661-5.

Nonaka, S; Hough, CJ; Chuang, DM. Chronic lithium treatment robustly protects neurons in the central nervous system against excitotoxicity by inhibiting N-methyl-D-aspartate receptor-mediated calcium influx. *Proc Natl Acad Sci USA,* 1998 95, 2642-7.

Obrenovitch, TP; Urenjak, J. Altered glutamatergic transmission in neurological disorders: from high extracellular glutamate to excessive synaptic efficacy. *Prog Neurobiol,* 1997 51, 39-87.

O'Brien, WT; Harper, AD; Jové, F; Woodgett, JR; Maretto, S; Piccolo, S; Klein, PS. Glycogen synthase kinase-3beta haploinsufficiency mimics the behavioral and molecular effects of lithium. *J Neurosci,* 2004 24, 6791-8.

Öngür, D; Jensen, JE; Prescot, AP; Stork, C; Lundy, M; Cohen, BM; Renshaw, PF. Abnormal glutamatergic neurotransmission and neuronal-glial interactions in acute mania. *Biol Psychiatry*, 2008 64, 718-26.

Ozbek, Z; Kucukali, CI; Ozkok, E; Orhan, N; Aydin, M; Kilic, G; Sazci, A; Kara, I. Effect of the methylenetetrahydrofolate reductase gene polymorphisms on homocysteine, folate and vitamin B12 in patients with bipolar disorder and relatives. *Prog Neuropsychopharmacol Biol Psychiatry*, 2008 32, 1331-7.

Pacher, P; Nivorozhkin, A; Szabó, C. Therapeutic effects of xanthine oxidase inhibitors: renaissance halfa century after the discovery of allopurinol. *Pharmacol Rev*, 2006 58, 87–114.

Pan, JQ; Lewis, MC; Ketterman, JK; Clore, EL; Riley, M; Richards, KR; Berry-Scott, E; Liu, X; Wagner, FF; Holson, EB; Neve, RL; Biechele, TL; Moon, RT; Scolnick, EM; Petryshen, TL; Haggarty, SJ. AKT Kinase Activity Is Required for Lithium to Modulate Mood-Related Behaviors in Mice. *Neuropsychopharmacology*, 2011 36, 1397-411.

Pap, M; Cooper, GM. Role of glycogen synthase kinase-3 in the phosphatidylinositol 3-Kinase/Akt cell survival pathway. *J Biol Chem*, 1998 273, 19929-32.

Park, MJ; Lee, SK; Lima, MA; Chung, HS; Cho, SI; Jang, CG; Lee, SM. Effect of alpha-tocopherol and deferoxamine on methamphetamine-induced neurotoxicity. *Brain Res,* 2006 1109, 176-82.

Phiel, CJ; Zhang, F; Huang, EY; Guenther, MG; Lazar, MA; Klein, PS. Histone deacetylase is a direct target of valproic acid, a potent anticonvulsant, mood stabilizer, and teratogen. *J Biol Chem*, 2001 276, 36734-41.

Polter, A; Beurel, E; Yang, S; Garner, R; Song, L; Miller, CA; Sweatt, JD; McMahon, L; Bartolucci, AA; Li, X; Jope, RS. Deficiency in the inhibitory serine-phosphorylation of glycogen synthase kinase-3 increases sensitivity to mood disturbances. *Neuropsychopharmacology*, 2010 35, 1761-74.

Quiroz, JA; Gray, NA; Kato, T; Manji, HK. Mitochondrially mediated plasticity in the pathophysiology and treatment of bipolar disorder. *Neuropsychopharmacology*, 2008 33, 2551-65.

Rao, JS; Harry, GJ; Rapoport, SI; Kim, HW. Increased excitotoxicity and neuroinflammatory markers in postmortem frontal cortex from bipolar disorder patients. *Mol Psychiatry,* 2010 15, 384-92.

Riegel, RE; Valvassori, SS; Moretti, M; Ferreira, CL; Steckert, AV; de Souza, B; Dal-Pizzol, F; Quevedo, J. Intracerebroventricularouabain administration induces oxidative stress in the rat brain. *Int J Dev Neurosci*, 2010 28, 233-7.

Roh, MS; Kang, UG; Shin, SY; Lee, YH; Jung, HY; Juhnn, YS; Kim, YS. Biphasic changes in the Ser-9 phosphorylation of glycogen synthase kinase-3beta after electroconvulsive shock in the rat brain. *Prog Neuropsychopharmacol Biol Psychiatry*, 2003 27, 1-5.

Rosa, AR; Fountoulakis, K; Siamouli, M; Gonda, X; Vieta, E. Is anticonvulsant treatment of mania a class effect? Data from randomized clinical trials. *CNS Neurosci Ther*, 2011 17, 167-77.

Rowe, MK; Wiest, C; Chuang, DM. GSK-3 is a viable potential target for therapeutic intervention in bipolar disorder. *Neurosci Biobehav Rev,* 2007 31 920-31.

Rucklidge, JJ; Gately, D; Kaplan, BJ. Database analysis of children and adolescents with bipolar disorder consuming a micronutrient formula. *BMC Psychiatry*, 2010 10, 74.

Rucklidge, JJ; Harrison, R. Successful treatment of bipolar disorder II and ADHD with a micronutrient formula: a case study. *CNS Spectr*, 2010 15, 289-95.

Sabioni, P; Baretta, IP; Ninomiya, EM; Gustafson, L; Rodrigues, ALS; Andreatini, R. The antimanic-like effect of tamoxifen: Behavioural comparison with other PKC-inhibiting and antiestrogenic drugs. *Prog Neuropsychopharmacol Biol Psychiatry*, 2008 32, 1927-31.

Santini, V; Gozzini, A; Ferrari, G. Histone deacetylase inhibitors: Molecular and biological activity as a premise to clinical application. *Curr Drug Metab,* 2007 8, 383-93.

Sawyer, DA; Julia, HL; Turin, AC. Caffeine and human behavior: arousal, anxiety, and performance effects. *J Behav Med,* 1982 5, 415–39.

Scarna, A; Gijsman, HJ; McTavish, SF; Harmer, CJ; Cowen, PJ; Goodwin, GM. Effects of a branched-chain amino acid drink in mania. *Br J Psychiatry,* 2003 182, 210-3.

Schroeder, FA; Lin, CL; Crusio, WE; Akbarian, S. Antidepressant-like effects of the histone deacetylase inhibitor, sodium butyrate, in the mouse. *Biol Psychiatry*, 2007 62, 55-64.

Schroeder, FA; Penta, KL; Matevossian, A; Jones, SR; Konradi, C; Tapper, AR; Akbarian, S. Drug-induced activation of dopamine D(1) receptor signaling and inhibition of class I/II histone deacetylase induce chromatin remodeling in reward circuitry and modulate cocaine-related behaviors. *Neuropsychopharmacology*, 2008 33, 2981-92.

Segal, M; Avital, A; Drobot, M; Lukanin, A; Derevenski, A; Sandbank, S; Weizman, A. CK levels in unmedicated bipolar patients. *Eur Neuropsychopharmacol*, 2007 17, 763-7.

Siegfried, E; Chou, T; Perrimon, N. wingless signaling acts through zeste-white 3, the Drosophila homolog of glycogen synthase kinase-3, to regulate engrailed and establish cell fate. *Cell*, 1992 71, 1167-79.

Soares, JC; Chen, G; Dippold, CS; Wells, KF; Frank, E; Kupfer, DJ; Manji, HK; Mallinger, AG. Concurrent measures of protein kinase C and phosphoinositides in lithium-treated bipolar patients and healthy individuals: a preliminary study. *Psychiatry Res*, 2000 95, 109-18.

Stambolic, V; Ruel, L; Woodgett, JR. Lithium inhibits glycogen synthase kinase-3 activity and mimics wingless signalling in intact cells. *Curr Biol,* 1996 6, 1664-8.

Steckert, AV; Valvassori, SS; Moretti, M; Dal-Pizzol, F; Quevedo, J. Role of oxidative stress in the pathophysiology of bipolar disorder. *Neurochem Res*, 2010 35, 1295-301.

Stork, C; Renshaw, PF. Mitochondrial dysfunction in bipolar disorder: evidence from magnetic resonance spectroscopy research. *Mol Psychiatry*, 2005 10, 900–19.

Streck, EL; Amboni, G; Scaini, G; Di-Pietro, PB; Rezin, GT; Valvassori, SS; Luz, G; Kapczinski, F; Quevedo, J. Brain creatine kinase activity in an animal model of mania. *Life Sci*, 2008 82, 424-9.

Sutherland, C; Cohen, P. The alpha-isoform of glycogen synthase kinase-3 from rabbit skeletal muscle is inactivated by p70 S6 kinase or MAP kinase-activated protein kinase-1 in vitro. *FEBS Lett,* 1994 338, 37-42.

Tanaka, C; Nishizuka, Y. The protein kinase C family for neuronal signaling. *Annu Rev Neurosci,* 1994 17, 551–67.

Tanji, C; Yamamoto, H; Yorioka, N; Kohno, N; Kikuchi, K; Kikuchi, A. A-kinase anchoring protein AKAP220 binds to glycogen synthase kinase-3beta (GSK-3beta) and mediates protein kinase A-dependent inhibition of GSK-3beta. *J Biol Chem*, 2002 277, 36955-61.

Tsankova, N; Renthal, W; Kumar, A; Nestler, EJ. Epigenetic regulation in psychiatric disorders. *Nat Rev*, 2007 8, 355–67.

Valvassori, SS; Petronilho, FC; Réus, GZ; Steckert, AV; Oliveira, VB; Boeck, CR; Kapczinski, F; Dal-Pizzol, F; Quevedo, J. Effect of N-acetylcysteine and/or deferoxamine on oxidative stress and hyperactivity in an animal model of mania. *Prog Neuropsychopharmacol Biol Psychiatry*, 2008 15 32, 1064-8.

Valvassori, SS; Rezin, GT; Ferreira, CL; Moretti, M; Gonçalves, CL; Cardoso, MR; Streck, EL; Kapczinski, F; Quevedo, J. Effects of mood stabilizers on mitochondrial respiratory chain activity in brain of rats treated with d-amphetamine. *J Psychiatr Res,* 2010 44, 903-9.

Vawter, MP; Tomita, H; Meng, F; Bolstad, B; Evans, S; Choudary, P; Atz, M; Shao, L; Neal, C; Walsh, DM; Burmeister, M; Speed, T; Myers, R; Jones, EG; Watson, SJ; Akil, H; Bunney, WE. Mitochondrial-related gene expression changes are sensitive to agonal-pH state: implications for brain disorders. *Mol Psychiatry*, 2006 11, 663-79.

Vecsey, CG; Hawk, JD; Lattal, KM; Stein, JM; Fabian SA; Attner, MA; Cabrera, SM; McDonough, CB; Brindle PK; Abel, T; Wood, MA. Histone deacetylase inhibitors enhance memory and synaptic plasticity via CREB: CBP dependent transcriptional activation. *J Neurosci*, 2007 27, 6128-40.

Verkhratsky, A; Kirchhoff, F. NMDA Receptors in glia. *Neuroscientist*, 2007 13, 28-37.

Versiani, M; Cheniaux, E; Landeira-Fernandez, J. Efficacy and Safety of Electroconvulsive Therapy in the Treatment of Bipolar Disorder A Systematic Review. *Journal of Ect*, 2011 27, 153-64.

Waldeck, B. Effect of caffeine on locomotor activity and central catecholamine mechanisms: a study with special references to drug interaction. *Acta Pharmacol Toxicol*, 1975 36, 1-23.

Wan, FJ; Tung, CS; Shiah, IS; Lin, HC. Effects of alpha-phenyl-N-tert-butyl nitrone and Nacetylcysteine on hydroxyl radical formation and dopamine depletion in the rat striatum produced by d-amphetamine. *Eur Neuropsychopharmacol*, 2006 16, 147–53.

Wang, HY; Friedman, E. Enhanced protein kinase C activity and translocation in bipolar affective disorder brains. *Biol Psychiatry*, 1996 40, 568-75.

Wang, HY; Friedman, E. Lithium inhibition of protein kinase C activation-induced serotonin release. *Psychopharmacology*, 1989 99, 213-8.

Watkins, JC; Evans, RH. Excitatory Amino Acid Transmitters. *Ann Rev Pharmacol Toxicol,* 1981 21, 165-204.

Watson, DG; Watterson, JM; Lenox, RH. Sodium valproate down-regulates the myristoylated alanine-rich C kinase substrate (MARCKS) in immortalized hippocampal cells: a property of protein kinase C-mediated mood stabilizers. *J Pharmacol Exp Ther*, 1998 285, 307-16.

Winslow, BT; Onysko, MK; Stob, CM; Hazlewood, KA. Treatment of Alzheimer disease. *Am Fam Physician*, 2011 83, 1403-12.

Woo, TU; Walsh, JP; Benes, FM. Density of Glutamic Acid Decarboxylase 67 Messenger RNA–Containing Neurons That Express the N-Methyl-D-Aspartate Receptor Subunit NR2A in the Anterior Cingulate Cortex in Schizophrenia and Bipolar Disorder. *Arch Gen Psychiatry*, 2004 61, 649-57.

Woodgett, JR. cDNA cloning and properties of glycogen synthase kinase-3. *Methods Enzymol*, 1991 200, 564-77.

Woodgett, JR. Molecular cloning and expression of glycogen synthase kinase-3/factor A. *EMBO J*, 1990 9, 2431-8.

Wu, X; Chen, PS; Dallas, S; Wilson, B; Block, ML; Wang, CC; Kinyamu, H; Lu, N; Gao, X; Leng, Y; Chuang, DM; Zhang, W; Lu, RB; Hong, JS. Histone deacetylase inhibitors up-regulate astrocyte GDNF and BDNF gene transcription and protect dopaminergic neurons. *Int J Neuropsychopharmacol*, 2008 11, 1123-34.

Yatham, LN; Liddle, PF; Lam, RW; Shiah, IS; Lane, C; Stoessl, AJ; Sossi, V; Ruth, TJ. PET study of the effects of valproate on dopamine D(2) receptors in neuroleptic- and mood-stabilizer-naive patients with nonpsychotic mania. *Am J Psychiatry*, 2002 159, 1718-23.

Yildiz, A; Guleryuz, S; Ankerst, DP; Ongür, D; Renshaw, PF. Protein kinase C inhibition in the treatment of mania: a double-blind; placebo-controlled trial of tamoxifen. *Arch Gen Psychiatry*, 2008 65, 255-63.

Yumru, M; Savas, H; Kalenderoglu, A; Bulut, M; Celik, H; Erel, O. Oxidative imbalance in bipolar disorder subtypes: a comparative study. *Prog Neuropsychopharmacol Biol Psychiatry,* 2009 33, 1070-4.

Zarate, C Jr; Machado-Vieira, R; Henter, I; Ibrahim, L; Diazgranados, N; Salvadore, G. Glutamatergic modulators: the future of treating mood disorders? *Harv Rev Psychiatry.* 2010 18, 293-303.

Zwyguizen-Doorenbos, A; Roehrs, T; Lipschutz, L; Timms, V; Roth, T. Effects of caffeine on alertness. *Psychopharmacology*, 1990 100, 36-9.

In: Advances in Psychology Research. Volume 88
Editor: Alexandra M. Columbus, pp. 25-48
ISBN: 978-1-62100-591-9

Chapter 2

SOCIAL ASPECTS OF MOOD DISORDERS

Tahany M. Gadalla*
Factor-Inwentash Faculty of Social Work, University of Toronto,
Toronto, Ontario, Canada.

ABSTRACT

Mood disorders are among the most prevalent mental disorders with almost twice as many women as men afflicted by them. They can lead to occupational impairment, disruption in interpersonal and family relationships, poor health and suicide. Thus, they represent a significant burden to individuals and society. Moreover, although effective interventions for the treatment of mood disorders are available, most individuals who suffer from them do not seek medical treatment.

In this chapter, data from nationally representative surveys are used to identify demographic and socioeconomic factors associated with mood disorders. Secondly, the comorbidity of mood disorders with other psychological conditions, e.g. eating disorders and with chronic physical illness are examined. Thirdly, effects of mood disorders, alone and in combination with anxiety disorders and/or physical illness on functional disability and quality of life are studied. Specifically, the hypothesis of a socioeconomic gradient in disability associated with mood disorders is explored. Lastly, Barriers to seeking medical help for mood disorders are examined and identified.

INTRODUCTION

Mood disorders are among the most common mental disorders in the general population. They include major depression, bipolar disorder, dysthymic disorder and perinatal depression. The 12-month prevalence and the lifetime prevalence of mood disorders in the US were estimated at 9.5% and 18.1% (Kessler et al., 2005). In Canada, 6.3% of women and 4.2% of men reported symptoms that met the criteria for a mood disorder in 2002 while 16.1% of

* Corresponding author: Tahany M Gadalla, MMath, MSc, PhD, Associate Professor, Factor-Inwentash Faculty of Social Work, University of Toronto, 246 Bloor Street West, Toronto, Ontario, Canada M5S 1A1, Telephone: (416) 946-0623, Email: tahany.gadalla@utoronto.ca

women and 10.5% of men reported having such symptoms at some point in their lifetime (Gadalla, 2008a).

Among mood disorders, major depression is the most prevalent in the population. Estimates from the US National Comorbidity Survey indicated that 17.1% of the population suffered from at least one major depressive episode at some point in their lives, and 10.3% had experienced one or more depressive episodes in the previous 12 months (Kessler et al., 2005). In Canada, an estimated 4.8% of Canadians aged 15 and over experienced at least one such episose in 2002 with almost twice as many women as men suffering from this debilitating condition (Statistics Canada, 2002). Reported estimates of lifetime dysthymic disorder range between 3% and 6% (Bland, 1997). About 10% of women experience depression during pregnancy while 10-15% experience it after giving birth (Herrick, 2002; Seyfried & Marcus, 2003).

Reasons for the discrepancy among reported prevalence rates of mood and anxiety disorders include the use of different methods to measure prevalence. Such methods range between self-report, diagnostic instruments and clinical assessment. Another reason for the discrepancy in reported rates is the number and type of specific disorders included in the reported prevalence. A third reason is the use of different reference time duration used by different researchers.

DEMOGRAPHIC AND SOCIOECONOMIC CORRELATES OF MOOD DISORDERS

Being female, having poor physical health, inadequate social support, poor socioeconomic conditions, lone parenthood, stress and traumatic and negative life events have been indicated as risk factors for depression (Leskela et al., 2004; Starkes et al., 2005; Stewart et al., 2004; Takeuchi et al., 1998). Research findings in many developed countries show that approximately twice as many women as men experience depression (Bierut et al., 1999; Weissman et al., 1996). Psychosocial factors such as different social roles, lower self-esteem and less favorable economic conditions (Stewart et al., 2004) as well as biological factors (Mazure et al., 2002) have been suggested as causes for the higher prevalence of depression among women.

An association between lower socioeconomic conditions and the prevalence of depression has been reported (Gadalla, 2008b; Hudson, 2005; Skapinakis et al, 2006; Vetter et al, 2006). In a meta analysis of the research conducted on socioeconomic status and depression (Lorant et al., 2003), the authors found the odds of reporting depression for people in the lower socioeconomic strata to be about 1.81 times higher than those in the higher socioeconomic strata. They also reported a dose response relation between depression and each of education and income levels. Similar results have been found in a national sample of South Africans (Myer, Stein, Grimsrud, Seedat, & Williams, 2008), a national sample of the Norway population (Dalgard, Mykletun, Rognerud, Johansen, & Zahl, 2007) and in a national sample of Finns (Talala, Huurre, Aro, Martelin, & Prattala, 2008).

Lorant and colleagues (2003) also reported a strong relationship between socioeconomic status and the course of depression, whereby once depressed, individuals at lower socioeconomic levels were almost twice as likely to persist in depression compared with

depressed individuals at higher socioeconomic levels. Goosby (2007) found that mothers' sense of mastery and depressive symptoms mediated the relationship between the duration of time they spent in poverty and their adolescent children's depressive symptoms. Hudson (2005) found a strong correlation between poor socioeconomic status and higher risk for mental disability and psychiatric hospitalization that was significant regardless of the particular indicator of socioeconomic status or type of mental illness examined.

Historically, two hypotheses have been used to explain the direction of the causal relationship between socioeconomic conditions and mental disorders, the social causation hypothesis, whereby unfavorable socioeconomic conditions increase the risk of depression and the selection hypothesis, whereby genetically predisposed depression leads to a downward drift in socioeconomic conditions (Wadsworth & Achenbach, 2005). For example, Ritcher and colleagues (2001) found low parental education to be associated with increased risk for offspring depression, even after controlling for parental depression, offspring gender and offspring age while neither parental nor offspring depression predicted later levels of offspring occupation, education or income. Dembling et al (2002), on the other hand, suggested that mentally ill individuals gravitated to low income communities as a result of their disability. In a 30-year longitudinal study of a British birth cohort, Power and colleagues (2002) found that both childhood and adulthood factors were involved in the development of a socio-economic gradient in psychological distress, which was not due to selection effects.

Other studies pointed to an interactive and reciprocal relationship with socioeconomic conditions influencing depression, which in turn, influences socioeconomic conditions. For example, Weich and Lewis (1998) combined elements of both hypotheses by acknowledging the genetic predisposition of mental illness and focusing on the role of socioeconomic conditions in triggering these predispositions or moderating their severity. These authors found that poverty and unemployment increased the duration of common mental disorders but did not trigger their initial occurrence. Recent reviews of epidemiological research indicate that the complexity of the causal pathways between socioeconomic factors and mental disorders, particularly depression, requires the inclusion of factors from both the social causation and selection hypotheses (Sullivan et al, 2000) and the use of multivariate, causal models that allow for the simultaneous estimation of reciprocal effects (Hudson, 2005).

Research evidence suggests that work stress as measured by high job demands combined with low control and low social support in the workplace are associated with elevated risk of depression and psychological distress (De Lange et al., 2004; Elovainio et al., 2007; Mathews et al, 2001; Power et al., 2002). Higher level of chronic stress was positively correlated with the prevalence of depression in the Canadian population (Gadalla, 2008b).

Poor physical health has also been associated with elevated risk of depression. Individuals' physical health and mental health are inextricably intertwined.

In Canada, in 2002, an individual with a chronic physical condition was twice as likely as an individual without such a condition to have a mood disorder (Statistics Canada, 2002). Depression often accompanies chronic illnesses such as heart disease, stroke, Parkinson's disease, cancer and HIV/AIDS (Evans et al, 2005).

Comorbidity between Mood Disorders and Physical Illness

Findings from comorbidity studies show the prevalence of mood disorders in individuals with chronic physical illness to be noticeably high compared to individuals with no such illness. Most of these studies, however, used clinical samples, which may lead to biased results. Clinical-based studies are vulnerable to several sources of sampling bias especially when studying patients with multiple health problems since these patients may seek treatment for either problem and thus, are more likely than patients with one health problem to be found in clinical settings (Berkson, 1946). Thus, comorbidity rates obtained in clinical studies may over estimate the actual comorbidity in the population. In addition, only in population-based samples can the whole range of symptom severity of psychiatric disorders be represented. Thus, researchers have highlighted the role of population-based studies in assessing the extent and nature of comorbidity between mental disorders and physical illness (Dansky et al., 2000).

Ferketich and colleagues(2000) analyzed data collected in a National longitudinal study and found that depressed men had a 71% greater risk of developing heart disease and were 2.34 times more likely than non-depressed men to die from this condition. Individuals with physical health problems often experience anxiety or depression, which affects their response to the treatment of their physical illness. On the other hand, individuals with mental illness can develop physical symptoms and illnesses, such as weight loss and biological disturbances associated with eating disorders.

In another population study and based on representative sample of individuals living in the province of Ontario, Canada, Gadalla (2008c) examined the relationship between socio-demographic characteristics and mood disorders in Ontarians with chronic physical conditions. Results indicate that individuals with chronic fatigue syndrome, fibromyalgia, bowel disorder or stomach or intestinal ulcers had the highest rates of mood disorders. The proportion of physically ill Canadians with mood disorders ranged from a minimum of 8% in individuals with high blood pressure to a maximum of 37% in individuals diagnosed with chronic fatigue syndrome (Gadalla, 2008b). The prevalence of mood disorders among men with chronic physical illness was 6.5% compared with 1.9% among men with no such illness. The prevalence of mood disorders among women with chronic physical illness was 10.5% compared with 3.8% among women with no chronic physical illness (Gadalla, 2008c). Individuals with comorbid mood disorders were more likely to be female, middle aged, poor, without a partner and born in Canada. These characteristics are similar to those of depressed individuals in the general population (Patten, 2000).

A bidirectional relationship between mood disorders and chronic physical illness that may explain their high comorbidity has been proposed (Evans et al., 2005). A diagnosis of a disabling physical illness and the associated decline in physical health may cause enough distress to trigger a depressive episode in vulnerable persons. On the other hand, research is discovering that depression itself may act as a risk factor for a variety of chronic illnesses. Goodman and Whitaker (2002) noted that patients with major depression had higher rates of unhealthy behaviors such as smoking and over-eating, which may lead to higher incidence of diabetes and heart disease. Depression has also been shown to be an independent risk factor for type 2 diabetes mellitus (Kawakami et al., 1999). Perretta and colleagues (1998) suggested that depression and mania may act as risk factors for HIV infection by promoting high-risk

behaviors. Large population studies indicate that depressed mood or stressful life events may increase the risk of cancer (Evans et al., 2005). In addition, the presence of depression can hinder compliance to treatment and weaken cognitive function, thus, adversely affect patients' prognosis and increase their morbidity. Ample research has focused on trying to understand the mechanisms of the relationship between depression and cardiovascular disease. In addition to promoting unhealthy behaviors and noncompliance with cardiac rehabilitation and medical regimens, some of the possible biologic mechanisms that may explain the increased risk associated with depression in heart disease patients are that depressed patients have decreased heart rate variability (Gormen and Sloan, 2000), increased platelet aggregation (Whyte et al., 2001) and higher levels of inflammatory risk markers (Miller et al., 2002). Other mood disorders may also act as risk factors for physical illnesses and/or adversely affect their prognosis; however, the underlying mechanisms are not as extensively researched as those of depression.

Comorbidity between Mood Disorders and Eating Disorders

The comorbidity of depression with eating disorders has also been the focus of a large number of research studies, most of which have reported high prevalence of depression in eating disordered individuals, and vise versa (e.g. Blinder et al., 2006, Courbasson et al, 2005; Geist et al., 1998; Godart et al., 2007). In a review of the literature on comorbidity of eating disorders and mood disorders, Godart and colleagues (2007) found that reported lifetime prevalence of depression ranged between 9.5% and 64.7% in restrictive anorexia patients and between 50% and 71.3% in patients having anorexia with bulimia subtype.

In a sample of 120 treatment-seeking Canadian adolescents with a range of eating disorder diagnoses, 45% were diagnosed with recurrent depression (Geist et al., 1998). In another sample of 135 male patients with eating disorders, 54% had lifetime diagnosis of depression (Carlat et al., 1997). Blinder and colleagues (2006) on the other hand, reported much higher rate of depression (86%) in female inpatients across all patterns of eating disorders.

Elevated levels of mood disorders in individuals with eating disorders have also been found in community-based samples (e.g. Dansky et al., 1998; Grucza et al., 2007; Telch and Stice, 1989). Significant associations between eating disorders and depression has been reported in men have been reported (Woodside et al., 2001). In another community-based sample of men and women, those who screened positive for binge eating disorder had significantly higher odds of depression compared with controls (Grucza et al., 2007). Significant association between eating disorders and depression has been found for both men and women in other community samples (John et al., 2006; Schuckit et al., 1996). In a national sample of US women, 36% of those meeting the criteria for bulimia nervosa, also met the criteria for a lifetime depression diagnosis (Dansky et al., 1998). Reviewing the literature on the association of mood disorders and eating disorders, Godart and colleagues (2007) concluded that in community samples, the lifetime prevalence of depression was 2.6 to 4 times higher in individuals with anorexia nercosa than that found in controls.

Gadalla (2008a) analyzed data from a national survey to explore the comorbidity of disordered eating symptomatology and selected mood disorders in adult men (N=16,773) and women (N=20,211). The author found both men and women with disordered eating symptomatology to have significantly elevated odds for major depression. The one-year prevalence of manic episodes was associated with risk of eating disorders for women but not for men. Being at risk for eating disorders was significantly associated with lifetime depression, manic episodes in women, and with lifetime depression in men.

COMORBIDITY BETWEEN MOOD DISORDERS AND OBESITY

In a review of four longitudinal studies and 20 cross-sectional studies of the effects of obesity on depression, Atlantis and Baker (2008) found longitudinal studies to provide consistent evidence that obesity may increase the odds of future depression or depressive symptoms. They also found most cross-sectional studies from the US to support the above association for women but not men. In contrast most cross-sectional studies from populations other than the US consistently failed to find such associations. On the other hand, Blaine (2008) conducted a meta-analysis of 16 longitudinal studies of the effect of depression on obesity in a meta-analysis. In five of the 16 studies, initial depression lead to weight loss but this association was statistically significant in only one study. After controlling for baseline body mass index (BMI) and background variables, depressed adults were at significantly higher risk for developing later obesity (OR=1.08) and the risk was particularly high for adolescent females (OR=2.57) compared to non-depressed people (Blaine, 2008). Yet, some studies found the relationship between obesity and depression non-significant (e.g. Faith et al., 2002) or positive (e.g. Jorm et al., 2003). Bruffaerts and colleagues (2008) analysed data from six European countries and found that obese individuals were more likely to have mood disorder (OR=1.3) compared with individuals of adequate weight. Similar findings were reported by Petry and colleagues (2008).

Scott and colleagues (2008) found obesity to be significantly associated with any mood disorder (OR=1.23), major depressive disorder (OR=1.27). However, when they adjusted for the comorbidity between anxiety and mood disorders, the association between obesity and anxiety disorders remained significant (OR=1.36) but the association between obesity and mood disorders became statistically insignificant (OR=1.05) (Scott et al., 2008). Similarly, Simon and colleagues (2006) found obesity to be associated with an approximately 25% increase in odds of mood and anxiety disorders.

Prior research also indicated that individual's socio-demographic characteristics moderated the relationship of obesity with mental disorders, especially that with mood disorders (Scott et al., 2008). McLaren and colleagues (2008) found the association between obesity and mental disorders to vary by type and severity of mental illness and by gender and age. For example, mood disorders were elevated among obese women compared to women of normal weight while subclinical depression was reduced among obese men compared to normal weight men and to women (McLaren et al., 2008). On the other hand, Simon and colleagues (2006) found no gender differences in the association between obesity and mood and anxiety disorders, but noted differences across racial groups and education levels. Gender

difference in the relationship between relative body weight and depression was also reported by Carpenter and colleagues (2003) who examined data on over 40,000 US adults and found a significant positive association between BMI and depression in women and a significant negative association in men. In the latter study, however, the authors compared prevalence of depression in obese persons to that in persons of normal or overweight. Yet, other researchers did not find such gender differences (e.g. Carr et al., 2007; Dong et al., 2004; Simon et al., 2006). Based on a review of the literature on the obesity-mood disorders relationship, McElroy and colleagues (2004) suggested that obesity is associated with depression in women while abdominal obesity may be associated with depression in both men and women. These findings highlight the importance of examining the relationship between obesity and each type of mental disorders separately while taking individual's socio-demographic characteristics into account.

Gadalla (2009a) reported that after controlling for demographic, socioeconomic and behavioural characteristics associated with obesity, the odds of obesity among those with mood disorders was 1.50 folds compared with the odds of obesity in those with no mental illness. The author also reported slight gender differences in the association between obesity and mood disorders. Adjusting for relevant socio-demographic and economic characteristics, the likelihood of obesity in women with mood disorders was 1.48 (95% CI=1.30, 1.68, $p<0.005$) and in men with mood disorders was 1.50. Additionally, after controlling for relevant demographic and socioeconomic factors, the odds of being overweight in persons with mood disorders were 1.23 times that in persons with no mental illness ($p<0.0005$).

A few conceptual models explaining the observed associations between obesity and mood disorders have been proposed. One explanation highlights the role of poor physical health, increased functional limitations and interpersonal stressors (Schwartz et al., 2003) experienced by obese persons as mediators in the obesity-poor mental health relationship. For example, Carr and colleagues (2007) reported that once these physical and interpersonal stressors were controlled for, obese persons had better psychological health, compared with persons of normal weight. A theoretical model, which stipulates a bidirectional causal pathway between obesity and depression and defines potential behavioral, cognitive, physiological, and social mediators, has also suggested (Markowitz et al., 2008). Additionally, a genetic susceptibility to both obesity and depression has been proposed, whereby both conditions share some common genes (Faith et al., 2002; Kendler et al., 1995; Stunkard et al., 2003). Stankard and colleagues (2003) emphasized the role of adverse childhood experiences in promoting both conditions. In their review of the literature on obesity and mood disorders, McIntyre and colleagues (2006) concluded that both conditions share aspects of phenomenology, comorbidity, family history and biology. More research examining this potential explanation is warranted.

The importance of comorbidy studies cannot be over-emphasized. Examination of comorbid psychiatric disorders in individuals with mood disorders is important because studies have shown that those with multiple disorders tend to have a worse prognosis, longer episodes and are less responsive to treatment. Further, they tend to be at increased risk for engaging in parasuicidal behaviours and suicide attempts (Wildman et al., 2004).

Association between Mood Disorders and Self-Reported Disability

Untreated, mental illness can lead to occupational impairment, disruption in interpersonal and family relationships, poor health and suicide (Kessler et al., 1998; Simon et al., 2001). As discussed above, research evidence show that individuals with mood disorders develop physical illness at higher rates compared with individuals with no such disorders. Additionally, the high prevalence of major depression in individuals 15-44 years old (Gadalla, 2008b) and its associated negative impact on their educational attainment and work productivity increases its impact on the whole population (Simon et al., 2008). Thus, depression has been indicated as the primary cause of disability in the Canadian workforce (Dewa et al., 2004).

Using data from a nationally representative sample of individuals living in Canada, Gadalla (2009b) examined the associations between mood and/or anxiety disorders and short-term disability, limitations in activities of daily living and work activities. Results are shown in Table 1. To isolate the relationship of mood disorders and quality of life from that of anxiety disorders that individuals may have had, measures of disability and suicidal ideation were estimated for survey participants with and without anxiety disorders (Table 1). As shown in the table, having a mood and/or anxiety disorders was significantly associated with short-term disability, requiring help with basic daily activities and reduction/modification in work activities was similar for men and women, albeit slightly stronger for men (Table 1).

Table 1[1]. Adjusted odds ratios of the relation between mood and anxiety disorders and disability and quality of life by gender

Mental disorder	Disability days in last 2 weeks(1) (95% CI)	Needed help with daily activities(2) (95% CI)	Reduced/modified work activity(3) (95% CI)
Women			
Sample size	58,135	58,135	34,263
Neither disorder	1	1	1
Any mood disorder	2.21*** (2.03, 2.41)	2.62*** (2.39, 2.87)	2.89*** (2.42, 3.45)
Any anxiety disorder	1.68*** (1.51, 1.87)	1.96*** (1.74, 2.21)	2.00*** (1.55, 2.57)
Mood and anxiety	3.16*** (2.83, 3.54)	4.48*** (3.95, 5.08)	5.58*** (4.51, 6.89)
Men			
Sample size	50,851	50,851	35,430
Neither disorder	1	1	1
Any mood disorder	2.80***(2.50, 3.13)	3.23*** (2.81, 3.66)	3.54*** (2.89, 4.33)
Any anxiety disorder	1.54*** (1.33, 1.79)	2.45*** (2.07, 2.90)	1.55** (1.16, 2.09)
Mood and anxiety	4.13*** (3.54, 4.82)	5.49*** (4.61, 6.54)	6.34*** (4.87, 8.26)

[1]Published with permission from Gadalla (2009b)

(1) Whether the participant stayed in bed for all or most of the day due to physical or emotional health issue during the two weeks prior to the interview

(2) Whether the participant required help with their usual daily activities, such as preparing meals, shopping for groceries and other necessities, getting to appointments, doing everyday housework, personal care or moving about inside their home.

(3) Whether the participants often had to reduce or modify their work activities because of health issues.

** p<0.005, *** P<0.0005.

The odds ratios presented in Table 1 were adjusted for age, marital status, income level, education level, immigration status and number of chronic physical conditions. Overall, for women, having a mood disorder was associated with more than double the odds of having disability days (OR=2.21, $p<0.0005$), 2.62 times ($p<0.0005$) the odds of requiring help with basic daily activities and almost triple (OR=2.89, $p<0.0005$) the odds of reducing/modifying work activities. Having an anxiety disorder was associated with a significant increases in the risk of disability (OR=1.68, $p<0.0005$), double the odds of requiring help with basic daily activities (OR=1.96, $p<0.0005$) and increases the risk of having to modify/reduce work activities (OR=2.00, $p<0.0005$). In men, having mood disorders was associated with significant increases in the odds of having disability days (OR=2.80, $p<0.0005$), the odds of requiring help with daily activities (OR=3.23, $p<0.0005$) and the odds of having to reduce or modify their work activities (OR=3.54, $p<0.0005$).

The likelihood of disability days, limitations in activities of daily living and reduction/modification of work activities were much higher in persons with both mood and anxiety disorders than in those with either anxiety or mood disorders alone. Women who suffered from both mood and anxiety disorders were three times more likely to have disability days (OR=3.16, $p<0.0005$), more than four times more likely to need help with basic activities of daily living (OR=4.48, $p<0.0005$) and almost six times more likely to reduce/modify their work activities compared with women with neither disorders (OR=5.58, $p<0.0005$). For men, the corresponding odds were 4.13, 5.49 and 6.34 respectively and were all highly significant ($p<0.0005$).

Disability Associated with Mood Disorders in Individuals with Physical Illness

High prevalence of mood disorders among individuals with chronic physical conditions represents a significant burden to individuals and society. At the individual level, mood disorders amplify the disability associated with the physical condition and adversely affect its course, thus, leading to occupational impairment, disruption in interpersonal and family relationships, poor health and suicide(Olfson and Klerman, 1992) Most of the research done in this field focuses on the impact of depression on quality of life after adjusting for the severity of physical illness (e.g. Vali and Walkup, 1998; Ades et al., 2002) rather than comparing the impact of comorbid mental disorders in individuals with and without physical illness. These studies usually find that depression adversely affect patients' quality of life after adjusting for severity of physical illness.

Simon and colleagues (2001) compared functional impairment on a clinical sample of depressed patients with and without chronic physical illness and concluded that depression and chronic physical illness produced differing patterns of impairment, and that comorbid depression created a substantial burden of additional functional impairment. Katon (2003) estimated medical costs for patients with major depression to be almost 50% higher than the costs of chronic physical illness alone. The associations between other mood disorders such as bipolar disorder or dysthymia and physical illness and their effect on the quality of life of the physically ill have not been examined.

At the national level, comorbid mood disorders can adversely affect the economy through reduced productivity and higher health care costs. Several studies have investigated the impact of comorbid depression on the cost of health services using patients with specific physical conditions such as arthritis (Vali and Walkup, 1998). In a study of the economic burden of mental health in Canada, Stephens and Joubert (2001) estimated work-related productivity losses due to mood disorders alone to be $4.5 billion annually.

Gadalla (2008d) analyzed data collected in the 2005 Canadian Community Health Survey (21,198 women and 20,478 men) to assess the impact of mood disorders on short-term disability and suicidal ideation in individuals with chronic physical illness. In light of the reported high comorbidity between mood and anxiety disorders (Kessler et al., 1999), and to isolate the relationship of comorbid mood disorders with disability from that of any anxiety disorders that the participant may have had, measures of disability and suicidal ideation were estimated for survey participants with and without anxiety disorders (Table 2). The negative effects of comorbid mood disorders on the quality of life of individuals with chronic physical conditions were independent from the effects of anxiety disorders. For example, 41.3% of chronically ill women with any mood disorder had disability days in the two weeks prior to the interview compared with 21.8% of women with neither anxiety nor mood disorders. Having any mood disorder without any anxiety disorder was associated with an increase of 15.7% in the proportion of women requiring help with basic daily activities, and 7.4% in the proportion of women having suicidal thoughts. More women than men with mood disorders reported having disability days in the two weeks prior to the interview (41.3% of women and 36.4% of men). Also, more women (40.5%) reported requiring help with activities of daily help compared with only 32.5% of men. Yet, 11.1% percent of men with comorbid mood disorders reported having suicidal thoughts compared with 8.1% of women.

Table 2[1]. Associations among comorbid mood and anxiety disorders and quality of life of individuals with chronic physical conditions by gender, Ontario 2005

Comorbid mental disorder	Sample size	Disability days in last 2 weeks Number (%)	Need help with daily activities Number (%)	Suicidal thoughts Number (%)
Women				
Physical illness only	10,725	2,338 (21.8)	2,660 (24.8)	75 (0.7) §
Any mood disorder	879	363 (41.3)	356 (40.5)	71 (8.1) §
Any anxiety disorder	469	144 (30.6)	153 (32.6)	10 (2.1) §§
Mood and anxiety	439	218 (49.7)	220 (50.1)	83 (18.9)
Men				
Physical illness only	9,168	1,595 (17.4)	1,375 (15.0)	83 (0.9) §
Any mood disorder	442	161 (36.4)	144 (32.5)	49 (11.1) §
Any anxiety disorder	279	78 (28.1)	67 (23.9)	14 (5.0) §§
Mood and anxiety	209	114 (54.6)	91 (43.3)	47 22.5)

[1] Published with permission from Gadalla (2008d).

(1) Whether the participant stayed in bed for all or most of the day due to physical or emotional health issue during the two weeks prior to the interview

(2) Whether the participant required help with their usual daily activities, such as preparing meals, shopping for groceries and other necessities, getting to appointments, doing everyday housework, personal care or moving about inside their home.

§ Marginal estimate of the true national rate, i.e. coefficient of variation is between 16.5% and 33.3%

§§ Unreliable estimate of the true Ontario rate, i.e. coefficient of variation > 33.3%

Socioeconomic Gradient of Functional Limitations Associated with Mood Disorders

The association between unfavorable socioeconomic conditions and higher prevalence of mood disorders has been well-established (Fryers et al., 2003; Gadalla, 2008b; Hudson, 2005; Leskela et al., 2004; Lorant et al., 2007; Skapinakis et al., 2006). The detrimental impact of mood disorders on disability is also well-established (Dewa et al., 2004; Gadalla, 2009; WHO, 2004). Less is known about the socioeconomic gradient of disability in individuals with mood disorders.

Few studies have examined the relationship between socioeconomic conditions and the disability associated with mood disorders. Among them, Trivedi and colleagues (2006) examined factors associated with health-related quality of life in a sample of outpatients with major depression. They found a significant negative association between health-related quality of life and education and income levels even after controlling for age and symptom severity. Isacson and colleagues (2005) found the burden of depression, measured as the decrease in health utility, to be unevenly distributed among depressed individuals, with a higher burden in low income individuals. In their study, persons with depression were identified as those who reported feeling depressed on the day of the survey.

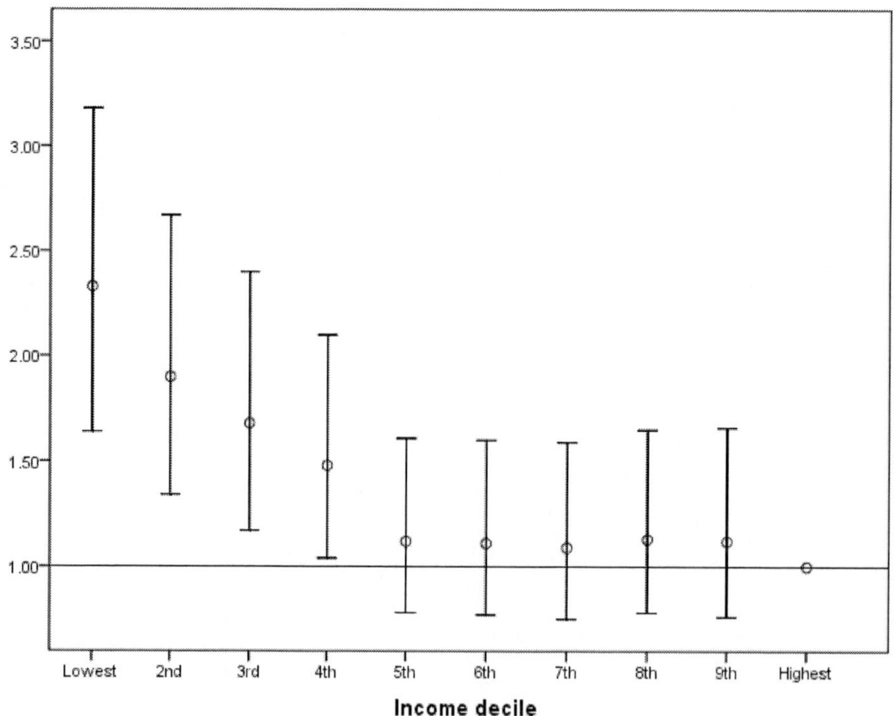

(1) Reprinted with permission from Gadalla (2009c)

(2) Odds ratios were adjusted for participant's age, marital status, number of chronic conditions and number of consultations with medical doctors.

Figure 1[(1)]. Adjusted[(2)] odds ratios and 95% confidence intervals (CI) for functional limitations by income decile for women with mood disorders, Canada 2005.

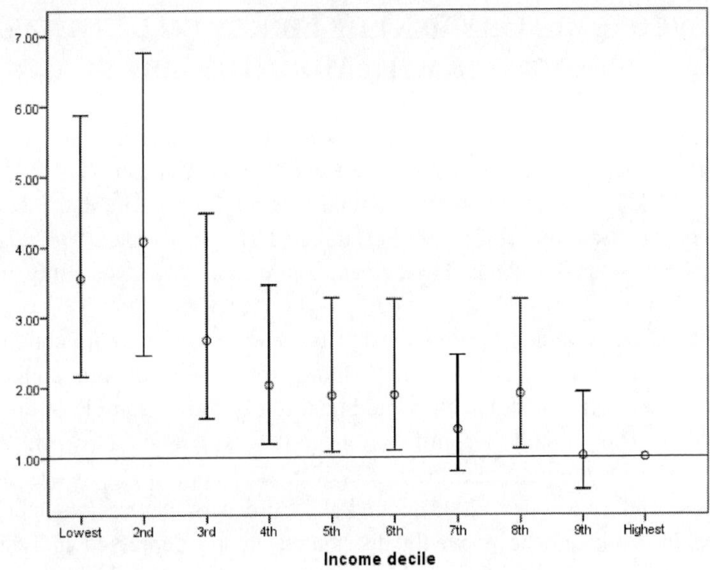

(1) Reprinted with permission from Gadalla (2009c)

(2) Odds ratios were adjusted for participant's age, marital status, number of chronic conditions and number of consultations with medical doctors.

Figure 2(1). Adjusted (2) odds ratios and 95% confidence intervals (CI) for functional limitations by income decile for men with mood disorders, Canada 2005.

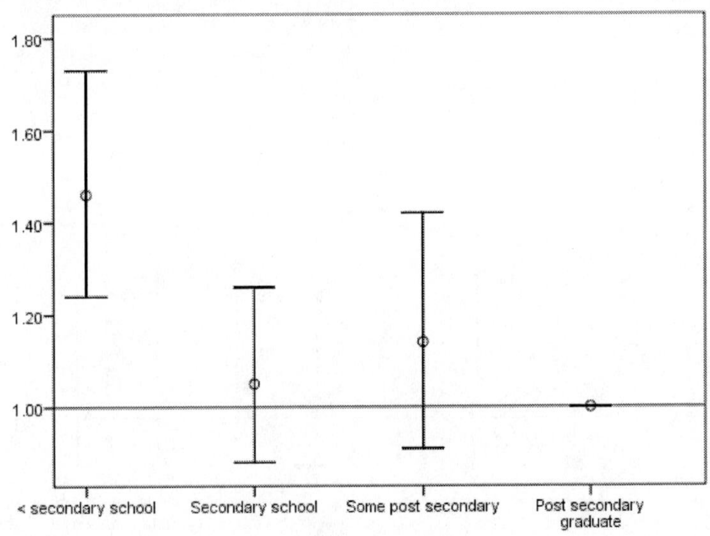

(1) Printed with permission from Gadalla (2009c)

(2) Odds ratios were adjusted for participant's age, marital status, number of chronic conditions and number of consultations with medical doctors.

Figure 3. (1). Adjusted (2) odds ratios and 95% confidence intervals (CI) for functional limitations by educational level for women with mood disorders, Canada 2005.

Based on secondary analyses of national data collected in the Canadian Community Health Survey in 2005 (Statistics Canada, 2006), and adjusting for age, number of chronic conditions and number of consultations with medical doctors, the odds of functional limitations were found to decline with increasing socioeconomic status (Gadalla, 2009c). This gradient was evident for both men and women and was more apparent with income level (Figures 1 and 2) than with education level (Figures 3 and 4). The odds of having functional limitations for women in the lowest income decile were 2.33 times the odds for women in the highest income decile. The corresponding odds for men were 3.56. Compared with post secondary graduates, women and men with less than high school education had 1.46 and 2.31 higher odds of functional limitations, respectively.

Unfavorable socioeconomic conditions may affect an individual's functional ability directly through inadequate housing and lack of economic resources to acquire helpful devices that can make daily activities easier (Lynch et al., 2008). Other explanations include the higher prevalence of health risk behaviors, such as smoking, high fat diets and excess drinking, among lower socioeconomic groups (House, 2002, Isaacs and Schroeder, 2004). On the other hand, Lantz and colleagues (2001) found that adjusting for the higher prevalence of cigarette smoking, alcohol consumption, physical inactivity and body mass index in lower socioeconomic groups to have a small effect on their odds of functional difficulties compared to the higher socioeconomic groups. More studies are needed to explore alternative explanations for the associations between lower socioeconomic conditions and functional difficulties.

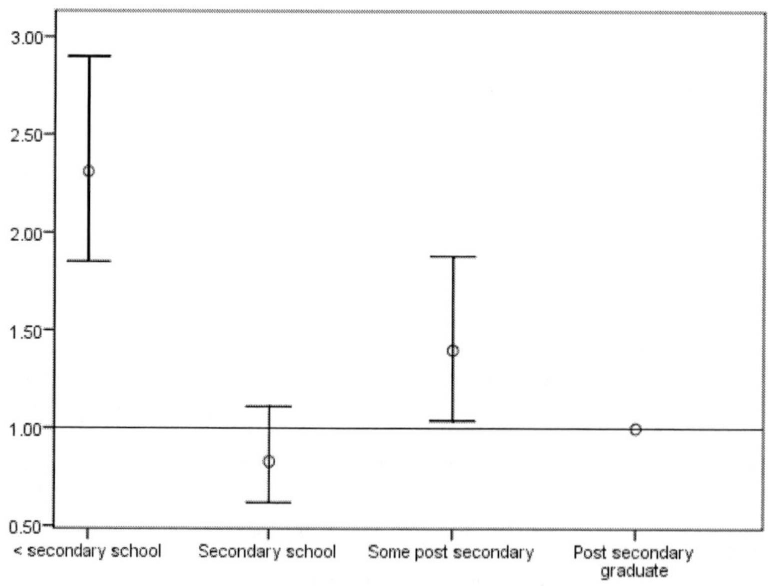

[(1)] Reprinted with permission from Gadalla (2009c)

[(2)] Odds ratios were adjusted for participant's age, marital status, number of chronic conditions and number of consultations with medical doctors.

Figure 4[(1)]. Adjusted [(2)] odds ratios and 95% confidence intervals (CI) for functional limitations by educational level for men with mood disorders, Canada 2005.

Barriers to Seeking Medical Help for Mood Disorders

Although effective interventions for the treatment of mood disorders are available (Roy-Byrne et al., 2004), the majority of individuals with mood disorders fail to consult health professionals. Mojtabai and Olfson (2006) analyzed data from the Joint Canada/United States Survey of Health, and reported similar help seeking rates for depression in the two populations (56% in Canada compared with 52% in the United States). Among participants who sought such help, Canadians were more likely than Americans to seek help from a mental health specialist. Similar results had been reported in studies conducted in other populations (Boyd and Amsterdam, 2004; Mann, 2005; Stewart et al., 2004).

Table 3[1]. Mental Health Care Utilization by Women with Major Depressive Disorder, 2002, CCHS 1.2

Socio-demographic characteristic	Psychiatrist care (%)	Primary care (%)	Non-medical professional (%)	Total number who received treatment (%)[1]
Age* (years) 15-29	64 (35.8)	78 (43.6)	37 (20.6§)	179 (48.1)
30-44	71 (28.1)	142 (56.1)	40 (15.8§)	253 (63.0)
45-59	53 (28.3)	116 (62.1)	18 (9.6§)	187 (59.5)
>=60	12 (37.5§§)	16 (50.0§)	4 (12.5§§)	32 (34.7)
Family type Unattached	60 (37.0)	83 (51.3)	19 (11.7§)	162 (56.4)
Partnered, no children	34 (33.7§)	51 (50.5§)	16 (15.8§§)	101 (51.8)
Two-parent family	52 (23.1§)	135 (60.0)	38 (16.9§)	225 (51.3)
Single-mother, child <25 years	47 (34.3§)	69 (50.4)	21 (15.3§)	137 (65.0)
Single-mother, child <24 years				13 (41.9§)
Length of time in Canada*** <10 years	1 (3.6§§)	13 (46.4§§)	14 (50.0§)	28 (52.8§)
>=10 years	24 (36.4§)	37 (56.1§)	5 (7.5§§)	66 (48.9)
Canadian born	174 (31.4)	302 (54.4)	79 (14.2)	555 (55.8)
Language skills*** English/French	198 (30.7)	350 (54.3)	96 (14.9)	644 (56.0)
Neither				2
Education Less than high school	45 (34.9§)	56 (43.4§)	28 (21.7§)	129 (43.3)
High school	43 (33.1§)	68 (52.3)	19 (14.6§)	130 (57.3)
Some post secondary	19 (33.3§)	29 (50.9§)	9 (15.8§§)	57 (53.8)
Post secondary	91 (27.8)	195 (59.7)	41 (12.5§)	327 (60.4)
Income adequacy* Low	48 (36.1§)	59 (44.4§)	26 (19.5§)	133 (61.9)
Middle/high	138 (29.1)	279 (58.9)	57 (12.0§)	474 (55.1)
Self-rated physical health*** Poor/fair	89 (41.0)	105 (48.4)	23 (10.6§)	217 (58.6)
Good/very good/excellent	111 (25.7)	246 (56.9)	75 (17.4)	432 (53.1)
Self-rated stress* Quite a bit/ a lot	137 (34.4)	210 (52.8)	51 (12.8§)	398 (57.9)
None/not much/ a bit	63 (25.1§)	141 (56.2)	47 (18.7§)	251 (50.5)
Chronic condition** Yes	195 (32.3)	324 (53.8)	84 (13.9)	603 (57.3)
No	5 (10.9§§)	27 (58.7§)	14 (30.4§)	46 (35.4)
Social support Low	141 (32.3)	235 (53.9)	60 (13.8§)	436 (54.8)
High	53 (26.5§)	111 (55.5)	36 (18.0§)	200 (56.2)
Number of MD episodes One	55 (26.3§)	123 (58.9)	31 (14.8§)	209 (47.7)
Two or more	101 (35.2)	148 (51.7)	38 (13.1§)	287 (55.4)
Total women	200 (30.7)	352 (54.1)	99 (15.2)	651 (54.9)
Total men *	130 (44.2)	130 (44.2)	34 (11.6)	294 (52.8)

[1] Printed with permission from Gadalla (2008b).

§ Marginal estimate of the true national rate, i.e. coefficient of variation is between 16.5% and 33.3%

§§ Unreliable estimate of the true national rate, i.e. coefficient of variation > 33.3%.

[1] Percentage of women receiving treatment among those with depression.

* $p<0.05$.

** $p<0.005$.

*** $p<0.0005$.

In Canada, despite a universal coverage of physician and hospital services, 45.1% of Canadian women with major depression did not consult a health professional regarding their mental health (Gadalla, 2008b). Among women with depression, the odds of not seeking treatment for depression were highest for single mothers with adult children, women with low social support and those with little formal education. While the proportion of depressed women who sought treatment (54.9%) was only slightly higher than that of men (52.7%), the type of care they sought varied significantly (Table 3). Fifty-four percent (352/651) of depressed women who sought treatment did so in a primary care setting and 30.7% (200/651) sought a psychiatrist help. Depressed men, on the other hand, were equally likely to seek treatment in a primary or a psychiatrist's care.

Among depressed women who used mental health services, the type of help sought was strongly associated with their self-rated physical health, chronic health conditions, length of time in Canada and language skills, and moderately associated with their age, income adequacy and stress level (Table 3). For example, 50% of recent immigrants reported contacting a non-medical professional, and 46.4% reported contacting a family doctor, while Canadian-born and immigrants who had lived in Canada for at least ten years were more likely to contact a psychiatrist. No significant difference was observed between the type of help sought by Canadian born and immigrants who had lived in Canada for at least ten years. Similar associations between language skills and help seeking were found. However, these two variables were confounded in that all women who were unable to communicate in English or French were recent immigrants. Middle aged (30-59 years) depressed women were more likely to seek primary care, while younger and older women were more likely to seek a psychiatrist's care. Women with middle to high income were more likely than women with low income to seek help in a primary care setting. Poor physical health, high stress level and chronic health conditions were associated with high rates of seeking help from psychiatrists. Family type, level of education, number of depression episodes and level of social support were not related to the type of health professional contacted.

Not much is known about the effect of ethnic/racial background on Canadians' tendency to seek treatment for depression. Racial/ethnic background can influence a person's tendency to seek mental health care in a number of ways. Having different cultural values may lead to feelings of isolation from the mainstream society. Persons in need of mental health care may not seek help because of cultural and/or religious specific beliefs on causes and cures of their mental illnesses (Hussain et al., 2002). They may be reluctant to seek treatment due to a perceived provider bias or a perceived lack of provider's understanding of their culture, a fact which is emphasized by the under-representation of people from culturally diverse backgrounds in health care professions (Hirschfeld et al., 1997; Miranda and Cooper, 2004). The stigma associated with mental illness and the shame it may bring upon families of patients promote their avoidance of mental health services. Low income, language barriers, perceived racism and unavailability of culturally sensitive services can further contribute to a persons' unwillingness to seek mental health treatment (Hunsley et al., 1999; Miranda & Cooper, 2004; Mojtabai & Olfson, 2006; Spencer and Chen, 2004). For example, Spencer and Chen (2004) examined the effect of discrimination on mental health service utilization among Chinese Americans and concluded that racial/ethnic discrimination resulting from speaking a different language was an important stressor that deterred immigrants from seeking treatment for their mental illness.

Most of the studies examining racial differences in seeking treatment for depression or for mental health in general have been conducted in the U.S. and have focused on comparing Blacks and Hispanics to Whites. Findings of these studies have been mixed and have led to inconsistent conclusions. For example, while several researchers reported that being white increased the rate of seeking treatment for depression (Olfson & Klerman, 1992; Cooper et al., 2003; Gallo et al., 1995; Hu et al., 1991), Diala and colleagues (2001) found that depressed African Americans had significantly more positive attitudes toward seeking mental health care than depressed Whites. Cooper and colleagues (2003) reported racial and ethnic differences in beliefs about various treatment modalities with African Americans and Hispanics less likely than Whites to find antidepressant medications acceptable and Hispanics more likely than Whites to find counseling acceptable. They also reported on the lack of differences among ethnic groups with regard to their perceptions of stigma and preference to see a mental health care professional of the same gender. Hu and colleagues (1991) reported significant differences in the selection of mental health providers among ethnic and racial minorities. In a study of help seeking patterns among Black, Hispanic and White women in primary care clinics, Van Hook (1999) concluded that barriers of stigma and separation between physical and mental health deter women from seeking help for depression. Strakes and colleagues (2005) reported that immigrants with MDE living in Atlantic Canada were significantly less likely than Canadian born to receive treatment.

Gadalla (in press) used data collected in the Health and Mental Health cycle of the Canadian Community Health Survey to assess the effects of ethnic background on seeking treatment for depression episodes and to investigate types of barriers to mental health care reported by members of different racial/ethnic groups. Results indicated that racial/ethnic background had a significant effect on treatment seeking rates, controlling for socio-economic, demographic and health factors. Gadalla (in press) found the proportion of depression sufferers who reported having unmet mental health care needs to vary significantly across racial/ethnic groups with the lowest rate reported among Blacks and the highest among South Asians. Findings also identified some access problems that were common across all racial/ethnic groups and some problems unique to members of specific groups. For example, two-thirds of depressed individuals of all racial/ethnic background with unmet needs reported personal barriers to treatment, i.e. they decided not to seek treatment. In contrast, rates of accessibility and availability barriers differed significantly across racial/ethnic groups.

The serious stigma attached to mental illness in general is one of the most recognized hurdles facing their diagnosis and treatment. Other factors associated with not seeking treatment for mental illness include being a lone mother, having low social support, lower education level, being a member of an ethnic/racial minority group and/or perceived separation between mental and physical health (Bristow & Patten, 2002; Lawrence et al., 2006; Miranda & Cooper, 2004; Mojtabai & Olfson, 2006; Patten & Beck, 2004).

Various reasons for the under treatment of depression include factors related to patients, health care providers and the health care system (Hirschfeld et al., 1997). Patient's gender, age, level of education, perceived social support, severity and duration of depression, comorbid physical or psychological illness were associated with seeking treatment for depression (Bristow & Patten, 2002; Hook, 1999; Mojtabai & Olfson, 2006; Patten & Beck, 2004). Ethnic/racial background was also a significant determinant of seeking treatment for depression (Miranda & Cooper, 2004; Mojtabai & Olfson, 2006), with members of ethnic/racial minorities less likely than Caucasians to seek treatment. Factors related to health

care providers such as limited training in interpersonal skills, inadequate time to diagnose and treat depression, and prescription of inadequate doses of antidepressant medication contribute to the under treatment of depression. Kouzis and Eaton (1998) reported a statistically significant association between insufficient health insurance and health care utilization in the general population, while Mojtabai & Olfson (2006) reported a marginally significant association between lack of health insurance coverage and seeking treatment among depressed individuals.

Over a quarter (26.1%) of women with major depression reported unmet mental health care needs. The majority (70%) of women with unmet need for mental health care cited reasons related to competing demand on their time, being afraid to ask, not thinking it was important or not believing it would help (Gadalla, 2008b).

Similar trends were reported in other studies. For example, Van Hook (1999) interviewed women who attended primary care clinics for a variety of medical concerns and found that women who were depressed did not seek help for their depression from clinic staff because of stigma and perceived separation between mental and physical health. Lawrence and colleagues (2006) reported similar results based on in-depth interviews with black Caribbean, South Asian and White older individuals living in the UK. Participants in these interviews felt that it was the individual's responsibility to combat depression, and many were reluctant to add more demands on their general practitioner's time. To fully understand the reasons behind not seeking help for mental health, all stages of the help-seeking process need to be examined. For example, the perception of need is an important element of the decision to seek help. Depressed individuals who do not seek mental health care, may do so because they underestimate the symptoms and consequences of depression, lack awareness of the importance of treating it, do not believe in the effectiveness of treatment, do not know how to get help, or want to void the stigma associated with having a mental health concern. It is also conceivable that at least some of these individuals experience less severe symptoms and hence, do not feel the need for seeking professional help.

REFERENCES

Ades P, Savage P, Tischler M, Poehlman E, Dee J, Niggel J. Determinants of disability in older coronary patients. *Am Heart J* 2002;143:151-156.

Atlantis E, Baker M. (2008). Obesity effects on depression: systematic review of epidemiological studies. *International Journal of Obesity*, 32(6):881-891.

Berkson J (1946). Limitations of the application of fourfold table analysis to hospital data. *Biometrics* 2: 47–53.

Bierut LJ, Heath AC, Andrew CD, Bucholz KK, Dinwiddle SH, Madden PA, Statham DJ, Dunne MP, Martin NG. (1999). Major depressive disorder in a community-based twin sample: are there different genetic and environmental contributions for men and women? *Archives of General Psychiatry*, 56(6):557-563.

Blaine B. (2008). Does depression cause obesity? A meta-analysis of longitudinal studies of depression and weight control. *Journal of Health Psychology*, 13(8):1190-1197.

Bland RC. Epidemiology of affective disorders: A review. *Can J Psychiatry*. 1997;42:367-77.

Blinder, B.J., Cumella, E.J., Sanathara, V.A. (2006). *Psychiatric comorbidities of female inpatients with eating disorders.* American Psychosomatic Society, 68(3), 454-462.

Boyd RC, Amsterdam JD. (2004). Mood disorders in women from adolescence to late life: An overview. *Clinical Obstetrics and Gynecology*, 47(3):515-526.

Bristow K, Patten S. (2002). Treatment-seeking rates and associated mediating factors among individuals with depression. *Canadian J Psychiatry*, 47:660-665.

Bruffaerts, R; Demyttenaere, K; Vilagut, G; Martinez, M; Bonnewyn, A; De Graaf, R; Haro, JM; Bernert, S; Angermeyer, MC; Brugha, T; Roick, C; Alonso, J. (2008). The Relation between Body Mass Index, Mental Health, and Functional Disability: A European Population Perspective. *Canadian Journal of Psychiatry*, 53(10):679-687.

Carlat DJ, Camargo CA, Jr., & Herzog DB. (1997). Eating disorders in males: a report on 135 patients. *American Journal of Psychiatry*, *154*, 1127-32.

Carpenter KM, Hasin DS, Allison DB, Faith MS. (2000). Relationships between obesity and DSM-IV major depressive disorder, suicide ideation and suicidal attempts: Results from a general population survey. *American Journal of Public Health*, 90(2):251-257.

Carr, D; Friedman, MA; Jaffe, K. (2007). Understanding the relationship between obesity and positive and negative affect: The role of psychosocial mechanisms. *Body Image*, 4(2):165-177.

Cooper, L.A., Gonzales, J.K., Gallo, J.J., et al. (2003). The acceptability of treatment for depression among African American, Hispanic and White primary care patients. *Medical Care*. 41(4):479-489.

Courbasson CM, Smith PD, Cleland PA. (2005). Substance use disorders, anorexia, bulimia, and concurrent disorders. *Can J Public Health* 2005; 96(2):102-6.

Dalgard, O. S., Mykletun, A., Rognerud, M., Johansen, R., & Zahl, P. H. (2007). Education, sense of mastery and mental health: results from a nation wide health monitoring study in Norway. BMC Psychiatry 2007. Article is available from: *http://www.biomedcentral.com/1471-244X/7/20*

Dansky, B.S., Brewerton, T.D. & Kilpatrick, D.G. (2000). Comorbidity of bulimia nervosa and alcohol use disorders: results from the National Women's Study. *International Journal of Eating Disorders, 27*, 180-190.

De Lange, A.H., Tarish, T., Kompier, M.A.J., Houtman, I. L.D. & Bongers, P. (2004). The relationship between work characteristics and mental health: Examining normal, reversed and reciprocal relationships in a 4-wave study. *Work & Stress, 18* (2), 149-166.

Dembling, B. P., Rovnyak, V., Macket, S., Blank, M. (2002). Effects of geographic migration on SMI prevalence estimates. *Mental Health Services Research*, 4:7-12.

Dewa, C.S., Lesage, A.D. Goering, P., & Caveen, M. (2004). Nature and prevalence of mental illness in the workplace. *Healthcare Papers*, 5, 12-25.

Diala CC, Muntaner C, Walrath C, et al. (2001). Racial/Ethnic differences in attitudes toward seeking professional mental health services. *Am J Public Health*. 91(5):805-807.

Dong C, Sanchez LE, Price RA. (2004). Relationship of obesity to depression: A family-based study. *International Journal of Obesity*, 28:780-795.

Elovainio M, Kivimaki M, Ek E, Vahtera J, Honkonen T, Taanila A, Veijola J, Jarvelin MR (2007). The effect of pre-employment factors on job control, job strain and psychological distress: A 31-year longitudinal study. *Social Science & Medicine,* 2007;65:187-199.

Evans DL, Charney DS, Lewis L, Golden RN, Gorman JM, Krishnan KR, Nemeroff CB, Bremner JD, Carney RM, et al. Mood disorders in the medically ill: Scientific review and recommendations. *Biol Psychiatry* 2005;58:175-189.

Faith MS, Matz PE, Jorge MA. (2002). Obesity-depression associations in the population. *Journal of Psychosomatic Research*, 53:935-942.

Ferketich A, Schwartzbaum J, Frid D, Moeschberger M. Depression as an antecedent to heart disease among women and men in the WHANES I study. National Health and Nutrition Survey. *Arch Intern Med* 2000;160:1261-1268.

Fryers, T., Melzer, D., & Jenkins, R. (2003). Social inequalities and the common mental disorders: A systematic review of the evidence. *Social Psychiatry and psychiatric Epidemiology*, 38, 229-237.

Gadalla, T. M. (in press). Ethnicity and seeking treatment for depression: A Canadian national study. *Canadian Ethnic Studies.*

Gadalla, T. M. (2009a). Association of obesity with mood and anxiety disorders in the adult general population. *Chronic Diseases in Canada*, 30(1):29-36.

Gadalla, T. M. (2009b). Association between mood and anxiety disorders and self-reported disability: results from a nationally representative sample of Canadians. *Journal of Mental Health,* 18(6):495-503.

Gadalla, T. M. (2009c). Socioeconomic gradient of functional limitations in individuals diagnosed with mood disorders. *Women & Health*, 49(1), 181-196.

Gadalla, T. M. (2008a). Psychiatric comorbidity in Eating Disorders: A comparison of men and women. *Journal of Men's Health*, 5(3), 209-217.

Gadalla, T. M. (2008b). Comparison of users and non-users of mental health services among depressed Women: A National Study. *Women & Health*, 47(1):1-19.

Gadalla, T. M. (2008c). Association of comorbid mood disorders and chronic illness on disability and quality of life in Ontario, Canada. *Chronic Diseases in Canada*, 28(4), 148-154.

Gadalla, T. M. (2008d). Disability associated with comorbid anxiety disorders in women with chronic physical illness in Ontario, Canada. *Women & Health*, 48(1), 1-20.

Gallo, J.J., Marino, S., Ford, D., et al. (1995). Filters on the pathway to mental health care, II. Socio-demographic factors. *Psychological Medicine*, 25(6):1149-1160.

Geist, R., Davis, R. & Heinmaa, M. (1998). Binge/purge symptoms and comorbidity in adolescents with eating disorders. *Canadian Journal of Psychiatry*, 43, 507-512.

Godart, N.T., Perdereau, F., Rein, Z., Berthoz, S., Wallier, J., Jeammet, Ph. Flament, M.F. (2007). Comorbidity studies of eating disorders and mood disorders. Critical review of the literature. *Journal of Affective Disorders*, 97, 37-49.

Goodman E, Whitaker R. A prospective study of the role of depression in the development and persistence of adult obesity. *Pediatrics* 2002;110:497-504.

Goosby, B. (2007). Poverty duration, maternal psychological resources, and adolescent outcomes. *Journal of Family Issues*, 28 (8), 1113-1134.

Gormen JM, Sloan RP. Heart rate variability in depressive and anxiety disorders. *Am Heart J* 2000;140(4 suppl):77-83.

Grucza, R.A., Przybeck, T.R., Cloninger, C.R. (2007). Prevalence and correlates of binge eating disorder in a community sample. *Comprehensive Psychiatry* 2007; 48:124-131.

Herrick H. *Postportum depression: who gets help?* State Centre for Health Statistics. Statistics Brief No. 24. Department of Health and Human Services. North Carolina Division of Public Health; 2002.

Hirschfeld, R.M., Keller, M.B., Panico, S., et al. (1997). The National Depressive and Manic-Depressive Association consensus statement on the undertreatment of depression. *J American Medical Association*, 277:333-40.

House JS. (2002). Understanding social factors and inequalities in health: 20th century progress and 21st century prospects. *Journal of Health and social Behaviors*, 43:125-142.

Hu, T., Snowden, L.R., Jerrell, JM, et al. (1991). Ethnic populations in public mental health: Services choice and level of use. *Am J Public Health*, 81(11):1429-1434.

Hudson, C. G. (2005). Socioeconomic status and mental illness: tests of the social causation and selection hypotheses. *American Journal of Orthopsychiatry*, 75(1):3-18.

Hunsley J, Lee CM, Aubry T. (1999). Who uses psychological services in Canada? *Canadian Psychology*, 40(3):232-240.

Hussain FA, Cochrane R. (2002). Depression in South Asian women: Asian women's beliefs on causes and cures. *Mental Health, Religion & Culture*, 5(3):285-311.

Isaacs SL, Schroeder, SA. (2004). Class – the ignored determinant of the nation's health. *New England Journal of Medicine*, 551:1137-1142.

Isacson, D., Bingefors, K., & von Knorring, L. (2005). The impact of depression is unevenly distributed in the population. *European Psychiatry*, 20, 205-212.

John U, Meyer C, Rumpf HJ, Hapke U. (2006). Psychiatric comorbidity including nicotine dependence among individuals with eating disorder criteria in an adult general population sample. *Psychiatry Research*, 2006;141: 71-79.

Jorm AF, Korten AE, Christensen H, Jacomb PA, Rodgers B, Parslow RA. (2003). Association of obesity with anxiety, depression, and emotional well-being: A community survey. *Australia and New Zealand Journal of Public Health*, 27:434-440.

Katon WJ. Clinical and health services relationships between major depression, depressive symptoms and general medical illness. Biol Psychiatry 2003;54:216-226.

Kawakami N, Takatsuka N, Shimizu H, Ishibashi H. Depressive symptoms and occurrence of type 2 diabetes among Japanese men. Diabetes 1999;22:1071-1076.

Kendler KS, Walters EE, Neale MC, Kessler RC, Heath AC, Eaves LJ. (1995). The structure of the genetic and environmental risk factors for six major psychiatric disorders in women: phobia, generalized anxiety disorder, panic disorder, bulimia, major depression and alcoholism. *Archives of General Psychiatry*, 52:374-83.

Kessler RC, Chiu WT, Demler O, Walters EE. (2005). Prevalence, severity and comorbidity of 12-month DSM-IV disorders in the National Comorbidity Survey replication. *Archives of General Psychiatry*, 62:617-627.

Kessler RC, Stang P, Wittchen HU, Stein M, Walters EE. (1999). Lifetime comorbidities between social phobia and mood disorders in the US National Comorbidity Survey. *Psychological Medicine*, 29:555-567.

Kessler RC, Walters EE, Forthofer MS. (1998). The social consequences of psychiatric disorders, III: Probability of marital stability. *American Journal of Psychiatry*, 155:1092-1096.

Kouzis, AC. and Eaton WW. (1998). Absence of social networks, social support and health services utilization *Psychological Medicine*, 28: 1301-1310.

Lantz PM, Lynch JW, House JS, Lepkowski JM, Mero RP, Musick MA, Williams DR. (2001). Socioeconomic disparities in health change in a longitudinal study of US adults: the role of health-risk behaviours. *Social Science and Medicine*, 53:29-40.

Lawrence V, Banerjee S, Bhugra D, Sangha K, Turner S,Murray J. (2006). *Coping with depression in later life*. Published Online July 20, 2006. Retrieved July 8, 2007.

Leskela US, Melartin TK, Lestela-Mielonen PS, Rytsala HJ, Sokero TP, Heikkinen ME, Isometsa ET. (2004). Life events, social support and onset of major depressive episode in Finnish patients. *The Journal of Nervous and Mental Disease*, 192(5):373-381.

Lorant V, Croux C, Weich S, Deliege D, Mackenbach J & Ansseau, M. (2007). Depression and socio-economic risk factors: 7-year longitudinal population study. *British Journal of Psychiatry*, 190, 293-298.

Lorant V, Deliege D, Eaton W, Robert A, Philippot P & Ansseau M. (2003). Socioeconomic inequalities in depression: A meta-analysis. *American Journal of Epidemiology*, 157(2), 98-112.

Lynch JW, Kaplan GA, Shema SJ. (2008). Cumulative impact of sustained economic hardship on physical, cognitive, psychological and social functioning. *New England Journal of Medicine*, 337(26):1889-1895.

Mann JJ. (2005). The medical management of depression. *New England Journal of Medicine,* 353:1819-34.

Markowitz, S; Friedman, MA; Arent, SM. (2008). Understanding the relation between obesity and depression: Causal mechanisms and implications for treatment. *Clinical Psychology-Science and Practice*, 15(1):1-20.

Matthews S, Power C, Stansfeld SA (2001). Psychological distress and work and home roles: a focus on socio-economic differences in distress. *Psychological Medicine*, 2001;31(4):725-736.

Mazure CM, Keita GP, Blehar MC. (2002). *Summit on Women and Depression: Proceedings and Recommendations*. Washington, D.C.: American Psychological Association Press.

McIntyre RS, Konarski JZ, Wilkins K, Soczynska JK, Kennedy SH. (2006). Obesity in bipolar disorder and major depressive disorder: Results from a National Community Health Survey on mental health and well-being. *Canadian Journal of Psychiatry*, 51:274-280.

McLaren L, Beck CA, Patten SB, Fick GH, Adair CE. (2008). The relationship between body mass index and mental health, A population-based study of the effects of the definition of mental health. *Society of Psychiatry and Psychiatric Epidemiology*, 43:63-71.

McElroy SL, Kotwal R, Malhorta S, Nelson EB, Keck PE, Nemeroff CB. (2004). Are mood disorders and obesity related? A review for the mental health professional. *Journal of Clinical Psychiatry*, 65:634-651.

Miller GE, Stetler CA, Carney RM, Freedland KE, Banks WA. Clinical depression and inflammatory risk markers for coronary artery disease. *Am J Cardiol* 2002;90:1279-1283.

Miranda J& Cooper LA. (2004). Disparities in care for depression among primary care patients. *J Gen Intern Med*, 19:120-128.

Mojtabai, R, Olfson M. (2006). Treatment seeking for depression in Canada and the United States. *Psychiatric Services*, 57:631-639.

Myer, L., Stein, D.J., Grimsrud, A., Seedat, S., & Williams, D.R. (2008). Social determinants of psychological distress in a nationally-representative sample of South African adults. *Social Science & Medicine*, *66*, 1828-1840.

Olfson M, Klerman GL. Depressive symptoms and mental health service utilization in a community sample. *Soc Psychiatry Psychiatr Epidemiol.* 1992;27(4):161-167.

Patten SB. (2000). Incidence of major depression in Canada. *Can Med Assoc J*;163:714-715.

Patten SB & Beck CA. (2004). Major depression and mental health care utilization in Canada: 1994 to 2000. *Canadian Journal of Psychiatry*, 49:303-309.

Petry NM, Barry D, Pietrzak RH, Wagner JA. (2008). Overweight and obesity are associated with psychiatric disorders: Results from the national epidemiologic survey on alcohol and related conditions. *Psychosomatic Medicine*, 70(3):288-297.

Perretta P, Akiskal HS, Nisita C, Lorenzetta C, Zaccagnini E, Della Santa M, Cassano GB. The high prevalence of bipolar II and associated cyclothymic and Hyperthymic temperaments in HIV-patients. *J Affect Disord* 1998;50:215-224.

Power C, Stansfeld SA, Matthews S, Mano O, Hope S (2002). Childhood and adulthood risk factors for socio-economic differentials in psychological distress: evidence from the 1958 British birth cohort. *Social Science & Medicine*, 2002;55:1989-2004. 11.

Ritcher JE, Warner V, Johnson JG, Dohrenwend BP (2001). Inter-generational longitudinal study of social class and depression: a test of social causation and social selection models. *The British Journal of Psychiatry*, 2001; 178: s84-s90

Schuckit MA, Tipp JE, Anthenelli RM, Bucholz KK, Hesselbrock VM, Nurnberger JI, Jr. (1996). Anorexia nervosa and bulimia nervosa in alcohol-dependent men and women and their relatives. *American Journal of Psychiatry, 153*, 74-82.

Scott KM, McGee MA, Wells JE, Browne MAO. (2008). Obesity and mental disorders in the adult general population. *Journal of Psychosomatic Research*, 64:97-105.

Seyfried LS, Marcus SM. Postpartum mood disorders. *International Review of Psychiatry*, 2003;15:231-42.

Simon GE, Ludman EJ, Unutzer J, Operskalski BH, Bauer MS. (2008). Severity of mood symptoms and work productivity in people treated for bipolar disorders. *Bipolar Disorders,* 10: 718-725.

Simon, GE; Von Korff, M; Saunders, K; Miglioretti, DL; Crane, PK; van Belle, G; Kessler, RC (2006). Association between obesity and psychiatric disorders in the US adult population. *Archives of General Psychiatry*, 63(7):824-830.

Simon G, Von Kroff M, Rutter C, Paterson D. (2001). Treatment process and outcomes for managed care patients receiving new antidepressant prescriptions from psychiatrists and primary care physicians. *Arch Gen Psychiatry* 2001;58:395-401.

Skapinakis, P., Weich, S., Lewis G., Singleton, N, Araya, R. (2006). Socio-economic position and common mental disorders. *British Journal of Psychiatry*, 189:109-117.

Spencer MS, Chen J. (2004). Effect of discrimination on mental health service utilization among Chinese Americans. *American Journal of Public Health*, 94(5):809-814.

Starkes J, Poulin C, Kisely S. Unmet need for the treatment of depression in Atlantic Canada. *Can J Psychiatry* 2005;50:580-90.

Statistics Canada. (2006). *Canadian Community Health Survey, cycle 3.1, 2005*. Public Use Microdata Documentation. Tunney's Pasture, Ottawa; 2006.

Statistics Canada. *Canadian Community Health Survey, Mental Health and Well Being. 2002.* Public Use Microdata Documentation. Tunney's Pasture, Ottawa; 2002.

Stunkard AJ, Faith MS, Allison KC. (2003). Depression and obesity. *Biological Psychiatry*, 54:330-337Skapinakis, P., Weich, S., Lewis G., Singleton, N, Araya, R. (2006). Socio-

economic position and common mental disorders. *British Journal of Psychiatry*, 189:109-117.

Stephens T & Joubert N. The economic burden of mental health problems in Canada. *Chronic diseases in Canada.* 2001;22(1):18-23.

Stewart D, Gucciardi E, Grace S. (2004). Depression. *BMC Women's Health*, 4(Suppl): Available from: *http://www.biomedicalcentral.com/1472-6874/4/S1/S19*

Sullivan, P., Neale, M. C. & Kendler, K. S. (2000). Genetic epidemiology of major depression: Review and meta-analysis. *American Journal of Psychiatry*, 157 (10), 1552-1562.

Takeuchi DT, Chung RC, Keh-Ming L, Shen H, Kurasaki K, Chun CM, Sue S. (1998). Lifetime and 12-month prevalence rates of major depressive episodes and dysthymia among Chinese Americans in Los Angeles. *The American Journal of Psychiatry*, 155:1407-1414.

Talala, K., Huurre, T., Aro, H., Martelin, T., Prattala, R. (2008). Socio-demographic differences in self-reported psychological distress among 25- to 64-year-old Finns. *Social Indic Research, 86*, 323-335.

Trivedi, M. H., Rush, A. J., Wisniewski, S. R., Warden, D., McKinney, W., Downing, M., Berman, S. R., Farabaugh, A., Luther, J. F., Nierenberg, A. A., Callan, J. A., & Sackeim, H. A. (2006). Factors associated with health-related quality of life among outpatients with Major Depressive Disorder: A STAR*D Report. *Journal of Clinical Psychiatry*, 67, 185-195.

Wadsworth, M.E. & Achenbach T.M. (2005). Explaining the link between low socioeconomic status and psychopathology: Testing two mechanisms of the social causation hypothesis. *Journal of Consulting and Clinical Psychology, 73* (6), 1146-1153

Weich, S. & Lewis, G. (1998). Poverty, unemployment, and common mental disorders: Population based cohort study. *British Medical Journal*, 317:115-119.

Weissman MM, Bland RC, Canino GJ, Faravelli C, Greenwald S, Hwu HG, Joyce PR, Karam EG, Lee CK, Lellouch J, Lepine JP, Newman SC, Rubio-Stipec M, Wells JE, Wickramaratne PJ, Wittchen HU, Yeh EK. (1996). Cross-national epidemiology of major depression and bipolar disorder. *JAMA*, 276(4):293-299.

WHO World Mental Health Survey Consortium. (2004). Prevalence, severity, and unmet need for treatment of mental disorders in the World Health Organization World Mental Health Surveys. *JAMA* 2004;291(21):2581-2590

Whyte E, Pollock B, Wagner W, Mulsant B, Ferrel R, Mazumdor S,, Reynolds C 3rd. Influence of serotonin-transporter-linked promoter region polymorphism on the platelet activation in geriatric depression. *Am J Psychiatry* 2001;158:2074-2076.

Wildman P, Lilenfeld LR, Marcus MD. (2004). Axis I comorbidity onset and parasuicide in women with eating disorders. *International J Eating Disorders* 2004;35:190-7.

Woodside DB, Garfinkel PE, Lin E, Goering P, Kaplan AS, Goldbloom DS, Kennedy SH. (2001). Comparisons of men with full or partial eating disorders, men without eating disorders, and women with eating disorders in the community. *American Journal of Psychiatry*, 158, 570-574.

Vali F, Walkup J. Combined medical and psychological symptoms: Impact on disability and health care utilization of patients with arthritis. *Med Care* 1998;36:1073-1084.

Van Hook MP. (1999). Women's help-seeking patterns for depression. *Social Work in Health Care*, 29(1):15-34.

Vetter, S., Endrass, J., Schweizer, I., Teng, H. M. Rossler, W., Gallo, W. T. (2006). The effects of economic deprivation on psychological well-being among working population of Switzerland. *BMC Public Health*, 6:223.

In: Advances in Psychology Research. Volume 88
Editor: Alexandra M. Columbus, pp. 49-73

ISBN: 978-1-62100-591-9

Chapter 3

INSIGHTS ON COMPETITION FROM A SCIENCE-BASED ANALYSIS

Theodore Modis*
Growth Dynamics, Massagno, Lugano, Switzerland.

ABSTRACT

The work presented here uses a science-based approach to obtain new understandings on the mechanisms and the ramifications of competition in everyday life. Assuming competition of a Darwinian nature we can deduce an S-shaped pattern for growth in most competitive environments. Examples range from a rabbit population growing in a fenced-off grass field to scientists competing for Nobel-Prize awards. There are secrets embedded in the mathematical law that describes growth in competition. The rate of growth being proportional to the amount of growth already achieved makes beginnings difficult and sheds light on such proverbial wisdom as "you need goal to make gold". It also argues for the necessity to engage teachers in the learning process. Other revelations are linked to the symmetry of a life-cycle pattern, which possesses predictive power and demystifies the easy-come-easy-go phenomenon. Predictive power characterizes the rapid-growth phase of the S-shaped pattern (rheostasis) as well as the end of the pattern when growth reaches a ceiling (homeostasis) where supply and demand are in equilibrium. The latter phenomenon is best exemplified by society's tolerance of deadly car accidents because deaths from car accidents have remained at an invariant level for many decades reflecting equilibrium. The mathematical equation for growth in competition when cast in discrete form reveals fluctuations of chaotic nature before and after the rapid-growth phase. This can illuminate the turbulent times before and after the formation of the USSR as well as the tumultuous times of the 1930s in America. Extending the quantitative approach to two species competing in the same niche involves introducing coupling constants that account for how one species impacts the growth rate of the other. A celebrated example is the predator-prey relationship, which is only one of six possible interactions all of which can be encountered in the marketplace where products and companies compete like species. There are six possible dimensions for action in a two-species competitive struggle that can be exploited toward managing

* Correspondence concerning this article should be addressed to Theodore Modis, Via Selva 8, Massagno 6900, Lugano, Switzerland. E-mail: tmodis@yahoo.com

competition and setting one's role/image in the marketplace. An example dealt in detail is the evolution of the number of American Noble-Prize winners whose numbers are not about to begin diminishing. Americans are involved in a win-win competitive struggle with non-American scholars, but Americans are drawing more of a benefit.

INSIGHTS ON COMPETITION FROM A SCIENCE-BASED ANALYSIS

The fisherman starting his day off the Adriatic coast was wondering whether it was going to be a day of big fish or smaller ones. He had seen this phenomenon often. He would start by catching a big fish in the morning and then for the rest of the day it would be one big fish after another. Other times it would be small catches all day long. He was reminded in passing of a biblical reference to periods of fat years and thin years, but he got down to work without further philosophizing. He had no time to waste; in the days following the Great War the sea was one place where food could still be found relatively easily.

Meanwhile, at the University of Siena, the biologist Umberto D'Ancona was making statistical studies of Adriatic fisheries. He found temporary increases in the relative frequency of the more voracious kinds of fish, as compared with the fish on which they preyed. Vito Volterra, a mathematician at the University of Rome, was preoccupied in his own way with the same phenomenon. He knew of D'Ancona's observations and believed he understood the reason for them. Since big fish eat small fish — and consequently depend on them for survival — some interchange in population dominance should be expected. The population of big fish would grow until small fish became scarce. At some point the big fish would starve and their diminishing numbers would give the small-fish survivors a chance to renew their numbers. Could this phenomenon be described mathematically?

Volterra succeeded in building a mathematical formulation that described well the fisherman's observations. A model for the growth of populations, it states that the rate of growth is limited by competition and that the overall size of the population (for example, the number of rabbits in a fenced-off grass field) slowly approaches a ceiling, the height of which reflects the capacity of the ecological niche. The model would serve as a foundation for modern biological studies of the competitive struggle for life. Alfred J. Lotka also studied such problems to some extent. Today, there are applications bearing both men's names.

Half a century later, Cesare Marchetti, a physicist at the International Institute of Applied Systems Analysis (IIASA) near Vienna, Austria, was given the task by the energy-project leader to forecast energy demands. Another kind of war had been shaking the West recently: the fierce competition for oil. The need for increased understanding of the future energy picture was becoming imperative. Marchetti approached the problem as a physicist, who sought answers through the use of the scientific method: observation, prediction, verification. In this approach predictions must be related to observations through a theory resting on hypotheses. When the predictions are verified, the hypotheses become laws. The simpler a law, the more fundamental it is and the wider its range of applications.

Marchetti had long been concerned with the "science" of predictions. In his work, he first started searching for what physicists call invariants. These are constants universally valid and manifested through indicators that do not change over time. He believed that such indicators represent some kind of equilibrium even if one is not dealing with physics but with human activities instead. He then suspected that the fundamental laws which govern growth and

competition among species may also describe human activities. Competition in the market place can be as fierce as in the jungle, and the law of the survival of the fittest becomes indisputable. Marchetti noted that growth curves for animal populations follow patterns similar to those for product sales. Could it be that the mathematics developed by Volterra for the growth of a rabbit population describe equally well the growth of cars and computers? Marchetti went on to make a dazzling array of predictions, including forecasts of future energy demands, using Volterra's equations.[1] But how far can the analogy between natural laws and human activities be pushed and how trustworthy are the quantitative forecasts based on such formulations?

In 1984 my professional lifeline crossed those of Volterra and Marchetti. I was passing from academia to industry, leaving fifteen years of research in elementary particle physics to work as a management-science consultant for DEC (Digital Equipment Corporation). My boss, an ex-physicist himself, tried to smooth the transition by showing me some of Marchetti's papers that described applications of laws from the natural sciences to a variety of human affairs. "See how we are also intellectually alert in industry" was the message. However, three weeks later, and in spite of my enthusiasm, the stern new message was: "Now leave all this aside and let's get down to work." It was too late, because the subject had intrigued me.

From then onward my involvement with natural growth in competition became my *raison d'être* and culminated with the publication of my first book *Predictions – Society's Telltale Signature Reveals the past and Forecasts the Future* (Modis, 1992), which begins the same way as this chapter.

The S-Curve

At the heart of competition lies the principle of survival of the fittest. If you put a pair of rabbits in a meadow and the average rabbit litter is taken as two, you can watch the rabbit population go through the successive stages of 2, 4, 8, 16, 32, 64, ..., 2^n in an exponential growth. There is a population explosion up to the time when a sizable part of the ecological niche is occupied. It is only after this time that limited food resources begin imposing constraints on the number of surviving rabbits and the population growth slows down as it approaches a ceiling — the capacity of a species' ecological niche. This slowdown may happen by means of increased kit mortality, diseases, lethal fights between overcrowded rabbits, or even other more subtle forms of behavior that rabbits may act out unsuspectingly. Nature imposes population controls as needed, and in a competitive environment, only the fittest survive.

Over time, the rabbit population traces an S-shaped trajectory. The *rate* of growth traces a curve that is bell-shaped and peaks when half the niche is filled. The S-shaped curve (S-curve) for the population and the bell-shaped curve for its rate of growth constitute a pictorial representation of the natural growth process — that is, how a species population grows into a limited space by obeying the law of survival of the fittest.

At the ceiling, we may witness oscillations as the rabbit population explores the possibility to go further and overshoots the niche capacity only to fall back later giving the

[1] See Marchetti's website: http://www.cesaremarchetti.org

grass a chance to grow back and feed more rabbits. At this point we may talk of a *homeostasis*, a stable state of equilibrium between the number of rabbits and the amount of grass.

An S-curve and the associated life cycle are two different ways of looking at the same growth process. The S-curve represents the size of the growth and points out (anticipates) the growth potential, the level of the final ceiling, how much could one expect to accomplish. The bell-shaped life-cycle curve represents the rate of growth and is more helpful when it comes to appreciating the growth phase you are traversing, and how far you are from the end. The S-shaped curve reminds us of the fact that competitive growth is capped. The bell-shaped curve reminds us that whatever gets born eventually dies. From an intuitive point of view, an S-curve promises a certain amount of growth that can be accomplished, whereas a bell-curve heralds the coming end of the process as a whole. Both curves possess predictive power.

At the ceiling of the S-curve (homeostasis) the level remains invariant and therefore it is trivial to forecast. But there is predictability also during the rapid-growth phase (rheostasis). You can easily anticipate where a fast-moving train will end up. A bicycle is stable only when in motion and the faster it is going the more stable it is, the easier it is to project its trajectory.

The Patterns of Natural Growth in Competition and Its Life Cycle

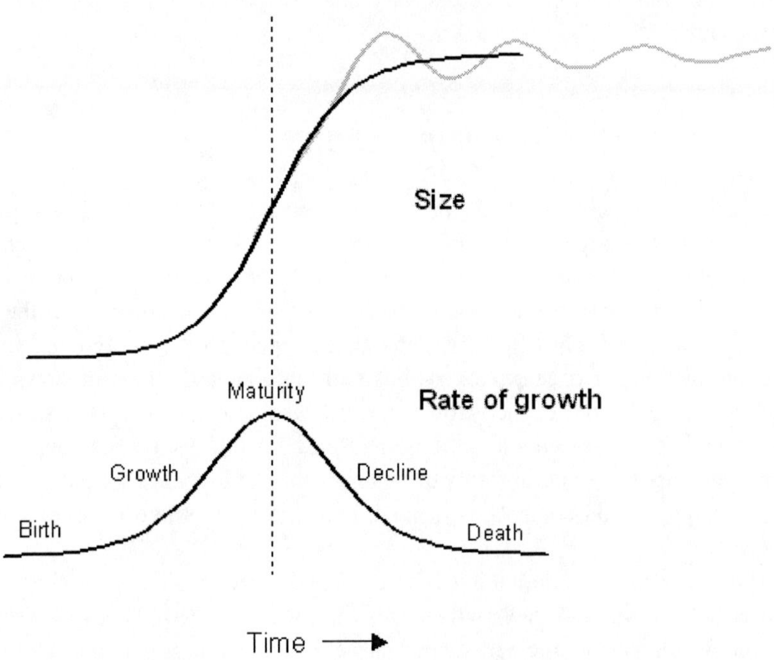

Figure 1. The S-shaped pattern above is the solution of the natural-growth equation. The bell-shaped curve below is used across disciplines as a template for the cycle of life. The gray line sketches the fluctuations of a rabbit population that has filled its ecological niche to capacity.

The predictive power of the bell-shaped life-cycle curve comes from its symmetry. A rapid rise will be followed by an equally rapid decline, echoing such expressions as "Easy come, easy go" and "Early ripe, early rot". Many business endeavors have experienced this the hard way in the marketplace.

The mathematical equation — the logistic equation — that describes the law of natural growth in competition and gives rise to the S-curve says in words that the rate of growth must be at all times proportional to two things:

- The amount of growth *already accomplished.*
- The amount of growth *remaining to be accomplished.*

If either one of these quantities is small, the rate of growth will be small. This is the case at the beginning and at the end of the process. The rate is greatest in the middle, where both the growth accomplished and the growth remaining are sizable. Furthermore, growth "remaining to be accomplished" implies a limit, a saturation level, a finite niche size. Competition is a consequence of a limited resource and therefore growth in competition cannot go on forever; it is necessarily capped. This ceiling of growth is assumed to be constant throughout the growth process. Such an assumption is a good approximation to many natural-growth processes, for example, plant growth, in which the final height is genetically pre-coded.

It is a remarkably simple and fundamental law. Besides used by biologists to describe species populations, it has also been used in medicine to describe the diffusion of epidemic diseases. J. C. Fisher and R. H. Pry refer to the logistic equation as a diffusion model and use it to quantify the spreading of new technologies into society (Fisher & Pry, 1971). One can immediately see how ideas or rumors may spread according to this law. Whether it is ideas, rumors, technologies, or diseases, the rate of new occurrences will always be proportional to how many people have it and to how many don't yet have it. At the end you will always be able to find — albeit in slowly diminishing numbers — the outcasts who never heard the rumor, or refused to adopt the new technology.

The S-curve has also being referred to as a learning curve in psychology as well as in industry. For example, the evolution of an infant's vocabulary has been shown to follow an S-curve that reaches a ceiling of about 2500 words by age six.[2] Acquiring vocabulary can be thought of as a competitive process where words in the combined active vocabulary of the two parents compete for the infant's attention. The words most frequently used will be learned first, but the rate of learning will eventually slow down because there are fewer words left to learn. This ceiling of 2500 words defines the size of the home vocabulary "niche," all the words available at home. Later, of course, schooling enriches the child's vocabulary, but this is a new process, starting another cycle, following probably a similar type of curve to reach a higher plateau.

The S-curve in Figure 1 is asymptotic, i.e. it approaches zero, the level of the ceiling continuously but reaches it only in time $-\infty$, $+\infty$ respectively. On the other hand the fact that growth is proportional to the amount of growth already achieved renders the beginning of every natural-growth process practically very difficult (theoretically impossible because zero growth achieved yields a null rate for growth and so things cannot be started!) This

[2] An S-curve has been fitted on the data found in Whiston (1974).

demystifies the known difficulty associated with beginnings. An ancient Greek proverb on achievement equates the beginning with half of the whole! The consequences on learning are enlightening. Theoretically learning cannot begin without outside help. The work of teachers becomes indispensable in this context. The teacher is the custodian of knowledge and oriental schools of thought preclude search for esoteric knowledge and personal development without a teacher.

The theoretical difficulty in getting growth in competition started touches upon philosophical questions akin to the genesis because of the requirement that some discontinuous intervention from an external agent (for example, a powerful intelligent entity) is necessary in order to get something going from nothing.

Fatal Car Accidents

The logistic equation has been successfully used to describe growth processes where the notion of competition has been raised to remarkable levels of abstraction. Marchetti has argued that primary-energy sources compete for consumers' favor and diseases compete for victims. In all cases there is a limited resource, which imposes the constraint that only the best-fit candidate wins. My favorite example is fatal car accidents (Marchetti, 1983). All possible accidents can be thought to compete for becoming realized and claim victims. Only the "best" of them will do so because here again there is a limited resource and contrary to what one may naively expect it is much smaller than the entire population.

Car safety has been a passionate subject frequently appearing in headlines. At some point in time cars had been compared to murder weapons. Still today close to two hundred thousand people worldwide die from car accidents every year, and up to ten times as many suffer injuries. Efforts are continually made to render cars safer and drivers more cautious. How successful have such efforts been? Can this rate be significantly reduced as we move toward a more advanced society?

To answer these questions, we must look at the history of car accidents, but in order to search for a fundamental law we must have accurate data and an appropriate indicator. Deaths are recorded and interpreted with less ambiguity than other accidents. Moreover, the car as a public menace is a threat to society, which may "feel" the pain and react accordingly. Consequently, the number of deaths per one hundred thousand inhabitants per year becomes a better indicator than accidents per mile, or per car, or per hour of driving.

The data shown in Figure 2 are for the United States starting at the beginning of the 20th century. What we observe is that deaths caused by car accidents grew along an S-shaped pattern with the appearance of cars until the mid 1920s, when they reached about twenty-four per one hundred thousand per year. From then onward they seem to have stabilized, even though the number of cars continued to grow. A homeostatic mechanism seems to emerge when this limit is reached, resulting in an oscillating pattern around the equilibrium position. The peaks may have produced public outcries for safety, while the valleys could have contributed to the relaxation of speed limits and safety regulations. What is remarkable is that for over sixty years there has been a persistent self-regulation on car safety despite major increases in car numbers and performance, and important changes in speed limits, safety technology, driving legislation, and education.

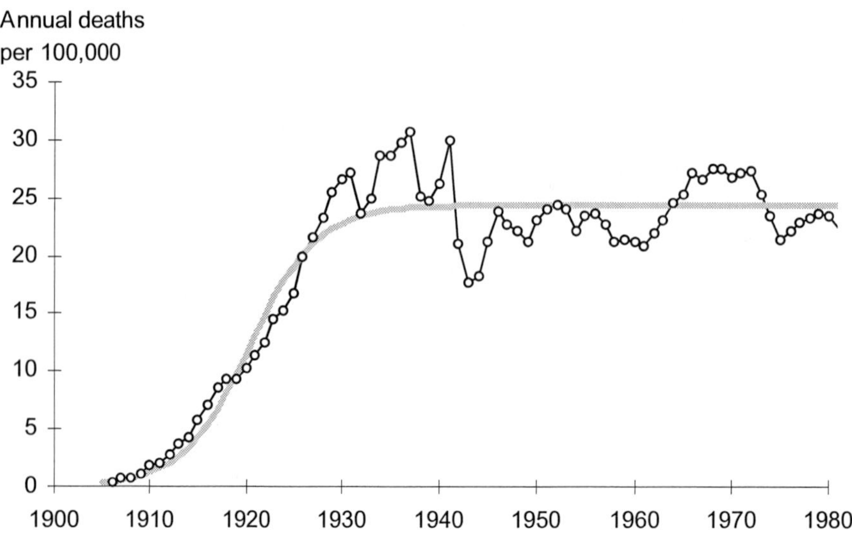

Figure 2. The annual number of deaths from motor-vehicle accidents per 100,000 population has followed an S-curve to reach a ceiling of 24 around which it has been fluctuating since the mid 1920s, not unlike the rabbit population sketched in gray in Figure 1. The peak in the late 1960s provoked a public outcry that resulted in legislation making seat belts mandatory.

Why the number of deaths is maintained constant and how society can detect excursions away from this level? Is it conceivable that some day car safety will improve so much that car accidents will be reduced to zero? American society has tolerated this level of accidents for more than half a century. A Rand analyst has described it as follows: "I am sure that there is, in effect, a desirable level of automobile accidents — desirable, that is, from a broad point of view, in the sense that it is a necessary concomitant of things of greater value to society" (Williams, 1958). Abolishing cars from the roads would certainly eliminate car accidents, but at the same time it would introduce more serious hardship to citizens.

An invariant (a homeostatic level) can be thought of as a state of well-being. It has its roots in nature, which develops ways of maintaining it. Individuals may come forward from time to time as advocates of an apparently well-justified cause. What they do not suspect is that they may be acting as agents to deeply rooted forces maintaining a balance that would have been maintained in any case. An example is Ralph Nader's crusade for car safety, *Unsafe at Any Speed*, published in the 1960s, by which time the number of fatal car accidents had already demonstrated a forty-year-long period of relative stability. But examining Figure 2 more closely, we see that the 1960s show a small peak in accidents, which must have been what prompted Nader to blow the whistle. Had he not done it, someone else would have. Alternatively, a timely social mechanism might have produced the same result; for example, an "accidental" discovery of an effective new car-safety feature.

During the last thirty years there has been evidence for a gentle downward trend not shown in Figure 2. One could argue that Nader's crusade for car safety was indeed effective. After all it was instrumental in making seat belts mandatory and lowering the speed limits

throughout the country. I seriously doubt such cause-and-effect reasoning. Seat belts and speed limits certainly had some effect, which among other things, made environmentalists shift their focus to other issues. But action taken forty years ago would not still keep reducing deaths from car accidents today. In fact speed limits have been significantly raised in most states since then. The state of Montana has even experimented with lifting some speed limits altogether.

As usually, there is a more deeply seated explanation for deviations from a natural-growth pattern. The airplane has been steadily replacing the automobile as a means of intercity transportation since the late 1960s. Despite the fact that the automobile still commands a dominant share of the transportation market today, Americans have in fact been giving up, slowly but steadily, their beloved cars, and the fatal accidents that go with them.

PERSONAL ACHIEVEMENT

Competition is abundant in the worlds of the arts and the sciences. But there is one aspect of competition that we are not familiar with. The fact that one's creative potential is finite, which results in a competitive squeeze for the realization of one's remaining creative impulses.

It was Marchetti again who first associated the evolution of a person's creativity and productivity with natural growth. He assumed that a work of art or science is the final expression of a "pulse of action" that originates somewhere in the depths of the brain and works its way through many intermediate stages to produce a creation. He then studied the number of these creations over time and found that their growth follows S-shaped curves. Each curve presupposed a final ceiling, a niche size, a perceived creative potential. "Perceived" because competition may prevent it from being reached. Marchetti proceeded to study hundreds of well-documented artists and scientists. In each case, he took the total number of known creations, graphed them over time, and determined the S-shaped curve that would best connect these data points. He found that most people died close to having realized their perceived potential. In his words:

"To illustrate further what I mean ... consider the amount of beans a man has in his bag and the amount left when he finally dies. Looking at the cases mentioned here ... I find that the leftover beans are usually five to ten percent of the total. Apparently when Mozart died at 35 years of age, he had already said what he had to say" (Marchetti, 1985).

The idea is intriguing. Obviously people's productivity increases and decreases with time. Youngsters cannot produce much because they have to learn first. Old people may become exhausted of ideas, energy, and motivation. It makes intuitive sense that productivity goes through a life cycle over a person's lifetime, slowing down as it approaches the end. The cumulative productivity — the total number of works produced — could very well look like an S-shaped curve over time.

So I looked up Mozart's compositions and was able to fit an S-curve on the evolution of his work volume, see Figure 3. I counted every composition as one unit, on the argument that a minuet at the age of six is no less a creative achievement than a requiem at the age of thirty-five.

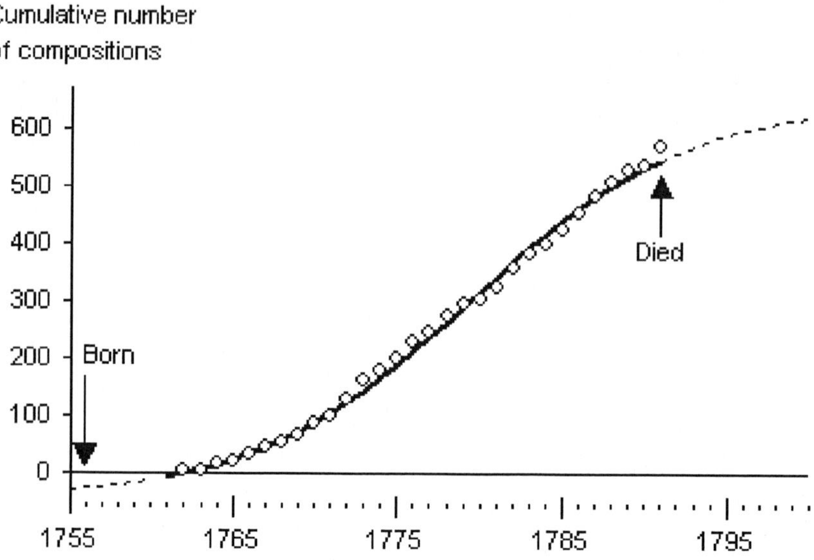

Figure 3. The best-fitting S-shaped curve implies 18 compositions "missing" between 1756 and 1762. The nominal beginning of the curve — the 1 percent level — points at Mozart's birthday. The nominal end — the 99 percent level — indicates a potential of 644 works.

The fit turned out to be successful. I found an S-curve that passed impressively close to all thirty-one yearly points representing the cumulative number of compositions. There were two little irregularities, however; one on each end.

The irregularity at the low end of the curve caused my computer program to include an early-missing-data parameter. The reason: better agreement between the curve and the data if 18 compositions are assumed to be missing during Mozart's earliest years. His first recorded composition was created in 1762, when he was six. However, the curve's nominal beginning — the 1 percent level of the ceiling — is around 1756, Mozart's birth date. Conclusion: Mozart was composing from the moment he was born. His first eighteen compositions, however, were never recorded due to "technical" difficulties — the fact that he could neither write nor speak well enough to dictate them to his father.

The second irregularity was at the high end of the curve, the year of Mozart's death: 1791 showed a large increase in productivity. In fact, the data point fell well above the curve, corresponding more to the productivity projected for the year 1793. What was Mozart trying to do during the last year of his life? With his creative potential determined as 644 compositions, his last composition would put him at the 91 percent level of exhaustion. Most people who die of old age have realized 90 percent of their creative potential. There was very little left for Mozart to do. His work in this world had been practically accomplished. The irregularity at the high end of his creativity curve indicated the sprint at the finish! What he had left to do was not enough to help him fight the illness that was consuming him. "Mozart died of old age" is the conclusion we would come to by looking at this graph. Yet there is a

popular belief that the world has been deprived of many musical masterpieces by his "premature" death.

In discussions with musicians, I have found that many are not shocked by the idea that Mozart may have exhausted his creative potential at the age of thirty-five. He had already contributed so much in every musical form of the time that he could no longer break new ground. Of course, he could have done more of the same: more concertos, more symphonies, more trios and quartets. But all this would have represented com-promised innovation. He himself wrote at the age of 21, "To live until one can no longer contribute anything new to music" (Massin, 1978).

From Order to Chaos and Back

When the logistic equation that describes growth in competition is cast into discrete form (necessary because everything in real life is discrete) it becomes the chaos equation. The latter is strikingly similar to the former — see Appendix — but whereas the former gives rise to the smooth S-curves, the latter, for certain values of its parameters, gives rise to states of chaos. The logistic equation emphasizes the presence of a trend and has become the tool to describe natural growth. The chaos equation emphasizes the lack of trend and has become the tool to describe chaotic states. Both equations originate with growth in competition of Darwinian nature.

The states of chaos appear on what corresponds to the ceiling of the logistic after the upward trend has died down. It has also been shown that chaotic-type fluctuations could be expected before as well as after the curve's steep rise (Modis & Debecker, 1992). An example in a large time frame is the world economy, as evidenced by the evolution of energy consumption. Per-capita energy consumption worldwide is more than seven times greater today than it was 150 years ago. This increase took place, not in a steady, uniform rate, or even in a random fashion, but in two well-defined S-shaped steps.

It is easy to see why energy consumption is a competitive process. Human appetite for energy is insatiable — they will use up all the energy they can get — but supply is limited because the procurement of energy is difficult (read expensive). From time to time technology and socioeconomic conditions permit/stimulate the opening up of new energy-supply niches. When this happens energy consumption increases to exhaust these niches in a natural way, namely along S-shaped patterns. At the end of the growth step energy consumption reaches a homeostasis; further growth is held back by other more urgent priorities.

In Figure 4 we see that the first step ended around 1920 with a period of stagnation that lasted for about two decades. The second energy consumption step was completed around 1975, and we have just witnessed the beginning of a third step. There can be little doubt that this indicator will go through another growth phase considering the dire need for industrial growth in the developing world.

Energy consumption correlates in an unambiguous way with industrial development and economic prosperity. The profile of the energy curve over time eloquently points out two chaotic low-growth periods, one centered on the mid-1930s and another one around 1990. These economic depressions echo Kondratieff's economic cycle (Kondratieff, 1935). Competition intensifies as we enter these periods. Remember the rabbits, they began feeling the squeeze when their ecological niche began filling up.

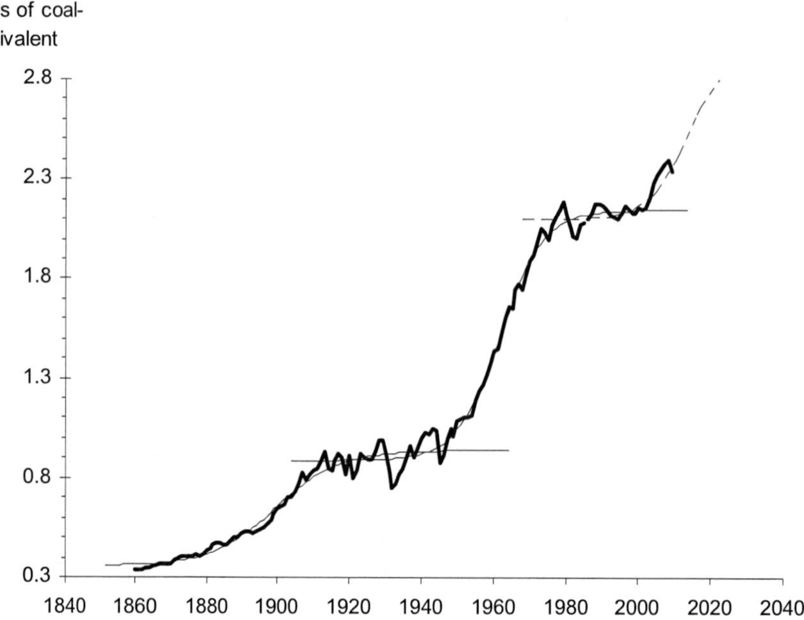

Figure 4. The data display sustained growth in terms of a succession of S-shaped steps. The two smooth solid lines are logistic fits to the data. The intermittent line is a scenario for the future suggested by analogy. The data pattern exemplifies the alternation between orderly growth and turbulent stagnation periods.

The Rise and Fall of the Communist Empire

The ultimate sin of a forecaster is to predict something after it has happened. Well, my work revolves around innovative forecasting techniques, and here I am about to present arguments demonstrating that the collapse of Communism could have been predicted with devilish precision as early as the 1960s. What makes me indulge in such an unprofessional exercise is the fact that recently one more person threw at me the by now classic remark: "Who could have ever predicted the fall of the Berlin wall?" His comment was the last straw.

We saw earlier that chaotic periods precede and follow the rapid-growth phase of a natural-growth process. At the same time, life cycles are generally symmetric. Communism and the USSR can be likened to a species whose life cycle began with the revolution of 1917. It peaked forty years later, in the mid-1950s, when the Soviet Union successfully competed and often surpassed the United States (for example, with Sputnik in 1957). A symmetric life cycle would position the end of communism another forty years later, the mid-1990s. The headline-making event, the collapse of the Berlin wall, took place in a sharp discontinuous way, reflecting the first large fluctuation of the chaotic state that sets in as the natural-growth process approaches completion. With the end of the process anticipated in the mid-1990s, chaotic tremors are to be expected several years earlier. These are rather accurate predictions for the collapse of communism and the fall of the Berlin wall. They ensue from a rigorous and precise reckoning. They could have been made as early as the 1960s, when it became clear

that the Soviet Union was already over its peak. The Soviets had begun losing, first in 1963 with the Cuban missile crisis, then in 1969 with the moon race that was doomed for lack of funds. The Soviets could not afford adequate testing of their superior rocket, and it exploded during the critical launch.

The Soviet Union Life Cycle

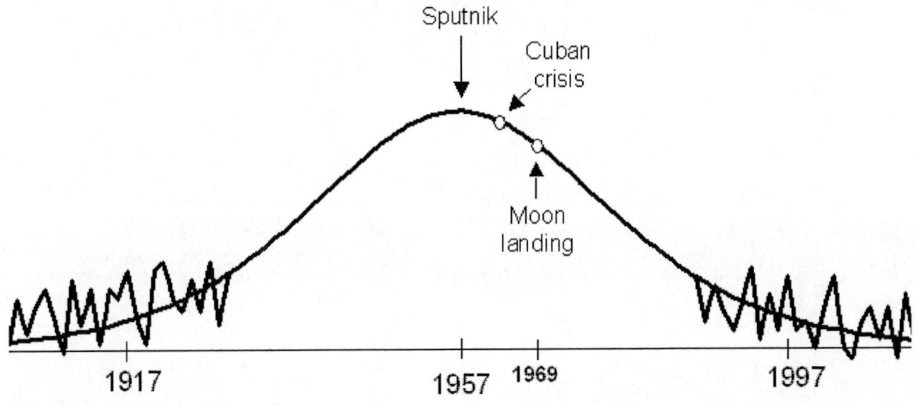

Figure 5. A pictorial representation of the making and the dismantling of the Soviet Union. Chaotic periods characterize the revolution of 1917 as well as the years following the fall of the Berlin wall.

The fall of the Berlin wall punctuated the end of the Communist growth curve and signaled the beginning of the chaotic phase. It should take a while for free market forces to become established there, however. If we divide the life cycle in four equal segments — according to the season metaphor, see *Conquering Uncertainty* — 20 years (one-fourth of the 80-year life cycle of the Soviet block) is how long the post-Berlin-wall chaotic period should last (Modis, 1998).

Competition Management

Extending the quantitative study of competition to more than one species requires the introduction of coupling constants. If there are two species in the niche, then two coupling constants are required to account for how one's presence impacts the growth rate of the other. The mathematical description then consists of two logistic equations each one augmented by one coupling parameters — see Appendix. The set of these equations are referred to as the Volterra-Lotka coupled equations. The usefulness of this formulation has been extended to describe competition outside biology and ecology. Indeed, the Volterra-Lotka model has opened the way to effectively managing competition in the marketplace. A set of elementary marketing actions has emerged that provide guidance when searching for a commercial image or an effective advertising message.

An intriguing aspect of the marketplace is that the nature of competition can change over time. A technology, company, or product does not need to remain prey to another forever. Competitive roles can be radically altered with technological advances or with the right

marketing decisions. External light meters, used for accurate diaphragm and speed setting on photographic cameras, enjoyed a stable, symbiotic (win–win) relationship with cameras for decades. As camera sales grew, so did light-meter sales. But eventually, technological developments enabled camera companies to incorporate light meters into their own boxes. Soon, the whole light-meter industry became prey to the camera industry. Sales of external light meters diminished while sales of cameras enjoyed a boost, and the relationship passed from win–win to predator–prey.

The Battle of the Pens

The struggle between fountain pens and ballpoint pens had a different ending, see Figure 6. The substitution of ballpoint pens for fountain pens as writing instruments went through three distinct stages. Before the appearance of ballpoint pens, fountain-pen sales grew undisturbed along an S-curve to fill the writing-instrument market. They were following an S-shaped curve when the ballpoint technology appeared in 1951. As ballpoint sales picked up, those of fountain pens declined in the period 1951 to 1973. Fountain pens staged a counterattack by radically dropping prices. But that effort failed. Fountain pens kept losing market share and embarked on an extinction course. By 1973, their average price had dropped to as low as 72 cents, to no avail.

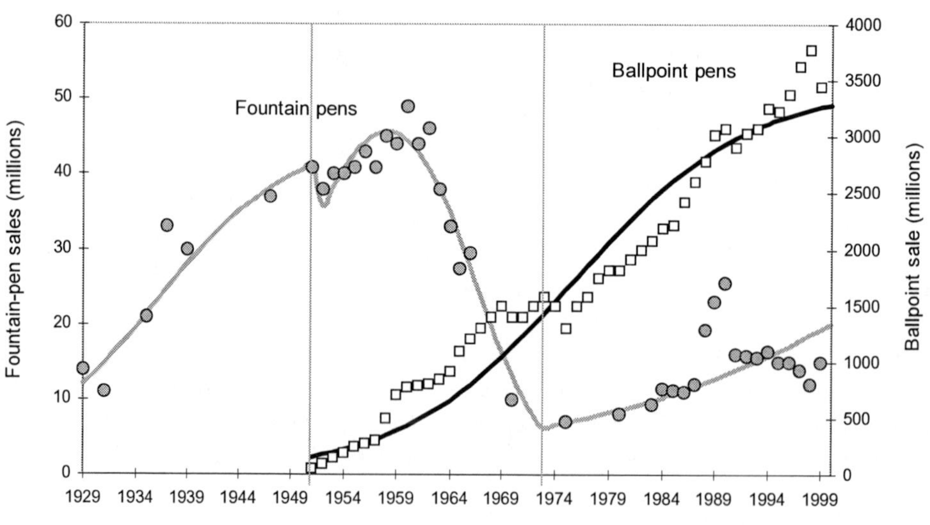

Figure 6. Fountain pen sales were following a classic S-shaped growth curve when ballpoint pens were introduced in 1951. Fountain pens counter attacked by dropping prices between 1951 and 1973, then retreated into noncompetition by entering a luxury niche.[3]

3 Data source: Writing Instrument Manufacturers Association, Mt. Laurel, NL 08054, and Farrell (1993).

Eventually, however, the prices of fountain pens began rising. The fountain pen underwent what Darwin would have described as a character displacement to the luxury niche of the executive-pen market. In the early 1970s, the strategy of fountain pens became a retreat into noncompetition. By 1988, the price of some fountain pens in the United States had climbed to $400. The Volterra-Lotka model indicates that today the two species no longer interact but each follows a simple S-shaped growth pattern. As a consequence, fountain pens have secured a healthy and profitable market niche. Had they persisted in their competition with ballpoint pens, they would have perished.

Handling Competition

Character displacement is a classical way to diminish the impact of competition. Another name for this is Darwinian divergence, sometimes also encountered among siblings. In his book *Born to Rebel: Birth Order, Family Dynamics, and Creative Lives*, Frank Sulloway shows that throughout history, first-born children have become conservative and later-borns revolutionaries. First-born children end up conservative because they do not want to lose any of the only-child privileges they enjoy. But this forces later-borns into becoming rebellious, to differentiate themselves and thus minimize competition with a sibling and optimize survival in the same family (Sulloway, 1996).

The attack of a new species against the defenses of an incumbent one lies at the heart of corporate marketing strategies. Christopher Farrell, director of scientific affairs at Baxter Healthcare Corp. (Deerfield, IL), defined an attacker's advantage and a defender's counterattack in terms of the coupling parameters in the Volterrra-Lotka model. A coupling parameter can be determined by data, and thus, it can assign a precise number to an attacker's advantage or a defender's counterattack.

The attacker's advantage quantifies the extent to which the attacker inhibits the ability of the defender to keep market share. The defender's counterattack quantifies the extent to which the defender can prevent the attacker from stealing market share (Farrell, 1993).

Under attack, the defender redoubles its efforts to maintain or improve its position. A high value for the defender's counterattack implies a face-on counterattack within the context "what they do, we do better." Kristina Smitalova and Stefan Sujan studied and classified the various coupling schemes by which two competitors might interact. They distinguished and labeled six ways in which two competitors can influence each other's growth rate, according to the sign of the two coupling parameters, Table 1 (Smitalova & Sujan, 1991). Pure competition occurs between rabbits and sheep. Each one diminishes the growth of the other but not necessarily with the same importance (sheep multiply more slowly but eat more). Market examples are the competition among mobile-telephone companies and among different-size computer models.

An example of predator–prey interaction is the case of cinema and television. The more movies made, the more television benefits; but the more television grows in importance, the more cinema suffers. Films made for TV are not shown in movie theaters. Without the legal protection that restricts permission to broadcast new movies, television would probably "eat up" the cinema audience.

Table 1. The six ways two competitors, A and B, can influence each other's growth rate can be summarized in terms of positive, negative, and neutral coupling parameters

MODE	DEFINITION	Coupling parameter	
		A	B
Pure competition	Both species suffer from each other's existence.	-	-
Predator-prey	One serves as food for the other.	+	-
Mutualism	Symbiosis; a win-win situation.	+	+
Commensalism	A parasitic type of relationship in which one benefits from the existence of the other, which nevertheless remains unaffected.	+	0
Amensalism	One suffers from the existence of the other, which remains impervious to what is happening.	-	0
Neutralism	No interaction whatsoever.	0	0

A typical case of mutualism is software and hardware. Sales of each trigger more sales for the other, as in the early relationship between external light meters and cameras. Add-ons and accessories such as vehicle extras illustrate commensalism. The more automobiles sold, the more car accessories will be sold. The inverse is not true, however; sales of accessories do not trigger automobile sales.

Amensalism can be found with ballpoint pens and fountain pens. The onslaught of ballpoint sales seriously damaged fountain pen sales, yet the ballpoint-pen population grew as if there were no competition.

Neutralism arises in all situations in which there is no market overlap, as happens between fountain pens and ballpoint pens today. Another example is a sports store that sells both swimwear and skiwear. Although sales of one may rise when sales of the other go down because of seasonal variation, sales of one product do not generally affect sales of the other (Modis, 1998).

Coupling Parameters

The S-shaped pattern evidenced in the evolution of a species population can in general be described with two parameters: one reflects the ability of the species to multiply (or a product's attractiveness), and the other reflects the size of the ecological niche (or a product's market niche). But what happens if more than one species of competitor is present? Besides rabbits and sheep, cows also eat grass. Worse yet, what happens if there are also foxes on the range? Competition between rabbits and sheep is not the same as between rabbits and foxes. Faced with a finite amount of grass, sheep would probably lament at the rapid multiplication of rabbits, whereas foxes would undoubtedly rejoice.

The main feature of the Volterra-Lotka equations is that they can deal with how one competitor influences the growth rate of the other. They do this by introducing a third parameter, the so-called coupling parameter. Sheep and rabbits have a negative effect on each other's population because they reduce each other's food supply. In contrast, foxes damage

rabbit populations, while rabbits enhance fox populations. The coupling parameter reflects how much one species affects another — in other words, how many sales you will lose or win because your competitor won one. The magnitude of the parameter measures your ability to attack, counterattack, or retreat.

Advertising Strategies

The Volterra-Lotka model has three parameters for each competitor — one reflecting the competitor's ability to multiply, the second the size of its niche, and the third the interference from the other competitor. Thus, there are three lines of marketing action, or six if we also consider the parameters of the other competitor, see Table 2. To increase our prospects for growth, we can try to influence one or more of the following:

- the product's attractiveness (increase ours or decrease theirs),
- the size of the market niche (increase ours or decrease theirs), and
- the nature of the interaction (increase our attack or decrease their defense).

Each line of action affects one parameter at a time, but it is not obvious which change will produce the greater effect at a given time or which parameter is easiest to change. It depends on the particular situation. The concrete actions may include performance improvements, price changes, image transformation, and advertising campaigns. Performance and price concern "our" products only, but advertising with an appropriate message can in principle influence all aspects of competition, producing an effect on all six parameters. The question is how much of an effect a certain effort (budget) will produce.

Table 2. Six basic advertising strategies are defined by increasing or decreasing the parameters: attractiveness, niche size, and competition

	ATTRACTIVENES	NICHE SIZE	COMPETITION
WE	Our products are good	You need our products	We are different
THEY	Their products are not good	You do not need their products	What they do, we do better

Some advertising messages have proven significantly more effective than others. Success is not necessarily due to whim, chance, or other after-the-fact explanations based on psychological or circumstantial arguments. The roles and positions of the competitors determine which advertising message will be most effective. Actual messages are often elaborate, but in principle, all successful advertising campaigns have exploited some combination of these six elements (Modis, 2003).

Carpet Wars

The effectiveness of advertising messages can be illustrated by a classical competitive technological substitution, that of synthetic fiber for natural fiber in the fabrication of carpets. For centuries, carpets were woven on a loom for which wool was well suited. But around the middle of the 20th century, a new tufting technique favored long, continuous filaments. At the same time, synthetic fibers such as nylon became available, and nylon-tufted carpets began replacing woven-wool rugs.

Solving the Volterra-Lotka equations for the carpet-sales data yields negative coupling constants for the two competitors, a typical situation of pure competition of the rabbit-sheep type. But the attacker's advantage was greater than the defender's counterattack, and so was its attractiveness. Therefore, the fate of the defender was eventual extinction. Today, woven-wool carpets represent less than 1% of carpet sales.

Could the makers of woven-wool carpets have secured a market niche the way fountain pens did? If so, what line of action should have they adopted? We can go back to 1979 and play out six scenarios exploring alternative lines of advertising — changing the six parameters one at a time by the same amount — to test their results. It turns out that effective campaigns would have been those that emphasized attractiveness and differentiation with messages such as "Wool is good" and "Wool is different from nylon" as opposed to a counterattack along the lines: "Wool is better than nylon." These conclusions could not have been arrived at by intuitive or other methods traditionally used by advertising agencies, and they could be completely different at another time or in another market (Modis, 2003).

Of crucial importance, of course, is the amount of effort required to achieve the targeted change. There is a way to estimate the size of the advertising investment needed. An advertising campaign along the line "Our product is good" affects the product's attractiveness just as a price cut does. The costs incurred from price dropping can thus be compared to those of an advertising campaign that achieves the same result. It should be noted, however, that if the survival of woolen carpets depended on price dropping alone, the price would have to be reduced to zero.

Effective Advertising

The Volterra–Lotka model accounts for the three fundamental factors that shape growth: the attractiveness of an offering, the size of its market niche, and its interaction with the competitor. When there is more than one competitor, the situation can be reduced to two by considering the major competitor only and by grouping all others together. Naturally, other factors influence growth, such as sales channels, distribution, market fragmentation, total market growth, market share, frequency of innovations, productivity, and organizational and human-resource issues. Many factors can be expressed as combinations of the three fundamental ones. Alternatively, the model could be elaborated — by adding more parameters — to take more phenomena into account.

As it stands, the model provides the baseline — the trend on top of which other, higher-order effects will be superimposed. It guides strategists through effective manipulations of a competitor's roles in the marketplace. It should be used before any discussions of investments, advertising tactics, or detailed planning take place. The model works equally

well for products, for corporations, technologies, and whole industries. Only the time frames differ. Strategists now have a quantitative, science-based way to understand the crux of the competitive dynamics and to anticipate the consequences of possible actions.

A typical first question is, "Should we differentiate or counterattack?" You can answer this question with a simulation on a computer using sales data and the Volterra-Lotka equations. Just think — at this very moment there may be a cost effective way to terminate the state of being prey to the voracious competitor that has been feeding persistently on your achievements.

COMPETITION FOR NOBEL PRIZES

It has been suggested that the competition for Nobel Prize awards can be described by logistic-growth curves (Marchetti, 1989). The reasoning behind it was that the limited resource was the total number of Nobel laureates that the US will ever claim. The implication was that this number is capped. In other words, there will be some time in the future when all Nobel Prizes will be awarded to nationals from other countries. Up to that time, Americans would be elbowing each other to win prizes and the fewer left in their "niche" the harder it would be to win one.

My first attempt to fit a logistic S-curve to the cumulative number of US Nobel laureates in 1988 concluded that the US Nobel niche was already more than half full and implied a diminishing annual number of Nobel Prizes for Americans from then onward (Modis, 1988). Ten years later I confronted those forecasts with more recent data in my book *Predictions – 10 Years Later* (Modis, 2002). The agreement was not very good. The forecasts fell below the actual data and despite the fact that there was agreement within the uncertainties expected for a 90% confidence level the discrepancy did not go unnoticed. A technical note published in the same journal in 2004 highlighted the inaccuracy of my forecasts and cast doubt in the use of logistics to forecast US Nobel laureates (Golden & Zantek, 2004). On my part, I refit the updated data sample with a new logistic pointing to a higher ceiling and began wondering whether there was evidence here for the known bias of logistic fits to underestimate the final niche size. The new forecast again indicated an imminent decline in the annual number of American Nobel laureates.

Years later while preparing a new edition for my book — *Predictions – 20 Years Later* — I once again confronted forecasts with data. The situation turned out to be the same as ten years earlier, namely the forecasts again underestimated reality and despite agreement with the result of ten years earlier within the uncertainties expected for a 90% confidence level there was now clear disagreement between recent actual numbers and the original forecasts of twenty years earlier. The situation was reminiscent of the celebrated Michele-parameter episode in experimental physics where a measurement repeated many times over the period of fifty years kept reporting an ever-increasing value always compatible with the previous measurement but finally ending up in violent disagreement with the very first measurement.

So I wanted to settle the question of the ever-growing ceiling of the logistic curve fitted to the US Nobel laureates once and for all. One explanation for the ceiling of the S-curve to be constantly increasing is the fact that the US population itself has also been increasing over the same historical period. An increasing population provides an increasing "niche" for Nobel

Prize winners. But in order to solve the logistic equation the size of the ceiling must remain constant throughout the growth process.

An obvious way to account for the growing American population would be to study the number of laureates per capita thus rendering the ceiling of the S-curve time-independent. When I repeated the previous analysis for Nobel Laureates normalized to population I obtained better fits and consistency, namely the S-curves for all three time periods had ceilings that agreed within the expected uncertainties from each other.

Yet, there was still some tendency for the ceiling to increase with time, which suggested that considering US Nobel laureates per capita did not fully account for the increase of the "niche" size over time. In fact, the niche of individuals qualified for Nobel-Prize candidature in America could be increasing faster than the average population. After all, in my study I classified laureates with double nationality as nationals of the nation where the research for which they were being distinguished was accomplished. America, as a rule, welcomes research scientists from all over the world while it thwarts immigration by the uneducated. It could very well be that the population sample capable of producing Nobel laureates in America is growing faster than the rest of the population. Also I obtained fits of decreasing quality in longer data sets, and counterintuitive forecasts for a dramatic decline of American Nobel laureates and/or a major increase of the American population by the second half of the 21st century. So there was a need for deeper understanding of the Nobel-Prize competition.

A Bigger Picture

Besides the competition among Americans there is also competition between Americans and nationals of other countries. To the extent that US Nobel laureates represent about half or more of all Nobel Prizes every year, it is a good approximation to consider a duopoly, namely a niche with only two species: Americans and all others grouped together. The species "all others" is rather inhomogeneous but with US Nobel laureates and all Nobel laureates both being well defined as species candidates, "all others" also becomes a well-defined species candidate.

The competition between two populations growing in the same niche renders itself for a description by the Volterra-Lotka system of equations mentioned earlier. A global fit to all the data turned out to be of acceptable quality. The results are graphed in Figure 7 and tabulated in Table 3. The American trajectory is S-shaped (but not a logistic S-curve) and the long-term forecast is roughly a 50-50 split of all Nobel Prizes between Americans and all other nationalities.

Of particular interest are the values of the coupling constants in the Competition column of Table 3. They are both positive indicating a win-win nature for the competition. In a symbiotic relationship each competitor benefits from the existence of the other, which is in line with the dynamics of scholarly research (each publication triggers more publications). But Americans benefit more when non-Americans win Nobel Prizes than vice versa. A ratio 1.5 implies that one Nobel Prize won by a non-American will trigger 1.5 times more Nobel Prizes for Americans than the other way around. This is counteracted to some extent by the smaller attractiveness constant for the Americans.

The attractiveness constant reflects the species' ability to multiply. For product sales it indicates how many new sales will be triggered by one sale.

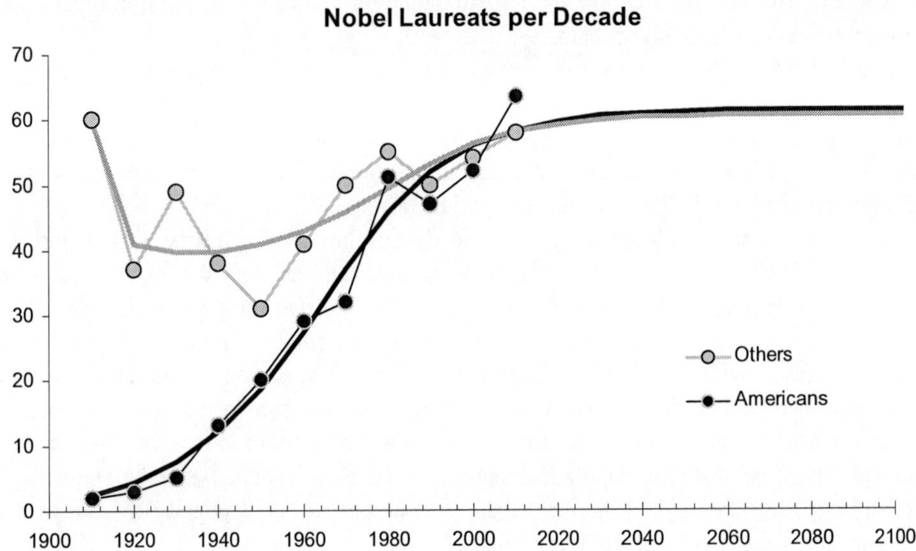

Figure 7. Decennial data points and solutions to the Volterra-Lotka equations. Despite its S-shaped form the black line is only approximately a logistic S-curve (Modis, 2010). This graph has been published in Modis (2010).

Table 3. Results for Volterra-Lotka Fits

	Attractiveness	Niche size	Competition
Americans	1.5	26	0.6
Others	1.7	37	0.4

In nature attractiveness represents the average litter size for a species (Modis, 1998). If it is greater than 1, the species population grows; if it is less than 1, it declines. The values in Table 3 shows attractiveness values for Americans and all others of 1.5 and 1.7 respectively. This means that each American Nobel laureate will "brood" 1.5 new American Nobel winners whereas for all others this number is 1.7. All in all, the number of American Nobel Laureates in the long run should stabilize around an average of 61.4 per decade barely higher than 60.6 for all others.

DISCUSSION

Competition arises when there are different entities vying for a limited resource. The two approaches considered here, i.e. logistic growth and Volterra-Lotka, correspond to different competitive struggles. In the first one the limited resource is the total number of Nobel laureates that the US will ever claim. The implication is that this number is capped. In other words, there will be a time when all Nobel Prizes will be awarded to nationals from other

countries. Up to that time, Americans will be elbowing each other to win prizes and the fewer left in their "niche" the harder it will be to win one.

Logistic growth descriptions have been successful when used with products filling their market niche, epidemics filling their niche of victims, and in general each time a niche is filled or emptied in competitive circumstances. The approach renders itself for fitting an S-curve on cumulated historical data.

In the second approach — Volterra-Lotka equations — the competition with another species is also taken into account. The niche now is all Nobel Prizes awarded annually, not only the ones destined for Americans. This competitive struggle can take many forms the most publicized of which is the predator-prey struggle in which the predator grows on expense of the prey but also depends on the prey so that when the latter diminishes in numbers the predator also diminishes and oscillations ensue. But with Nobel Prizes no oscillatory behavior is observed. The competitive struggle turns out to be a win-win relationship and following some substitution in the early 20th century the two species grow in parallel to a peaceful and stable coexistence in a symbiotic relationship.

Interestingly the US trajectory is S-shaped, which suggests that a logistic fit could have been a reasonable approximation but not on the cumulative numbers. The fit should have been on the numbers per unit of time. The limiting resource in this case would have been the annual number of American laureates. This number was zero at the turn of the 20th century and progressively grew to 8 by 2009 (6.4 on the average during the nine years 2001-2009). The meaning of competition in this picture would be that Americans elbow each other every year for one of their "quota" prizes that grew along an S-curve and in the 21st century reached a ceiling of 6.1.

Recapitulating

Logistic S-curves are special cases of solutions to the Volterra-Lotka system of equations. The Volterra-Lotka Equations reduce to the logistic Equation whenever the coupling constants become null. Whereas logistic growth describes competition only among the members of one species, the Volterra-Lotka system of equations handles competition also with other species. It is advisable to consult the Volterra-Lotka approach — whenever possible — even if one is interested only in logistic growth because it can shed light on how to apply the logistic-growth equation. In the US Nobel-laureates study the Volterra-Lotka solution dictates that a logistic S-curve should be fitted on the annual numbers and not on cumulative numbers. Had we done so we would have obtained an answer very close to the black S-shaped curve of Figure 7.

Deciding whether to fit S-curves on cumulative or on per-unit-of-time data is a crucial first step for all logistic-growth applications and constitutes treacherous terrain for inexperienced S-curve enthusiasts. I myself mastered it only later in my career (Modis, 2007).

The forecasts for American Nobel laureates from the Volterra-Lotka approach are stable around an annual average of 6.1, comparable to the number of Nobel laureates won by all other nationalities together. Moreover the fitted parameters give rise to some interesting insights. The competition between Americans and all others for Nobel Prizes is of the win-win type. Locked in a symbiotic relationship both sides are winning but Americans are profiting more by 50%. At the same time, the ability of Nobel laureates to "multiply", i.e. the

extent to which a Nobel laureate incubates more laureates, is lower for Americans than it is for other nationalities. One may ponder whether the roots of this last observation have something to do with the fact that chauvinistic traits tend to be more endemic in cultures with longer traditions.

All conclusions need to be interpreted within the uncertainties involved. The quality of the logistic fits worsens as the time window increases. Normalizing to the population improves the quality of the fits. A confidence level of 72% indicates that there is 7 out of 10 chances that the Volterra-Lotka description is the right way to analyze this competition, not very different from the S-curve fit on the data normalized to population. For the intermediate future — ten to twenty years — the logistic normalized to reasonable population projections would result in forecasts compatible with those of the Volterra-Lotka approach. Still, I would choose Volterra-Lotka because it addresses a more general type of competition. In any case, long-term forecasts cannot be reliable and the whole exercise must be repeated with updated data sets in a couple of decades, by which time it may be appropriate to consider more than just two players.

CONCLUSION

The natural law describing growth in competition has a very simple formulation, the logistic equation. The simpler a law the more fundamental it is and the wider its range of applications. The successful scientific description of competition in the cases considered in this chapter yields unexpected insights that include:

- All natural growth is capped. Sustained growth can only take place in successive well-defined natural-growth steps.
- Demystification of popular wisdom such as "easy come, easy go" and "you need gold to make gold."
- The indispensable role of teachers and the inherent difficulty in every beginning.
- Car fatal accidents are maintained at a "desirable" level by society as a concomitant of things of greater value.
- Death correlates with the end of one's productivity/creativity; Mozart may have died exhausted of creative musical potential.
- There is no universally best way to compete; the appropriateness of counterattack, cooperation, or differentiation depends on the particular situation.
- Americans are likely to continue dominating Nobel Prizes awards because they better leverage the win-win relationship they enjoy with Nobel Prizes won by non-Americans.
- The extent to which a Nobel laureate incubates more laureates, is lower for Americans than it is for other nationalities. One may ponder whether the roots of this have something to do with the fact that chauvinistic traits tend to be more endemic in cultures with longer traditions.

Europeans were first to reach the New World thanks to their physical proximity and their mastering of the maritime and navigation sciences. But the transfer of Nobel awards from

Europeans to Americans during the first half of the 20th century makes one wonder whether the blossoming of the New World was not due to a competitive advantage stemming from a science-based culture.

Appendix – The Mathematical Formulations Behind Natural Growth in Competition

A1. The Logistic and the Chaos Equations

Logistic growth describes how a species population grows to fill its ecological niche under conditions of natural competition (survival of the fittest). The same law also describes how we learn, and how rumors and epidemic diseases spread. The law is cast in the following differential equation:

$$\frac{dX}{dt} = aX(1-X) \text{ where } a \text{ is a constant} \qquad (1)$$

But when Equation (1) is put in the form of a difference equation, it becomes

$$X_{n+1} = r\,X_n(1-X_n) \text{ where } r \text{ is a constant} \qquad (2)$$

This equation is strikingly similar to Equation (1), but whereas Equation (1) gives rise to the smooth S-shaped logistic pattern, Equation (2) for certain values of r gives rise to states of chaos. The former emphasizes the presence of a trend and has become the tool to describe natural growth. The latter emphasizes the lack of trend and has become the tool to describe chaos. The chaotic fluctuations appear on what corresponds to the ceiling of the logistic after the upward trend has died down.

A2. The Solutions

The solution of Equation 1 (obtained by integration) is given below; it yields the S-shaped pattern of the S-curve.

$$X(t) = \frac{M}{1+e^{-a(t-t_0)}} \qquad \text{where } t_0 \text{ is an integration constant}$$

The solution of Equation 2 (obtained by iteration) for $r > 3.7$ gives the following pattern:

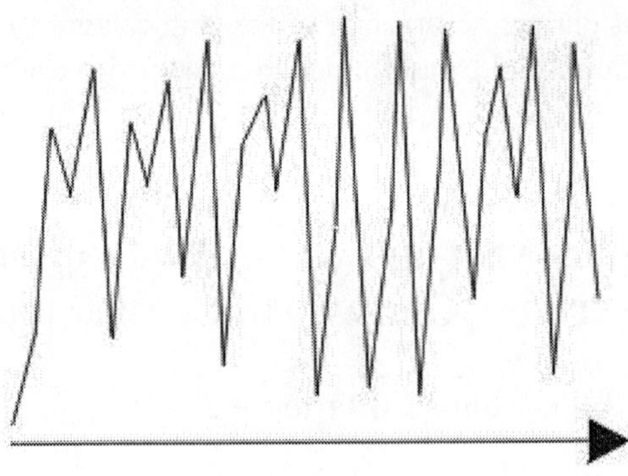

REFERENCES

Farrell, C. (1993) Theory of Technological Progress. *Technological Forecasting and Social Change*, 44, (2), 161- 178.

Farrell, C. (1993). Survival of the Fittest Technologies. *New Scientist*, 137, 35-39.

Fisher, J. C., Pry, R. H. (1971). A Simple Substitution Model of Technological Change. *Technological Forecasting and Social Change*, 3, 75-88.

Golden, B . L., Zantek, P. F. (2004). Inaccurate Forecasts of the Logistic Growth Model for Nobel Prizes. *Technological Forecasting & Social Change*, 71, (4), 417–422.

Jean and Brigitte Massin J., Massin B. *Wofgang Amadeus Mozart*. Paris: Fayard.

Kondratieff, N. D. (1935). The Long Wave in Economic Life. *The Review of Economic Statistics*, 17,105–115.

Marchetti, C. (1983). The Automobile in a Systems Context, the Past 80 Years and the Next 20 Years. *Technological Forecasting & Social Change*, 23, 3-23.

Marchetti, C. (1985). Action Curves and Clockwork Geniuses. International Institute of Advanced System Analysis. *Working Paper-85-74*, Laxenburg, Austria.

Marchetti, C. (1989). (Italian edition). La Saga dei Nobel. *Technol. Rev*., 13, 8–11.

Modis, T. (1988). Competition and Forecasts for Nobel Prize Awards. *Technological Forecasting & Social Change*, 34, (2), 95–102.

Modis, T. (1992). *Predictions: Society's Telltale Signature Reveals the Past and Forecasts the Future.* New York: Simon & Schuster.

Modis, T. (1998). *Conquering Uncertainty*. New York: McGraw-Hill.

Modis, T. (1998). Genetic Re-Engineering of Corporations. *Technological Forecasting & Social Change*, 56, (2), 107-118.

Modis, T. (2002). *Predictions – 10 Years Later*. Geneva, Switzerland: Growth Dynamics.

Modis, T. (February/March, 2003). A Scientific Approach to Managing Competition. *The Industrial Physicist*, 9, (1), 25-27.

Modis, T. (2007). Strengths and Weaknesses of S-Curves. *Technological Forecasting & Social Change*, 74, (6), 866-872.

Modis, T. (2010). US Nobel Laureates: Logistic Growth versus Volterra-Lotka. *Technological Forecasting & Social Change*, xxx, xxx-xxx.

Modis, T., Debecker, A. (1992). Chaoslike States Can Be Expected Before and After Logistic Growth. *Technological Forecasting & Social Change*, 41, 111-120.

Smitalova, K., Sujan, S. (1991). *A Mathematical Treatment of Dynamical Models in Biological Science*. West Sussex, England: Ellis Horwood.

Sulloway, F. (1996). *Born to Rebel.* Boston: Pantheon, Harvard University Press.

Whiston, T.G. (1974). Life Is Logarithmic. In J. Rose (Ed.), *Advances in cybernetics and systems.* London: Gordon and Breach.

Williams, J.D. (September 1958). The Nonsense about Safe Driving. *Fortune*, vol. LVIII, no. 3, 118–19.

In: Advances in Psychology Research. Volume 88
Editor: Alexandra M. Columbus, pp. 75-94
ISBN: 978-1-62100-591-9

Chapter 4

MOOD DISORDERS: CLASSIFICATION, HEALTH EFFECTS, AND SOCIETAL IMPACT

***Gianluca Serafini*[*1], *Maurizio Pompili*[1,2], *Marco Innamorati*[1,3], *Gloria Giordano*[1], *Roberto Tatarelli*[1] and *Paolo Girardi*[1]**

[1] Department of Neurosciences, Mental Health and Sensory Functions; Suicide Prevention Center, Sant'Andrea Hospital, "Sapienza" University of Rome, Italy.
[2] McLean Hospital, Harvard Medical School, U.S.A.
[3] Università Europea di Roma, Via degli Aldobrandeschi, Rome.

ABSTRACT

Mood disorders (MD) affect approximately 10% of the general population determining significant functional impairment in sufferers and often leads to adverse social outcomes. Two main groups of MD are broadly recognized: the unipolar and the bipolar types. Major depressive disorder is the most common mood disorder being one of the leading sources of premature death and disability among all diseases and accounting for enormous health service utilization. Comorbid anxiety and depression occurs at a high rate, and is associated with higher costs from both an individual and societal perspective. Patients with MD most often present in primary care settings, have more severe symptoms, and require health care resources. Case identification and correct assessment are crucial steps. MD pose complicated diagnostic and treatment challenges, often leading to inadequate diagnosis and treatment resulting in unnecessary patient distress and increased utilization of health care services. Effective assessment, correct evaluation, diagnosis and treatment can lead to better treatment outcomes and improved quality of life (QOL) in care patients.

Keywords: mood disorders; health service utilization; societal impact; assessment; treatment.

---

* Corresponding author: Gianluca Serafini, Department of Neuroscience, Mental Health and Sensory Function, "Sapienza" University of Rome, Faculty of Medicine and Psychology, Sant'Andrea Hospital, Via Grottarossa 1035-1039, 00189, Rome, Italy. Tel.: +39 06 33775675. Fax: +39 06 33775342; E-mail: gianluca.serafini@uniroma1.it

INTRODUCTION

MD are common and invalidating mental health problems in the general population (Bijl and Ravelli, 1998). Major depressive disorder (MDD) is the most common type of unipolar MD, characterized by single or recurrent major depressive episodes and classified as a mood disorder in the DSM-IV-TR (American Psychiatric Association, 2000). MDD was reported to be actually the second most common and costly mental health problem in clinical practice (Stewart et al, 2003) associated with relevant reduction in the patients QOL due to its multifaceted impact on physical, social, emotional functioning, and wellbeing (Bijl and Ravelli, 2000; Kruijshaar et al, 2003). From 2020, it was estimated that, depression will represent the second relevant contributor to the global burden of disease (Murray and Lopez, 1997). Several lines of evidence suggested that economic burden of depression is relevant (Cuijpers et al, 2007; Slobbe et al, 2003; Luppa et al, 2007). MDD significantly affects the familiar and personal relationships, work or school life, sleeping and eating habits, and general health. Individuals with MDD feel depressed, lose interest in their common activities, experience a change in appetite, suffer from disturbed sleep or have low energy.

Instead, bipolar disorder (BD) or manic-depressive disorder is a psychiatric illness characterized by the presence of one or more episodes of abnormally elevated energy levels, cognition, and mood with or without one or more depressive episodes (American Psychiatric Association, 2000). BD is characterized by episodes of mania and depression separated by periods of remission, with a lifetime prevalence of 1.5–3% (Angst, 1998; Narrow et al, 2002; Keller et al, 2005). Subjects with mania are overly energetic, with symptoms characterized by spending very freely and acquiring debt, reeking the law or showing lack of judgement in sexual behaviour.

Subjects with MD suffer relevant distress or severe impairment in social, occupational, educational and other significant areas of functioning. Moreover, MD are often associated with several medical conditions such as migraine, diabetes, heart disease and chronic obstructive pulmonary disease (Wells et al, 1988). Comorbid MDD has been demonstrated to enhance symptom burden, functional impairment and medical costs and induced to consider further additional treatment strategies (Trivedi et al, 2007). Additionally, several lines of evidence (Kessler et al, 1999; Ormel et al, 1994; Simon et al, 2000; Olfson et al, 1997; Zwerling et al, 2002; Wells et al, 2000; Simon, 2003) have investigated the impact of depression on the workplace. Subjects with depression were more likely (at least twice) to loss occupational activities or miss work due to disability (Simon, 2003).

The remarkable impact of MD on the patients suffering, lifetime disability and suicidality underlines the importance of the research in discovering new treatment and prevention strategies as well as more reliable classification systems. In fact, modern classifications of MD such as DSM-IV-TR were based on a categorical model may be helpful in terms of reliability and communication among clinicians and researchers (American Psychiatric Association, 1994) but raised serious concerns about the diagnostic validity. However, actually these classifications can be used across a variety of cultures and permit a reliable comparison of clinical definitions used in studies coming from all around the world. Many authors proposed different diagnostic criteria from DSM-IV-TR in order to introduce symptoms dimensions as a useful complement to categorical diagnosis. Considering this controversial background, we aimed to critically analyze and overview the current literature

trying to identify the advantages and limitations of the current diagnostic classification systems, health effects, and societal impact of MD.

METHODS

In order to provide a selected overview about MD in terms of classification, health effects, and societal impact we performed a MedLine, Excerpta Medica, PsycLit and PsycInfo and Index Medicus search to identify to identify all papers and book chapters in English language during the period between 1980 to 2010.

The following search terms were used: “Mood disorders” OR “Affective disorders” OR “Mania”, OR “Mixed states” AND “Classification” OR “Categorial classification system” OR “DSM-IV-TR” AND “Comorbidity” AND “Health effects” AND “Social impact” OR “Social impairment” AND “Economic burden” OR “Direct costs” OR “Indirect costs”. We included in the present review only those articles published in peer-reviewed journals. The combined search strategies yielded a total of 160 articles, of which after a complete analysis 120 full-text articles were reviewed and approximately 100 included in the present review. We excluded articles without abstract, abstract that did not explicitly mention MD and health effects or societal impact, studies with publication date under 1980, and articles not in the english language. We identified as specific fields of interest in the analysis MD and health, societal and economic effects.

RESULTS

Categorical Versus Dimensional Approaches in the Classification System of MD

According to the Diagnostic and Statistical Manual of Mental Disorders 4th Edition (DSM-IV), MD are divided into two categories: the unipolar and the bipolar disorders. The first group includes: a) Major Depression Disorder (MDD) that consists of one or more episodes of major depression with or without full recovery between these episodes; b) Dysthymic disorder in which depressed mood (less episodic) is associated with depressive symptoms for at least 2 years during which a major depressive episode has not occurred; c) Depression not otherwise specified that includes all depressed subjects who do not meet the diagnostic criteria for either MDD or dysthymia. MDD is characterized by the presence of at least five of the following symptoms, that have to be present during all the day, daily, for at least 2 weeks: depressed mood, markedly diminished interest or pleasure in almost activities, significant weight loss/gain, insomnia/hyperinsomnia, psychomotor agitation/retardation, fatigue (loss of energy), feelings of worthlessness (guilt), impaired concentration (indecisiveness), recurrent thoughts of death or suicide.

The second group includes: a) BD type I (BD-I) that requires at least one manic episode along with MDD episodes; b) BD type II (BD-II) characterized by hypomania plus episodes of depression; c) Cyclothymic Disorder, with frequent recurrent episodes of mild depression and episodes of hypomania. The criteria for a manic episode are: a period of abnormal,

persistent elevated, expansive or irritable mood and the presence of at least three of the following symptoms in the same period: overstated self-esteem or grandiosity, marked decrease in need for sleep, increased talk, flight of ideas, marked distractibility, increased acidity or psychomotor agitation, excessive involvement in pleasurable activities without regard for negative consequences (for example unrestrained buying, sexual indiscretions, foolish business adventures). According to DSM-IV-TR (APA, 2000), symptoms must be severe enough to impair function or required hospitalization to prevent self harm to self or others and not caused by schizophrenia, schizoaffective disorder or substance abuse.

Although criteria for the diagnosis of depression and mania have remained more or less unmodified for the past 35 years (Feighner et al, 1972; American Psychiatric Association, 1980, 1987, 1994, 2000) many authors (Akechi et al, 2003; Kathol et al, 1990; Koenig et al, 1997; Zimmerman et al, 2006) have harshly criticized their utilization.

Zimmerman et al. (2006) criticized the DSM-IV assumption of no difference between depressed patients who do and do not report low mood comparing the socio-demographic and clinical characteristics of 839 patients meeting the DSM-IV criteria for major depressive episode (MDE) with 69 who did not present low mood. Although in their study, patients without depressed mood were younger, had current shorter and less important affective episodes, less suicidality and less psychosocial impairment compared to patients with depressed, they found that diagnostic mood criteria are lengthy and difficult to remember.

Akechi et al. (2003) have expressed doubts regarding the utilization of DSM depression and mania criteria in patients with medical comorbidities. They retrospectively reviewed all psychiatric consultations referred to the Psychiatric ward of the National Cancer Center Hospital and its East Division in Japan from 1996 to 1999 using a database to identify patients with MDD. They identified a total of 1721 cancer patients referring during the study period of which 220 (12.8%) were diagnosed as having MDD according to the DSM-IV criteria and found, after logistic regression analyses, that weight loss or appetite change, a reduced ability to think or concentrate, was positively associated with a reduced interest or pleasure. Subjects having weight loss or appetite change among all somatic symptoms (also sleep disturbance, fatigue, reduced ability to think were analyzed) showed a significantly higher severe MDD compared with subjects without this symptom, differently from patients having the other three somatic symptoms. Therefore, they suggested that somatic criteria like fatigue and sleep disturbances can be the consequence of the medical illness rather than MDD.

Other lines of evidence (Kathol et al, 1990; Koenig et al, 1997) have demonstrated that DSM-IV depression criteria may be directly applied without making any adjustment based on medical illness. Kathol et al. (1990) suggested that diagnoses of MDD in 152 cancer patients may differ of 13% based on the diagnostic system which was utilized. Additionally, they reported that although the Beck Depression Inventory and the Hamilton Rating Scale for Depression were useful tools for screening patients with depressive symptoms, these two psychometric tools could not be able to identify subjects who had no major depression episode based on the diagnostic systems criteria.

Koenig et al. (1997) studied 460 consecutive patients aged 60 years or older and with cognitive impairments admitted to the general medical wards (medicine, cardiology, neurology services) of Duke Hospital. They reported that the prevalence of MDD may vary from 10% to 21% according to the different diagnostic criteria which were used whereas minor depression may vary from 14% to 25%. They also found that the diagnostic strategy

that best identified a severe and persistent MDD was the exclusive-etiologic approach consisting in a diagnostic scheme where symptoms are counted etiologically. Unfortunately, the exclusive-etiologic approach missed 49% of patients with MDD identified by the inclusive approach, of which approximately 60% continued to report persistent depressive symptoms for different weeks after discharge. Also, Parker (2005) although recognized initial perceived advantages in the assumption of MDD, then questioned the validity of the DSM criteria reporting its limited utility in clinical practice. He stated that aetiological models and treatment efficacy studies had generated additional limited information and that the assumption of MDD has produced sterility in either the research and clinical practice.

Another controversial point was that weather psychopharmacological drugs may determine different effects on different individuals with depressive symptoms. Trying to pass these limitations, some authors (Nelson et al, 2005) moved to demonstrate the eventual differential response to antidepressant medications acting through different mechanisms of actions.

Nelson et al. (2005) randomized, in a 8-week, double-blind study and compared 253 subjects taking a norepinephrine selective agent (reboxetine) with 168 subjects taking a serotonin selective agent, fluoxetine. They found that in both subjects taking reboxetine and fluoxetine, depressed mood, reduced interest, and anxiety had the greatest change but the effect sizes for all Hamilton Depression Rating Scale (HAM-D) symptoms were similar for the two groups. So, they concluded that they did not support the assumption that symptom differences are useful for antidepressant selection. They stated that the prediction of treatment response is not useful for identifying a more valid symptoms pathway of depression. Also, Vieta and Phillips (2007) proposed to modify DSM-IV diagnostic criteria for BD suggesting that bipolar subjects frequently were treated when are depressed but are often classified as unipolar depressed individuals leading to inadequate treatment and poor outcome. In their opinion, most patients do not fit in any diagnostic categories due to artificial borders and gaps between them or they do not fulfil the DSM-IV criteria for severity or duration of symptoms. So, they identified some differential biomarkers underlying the pathophysiology of the illness including the impaired emotion regulation, the impaired attention, and distractibility persisting during depression and remission and not frequent in unipolar depression. They also focused on functional abnormalities in amygdala systems underlying emotion processing and dorsolateral prefrontal cortex underlying working memory, and attention dysfunctions.

In addition, a frequent overlap (comorbidity) of affective symptoms may be observed among patients with psychiatric disorders. Not infrequently, affective symptoms occur in many different psychiatric and medical populations. Presicci et al, (2010) reported that the differential diagnosis is one of the major problem in clinical practice because it is not much addressed during the clinical investigation. They retrospectively analyzed 60 patients with depressive disorder and adjustment disorder and found that a significant association between prevalent symptoms, treatment, and family history with the single diagnostic categories supporting the construct validity of the 2 diagnostic categories, but criticized the assumption that they can be considered as diagnostic predictors. They also added that the spectrum approach could unify the categorical with the dimensional approaches and suggested a combination of dimensional and categorical principles for classifying affective disorders may help to reduce the underdiagnosis and undertreatment of MD.

According to many lines of evidence (Vieta and Phillips, 2007; Presicci et al, 2010; Henry and Etain, 2010; Parker, 2010) DSM-IV would needs a significant conceptual step

forward. In the absence of an aetiological classification and a huge overlapping of symptoms in psychiatric diseases, a dimensional approach could be the most desirable. Vieta and Phillips (2007) suggested that there is a deep need to improve and refine the current diagnostic criteria for the DSM-V, but also to introduce diagnostic dimensions, not as an alternative but rather than as a useful complement to categorical diagnosis. They proposed a modular system which may integrate categorical and dimensional issues, laboratory data, associated non-psychiatric medical conditions, psychological assessment and social issues in a comprehensive and practical approach. Henry and Etain (2010) reported that the predominant polarity, lifetime psychotics symptoms, substance abuse, suicidal risk and social impairment should be included as specific diagnostic dimensions in the BD diagnosis. The same authors suggested that the "bipolar spectrum disorders" category should be introduced in order to reflect the heterogeneity of the clinical presentation, course and comorbid patterns of the increasing and emerging bipolar subtypes. Parker (2010) suggested the salience of the stressors and the precipitant events in the onset of depression and underlined the importance in distinguishing between endogenous and exogenous depression. "It may be the time to design a psychiatric toolbox", said Vieta and Phillips (2007), suggesting that the psychiatric toolbox will presumably include genotyping, neurophysiologic, neuroimaging and neuropsychological tests, which could help to recognize persistent rather than trait dependent biomarkers, to improve the validity of psychiatric diseases classification and its pathophysiological basis.

These data, taken together, suggested that the categorial DSM-IV diagnostic criteria of both unipolar and bipolar depression had currently several limitations; however, research has not univocally demonstrated that the current diagnostic criteria validity is compromised (Zimmermann et al, 2006); however, a dimensional approach could integrate most of the limitations of the current categorical diagnostic system. More recent neurobiological advances are needed in order to clarify the validity of psychiatric diseases classification.

Health and MD: The Burden of Comorbidity

The World Health Organization (WHO) attributed 31% of all years lived-with-disability to neuropsychiatric disorders (of which 11% to unipolar depression and 2.4% to BD) and announced that unipolar depressive disorder will be the leading cause of the total disease burden within 2030 (Mathers and Loncar, 2006; WHO, 2008). Wells et al. (1988) have suggested that subjects with MD frequently had comorbid additional physical and psychological diseases that negatively impact on QOL. More recently, Grandes et al. (2011) in a cross-sectional multilevel analysis of 2539 subjects referred to eight primary care centres in different regions of Spain, found that mood disorders were the most common, with one-year prevalence of 10% and were associated with the greatest annual quality-adjusted life-years loss.

Affective disorders are often comorbid with other several psychiatric disorders. The comorbidity with substance abuse is relevant: several studies (Rodriguez-Llera et al, 2005; Hasin et al, 2002; Khantzian et al, 1985; Di Nicola et al, 2010; Mirin and Weiss, 1986; Maremmani et al, 2008) have demonstrated that subjects with a diagnosis of MD were more frequently substance abusers, above all cocaine and heroin abusers. Chronic cocaine or heroin

abusers may develop several health problems. Several lines of evidence (Egred and Davis, 2005; Dressler et al, 1990; Karch and Billingham, 1995; Frishman et al, 2003) suggest that they present an higher risk of myocardithis, sudden cardiac death and perivascular fibrosis. Other research (Tashkin, 2009; Tan et al, 2009; Mehra et al, 2006) showed an higher risk in these subjects of emphysema, chronic obstructive pulmonary disease, pneumothorax and lung cancer. Hepatitis (Paties et al, 1987) and glomerulonephritis (Rao et al., 1974) are also frequent. Cocaine use has been associated with choreoatetosis, akatisia, Parkinsonism and *gran mal* seizures (Nnadi et al, 2005; Catalano et al, 1997).

MD, especially depression, are also associated with a higher alcohol abuse (Saatchoglu et al, 2008) which increased the risk of dementia (Weyerer et al, 2011) and hepatic steatosis (Smathers et al., 2011). In the USA it has been demonstrated that the 35-65% of subjects with a diagnosis of mood disorder are active smokers (Diwan et al, 1998; Kessler, 1995). Ozasa et al. (2008) analyzing 140026 males and 156810 females aged 40-79 years included in large-scale cohort studies in Japan started from 1990 found that in both sexes, the age by which half of the current smokers had died was approximately 4 years younger than that for never-smokers. About 1/3 of subjects with bipolar disorders (Grant et al, 2005; Ostacher et al, 2006) and 1/4 of subjects with major depression (McEachin et al, 2010) were actively smokers.

MD are more frequent in subjects with chronic physical illness compared to other subjects not having these disturbances. The rate of comorbid depression and medical illness varies from 10 to 40% (Goodnick and Hernandez, 2000). MD increased the disability associated with physical conditions and negatively impact its course, contributing to psychosocial impairment, alterations in interpersonal and familiar relationships, poor health and finally suicide. The new National Institute for Health and Clinical Excellence (NICE) guidance about adult depression with comorbid chronic physical illness now emphasized the identification rather than the screening (NICE, 2009).

Several authors have reported higher rates of comorbid medical illness in depressed patients. Gadalla (2008) using data of the Canadian Community Health Survey of 2005 reported highest rates of MD in subjects with chronic fatigue syndrome, fibromyalgia, bowel disorder or stomach or intestinal ulcers. Comorbid medical illness resulted higher among single women, living in poverty and significantly associated with short-term disability and suicidal ideation.

Bland (2010) suggested that patients with chronic physical illness were two to three times more likely to be depressed than the general population and that this kind of depression is less likely to be recognised. He also sustained that the DSM-IV classification of major depression leads to overdiagnose patients with a chronic condition, in case of somatic symptoms are caused by the illness, rather than depression. Harpole et al. (2005) investigating 1801 depressed older adults in a randomized controlled trial in 18 primary care clinics in 5 states across the United States from 1999 to 2001 have found that patients had al least 3.8 chronic comorbid medical conditions although the presence of multiple medical illnesses did not significantly impact patient response to a multidisciplinary depression treatment program. Iosifescu et al. (2004), investigated 128 subjects meeting DSM-III-R MDD criteria achieved in clinical remission, found that greater medical comorbidity was associated with higher increases in self-reported symptoms of depression, anxiety, and anger during during the 28-week of follow-up. Koike et al. (2002) examining 1356 patients with major depression, dysthymia, or subthreshold depression referred to 46 managed primary care clinics found that depressed patients with comorbid medical disorders tend to have similar types of treatment

but worse depression outcomes compared to depressed patients without comorbid medical illness. Finally, Kumar and collegues (1999) using magnetic resonance imaging techniques in 28 subjects with late life MDD compared with 29 healthy control subjects and 34 subjects with probable dementia of the Alzheimer type found that after logistic regression analysis, either brain atrophy and medical illness are associated with an increased risk of MDD. They concluded that both atrophy and comorbid medical illness significantly contributed to the developing of late life MDD.

MD associated to chronic physical illness also confer a higher vulnerability to pain (Tsang et al, 2008). Approximately 52% of subjects with chronic pain had a concomitant diagnosis of MDD, while the 64% of subjects with MDD present chronic pain (Bair et al, 2003). Comorbid depression associated with pain resulted in a greater functional impairment and reduced QOL (Bland, 2010). Analyzing a sample of 573 depressed subjects in primary care, DeVeaugh-Geiss et al. (2010) found that compared to patients with no pain at baseline, those with severe pain were less likely to achieve remission and partial response. Instead, patients with early improvement in pain were more likely to achieve remission. Nicolson et al. (2008) stated that not infrequently psychiatrists were asked to investigate patients with pain because due to the onset of pain patients showed comorbid depression and increased suicidal risk. They also suggested that treatment strategies of patients with physical pain and psychiatric illness are rapidly changing due to the complex interplay of the various aspects of pain. Emptage et al. (2005) have investigated over six years a large population of nationally representative cohort of 8280older subjects finding that 6.6% reported depression associated with mild or moderate pain, and 2.6% had depression associated with severe pain. These subjects, having depression associated with comorbid pain, had worse clinical outcomes and greater was the pain greater were the decrements in outcomes levels. These results were also replicated after two to six years from baseline, when subjects with severe pain associated with depression were more likely to have functional limitations, to lose employment and private health insurance compared with other subjects having depression or pain alone.

In addition, MD particularly depression, is frequently associated with higher cardiovascular risk (Huang et al, 2009). In a recent 4-year cross-sectional survey performed using the Taiwan National Health Insurance Research Database from 2000 to 2003, Huang et al. (2009) investigated a total sample of 1031557 patients with MD, including 76430 cases of MDD and 41557 of BD. They found that the relative risk (RR) of developing ischemic heart disease was 2.0 and the RR of developing hypertensive disorders was 2.05 in the study participants compared with 21356304 subjects without mood or anxiety disorders; individuals under 20 years had also the highest RR (4.74 for ischemic heart disease and 4.08 for hypertensive disorders, respectively). Carney et al. (2002) in a review article have also reported that 1/5 of subjects with heart attack has a diagnosis of depression and tried to explain how depression increases the risk for incident coronary disease and subsequent cardiac morbidity and mortality. They suggested as potential pathophisiological mechanisms involved in the increased risk for incident coronary: antidepressant cardiotoxicity; association between depression and cardiac risk factors such as cigarette smoking, hypertension, diabetes, and reduced functional capacity; association between depression with greater coronary disease severity; nonadherence to treatment medications; lower heart rate variability; increased platelet aggregation and inflammatory disease.

Additional lines of evidence (Alosaimi et al, 2009; Huang et al, 2009; Grippo et al, 2009) have demonstrated that depression increase the risk of coronaric atherosclerosis, arrhythmias,

hypertension and ictus. Himmerlich et al. (2008) showed that either subjects with unipolar and bipolar depression have an higher risk of chronic inflammatory diseases. They tried to investigate the association between a medical history of depression, medical comorbidities and cytokine plasma levels citing the inflammatory theory of depression: higher levels of inflammatory cytokines, such as TNFα, IL-1, IL-6, IL-10 producing a reduction in serotonin levels would be involved in the pathophysiology of depressed subjects. This alteration would also explain why depression is often associated to autoimmune diseases (Carta et al, 2002), such as celiac disease, autoimmune atrophic gastritis, Hashimoto's thyroiditis and Systemic Lupus Erythematosus (SLE) (Carta et al, 2005; 2002; Nery et al, 2007). According to this assumption, Padmos et al. (2004) found that subjects with BD had a higher prevalence of thyroid peroxidise antibodies, adenosine triphosphate antibodies and glutamic acid decarboxylase antibodies, respectively related to an increasing risk for autoimmune thyroiditis, autoimmune atrophic gastritis and diabetes mellitus type I. Also, Carta et al. (2002) have demonstrated that depression was strongly correlated to celiac disease, Hashimoto's thyroiditis and SLE. Finally, other authors (Addolorato et al, 2008; Himmerich et al, 2008) have found an association between anxiety, depression and Helicobacter Pylori infection, food allergies, irritable bowel syndrome, peptic ulcer, SIBO (small intestinal bacterial overgrowth), celiac disease, Chron's disease and rectocolitis.

These data, taken together, suggest that subjects with MD frequently showed higher rates of comorbid medical illness; these subjects with comorbities had also a lower QOL and more health problems compared to subjects without MD and subjects with MD alone. More researchers and future contributions are needed in order to understand the exact role of comorbidity in increasing the burden of health problems in patients with MD.

The Societal and Economic Impact of Functional Impairment in MD

Mental disorders are a growing public health problem, affecting hundreds of millions of people and creating an enormous charge of suffering, disability and economic loss (WHO, 2008).

Subjects with MD frequently showed a relevant functional impairment in several important social areas: as a result, the effects of MD extend beyond internal distress to a wider range of consequences on family members, employers and health care systems (Simon, 2003). The DSM-IV states that symptoms must cause "clinically significant distress or impairment in social, occupational or other important areas of functioning" to make a psychiatric diagnosis (American Psychiatric Association, 1994). Therefore, MD resulted frequently associated severe functional impairment, relevant disability, lost of work productivity and increased use of health service (Simon, 2003).

Robust lines of evidence (Goldberg and Harrow, 2005; Rosa et al, 2010; Daly et al, 2010; Schoeyen et al, 2011) demonstrate a strong cross-sectional association between depression and decreasing self-reported functional status and QOL. Studies reported that outpatients with depressive disorders have been affected by severe functional impairment and lower well-being compared to (Wells et al, 1989; Hays et al, 1995) or greater (Spitzer et al, 1995; Grandes et al, 2011) patients with chronic conditions like hypertension, diabetes or heart

disease. Ormel et al. (1994) have demonstrated in a total of 25916 consecutive subjects screened for psychopathology that the association between depression and social impairment was consistent across 14 countries with different culture, socioeconomic development and health care systems. They reported that after controlling for physical disease severity, psychopathology was consistently associated with increased disability and a dose-response relationship exist between the severity of psychopathology and the level of disability which was prevalent in patients with major depression and other psychiatric conditions.

More recent evidences (Sanchez-Moreno et al, 2010; Rosa et al, 2010; Kilzieh et al, 2010; Rhebergen et al, 2010; Gadalla, 2009; Kauer-Sant'Anna et al, 2009; Gayman et al, 2008) confirmed higher functional impairment and disability in patients with both unipolar and bipolar disorders. Scientific literature (Coulehan et al, 1997; Katzelnick et al, 2000; Unutzer et al, 2002; Araya et al, 2003) have also found that improving the quality of depression treatment using antidepressant drugs or structured psychotherapy, leads to significant improvements in functional status and QOL.

BD, no doubt, represent one of the most stigmatized and invalidating disease among MD. The WHO ranks BD as the sixth leading cause of years lost due to disability in young adults (Murrey and Lopez, 1997). Subjects with BD had higher health care expenses, job absenteeism and short term disability payments than controls (Gardner et al, 2006). The QOL in patients with BD appears poorer compared to that of the general population (Arnold et al, 2000) or in schizophrenic patients (Atkinson et al, 1997) and similar to that observed among the chronically medically ill patients (Arnold et al, 2000; Cooke et al., 1996; Robb et al, 1997, 1998). Diminished satisfaction with life in BD continues even during periods of sustained euthymia (Cooke et al, 1996; Robb et al, 1997, 1998). Vojta et al. (2001) have found that patients with mania had a reduced QOL compared with euthymic patients, contrasting the conventional wisdom that mania is a more desirable state than other mood states. Rosa et al. (2010) demonstrated that higher functional impairment may be observed among depressed subjects, followed by subjects having a hypomanic and manic episode and finally the euthymic group. Berlim et al. (2004) have found that subjects with BD presented a lower psychological QOL compared with subjects with MDD: the authors suggested that this difference is presumably related to the higher rates of suicide observed in bipolar population, regardless to the severity of the mood disturbance. These data are in contrast with those reported by Goldberg et al. (2005). They found that QOL did not significantly differ among bipolar and unipolar subjects, due to the presumable fact that self reported life satisfaction may not consistently reflects objective functioning.

In addition, many studies (Kessler et al, 1999; Ormel et al, 1994; Simon et al, 2000; Olfson et al, 1997; Zwerling et al, 2002; Wells et al, 2000) demonstrated a strong association between MD and lost work productivity or absenteeism from job confirming higher level of disability and reduced QOL in patients with MD. Olfson et al. (1997) investigating a sample of 1001 primary care patients aged 18-70 years have found that the bipolar patients a higher risk (sevenfold) of missing work because of illness compared to patients having phobias (7.7%), major depressive disorder (7.3%), alcohol use disorders (5.2%), generalized anxiety disorder (3.7%), and panic disorder (3.0%). Bipolar patients exhibit significantly increased level of disability. Zwerling et al. (2002) using the National Health Interview Survey Disability Supplement of 1994 to 1995, showed that self-reported BD was associated with a 40% reduction in the likelihood to be employed. Lost productivity is an important issue in

MD, because these illness often strikes during working age and their chronic nature leads to an increase of lost productivity lost to society.

Recently, Birnbaum et al. (2010) using National Comorbidity Survey-Replication (2001-2002) data, investigated 539 US workforce with MDD, of which 13.8% were classified as mild, 38.5% as moderate, and 47.7% as severe. Mental health services utilization significantly increased with severity, and average treatment costs higher for severe compared to mild depression. MDD severity was directly related to the prevalence rates of unemployment/disability and workers with severe/moderate depression missed more work than non-depressed workers. Laxman (2008) in a systematic literature review focused on the impact of BD in employed populations found that from the results of the 17 studies included in the review, data suggested that BD significantly affects employers, costing more than twice as much as depression per employee. However, he also highlighted that most of the total cost of BD is derivable from indirect costs related to lost productivity, particularly from absenteeism and presenteeism. He concluded that comorbid medical conditions and stigma in the workplace often lead to delays in adequate diagnosis and correct management of BD.

In addition, there are considerable economic consequences that negatively impact on the outcome of subjects with MD. Investigators typically separate direct costs, which are due to the impact of MD, such as loss of work productivity (work absenteeism and reduction of productivity within the work place) and suicide (Thomas and Morris, 2003; Kind and Sorensen, 1993; Greenberg et al, 1993) with indirect costs. Economists usually try to take a "societal perspective", also taking into consideration the consequence on societal areas other than the health care sector. One of the most important consequence of MD regards the difficulties in find a adequate employment and particularly, the inability to work, the increased absenteeism and impaired performance (Tierney, 2007; Patel, 2008).

As mentioned above, Ornel et al. (1994) have found that depressive disorder was associated with an increased risk (twofold) of days lost due to the illness disability. Lepine et al. (1997) have found that in a 6 months periods, subjects with a diagnosis of major depression took an average of 13 days off work due to the illness, compared with 2,5 days off work for those without depression. Kessler et al. (1999) have demonstrated that depressed subjects were more likely (2,5 fold) in missing work due to the illness consequences and in increasing the time lost (50%) at work. Simon et al. (2000) in a 24 months secondary analysis of data from a randomized trial in seven primary care clinics of Seattle, found that, after adjustment for depression severity and medical baseline comorbidity, patients with greater clinical improvement were more likely to maintain paid employment and reported fewer days missed from work due to illness.

Finally, several lines of evidence (Simon et al, 1995; Henk et al, 1996; Unutzer et al, 1997; Simon, 2003) have demonstrated a robust association between depression and increasing utilization of general medical services. Simon et al. (1995) investigated 6257 consecutive primary care depressed patients compared with a sample of 6257 primary care patients with no depression diagnosis. They found that depressed patients had higher annual health care costs and higher costs than non-depressed patients and that twofold cost differences persisted for at least 12 months after initiation of treatment. The authors reported no difference between patients treated with antidepressants, patients not treated with antidepressants. Also, Henk et al. (1996) following 50000 patients enrolled in the DeanCare health maintenance organization for 2 consecutive years found that depressed high services utilizers were more likely than non-depressed high services utilizers to have higher medical

costs during 1994. Among high utilizers, depressed patients 1994 costs were significantly higher. Similarly, Unützer et al. (1997) in a total of 2558 subjects older than 65 years found that depressive symptoms were common, persistent, and associated with a significant increase in the cost of general medical services; this association remained significant after adjusting for differences in age, sex, and chronic medical illness. Similarly to the study of Henk et al. (1996), this increase was observed for every component of health care costs. As suggested by Simon (2003), most important increases in health services costs associated with depression are not due to depression treatment (antidepressant medication, specialty mental health care and primary care visits with depression diagnoses) that account for only 5%-10% of the total health care costs.

Finally, it is crucial to investigate the effects, in term of health care costs, of specific types of depression like Treatment Resistant Depression (TRD) which affects approximately 60-70% of patients with MDD (Fostick et al, 2010) and results in a substantial burden of growing medical mental health costs and huge suffering for patients (Fostick et al, 2010).

Several studies have investigated both direct healthcare costs and indirect (disability and medical-related absenteeism) associated with the TRD. Ivanova et al. (2010) analyzing 2312 TRD employees compared with a control group (age- and sex-matched employees with MDD but without TRD) during the 6-month pre-index (baseline) and 24-month post-index (study) period found that compared with MDD controls, TRD employees reported significantly higher rates of chronic pain, fibromyalgia, and comorbidity. TRD employees were assocated with higher direct 2-year costs and indirect costs were also higher for TRD employees than MDD controls. Fostick et al.(2010) investigated 107 unipolar MDD patients treated for at least 4 weeks and found that 39.3% patients with TRD had a more severe type of depressive disorder determining higher costs for imaging tests, physician visits, psychiatric hospitalizations and number of working days lost compared to non-TRD patients. In addition, higher MDD severity was found to be associated with higher costs. The authors concluded that either resistance and severity features were related to higher direct and indirect costs, but TRD may be the main factor involved in determining the economic burden of depression. A data analysis of 1692 MDD employees was conducted by Greenberg et al. (2004); the authors reported that the average annual cost of TRD employees was higher (twice) per single employee, compared to that of non-TRD employees. They also suggested that TRD subjects used more than twice as many medical services than non-TRD patients, and showed significantly greater work loss costs. Similarly, Corey-Lisle et al. (2002) performed a study in which were investigated 4186 MDD subjects and reported that 12% of them may be considered TRD-likely. Average annual costs were higher for TRD-likely patients compared to non-TRD subjects. They also found that TRD-likely patients used almost twice as many medical services compared to non-TRD subjects and had significantly greater indirect costs.

Conclusion

MD affect approximately 10% of the population and represent a growing and invalidating public health problem creating an enormous charge of suffering, disability and economic loss. MD determine increased health problems (elevated comorbidity with either several medical and psychiatric conditions), elevated social and economic burden and higher level of

functional impairment (WHO, 2008). According to the WHO (2008), unipolar depressive disorder will be the leading cause of the total disease burden in 2030 characterized by a severe disability, a huge lost of work productivity and increased use of health service.

Unfortunately, the current categorical approach and the modern classification systems like DSM-IV-TR did not adequately held clinicians to correctly diagnose and manage both the unipolar and bipolar types of MD in both short and long term period. Dimensional criteria have been often proposed trying to pass these limitations. However, actually research has not univocally demonstrated that the current diagnostic criteria validity is compromised.

Early intervention and correct management of patients with MD are critical to minimize the long term negative consequences such as poor outcome and increased risk of suicide. Although standard treatment may yield some benefit, further prospective studies may reveal which aspects of the intervention are salient, particularly in specific high risk populations like TRD patients. It was clearly demonstrated that these specific subgroups are more likely (almost twice) to use medical services and negatively impact on either direct and indirect costs. Specific medications and adequate psychosocial interventions may play a role, offering complementary benefits, but this needs to be examined further. More research is also needed in order to improve prevention and treatment strategies.

REFERENCES

[1] Addolorato G, Mirijello A, D'Angelo C, Leggio L, Ferrulli A, Abenavoli L, Vonghia L, Cardone S, Leso V, Cossari A, Capristo E, Gasbarrini G. State and trait anxiety and depression in patients affected by gastrointestinal diseases: psychometric evaluation of 1641 patients referred to an internal medicine outpatient setting. *Int J Clin Pract* 2008; 62(7): 1063-1069.

[2] Afonso L, Mohammad T, Thatai D. Crack whips the heart: a review of the cardiovascular toxicity of cocaine. *Am J Cardiol* 2007; 100: 1040–1043.

[3] Akechi T, Nakano T, Akizuki N, Okamura M, Sakuma K, Nakanishi T, Yoshikawa E, Uchitomi Y. Somatic symptoms for diagnosing major depression in cancer patients. *Psychosomatics* 2003; 4:244 –248.

[4] Alosaimi F, Hawa R. Broken heart: Broken mind. *J Psychosom Res* 2009; 67: 285-287.

[5] American Psychiatric Association. *Diagnostic and Statistical Manual of Mental Disorders* (3rd ed). Washington DC: American Psychiatric Association, 1980.

[6] American Psychiatric Association. *Diagnostic and Statistical Manual of Mental Disorders* (3rd revised ed). Washington DC: American Psychiatric Association,1987.

[7] American Psychiatric Association. *Diagnostic and Statistical Manual of Mental Disorders* (4th ed). Washington DC: American Psychiatric Association, 1994.

[8] American Psychiatric Association. *Diagnostic and Statistical Manual of Mental Disorders, Text Revision* (4th ed). Washington DC: American Psychiatric Association, 2000.

[9] Angst J. The emerging epidemiology of hypomania and bipolar II disorder. J Affect Disord 1998; 50: 143–151.

[10] Araya R, Rojas G, Fritsch R, Gaete J, Rojas M, Simon G, and Peters TJ. Treating depression in primary care among low-income women in Santiago, Chile: A randomised controlled trial. *Lancet* 2003; 361:995–1000.

[11] Arnold LM, Witzeman KA, Swank ML, McElroy SL, Keck Jr PE. Health-related quality of life using the SF-36 in patients with bipolar disorder compared with patients with chronic back pain and the general population. *J Affect Disord* 2000;57: 235–259.

[12] Atkinson M, Zibin S, Chuang H. Characterizing quality of life among patients with chronic mental illness: a critical examination of the self-report methodology. *Am J Psychiatry* 1997;154: 99– 105.

[13] Bair M., Robinson R, Katon W, Kroenke K. Depression and pain comorbidity: a literature review. *Arch Intern Med* 2003; 163: 2433-2445.

[14] Berlim MT, Pargendler J, Caldieraro MA, lmeida EA, Fleck MPA, Joine TE. Quality of Life in Unipolar and Bipolar Depression: Are There Significant Differences? *J Nerv Ment Dis* 2004;192(11):792-795.

[15] Bijl RV, Ravelli A, van Zessen G: Prevalence of psychiatric disorder in the general population: Results of the Netherlands Mental Health Survey and Incidence Study (NEMESIS). Soc Psychiatry Psychiatr Epidemiol 1998, 33(12):587-595.

[16] Birnbaum HG, Kessler RC, Kelley D, Ben-Hamadi R, Joish VN, Greenberg PE. Employer burden of mild, moderate, and severe major depressive disorder: mental health services utilization and costs, and work performance. *Depress Anxiety* 2010;27(1):78-89.

[17] Bland P. Tackling depression in patients with chronic conditions. *Practitioner* 2010; 254(1725): 28-32.

[18] Carney R, Freedland K, Miller E, Jaffe A. Depression as a risk factor for cardiac mortality and morbidity : a review of potential mechanisms. *J Psychosom Res* 2002; 53: 897-902.

[19] Carta MG, Hardoy MC, Boi MF, Mariotti S, Carpiniello B, Usa P. Association between panic disorder, major depressive disorder and celiac disease. A possible role of thyroid autoimmunity. *J Psychosom Res* 2002; 53: 789-793.

[20] Carta MG, Hardoy MC, Carpiniello B, Murru A, Marci AR, Carbone F, Deiana L, Cadeddu M and Mariotti S. A case control study on psychiatric disorders in Hashimoto disease and euthyroid goitre: not only depressive but also anxiety disorders are associated with thyroid autoimmunity. *Clin Pract Epidemiol Ment Health* 2005; 1: 23.

[21] Catalano G, Catalano MC, Rodriguez R. Dystonia associated with crack cocaine use. *South Med J* 1997; 90; 1050–1052.

[22] Cooke RG, Robb JC, Young LT, Joffe RT. Wellbeing and functioning in patients with bipolar disorder assessed using the MOS-20 item short form (SF-20). *J Affect Disord* 1996; 39: 93–97.

[23] Coulehan J, Schulberg H, Block M, Madonia M, Rodriguez E. Treating depressed primary care patients improves their physical, mental, and social functioning. *Arch Intern Med* 1997; 157:1113–1120.

[24] Cuijpers P, Smit F, Oostenbrink J, de Graaf R, ten Have M, Beekman A: Economic costs of minor depression: a population-based study. Acta Psychiatrica Scandinavica 2007, 115:229-236.

[25] Daly EJ, Trivedi MH, Wisniewski SR, Nierenberg AA, Gaynes BN, Warden D, Morris DW, Luther JF, Farabaugh A, Cook I, Rush AJ. Health-related quality of life in depression: a STAR*D report. *Ann Clin Psychiatry* 2010;22(1):43-55.

[26] DeVeaugh-Geiss AM, West SL, Miller WC, Sleath B, Gaynes BN, Kroenke K. The adverse effects of comorbid pain on depression outcomes in primary care patients: results from the ARTIST trial. *Pain Med* 2010;11(5):732-41.

[27] Di Nicola M, Tedeschi D, Mazza M, Martinotti G, Harnic D, Catalano V, Bruschi A, Pozzi G, Bria P, Janiri L. Behavioural addictions in bipolar disorder patients: Role of impulsivity and personality dimensions. Journal of affective disorders. *J Affect Disord* 2010;125 (1-3):82-88.

[28] Diwan A, Castine M, Pomerleau CS, Meador-Woodruff JH, Dalack GW. Differential prevalence of cigarette smoking in patients with schizophrenic vs mood disorders. *Schizophr Res* 1998; 33: 113-118.

[29] Dressler FA, Malekzadeh S, Roberts WC. Quantitative analysis of amounts of coronary arterial narrowing in cocaine addicts. *Am J Cardiol* 1990; 65; 303–308.

[30] Egred M, Davis GK. Cocaine and the heart. *Postgrad Med J* 2005; 81; 568–571.

[31] Emptage NP, Sturm R, Robinson RL. Depression and comorbid pain as predictors of disability, employment, insurance status, and health care costs. *Psychiatr Serv* 2005;56(4):468-474.

[32] Feighner JP, Robins E, Guze SB, Woodruff RA, Winokur G, Munoz R Diagnostic criteria for use in psychiatric research. *Arch Gen Psychiatry* 1972; 26:57– 67.

[33] Frishman WH, Del Vecchio A, Sanal S, Ismail A. Cardiovascular manifestations of substance abuse part 1: cocaine. *Heart Dis* 2003; 5; 187–201.

[34] Gadalla T. Association of comorbid mood disorders and chronic illness with disability and quality of life in Ontario, Canada. *Chronic Dis Can* 2008;28(4):148-54.

[35] Gadalla TM. Socioeconomic gradient of functional limitations in individuals diagnosed with mood disorders. *Women Health* 2009;49(2-3):181-96.

[36] Gayman MD, Turner RJ, Cui M. Physical limitations and depressive symptoms: exploring the nature of the association. *J. Gerontol B Psychol Sci Soc Sci* 2008;63(4):S219-S228.

[37] Gardner HH, Kleinman NL, Brook RA, et al. The economic impact of bipolar disorder in an employed population from an employer perspective. *J. Clin. Psychiatry* 2006;67:1209–18.

[38] Goodnick PJ, Hernandez M. Treatment of depression in comorbid medical illness. *Exp Opin Pharmacother* 2000;1(7):1367-84.

[39] Goldberg JF., Harrow M. Subjective life satisfaction and objective functional outcome in bipolar and unipolar mood disorders: A longitudinal analysis. *J. Affect Dis* 2005; 89: 79–89.

[40] Grandes G, Montoya I, Arietaleanizbeaskoa MS, Arce V, Sanchez A, on behalf of the MAS group. The burden of mental disorders in primary care. European Psychiatry (2011) 2011 Feb 7. [Epub ahead of print]

[41] Grant BF, Hasin DS, Chou SP, Stinson FS, Dawson DA. Nicotine dependence and psychiatric disorders in the United States: results from the national epidemiologic survey on alcohol and related conditions. *Arch Gen Psychiatry* 2004; 61: 1107-1115.

[42] Greenberg PE, Stiglin LE, Finkelstein SN, Berndt ER. The economic burden of depression in 1990. *J Clin Psychiatry* 1993; 54 (11): 405–418.

[43] Greenberg P, Corey-Lisle PK, Birnbaum H, Marynchenko M, Claxton A. Economic implications of treatment-resistant depression among employees. *Pharmacoeconomics* 2004;22(6):363-73.

[44] Grippo A, Johnson A. Stress, depression, and cardiovascular dysregulation : a review of neurobiological mechanisms and the integration of research from preclinical disease models. *Stress* 2009; 12(1): 1-21.

[45] Guo JJ., Keck Jr PE., Li H, Jang R, Kelton CML. Treatment Costs and Health Care Utilization for Patients with Bipolar Disorder in a Large Managed Care Population. *Value in Health* 2008; 11(3): 416-423.

[46] Harpole LH, Williams JW Jr, Olsen MK, Stechuchak KM, Oddone E, Callahan CM, Katon WJ, Lin EH, Grypma LM, Unützer J. Improving depression outcomes in older adults with comorbid medical illness. *Gen Hosp Psychiatry* 2005;27(1):4-12.

[47] Hasin D, Liu X, Nunes E, McCloud S, Samet S, Endicott J. Effects of Major Depression on Remission and Relapse of Substance Dependence. *Arch Gen Psychiatry* 2002; 59: 375-380.

[48] Hays R, Wells K, Sherbourne C, Rogers W, Spritzer K: Functioning and well-being outcomes of patients with depression compared with chronic medical illness. *Arch Gen Psychiatry* 1995; 52:11–19.

[49] Henk H, Katzelnick DJ, Kobak KA, Greist JH, Jefferson JW. Medical costs attributed to depression among patients with a history of high medical expenses in a health maintenance organization. *Arch Gen Psychiatry* 1996; 53:899–904.

[50] Henry C, Etain B. New Ways to Classify Bipolar Disorders: Going from Categorical Groups to Symptom Clusters or Dimensions. *Curr Psychiatry Rep* 2010; 12:505–511.

[51] Himmerich H, Fulda S, Linseisen J, Seiler H, Wolfram G, Himmerich S, Gedrich K, Kloiber S, Lucae S, Ising M, Uhr M, Holsboer F, Pollmächer T. Depression, comorbidities and the TNF-a system. *Eur Psychiatry* 2008; 23: 421-429.

[52] Huang KL, Su TP, Chen TJ, Chou YH, Bai YM. Comorbidity of cardiovascular diseases with mood and anxiety disorder : a population based 4 year study. *Psychiatry and Clin Neurosci* 2009; 63: 401-409.

[53] Iosifescu DV, Nierenberg AA, Alpert JE, Papakostas GI, Perlis RH, Sonawalla S, Fava M. Comorbid medical illness and relapse of major depressive disorder in the continuation phase of treatment. *Psychosomatics* 2004;45(5):419-25.

[54] Ivanova JI, Birnbaum HG, Kidolezi Y, Subramanian G, Khan SA, Stensland MD. Direct and indirect costs of employees with treatment-resistant and non-treatment-resistant major depressive disorder. *Curr Med Res Opin* 2010;26(10):2475-84.

[55] Karch SB, Billingham ME. Coronary artery and peripheral vascular disease in cocaine users. *Coron Artery Dis* 1995; 3; 220–225.

[56] Kathol R, Mutgi A, Williams J, Clamon G, Noyes R Jr. Diagnosis of major depression in cancer patients according to four sets of criteria. *Am J Psychiatry* 1990; 147:1021–1024.

[57] Katzelnick D, Simon G, Pearson S, Manning W, Helstad C, Henk H, et al: Randomized trial of a depression management program in high utilizers of medical care. *Arch Fam Med* 2000; 9:345–351.

[58] Kauer-Sant'Anna M, Bond DJ, Lam RW, Yatham LN. Functional outcomes in first-episode patients with bipolar disorder: a prospective study from the Systematic

Treatment Optimization Program for Early Mania project. *Compr Psychiatry* 2009;50(1):1-8.

[59] Kessler DA. Nicotine addiction in young people. N Engl *J Med* 1995; 333: 186-189.

[60] Kessler RC, Barber C, Birnbaum HG, Frank RG, Greenberg PE, Rose RM, Simon GE, Wang P. Depression in the workplace: Effects on short-term disability. Health Aff (Millwood) 1999;18:163–171.

[61] Kessler RC, Berglund P, Demler O, Jin R, Merikangas KR, Walters EE. Lifetime prevalence and age-of-onset distributions of DSM-IV disorders in the National Comorbidity Survey Replication. Arch Gen Psychiatry 2005; 62: 593–602.

[62] Khantzian EJ. The self-medication hypothesis of addictive disorders: focus on heroin and cocaine dependence. *Am J Psychiatry* 1985; 142: 1259-1264.

[63] Kilzieh N, Rastam S, Ward KD, Maziak W. Gender, depression and physical impairment: an epidemiologic perspective from Aleppo, Syria. *Soc Psychiatry Psychiatr Epidemiol* 2010;45(6):595-602.

[64] Kind P, Sorensen J. The costs of depression. *Int Clin Psychopharmacol* 1993;7 (3–4): 191–195.

[65] Koenig H, George L, Peterson B, Pieper C. Depression in medically ill hospitalized older adults: Prevalence, characteristics and course of symptoms according to six diagnostic schemes. *Am J Psychiatry* 1997; 154:1376–1383.

[66] Koike AK, Unützer J, Wells KB. Improving the care for depression in patients with comorbid medical illness. *Am J Psychiatry* 2002;159(10):1738-45. Erratum in: *Am J Psychiatry* 2003;160(1):204.

[67] Kruijshaar ME, Hoeymans N, Bijl RV, Spijker J, Essink-Bot ML: Levels of disability in Major Depression. Findings from the Netherlands Mental Health Survey and Incidence Study (NEMESIS). J Affect Disord 2003, 77(1):53-64.

[68] Laxman KE, Lovibond KS, Hassan MK. Impact of bipolar disorder in employed populations. *Am J Manag Care* 2008;14(11):757-764.

[69] Lepine JP, Gastpar M, Mendlewicz J, Tylee A. Depression in the community: the first pan-European study DEPRES (Depression Research in European Society). *Int Clin Psychopharmacol* 1997; 12:19–29.

[70] Luppa M, Heinrich S, Angermeyer MC, König HH, Riedel-Heller SG: Cost-of-illness studies of depression. A systematic review. Journal of Affective Disorders 2007, 98:29-43.

[71] Maremmani e al. Cocaine abuse and the bipolar spectrum in 1090 heroin addicts: Clinical observations and a proposed pathophysiologic model. *JAffect Dis* 2008; 106: 55-61.

[72] Mathers CD, Loncar D. Projections of global mortality and burden of disease from 2002 to 2030. *PLoSMed* 2006;3:e442.

[73] McEachin et al. Modeling complex genetic and environmental influences on comorbid bipolar disorder with tobacco use disorder. *BMC Medical Genetics* 2010:11:14

[74] Mehra R, Moore BA, Crothers K, Tetrault J, Fiellin DA. The association between marijuana smoking and lung cancer: a systematic review. *Arch Intern Med* 2006; 166; 1359–1367.

[75] Mirin SM,Weiss RD. Affective illness in substance abusers. Psychiatr. *Clin North Am* 1986; 9: 503-514.

[76] Murray CJ, Lopez AD. Global mortality, disability, and the contribution of risk factors: Global Burden of Disease Study. Lancet 1997;349:1436–42.

[77] Narrow WE, Rae DS, Robins LN, Regier DA. Revised prevalence estimates of mental disorders in the United States: using a clinical significance criterion to reconcile 2 surveys_ estimates. Arch Gen Psychiatry 2002; 59: 115–123.

[78] National Institute for Health and Clinical Excellence. Depression: the treatment and management of depression in adults (update). 2009. http://guidance.nice.org.uk/ CG90.

[79] Nelson J, Portera L, Leon A. Are there differences in the symptoms that respond to a selective serotonin or norepinephrine reuptake inhibitor? *Biol Psychiatry* 2005; 57:1535–1542.

[80] Nery FG, Borba EF, Hatch JP, Soares JC, Bonfa´E, Lotufo Neto F. Major depressive disorder and disease activity in systemic lupus erythematosus. *Compr Psychiatry* 2007; 48: 14-19.

[81] Nicolson SE, Caplan JP, Williams DE, Stern TA. Comorbid pain, depression, and anxiety: multifaceted pathology allows for multifaceted treatment. *Harv Rev Psychiatry* 2009;17(6):407-20. Review. Erratum in: *Harv Rev Psychiatry* 2010;18(2):141.

[82] Nnadi CU, Mimiko OA, McCurtis HL, Cadet JL. Neuropsychiatric effects of cocaine use disorders. *J Natl Med Assoc* 2005; 97; 1504–1515.

[83] Olfson M, Fireman B, Weissman M, Leon A, Sheehan D, Kathol R, et al: Mental disorders and disability among patients in a primary care group practice. *Am J Psychiatry* 1997;154:1734–1740.

[84] Ormel J, VonKorff M, Ustun TB, Pini S, Korten A, Oldehinkel T: Common mental disorders and disability across cultures. *JAMA* 1994; 272:1741–1748.

[85] Ostacher MJ, Nierenberg AA, Perlis RH, Eidelman P, Borrelli DJ, Tran TB, Marzilli Ericson G, Weiss RD, Sachs GS. The relationship between smoking and suicidal behavior, comorbidity, and course of illness in bipolar disorder. *J Clin Psychiatry* 2006; 67: 1907-1911.

[86] Ozasa K, Katanoda K, Tamakoshi A, Sato H, Tajima K, Suzuki T, Tsugane S, Sobue T. Reduced life expectancy due to smoking in large-scale cohort studies in Japan. *J Epidemiol* 2008;18(3):111-8.

[87] Padmos Roos C, Bekris L, Knijff EM, Tiemeier H, Kupka RW, Cohen D, Nolen WA, Lernmark Å and Drexhage HA. A High Prevalence of Organ-Specific Autoimmunity in Patients with Bipolar Disorder. *Biol Psychiatry* 2004; 56: 476-482.

[88] Parker G Beyond major depression. *Psychol Med* 2005; 35:467– 474.

[89] Parker G. The contribution of precipitants to depression onset, diagnostic sub-type, and treatment paradigm: a ''mix and match'' model. *Depression and Anxiety* 2010; 27: 787–790.

[90] Paties C, Peveri V, Falzi G. Liver histopathology in autopsied drug-addicts. *Forensic Sci Int* 1987; 35: 11–26.

[91] Presicci A, Lecce P, Ventura P, Margari F, Tafuri S, Margari L. Depressive and adjustment disorders – some questions about the differential diagnosis: case studies. *Neuropsych Dis Treat* 2010:6 473–481.

[92] Rao TK, Nicastri AD, Friedman EA. Natural history of heroin associated nephropathy. *N Engl J Med* 1974; 290; 19–23.

[93] Rhebergen D, Beekman AT, de Graaf R, Nolen WA, Spijker J, Hoogendijk WJ, Penninx BW. Trajectories of recovery of social and physical functioning in major

depression, dysthymic disorder and double depression: a 3-year follow-up. *J Affect Disord* 2010; 124(1-2):148-56.
[94] Robb JC, Cooke RG, Devins GM, Young LT, Joffe RT. Quality of life and lifestyle disruption in euthymic bipolar disorder. *J Psychiatr Res* 1997; 31, 509–517.
[95] Robb JC, Young LT, Cooke RG, Joffe RT. Gender differences in patients with bipolar disorder influence outcome in the medical outcomes survey (SF-20) subscale scores. *J Affect Disord* 1998; 49: 189–193.
[96] Rodriguez-Llera et al. Psychiatric comorbidity in young heroin users. *Drug and Alcohol Dependence* 2006; 84: 48-55.
[97] Rosa AR, Reinares M, Michalak EE, Bonnin CM, Sole B, Franco C, Comes M, Torrent C, Kapczinski F, Vieta E. Functional impairment and disability across mood states in bipolar disorder. *Value Health* 2010;13(8):984-8.
[98] Weyerer S, Schäufele M, Wiese B, Maier W, Tebarth F, Van Den Bussche H, Pentzek M, Bickel H, Luppa M, Sg. Riedel-Heller For The German Agecode Study Group. Current alcohol consumption and its relationship to incident dementia: results from a 3-year follow-up study among primary care attenders aged 75 years and older. *Age and Ageing* 2011; 0: 1–7.
[99] Sanchez-Moreno J, Martinez-Aran A, Gadelrab HF, Cabello M, Torrent C, Bonnin Cdel M, Ferrer M, Leonardi M, Ayuso-Mateos JL, Vieta E. The role and impact of contextual factors on functioning in patients with bipolar disorder. *Disabil Rehabil* 2010;32 (Suppl 1): S94-S104.
[100] Saatcioglu O, Celikel FC, Cakmak D. Depression and Anxiety in Alcohol Dependent Inpatients Who Smoke. *Isr J Psychiatry Relat Sci* 2008; 45: 33-38.
[101] Schoeyen HK, Birkenaes AB, Vaaler AE, Auestad BH, Malt UF, Andreassen OA, Morken G. Bipolar disorder patients have similar levels of education but lower socio-economic status than the general population. *J Affect Dis* 2011; 129: 68–74.
[102] Simon G, VonKorff M, Barlow W. Health care costs of primary care patients with recognized depression. *Arch Gen Psychiatry* 1995; 52:850–856.
[103] Simon GE, Revicki D, Heiligenstein J, Grothaus L, VonKorff M, Katon WJ, Hylan TR. Recovery from depression, work productivity, and health care costs among primary care patients. *Gen Hosp Psychiatry* 2000; 22:153–162.
[104] Simon GE. Social and Economic Burden of Mood Disorders. Biol Psychiatry 2003;54:208–215.
[105] Slobbe LCJ, Kommer GJ, Smit JM, Groen J, Meerding WJ, Polder JJ: Kosten van Ziekten in Nederland 2003; Zorg voor euro's – 1 Bilthoven, Rijksinstituut voor Volksgezondheid en Milieu; 2006.
[106] Smathers RL, Galligan JJ, Stewart BJ, Petersen DR. Overview of lipid peroxidation products and hepatic protein modification in alcoholic liver disease. *Chem Biol Interact* 2011 Feb 24.
[107] Spitzer RL, Kroenke K, Linzer M, Hahn SR, Williams JB, deGruy FV 3rd, Brody D, Davies M. Health-related quality of life in primary care patients with mental disorders. *JAMA* 1995; 274:1511– 1517.
[108] Stewart WF, Ricci JA, Chee E, Hanh SR, Morganstein D: Cost of lost productive work time among US workers with depression. JAMA 2003, 289(23):3135-3144.
[109] Tan WC, Lo C, Jong A, Xing L, Fitzgerald MJ, Vollmer WM, Buist SA, Sin DD; Vancouver Burden of Obstructive Lung Disease (BOLD) Research Group. Marijuana

and chronic obstructive lung disease: a population-based study. *Can Med Assoc J* 2009; 180; 814–820.

[110] Tashkin DP. Does smoking marijuana increase the risk of chronic obstructive pulmonary disease? *Can Med Assoc J* 2009; 180; 797–798.

[111] Thomas CM, Morris S. Cost of depression among adults in England in 2000. *Br J Psychiatry* 2003;183: 514–519.

[112] Tierney JG. Treatment-resistant depression: managed care considerations. J. Manag. *Care Pharm* 2007;13 (6 Suppl A), S2–S7.

[113] Tsang A, Von Korff M, Lee S, Alonso J, Karam E, Angermeyer MC, Borges GL, Bromet EJ, Demytteneare K, de Girolamo G, de Graaf R, Gureje O, Lepine JP, Haro JM, Levinson D, Oakley Browne MA, Posada-Villa J, Seedat S, Watanabe M. Common Chronic Pain Conditions in Developed and Developing Countries: Gender and Age Differences and Comorbidity With Depression-Anxiety Disorders. *The Journal of Pain* 2008; 9(10): 883-891.

[114] Trivedi MH, Clayton AH, Frank E. Treating depression complicated by comorbid medical illness or anxiety. *J Clin Psychiatry* 2007;68(1):e01.

[115] Unützer J, Katon W, Callahan CM, Williams JW Jr, Hunkeler E, Harpole L, Hoffing M, Della Penna RD, Noël PH, Lin EH, Areán PA, Hegel MT, Tang L, Belin TR, Oishi S, Langston C; IMPACT Investigators. Improving Mood-Promoting Access to Collaborative Treatment. Collaborative care management of late-life depression in the primary care setting: A randomized controlled trial. *JAMA* 2002; 288:2836–2845.

[116] Vieta E and Phillips ML. Deconstructing Bipolar Disorder: A Critical Review of its Diagnostic Validity and a Proposal for DSM-V and ICD-11. *Schizophrenia Bulletin* 2007;33(4): 886–892.

[117] Vojta C, Kinosian B, Glick H, Altshuler L, Bauer M: Self-reported quality of life across mood states in bipolar disorder. *Compr Psychiatry* 2001; 42:190–195.

[118] Wells KB, Stewart A, Hays RD, Burnam MA, Rogers W, Daniels M, Berry S, Greenfield S, Ware J. The functioning and well-being of depressed patients: Results from the Medical Outcome Study. *JAMA* 1989; 262:914–919.

[119] Wells KB, Golding JM, Burnam MA. Psychiatric disorder in a sample of the general population with and without medical disorder. *Am J Psychiatry* 1988, 145:976–981.

[120] World Health Organization. World Organization of Family Doctors. Integrating mental health in to primary care: a global perspective. Geneva: WHO press; 2008.

[121] World Health Organization. The global burden of disease: 2004 up date. Geneva: World Health Organization; 2008, http://www.who.int/evidence/ bod.

[122] Zimmerman M, McGlinchey JB, Chelminski I, and Young D. Diagnosing Major Depressive Disorder X: Can the Utility of the DSM-IV Symptom Criteria Be Improved? *J Nerv Ment Dis* 2006;194: 893–897.

[123] Zimmerman M, Galione J. Psychiatrists reported use of the DSM-IV criteria for major depressive disorder. *J Clin Psychiatry* 2010;71:235-238.

[124] Zwerling C, Whitten PS, Sprince NL, Davis CS, Wallace RB, Blanck P, Heeringa SG. Workforce participation by persons with disabilities: The National Health Interview Survey Disability Supplement, 1995 to 1995. *J Occup Environ Med* 2002; 44:358– 364.

In: Advances in Psychology Research. Volume 88
Editor: Alexandra M. Columbus, pp. 95-115
ISBN: 978-1-62100-591-9

Chapter 5

The Role of Parental Disciple and Family Environment During Childhood and in Cluster B Personality Symptoms in Adulthood

***Lisa Milne**, *Kevin Peel*[1] *and Philip Greenway*[2]**
[1]Australian Catholic University,
[2]Monash University

Abstract

The present study sought to establish that negative parental discipline practices, parental bonding, and family conflict would be associated with self esteem, emotional dysregulation, guilt and shame in predicting Cluster B personality disorder (PD) features, i.e.Histrionic (HPD), Narcissistic (NPD) Borderline (BPD) and Antisocial (ASPD). The predictor measures were the Parental Bonding Instrument, PBI, two brief measures of parental discipline, the Family Environment Scale, the Rosenberg Self Esteem Scale, the Test of Self-Conscious Affect–3, the General Emotional Dysregulation Measure, and the dependent variables were the Cluster B disorder features as measured by the Personality Diagnostic Questionnaire4+ (PDQ). The PDQ was not used as specifically diagnostic, but as an estimate of personality disorder symptoms. Multiple regressions to find the best fit models were run with the above variables regressed onto each personality disorder. The criterion for each was taken as a measure of the presence of more severe symptoms in GLM analyses of the four PDs with the same dependent variables as were predictors in the regression analyses. The main findings were that emotional dysregulation was a significant predictor for all disorders except ASPD in females. Maternal negative discipline was mostly associated with it, but the pattern of other significant predictors differed for the four personality disorders. The findings suggested that emotional dysregulation varies in quality according to other influencing factors such as parental discipline style. There were some gender differences in variables that suggested that, in this sample, recollections of early bonding experiences were influenced by gender.

* Corresponding Author: Dr Lisa Milne, Australian Catholic University, 115 Victoria Parade, Fitzroy, Victoria, 3065, lisa.milne@acu.edu.au

Personality disorders (PDs) have received considerable attention over the past few decades because they have a chronic and major, negative impact on the individuals affected by them (e.g. Simonsen, Ronningstam, & Millon, 2008). With a prevalence rate estimated between 10 to 14.8% for the general population, they have extensive ramifications for society (e.g. Grant et al., 2004). Cluster B PDs account for some 50% of the prevalence of all PDs (Samuels et al., 2002) with the greatest impact on the health care system and society in general (Simonsen et al.). BPD has been the most extensively researched (Zimmerman & Mattia, 1999), and is the most costly to the health care system (Frankenburg & Zanarini, 2004). ASPD has been shown to be expensive to both the health care and justice systems (Moran, 1999). However, a recent study found that HPD results in most healthcare costs (Soeteman, Roijen, Verheul, & Busschbach, 2008). By contrast, NPD may not present a large cost to health care when compared to other PDs but it can present significant costs to society and/or the workplace as a result of poor decisions and productivity losses (Campbell, Goodie, & Foster, 2004).

Prevalence of Cluster B Personality Disorders and Gender Differences

Differential prevalence rates for BPD and ASPD have been commonly observed in both clinical and community populations, where ASPD is more often diagnosed in males than in females, and the opposite gender ratio has been observed for BPD (Looper & Paris, 2000). For ASPD the male to female ratio is approximately three to one and conversely for BPD one to three (Kraus & Reynolds, 2001). Corbitt and Widiger (1995) reviewed 12 studies and found substantial variation in the magnitude of gender differences (Corbitt & Widiger). They explained this variation both in terms of the gender bias in the diagnostic criteria pertaining to each PD, and bias in diagnosing clinicians. For example, the proportions of females diagnosed with BPD ranged from 50 to 100% in samples drawn from inpatient and outpatient populations, using a variety of assessment instruments from structured interview to self-report. By contrast, some of the same studies found that the proportions of males diagnosed with ASPD ranged from 71 to 81%. More recently, Paris' (2007) review noted that similar gender ratios for BPD and ASPD diagnoses had occurred in clinical samples, and that HPD had an even gender ratio, as did NPD in community samples. However, when Samuel and Widiger (2009) investigated diagnostic bias using the dimensional five factor model of personality, FFM, the gender bias with respect to ASPD, while similar, was much less marked than in previous studies. As a partial explanation of these varied findings, Looper and Paris drew attention to the different ways in which males and females may express common factors. For example, females may express their aggression indirectly or verbally, while males may do so directly and physically. Such differences render gender differences in the expressions of symptoms in personality disorders extremely complex.

Parental Bonding. In families where both mothers and fathers are warmly supportive and involved, children develop into well-adjusted adults (Amato, 1994). Studies using the Parental Bonding Instrument (PBI) have consistently shown that optimal parenting combines a high level of care and a low level of overprotection (Parker, Tupling and Brown, 1979). Where poor parenting practices along with conflict in families prevail, individuals risk developing a variety of psychological problems in adulthood (Krishnakumar & Buehler, 2000). The opposite PBI combination, low parental care and high overprotection has been

shown to be associated with anxiety and depression (Parker et al., 1979; Parker, 1983; Gerlsma, Kramer, Scholing, & Emmelkemp, 1990; Parker, Hadzi-Pavlovic, Greenwald, & Weissman, 1995). Adverse conditions in an individual's family of origin have been found to relate particularly to Cluster B psychopathology (Linehan, 1993; Otway & Vignoles, 2006; Bender, Farber, & Geller, 2001; Weston & Riolo, 2007). Although there have been few studies on HPD and NPD. Horton, Bleau and Drwecki (2006) found that parental warmth and psychological control predicted unhealthy narcissism in high school students, as did withdrawal of love and guilt induction by parents. Timmerman and Emmelkamp (2005) demonstrated that low parental care and high overprotection were associated with BPD, and ASPD as had Norden, Klein, Donaldson, Pepper, and Klein (1995). The development of BPD has been linked to verbal, emotional, physical abuse or neglect in childhood (Zanarini et al., 1997), confirming the finding of Nickell et al. (2002) that parental care and overprotection scores for both parents correlated with BPD scores . However, once Nickell et al. entered gender, attachment scores and other axis I and II pathology scores into a hierarchical regression, only maternal scores remained significant for parental care and overprotection. This is in contrast to previous research by Paris and Frank (1989) that found significant effects for care from both parents on borderline status, but not for parental overprotection, although their sample size was substantially smaller. Combining the positive findings from Nickell et al. and those from Paris and Frank, it would appear that parental care and maternal overprotection, but not paternal overprotection, are important in BPD.

Parental Discipline. Baumrind's (1966) authoritative model of parenting as a balance between the extremes of the authoritarian and permissive parenting was characterized by both high levels of demand and of responsiveness from the parent, i.e. positive and negative reinforcement of behaviour, and the parent's capacity to explain and reason when disciplining. This model of parenting enables children to behave in socially acceptable ways, reason autonomously, respect adult authority, and learn how to think independently (Baumrind, 1967; Baumrind, 1996; Chapell & Overton, 1998). Children, whose parents provide reasons for them, internalize parental values more readily than children whose parents rely on power-assertion or withdrawal of love techniques alone (Hoffman, 1983).

Family Conflict

Many studies in the family research literature have dealt with the impact of parental separation and divorce on offspring (Amato & Keith, 1991). While marital separation often causes hardship for offspring in the short term, the long term effects on psychological adjustment are small. Family conflict, however, has been identified as having the most detrimental impact (Amato & Keith), particularly on the developing child's self-concept (Nelson, Hughes, Handal, Katz, & Searight, 1993; Richardson & McCabe, 2001), The incidence of depression and anxiety, and less life satisfaction overall often result (Richardson & McCabe, 2001). Additionally, family conflict is also associated with lower attachment to one or both parents (Feenstra, Banyard, Rines, & Hopkins, 2001; Hannum & Dvorak, 2004). With regard to personality pathology, conflict in the family of origin was found to be significantly associated with dissocial behaviour and emotional dysregulation, crucial aspects of Cluster B pathology (Jang, Vernon, & Livesley, 2000). A study by Weaver

and Clum (1993) that found a moderate correlation between family conflict and dimensional BPD scores, but the sample was small and entirely female. Further, Klonsky Serrita, Turkheimer, and Oltmanns (2000) findings of a modest correlations between family conflict and PDs in general seem to downplay the relative importance of this factor. Other studies (e.g. Simons, Robertson, & Downs, 1989) have generated findings that, if extrapolated, would suggest that family conflict is in fact an important factor in personality pathology. For example, Simons et al.'s study explored the effect of parental rejection on adolescent delinquency and found that family conflict was significantly involved. As adolescent delinquency has been found to be a precursor to adult antisocial behaviour (Weston & Riolo, 2007), family conflict appears to be important in the development of ASPD. While there is evidence that family conflict impacts on general psychopathology, not much evidence links explicitly it to Cluster B pathology.

Parental Influence and Individual Factors Related to Cluster B Patholog

Self-conscious affects, such as shame and guilt (Mills, 2005), self esteem, emotional dysregulation (Eisenberg, 2000), and parental influence have been associated with Cluster B pathology. Some recent studies have focused on shame and guilt, in relation to psychopathology generally and specifically to axis II disorders (Eisenberg, 2000; Mills, 2005; Stuewig & McCloskey, 2005). Paulhus, Robins, Trzesniewski, and Tracy (2004) found that shame and guilt strongly correlated possibly due to their sharing a "generalized negative self-consciousness" (p 313). They differ, however, in that in feelings of shame, one's sense of self is diminished and impoverished, whereas in guilt a specific behaviour is evaluated negatively, leaving intact one's sense of self (Gramzow & Tangney, 1992; Tangney, Wagner, & Gramzow, 1992; Covert, Tangney, Maddux, & Heleno, 2003). Further, shame is central to narcissism as a disorder of the self-system, especially in relation to the regulation of self esteem and the integration of the different aspects of self (Gramzow & Tangney; Martens, 2005). Tracy and Robbins (2007) suggested that narcissistic features such as compensatory grandiosity, hypersensitivity to criticism, and need for admiration, may protect individuals from experiencing the discomfort of shame. Gramzow and Tangney, examined shame and guilt-proneness in relation to narcissism, although not pathological narcissism. They found in a sample of college students, that, although shame-proneness was negatively associated with narcissism as measured by the Narcissistic Personality Inventory as a whole (NPI; Raskin & Hall, 1979), it was positively associated with the maladaptive components of the NPI. Shame-proneness has also been associated with several negative aspects of personal and interpersonal adjustment, such as anger, hostility, social anxiety, self-consciousness, and a diminished capacity for empathy (Covert, Tangney, Maddux, & Heleno).

Leith and Baumeister (1998) observed that both guilt and shame are used in socializing children to comply with social norms and to behave in acceptable ways. They further suggested that in shame one focuses on one's own distress and the only responses that seem to manage it are, to deny responsibility, or to attack and blame others. Guilt, however, involves negative feelings of remorse or regret, that motivate individuals to make amends for behaviours experienced as reprehensible (Gramzow & Tangney, 1992). Consequently guilt tends to be absent in individuals with ASPD (Hare & Neumann, 2006). Moreover, Tangney and Dearing (2002) found guilt to be related to positive indicators of wellbeing. Paulhus et al.

(2004) speculated that in having 'bad behavior' as its focus rather than a bad self, guilt enables individuals to accept responsibility for their behaviour while maintaining their self concept. In their study of empathy, shame, guilt and interpersonal conflict, Leith and Baumeister found that guilt-proneness was associated with a greater ability to appreciate another's perspective thereby mediating the effects of empathy, whereas shame-proneness was not involved at all.

Stuewig and McCloskey (2005) in their longitudinal study reported that parental rejection and harshness in childhood was associated with shame proneness in adolescence. Rüsch et al., (2007a) explored shame and guilt-proneness and self-concept in females with BPD. They found that while both had significant zero-order correlations with self-esteem, when entered into a regression analysis, only shame-proneness was significant. Efthim, Maureen, Kenny, and Mahalik (2001) found evidence that it was in females associated with failing to live up to gender role expectations along with externalization, i.e. the tendency to shift blame to others. They linked this with previous findings that caregivers and peers shame children for violating cultural expectations for their gender group (Zahn-Waxler, Cole, & Barrett, 1991). They also argued that the negative consequences of violating internalized gender roles results in self devaluation. They cited the work of theorists in the shame literature who suggest that repeated failures gradually lead to shame (Morrison, 1989).

Emotional Dysregulation, Cluster B Pathology and Parental Bonding

Linehan (1993) originally characterized vulnerability to emotional dysregulation in terms of three major facets, "high sensitivity to emotional stimuli, emotional intensity, and slow return to emotional baseline" (p. 43). Emotional dysregulation is now accepted as an essential component of Cluster B pathology (Looper & Paris, 2000; Sarkar & Adshead 2006). It is one of the main features of BPD in which it leads to mood reactivity, dysphoria, irritability and feelings of abandonment and emptiness (Looper & Paris). This emotional turmoil further leads to self-destructive behaviours such as self-mutilation, substance abuse and suicide attempts.

In a large study involving, general population participants (N=939), personality disordered patients (N=656), and a volunteer twin pair sample (N=686), Livesley, Jang and Vernon's (1998) factor analysis found emotional dysregulation to be the largest of four major factors, the others being dissocial behavior, inhibitedness, and compulsivity. The authors described it as "a general factor of personality pathology organized around affective traits" (p. 945) similar in clinical and nonclinical samples. They found it to be a higher order, personality trait dimension, consisting of reactive tendencies, dissatisfaction with the self and life experiences, and interpersonal problems (Livesley, Jang, & Vernon). They further identified it as including a Cluster of lower order traits, anxiousness, submissiveness, cognitive distortion, identity problems, suspiciousness, insecure attachment and social avoidance. They recognised its similarity to Eysenck's concept of neuroticism, (Larstone, Jang, Livesley, Vernon, & Wolf, 2002) except that emotional dysregulation is broader, including identity problems, cognitive dysregulation, insecure attachment, oppositionality, suspiciousness and narcissism. The breadth of the factor suggested that it resembled Linehan's description of BPD. Miller & Pilkonis (2006) largely concurred with these findings. They suggested that neuroticism is mainly associated with an anxious avoidant

interpersonal style, together with a lowered sense of competence leading to a reliance on others for emotional support. Affective instability they conceived as mainly associated with an interpersonal style characterized by acting out in an egocentric, unpredictable way leading to aggression, and an unsocial, dramatic style of acting, characteristic of Cluster B behavioural expressions.

Bender, Farber and Geller (2001) in a study of outpatients, found that difficulties associated with less secure attachment were associated with all four Cluster B PDs. They concluded that participants with these PDs seemed to construct images of others as unavailable. At the same time, they wanted to be closer, feared separation and loss of the important other. Yu, Wang, Qian, Jang, et al., (2007) likewise concluded in line with previous studies that parental bonding as measured by the PBI and the kind of emotional personality functioning just described are related. Specifically, they reported that patients with personality disorders remembered less parental care than did a sample of adolescents and adult students. Moreover, the PBI scales were predictive of scores on the Dimensional Assessment of Personality Pathology - Basic Questionnaire in all of their three samples, patients, adolescents and students. For example, in patients, maternal Autonomy Denial, Care and Freedom Control, and paternal Care and Freedom Control in combination accounted for 14% of the variability in the scale Cognitive Distortion. The authors noted that low maternal Care had been associated previously with BPD (Nickell Waudby, & Trull, 2002; Zweig-Frank & Paris, 1991).

Self-Esteem and Emotional Dysregulation

The development of the self in childhood has been extensively investigated in relation to parenting (e.g., Roberts & Bengtson, 1993; Steinberg, Elmen, & Mounts, 1989). Bender and Skodol, (2007) have suggested that emotional dysregulation is secondary to a self-other disturbance that negatively impacts on interpersonal relations. How self-esteem and emotional dysregulation are associated with Cluster B personality pathology is thus a pivotal issue. According to Rosenberg (1979), self-concept is defined as "the totality of the individual's thoughts and feelings with reference to himself as an object" (p. 8), whereas self-esteem is the orientation toward that object. It concerns the degree to which individuals have respect for themselves, or consider themselves to be worthy (Rosenberg). Self-esteem has been associated with adjustment and subjective well being, in adolescence and adulthood (Diener, Emmons, Larsen, & Griffin, 1985; Roberts & Bengtson). Additionally, Parker's (1993) study found higher self-esteem to be significantly associated with maternal care and negatively so with maternal overprotection. No significant effect was observed between self-esteem and paternal care, though there was a significant but small negative relationship between paternal overprotection and self-esteem.

In relations to Cluster B personality pathology the role of the self-esteem has received mixed attention. It has been extensively investigated in NPD (e.g. Sedikides, Rudich, Gregg, Kumashiro, & Rusbult, 2004; Tracy, Cheng, Robins, & Trzesniewski, 2009; Zeigler-Hill, 2006), to a lesser extent in BPD (e.g. Rüsch et al., 2007b) and ASPD (Leary, Schreindorfer, & Haupt, 1995), and hardly at all in HPD (Apt & Hurlbert, 1994). With the exception of NPD, with which self-esteem is positively correlated (e.g. Zeigler-Hill), most studies have

reported negative associations between self-esteem and Cluster B pathology (e.g. Rüsch et al.; Leary et al.; Apt & Hurlbert).

The present study aimed at identifying which PBI, discipline and family conflict variables would be associated with emotional dysregulation, self esteem, guilt, and shame measures as predictors of each of the Cluster B disorders. A community sample seemed appropriate for two main reasons. First, it reduces the possibility of extreme expressions of the PDs, common in clinical samples. Second, it allows one to focus on PD symptoms as expressed in a nonclinical population, reducing the stress on diagnosis, and conversely putting it on personality related variables. If the number of symptoms endorsed by a participant indicates severity of symptoms then it is further useful to compare the participants who met the criterion for having a significantly large number of symptoms with those who did not. Finally, since personality pathology attenuates over time, age was added to the predictors.

The present study used the PDQ-4 as a screening measure for PD symptoms associated with Cluster B. The use of the PDQ-4 has been disputed in the assessment and screening for personality disorders, because of its modest correlation with other diagnostic instruments, such as structured interviews and self-report questionnaires in both clinical and nonclinical populations. (Bagby & Farvolden, 2004; Wilberg, Dammen, & Friis, 2000). It also has high sensitivity and low specificity, making it suitable as a screening measure (Wilberg, Dammen, & Friis, 2000). Nevertheless, the PDQ-4 does identify symptoms associated with specific PDs and in this study it was used for that purpose.

METHOD

Participants

The sample consisted of 530 adults from the non-clinical population, 265 women (M = 28.57, SD = 12.11) and 265 men (M = 32.27, SD = 13.57), ranging from 18 to 82 years old, with an overall mean age of 30.40 years (*SD* = 12.97). The data was collected from undergraduate students participating for course credit; and an advertisement on the social networking website Facebook®.

Measures

The Parental Bonding Instrument (PBI; Parker, Tupling & Brown, 1979), a widely used test has acceptable stable test-retest reliability (Wilhelm, Niven, Parker, & Hadzi-Pavlovic, 2005) and convergent validity with other attachment-related measures (Manassis, Owens, Adam, West, & Sheldon-Keller, 1999). It is a 25 item measure of retrospective perceptions of parental bonding experiences. It has two factors, Care, (Mcare for mother's Care, Fcare for father's Care) 13 items, assessing parental care and warmth as against rejection, and Overprotection, (Mov for mother's overprotection, Fov for father's overprotection) 12 items, assessing parental overprotection and control as against the allowance of independence and autonomy (Randolph & Dykman, 1998).

Parental Discipline: Adapted from Hoffman's (1970) categories of discipline, participants rated, separately for each parent, the following statements on a 4-point scale (never, rarely, often, always): *As a child, when I was naughty my mother/father smacked, hit, or spanked me. As a child, when I was naughty my mother/father ignored me for a while, and it was clear she was cross with me. As a child, when I was naughty my mother/father removed privileges, such as toys being confiscated, or being grounded.* Ratings were summed to form variables, Mother Negative, and Father Negative (MNeg/FNeg). The statement, *As a child, when I was naughty, my mother/father tried to reason with me and pointed out the harmful consequences of what I had done wrong,* formed a variable Mother Reasoned/Father Reasoned (MRea/FRea).

Family Conflict: Conflict in the participant's family of origin was measured using the conflict subscale of the Family Environment Scale, (FES; Moos & Moos, 1994), a 9 item (true =2/false = 1) self report scale. Cronbach's α ranged from 78 to .82 in previous studies (Sanford, Zucker, & Bingham, 1999; Saucier, Wilson, & Warka, 2007) and was .80 in the present sample. It measures remembered hostility in an individual's family of origin.

Self-esteem: The Rosenberg Self-Esteem Scale, (SE) 10 items on a 4 point scale, strongly agree to strongly disagree, α = .86 (RSES; Rosenberg, 1965) and .91 in the present study, measures self-esteem.

Guilt and Shame: The Test of Self-Conscious Affect–3 (TOSCA-3; Tangney, Dearing, Wagner, & Gramzow, 2000), has 16 items rated on a 5 point scale, not likely to very likely, assessing externalisation of blame, detachment, shame-proneness and guilt-proneness. The current study used the 11 item version (Tangney et. al, 2000) that utilises only negative scenarios. Only items for guilt and shame were administered. The items depict scenarios of socially difficult situations. TOSCA-3 has good validity and reliability (Ferguson & Crowley, 1997; Rüsch et al., 2007a; Tangney, 1996; Tangney et al., 1992). In the current sample, for shame-proneness α = .76 and guilt-proneness α = .72.

Emotional dysregulation: The General Emotional Dysregulation, (Emo), Measure assesses affect intensity and negative affect. It has 13 items, on a 5 point scale from strongly disagree to strongly agree, test-retest stability r = .81; (GEDM; Newhill, Mulvey, & Pilkonis, 2004), α = .87; (Newhill, Eack, & Conner, 2009) and in the present study α = .92.

The Cluster B personality disorders: These were assessed using the HPD, 8 items, NPD, 9 items, BPD, 9 items, ASPD 8 items from the fourth edition of the Personality Diagnostic Questionnaire (PDQ-4+; Hyler, 1994) based on the DSM-IV-TR (APA, 2000). All items in each subscale are endorsed as *true* or *false* (scored 1 or 0 respectively). Validity has been confirmed empirically, both in the clinical (Wilberg, Dammen, & Friis, 2000) and the non-clinical populations (Bagby, Marshall, & Georgiades, 2005).

Procedure

The present study was approved by the Australian Catholic University's Human Research Ethics Committee. Participants were recruited through the University, social networking, and through a Facebook® completed the battery of questionnaires through an online database.

RESULTS

Of the 254 males and 254 females 5.1% of males and 5.3% of females met the PDQ-4 criterion for HPD, 10.6% of males and 4.2% of females for NPD, 18.1% of males and 18.2% of females for BPD and 5.1% of males and 1.5% of females for ASPD. McNemar's *chi-square* suggested that there were no significant differences in the percentages for HPD and BPD in respect of gender. However, a significantly lower percentage of females met the PDQ-4 criterion for NPD and for ASPD.

GLM Analysis of the Cluster B PDs Using the PDQ-4 Criteria as an Indication of High End Symptom Scores

A series of GLMs were run in which Gender and each of the Cluster B PDs were fixed factors and Fov, Mov, Fcar, Mcar, Frea, Mrea, Fneg, Mneg, Fes, SE, Emo, Guilt and Shame were the dependent variables. In all these analyses the PD x Gender interaction was not significant. There was however a main effect for Gender in all. To assess how Gender affected the all the variables, including the four PDs, a separate analysis was run on the whole sample. The descriptive statistics are contained in Table 1. The effect for Gender explained 27% of variance, (Wilk's Λ =.73, $F(18/511) = 9.56$, $p < .0001$, $\eta^2 = .27$). In the univariate analyses the following variables were significant: NPD, $F(1/528) = 12.46$, $p < .0001$, $\eta^2 = .02$); ASPD, $F(1/528) = 32.62$, $p < .0001$, $\eta^2 = .02$); Guilt, $F(1/528) = 53.40$, $p < .0001$, $\eta^2 = .09$); Shame, $F(1/528) = 32.81$, $p < .0001$, $\eta^2 = .06$); Fneg, $F(1/528) = 14.00$, $p < .0001$, $\eta^2 = .03$); Fcare, $F(1/528) = 9.79$, $p < .002$, $\eta^2 = .02$); Emo, $F(1/528) = 9.20$, $p < .003$, $\eta^2 = .02$); Mov, $F(1/528) = 4.50$, $p < .034$, $\eta^2 = .01$).

Table 1. Descriptive Statistics for the Variables Significantly Affected by Gender

	Male *n=265*		Female *n=265*		*p*
	M	SD	M	SD	
HPD	2.26	1.68	2.52	1.74	*ns*
NPD	3.19	1.90	2.65	1.63	<.0001
BPD	3.37	2.22	3.33	2.31	*ns*
ASPD	2.22	1.83	1.39	1.50	<.0001
Mov	15.91	8.04	14.45	7.81	<.034
Fcare	19.55	3.82	18.57	3.42	<.002
Fneg	6.85	2.23	6.11	2.32	<0001
Shame	32.00	7.82	35.90	7.83	<.0001
Guilt	44.00	6.20	47.54	4.87	<0001
Emo	38.47	11.69	41.51	11.33	<.003

Note: Fov, Paternal overprotection, Mov, Maternal overprotection, Fcare, Paternal Care, Shame, Shame proneness scale, Guilt, Guilt proneness scale, SE, Self esteem, Emo, Emotional dysregulation.

Following the gender GLM, separate analyses were run with each of the four PDs as the fixed factor with the same variables as were in gender analysis as dependent variables. Table 2 contains the descriptive statistics for each of the four analyse.

Table 2. The Descriptive Statistics for each of the four GLM analyses.

		HPD		NPD		BPD		ASPD	
		0	1	0	1	0	1	0	1
		n=511	*n=19*	*n=489*	*n =41*	*n=433*	*n=97*	*n=530*	*n=30*
Fov	M	12.94	15.73	13.06	13.46	12.49	15.78	12.95	17.05
	SD	*7.06*	*8.75*	*7.15*	*7.66*	*7.01*	*7.39*	7.08	*8.87*
Mov	M	14.92	19.57	15.04	16.88	14.62	17.69	14.97	20.84
	SD	*7.98*	*6.09*	*7.90*	*8.40*	*7.85*	*7.96*	*7.82*	*9.43*
Fcare	M	19.05	19.27	19.06	19.00	19.07	18.99	19.00	20.53
	SD	*3.71*	*2.56*	*3.73*	*2.59*	*3.61*	*3.85*	*3.62*	*4.39*
Mcare	M	18.48	17.83	18.51	17.71	18.58	17.84	18.46	18.11
	SD	*3.17*	*4.08*	*3.26*	*2.62*	*2.95*	*4.19*	*3.13*	*5.20*
Frea	M	2.50	2.47	2.49	2.59	2.55	2.25	2.52	2.00
	SD	*1.09*	*1.14*	*1.09*	*1.16*	*1.09*	*1.08*	*1.09*	*1.05*
Mrea	M	3.10	3.30	3.10	3.20	3.13	3.00	3.12	2.74
	SD	*.92*	*.95*	*.94*	*.68*	*.90*	*1.04*	*.91*	*1.24*
Fneg	M	6.44	7.27	6.44	7.05	6.40	6.87	6.49	6.26
	SD	*2.25*	*2.94*	*2.30*	*2.34*	*2.19*	*2.74*	*2.30*	*2.45*
Mneg	M	7.29	7.23	7.23	8.02	7.15	7.93	7.28	7.68
	SD	*2.03*	*2.06*	*2.03*	*1.86*	*1.99*	*2.08*	*2.00*	*2.83*
Fes	M	13.10	14.30	13.14	13.54	12.90	14.38	13.09	15.26
	SD	*2.67*	*2.72*	*2.69*	*2.66*	*2.64*	*2.54*	*2.67*	*2.31*
Shame	M	33.73	37.67	34.01	33.20	32.87	38.76	33.93	34.47
	SD	*8.07*	*7.07*	*8.01*	*8.70*	*7.75*	*7.66*	*7.97*	*10.47*
Guilt	M	45.78	45.57	46.08	42.05	45.91	45.13	45.94	41.32
	SD	*5.87*	*5.53*	*5.57*	*7.62*	*5.64*	*6.70*	*5.60*	*9.67*
SE	M	19.23	17.50	19.15	18.95	20.34	13.72	19.31	14.47
	SD	*6.10*	*5.39*	*6.06*	*6.27*	*5.62*	*4.93*	*6.02*	*5.72*
Emo	M	39.32	51.20	39.48	46.00	37.31	51.96	39.71	47.58
	SD	*11.43*	*8.24*	*11.62*	*9.57*	*10.48*	*8.35*	*11.60*	*8.99*
Age	M	30.71	25.50	30.78	26.17	30.89	28.32	30.62	25.05
	SD	*13.04*	*10.95*	*13.12*	*10.31*	*13.52*	*10.00*	*12.95*	*17.05*

Note: Fov, Paternal overprotection, Mov, Maternal overprotection, Fcare, Paternal Care, Mcare, Maternal Care, Frea, Father reasoning as discipline style, Mrea, Mother reasoning as discipline style, Fneg, Negative paternal discipline, Mneg, Negative maternal discipline, Fes, Family environment scale, Shame, Shame proneness scale, Guilt, Guilt proneness scale, SE, Self esteem, Emo, Emotional dysregulation.

HPD. The HPD factor was significant, Wilk's $\Lambda = .89$, $F(14/515) = 4.23$, $p <.0001$, $\eta^2 = .11$). In the univariate analyses, the following variables were significant; Emo, $F(1/528) = 31.41$, $p < .000$, $\eta^2 = .06$; Mov, $F(1/528) = 9.83$, $p < .002$, $\eta^2 = .02$; Shame, $F(1/528) = 6.84$, $p < .007$, $\eta^2 = .01$; Fov, $F(1/528) = 4.32$, $p <.038$, $\eta^2 = .01$;*r*

NPD The NPD factor was significant (Wilks' $\Lambda =.91$, $F(14/515) = 2.78$, $p <.0001$, $\eta^2 = .09$). In the univariate analyses, the following variables were significant: Emo, $F(1/528) =$

12.18, $p <.001$, $\eta^2 = .02$; Guilt F (1/528) = 18.61, $p <.0001$,$\eta^2 = .03$; 02; Mneg F(1/528) = 5.86, $p < .016$, $\eta^2 =.01$; and Age, F(1/528) = 4.80, $p < .028$, $\eta^2 =.01$

BPD. The BPD was significant (Wilks' Λ =.69, F(13/514) = 17.63, $p <.0001$, $\eta^2 = .30$). In the univariate analyses the following variables were significant: Emo, F (1/528) = 165.78, $p < .0001$, $\eta^2 =.24$; SE, F(1/528) = 114.74, $p < .0001$, $\eta^2 = .18$; Shame, F(1/528) = 45.94, $p < .0001$, $\eta^2 =.08$; Fes, F(1/528) = 25.52, $p < .0001$, $\eta^2 = .05$; Fov, F(1/528) = 17.17, $p <.0001$, $\eta^2 = .03$; Mov, F(1/528) = 12.18, $p <.001$, $\eta^2 = .02$; Mneg,, F(1/528) = 11.89, $p < .001$, $\eta^2 = .02$; Mcar, F(1/528) = 4.26, $p < .004$, $\eta^2 =.01$; Frea, F(1/526) = 6.31, $p <.012$, $\eta^2 = .01$;

ASPD. In this analysis only since four females met the PDQ-4 criterion for antisocial personality disorder, gender was dropped as a factor. The ASPD factor was significant (Wilks' Λ =.92, F(14/515) = 3.13, $p <.0001$, $\eta^2 = .08$) factor was significant. In the univariates analyses the following variables were significant: SE, F(1/528) = 11.85, $p < .001$, $\eta^2 =.02$; Guilt, F (1/528) = 11.67, $p< .001$, $\eta^2 =.02$; Emo ,F (1/528) = 8.55, $p< .004$, $\eta^2 =.02$; Fes, F(1/528) = 12.26, $p < .001$, $\eta^2 =.02$; Mov, F(1/528) = 10.16, $p < .002$, $\eta^2 =.02$; Frea, F(1/528) = 4.13, $p < .043$, $\eta^2 =.01$;and Fov, F(1/528) = 6.04, $p < .014$, $\eta^2 =.01$;

Regression Analyses

Each personality disorder was analysed following the method of Gagné and Dayton (2002). All independent variables, correlating significantly with a specific personality disorder, with gender as an additional variable were regressed initially onto that disorder. Then, a series of multiple regression analyses were run to identify a best fit model with a reduced number of variables. A backward elimination procedure was used with the following criteria for dropping an independent variable. Loss in R^2 was not greater than 5%. The variable to be eliminated was that with the highest probability value greater than .05 for the t-test associated with it. Mallow's Cm statistic had to approximate to the number of independent variables+1, and Akaike's information criterion of each successive model had to decrease. The elimination procedure continued until all the remaining variables were significant. This result was accepted as the model best fitting the data. Only the reduced models are reported here. Gender was a significant predictor for NPD, BPD and ASPD but not for HPD. For NPD, BPD and ASPD the regressions were re-run separately for each gender. Table 3 shows the zero order correlations between all the variables in the analyses for males and females.

HPD. The best fit model, for the whole sample, Mallow's Prediction Criterion = 5, accounted for 23% of variance as compared with 23% for the initial analysis, and included the variables Emo ($\beta = .48$, $t = 10.51$, $p < .0001$), Age ($\beta = -.16$, $t = 4.09$, $p < .0001$), SE ($\beta = .12$, $t = 2.67$, $p < .008$), and Mrea, ($\beta = .09$, $t = 2.38$, $p < .018$).

NPD: For males, the best fit model, Mallow's Prediction Criterion = 4, accounted for 14% of variance as compared with 14.8% for the initial analysis and included four variables Emo ($\beta = .23$, $t = 4.03$, $p < .0001$), Age, ($\beta = -.20$, $t = -3.41$, $p < .001$), and Mneg, ($\beta = .16$, $t = 2.81$, $p < .005$).

For females, the best fit model, Mallow's Prediction Criterion = 4, accounted for 15.4% of variance as compared with 15.7% for the initial analysis and included three variables Emo ($\beta = .28$, $t = 4.80$, $p < .0001$), Guilt, ($\beta = -.20$, $t = 3.45$, $p < .001$, and Age, ($\beta = -.14$, $t = -2.35$, $p < .019$).

Table 3. Zero order Correlations between all the Variables in the study except Gender.

1.Fov	1.00	.39	.40	.14	-.02	.01	-.03	.05	.01	-.03	.05	-.03	.02	-.09	-.12	-.03	-.02	.24
2.Mov	.20	1.00	.09	.35	.00	-.08	.01	.00	-.07	-.04	-.01	.08	-.07	-.16	-.19	-.14	-.21	.25
3. Fcare	.47	.11	1.00	.15	.00	.09	.06	-.06	.00	-.04	.00	.13	-.17	-.11	-.13	-.14	.03	.05
4. Mcare	.02	.47	.15	1.00	.08	-.04	.04	-.14	-.08	-.04	-.15	.09	-.07	-.16	-.09	-.16	-.13	.03
5. Frea	-.26	-.01	-.17	.10	1.00	.30	.12	-.04	-.25	-.08	-.05	.26	-.09	-.07	-.06	-.16	-.15	-.09
6. Mrea	-.03	-.06	-.09	-.07	.29	1.00	.08	-.24	-.24	-.08	.14	.19	-.04	.08	-.05	-.11	-.14	-.16
7. Fneg	-.03	.05	-.17	.11	-.02	-.09	1.00	.25	.14	.15	-.02	-.14	.08	-.03	.04	.12	.07	.03
8. Mneg	.07	.05	.04	.01	-.01	.05	.28	1.00	.23	.19	.07	-.18	.16	.08	.10	.29	.21	.07
9. Fes	.01	.02	.07	.04	-.26	-.30	.19	.26	1.00	.08	-.07	-.21	.12	.13	.08	.25	.26	.00
10. Shame	.02	.05	.13	.16	.02	.00	.04	.05	.03	1.00	.29	-.46	.42	.19	.12	.47	.12	-.10
11. Guilt	-.01	.04	-.03	.00	.14	.11	.11	-.08	-.16	.33	1.00	-.02	.05	-.04	-.20	-.03	-.15	.16
12. SE	-.03	.11	.01	-.01	.18	.19	-.01	-.05	-.20	-.38	.06	1.00	-.51	-.15	-.09	-.62	-.27	.03
13. Emo	-.02	-.18	-.05	-.07	-.11	-.02	.16	.09	.29	.34	.04	-.56	1.00	.42	.28	.61	.16	-.10
14. HPD	-.03	-.17	-.03	-.06	.04	.16	.05	.02	.10	.13	.03	-.10	.42	1.00	.41	.47	.36	-.29
15. NPD	-.12	-.20	.01	-.09	.10	.09	.05	.21	.12	.01	-.14	.02	.25	.40	1.00	.34	.34	-.18
16. BPD	-.05	-.18	-.05	-.10	-.09	-.04	.11	.20	.27	.31	-.12	-.61	.67	.45	.32	1.00	.43	-.20
17. ASPD	-.12	-.08	-.06	-.12	-.11	-.08	.12	.26	.23	-.04	-.22	-.21	.32	.24	.31	.48	1.00	-.14
18. Age	.23	.16	.13	-.02	-.17	-.03	.06	-.11	-.09	.03	.16	.06	.00	-.09	-.22	-.15	-.19	1.00

Note: Fov, Paternal overprotection, Mov, Maternal overprotection, Fcare, Paternal Care, Mcare, Maternal Care, Frea, Father reasoning as discipline style, Mrea, Mother reasoning as discipline style, Fneg, Negative paternal discipline, Mneg, Negative maternal discipline, Fes, Family environment scale, Shame, Shame proneness scale, Guilt, Guilt proneness scale, SE, Self esteem, Emo, Emotional dysregulation

BPD. For males, the best fit model, Mallow's Prediction Criterion = 5, accounted for 54 % of variance as compared with 55.5% for the initial analysis and included four variables Emo, ($\beta = .48$, $t = 9.65$, $p < .0001$, SE ($\beta = -.33$, $t = -6.70$, $p < .0001$), and MNeg, ($\beta = .13$, $t = 3.12$, $p < .002$) and Age, ($\beta = -.11$, $t = -2.98$, $p < .008$).

BPD: For females, the best fit model, Mallow's Prediction Criterion = 7, accounted for 56% of variance as compared with 57% for the initial analysis. There were six significant variables; Emo, ($\beta = .34$, $t = 6.78$, $p < .0001$), SE, ($\beta = -.35$, $t = -6.55$, $p < .0001$), Age, ($\beta = -.15$, $t = -3.62$, $p < .0001$), Shame, ($\beta = .13$, $t = 2.73$, $p < .007$) Mneg, ($\beta = .13$, $t = 3.11$, $p < .002$), and. Fes, ($\beta = .10$, $t = -2.29$, $p < .023$)

ASPD: For males, the best fit model, Mallow's Prediction Criterion = 5 accounted for 23.4% of variance as compared with 24% for the initial analysis and included five variables Emo, ($\beta = .31$, $t = 5.58$, $p < .0001$), MNeg, ($\beta = .21$, $t = 3.73$, $p < .0001$), Guilt, ($\beta = -.19$, $t = -3.49$, $p < .001$), and Age, ($\beta = -.13$, $t = -2.41$, $p < .017$).

For females, the best fit model, Mallow's Prediction Criterion = 5, accounted for 16.8 % of variance as compared with 15.4% for the initial analysis and included five variables SE ($\beta = -.19$, $t = -3.17$, $p < .002$), Mov, ($\beta = -.18$, $t = -3.04$, $p < .003$, Fes, ($\beta = .18$, $t = 3.11$, $p < .002$), and Age, ($\beta = -.13$, $t = -2.30$, $p < .022$).

If the GLM analysis identified variables associated with high end scores on the Cluster B PDs, the regression analyses identified variables current in the rest of the sample that are subclinical expressions of personality that, when extreme, manifest as PD symptoms. Largely, the results of the two kinds of analysis overlapped.

It is generally accepted that emotional dysregulation is associated with Cluster B PDs and the present study clearly confirmed this. In the regression analyses, it predicted scores on all the PDs for males and females, with the exception of ASPD in females. Likewise, in the four GLM analyses it had significant effects in all PDs. Further, its negative correlations with maternal overprotection, and paternal reasoning, and its positive correlations with paternal negative discipline, and family conflict suggest that these factors combined readily elicit emotional disturbance. Livesley et al., (1998) described emotional dysregulation as a mixture of reactive tendencies, dissatisfaction with the self, life experiences, and interpersonal problems. The present findings are consistent this description, and further link it with parental discipline variables. That differing variables were associated with emotional dysregulation suggests variations in dysregulation. In the BPD analysis it accounted for 24% of variance, but only 2% in ASPD. Perhaps this difference points to some process, such as suppression in ASPD not present in BPD.

For the histrionic group, those meeting the categorical criterion had higher paternal and maternal overprotection, emotional dysregulation and shame scores. In the regression analysis emotional dysregulation, self esteem and maternal reasoning as a discipline style, were positive predictors. Previous studies have shown that low maternal care and high overprotection are associated with psychopathology, especially in clinical samples (Gerlsma, Emmelkamp, & Arrindell, 1990; Parker, 1983) such as neuroticism and harm avoidance (Reti, et al., 2002). Little is known of the relationship of parenting variables to HPD, but the present findings suggest parenting characterized by parental overprotection and the maternal use of explanations as a disciplinary strategy are important. In context of emotional dysregulation, this may lead to high but not well founded self esteem with a proneness to experience shame, and exaggerated emotional expression.

For the narcissistic group, although emotional dysregulation appeared positively related to NPD in both, the dimensional and categorical findings differed. In the regression analyses, for males, it was associated with negative maternal discipline, while in females it was associated with a lower level of guilt-proneness. In the GLM analysis, it was associated with emotional dysregulation, negative maternal discipline and lower guilt-proneness. The finding of lower guilt is consistent with that found in Gramzow & Tangney's (1992) study of narcissism. If empathy comes with feelings of guilt, these findings suggest that a punitive maternal style of parenting leads to less empathic feelings towards mother, a perception of her as negative and greater emotional disturbance as part of the basis for a narcissistic style.

In the regression analyses for BPD, emotional dysregulation, self and negative maternal discipline were significant positive predictors, and self esteem a negative predictor for both genders. In the GLM analysis, BPD was associated with lower maternal care and higher overprotection, a finding often found in previous studies (Parker et al., 1979; Parker, 1983; Gerlsma, Kramer, Scholing, & Emmelkemp, 1990; Parker, Hadzi-Pavlovic, Greenwald, & Weissman, 1995). It was also associated with lower scores for paternal reasoning, higher negative maternal discipline and family conflict. This configuration of factors was further associated with shame-proneness, low self esteem and emotional dysregulation. The overall pattern is characteristic of BPD as has been frequently described, with features of suboptimal, negative parenting, inadequate caregiving, emotional instability and intensity (Cole, Llera & Pemberton, 2009). These authors stressed the importance of the proximal emotional environment for the development healthy emotional processing. They pointed out that child directed anger and a problematic family environment may lead to poor emotional awareness and a tendency not to expect emotional support. In the present study, the discipline variables, along with a negative maternal style, low use of paternal explanations, and family conflict would provide an environment in which emotional processing is likely to be distorted. As Cole et al. observed the experience of shame would be expected in such an environment.

Only four females met the criterion for antisocial personality, ruling out any categorical analysis using gender as a variable. In the GLM analysis for the whole sample, those meeting the criteria on the PDQ-4 reported higher levels of both paternal and maternal overprotection, family conflict and emotional dysregulation, and lower levels of paternal reasoning and self esteem. In the regression analyses, males reported higher levels of negative maternal disciplining, emotional dysregulation and lower guilt-proneness. Females reported higher levels of family conflict and maternal overprotection and lower levels self esteem.

Gender played a significant role in the study. In NPD, ASPD, maternal overprotection and paternal care, males scored significantly higher than females. Conversely, females scored higher on negative paternal discipline, shame, guilt and emotional dysregulation. The findings for NPD and ASPD fit with those described by Looper and Paris (2000), in that both PDs are more commonly diagnosed in men than in women. The differences in maternal overprotection and paternal care contradict Kay et al.'s (2007) findings that recollections of one's parental environment are not substantially affected by gender. With regard to shame, Efthim et al. (2001) found that women were prone to shame due to gender role stress, especially around relationship issues. These authors also referred to the body of literature linking the feminine gender role to guilt and empathy. In the present study, guilt and shame were associated with a negative family environment in which gender roles would be inevitably involved (Cole et al., 2009). As Efthim et al. commented the relationship between gender role stress and guilt and shame is complex and in need of further investigation for both males and females.

The primary aim of this study was to use the PDQ-4 as a measure of symptoms rather than diagnostically. The prevalency rates of Cluster B PDs in this study should be taken in the light of the earlier PDQ/R's having high sensitivity and somewhat lower specificity in diagnostic situations (Wilberg, Dammen, & Friis, 2000). When compared with the rates, reported for college students using the Peer Inventory for Personality Disorders, the prevalencey rates in the present study are roughly comparable, except for Borderline PD. The percentages in the present study were approximately 18% for both genders in the present study compared with previous findings of 3.7% for males and 1.85 for females (Klonsky, Serrita, Turkheimer, & Oltmanns, 2002). These authors remarked that self report participants were probably more liberal in their reporting of symptoms. The same may well be so for the present sample. The interest in the present study however was not in the diagnostic value of the PDQ-4, but in its listing Cluster B symptoms that might be associated with personality related variables.

Limitations

The sample was mostly of undergraduates and individuals who responded to a social networking site advertisement. Consequently, the demographic information about the sample was sparse. Given that much more information would have improved the study, the findings have limited generalizability. The sample was also non-clinical, although there was no way of being certain about this, given the method of recruitment. While this allowed for the examination of the contribution of common personality related variables, it did not allow for a strict diagnostic analysis. The use of the PDQ-4 likewise is only of use for screening purposes. Nevertheless, it does permit symptoms associated with PDs to be examined and related to variables such as emotional dysregulation, self esteem and recollections of early parental experiences.

REFERENCES

Amato, P. R. (1994). Father-child relations, mother-child relations, and offspring psychological well-being in early adulthood. *Journal of Marriage and the Family, 56*, 1031-1042.

Amato, P. R., & Keith, B. (1991). Parental divorce and adult well-being: A meta-analysis. *Journal of Marriage & the Family, 53*, 43-58.

American Psychiatric Association. (2000). *Diagnostic and statistical manual of mental disorders* (4th ed.). Washington, DC: Author.

Apt, C., & Hurlbert, D. F. (1994). The sexual attitudes, behavior, and relationships of women with histrionic personality disorder. *Journal of Sex and Marital Therapy, 20*, 125-133.

Bagby, R. M. & Farvolden, P. (3004). *The Personality Diagnostic Questionnaire – 4. (PDQ-4)* In M. J. Hilsenroth & D. L. Segal (Eds), *Comprehensive Handbook of Psychological Assessment: Vol. 2. Personality Assessment, 122-133. New York: Wiley.*

Bagby, R. M., Marshall, M. B., & Georgiades, S. (2005). Dimensional personality traits and the prediction of DSM-IV personality disorder symptom counts in a nonclinical sample. *Journal of Personality Disorders, 19*, 53-67.

Baumrind, D. (1966). Effects of authoritative parental control on child behavior. *Child Development, 37,* 887-907.

Baumrind, D. (1967). Child care practices anteceding three patterns of preschool behaviour. *Genetic Psychology Monographs, 75, 43-88.*

Baumrind, D. (1996). Parenting: The discipline controversy revisited. *Family Relations, 45*, 405-414.

Bender, D. S., Farber, B. A., & Geller, J. D. (2001). Cluster B personality traits and attachment. *Journal of the American Academy of Psychoanalysis, 29*, 551-563.

Bender, D. S., & Skodol, A. E. (2007). Borderline personality as a self-other representational disturbance. *Journal of Personality Disorders, 21*, 500-517.

Campbell, W. K., Goodie, A. S., & Foster, J. D. (2004). Narcissism, confidence, and risk attitude. *Journal of Behavioral Decision Making, 17*, 297-311.

Chapell, M.S., & Overton, W.F. (1998). Development of logical reasoning in the context of parental style and test anxiety. *Merrill-Palmer Quarterly, 44*, 141-156.

Cole' P. M., Llera, S. J. & & Pemberton, C. K. (2009). Emotional instability, poor emotional awareness, and the development of borderline personality, *Development and Psychopathology, 21*, 1293-1310.

Corbitt, E. M., & Widiger, T. A. (1995). Sex differences among the personality disorders: An exploration of the data. *Clinical Psychology: Science and Practice*, , 225-238.

Covert, M. V., Tangney, J. P., Maddux, J. E., & Heleno, N. M. (2003). Shame-proneness, guilt-proneness, and interpersonal problem solving: A social cognitive analysis. *Journal of Social and Clinical Psychology, 22*, 1-12.

Diener, E., Emmons, R. A., Larsen, R. J., & Griffin, S. (1985). The Satisfaction with Life Scale. *Journal of Personality Assessment, 49*, 71-75.

Efthim, P. W. Maureen E. Kenny, M. E., & Mahalik, J. R. (2001). Gender Role Stress in Relation to Shame, Guilt, and Externalization, *Journal of Counseling and Development, 79*, 430-438.

Eisenberg, N. (2000). Emotion, regulation, and moral development. *Annual Review in Psychology, 51*, 665-697.

Feenstra, J. S., Banyard, V. L., Rines, E. N., & Hopkins, K. R. (2001). First-year students' adaptation to college: The role of family variables and individual coping. *Journal of College Student Development, 42*, 106-113.

Ferguson, T. J., & Crowley, S. L. (1997). Measure for measure: A multitrait-multimethod analysis of guilt and shame. *Journal of Personality Assessment, 69*, 425-441.

Frankenburg, F. R., & Zanarini, M. C. (2004). The association between borderline personality disorder and chronic medical illnesses, poor health-related lifestyle choices, and costly forms of health care utilization. *The Journal of clinical psychiatry, 65*, 1660.

Gagné, P. & Dayton, C. M. (2002) Best regression model using information criteria. *Journal of Modern Applied Statistical Methods, 1*, 479-488.

Gerlsma, C., Emmelkamp, P.M.G., & Arrindell, W.A. (1990). Anxiety, depression and perception of early parenting: A meta-analysis. *Clinical Psychology Review, 10*, 251–277.

Gramzow, R., & Tangney, J. P. (1992). Proneness to shame and the narcissistic personality. *Personality and Social Psychology Bulletin, 18*, 369-376.

Grant, B. F., Hasin, D. S., Stinson, F. S., Dawson, D. A., Chou, S. P., Ruan, W. J., et al. (2004). Prevalence, correlates, and disability of personality disorders in the United States: Results from the National Epidemiologic Survey on Alcohol and Related Conditions. *The Journal of Clinical Psychiatry, 65*, 948-958.

Hannum, J. W., & Dvorak, D. M. (2004). Effects of Family Conflict, Divorce, and Attachment Patterns on the Psychological Distress and Social Adjustment of College Freshmen. *Journal of College Student Development, 45*, 27-42.

Hare, R. D., & Neumann, C. N. (2006). The PCL-R Assessment of Psychopathy: Development, Structural Properties, and New Directions. In C. Patrick (Ed.), *Handbook of Psychopathy* (pp. 58-88). New York: Guilford.

Hoffman, M.L. (1970). Moral development. In P.H.Mussen (Ed.). *Carmichael's manual of child psychology* (Vol. 2, pp. 261-359). New York: Wiley.

Hoffman, M.L. (1983). Affective and cognitive processes in moral internalization. In E.T. Higgins, D.N. Ruble, & W.W. Hartup (Eds.). *Social cognition and social development: A sociocultural perspective* (pp. 236-274). Cambridge: Cambridge University Press.

Horton, R. S., Bleau, G., & Drwecki, B. (2006). Parenting Narcissus: What are the links between parenting and narcissism? *Journal of Personality, 74*, 345-376.

Hyler, S. E. (1994). *Personality diagnostic questionnaire 4+ (PDQ-4+)*. New York: New York State Psychiatric Institute.

Jang, K. L., Vernon, P. A., & Livesley, W. J. (2000). Personality disorder traits, family environment, and alcohol misuse: A multivariate behavioural genetic analysis. *Addiction, 95*, 873-888.

Klonsky, E. D., Oltmanns, T. F., Turkheimer, E. N., & Fiedler, E. R. (2000). Recollections of conflict with parents and family support in the personality disorders. *Journal of Personality Disorders, 14*, 327-338.

Klonsky, E. D., Serrita, J., Turkheimer, E. N., & Oltmanns, T. F. (2002). Gender role and personality disorders. *Journal of Personality Disorders, 16,* 464 476.

Kraus, G., & Reynolds, D. J. (2001). The "A-B-C's" of the Cluster B's: Identifying, understanding, and treating Cluster B personality disorders. *Clinical Psychology Review, 21*, 345-373.

Krishnakumar, A., & Buehler, C. (2000). Interparental conflict and parenting behaviors: A meta-analytic review. *Family Relations. 49*, 25-44.

Larstone, R. M., Jang, K. L., Livesley, W. J., Vernon, P. A., & Wolf, H. (2002). The relationship between Eysenck's P–E–N model of personality, the Five-Factor Model of personality, and traits delineating personality disorder. *Personality and Individual Differences, 33*, 25–37.

Leary, M. R., Schreindorfer, L. S., & Haupt, A. L. (1995). The role of low self-esteem in emotional and behavioral problems: Why is low self-esteem dysfunctional? *Journal of Social and Clinical Psychology, 14*, 297-314.

Leith, K. P., & Baumeister, R. F. (1998). Empathy, shame, guilt, and narratives of interpersonal conflicts: Guilt-prone people are better at perspective taking. *Journal of Personality, 66*, 1-37.

Linehan, M. (1993). *Cognitive-behavioral treatment of borderline personality disorder*. New York: The Guilford Press.

Livesley, W. J., Jang, K. L., & Vernon, P. A. (1998). The phenotypic and genetic structure of traits delineating personality disorder. *Archives of General Psychiatry, 55*, 941–948.

Looper, K. J., & Paris, J. (2000). What dimensions underlie Cluster B personality disorders? *Comprehensive Psychiatry, 41*, 432-437.

Lynam, D. R., & Widiger, T. A. (2001). Using the five-factor model to represent the DSM-IV personality disorders: An expert consensus approach. *Journal of abnormal psychology, 110*, 401-412.

Manassis, K., Owens, M., Adam, K. S., West, M., & Sheldon-Keller, A. E. (1999). Assessing attachment: Convergent validity of the adult attachment interview and the parental bonding instrument. *Australian and New Zealand Journal of Psychiatry, 33*, 559-567.

Martens, W. (2005). A multicomponential model of shame. *Journal for the Theory of Social Behaviour, 35*, 399-411.

Miller, J. D., & Pilkonis, P. A. (2006). Neuroticism and affective instability: The same or different? *American Journal of Psychiatry*, 163, 839-845.

Mills, R. S. L. (2005). Taking stock of the developmental literature on shame. *Developmental Review*, 25, 26-63.

Moos, R. H., & Moos, B. S. (1994). *Family Environment Scale Manual: Development, Applications, Research* (3rd ed.). Palo Alto, CA: Consulting Psychologists Press.

Moran, P. (1999). The epidemiology of antisocial personality disorder. *Social Psychiatry and Psychiatric Epidemiology, 34*, 231-242.

Morrison, A. P. (1989). Shame. The underside of narcissism. Hillsdale, NJ: The Analytic Press.

Nelson, W. L., Hughes, H. M., Handal, P., Katz, B., & Searight, H. R. (1993). The relationship of family structure and family conflict to adjustment in young adult college students. *Adolescence, 28*, 29-40.

Newhill, C. E., Eack, S. M., & Conner, K. O. (2009). Racial differences between African and White Americans in the presentation of borderline personality disorder. *Race and Social Problems, 1*, 87-96.

Newhill, C. E., Mulvey, E. P., & Pilkonis, P. A. (2004). Initial development of a measure of emotional dysregulation for individuals with Cluster B personality disorders. *Research on Social Work Practice, 14*, 443-449.

Nickell, A. D., Waudby, C. J., & Trull, T. J. (2002). Attachment, parental bonding and borderline personality disorder features in young adults. *Journal of Personality Disorders, 16*, 148-159.

Norden, K.A., Klein, D.N., Donaldson, S.K., Pepper, C.M., & Klein, L.M. (1995). Reports of the early home environment in DSM-III-R personality disorders. *Journal of Personality Disorders, 9*, 213–223.

Otway, L. J., & Vignoles, V. L. (2006). Narcissism and childhood recollections: A quantitative test of psychoanalytic predictions. *Personality and Social Psychology Bulletin, 32*, 104-116.

Paris, J. (2007). An overview on gender, personality and mental health. Personality and Mental Health, 1, 14-20.

Paris, J., & Frank, H. (1989). Perceptions of parental bonding in borderline patients. *The American Journal of Psychiatry, 146*, 1498-1499.

Parker, G. (1993). Parental rearing style: examining for links with personality vulnerability factors for depression. *Social Psychiatry and Psychiatric Epidemiology, 28*, 97-100.

Parker, G. P. (1983). Parental 'affectionless control' as an antecedent to adult depression: A risk factor delineated. *Archives of General Psychiatry, 40*, 956-960.

Parker, G. P., Tupling, H., & Brown, L. B. (1979). A parental bonding instrument. *British Journal of Medical Psychology, 52*, 1-10.

Parker, G., Hadzi-Pavlovic, D., Greenwald, S., & Weissman, M. (1995). Low parental care as a risk factor to lifetime depression in a community sample. *Journal of Affective Disorders, 33*, 173-180.

Paulhus, D. L., Robins, R. W., Trzesniewski, K. H., & Tracy, J. L. (2004). Two replicable suppressor situations in personality research. *Multivariate Behavioral Research, 39*, 303-328.

Randolph, J. J., & Dykman, B. M. (1998). Perceptions of parenting and depression-proneness in the offspring: Dysfunctional attitudes as a mediating mechanism. *Cognitive Therapy and Research, 22*(4), 377-400.

Raskin, R. N., & Hall, C. S. (1979). A narcissistic personality inventory. *Psychological Reports, 45*, 590.

Reti, I. M., Samuels, J. F., Eaton, W. w., Bienvenu, O. J., Costa, P. T., & Nestadt, G. (2002). Influences of parenting on normal personality traits. *Psychiatry Research, 111*, 55-64.

Richardson, S., & McCabe, M. P. (2001). Parental divorce during adolescence and adjustment in early adulthood. *Adolescence, 36*, 467-489.

Roberts, R. E. L., & Bengtson, V. L. (1993). Relationships with parents, self-esteem, and psychological well-being in young adulthood. *Social Psychology Quarterly, 56*, 263-277.

Rosenberg, M. (1979). *Conceiving the self.* New York: Basic Books.

Rosenberg, M. (1965). *Society and the adolescent self-image.* Princeton, NJ: Princeton University Press.

Rüsch, N., Corrigan, P. W., Bohus, M., Jacob, G. A., Brueck, R., & Lieb, K. (2007a). Measuring shame and guilt by self-report questionnaires: A validation study. *Psychiatry Research, 150*, 313-325.

Rüsch, N., Lieb, K., Gottler, I., Hermann, C., Schramm, E., Richter, H., et al. (2007b). Shame and implicit self-concept in women with borderline personality disorder. *American Journal of Psychiatry, 164*, 500-508.

Samuel, D.B., & Widiger, T.A. (2009). Comparative gender biases in models of personality disorder. *Personality and Mental Health, 3*, 12-25.

Samuels, J., Eaton, W. W., Bienvenu, J. O., Brown, C. H., Coata, P., & Nestadt, G. (2002). Prevalence and correlates of personality disorders in a community sample. *The British Journal of Psychiatry, 180*, 536-542.

Sanford, K., Zucker, R. A., & Bingham, C. R. (1999). Validity issues with the Family Environment Scale: Psychometric resolution and research application with alcoholic families. *Psychological assessment, 11*, 315-325.

Sarkar, J., & Adshead, G. (2006). Personality disorders as disorganisation of attachment and affect regulation. *Advances in Psychiatric Treatment, 12*, 297-305.

Saucier, G., Wilson, K. R., & Warka, J. (2007). The structure of retrospective accounts of family environments: Related to the structure of personality attributes. *Journal of Personality Assessment, 88*, 295-308.

Simons, R. L., Robertson, J. F., & Downs, W. R. (1989). The nature of the association between parental rejection and delinquent behavior. *Journal of Youth and Adolescence, 18*, 297-310.

Simonsen, E., Ronningstam, E., & Millon, T. (2008). A synopsis of the WPA educational program on personality disorders. *World Psychiatry*, *7*, 119–125.

Soeteman, D. I., Roijen, L. H., Verheul, R., & Busschbach, J. J. V. (2008). The economic burden of personality disorders in mental health care. *Journal of Clinical Psychiatry*, *69*, 259-265.

Sedikides, C., Rudich, E. A., Gregg, A. P., Kumashiro, M., & Rusbult, C. (2004). Are normal narcissists psychologically healthy?: Self-esteem matters. *Journal of Personality and Social Psychology, 87*, 400-416.

Steinberg, L., Elmen, J. D., & Mounts, N. S. (1989). Authoritative parenting, psychosocial maturity, and academic success among adolescents. *Child Development*, 1424-1436.

Stuewig, J. & McCloskey, L. A.(2005). The Relation of Child Maltreatment to Shame and Guilt Among Adolescents: Psychological Routes to Depression and Delinquency *Child Maltreat. 10*: 324-336.

Tangney, J. P. (1996). Conceptual and methodological issues in the assessment of shame and guilt. *Behaviour Research and Therapy, 34*, 741-754.

Tangney, J. P., Dearing, R. L. (2002). *Shame and Guilt*. New York: The Guildford Press.

Tangney, J. P., Dearing, R. L., Wagner, P. E., & Gramzow, R. (2000). *The Test of Self-Conscious Affect–3 (TOSCA-3)*. Fairfax, VA: George Mason University.

Tangney, J. P., Wagner, P., & Gramzow, R. (1992). Proneness to shame, proneness to guilt, and psychopathology. *Journal of Abnormal Psychology, 101*, 469-478.

Timmerman, I. G. H., & Emmelkamp, P. M. G. (2005). Parental rearing styles and personality disorders in prisoners and forensic patients. *Clinical Psychology and Psychotherapy, 12*, 191–200.

Tracy, J. L., Cheng, J. T., Robins, R. W., & Trzesniewski, K. H. (2009). Authentic and hubristic pride: The affective core of self-esteem and narcissism. *Self and Identity, 8*, 196-213.

Tracy, J. L., & Robins, R. W. (2007). Self-conscious emotions: Where self and emotion meet. In C. Sedikides & S. Spence (Eds.), *Frontiers of social psychology: The self* (pp. 187–209). New York: Psychology Press.

Weaver, T. L., & Clum, G. A. (1993). Early family environments and traumatic experiences associated with borderline personality disorder. *Journal of Consulting and Clinical Psychology*, *61*, 1068-1074.

Weston, C. G., & Riolo, S. (2007). Childhood and adolescent precursors to adult personality disorders. *Psychiatric Annals*, *37*, 114-120.

Wilberg, T., Dammen, T., & Friis, S. (2000). Comparing Personality Diagnostic questionnaire-4+ with Longitudinal, Expert, All Data (LEAD) standard diagnoses in a sample with a high prevalence of axis I and axis II disorders. *Comprehensive Psychiatry, 41*, 295-302.

Wilhelm, K., Niven, H., Parker, G., & Hadzi-Pavlovic, D. (2005). The stability of the Parental Bonding Instrument over a 20-year period. *Psychological Medicine, 35*, 387-393.

Yu, R., Wang; Z., Qian, F., Jang, K., et al. (2007). Perceived parenting styles and disordered personality traits in adolescent and adult students and in personality disorder patients. *Social Behavior and Personality;*, 35, 587-598.

Zahn-Waxler, C, Cole, P. M., & Barrett, K. C (1991). Guilt and empathy: Sex differences and implications for the development of depression. In J.Garber & K. A. Dodge (Eds.), The

development of emotion regulation and dysregulation (pp. 243-272). Cambridge, MA: Cambridge University Press.

Zanarini, M.C., Williams, A.A., Lewis, R.E., Reich, R.B., Vera, S.C., Marino, M.F. et al. (1997). Reported pathological childhood experiences associated with the development of borderline personality disorder. *American Journal of Psychiatry*, *154*, 1101-1106.

Zeigler-Hill, V. (2006). Discrepancies between implicit and explicit self-esteem: Implications for narcissism and self-esteem instability, *Journal of Personality 74*, 119-143.

Zweig-Frank, H., & Paris, J. (1991). Parents' emotional neglect and overprotection according to the recollections of patients with borderline personality disorder. *American Journal of Psychiatry*, *148*, 648 – 651.

Zimmerman, M., & Mattia, J. I. (1999). Axis I diagnostic comorbidity and borderline personality disorder. *Comprehensive Psychiatry*, *40*, 245-252.

In: Advances in Psychology Research. Volume 88
Editor: Alexandra M. Columbus, pp. 117-139
ISBN: 978-1-62100-591-9

Chapter 6

MANIA: NEW RESEARCH

Gianluca Serafini*[*1], *Maurizio Pompili*[1,2], *Gloria Giordano*[1], *Marco Innamorati*[1] and *Paolo Girardi*[1]

[1] Department of Neurosciences, Mental Health and Sensory Organs; Suicide Prevention Center, Sant'Andrea Hospital, "Sapienza" University of Rome, Italy.

[2] McLean Hospital, Harvard Medical School, U.S.A.

ABSTRACT

Mania has long been considered as an abnormal behaviour indicative of mental illness. Manic states are generally characterized by abnormal elevated mood (euphoria) also including hyperactivity, hypersexuality, irritability, reduced need for sleep and cognitive deficits associated with negative functional outcome. According to the Diagnostic and Statistical Manual of Mental Disorders, Fourth Edition, Text Revision (DSM-IV-TR), a subject experiencing a state of elevated or irritable mood, as well as other invalidating symptoms for at least one week may be diagnosed as affected by bipolar disorder. However, manic symptoms and hypomanic symptoms challenge conventional diagnostic nomenclature and are often not adequately recognized in clinical practice. Individuals are commonly misdiagnosed due to the frequent coexisting psychiatric conditions such as frequent substance abuse.

Recently, the fifth edition of the DSM proposes modifications of the actual diagnostic system. Overall, despite recent advances, efficacy and tolerability of current treatments are limited and additional interventions strategies are needed in order to develop new treatment strategies. Combining psychological, psychosocial and psychopharmacological approaches will presumably offer new operative models to better manage patients with different bipolar subtypes. [**key words:** mania, bipolar disorder, diagnostic nomenclature, treatment, intervention]

---

* Corresponding author: Gianluca Serafini, Department of neurosciences, Mental Health and Sensory Organs, Sant'Andrea Hospital, Faculty of Medicine and Psychology, Suicide Prevention Center, "Sapienza" University of Rome, 1035 Via di Grottarossa, 00189 Roma Italy Tel.: +390633775675. Fax: +390633775342; e.mail: gianluca.serafini@uniroma1.it

INTRODUCTION

The term ''mania'' was first used in ancient Greece (Koukopoulos and Ghaemi, 2009) and it's actually used to identify a mood disorder characterized by the occurrence of euphoric or irritable mood with hyperactivity, decreased need for sleep, and other invalidating symptoms occurring episodically and including restlessness, inflated self confidence, a marked decrease in the need for sleep, rapid and loud speech that is difficult to interrupt, racing thoughts and high distractibility. An episode of mania had to last at least one week determining significant psychosocial and functional impairment. Over time, manic episodes are usually preceded or followed by depressive episodes and mania is often recognized as part of bipolar or manic-depressive disorder (Cousins et al, 2009).

Currently, DSM-IV-TR do not include mania or manic disorder as a separate diagnostic disorder although, over decades, several researchers have questioned whether mania may be experienced without the presence of depressive episodes distinguishing as a distinct illness from bipolar disorder (BD). Recent evidence indicated that the concept of mania as a distinct disorder merits further investigation (Koukopoulos and Ghaemi, 2009; Mahli et al, 2010) and DSM-V which should be published on May 2013 has proposed new criteria to describe the spectrum of mania (for more details, see below).

BD is a common and invalidating psychiatric disorder widely recognized as one of the leading cause of ill health among all psychiatric conditions (Dean et al, 2004; Kleinman et al, 2003; Kupfer, 2005, Simon et al, 1999; Begley et al, 2001; Peele et al, 2003). It has been reported that approximately 25-60% of individuals with BD will attempt suicide at least once in their lives and between 4% and 19% will complete suicide (Goodwin et al, 1990). Additionally, severe cognitive impairments and impaired functional status were found in bipolar patients (Harvey et al, 2010). Cognitive deficits were reported both in patients with bipolar disorder, type I (BD-I) (generally more severe than in other illness subtypes) and in bipolar disorder, type II (BD-II) but also during euthymia (Torrent et al, 2006; Simonsen et al, 2008). Although relevant advances in the neurobiology and treatment of BD, the pathophysiology of this complex condition remains relatively unknown. Recent research has suggested that alterations in different brain regions and neural connectivity may play a critical role in BD and neuroimaging techniques, no doubt, are currently revealed new research directions in mania and BD. Additionally, new treatment strategies will presumably highlight molecular aspects underlying the illness with relevant implications in clinical practice.

With these considerations in mind, we aimed to provide an updated review chapter about mania and new research in BD critically discussing the significance of new neuroimaging and treatment findings such as the role of anterior cingulate cortex abnormalities.

METHODS

In order to provide a new and timely review chapter about mania and BD, we performed a careful MedLine, Excerpta Medica, PsycLit, PsycInfo and Index Medicus search to identify all papers and book chapters in English for the period between 1980 to 2011. The following search terms were used: "Mania" OR "Manic episode" OR "Manic symptoms" AND "Hypomania" OR "Hypomanic symptoms" AND "Bipolar Disorder I" OR "Bipolar Disorder

II" OR "Manic-depressive illness" AND "New research" OR "Current investigations" AND "Neurobiological aspects" AND "Neuroimaging studies". Textbooks on psychiatry were also consulted. We included only those articles that added an original contribution to the literature. Approximately 60 contributions met our inclusion criteria and were considered for the inclusion in the present review. We excluded studies that reported data related to mania or BD but were not clear about follow-up times, methodology, statistical analysis, diagnostic criteria and sample of patients recruited.

Historical Overview

Over centuries, mania has been considered as one of the most relevant and common mental illness (Berrios et al, 1995; Berrios et al, 2004). According to Pinel (1801), mania is the most common type of mental illness. Heinroth (1818) expressed mania as "the fundamental affection of the psyche". Griesinger (1861) focused on mood elevation as cause of depressive states. Kraepelin (1913) reported the importance of mixed states and affective temperaments in the diagnosis of mania: he proposed broad diagnostic criteria for mania suggesting that mixed states are fundamental conditions of excitement and the analysis of affective temperaments is crucial to understand the pathogenesis of mania and mood elevation states. After Kraepelin, clinical interest moved from mania to other psychiatric diseases such as schizophrenia and psychotic disorders (Shorter, 1997) while unipolar major depressive disorder was included in DSM-III (Angst, 1966; Perris, 1966; Shorter, 1997) gradually assuming major clinical significance. Recently, several authors proposed a clinical reconsideration of mood disorders and broader criteria to diagnose bipolar spectrum disorders (Akiskal, 1983; Winokur et al, 1993; Schatzberg, 1998; Cassano et al, 2004; Goodwin et al, 2007).

DSM-IV-TR Current Nosography, Section Mood Disorders

According to DSM-IV-TR, mood disorders were divided into two categories: the unipolar and the bipolar disorders. The first group included: a) Major Depression Disorder (MDD) that consists of one or more episodes of major depression with or without full recovery between episodes; b) Dysthymic disorder characterized by low grade, more constant (less episodic) depressed mood associated with several symptoms occurring for at least 2 years during which a major depressive episode has not occurred; c) Depression Not Otherwise Specified that includes all those subjects with symptoms and signs of depression that do not meet the criteria for either MDD or dysthymia.

The second group includes: a) BD-I requiring at least one manic episode together with major depressive episodes; b) BD-II characterized by hypomania associated with depressive episodes; c) Cyclothymic Disorder in which frequent recurrent episodes of mild depression and hypomania were reported.

Criteria for a manic episode included: a period of abnormal, persistent elevated, expansive or irritable mood with at least three of the following symptoms in the same period: 1) hypertrophic self-esteem or grandiosity; 2) marked decrease in need for sleep; 3) increased

talk that is difficult to interrupt; 4) flight of ideas; 5) marked distractibility; 6) increased psychomotor agitation; 7) excessive involvement in pleasurable activities without regard for negative consequences (i.e., unrestrained buying, sexual indiscretions, foolish business adventures). These symptoms are enough severe to impair daily functioning or require hospitalization and are not caused by schizophrenia, schizoaffective disorder, substance abuse or other Axis I disorders.

Table 1. DSM-V diagnostic categories including in the section Bipolar and related Disorders

Bipolar I Disorder	Subtypes: Current or Most Recent Episode Hypomanic A. Currently (or most recently) in a Hypomanic Episode (see Criteria for Hypomanic Episode). B. There has previously been at least one Manic Episode (see Criteria for Manic Episode). C. The mood symptoms cause clinically significant distress or impairment in social, occupational, or other important areas of functioning. D. The mood episodes in Criteria A and B are not better accounted for by Schizoaffective Disorder and are not superimposed on Schizophrenia, Schizophreniform Disorder, Delusional Disorder, or Psychotic Disorder Not Otherwise Specified. Specify if: 1. With Psychotic Features 2. With Mixed Features 3. With Catatonic Features 4. With Rapid Cycling 5. With Anxiety, mild to severe 6. With Suicide Risk Severity 7. With Seasonal Pattern 8. With Postpartum Onset
	Current or Most Recent Episode Manic A. Currently (or most recently) in a Manic Episode (see Criteria for Manic Episode). B. There has previously been at least one Manic Episode(see Criteria for Manic Episode). C. The mood episodes in Criteria A and B are not better accounted for by Schizoaffective Disorder and are not superimposed on Schizophrenia, Schizophreniform Disorder, Delusional Disorder, or Psychotic Disorder Not Otherwise Specified. Specify if: 1. With Psychotic Features 2. With Mixed Features 3. With Catatonic Features 4. With Rapid Cycling 5. With Anxiety, mild to severe 6. With Suicide Risk Severity 7. With Seasonal Pattern 8. With Postpartum Onset

<table>
<tr><td></td><td>Current or Most Recent Episode Depressed

A. Currently (or most recently) in a Major Depressive Episode or there are at least 3 symptoms of Major Depression (see Criteria for Major Depressive Episode) of which one of the symptoms is depressed mood or anhedonia.
B. There has previously been at least one Manic Episode (see Criteria for Manic Episode).
C. The mood episodes in Criteria A and B are not better accounted for by Schizoaffective Disorder and are not superimposed on Schizophrenia, Schizophreniform Disorder, Delusional Disorder, or Psychotic Disorder Not Otherwise Specified.

Specify if:

1. With Psychotic Features
2. With Mixed Features
3. With Catatonic Features
4. With Rapid Cycling
5. With Anxiety, mild to severe
6. With Suicide Risk Severity
7. With Seasonal Pattern
8. With Melancholic Features
9. With Atypical Features
10. With Postpartum Onset</td></tr>
<tr><td></td><td>Current or Most Recept Episode Unspecified

A. Criteria, except for duration, are currently (or most recently) met for a Manic (see Criteria for Manic Episode), a Hypomanic (see Criteria for Hypomanic Episode), or a Major Depressive Episode (see Criteria for Major Depressive Episode).
B. There has previously been at least one Manic Episode (see Criteria for Manic Episode).
C. The mood symptoms cause clinically significant distress or impairment in social, occupational, or other important areas of functioning.
D. The mood symptoms in Criteria A and B are not better accounted for by Schizoaffective Disorder and are not superimposed on Schizophrenia, Schizophreniform Disorder, Delusional Disorder, or Psychotic Disorder Not Otherwise Specified.

The mood symptoms in Criteria A and B are not due to the direct physiological effects of a substance (e.g., a drug of abuse, a medication, or other treatment) or a general medical condition (e.g., hyperthyroidism).</td></tr>
<tr><td>Bipolar II</td><td>Subtypes:
Current or Most Recent Episode Hypomanic

A. Presence (or history) of one or more Major Depressive Episodes (see Criteria for Major Depressive Episode).
B. Presence (or history) of at least one Hypomanic Episode (see Criteria for Hypomanic Episode).
C. There has never been a Manic Episode (see Criteria for Manic Episode).
D. The mood symptoms in Criteria A and B are not better accounted for by Schizoaffective Disorder and are not superimposed on Schizophrenia, Schizophreniform Disorder, Delusional Disorder, or Psychotic Disorder Not Otherwise Specified.
E. The symptoms cause clinically significant distress or impairment in social, occupational, or other important areas of functioning.</td></tr>
</table>

(Continued).

	Specify if: 1. With Mixed Features 2. With Rapid Cycling 3. With Anxiety, mild to severe 4. With Suicide Risk Severity 5. With Seasonal Pattern 6. With Postpartum Onset
	Current or Most Recent Episode Depressed A. Presence (or history) of one or more Major Depressive Episodes (see Criteria for Major Depressive Episode). B. Presence (or history) of at least one Hypomanic Episode (see Criteria for Hypomanic Episode). C. There has never been a Manic Episode (see Criteria for Manic Episode). D. The mood symptoms in Criteria A and B are not better accounted for by Schizoaffective Disorder and are not superimposed on Schizophrenia, Schizophreniform Disorder, Delusional Disorder, or Psychotic Disorder Not Otherwise Specified. E. The symptoms cause clinically significant distress or impairment in social, occupational, or other important areas of functioning. Specify if: 1. With Psychotic Features 2. With Mixed Features 3. With Catatonic Features 4. With Rapid Cycling 5. With Anxiety, mild to severe 6. With Suicide Risk Severity 7. With Seasonal Pattern 8. With Melancholic Features 9. With Atypical Features 10. With Postpartum Onset
Cyclothymic Disorder	A. For at least 2 years, the presence of numerous periods with hypomanic symptoms (see Criteria for Hypomanic Episode) and numerous periods with depressive symptoms that do not meet criteria for a Major Depressive Episode. Note: In children and adolescents, the duration must be at least 1 year. B. During the above 2-year period (1 year in children and adolescents), the person has not been without the symptoms in Criterion A for more than 2 months at a time. C. No Major Depressive Episode (Criteria for Major Depressive Episode), or Manic Episode (Criteria for Manic Episode) has been present during the first 2 years of the disturbance. Note: After the initial 2 years (1 year in children and adolescents) of Cyclothymic Disorder, there may be superimposed Manic Episodes (in which case both Bipolar I Disorder and Cyclothymic Disorder may be diagnosed) or Major Depressive Episodes (in which case both Bipolar II Disorder and Cyclothymic Disorder may be diagnosed). D. The symptoms in Criterion A are not better accounted for by Schizoaffective Disorder and are not superimposed on Schizophrenia, Schizophreniform Disorder, Delusional Disorder, or Psychotic Disorder Not Otherwise Specified. E. Symptoms are not due to the direct physiological effects of a substance (e.g., a drug of abuse, a medication, or other treatment).

	F. The symptoms cause clinically significant distress or impairment in social, occupational, or other important areas of functioning. Specify if: 1. With Mixed features 2. With Rapid Cycling 3. With Anxiety, mild to severe 4. With Suicide Risk Severity 5. With Seasonal Pattern 6. With Postpartum Onset
Substance-Induced Bipolar Disorder	A. A disturbance that meets full criteria for a relevant bipolar disorder B. There is evidence from the history, physical examination, or laboratory findings of (1) and (2): [1] The criteria for the bipolar disorder developed during or within a month after severe intoxication or withdrawal. [2] The involved substance is capable of producing mania. C. The bipolar disorder is not better accounted for by a disorder that is not substance-induced. Such evidence of an independent mood disorder includes the following: [1] The bipolar disorder preceded the onset of severe intoxication or withdrawal; Or [2] The full bipolar disorder persisted for a substantial period of time (e.g., about a month or more) after the cessation of severe intoxication or withdrawal. D. The bipolar disorder does not occur exclusively during the course of a delirium. E. The bipolar disorder causes clinically significant distress or impairment in social, occupational, or other important areas of functioning. Note: This diagnosis should be made instead of a diagnosis of Substance Intoxication or Substance Withdrawal only when the symptoms fulfill full criteria for a DSM-5 disorder and when the disorder is sufficiently severe to warrant clinical attention. Code: [Specific Substance]-Induced Bipolar Disorder: Alcohol; Amphetamines; Cocaine; Hallucinogen; Opioid; Phencyclidine-like substance; Sedative, Hypnotic, or Anxiolytic; Other (or Unknown) Substance. Specify: 1. With Onset During Intoxication 2. With Onset During Withdrawal
Bipolar Disorder Associated with a Known General Medical Condition	The work group has not yet proposed criteria for this disorder. Please continue to check this Web site for updates, as the criteria will be forthcoming.
Bipolar Conditions Not Elsewhere Classified	This group of diagnoses is reserved for individuals that have symptoms that do not meet diagnostic criteria for any other mood disorder, that are associated with moderate or severe psychosocial dysfunction or distress (i.e., coded 3 or 4 on the dysfunction scale), and that are not due to the direct physiological effects of a substance or a general medical condition. The condition must be categorized into one of the four sub-categorical diagnosis listed below based on the characteristics of the episode.

(Continued).

	In the Bipolar Disorder Not Elsewhere Classified category, characteristic symptoms of hypomania/mania or depression are present during separate time periods and cause distress or dysfunction but are not of sufficient duration and/or intensity to meet criteria for a specific bipolar diagnosis. Note: mood symptoms that occur concurrently should be captured by the with Mixed Features episode specifier. If the individual meets criteria for one of the following subcategories the corresponding code should be employed.
05 00 Subsyndromal Hypomania - Short Duration	Those who report the lifetime experience of syndromal depressive episodes (sufficient number of criterion symptoms and sufficient duration) and hypomanic episodes consisting of a sufficient number of criterion symptoms but of insufficient duration (≥2 and < 4 consecutive days).
05 01 Subsyndromal Hypomania - Insufficient Symptoms	Those who report the lifetime experience of syndromal depressive episodes (sufficient number of criterion symptoms and sufficient duration) and hypomanic episodes consisting of sufficient duration but an insufficient number of criterion symptoms (≥2 (3 if mood is only irritable).
05 02 Other Bipolar CNEC	This includes atypical presentations of bipolar symptoms not considered above that cause significant distress or psychosocial dysfunction.
05 03 Bipolar CNEC with insufficient information to make a specific diagnosis	This diagnosis is used for patients with bipolar symptoms that have resulted in distress or psychosocial dysfunction when there is not sufficient information available to make a specific diagnosis. It includes, but is not limited to, the following situations: 1. Uncertainty about primary versus secondary nature of Bipolar Disorder. Meets symptomatic and duration criteria of Bipolar Disorder but the clinician is unable to determine whether it is primary or due to a general medical condition (GMC) or substance induced. 2. Patient is unable or unwilling to provide information about symptoms and/or history. Bipolar symptoms are observed and associated with distress or dysfunction but detailed information needed for a specific diagnosis cannot be obtained due to communication difficulties, mental retardation, uncooperativeness, or similar reasons. 3. Clinician does not have the time or training needed to conduct a detailed examination. Specify if: 1. With Mixed Features 2. With Anxiety, mild to severe 3. With Suicide Risk Severity 4. With Seasonal Pattern 5. With Postpartum Onset
Unspecified Bipolar Disorder	The work group has not yet proposed criteria for this disorder. Please continue to check this Web site for updates, as the criteria will be forthcoming.

Source: http://www.dsm5.org/ProposedRevision/Pages/BipolarandRelatedDisorders.aspx, accessed on June 9, 2011

It has been suggested to delete mixed episodes in favor of a "mixed features" specifier, which would apply to manic, hypomanic, and depressive episodes. However, there have been other several proposals to include further and more accurate subtypes of BD (Akiskal and Ghaemi, 2006). A modification of the symptom set for mixed mania diagnosis/specifier has been recommended, including a long-overdue deletion of nonspecific symptoms. Five of the planned six symptoms for the criteria set (depressed mood, suicidality, guilt, anhedonia, and fatigue) have faced validity and internal consistency (Cassidy et al, 1997; Cassidy et al, 2000). However, the current diagnostic scheme for mania proposed by DSM-V is likely to

endure further revisions and additional refinements (Cassidy, 2010). The substitution of anxiety to psychomotor retardation and the adoption of a diagnostic threshold of two or more symptoms would be a better starting point for diagnostic change set out by DSM-V nomenclature (Kendler et al, 2009). These present and future revisions as well as the new proposed criteria are based on a decade of research on severe mood dysregulation and may help clinicians to better understand patients symptoms in clinical practice.

DSM-V: The Future of Psychiatric Disorders, Section Bipolar and Related Disorders

The elaboration of the fifth edition of Diagnostic and Statistical Manual of Mental Disorders (DSM-5) by several task force members designated by the American Psychiatric Association (APA) represents one of the most anticipated events in the mental health field. Revisions are also expected in the manual section of Mood Disorders. The most relevant diagnostic categories proposed by the DSM-V section of bipolar and related disorders are: bipolar I disorder (c 00); bipolar II disorder (c 01); cyclothymic disorder (c 02); substance-induced bipolar disorder (c 03); bipolar disorder associated with a known general medical condition (c 04); other specified bipolar disorder; c 06 unspecified bipolar disorder (c 05) (see Table 1).

Criticism of DSM-V

One of the most relevant criticism of DSM-V is relative to the validity and reliability of the proposed diagnostic categories. The debate, first raised by the Rosenhan experiment (1970), is predominantly about the existence in the real world of the different mental disorders and their subtypes defined by DSM criteria.

Although DSM-V promoters stated that the diagnostic categories have a good inter-rater reliability through the Structured Clinical Interview for DSM-IV (SCID) and that they are linked to specific patterns of mental, behavioural or neurological dysfunctions, their validity continued to remain unclear also considering the general lack of diagnostic laboratory or neuroimaging tests as well as reliable biomarkers.

Another limitation was about the lack of an agreed scientific model underlying mental disorders that negatively affects DSM-V reliability as demonstrated by the fact that different diagnoses share many DSM criteria and often originate by the same theoretical assumptions. Sometimes clinicians decide to allocate a specific diagnosis instead of another to a patient as a result of individual prejudices or according to personal background.

Also, in order to develop credibility, transparency in conducting the whole process of elaboration of DSM-V diagnoses has been requested to task force members by some authors such as Robert Spitzer, the head of the DSM-III. Focusing on the same controversial credibility, other authors like Allen Frances, the head of the DSM-IV task force, have suggested that the work on DSM-V could display a dangerous combination between increasing ambition and weak methodology and expressed worries about the future clinical consequences related to the current debate.

DSM was primarily based on the statistical and clinical collection of different signs and symptoms of mental disorders rather than on underlying neurobiological causes. This lack of a adequate explanatory model generally reflects our difficulty to understand the pathophysiological mechanisms underlying the most common psychiatric conditions.

Therefore, symptom patterns makes actually sense to the DSM structure that remained negatively affected by the main limitation of its current design and by the lack of a specific etiological model.

The Contribution of Neuroimaging Techniques: Focus on the Role of Cingulate Cortex

After thirty years of neuroimaging studies, it has been widely demonstrated that BD is associated with morphological brain alterations. Computed tomography (CT) and magnetic resonance imaging (MRI) studies have found that bipolar subjects have enlarged third and lateral ventricles (McDonald et al, 2004; Kempton et al, 2008), smaller volume of corpus callosum (Kempton et al, 2008), and increased rates of white matter hyperintensities (WMHs) revealed by T2-weighted MRI (Kempton et al, 2008; Altshuler et al, 1995; Videbech, 1997) compared with healthy controls. Nevertheless, despite the strength of such results, the etiology of these structural neurobiological changes reported in BD remains still poorly understood (Vita et al, 2009).

MRI studies on subjects having a first bipolar episode have showed a pattern of brain alterations which was similar to the most replicated findings in samples of chronic patients: enlargement of the ventricular system (Strakowsky et al, 1993), smaller area of the corpus callosum (Atmaca et al, 2007), and the presence of WMHs (Zanetti et al, 2008). However, other MRI studies have described important different cortical and subcortical brain abnormalities at illness onset that are not found in chronic subjects, such as decreased volumes of frontal lobe and temporal gyrus gray matter (GM) (Farrow et al, 2005), reduction in neocortical (Nakamura et al, 2007) and cingulated gyrus (Farrow et al, 2005; Yatham et al, 2007) GM volume, smaller amygdala volume (Rosso et al, 2007) and larger volume than normal striatum (Strakowski et al, 2002). Unfortunately, definitive conclusions about the time of onset and course of brain abnormalities in BD cannot be extrapolated due to the limited existing literature. Studies on first-episode BD demonstrate changes in brain total volume in the first years of illness with a progression over time and a reduction in the GM volume of the cingulate cortex (Farrow et al, 2005; Koo et al, 2008). Other authors found an increase in volume of neocortical GM (Nakamura et al, 2007), ventriculomegaly (Strakowski et al, 2002) and cerebellar vermis atrophy (DelBello et al, 1999) in multiple-episode BD subjects.

During the last years, researchers have tried to define the neurobiological substrates of deficient emotional regulation in BD. Studies (Swanda et al, 2000) have demonstrated the role of the anterior cingulate cortex (ACC) (including ventral system, amygdala, insula, ventral striatum, and prefrontal cortex) in the recognition of the emotional significance of stimuli, in the production of affective states, and automatic regulation of emotional responses. A simplified neurobiological model suggest that 'mood' presumably originates from processes largely taking part in the amygdala and the insula, while 'emotion' is mainly created in the ACC, specifically in area 25 (Anderson and Phelps, 2002). The regulation of

patterns. When treated with lithium, subjects displayed an increased activation of Brodmann area 24 compared to subjects treated with valproate showing decreased metabolic rates in this area (Kruger et al, 2006).

However, these studies have a limited generalizability because the samples included may not be representative of patients commonly treated in clinical settings (Tohen and Vieta, 2008). Finally, despite the available number of pharmacological options, bipolar mania still remains difficult to treat (Tohen, 1997; Van Riel et al, 2008), especially at first manic episode (Tohen et al, 2003).

Psychological and Psychosocial Treatments

Before the pharmacological era, psychotherapy had been proposed as the primary treatment for bipolar illness (Cohen et al, 1954). After the rise of genetic and neurobiological models about BD (Smoller et al, 2003; Menji et al, 2003), the introduction of lithium and other mood stabilizing medications took place (Miklowitz et al, 2009).

Studies demonstrated that adaptations of cognitive-behavioural therapy (CBT), family-focused therapy (FFT), group psychoeducation, interpersonal and social rhythm therapy (IPSRT) and systematic care management programs may be effective in hastening stabilization, delaying relapses, reducing symptom severity over time, and enhancing psychosocial and family functioning (Miklowitz, 2008; Scott, 2006). A lot of psychosocial treatments are described as cost-effective even because they are cheap to administer. Other treatments have been shown to reduce costs associated with multiple hospitalizations (Rea et al, 2003; Bauer et al, 2003; Scott et al, 2009).

Lam et al. (2009) demonstrated that a particular psychotherapy specific for BD is effective in preventing or delaying relapses. Miklowitz et al. (2007) showed that, adding a disorder-specific psychotherapy to standard pharmacotherapy, symptomatic outcomes and relational functioning significantly improve in the treatment of acute bipolar depression. The existing evidence about relapse prevention only supports efficacy for subjects with residual symptoms (Lam et al, 2003) and research in adjunctive psychological therapies to medication in BD is still at an early stage. It is still largely unclear whether, such as for drugs, also psychotherapy could determine the onset of adverse effects for some bipolar individuals (Miklowitz and Scott, 2009).

It is also very important to understand what are those variables, such as the number of prior episodes, which generally resulted significantly associated with other poor prognostic indicators, that could predict a poor response to psychotherapy. In fact it is crucial to identify those predictors of good outcome among all combined treatments (Miklowitz and Scott, 2009).

The current therapeutic models should be modified in relation to the particular needs of special population of bipolar patients, especially those with extensive histories of relapse, BD-II with high levels of intermorbid depression and higher suicidality, rapid cycling, early-onset, or poor prognostic comorbidites (i.e., anxiety, substance abuse, and Axis II disorders) (Miklowitz et al, 2006).

However, whether psychological therapies alone may show better evidence of benefits in specific subgroups of bipolar patients rather than combined to medications is still unclear;

therefore, clinicians should be actually use cautious to totally replace pharmacotherapy with psychological therapy. Draw definitive conclusions about the efficacy of the different types of interventions is especially difficult in subjects with BD-II, since most studies actually included few patients with this type of diagnosis (Lam et al, 2009).

Finally, the real efficacy of psychotherapy in BD may be further investigated because our current understanding of the psychological processes underlying mania is extremely limited. The impact of the development of effective psychological therapies is hampered by the lack of a adequate understanding of the changes in cognition and behaviours accompanying and interacting with the changes of mood states.

CONCLUSION

BD is a common psychiatric illness characterized by severe cognitive impairments and functional disabilities. Many of bipolar subjects present relevant psychosocial impairments negatively affecting their quality of life and persisting throughout the disease course (Harvey et al, 2010). Although cognitive impairments and functional disabilities are common in BD, we know very little about the course and correlates of cognitive impairments, particularly about potential stable markers of vulnerability or risk-enhancing factors and their impact on functional status (Harvey et al, 2010). Although the available number of current treatment options, the treatment of mania and BD remains difficult and new pharmacological and rehabilitative strategies focused on the improvement of both cognitive impairments and functional status are requested.

DSM-V proposed modifications within the BD section that will presumably have relevant implications in the clinical practice but the diagnostic nomenclature for mania and BD is likely to undergo further additional revisions before 2013.

Currently, there are very few studies investigating the correlation between functional status in bipolar patients and demographic, clinical, treatment, environmental, and motivational variables. Such studies are crucial for understanding the clinical determinants of disability in the different BD phases and subtypes. Also, several neuroimaging studies have reported the presence of qualitative and quantitative structural abnormalities as well as functional brain changes in BD, particularly focusing on the role of ACC. However, although their theoretical interest, they did not satisfy early expectations and need to be replicated in more homogeneous samples. Additionally, molecular background underlying the neuroimaging and neuropathological changes occurring in ACC of bipolar subjects should be carefully investigated.

Further studies are needed in order to clarify the pathophysiological mechanisms underlying this complex condition as well as to face the multifaced diagnostic and treatment challenges.

REFERENCES

Akiskal H, McKinney W. Depressive disorders: toward a unified hypothesis. *Science* 1973; 182 (107), 20-29.

Akiskal HS. *The bipolar spectrum: new concepts in classification and diagnosis*. In: Grinspoon L, editor. Washington DC. Psychiatry update; the American Psychiatric Association Annual Review, vol. 2. American Psychiatric Press, pp. 271-292, 1983.

Altshuler LL, Curran JG, Hauser P, Mintz J, Denicoff K, Post R. T2 hyperintensities in bipolar disorder: magnetic resonance imaging comparison and literature meta-analysis. *Am J Psychiatry* 1995; 152: 1139–1144.

Amann B, Sterr A, Mergl R et al. Zotepine loading in acute and severely manic patients: a pilot study. *Bipolar Disord* 2005; 7: 471–476.

Anderson AK, Phelps EA. Is the human amygdala critical for the subjective experience of emotion? Evidence of intact dispositional affect in patients with amygdala lesions. *J Cogn Neurosci* 2002; 14 (5), 709–720.

Angst J. On the etiology and nosology of endogenous depressive psychoses: a genetic, sociologic, and clinical study. *Monogr Gesamtgeb Neurol Psychiatr* 1966;112:1-118.

Atmaca M, Ozdemir H, Yildirim H. Corpus callosum areas in first-episode patients with bipolar disorder. *Psychol Med* 2007; 37: 699–704.

Ballantine Jr, HT, Bouckoms AJ, Thomas EK, Giriunas IE. Treatment of psychiatric illness by stereotactic cingulotomy. *Biol Psychiatry* 1987; 22 (7): 807–819.

Bauer MS, McBride L, Williford WO, et al. Collaborative care for bipolar disorder: Part II. Impact on clinical outcome, function, and costs. *Psychiatric Serv* 2006; 57: 937–945.

Bech P. *Rating Scales for Psychopathology, Health Status and Quality of Life*. Heidelberg, Springer Verlag, 1993.

Begley CE, Annegers JF, Swann AC et al. The lifetime cost of bipolar disorder in the US: an estimate for new cases in 1998. *Pharmacoeconomics* 2001; 19: 483–495.

Berrios G, Porter R, editors. *A history of clinical psychiatry*. New York: New York University Press, 1995.

Berrios GE. Of mania: introduction (Classic text no. 57). *Hist Psychiatry* 2004;15(57 Pt 1):105-124.

Bowden CL. Predictors of response to divalproex and lithium. *J Clin Psychiatry* 1995; 56 (Suppl. 3): 25–30.

Caetano SC, Kaur S, Brambilla P, Nicoletti M, Hatch JP, Sassi RB, Mallinger AG, Keshavan MS, Kupfer DJ, Frank E, Soares JC. Smaller cingulate volumes in unipolar depressed patients. *Biol Psychiatry* 2006; 59 (8), 702–706.

Cassano GB, Rucci P, Frank E, Fagiolini A, Dell'Osso L, Shear MK, et al. The mood spectrum in unipolar and bipolar disorder: arguments for a unitary approach. *Am J Psychiatry* 2004;161(7):1264-1269.

Cassidy F, Ahearn E, Murry E, Forest K, Carroll BJ. Diagnostic depressive symptoms of the mixed bipolar episode. *Psychol Med* 2000; 30: 403–411.

Cassidy F, Murry E, Forest K, Carroll BJ. The performance of DSM-III-R major depression criteria in the diagnosis of bipolar mixed states. *J Affect Disord* 1997; 46: 79–81.

Cassidy F. Anxiety as a symptom of mixed mania: implications for DSM-5. *Bipolar Disord* 2010: 12: 437–439.

Chow T, Cummings J. Neuropsychiatry: clinical assessment and approach to diagnosis. In: Sadock, B., Sadock, V. (Eds.), *Comprehensive Textbook of Psychiatry*. Lipppincott Williams & Wilkins, Philadelphia, pp. 221–242, 2000.

Cohen M, Baker G, Cohen RA, Fromm-Reichmann F, Weigert V. An intensive study of 12 cases of manic-depressive psychosis. *Psychiatry* 1954; 17: 103–137.

Conca A, Fritzsche H, Peschina W, Konig P, Swoboda E, Wiederin H, Haas C. Preliminary findings of simultaneous 18F-FDG and 99mTc-HMPAO SPECT in patients with depressive disorders at rest: differential correlates with ratings of anxiety. *Psychiatry Res* 2000; 98 (1), 43–54.

Cousins DA, Butts K, Young AH. The role of dopamine in bipolar disorder. *Bipolar Disord* 2009; 11: 787–806.

Dean BB, Gerner D, Gerner RH. A systematic review evaluating health-related quality of life, work impairment, and healthcare costs and utilization in bipolar disorder. *Curr Med Res Opin* 2004; 20: 139–154.

Delay J, Deniker P, Harl J. Utilization therapeutique psychiatrique d'une phenothiazine d'action cetrale elective (4560RP). *Ann Med Psychol* 1952; 110: 112–117

DelBello MP, Strakowski SM, Zimmerman ME, Hawkins JM, Sax KW. MRI analysis of the cerebellum in bipolar disorder: a pilot study. *Neuropsychopharmacology* 1999; 21: 63–68.

Dunn RT, Willis MW, Benson BE, Repella JD, Kimbrell TA, Ketter TA, Speer AM, Osuch EA, Post RM. Preliminary findings of uncoupling of flow and metabolism in unipolar compared with bipolar affective illness and normal controls. *Psychiatry Res* 2005; 140 (2): 181–198.

Farrow TF, Whitford TJ, Williams LM, Gomes L, Harris AW. Diagnosis-related regional gray matter loss over two years in first episode schizophrenia and bipolar disorder. *Biol Psychiatry* 2005; 58: 713–723.

Fountoulakis K, Iacovides A, Nimatoudis I, Kaprinis G, Ierodiakonou C. Comparison of the diagnosis of melancholic and atypical features according to DSM-IV and somatic syndrome according to ICD-10 in patients suffering from major depression. *Eur Psychiatry* 1999; 14 (8): 426–434.

Fountoulakis KN, Vieta E, Bouras C, Notaridis G, Giannakopoulos P, Kaprinis G, Akiskal H. A systematic review of existing data on long-term lithium therapy: neuroprotective or neurotoxic? *Int J Neuropsychopharmacol* 2007b; 1–19.

Fountoulakis KN, Vieta E, Siamouli M, Valenti M, Magiria S, Oral T, Fresno D, Giannakopoulos P, Kaprinis GS. Treatment of bipolar disorder: a complex treatment for a multi-faceted disorder. *Ann Gen Psychiatry* 2007c; 6: 27.

Fountoulakis KN, Grunze H, Panagiotidis P, Kaprinis G. Treatment of bipolar depression: an update. *J Affect Disord* 2008; 109(1-2):21-34.

Friedman SD, Dager SR, Parow A, Hirashima F, Demopulos C, Stoll AL, Lyoo IK, Dunner DL, Renshaw PF. Lithium and valproic acid treatment effects on brain chemistry in bipolar disorder. *Biol. Psychiatry* 2004; 56 (5): 340–348.

Garfinkle PE, Stancer HG, Persad E. A comparison of haloperidol, lithium carbonate and their combination in the treatment of mania. *J Affect Disord* 1980; 2: 279–288.

Gobbi G, Janiri L. Sodium- and magnesium-valproate in vivo modulate glutamatergic and GABAergic synapses in the medial prefrontal cortex. *Psychopharmacology* (Berl) 2006; 185 (2): 255–262.

Goodwin F, Jamison K. *Manic depressive ill*ness. 2nd ed. New York: Oxford University Press; 2007.

Goodwin FK, Jamison KR. *Manic-Depressive Illness*. New York: Oxford University Press, 1990.

Griesinger W. *Pathologie und Therapie der psychischen Krankheiten*. Struttgart: Adolf Krabbe Verlag; 1861.

Gur R, Mozley H. Sex differences in regional cerebral glucose metabolism during a resting state. *Science* 1995; 267: 528–531.

Hajek T, Carrey N, Alda M. Neuroanatomical abnormalities as risk factors for bipolar disorder. *Bipolar Disord* 2005; 7 (5): 393–403.

Haldane M, Frangou S. New insights help define the pathophysiology of bipolar affective disorder: neuroimaging and neuropathology findings. *Prog Neuropsychopharmacol Biol Psychiatry* 2004; 28 (6): 943–960.

Harrison PJ. The neuropathology of primary mood disorder. *Brain* 2002; 125 (Pt 7): 1428–1449.

Harvey PD, Wingo AP, Burdick KE, Baldessarini RJ. Cognition and disability in bipolar disorder: lessons from schizophrenia research. *Bipolar Disord* 2010: 12: 364–375.

Hasler G, Drevets WC, Gould TD, Gottesman II, Manji HK. Toward constructing an endophenotype strategy for bipolar disorders. *Biol. Psychiatry*. 2006. 60(2):93-105.

Heinroth J. *Lehrbuch der Stroerungen des Seelenlebens*. Leipzig: Vogel; 1818

Himmelhoch JM, Mulla D, Neil JF, Detre TP, Kupfer DJ. Incidence and significance of mixed affective states in a bipolar population. *Arch Gen Psychiatry* 1976; 33: 1062–1066.

Hirschfeld RM, Clayton PJ, Cohen I, et al. Practice guideline for the treatment of patients with bipolar disorder. *Am J Psychiatry* 1994; 151 (Suppl. 1): 1–36.

Keller MB, Lavori PW, Coryell W, et al. Differential outcome of pure manic, mixed/cycling, and pure depressive episodes in patients with bipolar illness. *JAMA* 1986; 255: 3138–3142.

Kempton MJ, Geddes JR, Ettinger U, Williams SC, Grasby PM. Meta-analysis, database, and meta-regression of 98 structural imaging studies in bipolar disorder. *Arch Gen Psychiatry* 2008; 65: 1017–1032.

Kendler D, Kupfer D, Narrow W, Phillips K, Fawcett J. *Guidelines for Making Changes to DSM-V*. Washington, D.C., American Psychiatric Association, 2009.

Kennedy SH, Javanmard M, Vaccarino FJ. A review of functional neuroimaging in mood disorders: positron emission tomography and depression. *Can J Psychiatry* 1997; 42 (5): 467–475.

Kleinman L, Lowin A, Flood E, Gandhi G, Edgell E, Revicki D. Costs of bipolar disorder. *Pharmacoeconomics* 2003; 21: 601–622.

Koo MS, Levitt JJ, Salisbury DF, Nakamura M, Shenton ME, McCarley RW. A cross-sectional and longitudinal magnetic resonance imaging study of cingulate gyrus gray matter volume abnormalities in first-episode schizophrenia and first-episode affective psychosis. *Arch Gen Psychiatry* 2008; 65: 746–760.

Koukopoulos AS, Ghaemi N. The primacy of mania: A reconsideration of mood disorders. *European Psychiatry* 2009; 24: 125-134.

Kraepelin E. *Psychiatrie*. Leipzig: JA Barth; 1913.

Kruger S, Trevor Young L, Braunig P. Pharmacotherapy of bipolar mixed states. *Bipolar Disord* 2005; 7: 205–215.

Krystal JH, Sanacora G, Blumberg H, Anand A, Charney DS, Marek G, Epperson CN, Goddard A, Mason GF. Glutamate and GABA systems as targets for novel antidepressant and mood-stabilizing treatments. *Mol Psychiatry* 2002; 7 (Suppl. 1): S71–S80.

Kupfer DJ. The increasing medical burden in bipolar disorder. *JAMA* 2005; 293: 2528–2530.

Kusumakar V, Yatham LN, Haslam DR, et al. Treatment of mania, mixed state, and rapid cycling. *Can J Psychiatry* 1997; 42 (Suppl. 2): 79S–86S.

Laeng P, Pitts RL, Lemire AL, Drabik CE, Weiner A, Tang H, Thyagarajan R, Mallon BS, Altar CA. The mood stabilizer valproic acid stimulates GABA neurogenesis from rat forebrain stem cells. *J Neurochem* 2004; 91 (1): 238–251.

Lam D, Watkins E, Hayward P, et al. A randomized controlled study of cognitive therapy of relapse prevention for bipolar affective disorder—outcome of the first year. *Arch Gen Psychiatry* 2003; 60: 145–152.

Lam DH, Burbeck R, Wright K, Pilling S. Psychological therapies in bipolar disorder: the effect of illness history on relapse prevention – a systematic review. *Bipolar Disord* 2009: 11: 474–482.

Lam RW, Kennedy SH, Grigoriadis S, McIntyre RS, Milev R, Ramasubbu R, Parikh SV, Patten SB, Ravindran AV; Canadian Network for Mood and Anxiety Treatments (CANMAT). Canadian Network for Mood and Anxiety Treatments (CANMAT) clinical guidelines for the management of major depressive disorder in adults. III. Pharmacotherapy. *J Affect Disord.* 2009;117 Suppl 1:S26-43.

Landmark CJ. Targets for antiepileptic drugs in the synapse. *Med Sci Monit* 2007; 13 (1): RA1–RA7

Lee SH, Sohn JW, Ahn SC, Park WS, Ho WK. Li+ enhances GABAergic inputs to granule cells in the rat hippocampal dentate gyrus. *Neuropharmacology* 2004; 46 (5): 638–646.

Li X, Ketter TA, Frye MA. Synaptic, intracellular, and neuroprotective mechanisms of anticonvulsants: are they relevant for the treatment and course of bipolar disorders? *J Affect Disord* 2002; 69 (1–3): 1–14.

Long CJ, Pueschel K, Hunter SE. Assessment of the effects of cinglulate gyrus lesions by neuropsychological techniques. *J Neurosurg* 1978; 49 (2): 264–271.

Malhi GS, Roy Chengappa KN, Gershon S, Goldberg JF. Hypomania: hype or mania? *Bipolar Disord* 2010: 12: 758–763.

Manji HK, Quiroz JA, Payne JL, et al. The underlying neurobiology of bipolar disorder. *World Psychiatry* 2003; 2: 136–146.

McDonald C, Bullmore ET, Sham PC, Chitnis X, Wickham H, Bramon E, Murray RM. Association of genetic risks for schizophrenia andbipolar disorderwith specific andgeneric brain structural endophenotypes. *Arch. Gen. Psychiatry* 2004; 61 (10): 974–984.

McDonald C, Zanelli J, Rabe-Hesketh S, et al. Metaanalysis of magnetic resonance imaging brain morphometry studies in bipolar disorder. *Biol Psychiatry* 2004; 56:411–417.

McIntyre R, Panagides J, Alphs L, et al. *Efficacy and tolerability of asenapine and olanzapine in acute mania: a double-blind extension study* (ARES 7501006). Presented at the 20th ECNP Meeting, Vienna, 13–17 October. 2007.

Miklowitz DJ, Johnson SL. The psychopathology and treatment of bipolar disorder. *Annu Rev Clin Psychol* 2006; 2: 199–235.

Miklowitz DJ, Otto MW, Frank E et al. Psychosocial treatment for bipolar depression. *Arch Gen Psychiatry* 2007; 64: 419–427.

Miklowitz DJ, Scott J. Psychosocial treatments for bipolar disorder: cost-effectiveness, mediating mechanisms, and future directions. *Bipolar Disord* 2009: 11 (Suppl. 2): 110–122.

Miklowitz DJ. Adjunctive psychotherapy for bipolar disorder: state of the evidence. *Am J Psychiatry* 2008; 165: 1408–1419.

Muzina DJ. Pharmacologic treatment of rapid cycling and mixed states in bipolar disorder: an argument for the use of lithium. *Bipolar Disord* 2009: 11 (Suppl. 2): 84–91.

Nakamura M, Salisbury DF, Hirayasu Y et al. Neocortical gray matter volume in first-episode schizophrenia and firstepisode affective psychosis: a cross-sectional and longitudinal MRI study. *Biol Psychiatry* 2007; 62: 773–783.

Overall J, Hollister L, Johnson M. Nosology of depression and differential response to drugs. *JAMA* 1966; 195, 946–950.

Peele PB, Xu Y, Kupfer DJ. Insurance expenditures on bipolar disorder: clinical and parity implications. *Am J Psychiatry* 2003; 160: 1286–1290.

Perris C. A study of bipolar (manic-depressive) and unipolar recurrent depressive psychoses. *Acta Psychiatr Scand* 1966;42(Suppl 194): 150-152.

Phillips ML, Drevets WC, Rauch SL, Lane R. Neurobiology of emotion perception I: the neural basis of normal emotion perception. *Biol Psychiatry* 2003a; 54 (5): 504–514.

Phillips ML, Drevets WC, Rauch SL, Lane R. Neurobiology of emotion perception II: implications for major psychiatric disorders. *Biol Psychiatry* 2003b; 54 (5): 515–528.

Phillips ML, Gregory LJ, Cullen S, Coen S, Ng V, Andrew C, Giampietro V, Bullmore E, Zelaya F, Amaro E, Thompson DG, Hobson AR, Williams SC, Brammer M, Aziz Q. The effect of negative emotional context on neural and behavioural responses to oesophageal stimulation. *Brain* 2003c; 126 (Pt 3): 669–684.

Pinel P. *Traite′ me′dicophilosophique sur l'alienation mentale ou la manie*. Paris: Richard Caille et Ravier; 1801.

Quiroz JA, Gray NA, Kato T, Manji HK. Mitchondrially mediated plasticity in the pathophysiology and treatment of bipolar disorder. *Neuropsychopharmacology* 2008; 33: 2551–2565.

Rea MM, Tompson M, Miklowitz DJ, Goldstein MJ, Hwang S, Mintz J. Family focused treatment vs. individual treatment for bipolar disorder: results of a randomized clinical trial. *J Cons Clin Psychol* 2003; 71: 482–492.

Rogers RD, Ramnani N, Mackay C, Wilson JL, Jezzard P, Carter CS, Smith SM. Distinct portions of anterior cingulate cortex and medial prefrontal cortex are activated by reward processing in separable phases of decision-making cognition. *Biol Psychiatry* 2004; 55 (6): 594–602.

Rosso IM, Killgore WD, Cintron CM, Gruber SA, Tohen M, Yurgelun-Todd DS. Reduced amygdala volume in firstepisode bipolar disorder and correlation with cerebral white matter. *Biol Psychiatry* 2007; 61: 743–749.

Roth M. The phenomenology of depressive states. *Can Psychiatr Assoc J* 1959; 4 (suppl): 32–52.

Schatzberg AF. Bipolar disorder: recent issues in diagnosis and classification. *J Clin Psychiatry* 1998;59 (Suppl. 6): 5-10.

Scott J, Colom F, Popova E, et al. Long-term mental health resource utilization and cost of care following group psychoeducation or unstructured group support for bipolar disorders: a cost-benefit analysis. *J Clin Psychiatry* 2009; 70: 378–386.

Scott J. Psychotherapy for bipolar disorders-efficacy and effectiveness. *J Psychopharmacol* 2006; 20: 46–50.

Shorter E. *A history of psychiatry*. New York: John Wiley and Sons; 1997.

Simon GE, Unutzer J. Health care utilization and costs among patients treated for bipolar disorder in an insured population. *Psychiatr Serv* 1999; 50: 1303–1308.

Simonsen C, Sundet K, Vaskinn A et al. Neurocognitive profiles in bipolar I and bipolar II disorder: differences in pattern and magnitude of dysfunction. *Bipolar Disord* 2008; 10: 245–255.

Smoller JW, Finn CT. Family, twin, and adoption studies of bipolar disorder. *Am J Med Gen C Semin Med Genet* 2003; 123: 48–58.

Strakowski SM, Adler CM, Holland SK, Mills NP, DelBello MP, Eliassen JC. Abnormal FMRI brain activation in euthymic bipolar disorder patients during a counting Stroop interference task. *Am J Psychiatry* 2005; 162 (9): 1697–1705.

Strakowski SM, DelBello MP, Zimmerman ME et al. Ventricular and periventricular structural volumes in firstversus multiple-episode bipolar disorder. *Am J Psychiatry* 2002; 159: 1841–1847.

Strakowski SM, Wilson DR, Tohen M, Woods BT, Douglass AW, Stoll AL. Structural brain abnormalities in first-episode mania. *Biol Psychiatry* 1993; 33: 602–609.

Swanda R, Haaland K, LaRue A. Clinical neuropsychology and intellectual assessment of adults. In: Sadock, B., Sadock, V. (Eds.), *Comprehensive Textbook of Psychiatry.* Lipppincott Williams & Wilkins, Philadelphia, pp. 689–702, 2000.

Tekin S, Cummings JL. Frontal-subcortical neuronal circuits and clinical neuropsychiatry: an update. *J Psychosom Res* 2002; 53 (2): 647–654.

Thomas P, Vieta E, for the SOLMANIA study group. Amisulpride plus valproate vs haloperidol plus valproate in the treatment of acute mania of bipolar I patients: a multicenter, open-label, randomized, comparative trial. *Neuropsychiatr Dis Treat* 2008; 4: 675–686.

Tohen M, Zarate CA, Hennen J, et al. The McLean Harvard first-episode mania study; prediction of recovery and first recurrence. *Am J Psychiatry* 2003; 160: 2099– 2107.

Tohen M, Zhang F, Taylor CC, et al. A meta-analysis of the use of typical antipsychotic agents in bipolar disorder. *J Affect Disord* 2001; 65: 85–93.

Tohen M. Mania. In: Sederer LI, Rothschild AJ eds. *Acute Care Psychiatry: Diagnosis and Treatment.* Baltimore, MD: Williams & Wilkins: 141–165, 1997.

Torrent C, Martìnez-Aràn A, Daban C, et al. Cognitive impairment in bipolar II disorder. *Br J Psychiatry* 2006; 189: 254–259.

Van Riel WG, Vieta E, Martìnez-Aràn A, et al. Chronic mania revisited: factors associated with treatment nonresponse during prospective follow-up of a large European cohort (EMBLEM*). World J Biol Psychiatry* 2008; 9: 313– 320.

VanPraag H, Uleman A, Spitz J. The vital syndrome interview. *Psychiatr Neurol Neurochir* 1965; 68: 329–349.

Videbech P. MRI findings in patients with affective disorder: a meta-analysis. *Acta Psychiatr Scand* 1997; 96: 157–168.

Vieta E, Berwaerts J, Nuamah I, et al. Randomized, placebo-active controlled study of paliperidone extended release for acute manic and mixed episodes in bipolar I disorder. *Eur Neuropsychopharmacol* 2008; 18 (Suppl. 4): S369.

Vita A, De Peri L, Sacchetti E. Gray matter, white matter, brain, and intracranial volumes in first-episode bipolar disorder: a meta-analysis of magnetic resonance imaging studies. *Bipolar Disord* 2009: 11: 807–814.

Whitty CW, Duffield JE, Tov PM, Cairns H. Anterior cingulectomy in the treatment of mental disease. *Lancet* 1952; 1 (10): 475–481.

Winokur G, Coryell W, Endicott J, Akiskal H. Further distinctions between manic-depressive illness (bipolar disorder) and primary depressive disorder (unipolar depression). *Am J Psychiatry* 1993; 150(8):1176-1181.

Yatham LN, Lyoo IK, Liddle P, et al.A magnetic resonance imaging study of mood stabilizer- and neuroleptic-naı¨ve first-episode mania. *Bipolar Disord* 2007; 9: 693–697.

Yildiz-Yesiloglu A, Ankerst DP. Neurochemical alterations of the brain in bipolar disorder and their implications for pathophysiology: a systematic review of the in vivo proton magnetic resonance spectroscopy findings. *Prog. Neuropsychopharmacol. Biol Psychiatry* 2006; 30 (6): 969–995.

Zanetti MV, Schaufelberger MS, de Castro CC, et al. White-matter hyperintensities in first-episode psychosis. *Br J Psychiatry* 2008; 193: 25–30.

In: Advances in Psychology Research. Volume 88
Editor: Alexandra M. Columbus, pp. 141-159
ISBN: 978-1-62100-591-9

Chapter 7

BEHAVIOR THERAPY IN TOURETTE SYNDROME

***Clare M. Eddy*[1] *and Andrea E. Cavanna**[1,2]

[1] Department of Neuropsychiatry,
BSMHFT and University of Birmingham,
United Kingdom.
[2] Institute of Neurology, UCL, London, United Kingdom.

ABSTRACT

Tourette syndrome (TS) is a chronic neurodevelopmental disorder characterized by the presence of multiple motor and phonic tics, and associated behavioural problems. While a range of pharmacological therapies have been shown to be effective in treating tic symptoms and co-morbid conditions such as obsessive compulsive disorder and attention-deficit hyperactivity disorder, drug treatment is complicated by side effects and potential toxicity in young individuals. Furthermore, some individuals with TS find that their symptoms do not respond favourably to such treatments, and exhibit difficulties for which behavioural treatments may be more appropriate or effective. Current behavioural treatments for tics include Habit Reversal Training, Exposure Response Prevention and Massed Negative Practice. Other approaches, such as hypnotherapy and self-monitoring have also been trialled in TS. Interventions including psychotherapy and cognitive behavioural therapy can be applied to assist with co-morbid conditions, and related social or self esteem difficulties which can impact quality of life. In this chapter, we review behavioural treatments available for the symptoms of TS, providing an evaluation of efficacy and associated limitations. We discuss factors influencing treatment response, such as attention, insight, sensory awareness and compliance which implicate cognitive, physiological and psychosocial domains. Future longitudinal studies are crucial in order to determine the long term efficacy of behavioural treatments in TS, and establish whether certain approaches are more appropriate for individuals exhibiting particular clinical and behavioural profiles.

---

* Correspondence: Dr Andrea E. Cavanna MD PhD, Department of Neuropsychiatry, University of Birmingham and BSMHFT, Barberry Building, 25 Vincent Drive, B152TT Birmingham, United Kingdom, Email: a.cavanna@ion.ucl.ac.uk

Keywords: Tourette syndrome; tics; behaviour; Habit Reversal Training; Exposure Response Prevention; Massed Negative Practice.

INTRODUCTION

Tourette syndrome (TS) is a neurodevelopmental disorder, involving tics: repetitive, stereotyped movements and vocalisations. Tics can be simple or complex and characteristically vary in severity over time. Patients with TS commonly experience symptoms associated with conditions such as obsessive compulsive disorder and attention deficit hyperactivity disorder. Mood and behavioural problems relating to emotional dysregulation and impulse control may also be present.

Some effective pharmacological agents are available for tics in TS [1]. The largest class of medications which appear effective in reducing tics are atypical antipsychotics. There are limitations with the use of these treatments, which commonly exert drowsiness as a side effect and have the potential to more serious problems, such as extrapyramidal motor symptoms. Tics are often at their worse during puberty and adolescence, a period when effective treatment may be crucial for both learning and social integration. Medication side effects are a particularly important issue in children, who are more susceptible to drug toxicity, and make up a large proportion of the population of individuals with TS. Furthermore, some patients trial many kinds of drugs and find them to be ineffective. Behavioural treatments are likely to be the most appropriate options for young children, drug-refractory patients and those who experience unacceptable medication side effects. In addition, by providing a patient with behavioural therapy you are more likely to equip them with coping mechanisms which can assist with long-term management of their condition, and their cognitive, emotional and physiological symptoms can be targeted simultaneously.

Some of the characteristics of tics which make behavioural therapy potentially helpful include the finding that patients often experience a preceding physiological sensation before they tic (often termed a premonitory urge). Such ‘premonitory sensations’ may be described as tension, pressure, tickling, or itching [2;3]. It has also been observed that tics can often be exacerbated by psychological stressors or emotional states, such as anxiety [4;5]. Because patients with TS commonly experience symptoms associated with OCD or ADHD, it is important to take these conditions into account when considering treatments for both tics and behavioural symptoms in TS. For some patients, the impact of these co-morbid conditions can be more detrimental than tics in terms of emotional experience and practical functioning.

In this chapter, we review a range of behavioural therapies which have been used to treat TS. These include habit reversal training (HR), exposure response prevention (ERP), massed negative practice (NP), biofeedback therapy, hypnotherapy, self-monitoring, relaxation therapy, psychotherapy and cognitive behavioural therapy (CBT). The main focus of treatment in this condition has been the improvement of tics, but some methods have been applied which can assist in dealing with a wider range of difficulties experienced by these individuals.

BEHAVIOURAL TREATMENTS FOR TOURETTE SYNDROME

Habit Reversal Training

Treatment Aims

Habit reversal (HR) training is perhaps the most extensively studied behavioural approach used for tics. HR is based on a competing response rationale first applied by Azrin and Nunn [6]. Patients first discuss their tics in a way that encourages awareness and understanding of their movement symptoms, and are then instructed to practice movements which are physiologically topographically incompatible with their tics. After practice, these consciously applied competing responses should become more automatic. Further therapy components can include relaxation techniques, contingency management, and social support interventions, although a simplified HR method consisting of only awareness and competing response training can be effective [7;8]. HR may work by interrupting tics, strengthening competing muscles and perhaps encouraging habituation to premonitory urges.

Method

Awareness training can include identification of situations associated with tics, increasing awareness of physiological sensations which may precede the tic, and performing and describing the tic in front of a mirror. During the competing response procedure, the patient learns how to exert isometric pressure from muscles opposed to the tic movement when experiencing the urge to tic. The competing response should be inconspicuous to an observer and easily compatible with normal daily behaviour. This can be achieved by practicing in front of a mirror and the therapist. The amount of tension exerted in opposing muscles should hold the body part in place in a way that prevents purposeful attempts to perform the tic. On feeling that a tic is likely to occur or has started to occur, the patient performs the competing response for perhaps 1-3 minutes, in addition to practicing the competing movements on a daily basis, preferably in front of a mirror. The competing response method is applied to individual tics. For example, for a shoulder jerk, the shoulders can be contracted by lowering the shoulders down as far as possible while keeping the arms close to the body. HR may appear most easily applied to motor tics; however, similar techniques can be applied to vocal tics, such as controlling breathing patterns for vocal tics.

Efficacy

Tested with 11 nonretarded outpatients, 4 of whom suffered from tics such as head shaking, head jerking, arm jerking, tongue thrusting, and shoulder jerking, the others suffering from other nervous habits [6]. The method, termed habit reversal, resulted in a mean decrease of 90% of the habit or tic on the first day, 95% after 1 month, and 99% after 3 months. The effectiveness of habit reversal training has been reviewed fairly recently [9]. Many studies have reported that HR can be successful in treating tics [10-13]. Azrin, Nunn and Franz [14] treated 10 adults with HR. Treatment reduced tic episodes by 84% on the first day of treatment, decreasing progressively by 92% by the fourth week, by 97% during the second month, 99% during the fourth, fifth, and sixth months and at the 18-month follow-up showed a 97% reduction. In a later study, Azrin & Peterson [15] showed that during the first month of treatment, many treated patients exhibited a reduction of at least 50% when tested in

clinic or at home, and this increased to 100% of the treatment group during the second month of treatment. The mean percentage reduction for all 10 subjects at the last month of treatment was 93.0% at home and 93.5% in the clinic, and tics were significantly less frequent in both environments than at baseline, and significantly less in comparison to a waiting list group. Furthermore, tic severity also appeared to reduce, according to video ratings. Woods and colleagues reported improvements of 89% to 96% in four children with motor tics [16], and another study indicated HR can be used successfully to treat vocal tics [17]. Four out of five children (aged 10-13 years) showed a reduction in vocal tic frequency of 38-96%, while untreated motor tics remained the same. Gains were maintained at three months. In relation to other treatments, HR can be more effective than massed negative practice [14] and supportive psychotherapy [18;19]. It may also be successful when combined with cognitive behavioural therapy [20]. Positive effects can also include improved self-esteem and feelings of self-control [21], while negative effects of treatment include tic worsening (shown by 4% of children in one study [22])However, treatment gains appear durable, with the latter study finding that 87% of available responders showed continued benefit 6 months following treatment.

Predictors of Treatment Response

Due to the technique needing to be applied to individual tics, the method may be easiest for patients who experience fewer different tics. HR seems effective in children and adults, and can be used for both motor and vocal tics. However, Azrin & Peterson [15] noted poor response in a patient with a whole body tic, highlighting the necessary ease of identification of a suitable competing response. The patients' awareness of premonitory or preceding physiological sensations could be important for effectiveness, and it has been suggested that younger children (perhaps below 10 years) may show less awareness of such factors [23].

Limitations

While increased attentional focus could serve to exacerbate tics, HR may be a method of directing attentional focus in a productive way. Patients with attentional difficulties may also find this method more difficult to master. A recent study further suggests that assessments of response inhibition may be of value for predicting treatment response to HR [18]. Compliance is also very important. Patients who fail to complete home-work in order for the competing response to become conditioned and easy to apply in all environments are likely to show poorer treatment response. Another possible limitation associated with this behavioural technique is that tics in one part of the body may be replaced by tics in another part [24]. Long-term evaluation of treatment outcome is needed in order to gain a full appreciation of the efficacy of this technique.

Exposure Response Prevention

Treatment Aims

In learning theory terms, tics can be viewed as conditioned responses to premonitory, interoceptive stimuli. It is assumed that repetition over time strengthens the power of the associative interaction between the sensations and the resultant tic behaviour. Exposure

Response Prevention (ERP) aims to interrupt this association, with a resulting reduction in tic frequency.

Method

During ERP, patients are aided in resisting performing their tics for a prolonged period of time, often by gradually increasing the time spent suppressing tics. This approach leads the patient to confront the tic related physiological sensations which precede or accompany the tic, with a view to reducing sensitivity over time. Patients learn to tolerate these generally unpleasant sensations, leading to habituation. Habituation in turn will lessen the urge to tic, as cues to tic disappear.

Efficacy

Although ERP may sound challenging, studies have revealed that this simple therapy can prove effective. Verdellen and colleagues reported a reduction in tics in treated patients with Tourette syndrome and that this treatment was equally effective to the more widely applied technique of habit reversal training [25]. Not only can ERP reduce tics, but it can also reduce premonitory sensations [26], as shown in a randomized controlled trial [27].

Predictors of Treatment Response

Preliminary results indicate that ER is effective for vocal and motor tics, for children as well as adults, for tic severity as well as tic frequency [27]. Since younger children are less aware of premonitory sensory motor phenomena it has to be clarified if there is an age effect respective an age limit for ER but also for HR [23]. Consistent compliance is likely to be essential in order to allow application of suppression responses to lead to habituation. The ability to suppress tics of clearly critical, and it would be useful for future research to investigate the relationship of treatment response using this technique and performance on cognitive tests of response inhibition and sustained attention. Patients likely to have difficulties with these factors e.g. patients with attention-deficit hyperactivity disorder, may find ERP less efficacious.

Limitations

Although focusing attention on tics may increase the inhibitory effort leading to exacerbation [24], Verdellen and colleagues reported no evidence for a rebound effect after exposure plus response prevention therapy sessions [27]. The patients' awareness of premonitory or preceding physiological sensations is likely to make a key contribution to the effectiveness, and the technique could be less effective with young children or patients who cannot identify such sensations [23]. Further investigations are needed.

Massed Negative Practice

Treatment Aims

Negative practice (NP) training [28] sometimes also termed 'massed negative practice', was one of the most common early behavioral treatments for tics. The idea behind this

therapy is that repeating the tics at a very high frequency will lead to muscle exhaustion and can help condition against having tics.

Method

An NP procedure described by Azrin et al [29] involved patients purposely performing the tic in a massed practice schedule in front of a mirror for 30-second periods over a1-hour period interspersed by brief rests. During this period, patients were instructed to say to themselves, "this is what I'm supposed not to do."

They were advised to continue this exercise daily until a few days after tics had subsided, after which they would gradually discontinue the practice over the following 2 weeks, resuming in the case of relapse. The repeated practice of the tics tires out the muscles involved in performing them and they have to rest. Over time and practice, behaviour is re-programmed, with the resting time after tic performance increasing, leading to a reduction in tic frequency outside practice.

Efficacy

Negative practice has been found to be at least somewhat effective for tics in Tourette Syndrome [31;31], multiple tics [32-34], and for specific tics such as eye blinking (Costello, 1963; Frederick, 1971), mouth grimacing [35], and head jerking [36]. Topoff [37] describe how a 13 year old boy recovered completely after 14 sessions, and Storms [38] reports on 2 more successful cases. However, in a comparative study with HR, Azrin and colleagues [29] showed that NP reduced tic episodes by about 1/3 during the 4-week follow-up in 12 adults. However, significantly greater improvement was reported with HR. Other studies have reported little improvement [39;40].

Predictors of Treatment Response

Little data is currently available in relation to factors that may be predictive of treatment response with this therapeutic approach.

One study reports little success with coprolalia [39] raising the possibility that particular tics may be more difficult to treat. Complex sequences of motor tics involving many muscle groups could be particularly challenging. A patient with a few simple motor tics is likely to show the greatest potential for improvement.

Limitations

It is difficult to fully evaluate the effectiveness of this technique as larger, controlled trials are needed. The available evidence for the efficacy of this technique is less than for HR or ERP, however, NP is not associated with limitations linked to attention and sensory awareness associated with these other techniques. Likely possible drawbacks include muscular discomfort associated with repetitive ticcing and the difficulty with practicing this technique in a range of everyday environments. This treatment could also not be applied to treat more severe tics likely to lead to self-damage.

Biofeedback Therapy

Treatment Aims

Biofeedback therapy provides the patient with information about automatic and unconscious physiological or neurological responses which are related to having tics. Training is then given in order to help the patient gain control over this physiological response using an operant conditioning approach, with a view to gaining control over tics and reducing their frequency or severity.

Methods

Forms of biofeedback involving feedback about heart or respiration rate or blood pressure may be closely related to relaxation therapy. A more recent technique used with patients with attention-deficit hyperactivity disorder (commonly co-morbid with TS) involves neurofeedback, and is aimed at self- modulation of defined parts of brain electrical activity. During a treatment session, physiological measures are used to collect biofeedback data, and when the patient modifies their physiological condition, this is immediately indicated through the biofeedback measure. For example, brain activity is assessed using metal discs placed on the scalp that pick up electrical signals from the brain. An attached computer processes the patients' brain waves and indicates when they are modulated by means of sounds and changing screen patterns. This method can provide a form of positive feedback when the physiological state is modified as required (e.g. lower heart rate, increased alertness etc). At first it is difficult for the patient to achieve the desired physiological change, but with practice this becomes easier. It is expected that after enough training the patient has much more control, perhaps even automatic control, over problem symptoms.

Efficacy

A study by Tansey [41] showed that biofeedback may be a successful treatment to reduce tics through increases in voluntary muscle control, but another study reported inconclusive results [42]. While few studies have reported the use of biofeedback with tics, a recent study suggests that this approach has the potential to be useful. Nagai et al [43] conducted a study involving 15 adult patients with TS. All patients performed arousal and relaxation biofeedback sessions for 5 minutes each followed by 2 minutes of baseline resting. Tic rates were recorded using a video camera. Significantly fewer tics were apparent during relaxation biofeedback compared to arousal biofeedback. Furthermore, tic frequency was positively correlated with sympathetic arousal during the arousal session, suggesting that training to reduce arousal and increase relaxation could encourage a reduction in the frequency of tics.

Predictors of Treatment Response

Factors relating to the success of this treatment in treating tics remain to be identified. However, some general hypotheses may be proposed. Firstly, patients with attentional difficulties may find it difficult to sustain effort in modifying their physiological responses through biofeedback methods. Secondly, individuals with anxiety disorders in addition to tics may also find this technique more difficult due to generally heightened signs of physiological stress, although they may also demonstrate the greatest potential for improvement through modification of these signs as they could play a more significant role in their tic symptoms.

Biofeedback would not be useful for those patients whose tics appear unrelated to identifiable physiological signs.

Limitations

Biofeedback appears to have a number of advantages. It is non-invasive and pain-free. After gaining the ability to recognise changes in their physiological state, patients are able to identify these problematic responses and control them independently. The patient is empowered, experiencing greater self-control. However, this process may take a long time in order for skills to be solidified and gains to be maintained raising issues of compliance and expense.

Hypnotherapy

Treatment Aims

The rationale for hypnotherapy is that the unconscious mind can gain control over aspects of behaviour that the conscious mind may not be able to. During deep hypnosis breathing rate and heart rate reduce, and the brain produces alpha-waves, which indicate deep relaxation and are also induced by meditation. Hypnotherapy could therefore help reduce the unconscious stress associated with particular behaviour leading to improvements in related symptoms.

Methods

The most common form of hypnotherapy is 'suggestion hypnotherapy', which aims to break patterns of thought and behaviour through positive suggestions and imagery. Initially the therapist will discuss the patients problems, intentions and motivation to resolve any problem. When the patient is ready to enter hypnotic trance, the therapist will encourage a state of relaxation often by asking the patient to visualise a place or scene, or using a counting method. During trance, the therapist will make encouraging and persuasive positive suggestions about the patient's ability to resist or overcome their difficulties. Some approaches may involve discussing techniques that can help in combating symptoms. The patient will then be gradually brought out of trance state.

Efficacy

A successful story using hypnotherapy on an adolescent with Tourette syndrome was reported by Culbertson [44]. The patient underwent 9 hypnosis sessions over 6-months. The model used involved a 4-step treatment process including progressive relaxation, finger-tip temperature feedback, Spiegel's eye-roll procedure, and imagery. Tics appeared to remit completely following treatment and gains were apparent at 6-month follow-up. It appeared that the hypnosis sessions helped reduce stress linked to the symptoms of TS.

In a recent study, Lazarus et al [45] tried a series of self-hypnosis techniques in a group of thirty-three participants with TS, aged 6-19 years, over two and a half months. Participants viewed a video featuring a young boy outlining self-hypnosis techniques. They were also given relaxation techniques and asked to focus on the feelings occurring prior to a tic (premonitory sensation) in addition to reducing tics. Participants were instructed to practice the self-hypnosis techniques at least three times per day. 46% of patients self-reported

improved tic control after 2 sessions, and all children reported significant benefit by the end of the therapy period. These promising results are limited by no inclusion of a control group or longer follow-up.

Predictors of Treatment Response

As with many of the behavioural therapies discussed, data according to factors linked to treatment response is unavailable for hypnosis. It may be that tics have the potential to benefit most from this treatment when a patient is very motivated and has faith in the technique. Some patients may be more susceptible to positive hypnotic suggestion, particularly if they have a good rapport with their therapist. When tics are related to unconscious stress, the relaxation associated with hypnosis could have a positive effect on symptoms and help to increase control over tic suppression.

Limitations

Hypnotic treatments will not work for people who find it difficult to enter a trance-state. Furthermore, motivation is considered to be particularly important, as patients cannot be encouraged to do anything they don't truly want to.

Self-Monitoring

Treatment Aims

The goal of self-monitoring (SM) is to identify when and in what situations tics occur. This offers further insight into the possible triggers of tics and may therefore help the patient in managing their occurrence. SM is often applied in multi-component HR packages.

Methods

SM can involve instructing the patient to describe their tics and record their occurence during a specified period by using a diary, or using a counting device to record the frequency of tics for a specified period [46]. The patient will become more aware of which environments and behaviours are related to increased tic frequency and severity. They may also begin to understand the physiological, cognitive and emotional mechanisms involved in their ticcing behaviour. Although self-monitoring is not a treatment as such, this information can be useful in adopting strategies to help reduce tic symptoms. The risk of tics may be lowered by modifying behaviours or activities which are determined as risk factors. For example, patients may be able to make early detection of stressful situations which have been shown to pose a risk for increased tics, and could attempt to modify their actions, cognitions or emotional responses to lower stress responses. Therapies such as HR, CBT and relaxation training could be used as mechanisms through which this control or modification may be achieved. It may be possible to almost completely avoid some known triggers for tics, if they are linked to unnecessary or maladaptive behaviours.

Efficacy

There is some evidence that SM can result in a reduction in tic frequency in some individuals, even when used without other behavioral therapies [16;47]. For example, Hutzell

et al [48] reported success in an 11-year-old male with TS. A five-step procedure of successively refining control was employed alongside SM. It was reported that symptoms were found to decrease in the therapeutic setting and in the patients' natural environment. However, very few studies have been conducted in which SM was used as the primary treatment procedure. In More research is needed in order to ascertain the generalizability and durability of any treatment gains.

Predictors of Treatment Response

Keeping a diary requires a degree of commitment and may appeal to individuals with more reflective personalities who already demonstrate good insight into their symptoms. Patients with memory difficulties would clearly struggle with this method. Studies have indicated that immediate, rather than delayed recording of tics, appears to be essential for ultimate treatment improvement [40;49]. More resourceful individuals who have greater belief in their ability to modify their behaviour may respond best to this kind of approach.

Limitations

It has been suggested that focusing attention on tics can lead to a worsening of tic symptoms [50;51]. Moreover, the outcome of SM is likely to be very dependent on patients' controlled reaction to identified triggers/risk factors. It is possible that some situations are unavoidable and therefore highlighting the risk of tics could in fact be detrimental, through leading to increased fear of ticcing and stress, which in turn exacerbate symptoms. It seems important that the patient is instructed to think about behaviours or activities which are more within their control to encourage self-efficacy and positive outcome, and are instructed in methods that will assist them in tackling the identified risk factors. Having said this, it is likely that SM documentation techniques will make a valuable contribution to the success of any therapy by providing critical insight into the mechanisms driving patients' symptoms.

Relaxation Therapy

Treatment Aims

The use of relaxation therapy (RT) in the treatment of tics is based on the observation that increases in stress and anxiety can result in concomitant increases in tic frequency and severity. Reducing stress and anxiety through applying relaxation techniques could therefore reduce this contributing/precipitating factor [4;5]. An additional useful aspect of relaxation is reduction in muscular tension, a physiological effect which may help reduce negative sensory feedback which could contribute to the urge to tic. In addition, adopting the physical state of a relaxed person may feedback important cues to the conscious mind enabling the patient to reduce their stress level.

Methods

RT can include deep or diaphragmatic breathing [52], progressive muscle training [53], imagery [54], and 'autogenic training': self statements of relaxation [55]. Electromyographic feedback can also be used to aid the patient to enter a relaxed state and to learn how to control themselves physiologically in order to achieve this [46]. RT is often applied as part of a

multi-component treatment, e.g. with HR (e.g. [15]). Patients are instructed in these procedures and advised to practice them on a daily basis for a set period (e.g. 10-15 minutes). They may also be applied during periods when tics are more problematic. Bergin et al [46] describe training in behavioral relaxation which first involved teaching patients to adopt 10 postures characteristic of a relaxed state (e.g., eyelids lightly closed, absence of eye movements, stillness of throat, and relaxed posture of body parts and a quiet breathing pattern) that have been shown to correlate with actual relaxation. Applied relaxation training was then used which instructed patients how to identify tics and apply a rapid relaxation technique, initially to cope with, and ultimately, to help reduce their symptoms. Homework assignments and electromyographic biofeedback were also used to facilitate treatment response.

Efficacy

Application of RT by Bergin et al [46] in 16 children with TS, led them to have an increased ability to relax. Tic ratings improved at 6 weeks according to both clinician rated scales and video ratings, and this improvement seemed much greater than for a minimal treatment control group. However, the noted differences did not reach clinical significance. In addition, increased relaxation did not significantly affect behavioral symptoms recorded using the Child Behavioral Checklist. Peterson and Azrin [47] found that RT resulted in an average tic decrease of 32% in six patients, which was less than the effect of HR (55% decrease) or SM (45% decrease).Other studies have reported that RT can be helpful, but tics often recur [37;40;56].

Predictors of Treatment Response

Some of the patients in the study conducted by Bergin et al [46] had ADHD which could have affected their compliance or ability to apply the recommended technique. Indeed, overall compliance was not very good for this study: on average, less than half of the advised time was spent by patients on training, which could help explain why gains failed to reach significance. Clearly, training in relaxation has the greatest potential to benefit those patients who experience stress and anxiety which is linked to their tics.

Limitations

There is difficulty in evaluating the effectiveness of RT due to small sample sizes, lack of evidence if technique was applied and mastered, and problems with reliance on self report scales for some studies [46]. These authors suggest that the implementation of behavioral training is limited by the need for a co-operative motivated patient, frequent training sessions, availability of an experienced teacher, and the financial cost of the therapist's time.

Psychotherapy

Treatment Aims

Psychotherapy does not tackle tics directly, but it may prove beneficial for some patients. Mood symptoms and self-esteem problems are common, and may play a mediating role in tic severity due to increased self-consciousness or negative cognitions about the self, which lead

to stress, feelings of helplessness and related symptom exacerbation. Psychotherapeutic treatment may benefit the patient by addressing contributing psychological problems. This in turn could help reduce tics to some degree.

Methods

Tourette's Syndrome can be associated with anxiety, anger, depression and internalising and externalising symptoms such as withdrawal or aggression. Psychotherapy may help patients understand the causes of these symptoms and offer insight into how behaviour and cognitions can be modified to improve wellbeing. The role of the therapist is to listen to the patient and support them in coping with their symptoms and the discomfort caused by the disorder, by assisting them in addressing social and emotional problems. Therapists can be non-directive, allowing the patient to select the therapy session topic, during which the focus will be on reflecting on and expressing feelings about current life issues and problem solving.

Efficacy

A randomised controlled trial by Wilhelm et al [19] involving 32 adults with TS compared the effectiveness of HR and supportive psychotherapy. HR led to significantly lower tic ratings post treatment, but psychotherapy did not. Similar findings were reported in another study of 30 adults with TS [18]. However, patients may report benefits in psychological status that can be unrelated to changes in tics. Deckersbach et al [18] reported improvement in life-satisfaction and psychosocial functioning.

Predictors of Treatment Response

As few studies have investigated the application of psychotherapy in TS, likely predictors of treatment outcome have not yet been examined. A few more general factors likely to influence the effectiveness of this treatment may be noted. The success of psychotherapy will partly depend on the patients' willingness to discuss problem issues and their beliefs in their ability to cope with these problems. Self-disclosure may in turn depend on having a good rapport with the therapist.

Limitations

There is no evidence that psychotherapy alone is likely to have a direct effect in terms of improving tic symptoms. However, positive effects in other areas of the patients functioning may be seen, which in turn lesser the burden of their condition. Conversely, if psychotherapy raises difficult issues that the patient is unable to deal with successfully, there could be the potential for a detrimental effect on tics. Further research is necessary to evaluate these possibilities.

Cognitive Behavioural Therapy

Treatment Aims

The cognitive component of the intervention consisted of mentally challenging and restructuring the way patients evaluate their expectations and actions in high-risk situations. CBT is often used in OCD, but has the potential to assist with tic symptoms.

Methods

CBT involves helping the patient understand the relationship and interactions between their feelings (including physiological sensations), thoughts, and behaviour. The patient is taught to recognize anxious and dysfunctional feelings and thoughts, and how these contribute to their symptoms (e.g. compulsions or tic exacerbation). The therapist assists the patient in learning how to challenge and modify these unhelpful thoughts and replace them with more productive coping thoughts. CBT may also involve learning relaxation techniques or conditioning strategies. This therapy can help reduce anxiety and problem symptoms through identifying specific unrealistic thoughts, replacing these with realistic beliefs, and encouraging the patient to address and confront fears in order to re-program their thought patterns. CBT could therefore assist patients with tics to reduce anxiety factors related to their symptoms, which could in turn help reduce tics.

Efficacy

One study compared CBT with HR in CTD and found comparable results for both treatments [20]. In another study, CBT combined with HR in CTD was found to improve tics when compared to waiting list control [57].

In a later study by O-Connor et al [58], CBT was administered to 76 people diagnosed with either TS or chronic tic disorder. Medicated and non-medicated groups were compared. Participants underwent four months of individualized, manual-based CBT. Both medicated and unmedicated groups' tics greatly improved from the CBT. The unmedicated group improved in terms of anxiety, and both groups' depressive symptoms decreased.

Lavoie et al [59] carried out a study in which 10 adults with Tourette syndrome and 14 adults with no neurological impairment completed a series of tasks which stimulated specific brain regions, while an electroencephalogram was used to assess brain activity. Six months later this assessment was repeated after the patients had received CBT. A quantifiable "normalization" of brain activity along with an improvement in tics was reported. Although further research is needed, this study suggests that CBT in TS could actually lead to neural changes which could be related to effectiveness in treating patients' symptoms.

Predictors of Treatment Response

The success of CBT is likely to be greater when the patient is motivated, shows insight into their condition, believes they can overcome their symptoms, and is compliant with directed homework tasks. As CBT is often used to combat OCD [60], individuals with this condition may benefit most from this form of behavioural therapy.

Limitations

CBT is likely to be less successful for patients who lack insight into their symptoms. It could be useful in tackling anxiety, OCD symptoms, and the cognitive factors that affect tics. However, it may have limited success because it does not address the physiological aspects of tics (i.e. premonitory sensations).

Other Therapies

Other specific therapies applied in TS have used reward related conditioning, such as response contingencies [61], token economy [62] and shock punishment [63]. Contingency management involves the manipulation of environmental contingencies, so that tic-free intervals are positively reinforced while tic behaviours are ignored. Using tokens to reinforce the absence of tics is an example of a CM-based intervention [64]. This method tends to be applied as part of multi-component treatment packages, therefore its effectiveness has not been evaluated independently. It may be more often used with patients with ADHD [65]. A more specific type of CM is known as 'function based interventions' (FBI). During FBI, factors specific to the patients' own environment are indentified which are thought to be associated with an increase or decrease in tics. These factors are then modified in order to lead to a reduction in tics. This technique has been applied in a few single-case studies [66].

Conclusion

Summary of Study Findings

Although some behavioural therapies are accompanied by greater evidence of efficacy, the most successful treatment for an individual will at least partly depend on the nature of tic symptoms, personality and motivation, presence of co-morbid conditions, environmental conditions, and the time scale focused on. HR may be effective at treating an identified problem tic but another may develop in its place. However, relaxation therapy may be less acutely effective but lead to milder, more generalizable and durable gains. MP may lead to short term improvements but cannot be applied for more physically damaging tics and is hard to practice in social environments. Hypnotherapy may be more effective in patients who are more suggestible, while psychotherapy may be more effective for patients with emotional issues which contribute to tic severity. CBT could be useful in teaching cognitive techniques to help with tic control, and could be particularly effective when paired with HR or biofeedback, which encourage control of physiological reactions. SM offers important insight as a basis for many other approaches. While those with OCD may be more equipped to profit from therapies which depend on insight, reflection and commitment, individuals with attentional difficulties may respond best to reward related conditioning. Overall however, it is likely that the most effective treatment packages will empower patients and encourage self-efficacy, while combining techniques designed to combat problem behaviours, movements, emotions and cognitions which interact in determining symptom severity.

Summary of Study Limitations

There are many difficulties in evaluating the effectiveness of available behavioural treatments for TS, including methodological problems with many existing studies. These include small numbers of participants, lack of inclusion of control groups, and potential concurrent medication confounds. Some therapies have been mainly explored in combination

with other behavioural treatments. Other limitations include the use of subjective report rather than more objective measures of outcome and drop-outs which can lead to inflated estimates of treatment effectiveness, as the individuals who withdraw from treatment may do so due to poor response. One critical difficulty in drawing comparisons across studies is that studies vary in the approach they employ to assess efficacy. For example, effectiveness may be considered in terms of the percentage of patients given treatment whose symptoms improve, or by the mean percentage improvement in tic severity or frequency shown by the treatment group. Another significant limitation is the lack of inclusion of QoL measures, which may be particularly useful in indicating which treatments lead to improved functioning in addition to symptom changes, and are most advantageous in a broader context according to the patient's perspective. While it is understandably difficult to achieve placebo control or blinded trials in this area, improved scientific rigour is needed for the advancement of our knowledge.

More fundamental problems arise due to the nature of TS. Long-term studies are encouraged by the finding that tics tend to follow a waxing and waning course, which could obscure treatment effects. In relation to tic severity, some interventions may be effective only in mild cases, whereas others may only show an effect in patients with more severe tics who have the potential to exhibit improvement across a wider scale.

FUTURE DIRECTIONS

Although individual patients' symptoms and characteristics are likely to affect the suitability and outcome of a particular therapy, overall this has been poorly explored. Initial indications suggest that factors that may be useful in selecting treatments and their ultimate effectiveness encompass cognitive, physiological and psychosocial domains. For example, attention and inhibitory functions, the ability reflect and achieve insight into symptoms, sensory or physiological awareness, motivation, self-efficacy and commitment, are all likely to make important contributions to therapy appropriateness and experience. Further research into the mechanisms by which symptoms can be improved for individuals exhibiting specific symptoms profiles and psychological characteristics will cement the role of behavioural therapies as safe and efficacious first-line options for this chronic neurodevelopmental condition.

REFERENCES

[1] Eddy, C. M., Rickards, H. & Cavanna, A.E. (2011). Treatment strategies for tics in Tourette syndrome. *Therapeutic Advances in Neurological Disorders*, 4, 25-45.

[2] Bliss, J. (1980). Sensory experiences of Gilles de la Tourette syndrome. *Archives of General Psychiatry*, *37*, 1343-1347.

[3] Bullen, J. G. & Hemsley, D. R. (1983). Sensory experience as a trigger in Gilles de la Tourette's syndrome. *Journal of Behavior Therapy and Experimental Psychiatry*, *14*, 197-201.

[4] Bornstein, R. A., Steft, M. E., & Hammond, L. (1990). A survey of Tourette syndrome patients and their families: The 1987 Ohio Tourette Survey. *Journal of Neuropsychiatry and Clinical Neurosciences*, *2*, 275-281.

[5] Robertson, M. M. (1989). The Gilles de la Tourette syndrome: The current status. *British Journal of Psychiatry*, 154, 147-169.

[6] Azrin, N. H., & Nunn, R.G. (1973). Habit reversal: A method of eliminating nervous habits and tics. *Behaviour Research and Therapy,* 11, 619-628.

[7] Miltenberger, R. G., Fuqua, R. W. & McKinley, T. (1985). Habit reversal with muscle tics: replication and component analysis. *Behavior Therapy*, 16(1), 39–50.

[8] Woods, D.W., Miltenberger, R.G. & Lumley, V. (1996). Sequential application of major habit reversal components to treat motor tics in children. *Journal of Applied Behavior Analysis*, 29, 483-493.

[9] Himle, M.B., Woods, D.W., Piacentini, J.C. & Walkup, J.T. (2006). Brief review of habit reversal training for Tourette Syndrome. *Journal of Child Neurology*, 21, 719-725.

[10] Azrin, N. H., & Peterson, A. L. (1988). Habit reversal for the treatment of Tourette Syndrome. *Behavior Research and Therapy, 26,* 347-351.

[11] Finney, J. W. Rapoff, M. A., Hall, C. H., & Christopherson, E. R (1983). Replication and social validation of habit reversal treatment for tics. *Behavior Therapy, 14,* 116-126.

[12] Franco, D. P. (1981). Habit reversal and isometric tensing with motor tics. *Dissertation Abstracts International, 42,* 3418B.

[13] Zikis, P. (1983). Habit reversal treatment of a 10-year-old school boy with severe tics. *Behavior Therapy, 6,* 50-51

[14] Azrin, N. H., Nunn, R.G. & Frantz, S.E. (1980). Habit Reversal Vs. Negative Practice: Treatment of Nervous Tics. *Behavior Therapy*, 11, 169-178.

[15] Azrin, N. H. & Peterson, A. L. (1990) Treatment of Tourette Syndrome by habit reversal: A waiting list control group comparison. *Behavior Therapy*, 21, 305-318.

[16] Woods, D. W, Miltenberger, R. G. & Lumley, V. (1996). Sequential application of major habit-reversal components to treat motor tics in children. *Journal of Applied Behavior Analysis*, 29, 483–493.

[17] Woods, D. W., Twohig, M. P., Flessner, C. A. & Roloff, T. J. (2003). Treatment of vocal tics in children with Tourette Syndrome: Investigating the efficacy of habit reversal. *Journal of Applied Behavior Analysis*, 36, 109-112.

[18] Deckersbach, T., Rauc, S., Buhlmann, U. & Wilhelm, S. (2006). Habit reversal versus supportive psychotherapy in Tourette's disorder: a randomized controlled trial and predictors of treatment response. *Behavior Research and Therapy*, 44(8), 1079-90.

[19] Wilhelm, S., Deckersbach, T., Coffey, B.J., Bohne, A., Peterson, A. L. & Baer, L. (2003). Habit reversal versus supportive psychotherapy for Tourette's disorder: A randomized controlled trial. *American Journal of Psychiatry*, 160, 1175–1177.

[20] O'Connor, K., Gareau, D. and Borgeat, F. (1997). A comparison of a behavioural and a cognitive behavioural approach to the management of chronic tic disorders. *Clinical Psychiatry and Psychotherapy*, 4, 105-117.

[21] Piacentini, J. & Chang, S. (2005). Habit reversal training for tic disorders in children and adolescents. *Behavior Modification*, 29, 803-822.

[22] Piacentini, J., Woods, D. W., Scahill, L., Wilhelm, S., Peterson, A. L., Chang, S., Ginsburg, G.S., Deckersbach, T., Dziura, J., Levi-Pearl, S. & Walkup, J.T. (2010). Behavior therapy for children with Tourette disorder: a randomized controlled trial. *Journal of the American Medical Association*, 303(19), 1929-37.

[23] Banaschewski, T., Woerner, W. & Rothenberger, A. (2003). Premonitory sensory phenomena and suppressibility of tics in Tourette Syndrome -developmental aspects in children. *Developmental Medicine and Child Neurology*, 45, 700–703.

[24] Robertson, M.M. and Stern, J.S. (2000). Gilles de la Tourette Syndrome: symptomatic treatment based on evidence. *European Journal of Child and Adolescent Psychiatry*, 9, 60-75.

[25] Verdellen, C. W. J., Keijers, G. P. J., Cath, D. C. & Hoogduin, C. A. L. (2004). Exposure and response prevention versus habit reversal in Tourette's Syndrome: a controlled study. *Behavior Research and Therapy*, 42, 501-511.

[26] Hoogduin, K., Verdellen, C. & Cath, D. (1997). Exposure and response prevention in the treatment of Gilles de la Tourette's syndrome: Four case studies. *Clinical Psychology and Psychotherapy*, 4, 125-137.

[27] Verdellen, C.W.J., Hoogduin, C.A.L. and Keijers, G.P.J. (2007) Tic suppression in the treatment of Tourette's Syndrome with exposure therapy: the rebound phenomenon reconsidered. *Movement Disorders* 22, 1601-1606.

[28] Dunlap, K. (1932). *Habits: Their making and unmaking.* New York, Liveright.

[29] Azrin, N. H., Nunn, R. G. and Frantz, S. E. (1980) Habit reversal versus negative practice treatment for nervous tics. *Behavior Therapy*, 11, 169-178.

[30] Savicki, V., & Carlin, A. S. (1972). Behavioral treatment of Gilles de la Tourette's syndrome. *International Journal of Child Psychotherapy,* 1, 97-109.

[31] Clark, D. F. (1966). Behavior therapy of Gilles de la Tourette's syndrome. *British Journal of Psychiatry,* 112, 771-778.

[32] Walton, D. (1961). Experimental psychology and the treatment of a tiqueur. *Journal of Child Psychology and Psychiatry,* 2, 148-155.

[33] Walton, D. (1964). Massed practice and simultaneous reduction in drive level--Further evidence of the efficacy of this approach to the treatment of tics. In H. J. Eysenck (Ed.), *Experiments in Behavior Therapy.* London, Pergamon Press.

[34] Yates, A.J. (1958). The application of learning theory to the treatment of tics. *Journal of Abnormal and Social Psychology,* 56, 175-182.

[35] Chapel, J.L. (1970). Behavior modification techniques with children and adolescents. *Canadian Psychiatric Association Journal,* 15, 315-318.

[36] Turner, S. M., Hersen, M., & Alford, H. (1974). Effects of massed practice and meprobamate on spasmodic torticollis: An experimental analysis. *Behaviour Research and Therapy,* 12, 259-260.

[37] Tophoff, M. (1973). Massed negative practice, relaxation and assertion training in the treatment of Gilles de la Tourette's syndrome. *Journal of Behavior Therapy and Experimental Psychiatry*, 4, 71-3.

[38] Storms, L. (1985). Massed negative practice as a behavioral treatment for Gilles de la Tourette's syndrome. *American Journal of Psychotherapy,* 39(2), 277-81.

[39] Hollandsworth, J. G. & Bausinger, L. (1978). Unsuccessful use of massed practice in the treatment of Gilles de la Tourette syndrome. *Psychological Reports*, 43(2), 671-677.

[40] Turpin, G. & Powell, G. E. (1984). Effects of massed practice and cue controlled relaxation on tic frequency in Gilles de la Tourette's syndrome. *Behavior Research and Therapy*, 22, 165-78.

[41] Tansey, M. A. (1986). A simple and a complex tic (Gilles de la Tourette's syndrome): their response to EEG sensorimotor rhythm biofeedback training. *International Journal of Psychophysiology*, 4(2), 91-97.

[42] Breteler, M. H. M, van Heeswijk, L., Arns, M. & Verdellen, C. (2008). Psychologische interventies bij het syndroom van Gilles de la Tourette [Psychological interventions in Gilles de la Tourette syndrome]. *Tijdschrift voor Neuropsychiatrie en Gedragsneurologie*, 7, 158-164.

[43] Nagai, Y., Cavanna, A. & Critchley, H. D. (2009). Influence of sympathetic autonomic arousal on tics: Implications for a therapeutic behavioral intervention for Tourette syndrome. *Journal of Psychosomatic Research*, 67, 599-605.

[44] Culbertson, F. M. (1989). A four-step hypnotherapy model for Gilles de la Tourette's syndrome. *American Journal of Clinical Hypnotherapy*, 31, 252–256.

[45] Lazarus, J. E. & Klein, S. K. (2010). Nonpharmacological treatment of tics in Tourette syndrome adding videotape training to self-hypnosis. *Journal of Developmental and Behavioural Pediatrics*, 31(6), 498-504.

[46] Bergin, A., Waranch, H. R., Brown, J., Carson, K. & Singer, H. S. (1998). Relaxation therapy in Tourette syndrome: A pilot study. *Pediatric Neurology*, 18, 136-142.

[47] Peterson, A.L. & Azrin, N.H. (1992). An evaluation of behavioral treatments for Tourette syndrome. *Behavior Research and Therapy*, 30, 167-74.

[48] Hutzell, R. R., Platzek, D., & Logue, P.E. (1974) Control of symptoms of Gilles de la Tourette's syndrome by self-monitoring. *Journal of Behavior Therapy and Experimental Psychiatry,* 5, 71-76.

[49] Billings, A. (1978). Self-monitoring in the treatment of tics: a single subject analysis. *Journal of Behavior Therapy and Experimental Psychiatry*, 9(4), 339-342.

[50] Burd, L. & Kerbeshian, J. (1987). Treatment generated problems associated with behavior modification in Tourette disorder. *Developmental Medicine and Child Neurology*, 29, 831-3.

[51] Silva, R. R., Munoz, D. M., Barickman, J.,&Friedhoff, A. J. (1995). Environmental factors and related fluctuation of symptoms in children and adolescents withTourette's disorder. *Journal of Child Psychology and Psychiatry*, 36, 305-312.

[52] Cappo, B. M., & Holmes, D. S. (1984). The utility of prolonged respiratory exhalation for reducing physiological and psychological arousal in non-threatening and threatening situations. *Journal of Psychosomatic Research, 28,* 265-273.

[53] Jacobson, E. (1938). *Progressive relaxation.* Chicago, University of Chicago Press.

[54] Suinn, R. M. (1975). Anxiety management training for general anxiety. In R M Suinn & R G. Welgel (Eds.) *The lnnovative Psychological Therapies. Critical and Creative Contributions*. New York, Harper & Row.

[55] Schultz, J., & Luthe, W. (1959). *Autogenic training: A psychophysiologic approach in psychotherapy.* New York, Grune & Stratton.

[56] Canavan, A. G. M. & Powell, G.E. (1981).The efficacy of several treatments of Gilles de la Tourette's syndrome as assessed in a single case. *Behavior Research and Therapy*, 19, 549-56.

[57] O'Connor, K. P., Brault, M., Robillard, S., Loiselle, J., Borgeat, F. & Stip, E. (2001). Evaluation of a cognitive-behavioural program for the management of chronic tic and habit disorders. *Behavior Research and Therapy*, 39(6), 667-681.

[58] O'Connor, K. P., Laverdure, A., Taillon, A., Stip, E., Borgeat, F. & Lavoie, M. (2009). Cognitive behavioral management of Tourette's syndrome and chronic tic disorder in medicated and unmedicated samples. *Behavior Research and Therapy*, 47(12), 1090-5.

[59] Lavoie, M. E., Imbriglio, T. V., Stip, E. & O'Connor, K.P. (2011). "Neurocognitive changes following cognitive-behavioral treatment in the Tourette syndrome and chronic tic disorder." *International Journal of Cognitive Psychotherapy* (4)1, 34-50.

[60] March, J.S. (1995). Cognitive-behavioral treatments for children and adolescents with OCD: a review and recommendations for treatment. *Journal of the American Academy of Child and Adolescent Psychiatry*, 34, 7-18.

[61] Barrett, B. H. (1962). Reduction in rate of multiple tics by free operant conditioning methods. *Journal of Nervous and Mental Disease,* 135, 187-195.

[62] Doleys, D. M., & Kurtz, P.S. (1974). A behavioral treatment program for the Gilles de la Tourette syndrome. *Psychological Reports,* 35, 43-48.

[63] Brierley, H. (1967). The treatment of hysterical spasmodic torticollis by behavior therapy. *Behaviour Research and Therapy,* 5, 139-142.

[64] Woods, D. W. & Himle, M. B. (2004). Creating tic suppression: comparing the effects of verbal instruction to differential reinforcement. *Journal of Applied Behavioral Analysis*, 37(3), 417–420.

[65] Pelham, W. E., Wheeler, T. & Chronis, A. (1988). Empirically supported psychosocial treatments for attention deficit hyperactivity disorder. *Journal of Clinical Child Psychology*, 27, 190-205.

[66] Watson, T. S. & Sterling, H. E. (1998). Brief functional analysis and treatment of a vocal tic. *Journal of Applied Behavior Analysis*, 31(3), 471–474.

In: Advances in Psychology Research. Volume 88
Editor: Alexandra M. Columbus, pp. 161-177
ISBN: 978-1-62100-591-9

Chapter 8

DEPRESSION AND ITS IMPACT ON OSTEOARTHRITIS OUTCOMES

Ray Marks*
School of Health and behavioral Sciences, Department of Health, Physical Education & Gerontological Studies and Services, City University of New York, York College and Department of Health and Behavior Studies, Program in Health Education, Columbia University, Teachers College, New York, U.S.A.

ABSTRACT

Psychological conditions are highly prevalent among adults in general, and among adults with chronic diseases, in particular. This chapter describes the literature and research evidence concerning the nature of depression, its prevalence among aging adults, and the impact of comorbid and/or concurrent depressive symptoms among adults with hip or knee osteoarthritis, a highly prevalent and painful disabling joint disease. It also advocates for improved efforts to identify and treat concomitant depression among adults with osteoarthritis in the context of the community as well as the surgical setting. To this end, the author reports data embedded in the relevant literature using PubMed, Scopus, Science Citation and PsychInfo data bases over the last twenty years, as well as data extracted from the records of 1,000 hip osteoarthritis surgical candidates and 100 community dwelling cases of knee osteoarthritis that highlight the magnitude and impact of the presence of a comorbid depression or depression/anxiety anxiety, as well as concurrent depressive symptoms on selected disease features and treatment outcomes. Based on this evidence, the author highlights the importance of comprehensive efforts to prevent, identify and treat comorbid depression among people with chronic pain due to osteoarthritis. The author's insights and analysis should be of specific interest to clinicians working in this area who seek to apply their skills towards reducing the immense burden of osteoarthritis and heightening their patients' life quality.

* Correspondence and requests for reprints should be sent to: Dr. Ray Marks, Department of Health and Behavior Studies, Columbia University, Teachers College, Box 114, 525W 120th Street, New York, NY 10027; Tel: 1-212-678-3445, Fax: 1-212-678-8259: e-mail: rm226@columbia.edu

INTRODUCTION

Osteoarthritis, the most common joint disease, causes appreciable pain and disability in a high percentage of people over the age of 55 [1-5]. Principally due to symptomatic pathological changes in the articular cartilage and underlying bone structures of one or more joints, [6-7] osteoarthritis can be extremely debilitating [8-9]. Often attributed to the wear and tear processes of aging, a variety of medical comorbidities and biological factors may contribute to its pathogenesis [10-14]. Moreover, the disease is likely to be influenced adversely by psychological factors, including mood disorders such as depression [15-22], a condition occurring frequently in the general population [23].

However, although depression occurs with a lifetime prevalence of approximately 20 percent in the general population [23], many of whom may suffer from painful disabling osteoarthritis, with few exceptions, there is very little specific information about the extent to which mood disorders occur in populations with osteoarthritis. Moreover, several existing studies on the topic have examined samples of osteoarthritis cases alongside cases of inflammatory arthritis, as well as other comorbid conditions. Hence, the precise role of depression in the natural history of osteoarthritis, and the degree to which health outcomes are uniquely impacted by depression among adults with osteoarthritis is not well understood. In addition, even though one report has stressed a need for the evaluation of a patients' mental health status at time of hip replacement surgery for end-stage hip osteoarthritis [17], and depression has been associated with a higher risk of moderate-severe activity limitations for up to 5 years post-surgery [24], another found no such existing relationship between these factors [25]. Similarly, even though depression may be related to elevated pain levels among adults with osteoarthritis [26], Riddle et al. [27] found no relationship between psychological predictors such as depression and the pain outcomes of cases who had undergone knee joint replacement surgery for their osteoarthritis.

Given the unrelenting personal and societal burden imposed by osteoarthritis among the older population, the goal of this review was to explore if depression is a common finding in adults with osteoarthritis, and if so, how depression impacts osteoarthritis health outcomes. By analogy, a second aim was to examine the potential role of intervening to minimize depression in the context of allaying or slowing the progression of osteoarthritis disability. To this end, this review examines the prevailing literature on osteoarthritis and depression. In addition, it details some recent data collected by the author that highlights the extent to which pre-morbid and/or concurrent symptoms of depression appear to prevail among adults with advanced hip joint disease about to undergo hip replacement or revision surgery for a failed hip replacement. It also presents recent findings observed among a cohort of community dwelling elders with mild to moderate knee osteoarthritis that is pertinent to this topic. More specifically, the association between the presence of a pre existing mood disorder, and the patients' pre and post surgical status observed among hip osteoarthritis cases is documented. As well, a summary of the relationship between depression and the knee osteoarthritis patient's clinical status is examined.

It was felt this information would be consistent with the need for ongoing efforts to broaden our knowledge base concerning factors that impact osteoarthritis disability, particularly with respect to the long term prognosis of this condition. The information was also deemed consistent with the goal of identifying what prevention/intervention strategies

other than those currently considered standard practice might prove efficacious in the future for maximizing the affected individuals' functional status. Commonly a neglected area of therapeutic concern, the author's purpose was to provide a firm rationale for supporting the role of heightened efforts to prevent, identify and treat depression among people diagnosed as having chronic disabling osteoarthritis.

In the first section of this chapter, some background information on depression is provided. Then some data from separate clinical observations of selected cohorts with hip and knee osteoarthritis is presented. The chapter concludes by summarizing the key findings from these data and by providing guidelines for clinical practice and future research endeavors.

Depression among Adults with Chronic Disease

It is well documented that a large proportion of older adults [28, 29], as well as adults with one or more chronic diseases suffer from clinical depression that can range from mild to severe, and this can occur at higher rates than that of the general population [30]. In the context of osteoarthritis, a chronic disabling joint disease, frequently associated with obesity [31] and cardiovascular problems including diabetes, related work by Khuwaja et al. [32] shows that depression, which is independently associated with symptoms of high blood pressure, blood glucose and blood triglyceride levels can potentially increase the burden of the disease quite significantly. In addition, high body mass indices, often associated with osteoarthritis disability, are found to be independently associated with depression, and can significantly limit the ability of the individual to carry out activities of daily living that affect wellbeing [33]. As well, among adults at risk for excess weight, a problem strongly associated with being overweight and knee osteoarthritis, older women with high rather than low rates of depressive symptoms were specifically affected [34].

Additional work by Hooten et al. [35] has also identified a link between depression and pain severity in patients with chronic pain. This linkage is especially important in the context of managing osteoarthritis because pain is commonly the most serious complaint of the individual with this condition, and can seriously interfere with one's ability to function both physically as well as socially. In turn, this added risk of activity limitations when mood disorders and osteoarthritis coexist, potentially heightens functional disability as well as pain and emotional distress. In addition, when controlling for other factors, osteoarthritis pain increases the risk for reactive depression. It is not surprising therefore, that these inter-related effects are found to exacerbate pain and disability over time [36], and have the potential to increase the risk of incurring predictable functional declines among knee and/or hip osteoarthritis sufferers [37].

The patient with severe osteoarthritis requiring joint replacement surgery who commonly has chronically painful advanced end-stage disease can consequently be expected to show a high prevalence of psychopathology, psychological distress, and poor pain scores, excess disability, limited function, and lower life quality than non-psychologically distressed patients [38]. Similarly, among patients with painful disabling osteoarthritis attending an outpatient clinic, up to 40 percent of cases had a mood disorder, and pain intensity, rather than radiological severity was found to be correlated with the patient's depression scores. In addition, those with depression had higher disability rates than those with no depression [20].

This was a high rate of clinically significant depression and anxiety and was higher than that recorded in a previous study by Abdel-Nasser et al. [14] of cases with rheumatoid arthritis, thought to be a more severe disease, where only 10% of the sample reported a prior medical history of depression and/or anxiety. Similarly, in a study by Stebbings et al. [39], osteoarthritis participants reported greater pain, disability, depression and sleeplessness than those with rheumatoid arthritis (all $p < 0.01$). In those with osteoarthritis, the correlates of fatigue, often not associated strongly with osteoarthritis, were older age ($p = 0.02$), sleep disturbances ($p = 0.03$), depression ($p = 0.04$), disability ($p = 0.04$) and lower C-Reactive Protein ($p = 0.001$).

Other research of osteoarthritis patients has shown these patients can exhibit progressive decreases in mental health over time ($p<.001$), and that those with generalized osteoarthritis suffer more disease-associated consequences with relatively lower health than those with knee or hip problems alone [19]. As previously mentioned, they also exhibit greater pain as well as reduced physical ability if they are depressed ($p<.05$), and this association is particularly common among women with the condition ($p<.05$). In turn, their disability, has been associated with a reduced ability to cope, and an increased risk of further depression and more pain ($p<.05$) [20]. Another related study of 171 patients with osteoarthritis who completed a pre treatment battery of questionnaires concerning their status before and after a pain coping skills intervention has suggested that those patients who are psychologically distressed are less likely to be optimistic about engaging in treatments that are crucial for minimizing this disability [40]. While depression is common in older populations, depression and its symptoms have been observed to occur readily in younger and less educated osteoarthritis cases, where the correlation between osteoarthritis and its impact, and depression is high [15].

Findings from Hip Osteoarthritis Cases

To examine whether cases with end-stage osteoarthritis may also be depressed, or have a depression history, an analysis of data extracted systematically from the pre-existing records of a cohort of 1,000 North American hip replacement surgical candidates depicting their baseline pre-operative status and their immediate post-surgical functional status and discharge destination was recently conducted. Preoperative measures included body mass index, walking ability, and self-reported subjective pain on a 5 point Likert scale ranging from 0 (no pain) to 4 (severe pain). Postoperative measures included walking distances, one and three days after surgery, and the discharge destination. Subjects were either classified as having a depression history, a depression and anxiety history (trait depression), or symptoms of state depression [see reference 41 for details].

Data analyses constituted a 2-phase process, wherein the first phase involved the calculation and recording of the descriptive information of interest. Thereafter, the data were disaggregated to garner an estimate of the prevalence of trait and state depression among the cohort. These sub-groups included patients with a prior depression history, patients with a conjoint depression and anxiety history, and patients reporting pre-surgical symptoms of depression.

To ascertain how mood disorders might specifically impact adults diagnosed as having debilitating hip joint osteoarthritis, a comparative analysis of the relationship between several

disease-associated characteristics of these sub-groups and a random sample of hip osteoarthritis surgical candidates from the same cohort with no evidence of any comorbid condition was conducted. In addition, to tease out factors of import that might guide practice, research or thinking about how to improve practice in the future, selected correlational analyses were carried out using chi-square, t-tests and analysis of variance and the SPSS statistical software package, version *12.0.*

The demographic results were reasonably typical of those expected from a similar group of patients as reported in other studies [24]. That is, the cohort had a mean age of 65±13.4 years, 60 percent were women, and 55 percent had at least one comorbid condition related to an insufficiency of the cardiovascular or respiratory systems. The average body mass index of the cohort was 27.5±5.6 $kg.m^{-2}$ indicating the group was overweight, on average.

In terms of their affective status, over 180 cases or 18% of the present cohort reported a prior affective disorder history, of either depression or anxiety or both, or were experiencing pre-surgical psychological distress. Of these cases, 50 or 5% specifically reported having a depression history, 2 or .2% had a bipolar disorder, and 20 or 2% had conjoint depression and anxiety histories. Importantly, among the sub-group with pre-existing depression, 28% reported their mental health status was impacted by their pending surgery, such that 12 said they felt anxious and two said they felt depressed, including one patient who had attempted suicide. Five additional patients with pre-existing depression and anxiety histories reported situational anxiety and one reported feeling depressed. Moreover, eight cases without any pre-existing affective disorder reported feeling depressed during the pre-operative period because of the pain they were experiencing and its detrimental impact on their functional ability, and one case who expressed feeling depressed, also expressed fear about being 'hurt' by the nurse.

The sub-group data clearly showed that regardless of sub-group allocation, the majority of those with depressive symptoms or histories were women. Those patients reporting a depression history were also older and weighed more on average than those with no depression history, and the majority in this group were obese. Moreover, this sub-group of hip osteoarthritis patients reported higher levels of pain on average than the controls with no such history (p=0.000), and 44% were experiencing severe pain prior to surgery. Similar to those with a depression history, those with anxiety and depression histories had histories of back pain in two cases, knee pain in four cases and rheumatoid arthritis in one case and on average patients in these groups consumed 3 prescribed medications daily, and this group had higher pain levels than the group with depression only as well as those with no health problems.

Numbers of comorbid conditions varied significantly among sub-groups with and without a mood history or symptoms of psychological distress (p=.000), and the two most commonly identified comorbid conditions in this subgroup were respiratory conditions and hypertension.

In terms of post-operative recovery rates, patients with a depression history walked an average of 7.14±11.60 foot compared to the controls with no depression history undergoing the same surgery who walked 13.46±21.72 foot on average (p=.000) on the first day after surgery. The group with depression and anxiety histories walked 7.47±13.11 foot on average, which was comparable to those with a depression history.

Three days after surgery, walking distance increased to 77.9 foot on average for those with depression histories, and 74.45±65.89 foot for the depressed and anxious cohort. Walking distance was 114 foot on average for matched subjects undergoing the same surgery but with no other health condition (p=.000). In addition, only 20% of those with state

depression could walk further than 100 foot, while 57% of those with no comorbid medical histories or affective symptoms could walk more than 100 foot. The walking distances were thus marginally lower for those with trait depression compared to those with no history of depression, both before and immediately after surgery.

In terms of discharge destination, recovery was better for those with no comorbid health problem (p=.009). That is, while 80% of those with depression histories were discharged to rehabilitation centers, 80% of those with no affective or comorbid history were discharged to their homes. Table 1 describes the variation in characteristics of a matched group of cases with and without depression histories as regards, discharge destination, rates of severe pain, plus functional outcomes.

Table 1. Table Showing Selected Comparisons Between Hip Osteoarthritis Surgery Candidates With and Without a Depression History

Factor	Depression History (N=47)	No Depression History (N=47)	p -value
Mean age [SD] years	65.54 +11.58	62.51+11.50	.209
Gender % female	66%	48%	.017
# Comorbid conditions	1.3 +.44	0	.000
Mean pain scores (0-4)	3.29+.83	2.84+.93	.088
% in severe pain (4 on 0-4 scale)	36.2%	6.4%	.000
Blocks walked pre-surgery	3.09+4.1	4.81+4.9	.089
Day 1 walking distance (ft)	7.76+12.03	13.46+21.7	.067
Day 3 walking distance (ft)	75.83 +59.37	117.11+69.81	.062
Discharged to home	20.8%	79.2%	.009

Findings from Knee Osteoarthritis Cases

To ascertain how frequently depression symptoms could be expected to occur among community dwelling individuals diagnosed as having osteoarthritis of one or both knee joints, and to examine whether variations in the disease prevail in the context of these factors as well as age, gender and body mass, a cross-sectional analysis of 100 community dwelling adults diagnosed as having knee osteoarthritis of one or both knees was conducted [see reference 73]. More specifically, this exploratory study examined the frequency with which depressive symptoms were reported in the sample, the magnitude of the depression, if present, and the strength of the relationship between pain, depression, levels of self-efficacy for pain and other-symptoms management, and ambulatory status. The sample including, 57 persons with unilateral and 43 persons with bilateral knee osteoarthritis, mean age, 69.9±1 years of age all underwent a standard assessment procedure on a single test occasion using several validated surveys and walking tests (See Table 2).

Table 2. Summary Table of Key Demographic and Disease Related Characteristics of the Sample of Knee Osteoarthritis Cases as adapted from [73]: (N=100)

	Mean	SD	Range
Age (years)	69.68	10.11	40-89
Body Mass Index ($w.h^{-2}$)	29.4	5.6	20-48
VAS Pain Score*	4.92	2.96	0-10
CESD (0-60)*	12.32	10.19	0-46
Unilateral cases	13.37	10.04	
Bilateral cases	10.93	10.33	
Fast Walk Test ($m.min^{-1}$)	52.853	15.35	13.6-84.7
6 Min Walk Test (m)	370.65	121.24	53.03-640.4

Abbreviations: Body mass index: 25-28.9=overweight; 29>=obese; CES-D=Center for Epidemiologic Studies Depression Scale (0=no depression, 60=many depressive symptoms); h=height; m=meters; min=minutes; No. Med. Conditions=Number of Medical Conditions; VAS=visual analogue scale (0=no pain, 10=severe pain); w=weight; *significantly correlated variables at p=0.01 level.

Of import to this present chapter topic, depression, which was assessed using the Center for Epidemiologic Studies Depression (CES-D) scale [72], occurred in 52% of cases and of these 52 cases, 27 had moderate or severe signs of depression. In addition, the bivariate and multiple regression analyses conducted on these data revealed significant relationships between pain and self-efficacy for managing other arthritis symptoms including pain and depression (r =-0.46, -0.54) (p < 0.001), which was found to predict walking speed (r = 0.30, 0.31) (p <0.001). In addition, there was a positive association between depression as measured by the CES-D and pain as measured on a visual analogue scale (r-0.280; p=.0009), and a trend towards significance was noted between body mass index and the depression score, suggesting those who are more depressed may be heavier than those who are not (r=.203; p=.061). When a separate analysis was conducted for those in the obese range, versus those in the normal or overweight category, being obese was associated with a significantly higher rate of depression as determined by their CES-D scores (p=0.05), and there was a trend towards exhibiting more severe depression on the CES-D if the subject was categorized as being obese rather than normal or overweight (p=0.032). When the data were analyzed separately for those of normal weight, overweight or obese groupings, more with depression were overweight, especially at the grade 3 level of severity (p=.016). Finally those who were depressed had poorer walking endurance scores than those who were not (r=-.261; p=015).

In another similar cross-sectional analysis conducted by Sullivan et al. [42] on cases with knee osteoarthritis requiring surgery, significant correlations were also recorded between pre-surgical pain severity measures, depression and pain-related fears of movement. In their further prospective analyses pre-surgical pain severity was a unique predictor of post-surgical pain severity, indicating that it may be extremely important to target pain-related psychological risk factors before surgery if optimal post-surgical outcomes are sought. Similarly, this group stressed that depression, a common feature of knee osteoarthritis cases who are obese should be addressed where possible as it is strongly related to poor function status [43].

Other related findings are depicted in Table 3.

Table 3. Summary of Key Study Findings in the Related Literature Implicating Depression in the Natural History of Osteoarthritis (OA)

Authors	Study Design	Findings
Allen et al. [16]	8 focus groups of men + women with hip or knee OA	Mental health affected fatigue and caused fatigue
Axford et al. [20]	54 cases of OA were studied	Depression is common in OA and is related to pain and disability
Dieppe et al. [74]	8 year prospective study of 349 OA cases	Outcomes were predicted by biological and psychological factors
Lin et al. [44]	Preplanned subgroup analysis of trial of depression care in 480 adults with arthritis	Intervention reduced depression and pain at 12 months
Salaffi et al. [75]	61 cases knee OA assessed with AIMS and Zung Depression Scale	Pain and disability was significantly influenced by psychosocial factors
Singh and Lewalien [24]	2-5 year follow-up of total hip arthroplasty cases	Those with depression h had 1.5 times odds of moderate to severe pain at 2 years. Narcotic use was also greater for these cases
Sharma et al. [70]	3 year study of knee OA cases	Protective factors for OA include mental health
Summers et al. [67]	65 outpatients with knee or hip OA were assessed radiographically and clinically	Psychological factors were predictors of pain and disability
Van Baar et al. [69]	200 cases with knee or hip OA were examined on one occasion	Kinesiological and psychological factors contribute to OA disability
Zautra and Smith [16]	Studied 101 cases with OA weekly for 12-20 weeks	Depression may be related to elevations in pain

DISCUSSION

As outlined above and highlighted in Table 3, in addition to physical correlates of disability, an increasing emphasis has recently been placed on psychological correlates of osteoarthritis disability in an effort to better understand factors contributing to its pathogenesis [44].

Because emotional health may have an important role to play in mediating and magnifying the extent of osteoarthritis-related disability [45, 79], but there is very little joint specific information on this topic, the present work sought to examine the related literature and to describe the prevalence and impact of depression among patients with advanced hip and/or knee joint osteoarthritis.

While the present focus was on whether the mood disorder of depression presenting either as a pre-morbid condition and/or a concurrent condition is likely to impact short-term functional outcomes adversely as outlined in Figure 1, it is well recognized that pain and unpredictable functional limitations can contribute to affective changes among these patients, and indirectly to the ability to cope with osteoarthritis [46].

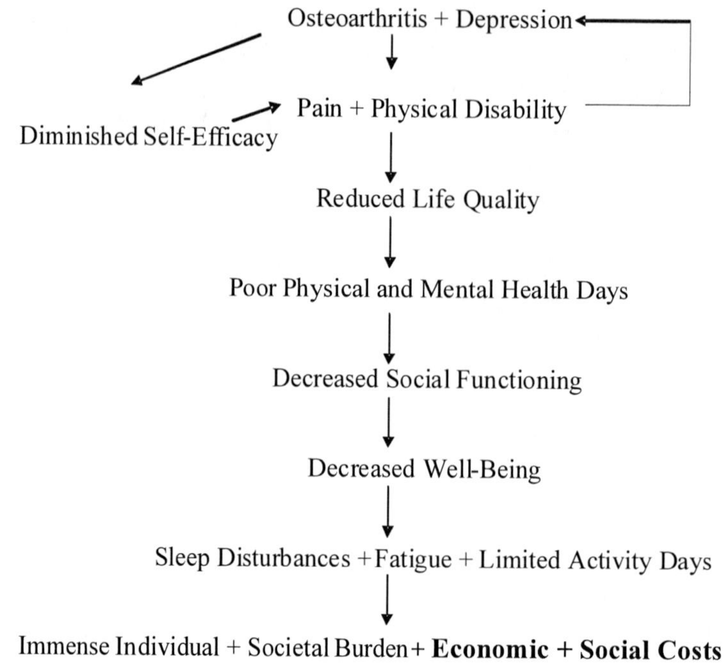

Figure 1. Figure showing, osteoarthritis and depression can lead to complex health related outcomes.

Although Maly et al. [71] found depression did not explain the variance in performance of adults with knee osteoarthritis, in general, and consistent with previous studies of hip or knee osteoarthritis [16, 47, 79], the current findings showed those who report depression histories are more likely to experience functional limitations and severe pain than those who are mentally healthy. There was also evidence that several patients exhibited clinically significant emotional distress prior to surgery that was not treated or evaluated, and that the presence of depression can influence recovery from surgery as outlined by Possley et al. [43]. Since depression may influence pain and lower extremity function quite significantly in adults with knee osteoarthritis [62] or osteoarthritis of the lower limb [79], and substantive research shows that pre-operative functional status is a significant predictor of functional post-operative status, minimizing the excess pain and disability related in part to emotional factors is arguably crucial for improving osteoarthritis treatment outcomes in general, as well as specifically after surgery, if this is indicated.

In addition, given that depressive symptoms are common in overweight cases of osteoarthritis as observed by Possley et al. [43] and Rosemann et al. [68], and those who are depressed tend to be heavier than those who are not [41], more needs to be done to address this associated determinant of poor osteoarthritis related outcomes. Being overweight places great stress on a damaged joint and could be due to treatments given to alleviate depression so this issue should be dealt with carefully by the attending physician. Having high rates of depressive symptoms may also reduce motivation for physical activity, and self-efficacy which influences physical performance in knee osteoarthritis [71], thus potentially contributing to a cycle or downward spiral of negative events as shown in Figure 1. Not surprisingly, patients with osteoarthritis who report depressive symptoms and/or histories do

appear to suffer severe pain and functional disability more readily than those with no depression, a finding also supported by Summers et al. [67] and Van Baar et al. [69]. Even if surgery is seen as the solution, since there is a higher risk of moderate-severe activity limitations 2-5 years after surgery if a patient is depressed [24], addressing both the mental as well as the physical health status of patients both in the clinical as well as surgical settings is strongly advocated as outlined by Sharma et al. [70]. In particular, women and younger less educated low-income patients who tend to suffer an excess burden of disability if depressed should be targeted. Moreover, rather than waiting until the adult with osteoarthritis requires surgery, the importance of assessing and treating pain plus any attendant depression among persons seeking clinical care for osteoarthritis as stressed as highlighted by Dexter and Brandt [15], Hill et al. [47] and Lin et al. [44] and Rolfson et al [48] is indicated. By contrast, since reactive depression can influence pain perception as well as functional ability quite markedly, preventing depression attributable to pain and physical dysfunction may have a strong bearing on the health of the joint and the overall health outcome as outlined by Calfas et al. [46]. As well, since the presently reported levels of distress, along with medication reports, may also be underestimates, and our cohorts were mostly middle class, more specific exploration and recording of these variables among indigent samples, who commonly exhibit a high prevalence of psychopathology [38] is indicated as well.

In addition, although the functional limitations experienced by people with end-stage osteoarthritis are likely to be largely due to physical disturbances and pain, and not to any specific affective comorbid condition[s] [78], pain can lead to depression as well as disability [35]. Additionally, both pain and disability as well as physical comorbidities such as cardiovascular diseases may clearly be amplified by depression, and since preoperative pain predicts a poor outcome of total hip replacement for osteoarthritis [52], interventions that specifically target pain-related psychological factors risk factors may yield more successful surgical outcomes than those that do not [42]. Teasing out this complex relationship between all these overlapping factors is especially important given that depressive symptoms could adversely affect disability outcomes, including narcotic medication usage [23], as was observed by Singh et al. [24] two years following hip replacement surgery.

This argument is further strengthened since neither age, gender, body mass, or disease status were able to account for the presently observed differences in short-term disability outcomes between the osteoarthritis cases with affective disorder histories and the controls. It is possible too that the mechanisms for this may be explained by a lower level of motivation for recovery, heightened fear about undertaking activity or rehabilitation post-surgery, and a lack of self-efficacy for undertaking prescribed functional recovery steps, which was a relationship demonstrated in the sample of moderately affected knee osteoarthritis cases studied. Moreover, the presence of clinical depression can adversely affect decision-making and effective self-management among people with arthritis [47]. The depressed group was also slightly more overweight than the non-depressed sample, and it is known that having a higher age and body mass index is likely to impact recovery rates after hip surgery quite negatively. This group also included patients who suffered from other joint related problems, a factor identified as affecting functional improvement after total hip replacement for osteoarthritis by Nilsdotter et al. [52]. Finally, a high percentage had asthma histories, which have been tied to poor exercise capacity [53], as well as high medication usage rates that could impact functional recovery after surgery adversely.

Some of the patients reporting depression histories also reported they were experiencing state anxiety [55], and this may be of significance in explaining the reduced post-operative function in those with affective comorbid histories compared to those with no such history. Although findings by Caracciolo and Giaquinto [18] suggest cases with hip osteoarthritis are not affected by their mental health status, the present findings were consistent with data from other sources that show depression can impact physical functioning quite negatively after hip joint surgery [e.g., 46], as well as knee osteoarthritis in the absence and presence of surgery [18]. As well, Salaffi et al. [75] found the pain and disability experience of knee osteoarthritis was strongly influenced by the prevailing degree of depression and anxiety, rather than radiographic score, as did Martin [77] for low-income black women, where depression explained the largest amount of variance in functional health. Because osteoarthritis in one joint can spread to other joints over time and can produce high levels of physical disability, anxiety and depression, high levels of healthcare resources utilization, including drugs and surgery [74], allaying the progression of the disease and its outcome may be paramount to treating osteoarthritis cases successfully as stated by Axford et al. [64]. Since depression is one factor in this cycle that is amenable to detection and treatment, concerted efforts to educate providers about how to limit depression and its consequences [77], plus encouraging them to routinely identify and treat depression among cases with osteoarthritis can be expected to markedly reduce the occurrence of depression, joint pathology, and physical immobility, as well as the immense societal burden of this condition.

Conclusion

Osteoarthritis, an important cause of disability among aging adults [58], has been linked to being overweight or obese [59] plus having hypertension [60]. Less well documented are related affective comorbid conditions such as depression that may influence disease outcomes adversely [44]. However, if pain and disability are truly more predictive of depression than any of the most prevalent medical illnesses [23], the presence of a modest to reasonably high prevalence of pre-morbid and/or concurrent mood disorders or emotional distress in sub-populations of osteoarthritis cases is more likely to occur than not, and has been evidenced in both men and women at comparable rates of approximately 19% among primary care patients [68]. Second, the presence of depression is likely to impact short-term as well as long-term health outcomes and is an important predictor of functional disability for osteoarthritis patients [68], efforts to prevent, identify and treat depression sooner, rather than later, should be forthcoming in order to minimize the burden of the disease as outlined by Lin et al. [44] and Rosemann et al [54, 61]. To better address the interactive elements that influence depression, such as disease knowledge, depression, pain, and physical ability [64], a multi-component program that accounts for both the physical and mental health status of the individual patient, may help to minimize both reactive, as well as trait depression, that can mediate the pathogenesis of osteoarthritis, as well as other comorbid conditions that can influence the onset of obesity, pain and anxiety as outlined in Figure 2.

Routinely assess patients for any associated depressive symptoms using valid instruments such as the Center for Epidemiologic Studies Depression Scale [72]*

Follow with individualized/multidisciplinary interventions, systemic depression management, a care program addressing both physical and emotional pain associated with OA and late life-depression, and/or cognitive behavioural, integrated depression care management and exercise, social support, or psychosocial interventions to relieve depression and re-assess.

↓

- Reduced pain severity and arthritis limitations in daily activities
- Better sleep patterns and diminished fatigue
- Higher health status
- Higher quality of life
- Improved short-and long term outcomes
- Less likelihood of developing other comorbid conditions that are influenced by depression
- Potentially reduced prevalence of disability and heightened life quality
- Improvements in self-efficacy
- Satisfaction with depression care
- Timed walking test improvements

*Target women, the elderly, those who are overweight/obese, those with generalized osteoarthritis, those who are younger and less educated, and those with additional comorbidities and other joint problems.

Sources: [15, 19, 22, 43, 44, 63, 64, 65, 66]

Figure 2. Theoretical Model Depicting Potential Outcome of Routine Assessment and Targeted Rehabilitation Efforts for Adults with Osteoarthritis (OA) of One or More Joints.

In this respect, according to Yohannes and Caton [22], there is some evidence that the intervention of Cognitive Behavioral Therapy, integrated depression care management, social support and exercise therapy can reduce depressive symptoms in the short term, even though the long-term benefits of depression management in patients with osteoarthritis with co-morbid depression are unknown. Depression can also impact weight status among cases with osteoarthritis [31] and lower leg function [62], pain and functional limitations [63] and this should be borne in mind in efforts to encourage activity, known to reduce joint stresses and pain severity, as well as depression.

As depicted in Figure 2, a comprehensive collaborative care approach that takes into account the complexity of the disease and its symptoms may lessen both the disability and aversive experiences of osteoarthritis, thus heightening the likelihood of achieving optimal health outcomes, regardless of whether clinical or surgical intervention approaches are employed as outlined by Axford et al.[64] and Lin et al. [44, 65]. Early intervention may also reduce symptoms of hypertension and heart disease and asthma caused by psychological distress, excess body weight and pain and disability,-which can cause depression [23, 26], plus excess disability. Finally, people with advanced osteoarthritis, the most common chronic

condition among older people, may benefit from joint replacement surgery to a greater extent - if at the time of hospital referral - those with depression histories and those who express pre-surgical depression are identified, and precautions are taken to offset these risks as discussed by Giraudet-Le Quintrec et al. [45].

REFERENCES

[1] Zhang Y, Jordan JM. Epidemiology of osteoarthritis. *Clin Geriatr Med.* 2010;26(3):355-369.

[2] Kwok WY, Vliet Vlieland TP, Rosendaal FR, Huizinga TW, Kloppenburg M. Limitations in daily activities are the major determinant of reduced health-related quality of life in patients with hand osteoarthritis. *Ann Rheum Dis*. 2011;70(2):334-336.

[3] Douglas J, Simon T, Aberman HM. Symptomatic articular cartilage degeneration: the impact in the new millennium. *Clin Orthop Rel Res*. 2001;391;S14-S25.

[4] Moskowitz RW. The burden of osteoarthritis: clinical and quality-of-life issues. *Am J Manag Care.* 2009;15:S223-229.

[5] Peat G, McCarney R, Croft P. Knee pain and osteoarthritis in older adults: a review of community burden and current use of primary health care. *Ann Rheum Dis*.2001;60:89-90.

[6] Martel-Pelletier J, Boileau C, Pelletier JP, Roughley PJ. Cartilage in normal and osteoarthritis conditions. *Best Pract Res Clin Rheumatol*. 2008;22:351-384.

[7] Kubota M, Ishijima M, Kurosawa H, Liu L, Ikeda H, Osawa A, Takazawa Y, Kawasaki T, Saita Y, Kimura Y, Kaneko K. A longitudinal study of the relationship between the status of bone marrow abnormalities and progression of knee osteoarthritis. *J Orthop Sci.* 2010;15:641-646.

[8] McDonough CM, Jette AM. The contribution of osteoarthritis to functional limitations and disability. *Clin Geriatr Med.* 2010;26:387-399.

[9] Edwards RR, Calahan C, Mensing G, Smith M, Haythornthwaite JA. Pain, catastrophizing, and depression in the rheumatic diseases. *Nat Rev Rheumatol.* 2011; Feb 1.

[10] Heliovaara M, Makela M, Impivaara O, Knekt P, Aromaa A, Sievers K. Association of overweight, trauma, and workload with coxarthrosis. A health survey of 7,217 persons. *Acta Orthop Scandinav*. 1993;64:513-518.

[11] Philbin EF, Groff GD, Ries MD, Miller TE. Cardiovascular fitness and health in patients with end-stage osteoarthritis. *Arthritis Rheum*. 1995;38:799-805.

[12] [Knoop J, Steultjens MP, van der Leeden M, van der Esch M, Thorstensson CA, Roorda LD, Lems WF, Dekker J. Proprioception in knee osteoarthritis: a narrative review. *Osteoarthritis Cart.* 2011 Jan 17.

[13] Ratzlaff CR, Steininger G, Doerfling P, Koehoorn M, Cibere J, Liang MH, Wilson DR, Esdaile JM, Kopec JA. Influence of lifetime hip joint force on the risk of self-reported hip osteoarthritis: a community-based cohort study. *Osteoarthritis Cart.* 2011 Jan 18.

[14] Tepper S, Hochberg MC. Factors associated with hip osteoarthritis: data from the First National Health and Nutrition Examination Survey (NHANES-I). *Am J Epidemiol.* 1993; 137:1081-1088.

[15] Dexter P, Brandt K. Distribution and predictors of depressive symptoms in osteoarthritis. *J Rheumatol*. 1994;21:279-286.

[16] Power JD, Badley EM, French MR, Wall AJ, Hawker GA. Fatigue in osteoarthritis. *BMC Musculoskel Disord*. 2008;9:63.

[17] [Bischoff-Ferrari HJ, Lingard EA, Losina E, Baron JA, Roos EM, Phillips CB, Mahamed NN, Bareett, Katz JN. Psychosocial and geriatric correlates of functional status after total hip replacement. *Arthritis Rheum*. 2004;51;829-835.

[18] Caracciolo B, Giaquinto S. Self-perceived distress and self-perceived functional recovery after recent total hip and knee arthroplasty. *Arch Gerontol Geriatr*. 2005;41:177-181.

[19] Okma-Keulen P, Hopman-Rock M. The onset of generalizes osteoarthritis in older women: a qualitative approach. *Arthritis Care Res*. 2001;45:183-190.

[20] Axford J, Butt A, Heron C, Hammond J, Morgan J, Alavi A, Bolton J, Bland M. Prevalence of anxiety and depression in osteoarthritis: use of the Hospital Anxiety and Depression Scale as a screening tool. *Clin Rheumatol*. 2010;29:1277-1283.

[21] Somers TJ, Keefe FJ, Godiwala N, Hoyler GH. Psychosocial factors and the pain experience of osteoarthritis patients: new findings and new directions. *Curr Opin Rheumatol.* 2009 21(5):501-6.

[22] Yohannes AM, Caton S. Management of depression in older people with osteoarthritis: A systematic review. *Aging Ment Health*. 2010;14:637-651.

[23] Wu LR, Parkerson GR Jr, Doraiswamy PM. Health perception, pain, and disability as correlates of anxiety and depression symptoms in primary care patients. *J Am Board Fam Pract*. 2002;15:183-190.

[24] Singh JA, Lewalien D. Age, gender, obesity, and depression are associated with patient-related pain and function outcome after revision total hip arthroplasty. *Clin Rheumatol*. 2009; 28:1419-1430.

[25] Croft P, Lewis M, Wynn Jones C, Coggon D, Cooper C. Health status in patients awaiting hip replacement for osteoarthritis. *Rheumatol*. 2002;41:1001-1007.

[26] Zautra AJ, Smith BW. Depression and reactivity to stress in older women with rheumatoid arthritis and osteoarthritis. *Psychosom Med.* 2001;63:687-696.

[27] Riddle DL, Wade JB, Jiranek WA, Kong X. Preoperative pain catastrophizing predicts pain outcome after knee arthroplasty. *Clin Orthop Relat Res*. 2010;468:798-806.

[28] Tas U, Verhagen AP, Bierma-Zeinstra SM, Hofman A, Odding E, Pols HA, Koes BW. Incidence and risk factors of disability: the Rotterdam Study. *Prev Med.* 2006 Dec 19

[29] Yarmo-Roberts D, Freak-Poli RL, Cooper B, Noonan T, Stolewinder J, Reid CM. The heart of the matter: health status of aged care clients receiving home- and community-based care. *J Aging Res*. 2010; Jul 12: 275303.

[30] Qiu WQ, Dean M, Liu T, George L, Gann M, Cohen J, Bruce ML. Physical and mental health of homebound older adults: an overlooked population. *J Am Geriatr Soc.* 2010;58:2423-2428.

[31] Wolf S, Foley S, Budiman-Mak E, Moritz T, O'Connell S, Jelinek C, Collins EG. Predictors of weight loss in overweight veterans with knee osteoarthritis who participated in a clinical trial. *J Rehabil Res Dev*. 2010;47:171-181.

[32] Khuwaja AK, Lalani S, Dhanani R, Azam IS, Rafique G, White F. Anxiety and depression among outpatients with type 2 diabetes: a multi-centre study of prevalence and associated factors. *Diabetol Metab Syndr*. 2010; 2:72.

[33] Currey SS, Callahan L. Helplessness, self-reported comorbid depression, and health-related quality of life in rheumatic disease. *Arthritis Rheum.* 2001;44:S382.

[34] Grossniklaus DA, Gary RA, Higgins MK, Dunbar SB. Biobehavioral and psychological differences between overweight adults with and without waist circumference risk. *Res Nurs Hlth.* 2010;33:539-551.

[35] Hooten WM, Shi Y, Gazelka HM, Warner DO. The effects of depression and smoking on pain severity and opioid use in patients with chronic pain. *Pain.* 2011;152:223-229.

[36] [Hawker GA, Gignac MA, Badley E, Davis AM, French MR, Li Y, Perruccio AV, Power JD, Sale J, Lou W. A longitudinal study to explain the pain-depression link in older adults with osteoarthritis. *Arthritis Care Res* (Hoboken). 2010 Jul 26.

[37] Dekker J, van Dijk GM, Veenhof C. Risk factors for functional decline in osteoarthritis of the hip or knee. *Curr Opin Rheumatol.* 2009;21:520-524.

[38] Howard KJ, Ellis HB, Khaleel MA, Gatchel RJ, Bucholz R. Psychosocial profiles of indigent patients with severe osteoarthritis requiring arthroplasty. *J Arthroplasty.* 2010 Apr 7.

[39] Stebbings S, Herbison P, Doyle TC, Treharne GJ, Highton J. A comparison of fatigue correlates in rheumatoid arthritis and osteoarthritis: disparity in associations with disability, anxiety and sleep disturbance. *Rheumatol* (Oxford). 2010;49:361-367.

[40] Broderick JE, Junghaenel DU, Schneider S, Bruckenthal P, Keefe FJ. Treatment expectation for pain coping skills training: relationship to osteoarthritis patients' baseline psychosocial characteristics. *Clin J Pain.* 2010 Dec 20.

[41] Marks R. Comorbid depression and anxiety impact hip osteoarthritis disability. *Disabil & Hlth.* 2009;2:27-35.

[42] Sullivan M, Tanzer M, Stanish W, Fallaha M, Keefe FJ, Simmonds M, Dunbar M. Psychological determinants of problematic outcomes following Total Knee Arthroplasty. *Pain.* 2009;143:123-129.

[43] Possley D, Rudiman-Mak E, O'Connell S, Jelinek C, Collins EG. Relationship between depression and functional measures in overweight and obese persons with knee osteoarthritis of the knee. *J Rehabil Res Dev.* 2009:46:1091-1098.

[44] Lin EH, Katon W, Von Korff M, Tang L, Williams JW Jr, Kroenke K, et al. Effect of improving depression care on pain and functional outcomes among older adults with arthritis: a randomized controlled trial. *JAMA* 2003;290:2428-2429.

[45] Giraudet-Le Quintrec JS, Coste J, Vastel L, Pacualt V, Jeanne L, Lamas JP et al. Positive effect of patient education for hip surgery: a randomized trial. *Clin Orthop Rel Res.* 2003;414:112-120.

[46] Calfas KJ, Ingram RE. Information processing and affective distress in osteoarthritis patients. *J Consult Clin Psychol* 1997;65:576-581.

[47] Hill CL, Gill T, Taylor AW, et al. Psychological factors and quality of life: a population-based study. *Clin Rheumatol.* 2007;26:1049-1054.

[48] Rolfson O, Dahlberg LE, Nilsson JA, Malchau H, Garellick G. Variables determining outcome in total hip replacement surgery. *J Bone Joint Surg Br.* 2009;91:157-161.

[49] Scott KM, Bruffaerts R, Tsang A, Ormel J, Alonso J, Angermeyer MC, et al. Depression-anxiety relationships with chronic physical conditions: results from the World Mental Health surveys. *J Affect Disord.* 2007;103:113-120.

[50] Sareen J, Jacobi F, Cox BJ, Belik SL, Clara I, Stein MB. Disability and poor quality of life associated with comorbid anxiety disorders and physical conditions. *Arch Int Med.* 2006;166:2109-2116.

[51] Sareen J, Cox BJ, Clara I, Asmundson GJ. The relationship between anxiety disorders and physical disorders in the U.S. National Comorbidity Survey. *Depress Anxiety.* 2005;21:193-202.

[52] Nilsdotter AK, Petersson IF, Roos EM, Lohmander LS. Predictors of patient relevant outcomes after total hip replacement: a prospective study. *Ann Rheum Dis.* 2003;62:923-930.

[53] Jette, AM, Lachman M, Giogetti MM, et al. Exercise-its never too late: the Strong-for-Life program. *Am J Public Hlth.* 1999;89:66-72.

[54] Rosemann T, Backenstrass M, Joest K, Rosemann A, Szecsenyi J, Laux G. Predictors of depression in a sample of 1,021 primary care patients with osteoarthritis. *Arthritis Rheum*. 2007;15:57:415-422.

[55] Salmon P, Hall GM, Peerbhoy D. Influence of the emotional response to surgery on functional recovery during 6 months after hip arthroplasty. *J Behav Med.* 2001;24:489-502.

[56] Spalding NJ. Reducing anxiety by pre-operative education: make the future familiar. *Occupational Ther Int*. 2003;10:278-293.

[57] Butler GS, Hurley CA, Buchanan KL, Smith-VanHorne J. Prehospital education: effectiveness with total hip replacement surgery patients. *Patient Educ Counsel.* 1996;29:189-197.

[58] Hochberg MC, Kasper J, Williamson J, et al. The contribution of osteoarthritis to disability: preliminary data from the woman's Health and Aging Study. *J Rheumatol.* 1995;43:S16-18.

[59] Oliveria SA, Felson DT, Cirillo PA, et al. Body weight, body mass index, and incident symptomatic osteoarthritis of the hand, hip, and knee. *Epidemiol*. 1999;10:161-166.

[60] Lawrence JS. Hypertension in relation to musculoskeletal disorders. *Ann Rheum Dis.* 1975;34:451-456.

[61] Rosemann T, Gensichen J, Sauer N, Laux G, Szecsenyi J. The impact of depression on quality of life and health service utilisation in patients with osteoarthritis. *Rheumatol Int.* 2007;Jan 23.

[62] Scopaz KA, Piva SR, Wisniewski S, Fitzgerald GK. Relationships of fear, anxiety, and depression with physical function in patients with knee osteoarthritis. *Arch Phys Med Rehabil.* 2009;90:1866-1873.

[63] Blixen CE, Kippes C. Depression, social support, and quality of life in older adults with osteoarthritis. *Image J Nurs Sch.* 1999;31:221-226.

[64] Axford J, Heron C, Ross F, Victor CR. Management of knee osteoarthritis in primary care: pain and depression are the major obstacles. *J Psychosom Res.* 2008;64:461-467.

[65] Lin EHB, Tang L, Katon W, Hegel MT, Sullivan MD, Unutzer J. Arthritis pain and disability: response to collaborative depression care. *Gen Hosp Psychiatr*. 2006;28:482-486.

[66] Unutzer J, Hantke M, Powers D, Higa L, Lin E, D Vannoy S, Thiele S, Fan MY. Care management for depression and osteoarthritis pain in older primary care patients: a pilot study. *Int J Geriatr Psychiatr*. 2008;23:1166-1171.

[67] Summers M, Haley W, Reveille J, Alarcon G. Radiographic assessment and psychologic variables as predictors of pain and functional impairment in osteoarthritis of the knee or hip. *Arthritis Rheum.* 1988;31;204-209.

[68] Rosemann T, Laux G, Szecsenyi J. Osteoarthritis: quality of life, comorbidities, medication and health service utilization assessed in a large sample of primary care patients. *J Orthop Surg Res*. 2007;2:12.

[69] van Baar ME, Dekker J, Lemmens JA, Oostendorp RA, Bijlsma JW. Pain and disability in patients with osteoarthritis of hip or knee: the relationship with articular, kinesiological, and psychological characteristics. *J Rheumatol*. 1998;1:125-133.

[70] Sharma L, Cahue S, Song J, Hayes K, Pai YC, Dunlop D. Physical functioning over three years in knee osteoarthritis: role of psychosocial, local mechanical, and neuromuscular factors. *Arthritis Rheum*. 2003;48:3359-3370.

[71] Maly MR, Costigan PA, Olney SJ. Contribution of psychosocial and mechanical variables to physical performance measures in knee osteoarthritis. *Phys Ther.* 2005;85:1318-1328.

[72] Radloff LS. The CES-D scale: a self report depression scale for research in the general population. *J Appl Psychol Measurement*. 1977;1:385-401.

[73] Marks R. Physical and psychological correlates of disability among a cohort of individuals with knee osteoarthritis. *Can J Aging*. 2007;26:367-377.

[74] Dieppe P, Cushnaghan J, Tucker M, Browning S, Shepstone L. The Bristol 'OA500 study': progression and impact of the disease after 8 years. *Osteoarthritis Cart.* 2000;8:63-68.

[75] Salaffi F, Cavaliera F, Nolli M, Ferraccioli G. Analysis of disability in knee osteoarthritis. Relationship with age and psychological variables but not with radiographic score. *J Rheumatol.* 1991;18:1581-1586.

[76] Currey SS, Calaghan LF. Helplessness, self-reported comorbid depression, and health-related quality of life in rheumatic disease. *Arthritis Rheum*. 2001;44:S382 .

[77] Martin JC. Determinants of functional health of low-income women with osteoarthritis. *Am J Prev Med.* 1996;12:430-435.

[78] Juhakoski R, Tenhonen S, Anttonen T, Kauppinen T, Aroski JP. Factors affecting self-reported pain and physical function in patients with hip osteoarthritis. *Arch Phys Med Rehabil.* 2008;89:1066-1073.

[79] Rosemann T, Kuehlein T, Laux G, Scecsenyi J. Factors associated with physical activity of patients with osteoarthritis of the lower limb. *J Eval Clin Pract.* 2008;14:288-293.

In: Advances in Psychology Research. Volume 88
Editor: Alexandra M. Columbus, pp. 179-196
ISBN: 978-1-62100-591-9

Chapter 9

OBSERVATIONAL INSTRUMENTS FOR THE STUDY OF COGNITIVE TECHNIQUES: DEVELOPMENT AND APPLICATIONS

Ana Calero-Elvira, María Xesús Froján-Parga, Montserrat Montaño-Fidalgo and Manuel Alpañés-Freitag
Universidad Autónoma de Madrid (Madrid, Spain).

ABSTRACT

Cognitive restructuring is a therapeutic tool that is widely used by clinicians, specially the Socratic Method, that is considered its main therapeutic component. There are many contradictions that accompany the application of the Socratic Method and the research studies on the processes of this technique have not been clear, so virtually no progress has been made since it was initially proposed by Ellis and Beck. Some years ago our group started a research line on the mechanisms of change that occur when cognitive-behavioral therapy is applied in clinical contexts. Therefore we believe that we must know *which* techniques works, but also we must research on *how* or *why* certain changes take place. In this sense we began a study on cognitive techniques, specifically on the cognitive restructuring technique, based on the observation and analysis of the interaction between therapist and client. The aim of this work is to present three measuring instruments that we have developed to study this technique: (1) the *Coding System for the Study of Therapist-Patient Interaction* (SISC-INTER), that allows the analysis of the therapist's and the client's verbal behavior and finally the interaction between them; (2) the *Coding System of Patient Verbal Behavior Based on Therapeutic Goals* (SISC-COT), that allows classifying the clients' verbalizations according to their degree of approximation to the therapeutic objectives pursued by the psychologist during the Socratic Method; (3) the *Assessment Scale of Effectiveness of the Socratic Method in Cognitive Restructuring* (*EVED-RC*), that allows to assign to each fragment of Socratic Method a single category based on its level of effectiveness. This work has two objectives: first, to present the process of developing the measuring instruments; second, to discuss their possible applications for the research giving examples of studies performed by our group. Therefore, although the chapter is devoted primarily to explain

the process of developing the observation instruments, we will briefly discuss some of the results already found with their application.

INTRODUCTION

The objective of *results research* is to ascertain the treatments of choice for different psychological problems. *Processes research* focuses on the mechanisms of therapeutic change, or in other words, the processes that explain why the therapy works and how the change is produced (Kazdin, 2008). While the first type of study deals with understanding *what* works, the second type analyzes *how* or *why* certain changes occur.

In the field of clinical psychology, the evaluation of psychotherapy results has become an important topic since the 1990s, and it has given rise to many guidelines and treatment manuals about effective and efficacious treatments. The works of the Society of Clinical Psychology (Division 12) of the American Psychological Association (APA) have led the movement toward *empirically validated treatments* (Chambless, Baker, Baucom et al., 1998; Chambless, Sanderson, Shoham et al., 1996; Task Force on Promotion and Dissemination of Psychological Procedures, 1995) and inspired the recent trend of *evidence-based psychological practice* (the APA Presidential Task Force on Evidence-Based Practice, 2006). In contrast to results research, processes research has received little attention from the scientific community. Different authors have commented on this fact and have brought attention to the need for studies related to the mechanisms of therapeutic change. On this subject, Kazdin (2008) emphasized that this would be a good way to decrease the gap between research and clinical practice because knowing these mechanisms would optimize therapeutic change. Additionally, Rosen and Davison (2003) discussed the need for establishing principles of change with empirical support that would stop the proliferation of therapeutic proposals that might not provide any mechanism of change other than those that are already established.

Despite a renewed interest in processes research over the last few years, it is difficult to extract clear conclusions from the available studies, which are characterized by conceptual confusion (Orlinsky, Rønnestad, & Willutzki, 2004), methodological plurality (Hill & Lambert, 2004), and a notable diversity of research objectives (Llewelyn & Hardy, 2001). These characteristics are specially pronounced in the field of cognitive techniques, where, since its origin nearly four decades ago, there have only been small advances with respect to our knowledge of the mechanisms of change underlying their application.

Regarding the cognitive restructuring technique (Beck, 1967; Beck, Rush, Shaw, & Emery, 1979; Ellis, 1962; Ellis & Grieger, 1977), which is widely used by clinicians of cognitive-behavioral and other orientations (PracticeNet, 2003), we find that processes studies have focused on the analysis of treatment components to identify the active ingredients of change and on the identification of the mediators and moderators of change. With respect to the first type of study, there has been debate regarding the differentiating effects of behavioral activation and cognitive therapy (Dimidjian et al., 2006; Dobson et al., 2008; Jacobson et al., 1996), but conclusive results have not been reached. Additionally, there have been dismantling studies that have pointed to different restructuring components as the most active in each case (Arnkoff, 1986; Bennett-Levy, 2003; Jarrett & Nelson, 1987; Zettle & Hayes, 1987). Furthermore, research on change mediators and moderators has not answered many of

the formulated questions, and some factors have been proposed to serve as moderators, such as active client participation, therapeutic alliance, and the adjustment and competency of the therapist with respect to the cognitive model (Whisman, 1993). However, different studies have found that variables, such as attribution style (Whisman, 1993) or thought modification (Garratt et al., 2007; Longmore y Worrell, 2007), could mediate in the results found when applying cognitive therapy. But the mechanisms that could explain the change produced by the application of the cognitive restructuring technique remain to be determined.

Over the last few years, our group has developed a branch of research for the study of the clinical phenomenon centered on the analysis of therapeutic interaction (Froján Parga, Montaño Fidalgo, & Calero Elvira, 2006, 2007, 2010; Froján-Parga, Montaño-Fidalgo, Calero-Elvira, & Ruiz-Sancho, 2011; Froján-Parga, Ruiz-Sancho, Montaño-Fidalgo, Calero-Elvira, & Alpañés-Freitag, in press). Specifically, we have studied cognitive techniques with a focus on cognitive restructuring (Froján Parga, Calero Elvira, & Montaño Fidalgo, 2006, 2009, in press). The distinguishing characteristic of this research has been the union of the following aspects: 1) a solid theoretical behavioral framework from which to conceptualize the study and interpret data; specifically, the basis of understanding behavioral therapy as the application of basic behavioral operations (Catania, 1992) for the treatment of psychological problems along the lines of Pérez (1996a, 1996b, 2004); 2) a clear definition of the phenomenon to be analyzed, the verbal interaction between the therapist and the client, and the research objectives; and 3) a rigorous working methodology that combines observational methods and the use of an informatics tool, *The Observer XT*, which allows for highly precise recordings.

One of most important decisions that must be made at the time of launching a study based on observational methodology relates to the measuring tools to be used for what is observed. There are two significant criteria when making this selection: first, the tool must take into account all the information required for the analysis and it must fit the object of study at the level of the description of interest, and second, it must meet the previous criterion with sufficient scientific reliability. If a tool that meets these requirements could be identified, it could be used for the analysis of our study object, which would represent a useful contribution to the solution of one problem that characterize processes research: the use of different measurement tools by different research groups, making the comparison of results between studies difficult (Hill and Lambert, 2004). However, in the case of the present study, scientific review has shown the lack of measurement tools for the analysis of one of the variables of interest. In the case of the other variables, there are multiple published tools that do not meet all of the requirements. For this reason, we decided to create the three measurement tools presented in this study for the analysis of cognitive techniques, specifically cognitive restructuring and the Socratic Method.

The first tool developed was the *Coding System for the Study of Therapist-Patient Interaction* (SISC-INTER in Spanish), which allows the analysis of the behavior of both groups and of the therapist-client interaction that takes place during application of the technique; it is composed of two subsystems: the *Coding Subsystem of the Therapist Verbal Behavior for the Study of Interaction* (SISC-CVT-I in Spanish) and the *Coding Subsystem of the Client Verbal Behavior for the Study of the Interaction* (SISC-CVC-I). The second tool that was developed in this study is the *Coding System of Patient Verbal Behavior Based on Therapeutic Goals* (SISC-COT in Spanish), which aims to codify each of the client's verbalizations during the therapeutic process of Socratic method as a function of its degree of

approximation to the psychologist's therapy objectives. Lastly, an assessment scale was developed called the *Assessment Scale of Effectiveness of the Socratic method in Cognitive Restructuring* (EVED-RC in Spanish), which allows us to assign a category to each Socratic Method fragment as a function of its level of efficacy.

The goal of this study was twofold: on the one hand, it was to show the process of the elaboration of the three measurement tools and, on the other hand, to describe their possible research applications by providing examples through previously conducted studies.

METHOD

Sample

We analyzed 46 fragments of clinical-session recordings during which the Socratic method was applied in therapy. Four cognitive-behavioral psychologists from Therapeutic Institute of Madrid (Spain) participated in the study. These fragments of the Socratic method were selected from 35 sessions that involved 13 individual clinical cases. In all cases, the persons in need of psychological help were upper-middle-class Caucasian adults. We used two procedures during the selection of fragments for the development of each tool: (1) randomized selection and (2) selection as a function of the objective at each step of the study, paying attention to criteria, such as the type of activity used or the therapist participating. Table 1 shows the characteristics of the recordings used, the main data pertaining to clients and therapists, and the recordings used for each measurement tool.

Table 1. Characteristics of the recordings used

Recording characteristics		Tool for which they were used: number of fragments				Therapist characteristics			Client characteristics		
Case	Number of fragments (total duration)	SISC-INTER SISC-CVT-I	SISC-CVC-I	SISC-COT	EVED-RC	Therapist	Gender	Experience (years)	Gender	Age	Problem
1	6 (1h 28’ 57’’)	4	4	5	3	1	F	14	M	29	Low mood
2	2 (1h 09’ 47’’)	1	2	2	1	1	F	15	M	30	Marital problems
3	7 (0h 29’ 21’’)	3	7	0	1	1	F	16	M	32	Marital problems
4	14 (1h 41’ 05’’)	4	2	2	11	1	F	16	M	34	Low mood
5	1 (0h 25’ 53’’)	1	0	0	0	1	F	16	M	53	Psychotic problem
6	1 (0h 06’ 03’’)	1	0	0	0	2	F	4	M	18	Eating disorder
7	2 (0h 12’ 22’’)	1	2	2	2	3	F	6	M	19	Choking fear
8	2 (0h 09’ 11’’)	1	1	1	2	2	F	8	M	16	Problems of adaptation to the environment
9	3 (0h 18’ 02’’)	1	2	1	1	2	F	6	H	34	Hypochondriac
10	2 (0h 18’ 17’’)	1	1	1	2	4	M	6	H	36	Hypochondriac
11	1 (1h 15’ 20’’)	0	1	0	0	4	M	5	M	44	Low mood
12	4 (0h 10’ 44’’)	0	0	1	4	2	F	9	M	35	Marital problems
13	1 (0h 07’ 53’’)	0	0	1	1	2	F	8	H	37	Marital problems

F= female; M= male.

In all cases, informed consent was obtained from the clients so that we could proceed with the recording and subsequent observation and analysis of the sessions (a procedure

approved by the Committee of Ethics of Research of the Universidad Autónoma de Madrid). Confidentiality and privacy was maintained throughout.

Instruments

The observation and coding of the sessions was performed with the aid of the informatics program *The Observer XT*© by Noldus Information Technology, version 6.0. For the *EVED-RC* scale, no coding was required for the efficacy evaluation of the Socratic method, which was recorded with pencil and paper. *The Observer XT*, version 7.0 and *SPSS*, version 15.0 were used to calculate the agreement between observers.

The recordings were recorded on a closed circuit television at the collaborating center with semi-hidden cameras located in the corners of the offices in which the clinical sessions were conducted.

Procedure

The following is a summary of the different phases of the elaboration process for the three measurement tools, specifying at certain points the unique features of the procedure.

1. The Initial Proposal of Categories and the First Decisions Regarding the Observation and Coding Procedures

The first step in the elaboration of the measurement tools presented here was the proposal of the different categories that were considered theoretically important by the research team members, specialist in behavior therapy.

Thus, in the case of the SISC-INTER in this first phase, our basis was that of previously conducted work with the SISC-CVT (Froján et al., 2008) based on the proposal of basic behavioral operations by Pérez (1996a, 1996b, 2004). With respect to the subsystem for the verbal behavior of the therapist, SISC-CVT-I, we proposed 16 categories that were grouped into 6 supra-ordinate categories (*discriminative topography, reinforcement topography, punishment topography, evocative topography, preparation, and instruction)* so that we specified aspects of the potential basic functions of the therapist's behavior that are relevant for a detailed analysis of the restructuring technique. In the case of the subsystem for client verbal behavior, SISC-CVC-I, we proposed eight categories based on the client's possible responses to the potential functions of the therapist's verbalizations: *provide information, show acceptance, show disagreement, follow instructions, verbal imitation, request information, verbalize achievement, and verbalize failure.* With respect to the SISC-COT, we initially proposed four categories, including three previously used by Karpiak and Benjamin (2004) and one intermediate variable that was considered important: *adaptive, non-adaptive, semi-adaptive, and neutral response.* Lastly, the proposal for the evaluation of the degree of effectiveness of the Socratic method with the EVED-RC scale consisted of four categories: *total success, partial success, failure, and abandonment.* These categories refer to the objectives achieved with the Socratic Method in the observed session, and they are not related to the clinical changes achieved by the client as a result of treatment.

Initial decisions were made regarding the coding units and other aspects of the observation and coding procedures. In the case of the SISC-CVT-I subsystem, we decided to analyze all of the verbal behavior produced by the psychologist during the development of each restructuring fragment. In the case of the SISC-CVC-I and SISC-COT subsystems, we decided to analyze verbal behavior corresponding to the client. In all cases, we established that non-verbal or paralinguistic behavior of both groups would not be analyzed, except in cases where taking this into account would aid in clarifying the coding of verbal behavior (for example, at times when intonation, voice volume o facial expression can help us understand the meaning of words). We also decided to exclude verbalizations by the therapist and client that were considered by the observers as unrelated to the cognitive restructuring technique from the recordings and analysis. Various possibilities were proposed for the evaluation of the effectiveness of the Socratic Method fragments according to the EVED-RC scale, such as considering only the last part of the video-recording or accounting for the duration of the Socratic method, but finally we decided to observe the complete fragment of Socratic method and attend to the client verbalizations according to their previous categorization with the SISC-COT independent of time. This means that for determining the degree of achieved effectiveness in the Socratic method, we will consider the degree of approximation to the therapeutic goals for all the client verbalizations in each fragment, and we will make a global judgment as a function of this analysis.

Table 2. Observed recordings and observers participating in phases 2 and 3 of measurement tool development

Measurement tool		Phases Phase of pilot observations	Phase of system improvement
SISC-INTER	SISC-CVT-I	Number of fragments observed (Cases): 3 (Case 1 and 2) Observers participanting: Observer 1, Observer 2	Number of fragments observed (Cases): 15 (Cases 1, 3-11) Observers participanting: Observer 1, Observer 2, Observer 3
	SISC-CVC-I	Number of fragments observed (Cases): 3 (Cases 1 and 2) Observers participanting: Observer 1, Observer 3, Observer 4	Number of fragments observed (Cases): 20 (Cases 1-11) Observers participanting: Observer 1, Observer 2, Observer 5
SISC-COT		Number of fragments observed (Cases): 3 (Cases 1 and 2) Observers participanting: Observer 1, Observer 3	Number of fragments observed (Cases): 13 (Cases 1, 2, 4, 7-10, 12 and 13) Observers participanting: Observer 1, Observer 5
EVED-RC		Number of fragments observed (Cases): 7 (Cases 1, 2, 7, 8 and 10) Observers participanting: Observer 1, Observer 5	Number of fragments observed (Cases): 21 (Cases 3, 4, 7-10, 12 and 13) Observers participanting: Observer 1, Observer 5

2. Pilot Observations: Trial of the Established a Priori Categories and Initially Proposed Categorization Criteria

In this phase, we observed and coded different cognitive restructuring fragments to test if the initially proposed categories were applicable to the objective of this study. These first observations allowed for a better definition of the categories and their inclusion or elimination in some tools as well as an initial proposal for operationalizing the categorization criteria, thus, allowing us to make a decision regarding the assignation of the different categories. The general work flow consisted of independent observation and coding of fragments by various observers as well as the comparison, analysis, and discussion of the similarities and differences found in the recordings. In the case of the two coding systems, we opted for recording and coding using transcriptions of the sessions, instead of automatic recording, to facilitate this first approximation. The five observers who participated in the process of measurement tool elaboration were experts in behavioral therapy. For the creation of the SISC-CVT-I subsystem for the categorization of therapist verbal behavior, the observers were trained in the previous system, the SISC-CVT. Table 2 displays observers who participated in this and the following phase of tool development and the fragments used in each phase.

3. Improvement and Final Proposal of Measurement Tools

Following the first definition of the categories and the categorization criteria, we tried to improve both through the observation and coding of many restructuring fragments by different independent judges. As in the previous phase, the work flow was always the same: comparison of recordings by different observers and analysis and discussion of similarities and differences found, while trying to reach consensus on the criteria that would facilitate future recordings until the final configuration of the tools was determined.

In the case of the coding systems SISC-INTER and SISC-COT, in this phase, we started with systematic observation and recording using *The Observer XT* software. We decided to keep *recordings activated by transition* (Quera, 1991, 1997) for therapist and client verbal behavior cases, which are recordings where the observer notes all of the occurrences and/or the duration of the behavioral units in the order in which they are produced by the observed subject and records only the moments in which the behavioral change occurs, despite continuous observation to detect such changes. In this case, the behavioral units correspond with recording units, both determined by the transition of some categories to others instead of being previously established. Given the possibilities for recording that the use of the informatics tool allow and our interest in knowing the duration of certain behaviors, we decided to register not only the occurrence but also the duration of behaviors in some categories of the therapist system SISC-CVT-I, thus establishing state categories (those for which we register the initial and final moments) against event categories (those for which we only register their occurrence). In the case of the client, we only took into consideration the occurrence, but not the duration, of behavior.

For the EVED-RC scale, in this phase we did not change the support used for the recordings, which continued to be performed with paper and pencil. However, as in the case of the coding systems, we did considerably expand the observed fragment sample, which we attempted to diversify with respect to the participating therapists. Thus, in all of the built tools, we began with the observation and coding of the sessions in which the therapist with

the most expertise participated, for the possibility that this would provide clarity at the beginning of the process. Later, we gradually began observing different therapists.

We calculated the degree of agreement between pairs of observers at each point throughout the improvement phase of tool development. We used different statistical indices for the coding systems and the assessment scale, given that for the former, we must report the *point-by-point* agreement (agreement in the recordings for each of the units throughout the observation sessions), and in the second case, we must search for a *global* agreement index (agreement in the global behavioral measures) (Quera, 1997). One of the most widely used indices for informing point-by-point agreement is the *percentage of agreement between observers,* although a main problem is that it does not correct for the possible effect of chance, something that is taken into account by the *Cohen Kappa coefficient* (Cohen, 1960), which is considered to be the best index of point-by-point agreement. For indices of global agreement, the *Berk intraclass correlation coefficient* (1979) is preferable and provides information regarding the proportion of the total variability of the data that is due to the variability in the observed phenomenon instead of variability in the criteria of the observers. For this last index, we tend to consider values greater than 0.80 as optimal (Quera, 1997), though, it is difficult to establish which Kappa values indicate acceptable degrees of agreement between observers (Bakeman, Quera, McArthur, & Robinson, 1997); it seems that Kappa values could be classified as *poor* (values lower than 0.40), *reasonable* (between 0.40 and 0.60), *good* (between 0.60 and 0.75), and *excellent* (values greater than 0.75) (Bakeman, 2000; Landis & Koch, 1977). Taking this into account, we concluded the improvement phase when, for each case, the categorization agreements had been maximally operationalized and an appropriate level of agreement had been reached in the comparisons of observer pairs. Specifically, it was finalized when a Kappa value greater than 0.50 for the SISC-INTER and SISC-COT was reached and maintained for more than three consecutive comparisons, and when, considering the total of the observations from the establishment of the definitive categorization criteria with the EVED-RC scale, we obtained an intraclass correlation coefficient value greater than 0.80.

RESULTS

Definitive Measurement Tools

In this section, we present the definitions of the categories that are part of the final version of the SISC-INTER systems (table 3 for therapist categories and table 4 for client categories) and SISC-COT (table 5) that, as shown, add a total of 18 categories grouped into 7 supra-ordinate categories for the therapist and 8 categories for the client in the first tool and 4 categories in the second. Table 6 presents the three levels of effectiveness that were finally included in the EVED-RC scale. Due to a lack of space, we did not include the complete measurement tools, which include definitions, categorization criteria, and diverse examples and counter examples. Table 7 shows examples of categories for the therapist and the client in the SISC-INTER system to illustrate, as much as possible, the object of analysis.[1]

[1] The authors will send a copy of the complete tools used to any reader who is interested in receiving one. They may also be found in Calero-Elvira (2009).

Table 3. Definition of categories of verbal behavior of the therapist: SISC-CVT-I

Categories	Definition
Discriminative Topography	Verbalization of the therapist that raises the client's behavior (verbal or not). (Event category) Possible variants: Not indicating the desired direction of the reply, Indicating the desired direction of the reply, Conversational discriminative topography, Failed discriminative topography and Discriminative topography "other".
Evocative Topography	Verbalization of the therapist that gives rise to an emotional response manifested in the client accompanied by verbalization or the verbalization of an emotional response that is taking place. (Event category)
Reinforcement Topography	Verbalization of the therapist showing approval, agreement and/or acceptance of the behavior issued by the client. (Event category) Possible variants: Conversational, Low, Medium, High reinforcement.
Punishment Topography	Verbalization of the therapist showing disapproval, rejection and/or non-acceptance of the behavior of the client. (Event category) Possible variants: Low, Medium, High punishment.
Preparation	Verbalization of the therapist who facilitates, but does not directly evoke, the emission of a determined response by the client, putting him/her in a place so that he/she may adequately answer a question by providing technical or clinical information or by emphasizing the positive or negative consequences of a certain client behavior. Possible variants: Preparation of the discriminative (Event category), Informative (State category), Motivating (State category).
Instruction	Verbalization of the therapist who proposes to the client the completion of therapeutic homework outside or within the clinical context. The consequences should not be mentioned explicitly, but the steps of the action it is promoting should be. (State category)
Others	Any verbalization of the therapist that cannot be included in any of the preceding categories. (Event category)

Table 4. Definition of categories of verbal behavior of the client: SISC-CVC-I

Categories	Definition
Provide information	A verbalization in which the client tries to give information to the therapist that is relevant to the evaluation and/or treatment.
Request information	Question, commentary, and/or request for information by the client towards the therapist.
Show acceptance	A verbalization by the client that shows agreement, acceptance, and/or admiration toward verbalizations emitted by the therapist.
Show disagreement	A verbalization by the client that indicates disagreement, disapproval, and/or rejection toward verbalizations emitted by the therapist.
Verbalization of negative emotions	Expression of negative emotions in the form of complaints that make reference to the clients' illness due to his/her behavioral problems. In addition, verbalizations that indicate a resistance to the homework proposed by the therapist as a result of the illness.
Verbalization of positive emotions	Expression of positive emotions that make reference to therapeutic achievements or to the situation that the client is experiencing or expects to experience in the future as a result of his/her therapeutic achievements or any other circumstance.
Follow instructions	Verbal behavior of the client that implies a complete or partial adherence to the instructions presented immediately before by the therapist.
Other	Any verbalization by the client that cannot be included within the previous categories.

Table 5. Definitions of categories in the SISC-COT system

Categories	Definition
VAT	Verbalizations that approximate the therapeutic objective of the Socratic Method.
VOT	Verbalizations that oppose the therapeutic objective of the Socratic Method.
VIT	Verbalizations intermediate with respect to the therapeutic objective of the Socratic method.
Unable to categorize	Any client's verbalization that cannot be included in any of the preceding categories.

Table 6. Levels of effectiveness of the Socratic Method according to the EVED-RC scale

Levels	Definition
Failure	This level will be selected when none of the client's verbalizations approaches the therapeutic goals, when they only approach the goals with respect to a secondary objective or when they do it once in a non-emphatic way with respect to a main objective and then express an opinion against.
Partial success	This level will be selected when the client expresses a verbalization that approaches one of the main objectives of the Socratic method, but he/she does it once in a non-emphatic way or more than once in a non-emphatic way followed by an opinion against, or only once in an emphatic way followed by an opinion against.
Total success	This level will be selected when the client expresses a verbalization that approaches one of the main objectives of the Socratic method at least once in an emphatic way or more than once in a non-emphatic way, but he/she must not express a contrary opinion during the afterward application of the Socratic method.

Table 7. Examples of the categories of therapis and client verbal behavior in the SISC-INTER system

Categories	Examples
Therapist	
Discriminative Topography:	
Indicating the desired direction of the patient's response:	E.g., Therapist: "Wouldn't you agree that, in addition to what you just said, there is a different way of understanding this situation?"
Not indicating the desired direction of the patient's response:	E.g., Therapist: "Do you think that there is another different way of understanding this situation?"
Conversational discriminative topography:	E.g., Therapist: "Do you understand what I mean?"
Failed discriminative topography:	E.g., Therapist: "What do you think about it" E.g., Patient: (no response)
Discriminative topography other":	E.g., Therapist: "Could you hand me the pen?"
Evocative Topography:	E.g., Therapist: "I would like for you to talk about your father" E.g., Patient: "(crying)… My father was a good person"
Reinforcement Topography:	
Conversational:	E.g., Patient: "I had never been able to do that without taking a pill, so I'm…" E.g., Therapist: "Proud" E.g., Patient: "Proud of myself"

Categories	Examples
Low level:	E.g., Patient: "I had never been able to do that without taking a pill, so I'm proud of myself" E.g, Therapist: "Good"
Medium level:	E.g., Patient: "I had never been able to do that without taking a pill, so I'm proud of myself" E.g, Therapist: "Very good"
High level:	E.g., Patient: "I had never been able to do that without taking a pill, so I'm proud of myself" E.g, Therapist: "Excellent"
Punishment Topography:	
Low level:	E.g., Patient: "I don't think I can" E.g, Therapist: "Lets start again"
Medium level:	E.g., Patient: "I don't think I can" E.g, Therapist: "No, that's not true"
High level:	E.g., Patient: "I don't think I can" E.g, Therapist: "Exactly, you can do this bad and everything bad, as always" (ironically)
Preparation:	
Preparation of the discriminative:	E.g., Therapist: "Before responding to this question, I would like for you to take into account what we have just discussed"
Informative:	E.g., Therapist: "Each person is different, but with respect to criteria of efficiency and performance, or appraisal, people do not end up all equal"
Motivating:	E.g., Therapist: "If you can change what you say to yourself, you will feel much more relaxed"
Instruction:	E.g., Therapist: "You need to practice this type of discussion each day and record these conversations so that we can discuss them in the next session"
Others:	E.g., Therapist: "Today is a gorgeous day"
Client	
Proporcionar información:	E.g., Therapist: "How many times did you call your husband on the phone this week?" E.g., Client: "Around five or six times"
Solicitar información:	E.g., Client: "Do I need to record this as last week?"
Mostrar aceptación:	E.g., Therapist: "What happened to you is the same as what happened one month ago" E.g., Client: "It is true"
Mostrar desacuerdo:	E.g., Therapist: "What happened to you is the same as what happened one month ago" E.g., Client: "I do not think so"
Verbalización de emociones negativas:	E.g., Client: "This week I felt worse than ever"
Verbalización de emociones positivas:	E.g., Client: "I am very happy with all of the progress I have made this week"
Seguir instrucciones:	E.g., Therapist: "I now want you to give me other possible reason why he did not call you" E.g., Client: "Because he did not have time, for example"
Others:	E.g., Client: "I was late because I got lost"

Calculation of the Achieved Degree of Interjudge Agreement

Table 8 shows the data for the levels of interjudge agreement from which we decided to finalize the improvement phase of the measurement tools. The comparisons of the degree of agreement were made between the pairs of observers who, in the case of each system, had participated for a longer time during the tool development phase, and as a result, were better trained in their use. In the case of the coding systems SISC-INTER and SISC-COT, the agreement percentages (AP) and the Cohen Kappa coefficient (*k*) for the last three conducted comparisons between the observer pairs are shown. Both indices were calculated with the program *The Observer XT* using a tolerance window of two seconds. The results for the SIS-INTER system are shown separately for the therapist and client subsystems because they are two different groups of exhaustive and mutually exclusive categories. The Berk interclass correlation coefficient (ICC) for the calculation of the degree of agreement in the total number of observations conducted with the EVED-RC scale was obtained with the *SPSS* program, assuming the parallel model and absolute agreement.

Table 8. The degree of agreement after improvement of the measurement tools

Tools		Degree of agreement (observer and indices)	
SISC-INTER	SISC-CVT-I	Pair of observers: Ob. 1 and Ob. 2	
		Fragments:	AP / Cohen Kappa:
		Case 3, S10	70% / k = 0,64, p = 0,00
		Case 10, S11	59% / k = 0,51, p = 0,00
		Case 3, S9	78% / k = 0,74, p = 0,00
	SISC-CVC-I	Pair of observers: Ob. 1 and Ob. 2	
		Fragments:	AP / Cohen Kappa:
		Case 1, S9	85% / k = 0,73, p = 0,00
		Case 11, S10	86% / k = 0,75, p = 0,00
		Case 9, S9	68% / k = 0,51, p = 0,00
SISC-COT		Pair of observers: Ob. 1 and Ob. 5	
		Fragments:	AP / Cohen Kappa:
		Case 7, S8	88% / k = 0,85, p = 0,00
		Case 13, S6	89% / k = 0,80, p = 0,00
		Case 4, S14	85% / k = 0,79, p = 0,00
EVED-RC		Pair of observers: Ob. 1 and Ob. 5 Fragments: Case 4, S7, S54a, S54b, S60, S68, S71; Case 12, S6a, S6b, S6c; Case 3, S10; Case 7, S5. ICC = 0,89, p = 0,001	

Ob. = observer; S= session.

As can be seen, in this last case, we completed the development of the assessment scale when we obtained an elevated ICC average value - 0.89 -, which can be considered an optimal value of agreement, and a statistical level of significance lower than 0.01, which allows us to reject the hypothesis that the population value of ICC is zero. In the case of the SISC-INTER (in the two subsystems) and SISC-COT coding systems, the Kappa values were always at least reasonable, and they were good or excellent overall in all cases associated with statistically significant levels lower than 0.01; this result allows us to reject the hypothesis that the agreement between observers in the compared recordings occurred by chance. The

highest values were obtained in the SISC-COT system between observers 1 and 5, with Kappa indices between 0.79 and 0.85, corresponding to agreement percentages between 85% and 89%. In the case of the subsystem for the categorization of therapist verbal behavior, SISC-CVT-I, the agreement Kappa values between observers 1 and 2 were between 0.51 and 0.74, which is equivalent to a range between 59% and 78% of agreement between these two judges. Lastly, in the system for the categorization of the client verbal behavior, SISC-CVC-I, the Kappa index varied between 0.51 and 0.75 in the last three recording comparisons between observers 1 and 2, corresponding to values between 68% and 86% of agreement between these two judges.

CONCLUSION

As stated in the introduction, when a measurement tool is used, it must have sufficient scientific quality. In addition, it must account for everything that we wish to analyze at the level of description that is of interest. With respect to scientific quality, it is typically understood that the tool is guaranteed as sufficiently valid and reliable.

The study of the validity of the tool is a continuous process that tends to begin once the tool has been developed; here, we provide a description of how the validation process will proceed. In the field of observation, validity tends to be studied in relation to three aspects or dimensions: *content validity,* which refers to whether the selection of gathered behaviors in a system is a representative sample of the phenomenon to be observed; *construct validity*, which indicates whether the defined behavioral units adequately reflect the constructs (or variables not directly observed) that we speculate that they represent; and *criteria-oriented validity,* which establishes the degree to which a code detects the possible variations of the phenomenon to be observed (León & Montero, 1997; Quera, 1997). As Quera indicated (1997), the construct validity cannot be considered valid if the behaviors are not intended to represent unobservable variables. In these cases, the defined units would be considered inherently valid. In our case, given that the developed tools are not intended to reflect hypothetical constructs, the construct validity of the tool should at some point be accepted. For content validity, the ideal would be to compare our tools with similar tools that have previously been successfully applied in order to confirm whether there is any aspect that has been overlooked and could be added; however, the scarcity, and in some cases, the absence, of tools to measure the dimensions of the behaviors studied here at the level of analysis described in this study makes such a comparison impossible. For this reason, additional studies with large samples should be conducted to confirm that the categories proposed here cover the range of therapist and client behaviors that are required for analysis. For such studies, a basic starting point would be to define the categories, examples, counter examples, and the operationalization of the categorization criteria that have been gathered in different documents related to the developed tools. This process would allow us to understand what each of the proposed categories refers to. A way of approaching the criteria-oriented validity would be to design studies in which the measurement tools are applied in order to determine, first, whether possible variations have occurred in the observed phenomenon between different cases or groups and, second, to test if the variations are theoretically coherent.

Studies that have been implemented with these tools, which will be discussed below, constitute the first step in the validation process for the presented tools.

Reliability is a fundamental aspect of research based on observation. Throughout this chapter, we have presented our approach to this issue, which consisted of the improvement of the measurement tools until appropriate levels of interjudge agreement were achieved. As explained before, in the case of the assessment scale, the index of choice is the Berk intraclass correlation coefficient, and its optimal level was reached in the development of the EVED-RC scale. The Cohen Kappa coefficient values that were obtained to calculate the agreement between observers in the SISC-INTER and SISC-COT coding systems also seem to be appropriate, although, as previously noted, the interpretation of values of this index is difficult, and different factors must be taken into account for their correct evaluation (Bakeman et al., 2007). In the present study, we should point out that the obtained Kappa values were found, in the majority of cases, to be in the range of good to excellent according to Bakeman (2000) and Landis and Koch (1977).

Despite the conclusions that we have reached, it is important to emphasize that future work should aim to confirm that the degree of interjudge agreement is maintained and/or improves, even when certain conditions vary. First, it would be favorable to continue with the improvement of category systems, especially that of the SISC-INTER, so that in every case and not only in the majority of cases, the precision of the observers is optimized when developing the recordings. Second, it would be beneficial to train inexperienced observers on the measurement tools and calculate their degree of agreement with the judges participating in this study and with other inexperienced independent judges. This process would determine whether those who did not participate in the development of the tools are capable of reliably recording their observations with them.

It would also be useful to determine whether these reliability results are found in the recordings of samples of different cases and with different therapists. In principle, although a good portion of the systems was developed with sessions led by therapist 1, the agreement between observers was not always lower when calculated in other therapists' sessions. We can see in table 8 that although the lowest Kappa values were found in two fragments of sessions with therapists other than therapist 1 (Case 10, S11; Case 9, S9), in three other fragments led by different therapists, the Kappa levels were good or excellent (Case 11, S10; Case 7, S8; Case 13, S6). Even in this case, we believe that it would be beneficial to confirm that these measurement tools are also applicable to the observation of therapists and clients that are different from the therapists and clients observed here and, if necessary, to further improve the differences found to finally conclude that these tools are applicable to any sample of clinical sessions.

As discussed at the beginning of this chapter, the goal of this study was twofold. In addition to showing the process of tool development, we intended to present possible applications for research. In an attempt to develop a useful contribution to the complex field of cognitive techniques research, we have conducted initial studies on this subject. Specifically, we began with two studies with smaller samples in which we applied a preliminary version of the SISC-INTER system, and we analyzed the behavior of the therapist at different phases of the Socratic Method in cognitive restructuring (Froján Parga, Calero Elvira et al., 2006, in press). We also conducted a study in which we applied this preliminary version of the SISC-INTER system to the development of an entire clinical case to analyze its evolution (Froján-Parga, Calero Elvira et al., 2009). More recently, three different types of

studies have been conducted in which the measurement tools presented here were applied: (1) an analysis of the verbal behaviors of therapists and clients using the SISC-INTER during different aspects of cognitive restructuring, including the Socratic Method as well as the explanation, proposal, and review of take-home work (Calero-Elvira, Froján-Parga, Ruiz-Sancho, & Vargas-de la Cruz, in press); (2) an analysis of two and three-term behavioral sequences during application of the Socratic Method in which attempts were made to identify possible mechanisms, such as shaping, responsible for the change produced. To this end, we applied the SISC-INTER system for the psychologist and the SISC-COT for the client for the recording of clinical sessions, and the differences between the Socratic Method fragments were studied with success defined according to the EVED-RC scale (Calero-Elvira, Froján-Parga, Ruiz-Sancho, & Alpañés-Freitag, under review); (3) an analysis of behavioral sequences in the therapist-client interaction during application of the Socratic Method to determine whether it would be advisable to suggest alternative verbalizations during this therapeutic procedure or if it is best to let the client generate them on his/her own. To this end, the same methods were used as in the previous study. Thus, the three measurement tools presented in this study were used (Calero-Elvira, Froján-Parga, Alpañés-Freitag, & Ruiz-Sancho, under review).

It was confirmed that these three measurement tools can be applied to approach different research objectives. As previously indicated, we are aware of the need to continue working towards improving the tools' scientific quality, and it is necessary to continue working to better understand how cognitive techniques and psychological treatment in general work. The study presented here represents another step on that path. Although improvements will be made, this work provides a small advancement in this field.

REFERENCIAS

American Psychological Association Practice Directorate (2003). *PracticeNet survey: Clinical practice patterns*. Retrieved February 14, 2009, from *http://www.apapracticenet.net/results.asp*

APA Presidential Task Force on Evidence-Based Practice (2006). Evidence-based practice in psychology. *American Psychologist, 61*, 271-285.

Arnkoff, D. B. (1986). A comparison of the coping and restructuring components of cognitive restructuring. *Cognitive Therapy & Research, 10*, 147-158.

Bakeman, R. (2000). Behavioural observation and coding. In H. T. Reis & C. M. Judd (Eds.), *Handbook of research methods in social and personality psychology* (pp. 138-159). Cambridge, England: Cambridge University Press.

Bakeman, R. & Gottman, J. M. (1986). *Observing interaction: An introduction to sequential analysis*. Cambridge, England: Cambridge University Press.

Bakeman, R., Quera, V., McArthur, D., & Robinson, B. F. (1997). Detecting sequential patterns and determining their reliability with fallible observers. *Psychological Methods, 2*, 357-370.

Beck, A. T. (1967). *Depression: Clinical, experimental, and theoretical aspects.* New York, NY: Hoeber.

Beck, A. T., Rush, A. J., Shaw, B. F., & Emery, G. (1979). *Cognitive therapy of depression: A treatment manual*. New York, NY: Guilford Press.

Bennett-Levy, J. (2003). Mechanisms of change in cognitive therapy: the case of automatic thought records and behavioural experiments. *Behavioral and Cognitive Psychotherapy, 31*, 261-277.

Berk, R. A. (1979). Generalizability of behavioral observations: A clarification of interobserver agreement and interobserver reliability. *American Journal of Mental Deficiency, 83*, 460-472.

Calero Elvira, A. (2009). *Análisis de la interacción entre terapeuta y cliente durante la aplicación de la técnica de reestructuración cognitiva* [*Analysis of interaction between therapist and client during the application of the cognitive restructuring technique*] (Unpublished doctoral dissertation). Universidad Autónoma de Madrid, Madrid, Spain.

Calero-Elvira, A., Froján-Parga, M. X., Alpañés-Freitag, M. & Ruiz-Sancho, E. M. (2011). *Change preparation during implementation of the Socratic Method: Observational study*. Manuscript submitted for publication.

Calero-Elvira, A., Froján-Parga, M. X., Ruiz-Sancho, E. & Alpañés-Freitag, M. (2011). *Descriptive study of the Socratic Method as a process of shaping*. Manuscript submitted for publication.

Calero-Elvira, A., Froján-Parga, M. X., Ruiz-Sancho, E. M. & Vargas-de la Cruz, I. (in press). Conducta verbal de terapeutas y pacientes durante la aplicación de los distintos componentes de la reestructuración cognitiva [Verbal behavior of therapists and patients during the application of the different components of the cognitive restructuring technique]. *Revista Mexicana de Psicología*.

Catania, A. C. (1992). *Learning* (3rd ed.). Englewood Cliffs, NJ: Prentice Hall.

Chambless D. L., Baker, M. J., Baucom, D. H., Beutler, L. E., Calhoun, K. S., Crits-Christoph, P.,…Woody, S. R. (1998). Update on empirically validated therapies, II. *The Clinical Psychologist, 51*(1), 3–16.

Chambless, D. L., Sanderson, W. C., Shoham, V., Johnston, S. B., Pope, K. S., Crits-Christoph, P.,...McMurray, S. (1996) An update on empirically validated therapies. *The Clinical Psychologist, 49*(2), 5-18.

Cohen, J. (1960). A coefficient of agreement for nominal scales. *Educational and Psychological Measurement, 20,* 37- 46.

Dimidjian, S., Dobson, K. S., Kohlenberg, R. J., Gallop, R., Markley, D. K., Atkins, D. C.,...Jacobson, N. S. (2006). Randomized trial of Behavioral Activation, Cognitive Therapy, and antidepresant medication in the acute treatment of adults. *Journal of Consulting and Clinical Psychology, 74*, 658-670.

Dobson, K. S., Dimidjian, S., Kohlenberg, R. J., Rizvi, S. L., Hollon, S. D., Schmaling, K. B.,…Gollan, J. K. (2008). Randomized trial of behavioral activation, cognitive therapy, and antidepressant medication in the prevention of relapse and recurrence in major depression. *Journal of Consulting and Clinical Psychology, 76*, 468-477.

Ellis, A. (1962). *Reason and Emotion in Psychotherapy.* New York, NY: Lile Stuart.

Ellis, A. & Grieger, R. (1977). *Handbook of rational emotive therapy.* New York: Springer.

Froján-Parga, M. X., Calero-Elvira, A., & Montaño-Fidalgo, M. (2006). Procesos de aprendizaje en las técnicas de reestructuración semántica [Learning processes in the cognitive restructuring techniques]. *Análisis y Modificación de Conducta, 32*, 287-305.

Froján-Parga, M. X., Calero-Elvira, A., & Montaño-Fidalgo, M. (2009). Analysis of the therapist´s verbal behavior during cognitive restructuring debates: A case study. *Psychotherapy Research, 19*, 30-41.

Froján-Parga, M. X., Calero-Elvira, A., & Montaño-Fidalgo, M. (in press). Study of the Socratic method during cognitive restructuring. *Clinical Psychology & Psychotherapy.*

Froján, M. X., Montaño, M., & Calero, A. (2006). ¿Por qué la gente cambia en terapia? Un estudio preliminar [Why do people change in therapy? A preliminary study]. *Psicothema, 18*, 797-803.

Froján, M. X., Montaño, M., & Calero, A. (2007). Why do people change in therapy? A preliminary study. *Psychology in Spain, 11*, 53-60.

Froján, M. X., Montaño, M., & Calero, A. (2010). Verbal behavior analysis: A descriptive approach to psychotherapeutic phenomenon. *Spanish Journal of Psychology, 13,* 914-926.

Froján, M. X., Montaño, M., Calero, A., García, A., Garzón, A., & Ruiz, E. (2008). Sistema de categorización de la conducta verbal del terapeuta [Therapist's verbal behavior coding system]. *Psicothema, 20*, 603-609.

Froján Parga, M. X., Montaño-Fidalgo, M., Calero Elvira, A. y Ruiz-Sancho, E. (2011). Aproximación al estudio funcional de la interacción verbal entre terapeuta y cliente durante el proceso terapéutico [An approach to the functional study of verbal interaction between therapist and client during the therapeutic process]. *Clínica y Salud, 22*, 69-85.

Froján Parga, M. X., Ruiz Sancho, E. M., Montaño Fidalgo, M., Calero Elvira, A. y Alpañés Freitag, M. (in press). Estudio de las diferencias durante la evaluación clínica según la experiencia del terapeuta [Study of the differences during the clinical assessment according to the therapist's experience]. *Anales de Psicología.*

Garratt, G., Ingram, R. E., Rand, K. L., & Sawalani, G. (2007). Cognitive processes in cognitive therapy: Evaluation of the mechanisms of change in the treatment of depression. *Clinical Psychology: Science and Practice, 14*, 224-239.

Hill, C. E. & Lambert, M. J. (2004). Methodological issues in studying psychotherapy process and outcome. In M. J. Lambert (Ed.), *Bergin and Garfield's Handbook of Psychotherapy and Behavior Change* (5th ed., pp. 84-135). Nueva York: John Wiley.

Jacobson, N. S. & Christensen, A. (1996). *Integrative couple therapy: Promoting acceptance and change.* New York, NY: Norton.

Jarrett, R. & Nelson, R. (1987). Mechanisms of change in cognitive therapy of depression. *Behavior Therapy, 18*, 227-241.

Karpiak, C. P. & Benjamin, L. S. (2004). Therapist affirmation and the process and outcome of psychotherapy: two sequential analytic studies. *Journal of Clinical Psychology, 60*, 659-676.

Kazdin, A. E. (2008). Evidence-Based treatments and practice. New opportunities to bridge clinical research and practice, enhance the knowledge base, and improve patient care. *American Psychologist, 63*, 146-159.

Landis, J. R. & Koch, G. G. (1977). The measurement of observer agreement for categorical data. *Biometrics, 33*, 159-174.

León, O. G. & Montero, I. (1997). Diseño de investigaciones. Introducción a la lógica de la investigación en Psicología y Educación [Research design. Introduction to research on Psychology and Education] (2nd ed.). Madrid, Spain: McGraw-Hill.

Llewelyn, S. & Hardy, G. (2001). Process research in understanding and applying psychological therapies. *British Journal of Clinical Psychology, 40*, 1-21.

Longmore, R. J. & Worrell, M. (2007). Do we need to challenge thoughts in cognitive behavior therapy? *Clinical Psychology Review, 27*, 173-187.

Orlinsky, D. E., Rønnestad, M. H., & Willutzki, U. (2004). Fifty years of psychotherapy process-outcome research: continuity and change. In M. J. Lambert (Ed.), *Bergin and Garfield's handbook of psychotherapy and behaviour change* (5th ed., pp. 307-389). New York, NY: John Wiley.

Pérez-Álvarez, M. (1996a). *La psicoterapia desde el punto de vista conductista [Psychotherapy from the behavioristic point of view]*. Madrid, Spain: Biblioteca Nueva.

Pérez-Álvarez, M. (1996b). *Tratamientos psicológicos [Psychological treatments]*. Madrid, Spain: Universitas.

Pérez-Álvarez, M. (2004). *Contingencia y drama. La psicología según el conductismo [Contingency and drama. Psychology from behaviorism]*. Madrid, Spain: Minerva Ediciones.

Quera, V. (1991). Muestreo y registro observacional [Observational sampling and coding]. In M. T. Anguera (Ed.), *Metodología observacional en la investigación psicológica. Volumen I: Fundamentación [Observational methodology in psychological research. Volume I: Basis]* (pp. 241-327). Barcelona, Spain: Promociones y Publicaciones Universitarias.

Quera, V. (1997). Los métodos observacionales en la Etología [Observational methods in Ethology]. In F. Peláez & J. Veà (Eds.), *Etología. Bases biológicas de la conducta animal y humana* [*Ethology. Biological basis of animal and human behavior*] (pp. 43-83). Madrid, Spain: Pirámide.

Rosen, G. M. & Davison, G. C. (2003). Psychology should list empirically supported principles of change (ESPs) and not credential trademarked therapies or other treatment packages. *Behavior Modification, 27*, 300-312.

Task Force on Promotion and Dissemination of Psychological Procedures (1995). Training in and dissemination of empirically-validated psychological treatments: Report and recomendations. *The Clinical Psychologist, 48*(1), 3-23.

Whisman, M. A. (1993). Mediators and moderators of change in cognitive therapy of depression. *Psychological Bulletin, 114*, 248-265.

Zettle, R. D. & Hayes, S. C. (1987). Component and process analysis of cognitive therapy. *Psychological Report, 61*, 939-953.

In: Advances in Psychology Research. Volume 88
Editor: Alexandra M. Columbus, pp. 197-211
ISBN: 978-1-62100-591-9

Chapter 10

GENDER DIFFERENCES IN BIPOLAR DISORDER

Laia Miquel[a], Judith Usall[b] and Josep Maria Haro[b]
[a] CAS Vall d'Hebron, Vall d'Hebron Hospital,
Universitat Autonoma de Barcelona, Spain.
[b] Parc Sanitari Sant Joan de Déu. Centro de Investigación
Biomédica en Red de Salud Mental (CIBERSAM), Spain.

ABSTRACT

Interest in epidemiological and clinical gender differences in bipolar disorder have increased over the past few years. Most studies have found that women are at a higher risk of starting the bipolar disorder with a depressive episode and have more depressive episodes during the course of illness. When psychotic symptoms are associated with pure or mixed manic episodes, women show more paranoid and reference delusions than men, and more hallucinations. Moreover, women have a greater risk of mixed episodes and more tendency to rapid cycling than men. Anxiety and eating co-morbid disorders are more frequent in women whereas substance abuse disorders are more common in men. However, women with bipolar disorder have more drug problems than women of the general population. Other differences are more controversial, some studies have found that the age of onset is later among women, whereas others have found no significant differences. More women are hospitalised for manic episodes and it is controversial if they need more days for recovering. Longitudinal studies have shown that in women depressive episodes are more frequent than manic, mixed or euthymic episodes during the course of the illness. Moreover, women are at higher risk of suffering from depression. Treatment strategies specific for women in bipolar disorder are still scarce and will be discussed.

INTRODUCTION

The influence of gender in bipolar condition has been moderately studied in the last years. However, evidence on some clinical characteristics, outcomes, prognosis, and

treatment responses is still lacking. In this chapter we will review the most relevant results about the relationship between gender and bipolar disorder (BD) in adult population.

Bipolar illness is divided into different subtypes, the most frequents are bipolar I and II, which have been the most studied. There seems to be an equal proportion of men and women with bipolar type I and more women suffering from bipolar type II disorder.

CLINICAL DIFFERENCES

Age at Onset

It is very difficult to establish if there are gender differences in the age at onset of bipolar disorders. Some possible explanations are that most study samples consist of bipolar I and II patients and do not analyse the two illnesses separately. Since course of illness of bipolar I and II disorders is different not separating the two disorders may provide misleading results. Moreover, data taken from retrospective studies are subject to bias because patients have trouble recognizing symptoms that appeared at the beginning of the illness. On the other hand, experts use different definitions for establishing when the disorder starts. For example, some studies consider the beginning of the illness to be when it is first being treated[1], or when the first symptom took place (manic or depressive)[2] or when patients first met full DSM criteria for an affective episode [3], and other authors only consider the beginning of the illness when manic or hypomanic symptoms occur [4]. This situation can explain the conflicting results observed. Some authors have described that first symptoms of bipolar I and II disorder appeared significantly earlier in women (19.9 ± 9.6 vs 24.9 ± 10 years) [5,6]. Others found the opposite (men: 29.4 ± 10.9 vs. women: 30.3 ± 10.7 years) [2,7,8]. Additionally, one study found that the first depressive episode started earlier in women (21.9 ± 10.3 vs 24.3 ± 10.8) [9]and the first manic episode happened at an older age in females (35.1 ± 16.2 vs 30 ± 13.4; Z=-2.72, p=0.007)[4]. A part from that, some authors did not find significant gender differences in age at onset [3,10,11].

Risk factors related with age at onset of BD have not been well studied and need more research. Some authors have observed that antisocial traits can be associated with a younger age at onset [4] as illness presenting with psychosis [12]. Furthermore, substance use disorder (SUD) can trigger the illness [13].

Comorbidity

Comorbidity in BD with axis I or II disorders is frequent. Different patterns of comorbidity due to gender have been described.

Drug and alcohol dependence are very common in BD with a prevalence around 58% [13]. All studies have found significantly more legal and illegal drug consumption in men than in women (34% vs 24%) [1,5,6] being alcohol the most used (48.4% vs 20.3%; χ^2=10.66, p=0.001) [14,15]. Although more men have SUD, bipolar women have 7.35 (3.32-16.26) times more risk of developing alcohol dependence compared with women of the general population [16]. Furthermore, worst consequences have been described in dual-

diagnosis women [17] even if no differences were found in the addiction severity index scale [13].

Furthermore, women have more comorbid anxiety disorders (46%women 29%men) [6], eating disorders like bulimia (12% vs 2%) [5,10] and borderline personality disorder [5]. Moreover, women reported more sexual abuse (51% vs 14%), physical abuse (59% vs 31%), and post-traumatic stress disorder (PTSD) (21-42% vs 9-17%) than men [10,13]. Women have to be aware that if they are in a manic episode, where the risk of sexual abuse is high, it increases the risk of unwanted pregnancy and sexually transmitted diseases [18]. About suicide attempts, in general studies did not find significant gender differences (men, 20.6%; women, 19.6%) [8,10,19].

Course of the Illness

Longitudinal, prospective and naturalistic studies have shown that most bipolar I and II patients spend more time in a depressed mood (33-47%) [18,20,21] than manic (7-11%) [20,21]. Large rates of depression may cause high rates of disability in those patients [22]. Gender has not been found as a predictor of time spent with depression during the course of the illness [5,6,21]. Consistently, similar proportions of bipolar illness-time in mania (42.2 vs. 42.4%) and in depression (57.8 vs. 57.6%) were found in both sexes [8]. Nevertheless, men spent significantly more time euthymic than women (44.81% vs 34.46%)[5].

With regard to polarity and gender it is difficult to set any evidence because of controversial data. Most studies asses that women tend to have more depressive and mixed episodes. In this sense, it has been suggested that more women have a depressive diathesis and this theory would explain why more women are diagnosed later in life with a BD. Even though some authors found that women were more likely to start the illness with a depressive episode (1.21 times more) [8], not all found gender differences in depression at onset [10]. Until now, the methodology used to asses bipolar diathesis has been inadequate because most studies are retrospective.

Even if no gender differences have been described in the total time spent in depression during the illness, it seems that women have more depressive episodes during its course [19,23]. Prospective studies have found that more women than men develop a new depressive episode (76.3% vs 57.5%) [5] at short (12 weeks) and long (12 months) follow-up [2]. Anixety and psychosis have been related with a major presence of depression [6,12] both of which conditions are more frequent in women. Women are more aware of psychosocial stressors and experience a higher number of life events than men before depressive episodes [23]. It has been hypothesized that depression is more frequent in women due to a better prophylactic effect of lithium in men than in women for depression [1,24]. However, some authors did not describe gender differences in number of depressive episodes [7,10,14]. Differences between study outcomes can be explained by differences in population studied. For example, some exclude patients with SUD which has been related with depression in bipolar I patients [13].

In general, no significant gender differences have been described in the severity of symptoms [6,7,25,26]. Only one study found higher BDI scores in women (20.9 ± 11.3 vs 25.2 ± 12.3) [5].

Respect to manic episodes most of them have been described in men (10.4 ± 4.3 vs 7.3 ± 3.1, Z=2.4, p<0.05) [7,23] but not all studies have done so [10,14]. No gender differences were found in BD type II patients in hypomanic episodes [9].

On the other hand, mixed episodes and atypical depression have been related to females independently of the definition criteria used [9,13,18,19]. In hospitalised patients larger rates of mixed mania were described in women [15]. People who had suffered sexual and physical abuse had 4 times more risk of developing a mixed episode [13]. This outcome could explain to a certain extent why mixed mania is more frequent in women..

Rapid-cycling has been also considered characteristic of female sex, even if studies are not conclusive enough. Reports with large samples did not find gender differences in rapid cycling [2,10], although other studies found more rapid-cyclers among women (21% vs 15%) [6,18]. Thyroidal dysfunction, gonadal steroids, sleep-wake cycle, antidepressant medication have been considered risk factors related with rapid cycling. However, there is not enough evidence to support any of those hypothesis [1,18].

Psychotic symptoms are frequent in BD. Hallucinations have been described in 21.9% of mixed episodes, 11.2% mania and in 10.5% of bipolar depression {{861 Baethge,C. 2005}}. History of psychosis was considerably more frequent in BD women than in males [3]. One study evaluated gender differences in the presence and type of psychotic symptoms and found that 60% women vs 40% men with pure or mixed mania presented with concomitant psychosis. Delusions and hallucinations were more frequent in women patients (66.9%, 59.3%) than in men (33.1%, 40.7%), being this differences statistically significant. Paranoid delusions and delusions of reference were more frequent in women [12].

Gender Differences in Use of Services

Most experts agree that women start their first contact with psychiatrist later than men [4]. It has been described that women averaged 5.49 years older than men at the start of long-term lithium maintenance treatment and their latency from illness onset to start of lithium maintenance was 24.4 months longer than in men [8]. This difference could be explained because people with depression usually ask for treatment later than those with mania [1]. However, Suominen et al found that women started treatment at a younger age (28.7 ± 9.9 vs 32.8 ± 12 years)[5]. More women were treated as outpatients than as inpatients (57.8% versus 51.9%, $\chi 2 = 5.8$, df = 1, p < 0.02) [15] but no gender differences were found in number of admissions [14]. Women stayed longer in hospital [15] and were admitted for mania [14]. Little differences have been found during time to remission, worsening, and recurrence between studies [2,5,27]. Only a slightly higher proportion of women achieved mania improvement over 12 months of follow-up (95.4% vs. 89.2%) [2]. On the other hand, some studies found that time to recurrence was longer in men and that women had more recurrent episodes independently of its type [5]. Moreover, a gender effect was observed in mania recurrence even after adjustment to substance abuse and PTSD [13].

Treatment Differences

Depression is the most common condition that occurs during the life-time of Bipolar Disorders. Moreover, it seems that women are at a higher risk of having more depressive episodes. However, psychopharmacological strategies for treating acute depression and its prevention are scarce. Nowadays, lithium, valproate sodium and most atypical antipsychotics have been demonstrated to be useful for acute pure or mixed mania and for maintenance treatment. They are recommended in all clinical guidelines but no gender distinction is made because little is known about differences in pharmacological strategies due to gender.

An individualized approach has to be made with respect to gender. Women of childbearing age must know about effective contraception and have to be warned of the interaction between antiepileptic drugs and oral contraceptives (carbamacepine, oxcarbamazepine and topiramate) [18,24]. Individual decisions, choosing the best treatment according to women's wishes during pregnancy and breastfeeding, will have to be made according to severity of illness, prior frequency of episodes and any past history of relapse in pregnancy and the post-partum period.

Treating Bipolar Depression

Moderate to severe bipolar depression has to be treated with antidepressants combined with lithium or an antiepileptic [29]. The combination of olanzapine/fluoxetine also has an indication in the FDA. They showed better results compared to placebo and lamotrigine, but improvements have been observed only in secondary outcomes such as sleep and appetite [30]. Prescription of antidepressants in monotherapy should be avoided, overall in women, because of the high risk of promoting rapid-cycling [24]. SSRI antidepressants (but not paroxetine in pregnant women) are recommended as first-line therapy because these are less likely than tricyclic antidepressants to be associated with mood switching [29]. Lamotrigine has been demonstrated to be effective for bipolar depression and the prevention of depressive episodes in bipolar disorder. However, it has a very slow titration schedule and may take up to 4 weeks to reach a therapeutic dosage due to its risk of causing Stevens-Johnson syndrome [30]. Furthermore, we have to take into account that women on oral contraceptives can have reduced plasma concentration levels of lamotrigine [31]. There is limited evidence on lithium for bipolar depression even if it is recommended in some clinical guidelines as a first-line treatment for acute depression [32].

In the last few years, atypical antipsychotics have been tested for treating acute depression. Quetiapine 600mg has been demonstrated to be superior to lithium and paroxetine for improving MADRAS scores in Bipolar I patients and was effective for rapid-cyclers too. However, it had the disadvantage that it caused a lot of dropouts [30]. Because of that, the FDA-approved for bipolar depression a dose of 400 mg/day of quetiapine, which it can be reached within 2–3 days [30]. Patients with bipolar II disorder appeared to be more refractory to treatment because improvements in clinical measurements did not reach statistical significance during follow-up [30]. Two meta-analyses were carried out, the first one reviewed the efficacy of quetiapine, olanzapine and aripiprazol and the second one included randomised clinical trials about antiepileptics and atypical antipshycotics. The first one,

conclude that all three antipshycotics tested, demonstrated significant efficacy from week 1 through week 6. From week 6 to endpoint (week 8) quetiapine and olanzapine maintained their superiority over placebo, but aripiprazole did not. However, we still can't answer whether monotherapy with antipsychotics for acute depression is superior to combination therapy [33]. Second one concluded that mood-stabilizers monotherapy was superior to placebo and equivalent to combination or antidepressant therapy in bipolar I patients. No individual agent was demonstrated to be superior to the others. They recommended lamotrigine and quetiapine as first-line treatment for bipolar depression followed by carbamazepine and olanzapine [32].

When acute depression, treated with antidepressants is remitted, stopping medication should be considered [29]. Evidence on treatment maintenance of bipolar depression is short. There is no published literature on antipsycothics monotherapy for maintenance of bipolar depression [30].

Mood Stabilizers

Pharmacodinamic response to mode stabilizers only has been systematically studied with lithium. In some cases it has been found that lithium blood levels can vary depending on the menstrual phase, but there is not enough evidence to say that those changes affect efficacy [1]. Viguera et al after reviewing 17 reports about bipolar patients in maintenance treatment with lithium monotherapy concluded that there are not statistically significant differences in both sexes in terms of response (time being ill, improvement in episodes, etc) and morbidity, although outcomes were slightly superior in women. Nevertheless, some differences were found like lower serum concentration requirements of lithium in women, or women remaining longer than men in treatment without discontinuing differently (52.6 vs. 58.3%; chi-sq=0.969, NS) [8]. Moreover, survival analysis of time to first recurrence showed significantly earlier recurrence in men than in women (10.0±1.91 vs. 16.0±1.89 months [$\chi 2$(1 df)=8.3, p=0.004]) [8]. No studies have been carried out to test gender differences in other mood stabilizers. However, data make us think that there are not substantial gender differences in terms of response and efficacy to them.

On the other hand, differences have been observed in adverse effects on mood stabilizers. Lithium was found to cause less tremor in women than in men (26% vs 54%, p<0.05). Weight gain (47% v. 18%, $p < 0.05$) and hypothirodism (37% v. 9%, $p < 0.05$) were more frequent in women [24,34]. More over, women are at higher risk of developing lithium induced thyroiditis [31]. It is thought that lithium releases the thyroid hormone and secondarily may inhibit hormone synthesis and induce de production of antithyroid antibodies. Two explanations of why thyroidal dysfunction is more frequent in women have to be considered. First, it is thought that women are at higher risk as a reflection of what happens on general population [1]. And second, developing hypothyroidism after lithium treatment has been associated with weight gain and not with sex [34].

Valproic has to be avoided, when ever it is possible, in women of child-bearing because menstrual disturbances associated with polycystic ovary syndrome (PCOS) [1,18,24] have been described. Moreover, hyperandorgenism [1,18,24], hyperinsulinemia which has been related to weight gain [24,31] and also alopecia [24] are very frequent in women. The

association between PCOS and sodium valproat has not been clarified yet, but it has been suggested that could be due to weight gain which has been at the same time related with hyperinsulinemia and low levels of insulin-like growth factor-binding protein 1 [31]. If valproat agent had to be prescribed in a women weight (BMI) should be monitored at the beginning of the treatment and in each visit, like menstrual cycle and hyperandrogenism signs (hirsutism, alopecia or acne). If necessary hormonal levels should be determined to diagnose side effects [35]. Other recommendations for treatment of premenopausal women taking valproate are numbered in table 1.

Table 1. Recommendations for treatment of premenopausal women taking valproat

	Baseline	Each visit	Annual
Measure body mass index (BMI)	x	x	
Menstrual cycle	x	x	
Ovarian structure (pelvic ultrasound)	x		x
Sex hormone concentration	x		x
Lipid profile	x		x
Signs of hyperandrogenism	x	x	
Dehydroepiandrosterone and testosterone	x		x
Councel on nutrition and exercice	x	x	

When carbamazepine is prescribed in women taking oral contraceptives they have to be aware of the potential reduction of their effectiveness because carbamacepine increases hormone clearance [1,31]. Doses of oral contraceptives have to be heightened to maintain their protective effect against pregnancy [1,24].

Antipsychotics offer some practical advantages over the other pharmacologic options because they do not require therapeutic blood monitoring and need a short amount of days to reach a therapeutic dose [30]. Information on dosages based on gender is lacking in clinical trials although antipsychotic kinetic differences have been described between males and females. The findings suggest that women may need less dose of medication because have a greater gastrointestinal absorption, higher rates of distribution in the body and different enzymatic activity and liver clearance [36]. Moreover, women are more sensible to side effects like tardive dyskinesia or weight gain [37]. Because of that, some adverse effects like hyperglycemia, dyslipidemia, and weight gain would need monitoring [24,30]. Additionaly, hyperprolactinemia is an adverse effect very relevant for women because increases the risk of sexual dysfunction and infertility [18,24]. Risperidone is the antipshycotic that has more risk to raise prolactine levels [18]. Menstrual dysfunction can appear but in lower rates (<1%) with quetiapine, clozapine, olanzapine, and ziprasidona [24].

PREGNANCY

Against what has been previously thought, pregnancy is not protective towards bipolar disorder. Almost 50% of pregnant women experience severe mood symptoms in relation to childbearing. There is evidence that postpartum is the most risky period during pregnancy in which severe symptoms like psychosis can appear [18,31].

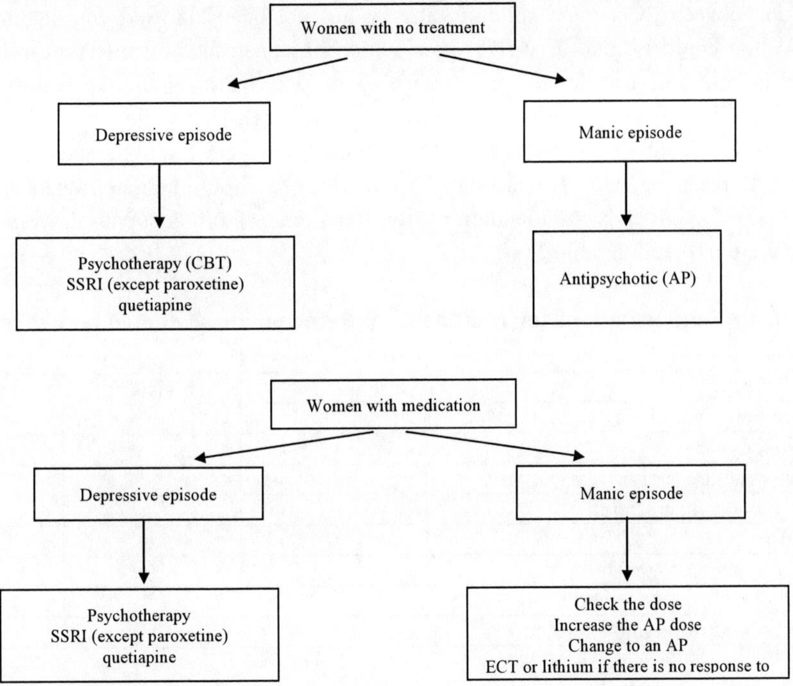

Figure1. Managing treatment during pregnancy in women with bipolar disorder.

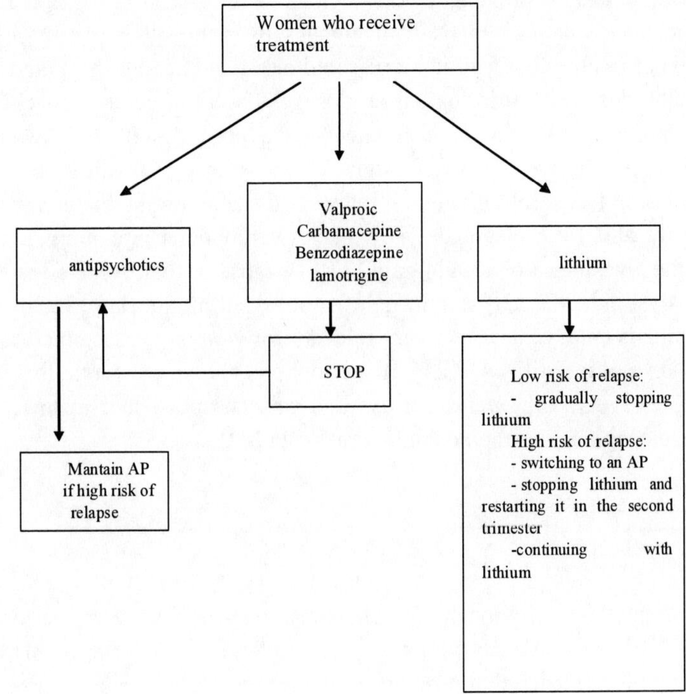

Figure 2. Treatment options in Bipolar Disorder while planning conception.

The problem is that no psychotropic drug has been specifically licensed for pregnancy [29], in deed most of them are considered category C or D [18].

Women who want to become pregnant need some counselling for a minimum of 3 months before the conception. They have to be aware of the risk of worsening during this period and which is the best treatment option to be chosen. It is very important to plan pregnancy because abrupt discontinuation of medication would strongly increase risk of recurrence [24,31,38]. Furthermore, folate supplementation (4-5mg/day) 3 months before conception and during 3 first months of pregnancy should be prescribed to minimize congenital abnormalities related with neural tube defects [31].

Nowadays, antipsychotics are considered the ones of least risk. Valproate, carbamacepine, lamotrigine, paroxetine and long-term treatment with benzodiazepines are not recommended during pregnancy and should be avoided if possible.

Depending on historical factors (previous course of the disease, duration of euthymia and treatment response, etc) medical decisions following the recommendations shown in fig1. and 2 would have to be taken with the mother's approval. As lithium may heighten the risk of congenital abnormalities (up to 20 to 40 times than the rate in the general population [38] it would be recommended to taper slowly the medication, when women have a low risk of relapse. The most common congenital alterations due to lithium are cardiovascular effects like Ebstein's anomaly [1,18,24], in which a risk of between 0.05% and 0.01% was identified following exposure in the first trimester [39], or neonatal toxicity like "floppy baby" syndrome (cyanosis and hypotonicity), neonatal hypothyroidism or nephrogenic diabetes insipidus [24]. When the risk of relapse is moderate psychiatrists have different choices. Lithium can be switched to an antipsychotic because it is known to be safe, or lithium can be avoided during the first trimester [31] and restarted during the second trimester if the women only has well responded to it compared to other pharmacological agents [18,24,29,31]. Some authors recommend starting treatment during the third trimester to prevent relapse because the postpartum period is one of the most risky ones [18]. Finally, in cases were women have had previous manic episodes during pregnancy, lithium can be maintained if woman respond well [29]. In the case that the mother decides to maintain treatment the lowest effective dose of medication should be used. In this case they would receive appropriate counselling, high-resolution ultrasound and foetal echocardiography at 16-18 weeks of gestation [18,38]. During the third trimester the dose should be checked, as plasma levels rise 50%, and it would be important to keep serum levels of lithium within the therapeutic range [29,31]. The recommendation is to monitor, serum lithium levels monthly, then weekly before childbirth, and less than 24 hours after childbirth [31].

Several studies have found that the use of lithium reduces the risk of relapse if re-instituted shortly before delivery (at about week 36), or within 48 hours of delivery and is continued into the post-partum period. As neonatal toxicity can occur, careful monitoring of maternal lithium levels needs to occur during and immediately after delivery [24]. If a woman maintained on lithium is at high risk of a manic relapse in the immediate postnatal period, augmenting treatment with an antipsychotic should be considered [29].

Of all mood-stabilizers, lithium is preferred over valproate and carbamazepine during the second and third trimester [24] because anticonvulsivants have shown that they increase the risk of malformations in pregnancy [39]. In the case that anticonvulsivants have to be prescribed women might be encouraged to take folate supplements to prevent the high risk of neural tube defects [18,24]. Prevalence of major congenital malformations due to valproate

has been determined between 6.2% and 16% [40]. Valproate is the antiepileptic agent which has been most associated with teratogenicity followed by carbamacepine 2.9% and lamotrigine 2.7% [39]. Valproate and carbamacepine have been associated with major congenital abnormalities involving neural tube defects, growth retardation, cardiac abnormalities and intrauterine growth retardation [18,24,39]. Carbamacepine can produce fetal vitamin K deficeny which increases the risk of neonatal bleeding and mid-facial abnormalities [38]. In neonats valproate has been associated with liver toxicity and hypoglycaemia. Additionally, carbamacepine can produce hepatic toxicity and hyperbilirubinemia [24,38]. If there is no alternative to valproate the woman should be informed of the increased risk to the fetus and the child's intellectual development. The lowest possible effective dose should be used being the maximum dosage about 1gram per day divided in doses [29]. Also it would be useful to consider augmenting its efficacy with additional antimanic medication (but not carbamazepine). However, it is recommended to avoid polytherapy as it has been associated with poorer neurodevelopmental outcomes [39]. Lamotrigine can cause abnormalities in 1.8% of cases a little bit more that those described in the general population [24]. The most frequent facial deficits described were oral clefts (cleft lip or palate) [40] although this observation was refuted in a report [39].

There is wide experience with first-generation antipsychotics during pregnancy and research has assessed its safety. Antipsychotics are recommended to treat manic relapse or to prevent recurrence during pregnancy when the woman has a history of frequent clinical worsening with mood-stabilizers like anticonvulsivants. Haloperidol was not found to increase major malformations compared with the group who was not exposed to it [41]. Few studies have been carried out to assess the teratogenic effects of second-generation antipsychotics. However, data reported did not show increased rates of fetus malformations compared with women of the general population [41].

When women have a depressive episode during pregnancy psychotherapy and antidepressives should be prescribed. For mild to moderate episodes psychotherapy like CBT, brief psychological interventions or antidepressant medication should be considered. Antidepressives like sertraline, fluoxetine and fluvoxamine are safe. However, some teratogenic abnormalities were assessed with paroxetine and tricyclic antidepressants which can cause anticholinergic effects in the neonate [24,29]. For moderate to severe depressive symptoms in pregnant women psychological intervention plus a combination of antidepressants with quetiapine or quetiapine alone should be prescribed. Because of the high risk of switching women would be monitored closely during treatment and antidepressants should be stopped if she develops manic or hypomanic symptoms [29]. In the case of psychosis or suicidal ideation appearing ECT should be considered [31].

BREASTFEEDING

Breastfeeding is not recommended in women taking lithium because 10-50% of maternal lithium serum levels can go through maternal breast milk and cause thyroid dysfunction [24,31]. It only would be safe when the child has more than 5 months. On the other hand, valproate and carbamacepine are compatible but they can cause hepatic dysfunction, anemia or thrombocytopenia[24,31]. There exists limited data on lamotrigine [24]. Atypical

antipsychotics, except clozapine, should be the first choice [29], although somnolence, tremor and rigidity have to be monitored in the baby [24]. The effects of antidepressant are not well known [18]. Tryciclic antidepressants are safe and SSIRs are recommended, except fluoxetine because a case of seizure-like activity was described and citalporam [29]. More studies are required [24]. Benzodiazepines, SSRI, older antipsychotic agents, clozpaine and lamotrigine appear in low concentrations in the milk but their long half-lives and metabolites can result in accumulation in plasma and tissues [31]. Sleep deprivation has to be taken into account after childbirth. It is recommended that women who take medication do so after breastfeeding and before the child sleeps [31].

Menstrual Cycle

Influence of menstrual cycle in modulation of symptoms in bipolar disorder has not been well studied but is receiving increased attention. Menstrual disturbances have been described 1.7 times more frequent in women with BD than women from the general population before the onset of the BD [42] and during the course of the illness while women take medication [43,44]. Nevertheless, we still do not know how neuroendocrine system disregulation can affect the pathophysiology of BD.

A recent study found premenstrual exacerbation in 65.2% of BD women showing more depressive episodes [45]. Moreover, premenstrual exacerbation was related with less time to relapse [45]. Conversely, a study carried out with 41 patients, 13 of which were in a depressive or manic episode, did not find any significant relationship between the phase of the menstrual cycle and the episodes [46]. In addition, even though some mood changes happened during the menstrual cycle no pattern was identified [43]. However, oestrogens administered exogenously have been related with manic symptoms and rapid-cycling. This results contrast with mixed findings observed between the influence of menstrual cycle and rapid-cycling [31].

Some experts have tried to investigate the relationship between pharmacokinetic changes in medication and hormonal changes but those studies have been carried out only in males [47,48].

Similarly, evidence of hormonal treatments for BD is limited. Some reports described mood stabilization in some cases, a better response of post-partum depression and good responses of refractory bipolar disorder in postmenopausal women [24]. In some cases, it has been recommended to use hormonal therapy to stabilize mood [1]and there is one study which found an improvement in manic symptoms in women receiving tamoxifen adjunct to a mood stabilizer compared with placebo [37]. However, we still do not know how steroid therapy can help to the course of BD.

Conclusions

Gender is a variable that has to be taken into account when treatment strategies for bipolar disorder are investigated. Solid findings about gender differences are that women are at higher risk of starting the bipolar disorder with a depressive episode and have more

depressive episodes during the course of illness. Women have a greater risk of mixed episodes and more tendency to rapid cycling than men. Anxiety and eating co-morbid disorders are more frequent in women.

An individualized treatment approach has to be made with respect to gender. Women of childbearing age must know about effective contraception and have to be warned of the interaction between antiepileptic drugs and oral contraceptives (carbamacepine, oxcarbamazepine and topiramate). Individual decisions, choosing the best treatment according to women's wishes during pregnancy and breastfeeding, will have to be made according to severity of illness, prior frequency of episodes and any past history of relapse in pregnancy and the post-partum period.

References

[1] Leibenluft, E. Women with bipolar illness: clinical and research issues. *Am J Psychiatry,* 1996;153:163-173.

[2] Miquel, L; Usall, J; Reed, C; Bertsch, J; Vieta, E; Gonzalez-Pinto, A; et al. Gender differences in outcomes of acute mania: a 12-month follow-up study. *Arch Womens Ment Health,* 2011;14:107-113.

[3] Carrus, D; Christodoulou, T; Hadjulis, M; Haldane, M; Galea, A; Koukopoulos, A; et al. Gender differences in immediate memory in bipolar disorder. *Psychol Med,* 2010;40:1349-1355.

[4] Kennedy, N; Boydell, J; Kalidindi, S; Fearon, P; Jones, PB; van Os, J; et al. Gender differences in incidence and age at onset of mania and bipolar disorder over a 35-year period in Camberwell, England. *Am J Psychiatry,* 2005;162:257-262.

[5] Suominen, K; Mantere, O; Valtonen, H; Arvilommi, P; Leppamaki, S & Isometsa, E. Gender differences in bipolar disorder type I and II. *Acta Psychiatr Scand,* 2009;120:464-473.

[6] Altshuler, LL; Kupka, RW; Hellemann, G; Frye, MA; Sugar, CA; McElroy, SL; et al. Gender and depressive symptoms in 711 patients with bipolar disorder evaluated prospectively in the Stanley Foundation bipolar treatment outcome network. *Am J Psychiatry,* 2010;167:708-715.

[7] Robb, JC; Young, LT; Cooke, RG & Joffe, RT. Gender differences in patients with bipolar disorder influence outcome in the medical outcomes survey (SF-20) subscale scores. *J Affect Disord,* 1998;49:189-193.

[8] Viguera, AC; Baldessarini, RJ & Tondo, L. Response to lithium maintenance treatment in bipolar disorders: comparison of women and men. *Bipolar Disord,* 2001;3:245-252.

[9] Benazzi, F. Gender differences in bipolar-II disorder. *Eur Arch Psychiatry Clin Neurosci,* 2006;256:67-71.

[10] Baldassano, CF; Marangell, LB; Gyulai, L; Ghaemi, SN; Joffe, H; Kim, DR; et al. Gender differences in bipolar disorder: retrospective data from the first 500 STEP-BD participants. *Bipolar Disord,* 2005;7:465-470.

[11] Young, RC; Kiosses, D; Heo, M; Schulberg, HC; Murphy, C; Klimstra, S; et al. Age and ratings of manic psychopathology. *Bipolar Disord,* 2007;9:301-304.

[12] Braunig, P; Sarkar, R; Effenberger, S; Schoofs, N & Kruger, S. Gender differences in psychotic bipolar mania. *Gend Med,* 2009;6:356-361.

[13] Meade, CS; McDonald, LJ; Graff, FS; Fitzmaurice, GM; Griffin, ML & Weiss, RD. A prospective study examining the effects of gender and sexual/physical abuse on mood outcomes in patients with co-occurring bipolar I and substance use disorders. *Bipolar Disord,* 2009;11:425-433.

[14] Hendrick, V; Altshuler, LL; Gitlin, MJ; Delrahim, S & Hammen, C. Gender and bipolar illness. *J Clin Psychiatry,* 2000;61:393-6; quiz 397.

[15] Kessing, LV. Gender differences in the phenomenology of bipolar disorder. *Bipolar Disord,* 2004;6:421-425.

[16] Frye, MA; Altshuler, LL; McElroy, SL; Suppes, T; Keck, PE; Denicoff, K; et al. Gender differences in prevalence, risk, and clinical correlates of alcoholism comorbidity in bipolar disorder. *Am J Psychiatry,* 2003;160:883-889.

[17] McDermott, BE; Quanbeck, CD & Frye, MA. Comorbid substance use disorder in women with bipolar disorder associated with criminal arrest. *Bipolar Disord,* 2007;9:536-540.

[18] Curtis, V. Women are not the same as men: specific clinical issues for female patients with bipolar disorder. *Bipolar Disord,* 2005;7 Suppl 1:16-24.

[19] Arnold, LM; McElroy, SL & Keck, PE,Jr. The role of gender in mixed mania. *Compr Psychiatry,* 2000;41:83-87.

[20] Keck, PE,Jr. Bipolar depression: a new role for atypical antipsychotics? *Bipolar Disord,* 2005;7 Suppl 4:34-40.

[21] Bopp, JM; Miklowitz, DJ; Goodwin, GM; Stevens, W; Rendell, JM & Geddes, JR. The longitudinal course of bipolar disorder as revealed through weekly text messaging: a feasibility study. *Bipolar Disord,* 2010;12:327-334.

[22] Frye, MA. Clinical practice. Bipolar disorder--a focus on depression. *N Engl J Med,* 2011;364:51-59.

[23] Christensen, EM; Gjerris, A; Larsen, JK; Bendtsen, BB; Larsen, BH; Rolff, H; et al. Life events and onset of a new phase in bipolar affective disorder. *Bipolar Disord,* 2003;5:356-361.

[24] Barnes, C; Mitchell, P. Considerations in the management of bipolar disorder in women. *Aust N Z J Psychiatry,* 2005;39:662-673.

[25] Benazzi, F. Gender differences in bipolar II and unipolar depressed outpatients: a 557-case study. *Ann Clin Psychiatry,* 1999;11:55-59.

[26] Benazzi, F. Classifying mood disorders by age-at-onset instead of polarity. *Prog Neuropsychopharmacol Biol Psychiatry,* 2009;33:86-93.

[27] Angst, J; Gamma, A; Sellaro, R; Lavori, PW & Zhang, H. Recurrence of bipolar disorders and major depression. A life-long perspective. *Eur Arch Psychiatry Clin Neurosci,* 2003;253:236-240.

[28] Baethge, C; Baldessarini, RJ; Freudenthal, K; Streeruwitz, A; Bauer, M & Bschor, T. Hallucinations in bipolar disorder: characteristics and comparison to unipolar depression and schizophrenia. *Bipolar Disord,* 2005;7:136-145.

[29] NICE clinical guideline. Bipolar disorder. The management of bipolar disorder in adults, children and adolescents, in primary and secondary care. 2006:4-76.

[30] Bogart, GT; Chavez, B. Safety and efficacy of quetiapine in bipolar depression. *Ann Pharmacother,* 2009;43:1848-1856.

[31] Burt, VK; Rasgon, N. Special considerations in treating bipolar disorder in women. *Bipolar Disord,* 2004;6:2-13.

[32] Van Lieshout, RJ; MacQueen, GM. Efficacy and acceptability of mood stabilisers in the treatment of acute bipolar depression: systematic review. *Br J Psychiatry,* 2010;196:266-273.

[33] Cruz, N; Sanchez-Moreno, J; Torres, F; Goikolea, JM; Valenti, M & Vieta, E. Efficacy of modern antipsychotics in placebo-controlled trials in bipolar depression: a meta-analysis. *Int J Neuropsychopharmacol,* 2010;13:5-14.

[34] Henry, C. Lithium side-effects and predictors of hypothyroidism in patients with bipolar disorder: sex differences. *J Psychiatry Neurosci,* 2002;27:104-107.

[35] Ernst, CL; Goldberg, JF. The reproductive safety profile of mood stabilizers, atypical antipsychotics, and broad-spectrum psychotropics. *J Clin Psychiatry,* 2002;63 Suppl 4:42-55.

[36] Usall i Rodie, J. Gender based psychopharmacology: gender influence in the pharmacological treatment of mental disorders. *Actas Esp Psiquiatr,* 2004;32:307-313.

[37] Kulkarni, J. Special issues in managing long-term mental illness in women. *Int Rev Psychiatry,* 2010;22:183-190.

[38] Yonkers, KA; Wisner, KL; Stowe, Z; Leibenluft, E; Cohen, L; Miller, L; et al. Management of bipolar disorder during pregnancy and the postpartum period. *Am J Psychiatry,* 2004;161:608-620.

[39] Galbally, M; Roberts, M; Buist, A & Perinatal Psychotropic Review Group. Mood stabilizers in pregnancy: a systematic review. *Aust N Z J Psychiatry,* 2010;44:967-977.

[40] Nguyen, HT; Sharma, V & McIntyre, RS. Teratogenesis associated with antibipolar agents. *Adv Ther,* 2009;26:281-294.

[41] Einarson, A; Boskovic, R. Use and safety of antipsychotic drugs during pregnancy. *J Psychiatr Pract,* 2009;15:183-192.

[42] Joffe, H; Kim, DR; Foris, JM; Baldassano, CF; Gyulai, L; Hwang, CH; et al. Menstrual dysfunction prior to onset of psychiatric illness is reported more commonly by women with bipolar disorder than by women with unipolar depression and healthy controls. *J Clin Psychiatry,* 2006;67:297-304.

[43] Rasgon, N; Bauer, M; Glenn, T; Elman, S & Whybrow, PC. Menstrual cycle related mood changes in women with bipolar disorder. *Bipolar Disord,* 2003;5:48-52.

[44] Kenna, HA; Jiang, B & Rasgon, NL. Reproductive and metabolic abnormalities associated with bipolar disorder and its treatment. *Harv Rev Psychiatry,* 2009;17:138-146.

[45] Dias, RS; Lafer, B; Russo, C; Del Debbio, A; Nierenberg, AA; Sachs, GS; et al. Longitudinal Follow-Up of Bipolar Disorder in Women With Premenstrual Exacerbation: Findings From STEP-BD. *Am J Psychiatry,* 2011;168:386-394.

[46] Shivakumar, G; Bernstein, IH; Suppes, T; Stanley Foundation Bipolar Network; Keck, PE; McElroy, SL; et al. Are bipolar mood symptoms affected by the phase of the menstrual cycle? *J Womens Health (Larchmt),* 2008;17:473-478.

[47] Hunter, R; Christie, JE; Whalley, LJ; Bennie, J; Carroll, S; Dick, H; et al. Luteinizing hormone responses to luteinizing hormone releasing hormone (LHRH) in acute mania and the effects of lithium on LHRH and thyrotrophin releasing hormone tests in volunteers. *Psychol Med,* 1989;19:69-77.

[48] Baptista, T; Alastre, T; Contreras, Q; Martinez, JL; Araujo de Baptista, E; Burguera, JL; et al. Effects of lithium carbonate on reproductive hormones in healthy men: relationship with body weight regulation--a pilot study. *Prog Neuropsychopharmacol Biol Psychiatry,* 1997;21:937-950.

In: Advances in Psychology Research. Volume 88
Editor: Alexandra M. Columbus, pp. 213-223
ISBN: 978-1-62100-591-9

Chapter 11

THE RELATION BETWEEN PREMENSTRUAL DYSPHORIC DISORDER, PANIC ATTACKS, AND PANIC DISORDER

Kelley Stevens and Kenneth Abrams*
Department of Psychology, Carleton College, Northfield, MN, U.S.A.

ABSTRACT

Premenstrual dysphoric disorder (PMDD) affects three to eight percent of women of reproductive age. The syndrome, which includes depressed mood, anxiety, irritability, mood fluctuations, and physical symptoms, occurs in the days prior to menstruation and remits a few days after the onset of menses. Women with PMDD suffer from a high rate of panic disorder (PD) and, like those with PD, demonstrate high fear reactivity to laboratory panic challenges. In this chapter, we examine prominent hypotheses for the high rate of panic attacks among women with PMDD. More specifically, we explore (a) physiological hypotheses, such as suffocation false alarm and neurotransmitter system dysfunction, and (b) psychological hypotheses, including those that invoke behavioral conditioning, catastrophic misinterpretation, and anxiety sensitivity. We conclude by proposing several lines of research that could shed additional light on this topic.

1. THE PREVALENCE, SYMPTOMS, AND CAUSES OF PMDD

Premenstrual Dysphoric Disorder (PMDD), a clinical syndrome associated with mood, somatic, and behavioral symptoms, affects approximately three to eight percent of women of reproductive age (Halbreich, Borenstein, Pearlstein & Kahn, 2003). An additional 13 to 18 percent of women meet enough of the criteria for PMDD to cause significant impairment or distress even if they do not meet the full DSM-IV research criteria (Halbreich et al., 2003).

* Correspondence concerning this chapter should be addressed to Kenneth Abrams, Department of Psychology, One North College St., Carleton College, Northfield, MN 55057 Phone: (507) 222-4380. Fax: (507) 222-7005. Email: kabrams@carleton.edu

The symptoms of PMDD occur during the last week of the luteal phase of the menstrual cycle (APA, 2000). (The luteal phase lasts from approximately day 14 of the cycle until menses; Carpenter, Upadhyana, LaRowe, Saladin, & Brady, 2005). Demonstrating the toll that PMDD often takes, Halbreich and colleagues found that luteal phase Social Adjustment Scale scores for women with PMDD were not significantly different from the scores of individuals with Major Depressive Disorder (MDD; Halbreich et al., 2003).

To meet proposed DSM-IV criteria for PMDD, a woman must have five or more of the following symptoms for most of the time during the last week of the luteal phase of the menstrual cycle, with at least one symptom being among the first four listed (APA, 2000):

1. Feeling sad or hopeless
2. Feeling tense, anxious, or on edge
3. Marked lability of mood interspersed with frequent tearfulness
4. Persistent irritability or anger, and increased interpersonal conflicts
5. Decreased interest in usual activities
6. Difficulty concentrating
7. Feeling fatigued or lethargic
8. Marked changes in appetite
9. Hypersomnia or insomnia
10. A subjective feeling of being overwhelmed or out of control
11. Physical symptoms such as breast tenderness or swelling, headaches, or sensations of "bloating" or weight gain

Although the causes of PMDD are still debated, a number of hypotheses have been proposed. One is that PMDD is partially caused by changes in progesterone levels during the luteal phase of the menstrual cycle, resulting in increased activation of the amygdala (Arehart-Treichel, 2007). Such activation can in turn affect a) the fusiform gyrus, a part of the limbic system that processes angry or fearful stimuli, b) the cingulate gyrus, which processes potential threats (Arehart-Treichel, 2007).

PMDD may also be caused by other hormonal abnormalities. For example, fluctuations in estrogen levels after ovulation have been shown to affect corticotrophin-releasing hormone (CRH) levels (Watson, Studd, Savvas, Barber, 1990). Low CRH levels are associated with seasonal depression and perhaps PMDD as well (Halenbreich, 2003). It is also possible that relative rather than absolute levels of particular hormones may promote PMDD. Perhaps it is the ratio of progesterone to estrogen that matters (Halenbreich, Edicott, Goldstein, Nee, 1986).

In a 2005 literature review, Guilio and Reissing (2006) explored the possibility that PMDD is caused in part by dysregulation of the serotonergic system. The authors postulated that low serotonin levels in women with PMDD could contribute to the anxiety, aggression, depression, irritability, and mood swings. This hypothesis is supported by selective serotonin reuptake inhibitor (SSRI) treatment studies. In one such study, SSRIs were seven times more effective than placebos in treating PMDD symptoms (Dimmock, Wyatt, Jones & O'Brien, 2000). Additionally, the serotonin agonists Dexfenfluramine and L-tryptophan have been found to decrease PMDD symptoms (Dimmock et al., 2000). These results suggest that low serotonin levels may contribute to the symptoms associated with PMDD.

Over the last two decades, increased attention has been directed toward the elevated rate of co-morbidity between PMDD and Panic Disorder (PD). For example, Fava (1992) found that 25% of women who were prospectively confirmed with Late Luteal Phase Dysphoric Disorder (the diagnostic precursor to PMDD) met criteria for PD. This rate was much higher than for healthy controls and than population estimates of PD (Myers et al., 1984).

Broadly speaking, there are two categories of hypotheses that attempt to explain the elevated rate of co-morbidity: a) physiological hypotheses, such as suffocation false alarm, GABA system dysfunction, and episodic functional endogenous opioid dysregulation; and b) psychological hypotheses, including those that invoke behavioral conditioning, catastrophic misinterpretation, and anxiety sensitivity.

2. Physiological Hypotheses

2.1. Suffocation False Alarm (SFA)

The SFA hypothesis, originally developed in 1993, posits that individuals who are hypersensitive to suffocation cues – such as increasing levels of arterial carbon dioxide – are especially likely to panic during respiratory challenges (Klein, 1993). Klein argued that a panic attack may occur when the brain's putative "suffocation monitor" erroneously signals that an individual has a scarcity of breathable air. This may lead to sympathetic arousal, respiratory distress, hyperventilation, and – potentially – a panic attack and strong desire to escape.

According to some theorists, if Klein's SFA hypothesis is accurate, then individuals with PMDD and PD are likely to share some of the same respiratory abnormalities that cause suffocation sensitivity (Vickers & McNally, 2004). However, there remains much debate about whether respiratory symptoms are diagnostically informative and whether meaningful conclusions can be drawn about the connection between respiratory abnormalities and panic. Regardless, Klein did address the connection between his SFA hypothesis and PMDD. He posited that a rise in blood progesterone levels following ovulation promotes hyperventilation and a corresponding drop in arterial carbon dioxide (CO_2) levels. Then, three to five days before menstrual discharge (when progesterone levels fall precipitously), arterial CO_2 levels and CO_2 sensitivity both rise. Such CO_2 hypersensitivity would occur at approximately the same time that dysphoria and panic tend to occur in women with co-morbid PMDD and PD.

A number of studies have examined respiratory abnormalities and CO_2 hypersensitivity among women with PMDD. In one, researchers examined the sensitivity of patients with PD, patients with PMDD, patients with MDD, and healthy controls to inhalations of 5% CO_2 and 7% CO_2 (Gorman, Kent, Martinez, Browne, Coplan & Papp, 2001). The PD and PMDD groups had the highest rates of panic though the physiological features of panic attacks (when they occurred) as measured by the Acute Panic Inventory were similar across all groups. The authors interpreted these results as indicating that there is nothing fundamentally abnormal about the respiratory physiology of individuals with PD or PMDD. Instead, they postulated that the high rate of panic among these groups is due to a "generalized fear response" that could be physiological, psychological, or both. On the other hand, Martinez et al. (2001)

found that patients with PD and patients with PMDD demonstrated greater respiratory variability at baseline than healthy controls and than patients with MDD.

Using animal models, Melchoir and colleagues proposed that respiratory variability in female Wistar rats originates from the estrus cycle (the rat equivalent of the menstrual cycle; Melchoir, Hoi-Por, Olsson, Annerbrink, Hedner, Eriksson, 2004). In one study, Wistar rats with estrus cycle-related aggression had greater breath-to-breath tidal volume variability than rats without cycle-related aggression. As such, a parallel can be drawn between the respiratory variability of these rats and the respiratory variability of women with PMDD. Rats with cycle-related behavior change exhibited respiratory abnormalities as do women (possibly) who have PMDD.

In summary, the SFA hypothesis provides a partial explanation for why individuals with PMDD have elevated levels of PD. Although animal studies have found respiratory variability in rats with estrus cycle-related aggression, evidence for abnormal respiratory patterns in humans with PMDD is mixed. Future research on the SFA hypothesis should focus on patterns of respiration in individuals with PMDD and PD across multiple types of biological challenges.

2.2. Episodic Endogenous Opioid Dysregulation

Episodic dysfunction of endogenous opioidergic regulation is one potential cause for panic attacks in individuals with PD (Preter & Klein, 2008). The opioidergic system regulates breathing, social-afflictive behaviors, and CO_2 sensitivity. In a recent study examining whether endogenous opioid regulation contributes to PD, 12 healthy individuals were provided an opioid antagonist (naloxone) prior to a sodium lactate challenge. The participants showed an increase in respiratory variability and general sensitivity to the lactate challenge relative to a placebo (Sinha, Goetz, & Klein, 2007). Perhaps, then, the acute withdrawal of endogenous opioids in the late luteal phase may contribute to the mood symptoms of PMDD (Elliott, 2002; Preter & Klein, 2008).

Inquiry into the role of opioids in the panic attacks of individuals with PMDD is quite new. Additional challenge studies using opioid antagonists should be conducted on women with PMDD across the menstrual cycle before firm conclusions can be drawn. Further, such challenge studies could examine whether responses are more severe for individuals with PD or PMDD than for individuals with other disorders (such as MDD or obsessive-compulsive disorder).

2.3. GABA System Dysfunction

GABA-system dysfunction has also been cited as a potential cause for the high rate of panic in women with PMDD (Le Mellédo, Van Driel, John Coupland, Lott & Jahangri, 2000). Among such women, low GABA plasma levels have been found, as have decreased cortical GABA levels during the follicular phase (relative to healthy controls; Halbreich et al., 1996). Further, particular metabolites of progesterone (such as allopregnanolone) bind to GABA-benzodiazepine receptors, causing anxiolysis. The levels of such metabolites would be expected to be higher during the mid-luteal phase (when progesterone levels peak) and lower

during the late luteal phase (when progesterone levels drop) and follicular phase (Smith et al., 1998). Of note, low levels of neurosteroids such as allopregnanolone have been found to cause tension and irritability.

Additional evidence for a GABA-related link between PD and PMDD includes the efficacy of benzodiazepines for treating both conditions. Benzodiazepines increase the efficiency of the synaptic transmission of GABA by binding to GABA receptors. Further, both individuals with PD and women with PMDD demonstrate diminished benzodiazepine-induced reductions in saccadic eye movements (Sundstrom et al., 1997).

Finally, individuals with PD or PMDD appear to be hypersensitive to GABA antagonists. In one study women with PMDD and healthy controls were injected with flumazenil (a GABA antagonist) during the luteal phase of the menstrual cycle. Those with PMDD experienced more panic symptoms than did the controls (Le Mellédo, 2000). This finding may indicate altered GABA sensitivity in individuals with PD. Of note, hypersensitivity to GABA antagonists has also been found in individuals with obsessive compulsive disorder. As such, abnormal GABA levels may not be unique to individuals with PD or PMDD (Vickers & McNally, 2004).

3. Psychological Hypotheses

3.1. Behavioral Conditioning

Learning theory, applied to PD, suggests that harmless somatic sensations can be conditioned to elicit panic (Vickers et al., 2009). One implication of this is that baseline anxiety levels should predict panic responding to lab challenges. In the case of PMDD, studies have not shown that baseline anxiety levels influence panic reactivity (Vickers et al., 2009). However, more challenge studies that examine the role of learning in PMDD are warranted.

3.2. Catastrophic Misinterpretation

The catastrophic misinterpretation hypothesis posits that individuals panic as a result of a catastrophic misinterpretation of harmless somatic sensations (Clark, 1986). Typical misinterpreted symptoms include heart palpitations, breathlessness, and dizziness. For example, a woman feeling breathless after walking up a flight of stairs may assume she is having a heart attack. According to this theory women with PMDD should be apt to misread their bodily sensations when put into a panic challenge study. This hypothesis has been tested only with PD patients, so further challenge studies involving participants with PMDD are necessary.

3.3. Anxiety Sensitivity

Anxiety Sensitivity is the fear of bodily sensations associated with anxiety or panic. Anxiety sensitivity is based on the belief that anxiety has negative consequences that last past the current moment (Donnell & McNally, 1989). High anxiety sensitivity is a known risk factor for panic. For example, Donnell and McNally (1989) found that, when asked to perform a hyperventilation task, individuals with high (vs. low) anxiety sensitivity experienced higher levels of anxiety, regardless of panic history.

An open question is whether women with PMDD exhibit high levels of anxiety sensitivity. One relevant study examined at different points in the menstrual cycle the psychophysiological symptoms of women, some of whom had PD (Sigmon, Dorhofer, Rohan, Hotovy, Boulard & Fink, 2000). In addition, participants were asked to imagine various anxiety-provoking scenes presented from a recording over headphones. As an example, one recording said, "You are sitting down to relax after a hectic day. Suddenly, you can't breathe, your chest feels tight, and you think, 'this is it, I am going to die'" (Sigmon et. al., 2000). High anxiety sensitivity was associated with increased menstrual distress and increased physical and psychological responding to the scenes. These results are consistent with the anxiety sensitivity hypothesis for panic; however, additional studies involving women with PMDD are needed.

4. Panic Challenge Studies

Researchers have used several biological agents to assess the factors that promote panic in women with PMDD. The most common agents used in challenge studies include cholecystokinin (CCK), flumazenil, carbon dioxide, and sodium lactate. Studies involving these panicogenic agents will now be discussed in the context of the aforementioned hypotheses.

4.1. Cholecystokinin (CCK)

CCK is a neuropeptide that binds with CCK-B receptors in the central nervous system and has shown to play a role in human anxiety (Brawman-Minzter et al., 1997). As such, challenge studies have been used to examine whether individuals with PD and PMDD have increased sensitivity to CCK. A few studies have found that individuals with PD panic at a high rate in response to CCK-4. For example, Bradwejn and colleagues (1992) found that, among individuals with PD given an injection of CCK-4, the rate of panicking was 17% at a 10-microgram dose, 64% at a 15-microgram dose, 75% at a 20-microgram dose, and 75% at a 25-microgram dose. By contrast, none of the participants panicked when given a placebo .

Researchers have also studied the potential connection between the CCK system and panic in women with PMDD (Mellédo et. al., 2009). In a placebo-controlled study, participants with PMDD and healthy female controls received one injection (CCK-4 or a placebo) during the luteal phase and one during the follicular phase. Participants with PMDD, relative to the healthy controls, exhibited a heightened sensitivity to the CCK-4 injection

during both phases, indicating that neurotransmitter system dysfunction may be present in individuals with PMDD.

The results of these studies suggest that individuals with PD and PMDD may share a common sensitivity to CCK-4. However, additional research into what mediates CCK-induced panic is needed. Of note, individuals with GAD also appear hypersensitive to CCK, indicating that this characteristic is not specific to individuals with PD and PMDD.

4.2. Flumazenil

Flumazenil is a GABA antagonist that binds to benzodiazepine receptors (Woods, Charney, Siler, Krystal & Heninger, 1990). Hence, flumazenil studies can examine whether individuals have an abnormal regulation of GABA-benzodiazepine receptor functioning. In one study the anxiety responses to a flumazenil infusion of 10 participants with PD and 10 healthy controls were compared (Nutt, Glue, Lawson & Wilson, 1990). Eight participants with PD had a panic attack but none of the controls did, suggesting that individuals with PD have an increased sensitivity to flumazenil and perhaps a dysregulation of $GABA_A$ receptor functioning.

Flumazenil challenge studies have also been used in women with PMDD. Le Mellédo and his team administered flumazenil to 10 women with PMDD and 11 healthy female controls during the late luteal phase of the menstrual cycles (Le Mellédo, 2000). Flumazenil induced panic more often in the women with PMDD than in the controls, suggesting a possible dysregulation of $GABA_A$ benzodiazepine receptor functioning. This conclusion is tempered a bit, though, by the range of panicogenic agents to which individuals with PMDD are hypersensitive (e.g., CCK-4 and sodium lactate).

4.3. Carbon Dioxide

The inhalation of CO_2 is known to provoke panic in patients with PD. In one study (discussed earlier), responses of individuals with PD, MDD, or PMDD to 5% and 7% CO_2 challenges were examined (Gorman et al., 2001). Participants were placed in a breathing canopy, and, in the first five minute block breathed room air, in the second (five minute) block breathed a 5% CO_2 gas mixture, in the third block breathed room air, in the forth block breathed a 7% percent CO_2 gas mixture, and in the fifth block breathed room air. Those participants with PD or PMDD spent the least amount of time in the canopy and tolerated the least amount of CO_2. PD patients had the highest rate of panic attacks, though participants with PMDD panicked at an elevated rate relative to those with MDD. These findings indicate that those with PD or PMDD are highly sensitive to CO_2 inhalations and highly susceptible to CO_2-induced panic attacks. Unfortunately, this study did not test women with PMDD in different phase of the menstrual cycle so no conclusions can be drawn about CO_2 sensitivity across phases.

In another study women with PMDD and healthy controls performed a double breath inhalation of both a 35% CO_2 gas mixture and a placebo (room air) gas at two times: once in the luteal phase and once in the follicular phase. The CO_2 breaths induced panic in 64% of the women with PMDD and in none of the controls (Harrison, Sandberg, Gorman, Fyer, Nee, Uy

& Edicott, 1987). Only six women with PMDD were willing to be tested on both occasions – of those four panicked during both phases of the menstrual cycle and another had a near panic during the follicular phase.

Generally, CO2 challenge studies support the notion that individuals with PD and PMDD may have an abnormal sensitivity to CO_2. Because CO_2 chemoreceptors are found in the locus ceruleus, this finding is consistent with dysregulation of the noradrenergic systems of those with PD or PMDD (Harrison et. al., 1987). However, another possibility is that those with PD or PMDD are hypersensitive to the somatic sensations produced though CO_2 inhalations.

4.4. Sodium Lactate

Sodium lactate infusions can produce physiological and psychological symptoms of anxiety in individuals with PD. In one study, 50 patients with PD with or without agoraphobia were administered sodium lactate at five-minute intervals (Cowley & Dunner, 1987). Of the PD patients without agoraphobia, 39% panicked, and of those with agoraphobia, 46% panicked. In addition, the study found that certain clinical characteristics of the participants (including age of onset of panic, frequency of spontaneous panic attacks, and impairment in social functioning) did not significantly correlate with the likelihood of panicking.

In another sodium lactate challenge study, 13 women seeking treatment for PMDD and 7 healthy female controls were compared (Sandberg et al., 1993). Those with PMDD were not currently taking birth control medication. All women were tested during the week before menses (i.e. during the late luteal phase of the menstrual cycle). After a 30-minute placebo infusion, participants were given for 20 minutes a 0.5 molar sodium lactate infusion. Examining Acute Panic Inventory and psychophysiological data, the authors concluded that 58% of the women with PMDD and none of the controls panicked. Limitations of the study include the small sample size and the absence of comparative data from the follicular phase. In addition, the mechanism by which participants panic in response to sodium lactate challenges remains unknown. Possibilities include both central nervous system dysfunction and the production and misinterpretation of somatic symptoms (Cowley et. al., 1988).

Conclusions and Future Research

Despite the amount of research that has been invested into the study of the elevated rate of panic in individuals with PMDD, few conclusions can be drawn with certainty. The high rate of panic in those with PMDD seems likely to be due in part to dysregulation of GABA receptor functioning, as flumazenil and GABA agonist studies suggest. However, because individuals with PMDD and PD panic at high rates to other panicogenic agents (e.g., CCK-4 and sodium lactate), it seems unlikely that GABA receptor dysfunction is the only relevant biological abnormality shared by these two disorders. In fact, several studies have found results consistent with noradrenergic or opioidergic system dysfunction among those with PMDD. By contrast, cognitive and behavioral links between PMDD and panic remain mostly theoretical, and additional research is needed that directly employs women with PMDD.

Regardless of specific research intent, researchers in this field are advised to adhere to the following principles to ensure maximum validity of approach and generalizability of results: 1) When conducting research on PD and/or PMDD, researchers should consider phase of the menstrual cycle. That is, women should be tested in the same phase (e.g., mid-luteal) or both phases to reduce extraneous variance. 2) Researchers should clearly differentiate between premenstrual syndrome (PMS) and PMDD in recruitment and analysis and use DSM-IV research criteria for assessing the latter. 3) Researchers should, if at all possible, assess PMDD prospectively as retrospective reports of PMDD symptoms are often erroneous. 4) Researchers should attend to their method of recruitment and recognize the inherent limitations of the method selected. That is, women with PMDD recruited from a women's health clinic or through a community advertisement offering treatment may not be representative of women with PMDD (i.e., they may be especially likely to have severe psychopathology or co-morbid diagnoses).

In conclusion it seems probable that none of the hypotheses as currently articulated can fully account for both the physiological and psychological symptoms of panic among women with PMDD, and it may be a combination of the physiological and psychological hypotheses that will ultimately provide the most robust explanation. Future studies that offer a therapeutic intervention for women with both PMDD and PD between panic challenges may shed light on the relative importance of cognitive and physiological factors. The ultimate aim of such research would be to gain insight into the etiology and treatment of the co-morbid condition.

References

Arehart-Treichel, J. (2007, September). Brain imaging suggests origin of premenstrual dysphoric disorder. *Psychiatric News, 43(18).*

Bäckström, T., Andrén, L., Bixo, M., Björn, I., Fernández, F., Johansson, I.,...Wang, M. (2008) Neuroactive steroids in brain and relevance to mood. In M.S. Ritsner & A. Weizman (Eds.), *Neuroactive steroids in brain function, behavior and neuropsychiatric disorders* (pp. 423-429). Netherlands: Springer.

Bradwejn, J., Koszycki, D., Annable, L., Couetoux du Tertre, A., Reines, S., & Karkanias, C. (1992). A dose-ranging study on the behavioral and cardiovascular effect of CCK-tetrapeptide in panic disorder. *Biological Psychiatry, 15*(10), 903-12.

Brawman-Mintzer, O., Lydiard, M.B., Bradwejn, J., Villarreal, G., Knapp, G., Emmanuel, N.,Ware, M.R., He, Q., & Ballenger, J.C. (1997). Effects of the cholecystokinin agonist pentagastrin in patients with generalized anxiety disorder. *American Journal of Psychiatry, 157,* 700-702.

Carpenter, M., Upadhyaya, H.P., LaRowe, S., Saladin, M., Brady, K.T. (2006). Menstrual cycle phase effects on nicotine withdrawal and cigarette craving: a review. *Society for Research on Nicotine and Tobacco annual meeting, Florida.*

Clark, D.M. (1986). A cognitive approach to panic. *Behavior Research and Therapy, 24*(2), 461-470.

Cowley, D.S., Dager, S.R., McClellan, J., Roy-Byrne, P.P., Dunner, D.L. (1988). Response to lactate infusion in generalized anxiety disorder. *Biological Psychology, 24,* 409-414.

Dimmock P., Wyatt K, Jones, P, & O'Brien P. (2000). Efficacy of selective serotoin-reuptake inhibitors in premenstrual syndrome: a systematic review. *Lancet, 356,* 1131-1136.

Donnell, C.D., McNally, R.J. (1989). Anxiety sensitivity and history of panic as predictors of response to hyperventilation. *Behavior Research and Therapy, 27*(4), 325-32.

Elliott, H. (2002). Premenstrual dysphoric disorder: a guide for the treating clinician. *North Carolina Medical Journal 63*(2).

Fava M, Pedrazzi F., Guaraldi GP., Romano G., Genazzani AR., Facchinetti F. (1992). Comorbid anxiety and depression among patients with late luteal phase dysphoric disorder. *J Anxiety Disorder, 6,* 325-327.

Gorman, J.M., Kent, J., Martinez, J., Browne, S., Coplan, J., & Papp, L.A. (2001). Physiological changes during carbon dioxide inhalation in patients with panic disorder, major depression, and premenstrual dysphoric disorder. *Archives of General Psychiatry, 58,* 125-131.

Halbreich, U., Borenstein, J., Pearlstein, T., & Kahn, L.S. (2003). The prevalence, impairment, impact, and burden of premenstrual dysphoric disorder (PMS/PMDD). *Psychoneuroendocrinology, 28*(3), 1-23.

Halenbreich, U., Eddicott, J., Goldstein, J., & Nee, J. Premenstrual changes and changes in Gonadal hormones. Acta Psychiatry Scand 1986 74 576-586.

Harrison, W.M., Sandberg, D., Gorman, J.M., Fyer, M., Nee, J., Uy, J., & Edicott, J. (1988). Provocation of panic with carbon dioxide inhalation in patients with premenstrual dysphoria. *Psychiatry Research, 27,* 183-192.

Kessler, R.C., McGonagle, K.A., Zhao, S., Nelson, C.B., Hughes, M., Eshleman, S., Wittchen, H.U., & Kendler K.S. (1994). Lifetime and 12-month prevalence of DSM-III-R psychiatric disorders in the United States: results from the National Comorbidity Survey. *Arch Gen Psychiatry, 51,* 8–19.

Kim, D.R., Gyulai, L., Freeman, E.W., Morrison, M.F., Baldassano, C., & Dube, B.(2004). *Archives of Women's Mental Health, 7,* 37-47.

Klein, D. (1993). False Suffocation alarms, spontaneous panics and related conditions. *Archives of General Psychiatry, 50,* 306-317.

LeMelledo, J.L., Van Driel, M., Coupland, J., Lott, P., & Jhangri, G.S. (2000). Response to flumazenil in women with premenstrual dysphoric disorder. *American Jounal of Psychiatry, 157,* 821-823.

Man, M.S., MacMillian, I., Scott, J., Young, A.H., 1999. Mood, neuropsychological function and cognitions in premenstrual dysphonic disorder. *Psychological. Med., 29,* 727-733.

Melchior, L.K., Ho, H., Olsson, M., Annerbrink, K., Hedner, J., & Eriksson, E. (2004). Association between estrus cycle-related aggression and tidal volume variability in female wistar rats. *Psychoneuroendocrinology, 29,* 1097-1100.

Nutt, D.J., Glue, P., Lawson, C., Wilson, S. (1990). Flumazenil Provocation of Panic AttacksEvidence for Altered Benzodiazepine Receptor Sensitivity in Panic Disorder. *Archives of General Psychiatry*, 47(10), 917-925.

Preter, M., Klein, D.F. (2008). Panic, suffocation false alarms, separation anxiety, and endogenous opioids.*Progress in Neuro- Psychopharmacology & Biological Psychiatry, 32,* 603-612.

Rapkin, A. (2003). A review of treatment of premenstrual syndrom & premenstrual dysphoric disorder. *Psychoneuroendocrinology, 28,* 30-53.

Signom, S.T., Dorhofer, D.M., Rohan, K.J., Hotovy, L.A., Boulard, N.E., Fink, C. (2000). Psychophsysiological, somatic, and affective changes across the menstrual cycle in women with panic disorder. *Journale of consulting and clinical psychology, 68*(3), 425-431.

Sinha, S.S., Goetz, R.R., & Klein, D.F. (2007). Physiological and behavioral effects of naloxone and lactate in normal volunteers with relevance to the pathophysiology of panic disorder. *Psychiatry Res, 149* (1-3), 309-14.

Van Ree, J.M, Schagen, Van Leeuwen, Koppeschaar, H.P., & Te Velde, E.R. (2005). Unexpected placebo response in premenstrual dysphoric disorder: implication of endogenous opioids. *Psychopharmachology, 182* (2), 318-319.

Vickers, K., McNally, R.J. (2004). Is premenstrual dysphoria a variant of panic disorder. Clinical Psychology Review, 24, 933-956.

Vickers K., McNally, R.,J. (2005). Respiratory symptoms and panic in the national comorbidity survey: a test of Klein's suffocation false alarm theory. Behavior Research and Therapy, 43, 1011-1018.

Watson, N.R, Studd JW, Savvass M, Barber, RJ. (1990). The long term effects of estradiol implant therapy for the treatment of premenstrual syndrom. *Gynecol `Edocrinol, 4*(2), 99-107.

Woods, S.W., Charney, D.S., Silver, J.M., Krystal, J.H., & Heninger, G.R. (1990). Behavioral, biochemical, and cardiovascular responses to benzodiazepine receptor antagonist flumazenil in panic disorder. *Psychiatry Research, 36,* 115-127.

In: Advances in Psychology Research. Volume 88
Editor: Alexandra M. Columbus, pp. 225-234
ISBN: 978-1-62100-591-9

Chapter 12

ASSESSMENT OF CRAVING TO PREDICT RELAPSE IN PATIENTS WITH SUBSTANCE ABUSE/DEPENDENCE

Yasukazu Ogai*[*1], Fumiyuki Chin[1,2] and Kazutaka Ikeda[1]
[1] Research Project for Addictive Substances,
Tokyo Metropolitan Institute of Medical Science, Setagaya-ku, Tokyo, Japan.
[2] Human Development and Family Studies, The Pennsylvania State University,
University Park, PA, U.S.A.

ABSTRACT

Clinical experts in drug dependence therapy must grasp patients' levels of craving to predict their propensity to relapse. Although craving is considered to lead to relapse, the findings have been mixed in supporting this hypothesis. The lack of robust associations may be attributable to (*i*) the inconsistency in the definition of craving across studies, (*ii*) limitations in measuring craving and drug use, and (*iii*) mismatched timeframes and timing in the measurement of craving. This chapter reviews the following possible solutions for these problems, including (*i*) multidimensional measurement of an extended concept of craving, (*ii*) methodological techniques to avoid response bias (e.g., social cognitive measurement), and (*iii*) real-time measurement of craving with Ecologically Momentary Assessment. Additionally, we developed the Relapse Risk Index (RRI), which is a set of assessment systems for predicting relapse. The use of conceptually and methodologically based assessments will lead to a more precise understanding of the directional relationship between a patient's level of craving and risk of relapse.

INTRODUCTION

Craving, one of the main factors of relapse, is generally understood to be a subjective motivational state in which an individual experiences an intense desire to use a drug.

* Corresponding author. Tel: +81-3-6834-2458; Fax: +81-3-6834-2390, E-mail address: ogai-ys@igakuken.or.jp, 1Research Project for Addictive Substances, Tokyo Metropolitan Institute of Medical Science, 2-1-6 Kamikitazawa, Setagaya-ku, Tokyo 156-8506, Japan

Although craving is considered closely related to relapse, study results have been inconclusive regarding this association.

Many investigators have claimed that craving precedes relapse, although conceptual and empirical criticisms have argued against this view (Sayette et al., 2000). Although an important relationship likely exists between craving and subsequent drug use (e.g., Killen and Fortmann, 1997; Shiffman et al., 1997a), previous reviews have concluded that the relationship between different measures of craving and between measures of craving and relapse are not strong (Rohsenow et al., 1990/1991; Tiffany, 1990). For example, Rohsenow and Monti (1999) found that the urge to drink does not necessarily increase the risk of relapse but may rather protect some drinkers against further drinking.

The present chapter first reviews the three major reasons for the inconsistency in the results on the relationship between craving and relapse (Fig. 1). Possible solutions to these problems are then discussed. Finally, the Relapse Risk Index (RRI) is presented, which is a set of assessment systems that aims to elucidate specific aspects of craving related to relapse.

Why are there inconsistencies in the findings on the relation between craving and relapse?

(1) The lack of consensus about the definition of craving
(2) Limitation in measuring craving and drug use
(3) Mismatched timeframe and timing of measurement of craving

Solution

(1) Multidimensional measurement of extended concept of craving
(2) Methodological techniques to avoid response bias such as social cognitive measurement
(3) Real-time measurement of craving with ecologically momentary assessment

Our attempt: The development of Relapse Risk Index

Figure 1. Outline of this chapter.

Reasons for Inconsistent Results on the Relationship between Craving and Relapse

The failure to find robust associations between craving and relapse may be attributable to (1) the lack of consensus regarding the definition of craving, (2) limitations in how craving and drug use are measured, and (3) mismatched timeframes and timing of measurement of craving.

Lack of Consensus Regarding the Definition of Craving

The inconsistent findings on the relationship between craving and relapse may be attributable to the lack of consensus regarding the definition of craving (Drummond, 2001). Craving and its generation process have been conceptualized in various ways. For example, the "expectancy theory" proposed by Jones et al. (2001) states that craving is a function of positive and negative expectancies for drug use.

Anton and colleagues (Anton, 2000; Anton et al., 1996) proposed the "obsessive compulsive theory," suggesting that drug craving is closely related to obsessive compulsive feelings about a drug that cannot be controlled. Other theories have focused on the behavioral aspects of craving. For example, Buydens-Branchey et al. (1997) assessed craving for alcohol by asking patients to estimate the chances that they would use alcohol if they were outside of the hospital and had unlimited financial resources. Marlatt (1985) suggested that the term "craving" should refer to the desire for the effects of a drug, whereas the term "urge" should indicate a behavioral intention to use a drug. Although each theory has some valid explanatory power, no theory to date can fully explain craving.

A person's craving for a drug is expressed in various ways, including desire, intention, expectancy, anticipation, and compulsivity. For example, Tiffany and Drobes (1991) suggested that the concept of "craving" should include the anticipation of a drug's reinforcing effects, intention to engage in drug use, and desire for the drug. However, critics (e.g., Kozlowski et al., 1996) of this view have stated that expressions other than desire are correlated with, but conceptually distinct from, craving. The previous investigations failed to sufficiently reveal aspects of craving, situation, and other antecedent factors of relapse.

Limitations in Measuring Craving and Drug Use

Based on the assumption of the current conceptualizations of craving, most studies have relied on self-report questionnaires to measure the subjective experience of craving. However, the measurement of craving using self-report questionnaires has limitations, including memory bias, misattribution, response style, and other types of craving-irrelevant factors that can affect ratings of craving (Kozlowski and Wilkinson, 1987; Drummond et al., 1990; Tiffany and Drobes, 1991; Bohn et al., 1995). Additionally, although the current collection of published questionnaires are understandable by those with at least a high school education, this does not prevent differences among respondents or between psychologists and respondents in their interpretation of the questions, response choices, and rating-scale anchors (Rosenberg, 2009).

Moreover, the participants may not be able to accurately assess their own internal states or may not report them honestly to the experimenter because of their defensiveness. For example, social desirability or self-consciousness may impact a person's response on a self-report measure (Baker and Brandon, 1990). Drug-dependent individuals tend to hide or deny their craving because the expression of drug craving is thought to be highly undesirable in society. Therefore, they may not respond honestly to the measurement of craving using a self-report questionnaire.

Mismatched Timeframe and Timing of Craving Measurement

Self-reports that involve retrospective recall or global summaries of prior experiences (e.g., "Please rate your strongest craving in the past 2 weeks," and "How much do you generally experience craving?") can be particularly subject to bias, sometimes without the respondent's awareness or intension to distort (Hammersley, 1994; Shiffman et al., 1997b). The issue of response bias generally applies to self-report measures and is not limited to craving ratings.

Shiffman et al. (1997b) found that the recall of cravings prior to a relapse was inaccurate and biased compared with concurrent recordings. Rather than a simple decay of memory stores, problems with autobiographical recall, including short-term recall, are likely to be attributed to cognitive processes that can result in distortions (Hammersley, 1994). Moreover, recall can be particularly biased if other craving-relevant events (e.g., drug use and other craving experiences) occur between the event and the time of recall.

SOLUTION

Multidimensional Measurement of Extended Concept of Craving

Although many craving theories have some valid explanatory power, no theory to date can wholly explain craving. To clarify the relationship between craving and relapse, understanding multiple factors, including craving, that are considered to induce relapse is necessary. Donovan (1996) suggested that relapse is best understood as a complex process that has multiple and interactive determinants that vary in their temporal proximity to and relative influence on relapse.

Miller et al. (1996) reported four potential antecedents to alcohol relapse that independently accounted for significant variance in drinking outcomes: (1) cognitive appraisal variables, including self-efficacy, alcohol expectancies, and motivation for change, (2) client coping resources, (3) craving experiences, and (4) affective/mood status. Therefore, to clarify the aspects of craving that are related to relapse among other antecedents, multidimensional scales have been frequently used to measure various aspects of craving.

Anton et al. (1995) developed the Obsessive Compulsive Drinking Scale (OCDS), which has three subscales: obsessions, drinking control and consequences, and alcohol consumption. Kranzler et al. (1999) suggested that the OCDS total score showed limited validity in predicting drinking during a posttreatment follow-up period. Furthermore, the only empirically derived factor that predicted drinking during this period was the alcohol consumption factor.

Paliwal et al. (2008) examined the predictive validity of the Cocaine Craving Questionnaire (CCQ-Now), which has five subscales: desire to use cocaine, intent and planning to use cocaine, anticipation of positive outcome from using cocaine, anticipation of relief from withdrawal or dysphoria from using cocaine, and lack of control over use. For 123 people who sought inpatient cocaine dependence treatment, the total score on the CCQ-Now predicted the time to cocaine relapse during a 90-day follow-up period after discharge.

Additionally, the anticipation of a positive outcome from cocaine use and intent and planning to use cocaine subscales of the CCQ-Now predicted the time to cocaine relapse.

Methodological Techniques to Avoid Response Bias, Such as Social Cognitive Measurement

Rosenberg et al. (2009) introduced a measurement with automatic cognitive tasks as one of the indirect measures of cravings. This measure of craving is assumed to eliminate self-report bias, be less subject to conscious self-control, and reflect craving that a person may not be able to express. Performance on attention-related tasks, such as the addiction-Stroop task and implicit association test, may serve as indirect measures of craving.

The addiction-Stroop task has been one of the most commonly used tasks to evaluate attentional bias in substance abusers (Cox et al., 2006). The task is a modified version of the classic Stroop task, which requires the participants to judge colors of ink independently from the written names of the colors (e.g., the color of the ink was red, although the stimulus word was "blue"). In this modified Stroop task, drug-related words and neutral words are used as stimuli instead of color names, but the task remains the same (i.e., to read the color of the ink in which the words are printed).

Based on their meta-analytic review of over 30 studies using some version of an addiction-Stroop task with drinkers, smokers, and illicit drug takers, Cox et al. (2006) concluded that a longer reaction time on the addiction-Stroop task reliably distinguished addiction-related words from neutral words, distinguished substance abusers from non-abusers, and predicted relapse following a period of abstinence.

The Implicit Association Test (IAT), which is a widely used task for investigating automatic affective associations in memory, has also been used as an indirect measure of craving. According to Waters et al. (2007), the IAT comprises two tasks. In Task 1, the participants are asked to respond rapidly with a specific key press to items that represent two concepts (e.g., *drug + positive*) and with a different key press to items from another pair of concepts (e.g., *not drug + negative*).

In Task 2, the assignments for one of the concept pairs are switched, such that, for example, *not drug + positive* shares a response and *drug + negative* shares a response. The key idea behind the IAT is that mapping two concepts onto a single response is easier when these concepts are more strongly associated in memory than when the concepts are unrelated or dissimilar (de Houwer, 2002).

The critical measure (i.e., IAT effect) is the difference in response times on Task 1 compared with Task 2. The magnitude of this automatic association between target (drug, alcohol, cigarette, etc.) and attributes (e.g., positive *vs.* negative words; approach *vs.* avoidance words) was interpreted as indirect craving. Houben et al. (2010) demonstrated that implicit affective associations with alcohol measured by the IAT predicted unique variance in drinking behavior above explicit cognition.

Real-Time Measurement of Craving with Ecologically Momentary Assessment

Ecological Momentary Assessment (EMA) facilitates the obtainment of valid data about behavior, thoughts, and feelings in real life situations over time. EMA involves repeated real-time administration of assessments using technologies such as electronic diaries with cell phones or palm-top computers in subjects' everyday lives and environments, which avoids problems associated with retrospective recall.

Shiffman (2009) suggested the promising use of EMA in future substance use research, noting that EMA could capture substance use patterns not measured by questionnaires or retrospective data. Unlike traditional assessments that are administered in clinical or laboratory settings, EMA allows researchers to evaluate the frequency and intensity of craving across contexts and study the relationships between drug use and the immediate experiences of urges and cravings (McKay et al., 2006; Shiffman and Waters, 2004).

For example, Chandra et al. (2007) found that individual differences, assessed by EMA, in patterns of smoking during the day predicted outcomes in subsequent smoking cessation. Using the same dataset, Shiffman (2007) compared the predictive power of EMA and questionnaire data on the negative affect associated with smoking and found that only the EMA-based measure (i.e., the individual subject's correlation between mood and smoking) predicted individual differences in relapse risk.

Cooney et al. (2007) used electronic diaries with alcoholics who were also being treated for smoking cessation and were assessed four times daily after being released from an inpatient program. The findings were surprising. Alcohol lapses were predicted by the urge to smoke but not by the urge to drink. Less surprisingly, lower abstinence self-efficacy in the immediately preceding observation period predicted the occurrence of a drinking lapse.

Development of the Relapse Risk Index

Our research team developed the RRI, which is a package of various assessments that predict relapse using multiple variables, including craving. This index consists of several measures, including the Visual Analogue Scale (VAS; to measure the subjective craving for drug), Stimulant Relapse Risk Scale (SRRS; Ogai et al., 2007) or Alcohol Relapse Risk Scale (ARRS; Ogai et al., 2009; to measure relapse risk), and other profile variables (e.g., date of last drug use, period of abstinence, number of years of drug use, other problems apart from drug, perceived stress, perceived social support, recent experience of contact with information, people, and situation related to drug). By measuring various dimensions of craving, the RRI is intended to clarify the aspects of craving that are specifically related to relapse among other antecedents of relapse.

The SRRS is a validated multidimensional measure of relapse risk for stimulants and includes five subscales: anxiety and intention to use drug, emotionality problems, impulsivity for drug use, positive expectancy and lack of control over drug, and lack of negative expectancy for drug use. The scores on these subscales can be interpreted as multiple or indirect expressions of cravings. The RRI with the SRRS was administered to drug-dependent outpatients to clarify which factors predict relapse in the case of drug dependence. Of the

SRRS subscales, the scores for anxiety and intention to use drug, positive expectancies and lack of control over drug, lack of negative expectancy for drug use, and total SRRS significantly correlated with relapse within 3 months. Moreover, the scores for positive expectancies and lack of control over drug and lack of negative expectancy for drug use significantly correlated with relapse within 6 months. These results indicate that higher scores on the SRRS subscales or total SRRS significantly related to a higher risk of relapse. In contrast, no significant correlations were found between relapse and craving measured by the VAS or between relapse and other antecedent factors, with the exception of the period of abstinence. This is consistent with the idea that relapse is triggered by the expectation of or anxiety associated with the risk situation related to drug use rather than the subjective desire for the drug (Drummond, 2001; Jones et al., 2001).

Based on the SRRS, the ARRS was developed and validated for predicting relapse among alcohol-dependent individuals. Similar to the SRRS, the ARRS has five subscales: stimulus-induced vulnerability, emotionality problems, impulsivity for alcohol use, positive expectancy for alcohol drinking, and lack of negative expectancy for alcohol drinking. Alcohol-dependent outpatients answered the RRI questionnaire package with the ARRS to clarify which factors predict relapse in the case of alcohol dependence. With regard to the ARRS, the scores for stimulus-induced vulnerability and total ARRS significantly correlated with relapse within 1 month, suggesting that these scores predict relapse risk. This was supported by the nearly significant prediction shown in the logistic regression analysis. In contrast, subjective craving measured by the VAS also significantly correlated with relapse within 1 month. No other significant correlations were found between relapse and the other antecedent factors, with the exception of the period of abstinence. The correlation between the scores for stimulus-induced vulnerability and relapse supports the hypothesis of a prior study of more than 900 individuals in which relapse was found to be triggered by social pressure, such as temptation from alcohol-drinking friends (Zywiak et al., 2006). Particularly in the Japanese collectivistic culture, refusing an offer to drink alcohol at a party is difficult. Thus, the cultural influence on stimulus-induced vulnerability (e.g., "It would be difficult for me to refuse if someone placed alcohol in front of me") may be a more prevalent risk factor in Japan. Interestingly, the logistic regression analysis showed that the lack of negative expectancy significantly predicted relapse. This result suggested that the lack of understanding the negative effects of alcohol drinking was an important factor that leads to relapse. This result was also consistent with a report in which relapsed alcohol-dependent individuals and their families reported that "reduced cognitive vigilance" was the most common sign of relapse (Malhotra et al., 1999).

Although preliminary, stimulus-induced vulnerability and lack of negative expectancy in the ARRS and craving measured by the VAS among alcohol-dependent individuals were significantly related to relapse within 1 month. Among stimulant abusers, in contrast, anxiety, intention, positive expectancy, and lack of negative expectancy were significantly related to relapse within 3 months. These results indicate that alcohol-dependent individuals express signs of relapse, such as craving for alcohol, more directly and appear to be easily influenced by the environment. In contrast, stimulant abusers express signs of relapse indirectly through inner feelings, such as anxiety and expectancy.

Studies on drug-dependent and alcohol-dependent individuals showed that the aspects of craving that trigger relapse depend on the type of substance and environmental factors. A multidimensional measurement such as the RRI, which considers various variables, including

craving and surrounding factors, would facilitate making more accurate predictions of relapse. Although multidimensional measurements enhance the prediction of relapse, more studies are needed to address the pitfalls of self-report questionnaires. For example, the current system of the craving index could be improved by adding indirect measures of craving using social cognitive methods and EMA. Using conceptually based multidimensional and multi-method measurements, a more precise understanding of the directional relationship between a patient's level of craving and relapse may become possible.

ACKNOWLEDGEMENTS

We are grateful to Dr. Céline Akiko Olivard and Mr. Michael Arends for fruitful discussions and proofreading. This work was supported by grants from the Ministry of Education, Culture, Sports, Science and Technology of Japan (government department; 20730467) and the Mitsubishi Foundation for Social Welfare Activities.

REFERENCES

Anton, R. F. (2000). Obsessive-compulsive aspects of craving: development of the Obsessive Compulsive Drinking Scale. *Addiction*, 95 (Suppl. 2), 211-217.

Anton, R. F., Moak, D. H., Latham, P. K. (1996). The obsessive compulsive drinking scale: a new method of assessing outcome in alcoholism treatment studies. *Archives of General Psychiatry*, 53, 225-231.

Baker, T. B., Brandon, T. H. (1990). Validity of self-reports in basic research. *Behavioral Assessment*, 12, 33-51.

Bohn, M. J., Krahn, D. D., Staehler, B. A. (1995) Development and initial validation of a measure of drinking urges in abstinent alcoholics. *Alcoholism: Clinical and Experimental Research*, 19, 600-606.

Buydens-Branchey, L., Branchey, M., Fergeson, P., Hudson, J., McKernin, C. (1997). Hormonal, psychological, and alcohol craving changes after m-chlorophenylpiperazine administration in alcoholics. *Alcoholism: Clinical and Experimental Research*, 21, 220-226.

Chandra, S., Shiffman, S., Scharf, D. M., Dang, Q., Shadel, W. G. (2007). Daily smoking patterns, their determinants, and implications for quitting. *Experimental and Clinical Psychopharmacology*, 15, 67-80.

Cooney, N. L., Litt, M. D., Cooney, J. L., Pilkey, D. T., Steinberg, H. R., Oncken, C. A. (2007). Alcohol and tobacco cessation in alcohol-dependent smokers: analysis of real-time reports. *Psychology of Addictive Behaviors*, 21, 277-286.

Cox, W. M., Fadardi, J. S., Pothos, E. M. (2006). The addiction-Stroop test: theoretical considerations and procedural recommendations. *Psychological Bulletin*, 132, 443-476.

de Houwer, J. (2002). The implicit Association Test as a tool for studying dysfunctional associations in psychopathology: strengths and limitations. *Journal of Behavior Therapy and Experimental Psychiatry*, 33, 115-133.

Donovan, D. M. (1996). Assessment issues and domains in the prediction of relapse. *Addiction*, 91 Suppl., S29-S36.

Drummond, D. C. (2001). Theories of drug craving, ancient and modern. *Addiction*, 96, 33-46.

Drummond, C. D., Cooper, T., Glautier, S. P. (1990). Conditioned learning in alcohol dependence: implications for cue exposure treatment. *British Journal of Addiction*, 85, 725-743.

Hammersley, R. (1994). A digest of memory phenomena for addiction research. *Addiction*, 89, 283-293.

Houben, K., Nosek, B. A., Wiers, R. W. (2010). Seeing the forest through the trees: a comparison of different IAT variants measuring implicit alcohol associations. *Drug and Alcohol Dependence*, 106, 204-211.

Jones, B.T., Corbin, W., Fromme, K. (2001). A review of expectancy theory and alcohol consumption. *Addiction*, 96, 57-72.

Killen, J. D., Fortmann, S. P. (1997). Craving is associated with smoking relapse: findings from three prospective studies. *Experimental and Clinical Psychopharmacology*, 5, 137-142.

Kozlowski, L. T., Pillitteri, J. L., Sweeney, C. T., Whitfield, K. E., Graham, J. W. (1996). Asking questions about urges or cravings for cigarettes. *Psychology of Addictive Behaviors*, 10, 248-260.

Kozlowski, L. T., Wilkinson, D. A. (1987). Use and misuse of the concept of craving by alcohol, tobacco, and drug researchers. *British Journal of Addiction*, 82, 31-45.

Kranzler, H. R., Mulgrew, C. L., Modesto-Lowe, V., Burleson, J. A. (1999). Validity of the Obsessive Compulsive Drinking Scale (OCDS): does craving predict drinking behavior? *Alcoholism: Clinical and Experimental Research*, 23, 108-114.

Malhotra, S., Malhotra, S., Basu, D. (1999). A comparison of the beliefs of Indian alcohol-dependent patients and their close family members on their reasons for relapse. *Addiction,* 94, 709-713.

Marlatt, G. A. (1985). Cognitive factors in the relapse process. In Marlatt, G. A., Gordon, J. R. (Eds). *Relapse Prevention: Maintenance Strategies in the Treatment of Addictive Behaviors*, Guilford Press, New York, pp. 128-200.

McKay, J. R., Franklin, T. R., Patapis, N., Lynch, K. G. (2006). Conceptual, methodological, and analytical issues in the study of relapse. *Clinical Psychology Review*, 26, 109-127.

Miller, W. R., Westerberg, V. S., Harris, R. J., Tonigan, J. S. (1996). What predicts relapse? Prospective testing of antecedent models. *Addiction*, 91 Suppl., S155-S172.

Ogai, Y., Haraguchi, A., Kondo, A., Ishibashi, Y., Umeno, M., Kikumoto, H., Hori, T., Komiyama, T., Kato, R., Aso, K., Asukai, N., Senoo, E., and Ikeda, K. (2007). Development and validation of Stimulant Relapse Risk Scale for drug abusers in Japan. *Drug and Alcohol Dependence*, 88, 174-181.

Ogai, Y., Yamashita, M., Endo, K., Haraguchi, A., Ishibashi, Y., Kurokawa, T., Muratake, T., Suga, R., Hori, T., Umeno, M., Asukai, N., Senoo, E., Ikeda, K. (2009). Application of the Relapse Risk Scale to alcohol-dependent individuals in Japan: comparison with stimulant abusers. *Drug and Alcohol Dependence*, 101, 20-26.

Paliwal, P., Hyman, S. M., Sinha, R. (2008). Craving predicts time to cocaine relapse: further validation of the Now and Brief versions of the cocaine craving questionnaire. *Drug and Alcohol Dependence*, 93, 252-259.

Rohsenow, D. J., Monti, P. M. (1999). Does urge to drink predict relapse after treatment? *Alcohol Research and Health*, 23, 225-232.

Rohsenow, D. J., Niaura, R. S., Childress, A. R., Abrams, D. B., Monti, P. M. (1990/1991). Cue reactivity in addictive behaviors: theoretical and treatment implications. *International Journal of the Addictions*, 25, 957-993.

Rosenberg, H. (2009). Clinical and laboratory assessment of the subjective experience of drug craving. *Clinical Psychology Review*, 29, 519-534.

Sayette, M. A., Shiffman, S., Tiffany, S. T., Niaura, R. S., Martin, C. S., Shadel, W. G. (2000). The measurement of drug craving. *Addiction*, 95 (Suppl. 2), S189-S210.

Shiffman, S. (2007). Designing protocols for ecological momentary assessment. In Stone, A. A., Shiffman S., Atienza A., Nebeling L. (Eds.). *The Science of Real-Time Data Capture: Self-Reports in Health Research.* Oxford University Press, New York, pp. 27-53.

Shiffman, S. (2009). Ecological momentary assessment (EMA) in studies of substance use. *Psychological Assessment*, 21, 486-497.

Shiffman, S., Engberg, J. B., Paty, J. A., Perz, W. G., Gnys, M., Kassel, J. D., Hickcox, M. (1997a). A day at a time: predicting smoking lapse from daily urge. *Journal of Abnormal Psychology*, 106, 104-116.

Shiffman, S., Hufford, M., Hickox, M., Paty, J. A., Gnys, M., Kassel, J. (1997b). Remember that? A comparison of real-time versus retrospective recall of smoking lapses. *Journal of Consulting and Clinical Psychology*, 65, 292-300.

Shiffman, S., Waters, A. J. (2004). Negative affect and smoking lapses: a prospective analysis. *Journal of Consulting and Clinical Psychology*, 72, 192-201.

Tiffany, S. T. (1990). A cognitive model of drug urges and drug-use behavior: role of automatic and nonautomatic processes. *Psychological Review*, 97, 147-168.

Tiffany, S. T., Drobes, D. J. (1991). The development and initial validation of a questionnaire on smoking urges. *British Journal of Addiction*, 86, 1467-1476.

Waters, A. J., Carter, B. L., Robinson, J. D., Wetter, D. W., Lam, C. Y., Cinciripini, P. M. (2007). Implicit attitudes to smoking are associated with craving and dependence. *Drug and Alcohol Dependence*, 91, 178-186.

Zywiak, W. H., Stout, R. L., Longabaugh, R., Dyck, I., Connors, G. J., Maisto, S. A., (2006). Relapse-onset factors in project MATCH: the Relapse Questionnaire. *Journal of Substance Abuse Treatment*, 31, 341-345.

In: Advances in Psychology Research. Volume 88
Editor: Alexandra M. Columbus, pp. 235-238
ISBN: 978-1-62100-591-9

Chapter 13

FAMILY RELATIONSHIPS AND ADHD: LITERATURE REVIEW AND STANDARDIZED ASSESSMENT

*H. Niederhofer**
Regional Hospital of Bolzano, Dep. of Pediatrics, Bolzano, Italia.

SUMMARY

Increased activity, poor attention and poorly modulated behaviour are important criteria of Attention deficit hyperactivity disorder (ADHD). Before a child with ADHD attends and complies, instructions often have to be repeated, sometimes even by different family members. The hyperkinetic child might result from from families with worse intrafamiliar relationships than healthy controls. We compared families of 15 boys (age 6 to 12 years) diagnosed with ADHD using the teacher`s form of the Conners Scale with a matched healthy control group of 15 boys. Parents completed a form assessing the intrafamiliar relationships. Results show that families of ADHD children have worse intrafamiliar relationships than healthy controls.

LITERATURE REVIEW

Early onset of increased activity, multiple attention deficits and a lack of perseverance (Jacob, O`Leary & Rosenblad, 1978; Cunningham & Barkley, 1979; Barkley, 1981; Döpfner & Lehmkuhl, 1995) increase Attention Deficit Hyperactivity disorder (ADHD). Furthermore, a low conflict potential, i.e., democratic decisions and fair discussions within the family (coherence) are very important. Instructions to the child over a long period and must be reinforced consistantly (Döpfner & Lehmkuhl, 1995). On the one hand, low family coherence, i.e. poor cooperation of the members of the family, may worsen ADHD symptomatology. On the other hand, children suffering from ADHD may strain the

* Regional Hospital of Bolzano, Dep. of Pediatrics, Via Guncina 54/A, I-39100 Bolzano, Italia, E-Mail. helmutniederhofer@yahoo.de

management of family conflicts (Barkley, 1981). This circular process could increase ADHD and lead to pathological coalitions of family members (Döpfner & Lehmkuhl, 1995).

The importance of the environment for a child`s psychopathology was described by Moos (1973). With lack of support, one may see psychotic exacerbation, ADHD and reactive attachment disorders. The environment may be monitored by a psychologist or by using standardized measures (Moos, 1974).

The characteristics of family relationships often increase the risk of antisocial behavior (Tolan, Gorman-Smith, Huesmann & Zelli, 1997). Family relationships can be observed during sessions (Stierlin, 1994). Interactions of the family members can be observed and analysed (Imber-Black, 1988). Objectivation of these interactions enables clinicians to work out standardized intervention recommendations (Tomm, 1994), which have to be specifized by analysis of the observed microstructure of the family (Mattejat & Scholz, 1994).

Objective Assessment of a family`s structure can be seen as a part of the observation method where the therapist defines himself as an expert more than an "equal" family member (Mattejat & Scholz, 1994; Tomm, 1994). His observations should be considered as influenced by his own experience as complete objectivity is impossible (Ludewig, 1992). The observations are the synthesis of all points of view of the individuals involved, including verbal and nonverbal statements (Tomm, 1994). The comparison of these points of view enables diagnosis of the family`s microstructure and giving therapeutic recommendations (Simon & Stierlin, 1994). The assessment of the different points of view - including that of the therapist - increases the likelyhood of activating a family`s resources (Ludewig, 1992), which are based on emotional relationships (Mattejat & Scholz, 1994) and on each individual`s autonomy (Oz & Fine, 1991). A sufficient fitting of these emotional relationships and individual autonomy enables a good developmental potential of the family (Ludewig, 1992) and avoids problems such as suicidal symptoms (Garber, Little & Weaver, 1998; Mattejat & Remschmidt, 1991). Several standardized instruments use to assess family relationships are the Family Relationship Index (Hoge, Andrews, Faulkner & Robinson, 1989), the Family Relations Inventory (Oz & Fine, 1991) and the "Subjectives Familienbild" (Mattejat & Scholz 1994). The "Subjectives Familienbild" (Mattejat & Scholz 1994) quantifies subjectively experienced relationships, which are divided into valence (emotional relationship) and potence (individual autonomy). These parameters describe the family`s structure, i.e. a system of relationships, which may induce individual actions. The higher the score of each assessed relationship, the more emotionally related and "stronger" a member of the family can be described. Significantly different estimations of the relationships may suggest therapeutic interventions (Mattejat & Scholz 1994).

The "Subjektives Familienbild" assessment battery is a screening instrument for assessing intrafamilial relationships, but it has to be supplemented by the therapist`s observation (Tomm, 1994).

STANDARDIZED ASSESSMENT

The purpose of our study is to assess the differences of ADHD children and healthy controls in a standardized way with respect to intrafamiliar relationships (assessed by the SFB).

We hypothesized, that ADHD children have worse intrafamilial relationships than healthy controls. In this study, we compared 15 boys with ADHD and 15 matched controls to assess whether coherence was related to types of interactions among family members (family features).

We assessed 15 6 to 12-year old boys (M=9.0 y, SD=1.0) boys in western Austria. In our outpatient clinic, they were diagnosed with ADHD according to the guidelines of the Conners Scale (Conners, Wells, Parker, Sitarenios, Diamond, & Powell, (1997), which includes 48 items, parent-rated on a 4-point scale with anchors of 0:never to 3:always. Scores exceeding 80 are considered indicative of ADHD. Children received no psychopharmacological treatment and lived in their families.

All participating families (father, mother and child, including brothers and sisters) had received psychotherapeutic treatment in our outpatient clinic (systematic family therapy; 1 session each two weeks for 6 months). The ADHD sample was compared with 15 healthy 6 - 12-year old (M=8.7 y, SD=0.89) boys, whom we recruited in a Grammar school. All parents were married. In 21 (approx.70%) of the families, at least one parent had finished college. In 9 (approx. 30%) of the families at least one parent had finished high school.

The relationships within the family were assessed by the "Subjektives Familienbild" (Mattejat & Scholz, 1994), completed by mother, father and child separately. Each individual had to estimate his or her relationship to the other members of the family by answering 6 items, rated on a 7step rating scale <-3=never, -2=very seldom, -1=seldom, 0=occasionally, +1=often, +2=very often, +3=always>, 3 of which referred to one of two “valence” and "autonomy" (uninterested, warm-hearted, appreciative, and independent, irresolute, secure respectively). Test completion took 10 minutes on average, range of 5 to 20 minutes.

The children`s mean age was 8.5 years (6-12y), that of their parents 38.3 (25-44y) years. No significant differences were found regarding the family`s socioeconomical state. All parents were married.

Autonomy of the mother was significantly lower in ADHD children (Table 1), as well as the ratings of the child`s valence.

Table 1. Family relationships and ADHD

Scale						*relationships*		
			valence/ father	valence/mot her	valence/c hild	autonomy/father	autonomy/ mother	autonomy/ child
			M/SD	M/SD	M/SD	M/SD	M/SD	M/SD
	ADHD		5,13+/-2,90	4,69+/-3,63	2,13+/- 4,44	4,90+/-2,37	2,67+/-2,69	3,04+/-4,08
	healthy controls		4,28+/-2,16	4,11+/-3,57	4,04+/- 3,98	4,05+/-2,19	4,98+/-2,21	2,21+/-3,57
	p		.005	.007	.002	.005	.002	.006

Our results strongly suggest, that the child`s empathy and the mother`s autonomy are less in ADHD children. These results suggest that psychotherapeutic interventions should focus the mother`s autonomy and the child`s empathy.

References

Barkley, R. (1981) *Hyperactive children: handbook for diagnosis and treatment.* New York: Guilford.

Conners, C. K., Wells, K. C., Parker, J. D., Sitarenios, G., Diamond, J. M., & Powell, J. W. (1997) A new self-report scale for assessment of adolescent psychopathology: factor structure, reliability, validity, and diagnostic sensitivity. *Journal of Abnormal Child Psychology*, 25(6), 487-497.

Cunningham, C. E. & Barkley, R. A. (1979) The interactions of hyperactive and normal children with their mothers during free play and structured task. *Child Development*, 50, 396-403.

Döpfner, M. & Lehmkuhl, G. (1995) Elterntraining bei hyperkinetischen Störungen. In H. C. Steinhausen (Ed.), *Hyperkinetische Störungen im Kindes- und Jugendalter*. Stuttgart: Kohlhammer pp 18-26.

Esser, G., Blanz, B., Geisel, B., & Laucht, M. (1989) *Mannheimer Elterninterview MEI.* Weinheim: Beltz Test GmbH.

Jacob, R. G., O`Leary, K. D., & Rosenblad, C. (1978) Formal and informal classroom settings: effects on hyperactivity. *Journal of Abnormal Child Psychology*, 6, 47-59.

Moos, R. H. (1973) Conceptualizations of human environments. *American Psychologist*, 45, 652-665.

Moos, R. H. (1974) *Family Environment Scale (FES): Preliminary manual.* Palo Alto, CA: Stanford Univ., Social Ecology Laboratory, Department of Psychiatry.

Saile, H., & Gsottschneider, A. (1995) Hyperaktives Verhalten von Kindern im familiären Kontext: Zum Stellenwert von mütterlicher Erziehung, Partnerschaftsqualität und Funktionsfähigkeit der Familie. *Psychologie in Erziehung und Unterricht*, 42, 206-220.

Saile, H., Röding, A., & Friedrich-Löffler, A. (1999) Familienprozesse bei Aufmerksamkeits- und Hyperaktivitätsstörung. *Zeitschrift für Kinder- und Jugendpsychiatrie*, 27(1), 48-52.

Schneewind, K. A., Beckmann, M., & Hecht-Jackl, B. (1985a). *The education of children test battery (Das Erziehungspraktiken gegenüber dem Sohn-Testsystem) manual.* München: Forschungsberichte 6.1

Schneewind K. A., Beckmann, M., & Hecht-Jackl, B. (1985b) *The family features (Das Familienklima-Testsystem) manual.* München: Forschungsberichte 8.1.

Schneewind, K. A., & Lortz, e. (1976) *Familienklima und elterliche Erziehungseinstellungen. Trier: Forschungsbericht* 9 des EKB-Projekts.

INDEX

A

B

C

D

E

F

G

H

I

J

K

L

M

N

O

P

Q

R

S

T

U

V

W

Y

Z